WORLD POLITICS
Trend and Transformation

WORLD POLITICS
TREND AND TRANSFORMATION

CHARLES W. KEGLEY, JR.
University of South Carolina

EUGENE R. WITTKOPF
University of Florida

St. Martin's Press   New York

For Pamela, Debra, and Jonathan

Library of Congress Catalog Card Number: 80–52381
Copyright © 1981 by St. Martin's Press, Inc.
All Rights Reserved.
Manufactured in the United States of America.
54321
fedcba
For information, write St. Martin's Press, Inc.,
175 Fifth Avenue, New York, N.Y. 10010

cover design: Tom McKeveny

typography: Bernard Klein

charts: Soho Studio, Inc.

cloth ISBN: 0–312–89246–2
paper ISBN: 0–312–89245–4

Contents

Preface

In what fundamental ways has the world changed since 1945? How has the traditional conduct of relations between and among nations been affected by the pace of change in today's world? To what extent has the transformation of world politics been inhibited by the strength of persistent global patterns?

These are the questions that provide the focus of *World Politics: Trend and Transformation.* Although attention to what is new and what is enduring is not unique in the study of world politics, the analysis presented here differs in a number of ways from that of earlier works on international relations. In addition to exploring conventional topics such as the evolving East-West controversy and the role of international law and organization in the management of conflict, the text gives detailed attention to the characteristics, interests, and objectives of Third World nations and delves into the growing significance of "nonstate actors," the varying organizations and movements that exercise influence in the global arena. Other unique features of this text include its special focus on the intersection of politics and economics and on transnational policy issues—for example, the relationship between growing population and dwindling food supplies, the energy crisis, the increase of arms transfers to Third World nations, and the impact of international terrorism on world political order.

In the examination of these complex and interrelated issues, *World Politics: Trend and Transformation* takes a macro or holistic view of the substance of international relations. Instead of concentrating narrowly on the nation-state, we attempt to discern trends and patterns that transcend national boundaries. The book is organized thematically, but in such a way that the reader is continually encouraged to consider how change within one policy area affects the probability of change in another.

World Politics: Trend and Transformation draws on a broad spectrum of research orientations. In doing so, we hope to make the reader aware of the different, often competing, visions of global political reality, for we believe it is important to stress that no single perspective is likely to provide an understanding of the kaleidoscopic changes affecting the world today.

No observer of the contemporary international scene can view it without a sense of urgency and alarm. Because the world's problems have become so intertwined, the challenges and dangers they present are unprecedented. The available choices for resolving these problems are confusing and quite often painful; but they are unavoidable. It is our hope that *World Politics: Trend and Transformation*, by attempting to capture the nature of change in global politics, will stimulate its readers to a more sophisticated contemplation of the destiny we all share.

No book is possible without the help of many people. Throughout the manuscript we have attempted to acknowledge the authors whose work proved especially valuable to the development of our own presentation. We also acknowledge with special thanks all those individuals who gave so generously of their time and wisdom examining earlier versions of the manuscript: Edward E. Azar, David Caufield, Timothy Duning, Albert Eldridge, James B. Holderman, Lee June Hevener, Stephen D. Hibbard, Lloyd Jensen, Robert S. Jordon, Paul M. Kattenburg, James A. Kuhlman, Thomas O'Donnell, Gregory A. Raymond, Neil P. Richardson, James N. Rosenau, Bruce M. Russett, Daniel Sabia, Steven E. Sanderson, Timothy Shank, J. David Singer, and Robert Trice. We also wish to thank Bertrand W. Lummus, Richard Steins, and Carolyn Eggleston, all of St. Martin's Press, for their continuing support of our work and for their professional assistance in bringing it to fruition.

To our wives, Pamela Kegley and Barbara Wittkopf, we owe a special debt of gratitude for their continuing understanding, support, and professional assistance.

As we look from the present to the future with hope, we dedicate this, our second coauthored book, to Pamela, Debra, and Jonathan.

Part I

THE INTERPLAY OF TRANSFORMING POLITICAL FORCES

One

World Politics in Transition: An Analytical Overview

> I say we had best look at our times and lands
> searchingly in the face, like a physician diagnosing
> some deep disease.
>
> Walt Whitman, 1888

> In the aftermath of the Second World War, there
> began a massive reorganization of the world. . . .
> We are living through an era of the most extensive
> and intensive political change in human history.
> . . . Our generation is living through a genuine
> global political awakening.
>
> Zbigniew Brzezinski, 1979

The spinning sphere we call earth is a planet in space approximately 8,000 miles in diameter and 25,000 miles in circumference. It is believed to be at least 4,000,000,000 years old. In the course of its evolution, it has undergone constant change. It is only in the last 3,000,000,000 years of its existence, for instance, that it is meaningful to speak of the earth possessing a biosphere—a system of life and of living organisms. And a sociosphere—a system of human beings in interaction—is, in the history of the planet, a relatively recent development. A cosmic calendar would tell us that the drama of human history commenced only in the last 340,000 years (Childe, 1962). Humankind has been a component of the earth's biosphere for merely 1/1,000th of its existence. And it is only for the past 5,000 years or so that we can speak of a meaningful record of human history.

Since Homo sapiens first began to roam the some 200,000,000 square miles of the earth's surface, human behavior has transformed the nature of the earth's terrestrial habitat. In the earth's ecosphere, the natural environment in which humans live, the quality of life has been influenced by the ways that humans have organized themselves politically for making decisions and managing disputes, how they have extracted from the earth resources to sustain and enhance life, and how they have exchanged and transferred those resources. These basic processes have conditioned the nature of human existence. And while the modes of human behavior on the planet defined by these processes have been relentlessly varied, they have been far from random. Since antiquity, patterns of political, economic, and social behaviors have been discernible. It is, therefore, possible to describe the characteristic ways in which peoples have acted toward one another and to trace continuities in political action. To understand the nature of contemporary global politics, therefore, we must be aware of the continuities in human interaction and look for historical legacies inherited from the past.

But if we are adequately to comprehend the present condition of global politics, we must be as sensitive to the magnitude of change as we are to the continuities. The global system is dynamic, not static; it is governed by movement as well as constancy. The contemporary world political system is a product of processes that are themselves susceptible to long-term evolutionary modification. Hence attention to both change and changelessness in the global forces that structure the world's present existence and future destiny is required if today's global politics are to be understood.

In what fundamental ways has the international political system changed or remained constant, especially since World War II? What do these changes and continuities tell us about the nature of contemporary global politics? What are the implications of emergent global trends—and persistent global arrangements—for the future of world politics? These are principal among the questions addressed in *World Politics: Trend and Transformation*.

At no time in history, perhaps, has a consideration of the changes taking place in world politics been more urgent than at present. This is not because the present age is unique, since every previous age has been one of transition. What makes attention to global trends so timely is the unprecedented *rapidity* with which so many facets of global politics appear to be undergoing transition. The dramatic, accelerating rate of change for humanity as a whole perhaps explains why those willing to think about the rapidity of change and its implications experience "future shock" (Toffler, 1970), a kind of disorientation and disillusionment—and even despair—encountered under frenzied conditions which disrupt traditions and long-established rituals. Confusion, uncertainty, and a sense of chaos accompany perceived discontinuity. Change, furthermore, almost always seems to be for the worse (especially for those in privileged circumstances). The fear and anxiety symptomatic of our times are therefore to be expected because fear and anxiety are often provoked by change. Coping with the anguish of change requires that we come to grips intellectually as well as emotionally with the nature of the changing world in which we live.

How can we best understand the world political transformations that seem to engulf us, and how can we best appreciate the significance of these changes for the future? At a minimum we must heed philosopher George Santayana's warning that those who ignore history are doomed to relive it. That we cannot live undisturbed in a disturbing world of explosive change must be confronted. Avoidance and denial will not shield us from forces that determine our destiny. Hence we must take seriously the need to comprehend the sources of change sweeping across world politics. Many present crises are extensions of forces not taken seriously yesterday.

To that end, *World Politics: Trend and Transformation* is concerned primarily with describing macropolitical processes. This in turn requires that we identify major changes which have occurred in the international system at least since 1945. Such an inventory cannot hope to be complete. It can only concentrate on developments in world politics which seem to be the most potent forces influencing the fundamental restructuring of the global environment which many observers perceive to be unfolding.

In an increasingly interdependent world, where nearly every change seems connected in one way or another to every other, a focus upon the major areas of movement is warranted. If we can detect the principal ways in which the characteristics of global politics are undergoing change, we can then begin to suggest how those changes stimulate or inhibit change in other less volatile features of global politics. But we cannot untangle this complexity without first selecting specific developments for analysis and treating them separately. Our first task in describing macropolitical processes, therefore, is to draw a separate analytical picture of certain aspects of our changed and changing globe, following these varied developments on different tracks. In our concluding chapters we will concern ourselves with how these are connected or might be fitted together.

Any inventory of the basic changes in global politics must establish its empirical bases. But because our subject of inquiry is change in the ways behavior flows across borders throughout the entire planet, we must recognize that we confront a difficult problem: How can we know what is new about world politics? How do we determine who is doing how much of what to whom? It is impossible to put the entire globe under a microscope or to measure movement in all global phenomena. Perhaps this explains why, in the midst of rapid change, we appear so often surprised by emerging developments.

Fortunately, social scientists, governments, and international institutions have devoted considerable effort over the past three decades to the collection of empirical evidence about the characteristics and changing attributes of the global environment. While these data possess limitations, they nevertheless provide empirical insight into what is occurring internationally and offer documentary evidence regarding many of the dominant trends in world politics. Thus, wherever possible, *World Politics: Trend and Transformation* will employ supporting data to demonstrate the extent to which global politics has ceased to be as it has been and to become what it was not before. Our inventory of global change is therefore intimately linked to our efforts to *describe* in operational and systematic terms the dimensions of transition in global politics.

The empirical quest for a description of contemporary international political reality necessitates looking at the international system as a whole. If the evolving nature of global politics is to be captured adequately, attention must concentrate on trends within the entire world environment and on developments and problems which transcend single nations or groups of nations. We must think globally and adopt a global vision. We seek to describe not so much change within any one *part* of the system (except in its context as a source of global change), but rather change *throughout* the world environment.

Such a macroscopic approach entails costs. Particular events, a particular nation's foreign policies, and particular foreign-policy-making processes are necessarily de-emphasized. In so doing, we lose sight of much that is the principal concern of social analysts. But a macropolitical approach is warranted if our purpose is to depict trends and behaviors which tend to cohere into general global patterns, patterns which in the long run have a substantial probability of shaping the future environment in which all of us will live. In other words, we seek to paint the larger picture of our globe by looking at the "forest" of planetary developments instead of the details that make up the "trees" of current international events and the national political processes which underlie them. Hence in this book we seek to identify the patterns that describe individual events and actions only insofar as they contribute to the macropolitical developments that condition and shape the present and future world. Rather than surveying limited, peculiar international problems and particular international political processes, our goal is to explore the kinds of global problems which are widespread in their impact and the kinds of issues which transcend local interests.[1]

Implicit in this approach to international relations is the necessity to observe world politics over an extended time period. If we want to discover the ways world politics are changing (and *if* they are changing), we must observe developments over prolonged periods. A long-term perspective helps differentiate a short-term fluctuation from a long-term trend. It also assists in distinguishing changes that occur over a brief period (and hence often of little ultimate significance) from trends or changes that persist over extended periods of time. And of course a long-term perspective enables us to appreciate the possibility that trends may reverse themselves.

Against the background of this perspective, the changes and continuities monitored in this book are inspected by reference to past developments. Of particular concern is the period since World War II. The reason for this focus is that World War II itself represented a significant breakpoint in the historical evolution of world political patterns. Power came to be concentrated in the hands of two states destined to become superpowers; Europe ceased to be the center of the international political system; self-determination became more than a slogan as the vast European colonial empires began to dismantle; and the atomic bomb set in motion a revolution in the development of weapons of mass destruction. In some instances we will find it useful in understanding contemporary global politics to examine developments prior to World War II. But because that global war was itself symbolic of a major transformation of world politics, attention will be concentrated on macropolitical processes since 1945. In this sense the question implicit in *World Politics: Trend and Transformation* is whether the world political system created in the aftermath of World War II is now undergoing another, equally profound transformation.

World Politics: Trend and Transformation is interested not only in describing underlying tendencies in contemporary international relations but also in projecting these tendencies through time in order to anticipate *future* trends and transformations. To anticipate what will happen, we must study what has already happened. The

1. This statement of purpose is in no way intended to denigrate the importance of examining political processes peculiar to individual national actors. Our own work on American foreign policy (Kegley and Wittkopf, 1979) demonstrates our commitment to understanding international politics from the viewpoint of individual actors and their foreign-policy-making processes. Instead, our intention here is to focus on global processes while inspecting intranational political processes insofar as they relate to macropolitical behavior.

past cannot be ignored in our desire to free the future from its paralyzing grip. It is from history that clues necessary to predict probable conditions in the years ahead can be extracted. As Winston Churchill once noted, "The further back you look, the farther forward you can see." A good prophet, it would seem, needs a good memory. Thus, by looking at the past in order to anticipate the shape of the future, we assert acceptance of one of the methodological cannons of social science expressed by the philosopher Leibniz in the eighteenth century: "The present is big with the future, the future might be read in the past, the distant is expressed in the near." This principle guides and provides rationales for much of the underlying approach we have taken to the analysis of the ways in which global politics have changed and are changing.

In summary, *World Politics: Trend and Transformation* is concerned with an empirical description of macropolitical processes, a concern that requires the use of history to understand how the world has come to be what it is and where it might be going in the future. These are its goals and conceptual boundaries.

But this book is also concerned with what such an inquiry might tell us about how we can best think about the nature of contemporary world politics. Even if we successfully discover patterns in international political behavior and describe the separate strands making up the transformation of world politics, we must still be concerned with what these changes signify about the best way to understand the often seemingly unrelated changes occurring around us. How, in short, should we make sense of the world that is evolving before our eyes? What concepts and models of reality render intellectually coherent and manageable the changes before us, and through what kinds of lenses can we visualize best the probable impact of the dynamic forces operating in contemporary world politics?

Two

Images of World Politics in Transition

> It's important that we take a hard, clear look . . .
> not at some simple world, either of universal good-
> will or of universal hostility, but the complex,
> changing, and sometimes dangerous world that
> really exists.
>
> Jimmy Carter, 1980

> We act according to the way the world appears to
> us, not necessarily according to the way it "is."
>
> Kenneth E. Boulding, 1975

We live in a world defined by our imagination. No one really "knows" what the world is like. Its characteristics can only be inferred from things perceived about it. Because international relationships and interactions in their totality are not directly observable, it is probable that many images about the political realities of the world are built upon illusions and misconceptions. Mental images are often fragmented and inaccurate. They also tend to become obsolete, because adjustments in the way we think about and visualize world politics tend to lag behind constantly shifting international circumstances.

It is precisely because the way we act is shaped so powerfully by what is perceived that attention must be paid to transformations in our *theories* of or systematic speculations about world politics. For the shape of the world's future will be determined not only by changes in the "objective" facts of world politics but also by the meaning people ascribe to those facts, the assumptions on which their interpretations are based, and the kinds of actions flowing from these assumptions and interpretations. Hence, to understand adequately the transformation of world politics, we must monitor not only the direction of change in world politics but also the variations in the way people view the world.

IMAGES OF "REALITY"

Everyone has some kind of mental model of world politics. The model may be explicit or perhaps only implicit. It may be a conscious model or only a subconscious one. Regardless of their nature, all models perform essentially the same function. They provide simplified versions of "reality" which exaggerate some features of the real world and ignore others.

There is, however, nothing pernicious about the tendency to view the world through simplifications called models. To make sense out of a confusing abundance of information, we all create "mental maps" of the world composed of categories into which we place information to facilitate understanding. These mental maps[1] might be thought of as "pre-theories" (Rosenau, 1966) because they provide an orientation toward world politics, and because they reflect "a point of view or philosophy about the way the world is." Perhaps our mental maps are better thought of as conceptual models, inasmuch as concepts are abstractions for the organization of perceptions. Regardless of what we call them, the important points are that there are alternative ways of viewing the world and that our images of the world determine the way we mentally map or model it. These characteristics derive from the tendency of people to

> respond [not] to the "objective" facts of the situation, whatever that may mean, but to their "image" of the situation. It is what we think the world is like, not what it is really like, that determines our behavior. . . . We act according to the way the world appears to us, not necessarily according to the way it "is." (Boulding, 1975: 348)

Before turning to an examination of the various models that have been used by scholars to understand the global system, it would be useful first to discuss briefly the sources of individuals'

---

1. We use the word *map* purposefully to signify the extent to which mental models of the globe are necessarily imperfect replicas of the global realities they are intended to portray. We speak not only of the kind of geography of the world that people carry in their heads about distance, size, and topography of the earth's surface, but also of maps people carry of the ways resources, military capabilities, power, diplomatic influence, populations, and the like are distributed throughout the globe, and the political meaning of such distributions. Having described mental models in these terms, it is perhaps axiomatic that the kinds of maps people carry in their heads about global attributes often bear little relationship to the realities of a shrinking, interdependent planet. For discussion of this thesis, see Sprout and Sprout (1971).

images of reality. Specifically, modes of thinking about politics can be influenced by any number of factors,[2] including:

- psychological needs and drives and the kinds of dispositions (e.g., trust or distrust) ingrained in personalities as a result of early childhood experiences;
- what we have been socialized into thinking about international relations as children (e.g., tolerance for cultural diversity, or fear of it) by parents, teachers, and peer groups and by the cultural system of which we are a part;
- opinions about world affairs articulated by those with whom we associate on a routine basis;
- attitudes expressed by authority figures, policy influentials, and others respected as experts;
- expectations (since what we expect to see often determines what we observe; expectations, or prophecies, have an uncanny way of becoming self-fulfilling[3]);
- positions we occupy and the kinds of roles we perform: what we see globally depends on where we sit (child, student, bureaucrat, policy maker, statesman, and so forth).

These principles from empirical research in perceptual psychology indicate that perception of the world is not a passive act.[4]

2. For elaborations on these multiple sources of influence, see DiRenzo (1974), McClosky (1967), Singer (1965), Bozeman (1960), Janis (1972), Asch (1951), Levinson (1964), Jervis (1969), and Lieberman (1965).

3. In international relations, many predictions seem to make themselves come true. For example, a forecast for the rapid economic development of a particular country may encourage multinational corporations to invest there and for other nations to negotiate trade agreements there, thus causing the forecast to be realized. Similarly, the perception of another country as a hostile enemy may encourage the conditions that confirm the impression; as George F. Kennan once observed, those who perceive themselves surrounded by hostile enemies often get their expectations fulfilled—they act aggressively, fearfully, and arm for "defense," and thus find themselves living in a world filled with enemies.

4. The study of psychology is important to the study of international relations because people differ in their reactions to conflicting or discrepant information. The general tendency of most people is to look for information which reinforces preexisting beliefs, to assimilate new data to familiar images, and to distort perceptions so as to deny those which fail to conform with prior expectations. Tolerance of ambiguity and willingness to consider new ways of organizing our thinking varies across individuals and personality types; some are more "open" and less rigid than others (Rokeach, 1960), and therefore more accepting of diversity and more able to revise perceptual habits to accommodate new realities. Nevertheless, all individuals are prisoners, to some extent, of the perceptual predispositions to which they have been conditioned. For an illuminating case study of the perceptual rigidities exhibited by a prominent American policy maker, John Foster Dulles, which demonstrates that leaders are not immune from such tendencies and that narrow belief systems by such leaders can have important international consequences, see Holsti (1975).

The mind is conditioned to select, screen, and filter what is perceived, organizing sensory sensations by accepting some cognitions (facts) and excluding others from consciousness. This means that what we "see" about world politics depends on what we look at, what we look for, and how we react to what we "find." The human tendency for selective perception (and selective recall) suggests that there is truth in the aphorism that what we see is what we get. Subconscious predispositions therefore also play a central role in the formation of thought. What we think about affects what we think. Hence all are to some extent captives of perceptual habits. What is seen in and thought about the world as a consequence of selective perception affects our views and corresponding mental images of world politics.[5]

These reminders of the factors which influence how people think about world politics do not imply that those thereby influenced are perceptual bigots (although apparently some people are). Although images of international relations are resistant to change, they are not incapable of change. Most people do have the capacity to reject cherished worldviews, or, more routinely, to revise and to refine how they think about the world. Mental maps tend to change when individuals experience punishment or discomfort as consequences of clinging to false assumptions. Dramatic events have also been shown to alter international images, sometimes drastically, changing thereafter how international relations are thought about (Deutsch and Merritt, 1965). The dropping of atomic bombs on Japan in 1945, the Korean and Vietnam conflicts, and the precarious brinkmanship experienced during the Cuban missile crisis in 1962 were learning experiences for many people, jolting them into awareness of vulnerabilities posed by international circumstances and leading them to modify previous images of international relations (see, e.g., Holsti and Rosenau, 1979). Often such consciousness-raising experiences provide occasions for the creation of new mental maps of the globe, new clusters of perceptual filters through which subsequent events are interpreted, and new criteria for "definitions of the situation" (Pruitt, 1965) when interpreting subsequent events.

Notice that such learning experiences do not necessarily lead to the creation of more "open" images, that is, models more receptive to incongruent information. They entail, more typically, the replacement of one frequently simplistic image with another often equally simplistic image. William James's adage that "most people think they are thinking when they replace one set of prejudices for another" perhaps describes this process of image alteration.

---

5. See Jervis (1976) for a review of the sources of perception and misperception in world politics.

Finally, although people's perceptual habits of thinking about international relations are generally not innovative, they have been shown to manifest long-term changes in response to growing awareness of fundamental changes in international conditions. This kind of change is more problematic than the others mentioned and is dependent on the amount of interest in, experience encountered, and information about international affairs of which the individual is cognizant.[6] The existence of long-term mood swings (see Klingberg, 1970 and 1979) and cycles of opinion regarding foreign policy suggest, nevertheless, that people do manage to rethink the basics of world politics, however reluctantly and belatedly. It is tempting to postulate that such rethinking will most likely occur under conditions of rapid change, since perceptions of change invite reconsideration of prevailing dogmas and conceptual orthodoxies. That we presently live in such an era is a distinct probability.

If we want to determine how mental models of world politics are shifting worldwide over time, we are presented with considerable analytic obstacles. It is not feasible to sample the beliefs about international relations held by the more than 4,000,000,000 people populating the globe. Nor is it possible to survey the opinions of world leaders to characterize the worldviews of these influential elites—even though it is self-evident that these elites also behave according to their mental models of politics, and their images are ultimately most important in determining the course of world affairs. What *is* possible to study are the images of international relations, and changes in them, held by scholars of international phenomena. Their concerns often reflect the policy issues dominant in different historical periods and decision makers' responses to them.

Because the definition of reality is a collective enterprise governed by group influences and supported by collective pressures, the study of international relations during different periods usually reflects a dominant viewpoint or orthodox worldview regarding the nature of global reality subscribed to by the majority of theorists and practitioners. Call it a common frame of reference, a prevalent school of thought, an organized belief system, or a paradigm[7]—

6. Opinion polls repeatedly demonstrate that the majority of people are inattentive to and uninformed about even the most elementary issues of world politics, despite the fact that these issues increasingly determine the quality of their lives and are directly relevant to their standards of living. See Kegley and Wittkopf (1979) for a discussion and documentation of these characteristics of mass attitudes in the American context.

7. The word *paradigm* is commonly employed to describe the dominant way of looking at a subject of inquiry, such as international relations. It was popularized by Thomas Kuhn's influential book *The Structure of Scientific Revolutions* (1970). Unfortunately, the term has been used in a variety of overlapping ways. But the general idea that thoughts about a particular area of inquiry tend to be structured by accept-

however we may refer to it, we can detect amidst intellectual diversity the existence of a modicum of consensus about how an international phenomenon should be characterized, what its central dimensions are, what basic questions should be asked, and how its study should be approached.

To a substantial extent, the various frameworks used by scholars to understand the behavior of policy makers and world politics generally are removed from the kinds of images of world politics the average "person in the street" carries in his or her head. However, the two are not entirely separated for precisely the reasons that mental maps are often drawn according to the messages portrayed by dominant sociological forces within different political systems. The role of the educational system in forging ideas and the mass media in transmitting them are critical in this process. Hence it is useful to examine the images of international relations held by professional students of international phenomena—regardless of how "esoteric" and removed from the "real world" they may on occasion seem.

To be sure, there have always existed scholars outside the intellectual paradigm dominant during any particular time, actively challenging it, questioning its relevance to world politics, and proposing alternative conceptions of reality and what knowledge about it should entail. Oftentimes those outside the paradigm come from countries other than those dominant in world politics itself, thus reinforcing the notion that scholars' views of "reality" to some extent reflect it. Marxist thinking has clearly been dominant in the scholarly work of those living in socialist societies, for example, but the ability of Marxist interpretations of reality to attain dominance worldwide has been constrained by the inability of communism as defined by Marx (i.e., a classless, stateless society) to become the preferred form of political and social organization in the world. But paradigms, nevertheless, appear and grow in strength as increasing numbers of observers accept their account of international phenomena. Such paradigms arise by the persuasiveness of their proponents' message, by the ability of paradigms to account for observed patterns in what is happening within and between nations, and by their ability to explain why and how particular causal forces rip and tear the course of world affairs. Particular paradigms flourish in

ance of particular aspects of the subject's characteristics as more important than others, and by agreement about the puzzles to be solved and the criteria that should govern investigation of those questions, has merit if we are to understand how images of world politics are shaped by sociological forces operating within the intellectual community as it seeks to assess the nature and meaning of global political developments.

particular international climates when they best meet needs to interpret the world, to guide research and thinking about it, to point to the data necessary best to describe it, and to provide the analytic categories by which the collected data can best be analyzed. Hence we can learn much about transformations in mental images concerning world politics by charting changes over time in the paradigms that have governed the study of international relations, particularly among the Western nations whose political influence has substantially conditioned the nature of international political reality as it is understood from the viewpoint of the Western world.[8]

Let us consider this thesis by tracing some of the ideas that have dominated thinking and theorizing about international affairs during the twentieth century. Such a chronological survey of the phases that have governed research in international relations enables us to capture how images of world politics have been transformed. Monitoring these changes enables us to capture as well some of the changing characteristics of the global environment.

THE STUDY OF INTERNATIONAL RELATIONS
PRIOR TO WORLD WAR I

As the Western world moved into the twentieth century it experienced a period of relative peace, prosperity, and stability. In those halcyon days, and perhaps because of them, the field of international relations could afford the luxury of pursuing largely academic questions about the world's past. Aside from some efforts to devise strategies for bringing about more adaptive world orders (such as the Hague peace conferences), the prevailing international atmosphere between the late 1800s and the outbreak of the world's first global war in 1914 fostered an emphasis on the study of *diplomatic history*. This approach consisted primarily of describing with as much detail and accuracy as possible the particulars of specific incidents in history. The approach was largely devoid of theoretical content.[9] Time and place were the dominant organizing concepts, and little effort was made to generalize about characteristics common to different incidents or to search for hypotheses relating

8. It is important to keep in mind, as we shall see, that a number of paradigms flourishing at one time may conflict or agree with one another. The interaction of these can be significant and is worth considering, inasmuch as in periods of rapid change the number of contending, interacting paradigms tends to increase.

9. There were some exceptions, of course. For instance, one of the major writers of the time, Sir Alfred Thayer Mahan, sought to generate broad theoretical propositions about the influence of geographic factors on national power and international relations.

cause to effect. Indeed, the methodology of diplomatic history was a "vacuum sweeper" approach: all available facts were gathered to describe what happened where, when, under what specific conditions, and within narrowly delimited time frames. The emphasis was on contextual detail and the unique. Absent was the explicit search for regularities and uniformities of behavior and for common denominators by which events could be compared, characteristics that would dominate later analytical approaches. Absent, too, was agreement on central problems or questions. Since the purpose of inquiry was faithful attention to fully detailed description, any and all aspects of reality were appropriate. This paradigm's legacy, therefore, was a series of pictures of past and present events similar to those found in today's newspapers. Missing was the quest for policy-relevant information that could be used to mold events to realize policy goals, for such information and theory require data-based generalizations about causal connections not bounded by time and place for their validity.

THE STUDY OF INTERNATIONAL RELATIONS BETWEEN TWO WORLD WARS

The advent of a catastrophic global war in 1914 stimulated the search for knowledge that could address contemporary problems in general and the problem of war in particular. This required a theoretical perspective with sustainable generalizations about the conditions under which war might be avoided and peace maintained. However interesting descriptions of past wars and the individuals who waged them might be, they were of little utility to a world looking for ways to prevent the disastrous consequences of wars of mass destruction. For that purpose a theory was needed that could predict the outbreak of future wars reliably and that could tell policy makers what factors could be manipulated to deter or perhaps prevent their occurrence. Such goals required a new analytical paradigm.

The diplomatic-historical perspective persisted in the period following World War I. Marxist-Leninist thought was becoming an increasingly challenging paradigm in the aftermath of the Bolshevik Revolution in Russia. Later, with the rise of Hitler and the Nazis in Germany, national socialism would also present a profound challenge to the thinking about international politics characteristic of the European-centered international political system. But emerging dominant between the two world wars in the Western world was a paradigm that came to be labeled (especially when it began to disappear) *political idealism.* Idealists held widely divergent viewpoints about world politics. What transformed their movement into a cohesive paradigm among Western scholars were the assumptions about reality they shared and the homogeneity of the conclusions their perspective elicited.

Collectively, idealists, representing the satisfied victors of World War I, projected a worldview usually resting upon the following axioms: (1) human nature is essentially "good" and capable of altruism, mutual aid, and collaboration; (2) the fundamental instinct of humans for the welfare of others makes progress possible (that is, the Enlightenment's faith in the possibility of advancing civilization was reaffirmed); (3) bad human behavior is the product not of evil people but of evil institutions and structural arrangements that create incentives for people to act selfishly and to harm others—including making war; (4) wars represent the worst feature of the international system; (5) war is not inevitable and can be eliminated by doing away with the institutional arrangements that encourage it; (6) war is an international problem that requires global rather than national efforts to eliminate it; and therefore (7) international society has to reorganize itself to eliminate the institutions that make war likely.[10]

To be sure, not all advocates of political idealism subscribed to each of these tenets with equal conviction. Many political idealists would probably disagree with some of them; perhaps all would be uncomfortable with the simplistic wording of these postulates of their convictions. Nevertheless, these tenets collectively describe the basic assumptions articulated in one way or another by the statesmen and theorists whose orientation toward world affairs captivated the discussion of world politics in the interwar period. Included in this discussion were strong strains of moralism, optimism, and internationalism.

Within the common framework of this paradigm there existed important differences and points of prescriptive departure. The solutions the idealists prescribed for international problems can be classified in three principal categories. One approach called for the creation of supranational institutions to replace the competitive and war-prone system of territorial states. Formation of the League of Nations and an emphasis on international cooperation in social matters as approaches to peace (see chapter thirteen for an elaboration) were symptomatic of idealists' institutional solutions to the problem of war.

A second approach emphasized the legal control of war. It called for new transnational norms to deter the initiation of war and, should it occur, its destructiveness. The Kellogg-Briand Pact of 1928, which "outlawed" war as an instrument of national policy (ex-

---

10. The alleged role of human nature in theories of international relations is controversial. For a review, see Nelson (1974).

cept—note the escape clause—"in self-defense"), represents the high point of the legal approach.

A third approach called for by the idealists was to eliminate weapons. The efforts toward global disarmament and arms control (the Washington naval conferences of the 1920s, for instance) were symbolic of this route to peace.

A number of idealists advocated the substitution of attitudes stressing the unity of humankind for narrow, parochial loyalties; the replacement of secret diplomacy by a system of "open covenants, openly arrived at"; and, above all, the end to interlocking bilateral alliances and the power balances they were supposed to achieve but seldom did. All these and more were part of the idealist paradigm's response to a world shocked by the horror and destructiveness that mass warfare posed.

These were the dominant ideas voiced by Western idealists from the victorious World War I powers, and their concepts dominated the academic discussions and policy rhetoric during this period. Other undercurrents of idealist thought in this period are also detectable, although they never achieved the prominence or symbolic success of those in the idealist paradigm who emphasized international law, organization, or arms control in their policy proposals. Some saw the path to peace and welfare in the restructuring of the international monetary system and in the elimination of barriers to international trade. A corollary view held by Marxist and neo-Marxist reformers was advocacy of economic systems to replace what were believed to be the imperialism-breeding consequences of international finance capitalism. Still others saw in the principle of self-determination the possibility to redraw the world's political geography (in order to make national borders conform to ethnic groupings), under the conviction that a world so arranged would be a peaceful world. Related to this was the call for democratic domestic institutions. Making the world safe for democracy, it was believed, would also make it secure and free of war.

Much of the idealist program for reform was never tried, and even less of it was ever achieved. But all of it died, at least temporarily, when the winds of international change again shifted and the world was confronted by the German, Italian, and Japanese pursuit of hegemony and even world conquest.

THE STUDY OF INTERNATIONAL RELATIONS SINCE WORLD WAR II

World War II further changed the way that statesmen and scholars viewed international politics and the way they thought politics should be managed. Marxist scholars retained their views about the inevitability of communism's victory over capitalism, but among the dominant powers in the West the events that led to World War II cast doubt on the worldview of the idealists and provoked strident criticism of the central assumptions of the idealist paradigm. Indeed, transformed perceptions of the realities of world politics generated a monumental shift of paradigms, one predicated on the rejection of idealist principles and one that obtained its identity and coherence largely from the critique of the idealists' conceptual lens for interpreting the world. A cleavage between them was being drawn.

Calling themselves *political realists*, advocates of the counter-paradigm coalesced into a self-conscious analytic movement. Among the principal prophets of the new worldview were E. H. Carr (1939) from the United Kingdom, and those writing in the United States, including Hans J. Morgenthau (1948), Kenneth W. Thompson (1958, 1960), Reinhold Niebuhr (1947), George F. Kennan (1954 and 1967), and later Henry A. Kissinger (1957 and 1964). These men were surrounded by many disciples, and their collective message about how world politics and inter-nation behavior ought to be viewed reads like an antithesis of the assumptions propounded by the idealists.

At the risk of oversimplifying their message, realists tended to make the following assumptions: (1) a reading of history teaches that humanity is by nature sinful and wicked; (2) of all of man's evil ways, no sin is more prevalent or more dangerous than his instinctive lust for power, his desire to dominate his fellowman; (3) if this inexorable and inevitable human characteristic is acknowledged, realism forces dismissal of the possibility of progress in the sense of ever hoping to eradicate the instinct for power; (4) under such conditions, international politics is a struggle for power, a war of all against all; (5) the primary obligation of every state in this environment—the goal to which all other national objectives should be subordinate—is to promote the national self-interest, defined in terms of the acquisition of power; (6) national self-interest is best served by doing anything necessary to ensure self-preservation; (7) the fundamental characteristic of international politics requires each state to trust no other, but above all never to entrust self-protection to international organizations or to international law; (8) the national interest necessitates self-promotion, especially through the acquisition of military capabilities sufficient to deter attack by potential enemies (read as "all others"); (9) the capacity for self-defense might also be augmented by acquiring allies, providing they are not relied upon for protection; and (10) if all states search for power, peace and stability will result through the operation of a balance of power propelled by self-interest and lubricated by fluid alliance systems.

Political realism fit the needs of a pessimistic age, where suspicion of the motives of others was the rule and where the prospects for peace seemed remote. The development of superpower rivalry between the United States and the Soviet Union, the expansion of that confrontation into a worldwide struggle between so-called East and West blocs, the development of atomic and thermonuclear weapons of mass destruction, the seemingly incessant turmoil around the globe—all these symptoms seemed to confirm the image of world politics described by political realists. The realists' belief that the structure of the international system determined the behavior of all nations was particularly convincing. To many, the view that, in a threatening international environment, foreign policy had to take primacy over domestic problems and policies was also cogent. The view of the world advanced in the paradigm created by the political realists in the immediate aftermath of World War II thus became dominant. The logic of *realpolitik* and the vocabulary of "power politics" structured the thoughts and perceptions of students and statesmen alike about the world and its evolving characteristics.

The realist paradigm, however, contained fissures that gradually splintered the school. While realists seemed to be in agreement about the essential properties of world politics, their conclusions were frequently at odds, even contradictory. Different conclusions could be, and often were, deduced from their assumptions. The underlying beliefs pointed to many paradoxes. Eventually the paradigm raised more questions than it could answer. Once analysis moved beyond the pithy notion that man was wicked and past the rhetoric requiring that foreign policy serve the national interest, important questions remained. Were alliances a force for peace or a factor for destabilization? Did arms contribute to security or encourage costly arms races that ultimately undermined the prospects for security? Was the United Nations merely another arena for the push and shove that was believed to characterize world politics or a tool for reforming national instincts for pure self-advantage? And more controversially, were the Cold War and the policies that sustained it a blessing or a curse? Did an ideological contest serve or undermine the national interest?[11]

11. Moral crusades were anathema to realist thinking. Moralism was seen as a wasteful and dangerous form of interference in the rational pursuit of national power. To the realist paradigm, therefore, questions about the relative virtues of this or that ism (ideological system) were irrelevant and should be kept outside policy thinking. Ideological preferences of national actors were immaterial, neither good nor bad—all that really mattered was whether one's national self-interest was being preserved.

Such questions are empirical ones. They require empirical methods for satisfactory answers. Political realism was found wanting in this respect. Possessing a distinctive perspective on international affairs but lacking a methodology for resolving competing claims, the realist paradigm lacked criteria for determining which data would count as significant information and which rules would be followed in interpreting the data. Thus criticism of realism began to mount.

Those within the movement and those outside it began to point to some disturbing deficiencies within the framework itself. Included were attacks on the logical consistency of the assumptions (if an inexorable law of history is that all actors always seek power, for example, then why is it necessary to advise states that they should quest for power?); challenges to some of the propositions (why is it that nearly every power balance has broken down and eventually resulted in war?); questions about some of the conclusions (for example, did not the realist paradigm, in advocating military vigilance and preparedness, rationalize perpetuation of arms races in a self-fulfilling manner?); and critiques of the paradigm's description of contemporary realities (for instance, was an approach focusing on the nation-state warranted in an age when national borders could be penetrated by a nuclear attack?). Even more disturbing, the paradigm failed to account in an acceptable way for some of the major international developments that were occurring in the post-World War II period. Realism failed to explain some of the collaborative and integrative ties that were being constructed in Western Europe, for instance, where the cooperative pursuit of mutual advantage rather than national self-interest seemed to dominate, at least in economic if not always in military affairs. Indeed, in an increasingly interdependent world, was it not in each nation's self-interest to seek confederation with others instead of struggling with them?

The failure of the realist paradigm to provide reliable descriptions of many political events as well as cogent policy prescriptions led to its challenge and eventual fall as the dominant paradigm. Amidst often contradictory and unverifiable propositions, systematic procedures were unavailable for determining which propositions had the most to recommend them. All too often, the vocabulary of realism degenerated into a set of concepts best suited for policy debate and policy advocacy (for example, "we should—or should not—give foreign aid, because it's in the national interest to do so"), but without criteria for policy planning. Although realism prescribed objectives which could be achieved through varying means, realists themselves could not agree on which policy alternatives best served the needs of the state. That their policy recommendations often failed to meet perceived policy needs underscored the uncertainty realism fomented (the same, of course, could often be said for their detractors).

But the shadow of political realism is still cast. Much of the world continues to think about international politics in terms of this mental model. Nor can its intellectual contributions be ignored. In the history of ideas about world affairs the ability of political realism to identify some of the major issues that divide nations, issues that still afflict the world; its demonstration that good intentions and moralistically inspired wishful thinking are not substitutes for rigorous inquiry; and its commitment to searching for generalizations and abstraction, rather than case-specific historical trivia, to explain international phenomena all assure realism a very special place. Its ideas were compelling and still compel. Nevertheless, its deficiencies and its frequent inability to extend its insight beyond reassertions of its fundamental assumptions led to its demise as the dominant paradigm. As the world entered the 1960s, the stage was set for a new phase in the study of international relations.

Realism prepared the way for serious theoretical thinking about conditions in the global arena and empirical linkages among them. Numerous hypotheses relating cause to effect have been posited. The analysis of world politics has grown haltingly into the kind of predictive science that seeks to inform policy makers about how more effectively to shape a more humane and less brutal world environment. Such efforts to advance grew out of the need for better theory and for the testing of hypotheses to ascertain their validity. The response to this need was largely in terms of method and language, for the paradigm that emerged dominant in place of political realism is defined in part by its worldview but especially by its approach to theory and by the logic and method of its inquiry (see Snyder, 1955; and Sondermann, 1957). The postrealist paradigm is appropriately labeled the *behavioral* approach to the study of international relations.

Actually, behavioralism in international relations was part of a larger movement spreading across the social sciences in general and political science in particular. Often called the scientific approach, behavioralism represented a challenge to preexisting modes of studying human behavior, and, more specifically, to the basis upon which truth-claims were derived by previous researchers, who came to be called "traditionalists." What ensued as this paradigm-shift occurred was an extensive and often heated debate over the principles and procedures most appropriate for investigating international phenomena. The debate centered on the meaning of theory, on the requirements for adequate theory, and on the methods best suited for testing existing theoretical propositions. The period of transition was one occupied as much by "theorizing about theory" (Singer, 1960) as theorizing about international relations.

Much of the debate between traditionalists and behavioralists was strident. A reading of the literature[12] in the period between 1955 and 1965 attests to the extent to which methodological issues— and not substantive ones—commanded the attention of professional journals and analysts, reflecting, perhaps, the uncertainty and immaturity of a "new" science in its incipient stages of development, one unsure about itself and its goals.

At the core of the behavioral movement were a number of shared assumptions and analytic prescriptions. The behavioral paradigm sought nomothetic or lawlike generalizations about international phenomena, that is, statements about patterns and regularities presumed to hold across time and place. Science, behavioralists claimed, is first and foremost a generalizing activity. The purpose of scientific inquiry therefore is to discover recurrent patterns of interstate behavior. From this perspective (a view incidentally consistent with that of many "traditional" realists and idealists), a theory of international relations should entail a statement of the relationship between two or more variables, specify the conditions under which the relationship(s) holds, and explicate why the relationship(s) should be expected to hold. To uncover such theories, behavioralists leaned to comparative cross-national analyses rather than to case studies of particular countries at particular points in time. They also acknowledged the necessity of systematically gathering data about the characteristics of nations and about how they interact with one another. Hence, the behavioral movement spawned, and is often synonymous with, the quantitative study of international relations.[13]

What made behavioralism innovative was not so much its reliance on controlled comparative techniques and quantitative analyses as was its temperament toward inquiry. Behavioralists sought greater rigor and precision in analysis. They sought to replace subjective belief with verifiable knowledge; to augment impressionism and intuition with testable evidence; and to substitute appeals to authority with data and irrefutable information as the bases on which to build cumulative knowledge. They pursued the goal of conduct-

12. For examples of the debate and illustrations of the tone of dialogue, see Knorr and Verba (1961), Wright (1955), Kaplan (1968), Knorr and Rosenau (1969), Tanter and Ullman (1972), and Hoffmann (1960). See also Lijphart (1974) for a review of the issues this debate entailed.

13. Exemplary discussions are found in Singer (1968), Zinnes (1976), Hoole and Zinnes (1976), LaBarr and Singer (1976), and Rosenau (1969 and 1971).

ing comparatively value-free research. They also sought to avoid the tendency of previous scholarship arbitrarily to select facts and cases that were consistent with preexisting models. Instead, all available data, that not supportive as well as that consistent with existing theoretical hypotheses, were to be examined. Moreover, behavioralists sought precision by replacing imprecise verbal definitions of concepts (such as power) with ones on which empirical tests could be conducted and whose meaning was easily communicated from one analyst to the next. Moreover, behavioralists argued that knowledge would advance best if a cautious, skeptical attitude toward any empirical statement were assumed. "Let the data, not the armchair theorist, speak," and "seek evidence, but distrust it" were slogans representative of the behavioral movement.

Armed with new tools for analyzing international relations, newly generated data for testing competing hypotheses that had been voiced over decades of traditional speculation, and sometimes with generous research support from governments and foundations, the behavioral paradigm commanded much of the attention in international relations research. Its early efforts were enthusiastic, and a generation of scholars was trained to study international relations with powerful new conceptual and methodological tools. In the process, some of these scholars addressed empirically questions at the core of some of the competing ideas about the social and political organization of national societies, including Marxist ideas and others relating to the persistent dependence of some states on others.

But cumulating verifiable knowledge is a difficult, even tedious, task. The early enthusiasm and optimism of the effort began to dissipate, and voices even within the behavioral movement itself began to ask sometimes embarrassing questions about the approach and its suitability. One of the early proponents of the behavioral movement, David Easton (1969), began to ask—in a self-fulfilling way—if the field was not moving into a "postbehavioral era." At the heart of this self-scrutiny was a common set of criticisms: that some devotees of the paradigm had become too preoccupied with method to the exclusion of real-world problems; that they had focused attention on testing interesting (and often the most readily quantified) hypotheses, but hypotheses that were largely trivial and meaningless to the policy maker interested in taking action to make the world a better place in which to live; and that the methodology of behavioralism, which sought to ground theories on hard data, necessarily relied on past human experience and patterns that did not describe linkages between variables holding constant in a rapidly changing world. Hence the findings might be historically accurate but unreliable for a changing world.

Also criticized was the behavioral paradigm's relative neglect of many of the ethical questions raised in a world of poverty, hunger, violence, and other forms of malaise. Hence the call for a postbehavioral era was a call for investigation of new types of issues and different kinds of hypotheses and reexamination of the philosophical implications from a multidisciplinary perspective of the trends and problems that were emerging in the world.[14] The perpetuation of an incredibly expensive worldwide arms race in the face of worldwide poverty, the rapid deterioration of the earth's ecological system, the depletion of the planet's natural resources, and the repeated outbreak of increasingly deadly wars—all called for a new research agenda and invited the creation of still newer mental models to deal with pressing world problems. In short, as the 1960s came to a close, the field of international relations as an academic discipline (as seen from the perspective dominant in the Western world) was undergoing yet another paradigmatic transformation.

THE STUDY OF INTERNATIONAL RELATIONS
IN A CHANGING WORLD

If new circumstances stimulate new modes of thought and focus perceptions on previously unexamined dimensions of reality, then it is understandable why a rapidly changing international environment has provoked new worldviews. As a field of study, international relations presently possesses no single, dominant paradigm for interpreting the world—nor has it for most of the past two decades. As the global agenda has expanded and the number and types of issues and actors proliferated, a rich variety of competing subparadigms has arisen to deal conceptually with each of them. The field is fragmented. Consensus about the nature of the global environment is absent. Looking at different elements of the global arena and different trends within it, students of international relations today are, like blind men each describing the elephant on the basis of the part they touch, observing the different facets of world politics to which they direct their attention. What we find, therefore, is a series of snapshots of world politics, with each picture colored by the way different conceptual cartographers choose to view the world.

14. Instructively, advocates of new approaches to studying international relations rarely recommended that scientific methods be jettisoned. More commonly they recommended that scientific methodologies be applied to new kinds of analytic problems.

In a sense this book reflects the heterogeneity characteristic of the study of world politics today. No single paradigm dominates *World Politics: Trend and Transformation.* Instead, our analysis reflects elements of many of the alternative perspectives on world politics competing for dominance and seeks to be responsive to the intellectual challenges of the worldviews expressed by competing paradigms (including some variants on Marxist interpretations). It also reflects some of the early approaches to world politics already discussed, including behavioralism and a sensitivity to postbehavioral criticism, political realism, and idealism, and even the diplomatic-historical paradigm. The intellectual heritage of *World Politics: Trend and Transformation* is therefore great. Subsequent chapters will demonstrate the depth and breadth of this heritage, and in particular the mental models to which we are indebted.

In the process of this analysis we will, of course, identify many of the key elements of the models currently competing for paradigmatic status in the study of world politics. It may be useful here, however, briefly to identify some current questions and theoretical foci guiding international relations inquiry as a way of introducing our subsequent topics and locating them intellectually.[15]

No aspect of global politics has more visibility than the issue of war and peace. And in the post-World War II period no contest better illuminates the most threatening challenge to global peace than the cleavage between the globe's most lethally armed countries, the United States and the Soviet Union. That embittered relationship touches the very fabric of every other dimension of world politics. To many, it has been *the* cleavage that matters. Hence it is no accident that there have arisen and persist two subparadigms focusing on the properties of the Soviet-American relationship. The first is *ideological,* the second *strategic.*

The ideological perspective focuses on the doctrinal differences between East and West and on the different "ways of life" that presumably shape how events, actions, and modes of economic and political organizations are to be interpreted. The strategic perspective,

---

15. The survey that follows touches on only some of the many contending approaches that exist today in the field. For more thorough reviews, see Morgan (1975), Taylor (1978), Sullivan (1976), Dougherty and Pfaltzgraff (1971), and Groom and Mitchell (1978).

It is important to emphasize that most of the perspectives we discuss are located historically in the post-World War II period and reflect overwhelmingly the predominantly North American and Western European orientation toward the study of world politics. Some are more recent in that period than others, but all can be seen as efforts to understand a world that has been changing for some time, for change is not something that has occurred only recently. What these foci share in common, however, is an effort to devise a better understanding of the world than those developed prior to and immediately after World War II, especially the paradigm of the political realists.

on the other hand, views the world in terms of military balances and of the relative equilibrium of weapons systems. It sees the future hinging on the quantitative and qualitative balance of destructive power and considers the national security policies most appropriate to deal with these global circumstances.

Both the ideological and strategic perspectives arose in the aftermath of World War II, when antagonism between the superpowers seemed inevitable and the quest for security via armament seemed (to some) more sane than suicidal. Adherents to these twin frames of reference persevere today. But, as we shall see in our examination of the transformation of the East-West confrontation in chapter three, the Soviet-American relationship has itself undergone substantial alteration over the past three decades, taking on new characteristics and twisting itself into new configurations and complexities. As Secretary of State Cyrus Vance once observed, "The unrelenting hostility of the Cold War has given way to a more complex relationship between East and West, with elements of both competition and cooperation." The ideological baggage and strategic assumptions accumulated in previous decades may therefore have been rendered partially obsolete. Some observers have adjusted, constructing more sophisticated and comprehensive mental models to account for more complex sets of interrelationships. Others have resisted adapting their viewpoints to new conditions. How the probability of war and peace, or of conflict and collaboration, has been transformed in our evolving globe will determine the wisdom of either choice.

The Soviet-American and East-West conflicts remain pervasive. But today an exclusive focus on the ideological and strategic relations between the superpowers and their clients runs the risk of hiding another issue dominating the attention of much of the world's population: the conflict between rich and poor. We live in a world of sharp contrasts, where a consumption-oriented minority lives in affluence, surrounded by a majority for whom life is brutal and short. The cleavage between the world's rich and poor continues to grow, and this widening disparity has generated a new debate on the global political agenda: the North-South conflict, which overlaps and affects other, more traditional differences.

The North-South conflict has gained prominence in part because of the disparities in global incomes and standards of living. It has gained prominence also because the number of independent nation-states has increased threefold since the end of World War II. The international system may thus have become a new system because it has many new members with entirely new kinds of foreign policy objectives, which derive from the new nations' relative lack of economic capabilities. Being relatively poor, the new nations seek to rise out of the inferior status they have inherited. They seek to restructure the international order thrust upon them, an order they perceive as contributing to their inferiority. Hence the era of global politics in which we live is populated by new actors with new foreign-policy goals.

The emergence of issues largely economic in nature and the shifting nature of the political conflict that has surfaced between rich and poor to resolve these issues have led to the use of concepts such as *neo-imperialism, dependence,* and *structural aggression,* among others, as theoretical foci for explaining these developments and their significance. We shall consider some of the worldviews associated with these terms when we examine the North-South conflict in chapters four, seven, and elsewhere.

Related to these developments has been a resurgent interest in the intellectual forerunner of political science, *political economy.* Political economy focuses on the interaction of economic and political forces and how these forces coalesce to allocate goods. In the context of international political inquiry, political economy specifically challenges the distinction between *high politics* (military-strategic issues) and *low politics* (economic issues). This distinction, reinforced by historical events since World War II, led political scientists to devote almost exclusive attention to political matters at the expense of economic ones (just as economists largely ignored political issues; see Spero, 1977). Reflecting the changing global environment, the political economy perspective seeks greater integration of politics and economics.

Another important global trend has been the ascendance of powerful new types of international actors. These include various types of nonstate actors, such as international organizations and multinational corporations. These actors often engage in actions that transcend national units, bridging nation-states into interlocking sets of economic, social, political, and even military ties. Nonstate actors have accelerated the pace with which the globe has become interdependent. They have made for a new international system because it is now composed of new types of actors pursuing new types of objectives through new modes of interaction. The emergence of the *transnational* perspective (see, e.g., Keohane and Nye, 1971 and 1977; and Feld, 1979) represents a theoretical effort to respond to the development of these global circumstances. The transnational subparadigm challenges the conventional *state-centric* view of international politics. That is, it challenges the view that the nation-state is the primary actor in world politics and hence the view that the nation-state ought to be the focal point of scholarly efforts to understand world politics.

Related to the transnational subparadigm is the convergence of theory and research around the concept of international *interdependence* as an organizing perspective for the study of global phenomena. In a world where the price of gasoline at American service stations is determined by people meeting in foreign capitals; where the availability of color television sets to the American consumer is governed, not simply by internal market forces, but also by agreements between Washington and Tokyo; where decisions reached in the Kremlin influence the level at which Americans are taxed and how revenues collected will be spent; where inflation abroad means inflation at home; where supplies elsewhere determine welfare everywhere—indeed, where everything appears to be connected to everything else, and everyone is linked in some way to everyone else—under these conditions new ways of thinking and new conceptual modes are needed. The fact that for more nations the links between conditions abroad and conditions at home are tighter and perhaps more pervasive now than at any time in history suggests the pressing need for new concepts to trace the interconnections between the various parts that collectively make up the global system.

These developments have even called into question the suitability of the nation-state as a unit for organizing political life on the planet and for making decisions appropriate to current global challenges. Given these circumstances, some have challenged the wisdom of thinking of the world in terms of national borders. This is not a radical thesis; it is a new theoretical posture for radically changing times. An observer as cautious as former Secretary of State Henry A. Kissinger has noted that "We are stranded between old conceptions of political conduct and a wholly new conception, between the inadequacy of the nation-state and the emerging imperative of global community" (cited in Falk, 1976).

We shall explore in part three the idea that much of the way the globe's political system is being transformed rests with changes occurring in the way the world's resources—its food, its energy, its goods—are distributed among the globe's exploding population. Adversity and divisiveness are endemic under conditions of global scarcity, where the demands of more people for a better life are taxing the ability of the global production and distribution systems to meet these demands. The problems are exacerbated by the fragility of a global environment that can neither yield unlimited supplies nor survive unrestrained pollution and other kinds of environmental degradation. Global problems appear unprecedented because of the huge numbers of mouths to feed and humans to sustain and because our environment is now recognized as one of finite resources. The transnational policy issues that are generated appear new because they transcend the issues of war and peace, the traditional concerns of nation-states.

These new kinds of global issues have generated a host of different analytical perspectives. One is reflected in the phrase *limits to growth* (e.g., Meadows et al., 1974), a perspective that strikes at the very heart of what *progress* has come to mean in the twentieth century to so many people the world over. The term *ecopolitics* has also been suggested (Pirages, 1978) as a concept designed to focus attention on a much broader range of transnational issues beyond the traditional focus of international relations on war and peace.[16]

Our changing world continues to be haunted by the specter of mass destruction and nuclear holocaust. We can characterize the problem that modern weapons pose to mankind as one of gargantuan proportions without fear of contradiction. What makes the present world environment new and so frightening is that it is now meaningful to talk about the vulnerability of all humankind to the actions of only one or two states. To speak of the prospects of human existence as precarious is no longer hyperbole. Chapters ten and eleven document these grim realities by examining global trends in the militarization of the entire world and in the incidence of international violence that these developments make possible. Efforts to account for these unpleasant features of a vigilant planet include a number of perspectives whose intent is to describe and explain the global consequences of militarism and violence. Included are variants of classical strategic theory emphasizing the dynamics of arms races and such important concepts as limited war and deterrence. The scientific study of war has also been part of the continuing efforts of social scientists to probe the causes of war in the contemporary war-prone environment (e.g., Singer and Small, 1972 and 1979).

Part of the response to the persistence of interstate violence has been revival of *peace research* (see the *Journal of Conflict Resolution* and the *Journal of Peace Research*, for example) as a distinct perspective on international phenomena. But approaches to the problem of war and the path to peace are divergent. In chapter twelve we will consider approaches which emphasize in one way or another the military dimensions of peace. Here we find some people looking

16. Percolating through the various perspectives relating to global disparities and the finiteness of the global ecosphere seems to be a heightened sensitivity to normative questions and ethical implications. On one hand, there seem to be some with a greater concern for alleviating the plight in which so much of humanity lives and for treating the delicate ecosystem with greater care. Others, however, seem to focus more on the advantages the current world predicament confers on some at the expense of others. From either point of view, normative considerations are probably the driving force that leads to emphasis on policy issues.

to theories of *armaments control* and others looking to ways of *balancing power with power*. Both views approach the problem from opposite directions and propose divergent solutions, but both pursue the same goal—searching for an arms-distribution formula that will reduce the incidence of violence.

The problems of global stability and world order have also generated concern for developing political controls of global violence. Included in this genre of research (much of which has a long heritage) are *functionalists, neofunctionalists, world federalists,* and *integration theorists* who contend that the gradual deterioration of national borders and the political consolidation or confederation of the globe's inhabitants will create "security zones" where peace will become probable and the prospects for war remote. Part of this logic suggests that learning the habits of peace will eventually culminate in the creation of supranational institutions capable of transcending the violence-prone nation-state system. In this sense we have witnessed revival of the transnational institution-building approach advocated by idealists in an earlier but equally insecure time.

The term *"futurology"* has been designated for another thrust sparked by the kinds of global problems now faced. Although "futurologists" take diverse approaches, as we would expect them to, a common element is concern for mapping the future with a possible view toward shaping it to fit preferred goals. Although the view of the future painted by these analysts ranges from forecasts of doom to faith in the capacity of technology to avert disaster, nearly all "futurologists" agree that civilization is living on borrowed time. The implication, then, is that tomorrow's problems must be dealt with today.

Among the "futurologists" are ethically concerned social scientists interested in providing a vision not of the world as it presently is, but of the desirable way international society might be organized in the future. Such a viewpoint begins by asking how we might act to make the world what we would like it to become (let's not simulate the world that exists, let's make the world look like our preferred simulations!). The World Order Models Project (WOMP) is exemplary of this mode of "futurology" (see Falk, 1975), as is the journal *Alternatives*, which asks its readers to think of different and alternative worlds.

INTERNATIONAL POLITICS IN A WORLD OF CHANGE

As this brief review has suggested, today's world is afflicted with a number of problems and corresponding political cleavages. It is divided ideologically. It is split economically. Its opposing divisions are armed militarily. And they often conflict violently. Yet alongside these divisions we also find unprecedented levels of transnational cooperation, and overlaying all of them have been increasing pressures on the world's delicate life-support systems.

Our changing world has changed how we must look at it; unfamiliar global circumstances require consideration of unfamiliar ways of viewing the world. We are compelled to look at our transforming world as Walt Whitman recommended: "searchingly in the face, like a physician diagnosing some deep disease." As President Gerald Ford noted with reference to the country whose destiny he once directed, "At no time in our peacetime history has the state of the Nation depended more heavily on the state of the world; and seldom, if ever, has the state of the world depended more heavily on the state of our Nation." That description holds for many other countries as well.

Will the world's complex metamorphoses outrun its ability to devise new mechanisms of political and social control? Will the world show the flexibility necessary to adjust perceptions to changing global realities? Will we be able to exchange conventional mental habits for ones more suitable for understanding unconventional circumstances? Let us turn to a more detailed examination of the trends underlying the transformation of world politics before we attempt, in our concluding chapters, to speculate on some answers.

Part II

THE INTERPLAY OF WORLD POLITICAL ACTORS

Three

The East-West Conflict: Evolution Of A Global Confrontation

The cold war has been a process of education of two rival elites, and détente is a new stage in that process.

Richard J. Barnet, 1977

It's time to stop pretending that détente with the Soviet Union is still alive. . . . The Soviets want peace and victory. They seek a superiority of military strength that, in the event of a confrontation, would leave us with an unacceptable choice between surrender or a conflict and defeat.

Ronald Reagan, 1980

As World War II drew to a close in 1945, it became increasingly apparent that one era of international politics was coming to an end and a new one was commencing. Unparalleled in scope and unprecedented in destructiveness, the second great war of the twentieth century unleashed forces promising to transform global politics. It brought into being a system dominated by two superstates, the United States and the Soviet Union, whose combined power and resources far surpassed those of all the rest of the world. It also speeded disintegration of the great colonial empires that had been assiduously assembled by imperialist nations in previous centuries, thereby augmenting the emancipation of many of the earth's people from foreign control. A new international system was unfolding, one that, unlike earlier systems, consisted of a large number of sovereign states that were dominated by the two most powerful.

These two characteristics—the number of states and the domination of the United States and the Soviet Union—define and delimit much of what we call the contemporary global system. More than anything else they have also colored the nature of contemporary global politics, for out of them have grown the two great conflicts of the second half of the twentieth century—the conflict between East and West and the conflict between the rich nations of the North and the poor nations of the South. Our purpose in this and the next chapter is to describe the foundations of these political contests whose evolution has not only defined contemporary world politics but will also affect its future.

In this chapter attention will be focused on the origins and evolution of the East-West conflict, and in particular on the rivalry between the United States and the Soviet Union. In chapter four we will focus on the bases of the North-South dichotomy and on the reasons for the contentious dialogue that has become one of its major characteristics.

Although relations between the ideologically antagonistic superpowers and relations between rich and poor countries are interwoven, our separate analytical treatment of them reflects the basic vocabulary that has arisen to describe the major divisions that afflict contemporary world politics. By convention, the labels "East" and "West" are used to differentiate, respectively, the communist nations in general, specifically the Soviet Union and its political and military allies in Eastern Europe, from the coalition of noncommunist nations led by the United States, whose principal partners are the advanced industrial societies of Western Europe, Japan, Canada, Australia, and New Zealand. The term "free world" is also sometimes used to describe the noncommunist world. As an anti-communist coalition led by the United States, the free world includes the West and several economically less developed nations linked to the United States in mutual defense arrangements.[1]

Some members of the western coalition share other characteristics, including a common cultural heritage, a commitment to varying forms of democratic political institutions and free-market economic principles, industrialized economies, and generally high standards of living. Reflecting their common economic characteristics in particular, these nations are known in the idiom of international diplomacy as "developed market economies." More popularly, they are referred to as the *First World*. The communist states comprise the *Second World*.[2] Characterized as "centrally planned

1. As a shorthand way of describing the anti-communist coalition, the term *free world* once enjoyed wide currency, but it is less widely used today, perhaps because some of the nations subsumed under the label practice policies otherwise associated with the most brutal authoritarian regimes of our time.

2. At one time the People's Republic of China was generally regarded as a member of the "Eastern camp," but by the 1980s, if not before, China had come to see the Soviet Union as a threat to, rather than guarantor of, its security. One result has been an increase in cooperative ties between China and various Western nations, including the United States.

economies" because of their preference for state-owned and -operated economic institutions, Second World nations are organized according to socialist principles and share an ideological commitment to the eventual victory of socialism over capitalism.

The East-West conflict between the First and Second Worlds has focused primarily on political controversies, in particular on the military and national security issues that divide East and West into contending factions. The rhetoric of debate in the North-South conflict, on the other hand, has tended to stress economic issues, even though the issues themselves are often intensely political in nature. The conflict pits First World nations and, somewhat less so, those of the Second World against the world's "have-not" nations. The have-nots are characterized by relative poverty, by a lack of economic development comparable to that experienced by First and Second World nations, and by their location largely in the Southern hemisphere of the globe. The have-nots are often referred to collectively as the *Third World*, a term we shall use throughout this book to refer to the economically underdeveloped or developing nations of the world.

Great diversity characterizes the Third World, however, a fact that has led some analysts to partition the Third World into Fourth and Fifth Worlds as well. Such distinctions among Third World nations are based primarily on disparities in their levels of economic development. Although the terms First, Second, and Third Worlds have grown pervasive in policy rhetoric throughout the globe, it should be noted that some observers find this vocabulary to be a repugnant symbol of the allegedly elitist mentality pervading the thinking of Western statesmen who largely coined the terminology.

The stratification of the nations of the world into different "classes" is intimately related to the way the East-West and North-South conflicts have been played out. The East-West conflict is essentially a struggle among those at the top of the international hierarchy for preeminent status, with each side seeking to protect its own position while gaining advantage in its relations with, and often at the expense of, the other. The North-South conflict, on the other hand, is essentially a struggle by those at the bottom of the hierarchy to improve their position in the international pecking order, which implies seeking advantage in their relations with the North, often at the North's expense. The North in turn has sought to "manage" the aspirations of the South in such a way as to preserve the advantages the North now enjoys.

Since this book is fundamentally about the relations between and among the various nations and peoples inhabiting the many "worlds" within the global environment, we shall be concerned throughout with the political objectives (and means for realizing them) of the nations of East and West, North and South. We shall also be concerned with the intersection of politics and economics underlying such analytical distinctions as those between the First, Second, and Third Worlds. We begin with an examination of the origins and evolution of the Cold War, as the East-West conflict has been known historically.

THE ORIGINS OF THE COLD WAR: THREE PERSPECTIVES

By May 1945 the Third Reich, which Hitler had predicted would survive a thousand years, was in ruins. But the victory by the Soviet, American, and British allies over the fascist threat to world conquest produced more than peace for a system that had been devastated by the ravages of total war. It produced as well a world fraught with uncertainty. Political arrangements that had been carefully built and maintained in order to survive in the common struggle against the Axis powers were quickly suspended. An international environment of chaos, of ill-defined borders, of altered allegiances and disentangling alliances, of power vacuums, of economic disarray, and of ambiguous rank and hierarchy emerged. The presumed consensus about goals, standards of behavior, and mutual obligations that had typified the allied efforts to defeat the common enemy was also uncertain. With victory came the loss of assurance.

Perhaps the most certain feature of an otherwise uncertain environment was the ascendency of the United States and the Soviet Union as its two dominant powers. World War II left both clearly preponderant in resources, military capabilities, and influence; in comparison, all other countries were dwarfed by the two giants. As Tocqueville had predicted in 1835, global politics and human destiny came to rest with how these nations would respond to each other.

Lending danger to an already dangerous international situation was the historic animosity of the emergent superpowers, which had recently been thrown together in a marriage of convenience, primarily for protection from a common enemy. Prior to World War II, relations between the two powers had been strained, to say the least. American troops had intervened in Russia in 1919 in an effort to turn back the Bolshevik Revolution; the United States had not even extended diplomatic recognition to the Soviets until 1933. Despite the cooperation between the two necessitated by the world war, traditional suspicions and distrust resurfaced in the immediate postwar period as the manifest and latent power of the two giants fueled their suspicions of each other.

Rivalry and distrust among great powers have been constants in global politics throughout history. Great powers have always found areas of vital interests over which to clash. They have always tended to perceive efforts by an opponent to resolve conflicts of interest as "aggrandizement." This historic tendency of great powers to become natural rivals has led analysts to conclude that conflict between the United States and the Soviet Union was inevitable as each pursued global leadership. But the possibility of a Cold War in the immediate aftermath of World War II was neither clear nor predetermined, and continued collaboration between the two superstates was by no means precluded. Interpretations of the inevitability of the Cold War are suspect because that contest was a product of the decisions made by the leaders of both nations. The capacity to devise policies aimed at cooperation rather than confrontation existed in both the United States and Soviet Union.

Cooperation was in fact envisioned by American and Soviet leaders, at least in their official discourse in the early phases of postwar negotiations. (See Gaddis, 1972, for a review and critique of thinking about this topic.) For instance, it was President Roosevelt's hope and expectation that wartime collaboration would persist in the aftermath of war. Roosevelt believed that flexible accommodation between the United States and the Soviet Union, based on mutual respect grounded on national interests, was possible. He envisioned that both nations would enjoy the benefits of power, but each within its *own sphere of influence.* An informal agreement was reached that each power would enjoy dominant influence and freedom in specified areas of the globe (see Morgenthau, 1969; Schlesinger, 1967). As John Foster Dulles, presidential policy adviser and later President Eisenhower's secretary of state, noted in January 1945, "The three great powers which at Moscow agreed upon the 'closest cooperation' about European questions have shifted to a practice of separate, regional responsibility." Also implicit was the agreement not to oppose each other in areas not vital to national security. Symbolic, too, of this implicit collaboration were the kinds of rules written into the United Nations charter, rules which obliged the United States and the Soviet Union to share, through the operation of the Security Council, responsibility for the preservation of world peace.

If these were the hopes and aspirations of the superpowers at the end of World War II, why, then, did they fail? Let us review three major interpretations.

Mutual Antagonism

One interpretation holds that the Cold War is best seen as a product of *mutual antagonism.* A month before Roosevelt died, he expressed to Stalin his desire to, above all, prevent "mutual distrust." Yet the history of the origins of the Cold War indicates that mistrust and consequent fear were the very foundations of the conflict. Stalin was as wary of the Americans as they were of him. Hostile initiatives by one power were responded to in kind by the other. Threats, and the suspicions they invariably bred, served as catalysts to further threats. Thus, according to this interpretation, the Cold War cannot be seen as simply the response of one peaceful nation to the aggressions of another. Nor can blame for the breakup of wartime cooperation be attributed exclusively to one side. Rather, the Cold War may be seen as a product of mutual fear and suspicion: once set in motion, a conflict developed which fed upon itself, breeding hostile interactions between both parties. From this perspective, the Cold War can be assessed as a conflict over reciprocal anxieties bred by the way officials of both sides elected to interpret the actions of the other. It can be seen as having originated in mistrust of the motives of the other side. Like a bad marriage that gets increasingly tense through constant bickering, the Cold War may have arisen, according to this view, as a result of the unwillingness of both powers to take initiatives to reduce tensions.

Ideological Incompatibilities

Another interpretation sees the Soviet-American conflict rooted in irreconcilable ideological incompatibilities. Secretary of State James F. Byrnes stated this thesis at the time when he contended that "there is too much difference in the ideologies of the U.S. and Russia to work out a long term program of cooperation" (cited in Paterson, 1979). What Byrnes was referring to was the revulsion and fear some Americans felt for Soviet communist doctrine. There was a particular fear that communism was an expansionist, crusading ideology intent on converting the entire world. Many Americans assumed that all communists were bound monolithically to the Soviet Union. As the spearhead of the presumed communist challenge, the Soviet Union itself was the ultimate symbol of the communist threat. The threat was reinforced, moreover, by the view that communism was necessarily totalitarian and anti-democratic and, therefore, posed a real threat to freedom and liberty throughout the world.[3] The fears evoked called, therefore, for a combative response. As President Eisenhower couched the mentality, "We face a hostile ideology—global in scope, atheistic in character, ruthless in purpose, and insidious in method." The enemy was evil incarnate.

Those who argue that ideological differences account for the origins of the Cold War attribute that conflict to more than just the real or imagined American fears of the "communist beast." They contend that, consistent with the proposition that every ideological movement breeds its antithesis, United States foreign policy became ideological in turn: the counter-ideology may be termed anticommunism. Thus, according to this perspective, the United States embarked upon a crusade of missionary proportions of its own, a crusade dedicated to the elimination of an alien set of ideas from the globe.[4] Henceforth, the United States would not be *for* something in the world so much as its policy would be *against* something: communism. The kinds of actions called for by this orientation were relentlessly competitive and confrontationist toward the Soviet Union. This interpretation thus sees the Cold War as fueled by historic antagonisms between diametrically opposed systems of belief. Like religious wars in the past, the Cold War is seen as a battle for the allegiance of men's minds. Like previous such battles, the conflict was exceedingly bitter, because ideological foes recognize no virtue in conciliation or cooperation with enemies.

3. Whether communist doctrine in fact constituted a real danger (what threats to national security are posed by *ideas* is unclear) is a question that cannot be answered empirically with certainty. The role of perceptions in defining political "reality" is nevertheless important. Moreover, it is important to emphasize that many Americans had good reasons for their fear of the Soviet Union, although hindsight shows many of these reasons to have been dubious. That communism is a cohesive force, for instance, is questionable. With the passage of time, communism has revealed itself to be increasingly polycentric; Communist party leaders have become vocal about their own divisions and disagreements about communism's fundamental beliefs. Also, the greatest fear of some communist states today appears to be fear of other communist states. The Sino-Soviet split, grounded fundamentally in national interest, not ideology, is the preeminent case in point. Moreover, if communism was expansionistic, it should be noted that its ideology showed itself to be more flexible and abstract than initially assumed, with no timetable for the conversion of nonbelievers and no requirement that revolution be exported to all quarters. But regardless, the impact of earlier assumptions in the American policy-making community was enormous. Policy makers defined a worldview which inevitably led to acceptance of the notion that successful opposition to communism was one of the most important interests of the United States, and the premise of communism's challenge contributed to the inception and intensity of the Cold War.

4. For reviews exploring this thesis further, see Gamson and Modigliani (1971), Kolko and Kolko (1972), Parenti (1969), and especially Gardner (1970).

Misperceptions

If the origins of the Cold War can be traced to mutual antagonisms and to ideological incompatibilities, they can also be attributed to the kinds of conflicts that are precipitated by *misperceptions*. This third alternative sees the Cold War between the United States and the Soviet Union rooted not in conflicting interests but in mutual misunderstanding. In the context of Soviet-American relations, the Cold War is explained in terms of a propensity of each party to see in its own actions only virtue and in those of the adversary only malice. These *mirror images* lead, of course, to conflict and distrust. Thus, some observers (e.g., Bronfenbrenner, 1975) have noted the proclivity of both Soviets and Americans to harbor the same perceptions of each other: *they* are the aggressors; *they* arm for war whereas *we* arm for peace; *they* intervene in others' territory to expand influence, whereas *we* do so to preserve the prospects for an acceptable way of life. Their *people* are good and peaceloving, but their *government* exploits its people; the mass of their people are really not sympathetic to the regime; *it* cannot be trusted; *its* policy verges on madness. To the extent that such mirror images became operative, as they probably did in the final stages of World War II and shortly thereafter, cooperation was precluded and hostility inevitable. According to this argument, prophecies became self-fulfilling. This interpretation of the origins of the Cold War is difficult to deny, given the perceptions that became accepted as dogma. Let us review briefly the opposing Soviet and American viewpoints.

The Soviet Image.   To the Soviets, reasons for doubting American intentions were abundant. The Soviets lived with the memory of the 1918–1919 American military intervention in Russia, which was designed to assist the overthrow of the Bolshevik Revolution. They were sensitive to the fact that the United States failed to recognize the Soviet Union diplomatically until 1933 in the midst of a depression, which was perceived to be a sign of capitalism's weakness and the beginning of its ultimate collapse. Moreover, the wartime experience had done little to remove Soviet suspicions of the United States. The Soviets recalled the United States procrastination before entering the war against the fascists; the American refusal to inform the Soviets of the Manhattan project to develop the atomic bomb; the delay in sending the Soviets promised Lend-Lease supplies; the failure to open up the second front (leading Stalin to suspect that American policy was to let the Russians and Germans destroy each other so that the United States could then pick up the pieces from among the rubble[5]); the American failure to inform the Soviets of wartime strategy to the extent that it informed Great Britain; and the use of the atomic bomb against Japan, perhaps perceived as a maneuver to prevent Russian involvement in the Pacific peace settlement (see Alperovitz, 1967 and 1970 and Alsop and Joravsky, 1980, for discussions of this thesis). These suspicions were later reinforced by the willingness of the United States to support previous Nazi collaborators in American-occupied countries, notably Italy, and by its pressure on the Soviet Union to abide by its promise to allow free elections in areas vital to Soviet national security, notably Poland. The Soviets were also resentful of the American decision abruptly to cancel promised Lend-Lease assistance to facilitate the postwar recovery of the Soviet Union. (The United States later framed the European recovery program known as the Marshall Plan in such a way as virtually to guarantee Soviet nonparticipation.) Thus Soviet distrust of American intentions was presumed to stem, at least in part, from fears of American encirclement buttressed by a historical record of demonstrated hostility.[6]

The American Image. To the United States, hostility toward the Soviet Union was considered more than justified. There seemed to be numerous indications of growing Soviet belligerence: Russian unwillingness to permit democratic elections in the territories they liberated from the Nazis; their refusal to assist in postwar reconstruction in regions outside Soviet control; their maintenance of an unnecessarily large postwar armed force; the stripping of supplies from Soviet areas of occupation; their selfish and often obstructive behavior in the fledgling new international organizations; and, perhaps most unacceptable, their anti-American propaganda and es-

5. Stalin's suspicions may not have been totally unfounded. While still a senator, for example, Harry Truman, on July 24, 1941, expressed the hope that following Hitler's invasion of Russia the Nazis and Communists would destroy each other. He stated flatly, "If we see that Germany is winning we ought to help Russia and if Russia is winning we ought to help Germany, and in that way let them kill as many as possible, although I don't want to see Hitler victorious under any circumstances." Although Truman was not speaking for President Roosevelt, such sentiments expressed publicly by a member of Congress are unlikely to be ignored by a foreign power.

6. Secretary of Commerce Henry A. Wallace, in a 1946 memorandum to the president, asked how American actions since V-J Day—especially American weapons production—looked to other nations. "These facts," Wallace concluded, "make it appear either (1) that we are preparing ourselves to win the war which we regard as inevitable or (2) that we are trying to build up a predominance of force to intimidate the rest of mankind. How would it look to us if Russia had the atomic bomb and we did not, if Russia had 10,000 mile bombers and air bases within 1,000 miles of our coastline, and we did not?" (cited in Horowitz, 1971: 68).

pousal of an alien ideology which promised to destroy the American type of economic and political system. The implied threats provoked more than an imaginary sense of fear on the part of Americans and were reinforced by the unwillingness of the Soviets to withdraw the Red Army from Eastern and Central Europe. The Soviet Union came to be perceived as a military rival straining at the leash to invade Western Europe and to acquire new satellites under Russian occupation. Thus, whereas Roosevelt had argued before the American people that postwar peace depended on Soviet-American collaboration, the actions and anti-American rhetoric of Soviet leaders led increasingly to the perception of the Soviet Union as the greatest threat to peace.

What even a cursory inspection of the Soviet and American images makes clear is that the leaders of the two countries saw the world differently. They imposed on events different definitions of reality. They became, in short, captives of their visions of reality. Expectations shaped the way developments were interpreted—what they looked for was what they got. Hence, even though both countries saw the adversary in remarkably identical images, the misperceptions involved became a source for conflict. In terms of mutual fears and suspicions, it is not difficult to comprehend why the actions of both sides were so often misunderstood. George F. Kennan, the American ambassador to the Soviet Union in 1952, noted that misread signals were common to both sides:

> The Marshall Plan, the preparations for the setting up of a West German government, and the first moves toward the establishment of NATO, were taken in Moscow as the beginnings of a campaign to deprive the Soviet Union of the fruits of its victory over Germany. The Soviet crackdown on Czechoslovakia (1948) and the mounting of the Berlin blockade, both essentially defensive . . . reactions to these Western moves, were then similarly misread on the Western side. Shortly thereafter there came the crisis of the Korean War, where the Soviet attempt to employ a satellite military force in civil combat to its own advantage, by way of reaction to the American decision to establish a permanent military presence in Japan, was read in Washington as the beginning of the final Soviet push for world conquest; whereas the active American military response, provoked by this move, appeared in Moscow . . . as a threat to the Soviet position in both Manchuria and in eastern Siberia. (Kennan, 1976: 683–689)

If we interpret the origins of the Cold War in terms of misperceptions, we can appreciate the role of mutual fear, oversensitivity about the motives of the other, and insensitivity about the impact of one's own action. It is therefore plausible to view the Cold War as a missed opportunity for cooperation. It may also be inappropriate to ask who was to blame for the deterioration of relations between the United States and the Soviet Union. Both were responsible because both were victims of their images and expectations. It was not simply an American response to communist aggression, which is the orthodox American view, nor was it simply a product of postwar American assertiveness, as many revisionist historians have recently argued (for a review of alternative interpretations, see Schlesinger, 1967). Each of the great powers felt threatened. And each had legitimate reasons to regard the other with suspicion.

Theories that explain the origins of the Cold War exclusively in terms of perceptual variables are, of course, only partially valid. They account for some aspects of Soviet-American rivalry, but not all. The origins of the Cold War are so multifaceted that no single interpretation contains it. Indeed, if an accurate picture of the sources of this conflict is ever to be constructed,[7] it will have to include reference to mutual antagonisms, to ideological incompatibilities, and to misperceptions. All three perspectives are relevant, and some combination of them is required to capture the essence of this global confrontation. So, too, are explanations that focus on such other factors as the emergence of "power vacuums" which invited the clash, the pressures exerted on foreign policies by interest groups within each society, the impact of shifts in the climate of domestic opinion on international issues, the effects of innovation in weapons technology and the shift in strategic balances they introduced, and the role played by military planners in each society in fomenting the conflict.[8]

Regardless of the reasons for the eruption, the Cold War very rapidly became perhaps the central fact of postwar international politics. Its shadow stretches across the entire spectrum of postwar world politics.

To better understand the impact of the Cold War on world politics, it is useful to examine the changing nature of the Soviet-American relationship, for even though this relationship remains a prominent fixture of global politics, it has undergone modification.

7. The abundance of authoritative but conflicting interpretations of the causes of the Cold War attests to the difficulties of resolving historical controversies of this complexity. See Welch (1970) for a review and assessment of the controversy in the American academic community.

8. See Sherry (1977) for an engaging and documented analysis which attributes the origins of the Cold War to the planning of American strategists during World War II for the postwar era. This thesis contends that much of the reasoning and rhetoric of the Cold War derived from American military planning during World War II, which rationalized a global policeman role for the United States and identified the Soviet Union as the "next" enemy.

Indeed, the extent to which the texture of Soviet-American interactions has evolved and changed over the course of thirty-five years constitutes one of the most fundamental ways in which the world political system has been transformed. Although international discourse remains littered with reminders that the Soviets and Americans once might have been pleased with the other's obliteration, a new vocabulary has arisen—the vocabulary of peaceful co-existence, of détente, and of interdependence—to reflect new images, and perhaps to acknowledge new realities and changed international circumstances.

THE EVOLUTION OF THE COLD WAR

Soviet-American relations have fluctuated sharply over time, with periods of heated confrontation followed, sometimes inexplicably, by bursts of cooperation. These relations have shifted in response to changing circumstances and emergent situations. Nonetheless, the record suggests a long-term but clear trend toward greater collaboration between the two superpowers over the 1949–1978 period, followed by a pronounced reassertion of hostility and even threats since. Consider, for instance, the quantitative evidence displayed in Figure 3.1. This chart shows rather vividly the high level of conflict which has typified Soviet-American interactions throughout much of the postwar era. It also suggests that periods of relative cooperation have been interspersed throughout. More importantly, it underscores the trend, especially between 1965 and 1978, toward détente, toward relaxed tensions, meaningful communication, and growing accommodation. It shows that habitual discord had been replaced by a norm of cooperative acts, wherein friendly exchanges became far more common than hostile ones. This represented a change of substantial proportions. Relations were said to have become "normalized"; the two superpowers were beginning to act toward each other in the usual give-and-take pattern that characterizes relations between most states. But in the late 1970s there was an abrupt deterioration of the relationship. Return to confrontation suggests that superpower conciliation and détente rest, as ever, on a fragile foundation. While the perpetuation is possible, it should not be thought of as permanent.

Following the trends depicted in Figure 3.1, it is possible for analytical purposes to divide the history of Soviet-American foreign policy interactions into six chronologically ordered phases.[9] Al-

9. See Gamson and Modigliani (1971), Quester (1971b), Brzezinski (1972), Kennan (1976), and Pastusiak (1978) for similar but variant treatments of Soviet-American interactions, which isolate portions of the postwar period into distinct phases or periods.

Figure 3.1
American-Soviet Relations, 1948–1978*

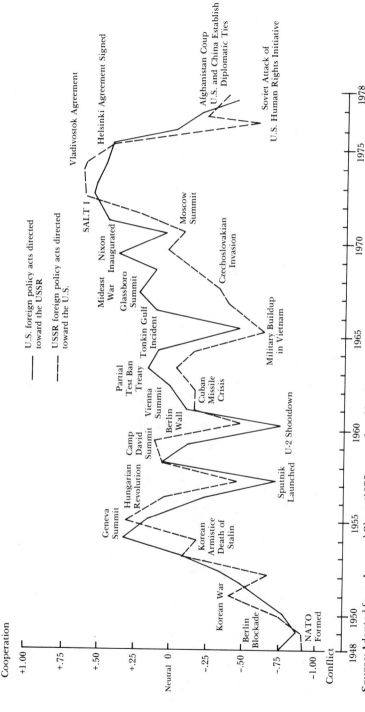

Source: Adapted from Azar and Sloan (1975), as updated by data supplied through the generous courtesy of Professor Azar. The data reported here are derived from Azar's Conflict and Peace Data Bank (COPDAB) project at the University of North Carolina.

*The net conflict index is obtained by summing the proportion of cooperative acts (+ %) and conflictual acts (− %) in a given year the United States sent 100 acts to the Soviet Union, with 75 being cooperative and 25 conflictual, then the index would be .75 − .25 = +.5. If no acts are initiated, or if the cooperative and conflictual acts are balanced (i.e., +50% and −50%), the index is zero, indicating a mixed, ambivalent relationship.

though the periods are necessarily somewhat arbitrary, the diplomatic record seems to suggest that such temporal boundaries in the relationship are reasonable.

Wary Friendship, 1945–1946

Immediately following the termination of World War II there began a brief but confusing period in Soviet-American relations which may be labeled *wary friendship*. This was a period characterized by uncertainty of each former ally about the other's intentions. Part of this period reflected the hope that Soviets and Americans would cooperate to safeguard world peace. Symptomatic of that hope was presidential adviser Harry Hopkins's description of the thinking of the Roosevelt administration: "The Russians had proved that they could be reasonable and farseeing and there wasn't any doubt in the minds of the President or any of us that we could live with them and get along with them peacefully for as far into the future as any of us could imagine" (cited in Ekirch, 1966). The spirit was evident as well at the San Francisco conference in the spring of 1945, which focused on establishment of the United Nations. But doubts began to spring forth, nonetheless, and to dominate discussion in Washington almost as soon as Truman assumed power in April,1945. Indeed, it appears in retrospect (Tugwell, 1971) that Truman jettisoned Roosevelt's policies aimed at maintaining postwar harmony with the Soviets. Typical of the shift in mood was Truman's statement that "if the Russians did not wish to join us they could go to hell." The Soviets likewise began to express their suspicions of American intentions. In short, vacillation, ambivalence, and uncertainty marked the behavior of the two powers during this brief interlude. Amidst occasional efforts at accommodation (for example, Stalin's advice to Greek insurgents either to stop their insurgency or carry on without Soviet assistance), overall both countries became increasingly pessimistic about the prospects for avoiding confrontation. The phase lasted little over a year, during which time the relationship underwent rapid deterioration.

Mutual Antagonism and Belligerence, 1946–1952

The second stage in Soviet-American relations is perhaps best characterized as one of *mutual antagonism and belligerence*. All pretense of collaboration ceased. It was an era in which the Cold War erupted and was in constant danger of becoming hot.

How did Soviet-American relations become so rapidly embittered? Some answers to this question have already been suggested.

Part of the reason undoubtedly stemmed from how each side interpreted the actions of the other. Consider, for example, the interpretation of intentions ascribed to the Soviet Union by American policy makers.[10] In February 1946, Stalin gave a speech in which he "spoke of the inevitability of conflict with the capitalist powers. He urged the Soviet people not to be deluded that the end of the war meant that the nation could relax. Rather, intensified efforts were needed to strengthen and defend the homeland" (Lovell, 1970). Shortly thereafter, George F. Kennan, then the number two civilian diplomat in the American embassy in Moscow, sent to Washington his famous "long telegram" assessing the motivations of the Soviet leadership. The conclusions of Kennan's assessment were ominous: "In summary, we have here a political force committed fanatically to the belief that with [the] U.S. there can be no permanent modus vivendi, that it is desirable and necessary that the internal harmony of our society be disrupted, our traditional way of life be destroyed, the international authority of our state be broken, if Soviet power is to be secure."

Kennan's assessment was widely circulated in Washington and presumably had an important bearing on the crystallization of thinking about Soviet postwar intentions. Somewhat later (when he became head of the State Department's policy-planning staff), Kennan's ideas received even wider circulation through the publication of his famous article in the influential journal *Foreign Affairs* (1947), which he signed "X" instead of identifying himself as its author. In it, Kennan argued that Soviet leaders would forever feel insecure about their political ability to maintain power against forces both within Soviet society itself and in the outside world. This insecurity would lead to an activist—and perhaps hostile—Soviet foreign policy. Yet it was in the power of the United States to increase the strains under which the Soviet leadership would have to operate, perhaps thus leading to a gradual mellowing or eventual breakup of Soviet power. Hence, Kennan made what eventually became an often-repeated and accepted view: "In these circumstances it is clear that the main element of any United States policy toward the Soviet Union must be that of a long-term, patient but firm and vigilant containment of Russian expansive tendencies" (Kennan, 1947). It was

10. It is easier to describe how American policy makers perceived themselves and the Soviet Union than to make similar statements about Soviet perceptions because the American record is not shrouded in the same secrecy as the Soviet record. We must also entertain the possibility, however, that American perceptions of itself and the Soviet Union may in part have been used to justify policies made for other reasons. Therefore, as implied earlier, to suggest that perceptions played a role in the evolution of Soviet-American competition is not to pass judgment on their accuracy.

not long before this intellectual assessment received such wide publicity that Truman made it the cornerstone of American postwar policy. Provoked in part by domestic turmoil in Turkey and civil war within Greece (which he and some others believed to be communist inspired), Truman stated "I believe that it must be the policy of the United States to support free peoples who are resisting attempted subjugation by armed minorities or by outside pressures."

Truman's declaration, eventually known as the Truman Doctrine, was based on a view of international politics as a contest for world domination, with the Soviet Union as an imperial power bent on world conquest. A crystallized American view that took on the characteristics of a "grand crusade" emerged.

> Whenever and wherever an anti-communist government was threatened, by indigenous insurgents, foreign invasion, or even diplomatic pressure (as with Turkey), the United States would supply political, economic, and most of all military aid. The Truman Doctrine came close to shutting the door against any revolution, since the terms "free peoples" and "anti-communist" were assumed to be synonymous. All . . . any dictatorship had to do to get American aid was to claim that its opponents were communist. (Ambrose, 1980:132)

The crusade laid out by the Truman Doctrine was, of course, the Cold War with the Soviet Union. The war became a national obsession, demanding the commitment of many of the nation's resources. (The same was true of the Soviet Union, of course.) Containment became the single foreign policy of the United States and colored everything else, including domestic politics, just as it colored the totality of international politics.

Whether the policy of containment was wise, necessary, or even justified at the time of its promulgation remains a matter of serious controversy among historians. Kennan was surprised and eventually alarmed at the way his famous statement was misinterpreted, abused, and ultimately distorted out of context. He has noted that, upon publication of his "X" article, containment soon became an "indestructible myth," a doctrine "which was then identified with the foreign policy of the Truman administration." But he has also noted the anguish he experienced with the way his assessment was interpreted.

> I . . . naturally went to great lengths to disclaim the view, imputed to me by implication . . . that containment was a matter of stationing military forces around the Soviet borders and preventing any outbreak of Soviet military aggressiveness. I protested . . . against the implication that the Russians were aspiring to invade other areas and that the task

of American policy was to prevent them from doing so. "The Russians don't want," I insisted, "to invade anyone. It is not in their tradition. They tried it once in Finland and got their fingers burned. They don't want war of any kind. Above all, they don't want the open responsibility that official invasion brings with it."(Kennan, 1967: 361)

Ten years after his "containment" metaphor had become American policy, Kennan reiterated that "the image of a Stalinist Russia poised and yearning to attack the West, and deterred only by our possession of atomic weapons, was largely a creation of the Western imagination." But Kennan's disclaimers notwithstanding, the "containment myth," as Kennan called it in his memoirs, "never fully lost its spell." It became, and remained, one of the guiding premises on which American action abroad was based for many years.

The emergence of this worldview and the attendant policy prescriptions associated with it helped to heighten the American tendency to view instability anywhere as Soviet conspiracy. It was not only the insurgency in Greece and the domestic strife in Turkey which were interpreted as part of a Soviet offensive. Nearly all other crises were put into this model as well.[11] The results were in part self-fulfilling, as a seemingly unending series of situations were defined as Cold War incidents, including the Soviet refusal to withdraw troops from Iran, the communist coup d'état in Czechoslovakia, the Berlin blockade, the formation of NATO in 1949 and the Warsaw Pact in 1955, and, most importantly, the acquisition of power by the Communist Chinese on the mainland and the Korean War and Taiwan Straits crises which followed. The Soviets inter-

---

11. Central to the propensity of each superpower to interpret crisis situations as the product of the other's aggressive efforts at global domination was their inability to maintain the "sphere-of-influence" posture tacitly agreed to earlier. When the Soviets moved into portions of Eastern Europe in a heavy-handed manner, this was interpreted by the Americans as a manifestation of Soviet ambitions for world conquest. Yet the Soviet Union perhaps had reason to think that the Americans would readily accede to Soviet domination in Eastern Europe. In 1945, for example, Secretary of State James Byrnes had commented that the "Soviet Union has a right to friendly governments along its borders," and Under Secretary of State Dean Acheson had spoken of "a Monroe Doctrine for Eastern Europe." Moreover, during the waning days of the fight against Nazi Germany, General Eisenhower refused to let the American army penetrate to Berlin and the eastern portion of Germany; instead, the Soviet army was permitted to liberate those areas as a prize for the sacrifices the Soviet Union had made in the war against the Nazis. To some this decision reflected the naiveté of the American government about the postwar structure of international politics in Europe that was being built by the way the war against Germany was terminated. But to the Soviet Union it may have reinforced the view that the Western powers would accept legitimate Soviet security needs, particularly the need for a buffer zone in Eastern Europe which had been the common invasion route into Russia for over three centuries. Hence, when the American government began to challenge Soviet supremacy in East Germany and elsewhere in Eastern Europe, the Soviet Union felt threatened by what it perceived to be Western "imperialist designs."

preted these same developments through a similar set of perceptual lenses, seeing American actions as a series of attempts to encircle the Soviet Union and eventually to attack. Hence, the relationship between the two states was not simply "cold"; it was one of open hostility and confrontation. Relations became frozen in an embittered quarrel with an ever-present danger of erupting into open warfare. Memorandums recently released indicate that in 1952 President Truman twice considered all-out war against the Soviet Union and China (*New York Times*, August 3, 1980).

To be sure, in the heat of confrontation there were moments of cooperation. In this period a few concessions, such as the lifting of the Berlin blockade, were interspersed with the hostile actions. But these were more "cooling" actions for the purpose of bargaining rather than true efforts at conciliation. Both the United States and the Soviet Union played the game of power politics with a vengeance, and both pursued the same goal: curtailing the influence of the other and stopping the adversary's presumed effort to conquer the world. The token acts of cooperation were little more than the kinds of communications between adversaries necessary to continue the contest. Basically, however, each side saw the world in terms of pure conflict: what one side won, the other necessarily lost. Compromise under such "zero-sum" conditions was impossible. Since each contestant projected a negative image onto its adversary, while maintaining a virtuous self-image, conflict was endemic. The strong kernel of truth in each others' perceptions of hostility reinforced and sustained the spiral of distrust and suspicion.

Rhetorical Hostility, Behavioral Accommodation, 1953–1962

The phase of Soviet-American relations described as mutual antagonism and belligerence was not only punctuated by the expectation of general war between the two states; it was also a phase during which the United States enjoyed a clear military superiority over the Soviet Union, for it alone possessed the atomic bomb and the means to deliver it. Then, in 1949, the American atomic monopoly was successfully cracked by the Soviet Union. For the next three decades the evolving strategic postures of the two superpowers permeated the entire range of their relations, and it ultimately altered their political postures toward each other.

The beginning of the convergence of Soviet and American military capabilities led to a third phase in American-Soviet relations (roughly 1953–1962): *rhetorical hostility and behavioral accommodation*. Both nations, but especially the United States, talked as if war was imminent, but in deeds (especially with the termination of the Korean War) both *acted* with increasing caution and restraint.[12] President Eisenhower and his secretary of state, John Foster Dulles, promised a "roll-back" of the iron curtain and the "liberation" of Eastern Europe. They criticized the allegedly "soft" and "restrained" containment doctrine of Truman, and they claimed to reject containment in favor of an ambitious "winning" strategy that would end the confrontation with godless communism for good. But communism was not rolled back in Eastern Europe and containment was not replaced by a bolder foreign policy strategy.

Thus, despite the threatening posture assumed by the United States toward the Soviet Union, more was promised than delivered. Contradictions between rhetoric and practice ran strong. And significantly, in the midst of this verbal confrontation, behavioral changes were beginning to occur. A first step toward détente, however halting and tentative, was taken with the Geneva summit meetings (1955), during which the two rivals established a precedent for mutual discussion of world problems. With hindsight, it is clear that Geneva represented more a pause in hostilities than a fundamental change in policy, since throughout the 1950s the Cold War remained an ever-present threat to peace. More symptomatic of this period was Dulles' advocacy of brinkmanship and his threat of "massive retaliation," through which he hoped to force the Soviets into submission. (See chapter ten for a further discussion of "massive retaliation" and other facets in the evolution of postwar Soviet-American strategic doctrine.) But the first attempts at wider communication between the antagonists were begun at the Geneva conference. And although hostility was endemic and reciprocal, warfare did not occur.

Competitive Cooperation, 1963–1968

A fourth discernible period in Soviet-American rivalry—*competitive cooperation*—can be said, rather arbitrarily, to run from 1963 to 1968. To be sure, the Cold War, ideological estrangement, and the assumptions that supported them (including the notion that the conflict between East and West was irreconcilable) endured, and the period began on the heels of the confrontation over missiles in Cuba and included the Vietnam conflict. And the ever-present, if restrained, hostility coincided with the eruption of an unrestrained

12. That the period was punctuated with a series of Cold War crises and confrontations (notably Suez, Hungary, the U-2 affair, Cuba) is undeniable. Noteworthy, however, was the fact that none of these threats to the peace culminated in war, and that steps toward improved relations (for example, the Camp David meeting of 1959) occurred in their midst.

arms race. But amidst these recurrences of Cold War politics were developments which may be interpreted as the origins of détente. All appear to have been tied to the convergence of American and Soviet military capabilities and the increasing dangers of modern warfare. Some of the major issues were resolved, for example, with tacit acceptance by the United States of a divided Germany and of Soviet hegemony in Eastern Europe. The precedent for communication established at Geneva and later at the 1959 Camp David meeting was followed by the installation of the "hot line" in 1963 linking the White House and the Kremlin with a direct communication line; the Glassboro summit meeting (1967); and negotiated agreements, such as the Antarctic Treaty (1959), the Partial Test Ban Treaty (1963), the Outer Space Treaty (1967), and the Nuclear Nonproliferation Treaty (1968).

At the American University commencement exercises in 1963, President Kennedy spoke about the necessity of reducing tensions:

> Among the many traits the people of [the United States and the Soviet Union] have in common, none is stronger than our mutual abhorrence of war. Almost unique among the major world powers, we have never been at war with each other. And no nation in the history of battle ever suffered more than the Soviet Union suffered in the course of the Second World War. At least twenty million lost their lives. . . .
>
> Today, should total war ever break out again—no matter how—our two countries would become the primary targets. It is an ironical but accurate fact that the two strongest powers are the two in the most danger of devastation. . . . We are both caught up in a vicious and dangerous cycle in which suspicion on one side breeds suspicion on the other and new weapons beget counterweapons.
>
> In short, both the United States and its allies, and the Soviet Union and its allies, have a mutually deep interest in a just and genuine peace and in halting the arms race. . . .
>
> So let us not be blind to our differences, but let us also direct attention to our common interests and to the means by which those differences can be resolved. And if we cannot end now our differences, at least we can help make the world safe for diversity. (*New York Times*, June 11, 1963)

Kennedy did not inaugurate a fundamental change in Soviet-American relations, but in tone and attitude he clearly signaled a shift in how the United States hoped to deal with a potentially hostile adversary. The Soviet Union by this time had also begun to change its political rhetoric. In particular, it emphasized the necessity for "peaceful coexistence" of capitalism and socialism, a view far different from the revolutionary thrust of traditional Marxist-Leninist principles. Admittedly those token moves were a far cry from sustained cooperation between the ideological antagonists, but they did signal a departure from the posture of confrontation that had previously typified Soviet-American relations. Cooperative behavior was evident, however intermittent and fleeting, amidst a pattern of continued competition for advantage and influence.

Détente, 1969–1978

Continuing a process now well under way, Soviet-American relations took a dramatic turn with the assumption of power by President Nixon and his national security adviser, Henry A. Kissinger. Their approach to Soviet-American relations was officially labeled *détente* in 1969. The Soviets also adopted the term to describe their policies toward the United States.[13]

As a peace strategy and diplomatic doctrine, détente was designed to create "a vested interest in cooperation and restraint" (Kissinger, 1973), "an environment in which competitors can regulate and restrain their differences and ultimately move from competition to cooperation" (Kissinger, 1974). As seen from the American viewpoint, the policy of relaxing tensions with the Soviets and of moving toward permanent accommodation and cooperation was based on a "linkage" theory: the development of economic, political, and strategic ties between the two nations, equally rewarding to both, would bind the two in a common fate, thereby lessening the incentives for conflict and war. Soviet global aspirations would be mollified, this view held, because Soviet peace and prosperity would depend on the continuation of peaceful links with the United States. The linkage theory rested on the premise that the Soviets were no longer militarily inferior to the United States.

As a path on the road to peace, the "age of détente" might, on one hand, be viewed as a step-level jump in the relations between the United States and the Soviet Union. On the other hand, because it marked a continuation of efforts by the superpower adversaries to reduce tensions, diminish distrust, and increase accommodation, détente might be viewed as simply the continuation of a process that was already well under way. As Kissinger himself noted:

> America's aspiration for the kind of political environment we now call détente is not new. The effort to achieve a more constructive relation-

---

13. Kennan (1976) suggests that what was to become known as détente actually could have commenced as early as 1965, had it not been victimized by (1) Soviet intervention in Czechoslovakia in 1968 and (2) American intervention in Vietnam: "It was not until the first could be forgotten, and the second brought into process of liquidation in the early 1970s, that prospects again opened up for further progress along the lines pioneered by Messrs. Johnson and Rusk some four to six years earlier."

ship with the Soviet Union . . . expresses the continuing desire . . . for an easing of international tensions. . . . What is new in the current period of relaxation of tensions is its duration, the scope of the relationship which has evolved, and the continuation and intensity of consultation which it has produced. (Kissinger, 1977: 147–148)

Détente represented an important shift of a critical global relationship. In diplomatic jargon, relations between the Soviets and Americans were said to have become "normalized." For the first time in several decades the expectation of war between the superpowers receded. As demonstrated in Figure 3.1, cooperative interaction became more commonplace than hostile relations. Visits, cultural exchanges, trade agreements, and cooperative technological ventures replaced threats, warnings, and confrontations as principal modes of interaction. Part of this change stemmed from the strategic necessity of avoiding suicidal war; part also presumably stemmed from awareness of the mutual advantages that could be derived from collaboration. Presumably good will could cement together a period of peace.

The change that transpired in this period can also be accounted for by growing sensitivity to and empathy for the security needs of the other, by tacit revival of the sphere-of-influence concept and the advantages it confers on the management of conflicts, and by shared concern for the aspirations of a potentially powerful China. The escalating costs of a continued arms race may also have contributed to the development of détente.

"Contestation," 1979–?

Despite these precedents and the careful nurturing of détente for nearly a decade, it was *not* perpetuated. Although the East-West rivalry may have waned between 1969 and 1978, competition between the superpowers for advantage and security (at the other's expense) was never wholly absent. Indeed, the historical ups and downs in the overall pattern of Soviet-American relations have been its most prominent and persistent characteristic. This was made evident as events unfolded in 1978, when a decided decline from the harmony of détente became distinct (see Figure 3.1). The words and deeds each state directed toward the other became more bitter and hostile. Secretary of State Vance's effort to deny, in 1977, that "U.S.-Soviet relations had reached their lowest point in years" was symptomatic of the shift, betraying the deterioration in the relationship that appeared to be under way.

As superpower relations in 1978 took a sudden turn toward confrontation, some observers began to ask if the two states were moving into a *postdétente* phase perhaps best characterized as Cold War II. Those seeing this development as the most probable noted that confrontation rather than accommodation had once again become the dominant mode of interaction between the two powers. Strains in the relationship undoubtedly prevailed. Recidivist outbreaks of threat and accusation occurred. Distrust persisted.

Other observers characterized the hardening of relations as merely a reaffirmation of their belief that the Cold War had never disappeared, even during the period of normalized relations that was called détente. The struggle had continued during détente, albeit on a new basis and in a new style; the differences that invariably divide great powers did not disappear. From this perspective, the terminology of détente tended to mask the enduring, fundamental rivalry between the superpowers. Hence, "détente [was] a part of the cold war, not an alternative to it" (Goodman, 1975).

Gelb (1976) cogently argued this thesis as seen from the American perspective, contending that the Nixon-Kissinger strategy sought "to evolve détente into a new form of containment of the Soviet Union—or, better still, self-containment on the part of the Russians." According to Kissinger's conception, détente represented an attempt to devise "new means to the old ends of containment." When the United States was in a strategic and military position of supremacy, according to this argument, containment and Cold War politics could be practiced by coercion and confrontation. But from a position of parity, confrontation is too risky and containment only achievable through seduction and collaborative linkages which would tie the Soviets in a web of cooperative arrangements, thereby prohibiting expansionism on their part. From the Soviet standpoint, this thesis suggests the possibility that the Soviets might have seen in trade, technological, and diplomatic exchanges a way of moderating the threat of the United States, thereby enabling them to concentrate attention on pressing domestic needs. It may also have been viewed as a means of minimizing the threat to the Soviet Union that impending rapprochement between the United States and China could pose.

At the center of the dialogue that détente entailed was the issue of arms control. The changing strategic balance between the superpowers was reflected in the importance each attached to the Strategic Arms Limitation Talks (SALT), which became the centerpiece of détente and the test of its viability. Initiated in 1969, the SALT negotiations attempted to restrain the threatening, extremely expensive, and spiraling arms race. SALT agreements were concluded in 1972 and 1979.[14] (See chapters ten and twelve for a further discussion of the substantive aspects of the SALT agreements.) With their signing, each of the superpowers appeared to have gained a principal objective it had sought through the process of détente. The Soviet Union gained recognition of its status as a coequal of the United States. And the United States appeared to gain a commitment of moderation on the Soviet Union's part in its attempt to achieve preeminent power in the world.

The difficulties encountered in reaching the SALT II agreement indicated, nevertheless, that substantial differences still separated the superpowers. By the end of the 1970s détente had lost nearly all of the momentum and much of the expectation associated with it only a few years earlier. The focus in the United States Senate during the SALT II ratification hearings on continued high levels of Soviet military spending, on Soviet "adventurism" in Africa and elsewhere, and on the presence of Soviet military forces in Cuba, hinted at the persistence of deep-seated American distrust of the Soviet Union. On the other hand, the threat that the Senate might unravel an agreement (especially after the Soviet intervention in Afghanistan) negotiated so as to satisfy the interests and objectives of *both* superpowers, not just one of them (i.e., the United States), was a matter of concern to the Soviet Union. In addition, the propensity of the Carter administration to champion the cause of human rights worldwide—including in the Soviet Union, which Soviet leaders viewed as a violation of the principle of noninterference in domestic affairs—gave the Soviet Union cause to question American intentions.

In short, the ideological differences between the United States and the Soviet Union, the military threat that each poses to the other, and the divergence of their interests and objectives throughout the world keep the conflict between East and West very much alive. The ability of the two states to bring strategic arms under control—the central issue during the period of détente—seems to have become hostage to the character of their overall diplomatic relationship.

Until the Soviet intervention in Afghanistan in late 1979, the relationship between the two powers was perhaps best described as *contestation*, a label coined by Zbigniew Brzezinski, President Carter's assistant for national security. What makes the term seem appropriate is that it emphasizes the enduring *contest* that remains

14. What is commonly known as SALT I, the 1972 agreement, actually contained two accords, one dealing with antiballistic missile systems, the other with strategic nuclear delivery systems. The SALT II treaty, signed in 1979, still had not been ratified by the U.S. Senate when this book went to press.

fundamental to Soviet-American relations. A contest involves elements of both conflict and cooperation. Contestation thus describes the superpowers' dual compulsion to oppose one another throughout the globe, but to cooperate out of necessity because of their common need to avoid nuclear devastation. The U.S. Department of State clarified this dual posture in an official policy statement released in early 1979:

> Soviet-American interests are competitive in important respects—militarily, politically, economically, and ideologically. Though controlled in some areas, the arms competition continues. . . . These elements of competition will remain for a long time and we must have no illusions about them. However, we and the USSR both have a strong interest in maintaining peace.
>
> Thus, Soviet-American relations will continue to be characterized by both competition and cooperation. The challenge of American foreign policy is to respond effectively to the former and encourage the latter, seeking to foster attitudes of restraint and respect for Western interests among the Kremlin leaders. The process is a long-term one since it involves the gradual modification of deeply ingrained political attitudes. . . . (U.S. Department of State, 1979c: 2)

If contestation described the relationship in early 1979, the Soviet intervention in Afghanistan challenged the appropriateness of the term. Secretary of State Cyrus Vance sounded the warning in early 1980: "Obviously, the bilateral relationship has received a severe blow as a result of what happened in Afghanistan." Shortly thereafter President Carter enunciated a new "doctrine" when he warned in his State of the Union address that "an attempt by any outside force to gain control of the Persian Gulf region will be regarded as an assault on the vital interests of the United States of America and such an assault will be repelled by any means necessary, including military force." The Soviet Union was clearly the intended target of the message, Afghanistan its prelude.[15] Then, in May 1980, Carter described the perceived Soviet threat in dramatic terms: "Soviet aggression in Afghanistan—unless checked—confronts all the world with the most serious strategic challenge since the Cold War began." By that time the United States had already initiated a series of countermoves, including an effort to organize a worldwide boycott of the 1980 Moscow Olympics, momentary suspension of American grain exports to the Soviet Union, and other

---

15. Soviet awareness of itself as the target (and its reaction) is indicated by its statement in *Sovetskaya Rossia* (January 26, 1980): "The 'new doctrine' contains dangerous old political elements."

limitations of the trade ties between the superpowers that had been nurtured during détente.

These developments were interpreted in different ways. To some, they suggested that détente was dead, perhaps irrevocably.[16] To others, they signaled the threat of another world war, or, as suggested by former President Richard M. Nixon (1980), they signified just another incident in the "third world war" claimed to have already been under way for decades. Still others responded with less alarm. George F. Kennan (in the *New York Times*, February 1, 1980), for example, attributed the Soviet invasion to "defensive rather than offensive impulses," and chided the Carter administration for mistaking the intervention as "a prelude to aggressive military moves against various countries and regions farther afield." But to all, the events served as a telling reminder that distrust between the two superstates is ever present, and discord can be overt as well as latent. The dangers to peace posed by the adverse turn in Soviet-American relations underscores why, in Jimmy Carter's words (June 7, 1978), "the relationship between the two greatest powers" is "one of the most important aspects of [the] international context." Its centrality is, indeed, axiomatic.

But its fate is uncertain. The Soviet Union's request (February 5, 1980) for a resumption of efforts to restore détente, joined by Secretary Vance's pledge (March 3, 1980) that the United States "seeks no return of the Cold War, of the indiscriminate confrontation of earlier times," suggests one path along which the future might unfold. But another possibility is suggested by President Carter's warning that "the Soviet Union can choose either confrontation or cooperation—the United States is adequately prepared to meet either choice." This reminds us that superpower peace is neither foreordained nor an immutable feature of our global future. The sequence of events over the past thirty-five years points to no inevitable climax.

THE SOVIET-AMERICAN RIVALRY IN WORLD POLITICS

The prominence of the United States and the Soviet Union in the international hierarchy, determined by the size and influence of their economies, the destructiveness of their weapons systems, and the stridency of their competition, has made their relationship with each other one of the most pregnant forces for change in the global

16. For example, the *Hong Kong Standard* (January 25, 1980) reacted to President Carter's policy departure by declaring that "President Carter's State of the Union Address [marked]. . . a return to the Cold War days."

environment—a relationship that has shaped the nature of world politics for the past thirty-five years. Affected by the conflict are the prospects for reducing global inequalities, for building new forms of political organization in the world, for restructuring the international political economy, and, most importantly, for maintaining global peace and order. Even the prospects for dealing meaningfully with the problems of population pressures, assuring adequate food supplies, and sharing and perhaps augmenting available energy supplies are, in varying degrees, touched by the conflict. In short, every theme and issue discussed in this book is influenced in one way or another, directly or indirectly, by the force and fact of the Soviet-American rivalry.

Identifying how Soviet-American competition is related to each of these themes and issues is necessarily the subject of later chapters. Here we can anticipate some of this subsequent analysis by briefly describing some of the linkages between the Soviet-American contest and other issues and actors on the global stage.

Perhaps the most obvious manifestation of the impact of the United States and the Soviet Union on the world political system is in the structural features that have come to be intimately tied to, and often defined by, the distribution of economic and military power between the two superpowers. The post-World War II era began with the United States the preeminent power in the world, but this situation changed quickly. The world power configuration came to be known as bipolar, with the United States and its allies constituting one pole, the Soviet Union and its allies the other. This power configuration roughly coincided with the periods of Soviet-American rivalry known as mutual antagonism and belligerence and rhetorical hostility and behavioral accommodation.

Periodic crises and the threat of war characterized these periods. By implication, then, we can suggest that the distribution of power between the United States and the Soviet Union not only defined the structural features of the international system; those features also determined Soviet and American behavior. And the behavior was often remarkably similar: both vehemently attacked the ideological beliefs of the other while perhaps becoming a prisoner of its own; both armed for defense and threatened to use the arms to settle the contest; and both sought, in an almost predatory fashion, allies who would assist in the struggle.[17]

17. One can perhaps also argue that the Cold War spurred industrialization and particularly scientific and technological competence in both the United States and the Soviet Union and thus, on these dimensions at least, the two countries became more alike. Some critics have argued, for example, that the policies of both superpowers are determined in part by the political power of their respective military- in-

The principal European allies of the superpowers were grouped into the North Atlantic Treaty Organization (NATO) and the Warsaw Pact Organization. Both alliances remain cornerstones of the superpowers' external policies, but neither may be as cohesive now as it once was.

During the 1950s European members of the Eastern and Western alliances willingly acceded to the leadership of their respective superpower patrons. In a hostile and potentially dangerous environment, the superpowers extended to their clients security from external threat. As the destructive capacity of U.S. and Soviet arsenals increased, however, and as the strategic doctrine governing the use of weapons of mass destruction changed, European members of the Cold War coalitions began to question whether their protectors would risk their own destruction in order to save one or more of their allies. Détente further undermined the once cohesive alliances, for it simultaneously laid to rest some of the most contentious issues of the Cold War era that had been left unresolved and further reduced the perception of an external threat on which the alliances had been formed in the first place.

Resurgent nationalism and renewed economic vigor also made European members of NATO and the Warsaw Pact more assertive on some matters, particularly economic issues. Thus, as the Soviet-American rivalry moved through the stage of competitive cooperation to détente, the international power configuration moved from bipolarity to what may be described as bipolycentrism. This concept draws attention not only to the continued dominance the United States and the Soviet Union exercised on military matters, but also to the far greater fluidity that came to characterize interactions between and among First and Second World nations on nonmilitary issues.

As diplomatic events between and among East and West unfolded, as the characteristics of the international system were defined and redefined by the capabilities of the major actors on the world stage, and, as these characteristics in turn influenced U.S. and Soviet behavior, the Third World found itself both an observer and a pawn in the Cold War contest. On the one hand, it had little in the way of capabilities that might have significantly affected the outcome of the East-West dispute. On the other hand, it neverthe-

---

dustrial complexes. A further extension of this argument can be found in the "convergence theory"—the argument that modern industrialization leads to similar social and political consequences—which sees the United States and the Soviet Union becoming more alike than dissimilar across a broad spectrum of socioeconomic and political arenas. See Brzezinski and Huntington (1964) for an elaboration and critique of the convergence theory.

less found itself the object of superpower courtship. The courtship assumed the form of competition for allies, of foreign-aid flows often designed more to serve the political interests of the donors than the economic development goals of the recipients, and frequently of massive amounts of military assistance. Although the Third World generally assumed a posture of noninvolvement in the East-West conflict, it nevertheless often found itself to be the territory on which some of the most violent conflicts in the postwar period were played out. Not all of these conflicts were immediate products of Soviet-American rivalry, but few were immune from it.

Like the European members of NATO and the Warsaw Pact (and also like Japan), the Third World has become more assertive on non-military matters that are otherwise on the periphery of the major political and military issues separating East and West. That they have been able to do so is in part a function of the evolving nature of the East-West conflict. The essential nuclear stalemate between the superpowers has produced greater fluidity in world politics because the superpowers, sensitive to the catastrophic consequences of a direct confrontation between them, have permitted ("been unable to control" is perhaps a better description) some political events to unfold without their direct intervention.

Another result of the East-West contest was the growth in the numbers of Third World nations (that very number one base of Third World political power). The decolonization process played out primarily since World War II was speeded by the political attacks of the Second World on First World imperialism and by the political alliance forged between the Second World and Third World nations, which effectively delegitimized colonialism as an acceptable form of political organization and control (see Kay, 1970b and Claude, 1967).

To recapitulate, the effect of the East-West conflict on world politics has been pervasive, and it remains one of the most significant factors on which the future of global politics hinges. But the future of world politics also hinges on the outcome of another explosive and divisive conflict—the confrontation between the rich and poor nations of the world. While the Soviet Union, the United States, and others continue to compete over the issues that divide East and West, the Third World has become more vocal and active in seeking to end its domination by the world's rich. The problems posed by global disparities in income and wealth, and the North-South confrontation such disparities have spawned, promises to propel in yet another way the transformation of world politics.

Four

Global Inequalities: Background to the North-South Conflict

> [There is a] ghastly resemblance of the world's present economic condition to an immense train, in which a few passengers, mainly in the advanced capitalist world, ride in first-class coaches, in conditions of comfort unimaginable to the enormously greater numbers crammed into the cattle cars that make up the bulk of the train's carriages.
>
> Robert L. Heilbroner, 1975

> Poverty levels may be more of a threat to the security of the world than anything else.
>
> Henry A. Kissinger, 1975

The drums began to roll on schedule when at precisely noon the Portuguese flag was lowered and the red, white, and yellow banner of Lilliput was unfurled to announce the arrival of the newest member of the international community. Visiting dignitaries from the United States, the Soviet Union, China, and elsewhere snapped to attention with the new prime minister as Lilliput's national security forces, a proud if small group of poorly trained and ill-equipped national militia, paraded before the reviewing stand. Over half of Lilliput's 200,000 inhabitants crowded the narrow, unpaved streets of their nation's capital to cheer the arrival of their new freedom from foreign rule. Little did they know the prime minister had already scheduled discussions with the visiting American, Chinese, and Russian dignitaries during which he hoped to secure their economic, military, and technical aid in coping with the poverty and squalor as well as military weakness that characterized Lilliput. Perhaps in the process he would find that overt foreign rule was being replaced by another, more subtle form of foreign dominance.

To most people in the world the skein of events in Lilliput went largely unnoticed. But their governmental representatives could not be so unconcerned. Already the Soviets and Americans had begun constructing new diplomatic offices in the capital, thus adding another channel to their already complex network of diplomatic linkages with the rest of the world. The decision to establish formal ties was motivated not only by the desire to maintain friendly political relations with Lilliput, whose geographical location made it of potential strategic significance to the major powers. It was also motivated by an economic concern. Potentially Lilliput could become a major source of chromium, a mineral of vital importance to industrialized nations.

The scenario depicted above is, of course, hypothetical. But the events and the issues are illustrative of real patterns that often have been repeated since World War II. Literally scores of new states have been created during the past three decades. They have often been courted by the older, more established nations for political reasons and, increasingly it seems, for economic reasons. Yet the new states often share little in common with those who do the courting. Born legally "sovereign" (while often their sovereign status is politically questionable), they find themselves thrust into an international system they had no voice in shaping but whose organization and operation they perceive to militate against their ability to compete effectively for realization of their own goals. And they are often beset by such overwhelming economic, social, and political problems at home that the likelihood of being able to rise above their underdog status is remote. We can better understand this as well as other implications contained in the story about Lilliput by examining the characteristics of the many new nations which have been created in the global trend toward decolonization of empires that has occurred since 1945.

ORIGINS AND EVOLUTION OF THE CONTEMPORARY STATE SYSTEM

The nomenclature for the description of various collectivities in world politics is imprecise. The terms *state*, *nation*, and *nation-state* are often used interchangeably, and this masks important differences. A *state* is a legal entity represented by a government empowered to make decisions and enforce rules for people residing on particular portions of territory. *Nation* refers to a collection of people who identify psychologically with one another on some basis, such as perceptions of ethnic or cultural uniformity. *Nation-states* are polities controlled by members of some nationality recognizing no authority higher than itself. To add to the confusion, *nonstate nations* are ethnic groupings, such as Indian tribes in the United States or Palestinians residing in the Middle East, composed of people without sovereign power over the territory they occupy. Thus, some nations are not states, and many states are made up of many nations.[1]

Countries of the world are today commonly referred to as nation-states. The term suggests a growing coincidence over time between states as legal entities and the psychological identification of people with particular pieces of territory. Although this convergence is of relatively recent origin, states as legal entities have been principal actors in world politics for over three centuries. Because they are legal entities, states are commonly assumed to possess a relatively permanent population, a well-defined territory, and a government possessing sovereignty, that is, supreme authority over its inhabitants as well as freedom from the interference of other states.

As a network of relationships among sovereign entities (and hence the term *international* relations), the state *system* is generally regarded to have been born in 1648 with the Peace of Westphalia, which ended the Thirty Years War in Europe. Thereafter European potentates refused to recognize the temporal authority of the papacy (that is, the Roman Catholic Church). A quasiworld polity (bounded, to be sure, by location) was replaced by a system of allegedly independent states recognizing no authority above them. Instead, relations between the sovereign political entities of Europe were to be conducted according to the rule of law, and disputes between them were to be settled without recourse to an institution transcending the states.

The state system born out of the Peace of Westphalia was essentially a European system rather than a truly global international system. Moreover, all states—the political units which the Westphalian treaties created—shared equally the same legal rights and duties conferred by their sovereign status: the territorial inviolability of the state, its freedom from interference, its right to conduct foreign relations with other states as it saw fit, and its ability to rule its own population. Of course, this conception also obligated all states to follow established rules for declaring and waging war, for making treaties and forming or dissolving alliances, for exchanging ambassadors, for the treatment of foreign diplomats, and the like.

Although states were assumed to be equal in law, they were not assumed to be equal in capabilities or power. In fact, the international law of the Westphalian system legalized the drive for power

1. See Bertelsen (1977) for a discussion of nonstate nations, and Gastil (1978) for a listing of peoples without a nation-state and peoples separated from existing nation-states. Gastil's listings suggest that perhaps three-quarters of a billion people fall into one or another of these categories.

and created rules by which states could compete with one another for rank in the international hierarchy. Hence, the states that were coequal in law were not coequal in their military and economic capabilities. There were great powers—England, France, Russia, Prussia, and Austria—and minor powers—various principalities in Germany and the Italian peninsula. Some of these major powers, as well as secondary powers like the Netherlands, Portugal, and Spain, began pushing beyond the European area, thus beginning the process of transforming the European state system into a truly global one. The rules of international law that in 1648 justified the pursuit of power by territorial acquisition rationalized imperialism and colonialism as well. The result was the eventual universalization of the European state system.

The Rise of European Empires

The first wave of European empire building began during the fifteenth century, as the English, French, Dutch, Portuguese, and Spanish used their military power to achieve commercial advantage overseas. Innovations in a variety of sciences made possible the adventures of European explorers.

> In their wake went Europe's merchants, quickly seizing upon opportunities to increase their business and profits. In turn, Europe's governments perceived the possibilities for increasing their own power and wealth. Commercial companies were chartered and financed, with military and naval expeditions frequently sent out after them to ensure political control of overseas territories. (Cohen, 1973: 20)

The economic strategy underlying the relationship between colonies and colonizers during this era of classical imperialism was known as *mercantilism*: "the philosophy and practice of governmental regulation of economic life to increase state power and security" (Cohen, 1973). State power was assumed to flow from the possession of national wealth, and gold and silver were regarded as important forms of wealth. One way to accumulate the desired bullion was to maintain a favorable balance of trade, that is, to export more than was imported.

> Colonies were desirable in this respect because they afforded an opportunity to shut out commercial competition; they guaranteed exclusive access to untapped markets and sources of cheap materials (as well as, in some instances, direct sources of the precious metals themselves). Each state was determined to monopolize as many of these overseas mercantile opportunities as possible. (Cohen, 1973)

By the end of the eighteenth century European powers had spread themselves, although thinly, throughout virtually the entire globe. But the colonial empires they had built were by that time already in rapid decay. Britain's thirteen North American colonies declared their independence in 1776, and most Spanish possessions in South America received their independence early in the nineteenth century.

Concurrent with this trend toward the breakup of colonial empires that produced increasing numbers of states, and a catalyst to it, was the waning of the mercantilist philosophy that had sustained the colonial system of classical imperialism. As argued by Adam Smith in his classic *Wealth of Nations*, national wealth was acquired not through the accumulation of gold and silver but rather through the capital and goods they could buy. A system of free international trade consistent with the precepts of laissez-faire economics (minimal governmental interference) eventually became the accepted philosophy governing international economic relations. European powers continued to hold numerous colonies, but the prevailing sentiment came to be more anti- than proimperialist.

Beginning about 1870 a new wave of imperialism swept the world. Western European nations (joined eventually by the United States and Japan) once more carved the world into a series of vast overseas empires. By the outbreak of World War I in 1914, nearly all of Africa was under the control of only seven European powers (Belgium, Britain, France, Germany, Italy, Portugal, and Spain); in all of the Far East and the Pacific only Siam (Thailand), China, and Japan remained outside the direct control of Europe or the United States. But in fact China had been divided into spheres of influence by foreign powers, and Japan had joined the imperialist wave with the acquisition of Korea and Formosa. In the Western Hemisphere the United States expanded across its continent, acquired Puerto Rico from the Spanish, extended its colonial reach westward to Hawaii and the Philippines, leased the Panama Canal Zone "in perpetuity" from the new state of Panama (generally regarded as an American creation), and came to exercise considerable political leverage over several Caribbean lands, notably Cuba (see Easton, 1964). The British Empire, built by the preeminent imperial power of the era, symbolized the imperial wave which in a single generation engulfed the world: by 1900 it covered a fifth of the land area of the globe and comprised perhaps a quarter of its population (Cohen, 1973: 30). It was an empire on which the sun, indeed, did never set.

In contrast to classical imperialism, the new imperialism of the late nineteenth century was marked by extraordinary competition among the imperial powers, for whom colonies became an important symbol of national power and prestige. In the course of this competition the local inhabitants of the conquered lands were often ruthlessly suppressed. As Benjamin Cohen observes in his book *The Question of Imperialism*:

> The imperial powers typically pursued their various interests overseas in a blatantly aggressive fashion. Bloody, one-sided wars with local inhabitants of contested territories were commonplace; "sporting wars," Bismarck once called them. The powers themselves rarely came into direct military conflict, but competition among them was keen, and they were perpetually involved in various diplomatic crises. In contrast to the preceding years of comparative political calm, the period after 1870 was one of unaccustomed hostility and tension. (Cohen, 1973: 30)

Numerous explanations of the causes of the new imperialism have been offered. They include Marxist explanations, such as V. I. Lenin's famous monograph *Imperialism, The Highest Stage of Capitalism*, which viewed imperialism as the "monopoly stage of capitalism." In general, Marxist interpretations saw imperialism as the result of capitalism's need for profitable overseas outlets for surplus capital ("finance capital"). From the Marxist perspective, the only way to end imperialism was to abolish capitalism. The Marxists' interpretations of imperialism differed from those of classical or liberal economists, who saw the new imperialism "not a product of capitalism as such, but rather a response to certain maladjustments within the contemporary capitalist system which, given the proper will, could be corrected" (Cohen, 1973).

Although Marxist and liberal economists differed in their explanations of the new imperialism and in their prescriptions for its elimination, they shared the view that it stemmed essentially from economic considerations.

> The fundamental problem was in the presumed material needs of advanced capitalist societies—the need for cheap raw materials to feed their growing industrial complexes, for additional markets to consume their rising levels of production, and for investment outlets to absorb their rapidly accumulating capital. The rush for colonies was supposed to be the response of these capitalist societies to one or another of these material needs. (Cohen, 1973: 34–35; see this source for an elaboration and critique of various economic interpretations of imperialism.)

But the new imperialism that engulfed the world in the last quarter of the nineteenth century can be explained by political as well as economic factors. In particular, it can be explained by the jockeying for power and prestige characteristic of the balance-of-power international political system which governed relations among European powers for more than two centuries following the Peace of Westphalia. During the nineteenth century in particular, Britain had assured effective operation of the European balance of power by acting as the "balancer," that is, by throwing its superior military power behind one or another of the other European states so as to guarantee that none would achieve hegemony on the continent, for the pursuit of hegemony would have likely resulted in open warfare.

By 1870, however, Britain's superiority was on the wane. Germany emerged on the continent as a powerful industrial nation, as did the United States in the Western Hemisphere. The rise of modern nationalism, which implied not only a sense of identification with and pride in the nation-state but also the quest for power and national self-fulfillment, further inhibited Britain's balancer role by reducing the flexibility that foreign-policy decision makers had traditionally enjoyed in choosing their friends and enemies. The Franco-Prussian War of 1870, which pitted the ascendant German nation against France, symbolized the growing importance of industrial might and nationalistic sentiment. Moreover, the annexation of the French territory of Alsace-Lorraine by Germany in 1871 solidified Franco-German antagonisms in a way that prevented normalization of relations between the two European powers. The stage was being set for the catastrophe of 1914.

As the European powers carried out their competition for power and prestige, not in Europe,[2] but in Asia and Africa, the political domination they imposed led to economic domination and exploitation.

> As in the days of mercantilism, colonies were integrated into an international economic system which was designed to serve the economic interests of the metropole [colonial power]. The political victors controlled investment and trade, regulated currency and production, and manipulated labor, thus establishing structures of economic dependency in their colonies which would endure far longer than their actual political authority. (Spero, 1977: 7)

2. Indeed, within the European subsystem itself, the trend was more toward the disintegration of political units into smaller ones than their integration into larger ones, as was occurring elsewhere in the world. (The unification of Germany and Italy are principal exceptions.) Europe consisted of about fifteen sovereign states in 1871, approximately twenty-five by the outbreak of World War I, and over thirty by the 1930s. The increase in the number of political entities was due partly to the independence movements created by rising nationalistic aspirations, a pattern for the expansion of the number of states that was to be emulated worldwide after World War II.

The State System in the Twentieth Century:
From World War I to World War II

The destructiveness of World War I (1914–1918) led to new demands for the creation of a more stable and peaceful international order. The war symbolized the breakdown of the European balance of power which statesmen for centuries had relied upon to maintain the integrity of the nation-state as the fundamental political unit in world politics. Now the very viability of the state was called into question.

In response to this threat, statesmen set about creating an alternative to the balance of power for purposes of preserving peace— the League of Nations, which was to operate according to the principle of collective security. In addition, World War I and its aftermath set in motion another world-shaping force. This was the principle of national self-determination, espoused by President Woodrow Wilson in justifying American participation in World War I and later incorporated into the Versailles peace settlement.[3] The principle of self-determination meant that nationalities would have the right to determine who would rule them. This freedom of choice was supposed to lead to nations and governments content with their territorial boundaries and therefore less inclined to make war. Self-determination would also mean a redrawing of the map of war-torn Europe so that borders would fit ethnic groupings as closely as possible.

The practical result of self-determination was that it accelerated the growth of new nation-states. The immediate consequence was the creation of six new states from the territory of the former Austro-Hungarian Empire (Czechoslovakia, Romania, Yugoslavia, Poland, Austria, and Hungary). Territorial adjustments were made elsewhere in Europe, many guided by the outcome of popular plebiscites.

The territorial clauses of the Versailles treaty deprived Germany of more than 25,000 square miles of territory and nearly seven million inhabitants in Europe (Carr, 1966). The settlement also deprived Germany of its overseas territories. This was accomplished through the League of Nations mandate system designed to transfer territories controlled by Germany and the Ottoman Empire to countries that would govern them as mandates pending their eventual

---

3. Self-determination was not really a new idea. The cry of ethnic groups to break away from larger entities in order to control their own destinies had been heard many times before among the ethnic nationalist movements of the nineteenth century. After World War I, however, the idea assumed new importance in international relations.

self-rule. In the Middle East, France was given the mandate for Syria, and Great Britain was given the mandate for Iraq, Transjordania, and Palestine. In Africa, most of the German colony of Tanganyika was mandated to Britain, the West African colonies of Cameroons and Togoland were divided between Britain and France, and the Union of South Africa was given the mandate for German South-West Africa. In the Pacific area, Australia, New Zealand, and Japan were given jurisdiction over German colonies.

Many of these territorial decisions were destined to shape the nature of world political conflicts for more than a half-century. Principal among them were the decisions relating to the Middle East, where the League called for the eventual creation of a Jewish national homeland in Palestine, and for the transfer of control over South-West Africa (now called Namibia) to what was to become the white-minority regime of South Africa. And in Europe the punitive elements of the Versailles treaty were legion. Hence the seeds of the next global war were planted by the way the first had been concluded (Carr, 1966).

In the 1930s and early 1940s the world was challenged by the expansionist drives of Germany, Japan, and Italy. With their defeat in World War II, the threat of worldwide empire building receded (although the threat of worldwide destruction increased with the advent of nuclear weapons), and the trend toward increasing the number of independent political units in the global arena gained momentum. The postcolonial era had begun, setting the stage for the North-South conflict as we know it today.

THE THIRD WORLD: PROFILES AND PROJECTIONS

The emergence of the Third World, as the term is commonly used today, is primarily a post-World War II phenomenon. Although most Latin American nations were independent prior to that time, it was not until 1946 that the floodgates of the decolonization process began to be opened. In the next thirty-five years a profusion of new states representing more than one and a half billion people joined the international community as sovereign entities. Nearly all of these new nations were the product of the breakup of the vast British, French, Belgian, Spanish, and Portuguese overseas empires. In many cases the areas granted independence had been colonized only since the late 1800s, when the wave of the new imperialism swept the world. In others the ties had existed for over 400 years, as in the case of Portugal's colony of Mozambique. Today, relatively few vestiges of colonialism remain. Perhaps as many as fifty remaining dependent territories may yet someday become independent members of the world community. But most of these territories have populations of less than 100,000 (Plischke, 1978). In short, decolonization is a distinctly contemporary phenomenon, but as a political process it has now largely been completed.

But the vestiges of colonialism remain, with important consequences for contemporary world politics. World politics today are significantly shaped by the presence of Third World states whose needs, circumstances, interests, and objectives are often quite dissimilar from the older and more established states. For a variety of reasons this dissimilarity stems from and is related to "the gap"— the enormous disparity in wealth and income between the world's rich nations and its emergent poor, between those who have advanced economically and those who have remained underdeveloped or may only now be developing economically. Differing perceptions of the causes of the gap with correspondingly different prescriptions for its cure also lie at the heart of contemporary world politics.

Global Disparities in Income and Wealth

The Third World comprises the poorer, economically less developed countries of the world. So numerous are they that it is easier to say who is developed than to say who is not. The underdeveloped countries include all of Asia and Oceania except Japan, Australia, and New Zealand, all of Africa except South Africa, and all of the Western Hemisphere except Canada and the United States.[4] Some formulations also include a few European nations in the class of developing economies (Portugal, Spain, Greece, Turkey, Yugoslavia, and Romania). The Third World thus contains about 75 percent of the world's population. But it accounts for only about 20 percent of the goods and services produced in the world, as measured by gross national product (GNP). On a per person or per capita basis (calculated by dividing the GNP of a country by the number of people living in it), this means that the average annual income for the Third World as a whole is less than $2,000, while the average income for the First (Western industrialized) and Second (socialist) Worlds is well in excess of this amount. Figure 4.1 and Table 4.1 depict these vast discrepancies in the distribution of the world's people and its wealth.

4. The oil-producing and -exporting nations of the world are still typically regarded as members of the Third World, despite the enormous increases in income they have realized in recent years, because they generally lack indigenous industrial capability and also have relatively low standards of living as measured by nonincome indicators. As these characteristics change, the appropriateness of the label "Third World" will become increasingly questionable.

Figure 4.1
The Geographic Distribution of World Population and per capita Gross National Product, 1976

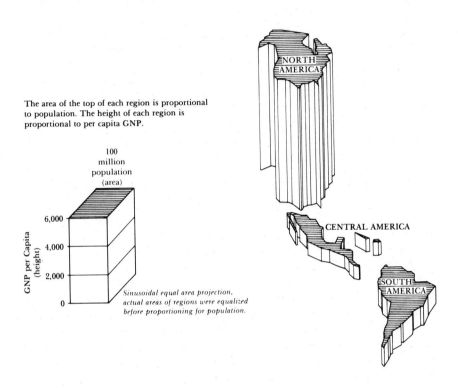

The area of the top of each region is proportional to population. The height of each region is proportional to per capita GNP.

Source: *World Bank Atlas* (Washington, D.C.: World Bank, 1978), pp. 12–13.

The actual discrepancies between various countries of the world are in fact much greater than these numbers suggest. One study puts the average per capita income in 1978 of twenty-nine developed countries (those with both per capita incomes of $2,000 annually and high standards of living[5]) comprising only a quarter of the world's population at $6,468. By contrast, the per capita income of 141 developing countries (those with either per capita incomes below $2,000 or low standards of living) comprising the rest of the world's population was only $597 (Sewell, 1980).

Least-developed countries. Included among these 141 countries are 28 designated by the United Nations as the "least developed" of the

5. Living standards are measured by the Physical Quality of Life Index (PQLI) discussed later in this chapter.

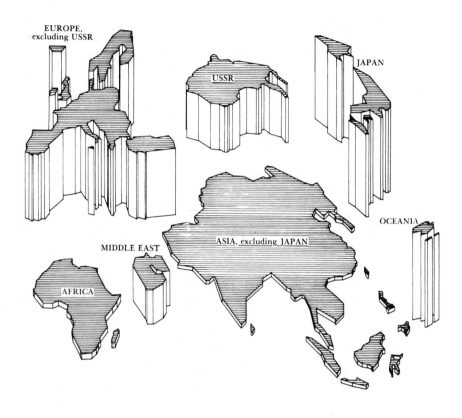

less developed countries (LLDC). Over half of these nations are in Africa; most of the rest are in Asia. As a group, their average per capita income in 1978 was only $233[6] (Sewell, 1980). In addition, they tend to be characterized by a small share of manufacturing in their GNP

6. Caution must be used in interpreting per capita income figures since they tend to understate the value of goods and services actually produced and consumed in poorer societies. It is absurd, for example, to think that an Indian could actually live by consuming no more goods and services in a single year than implied by India's 1976 per capita income of only $150. Part of the problem is that the GNP measures only those goods and services that enter the monetary sector of a society. Yet in many developing societies much economic activity exists outside the exchange economy, particularly in the agricultural sector, where much production and consumption occurs without ever entering the monetary marketplace (for instance, through barter). The problem is compounded by the fact that gross national products valued in domestic currencies are typically converted for international comparative purposes to a single currency unit, such as the U.S. dollar, using fixed rates of exchange (the rate

Table 4.1
The Geographic Distribution of World Population and per Capita Gross National Product, 1976

Region or country	GNP per capita 1976 (U.S. dollars)	GNP 1976 (U.S. dollars, hundred millions)	Population mid-1976 (millions)
North America	7,880	1,877	238
Japan	5,090	574	113
Oceania	5,320	115	22
Europe, excluding U.S.S.R.	4,280	2,215	518
U.S.S.R.	2,800	718	257
Middle East*	2,250	176	78
South America	1,230	270	219
Central America, including Mexico	1,000	109	109
Africa	420	180	426
Asia, excluding Japan and Middle East	290	586	2,040

Source: Adapted from *World Bank Atlas* (Washington, D.C.: World Bank, 1978), pp. 12–13. Figures used are rounded.

*Consists of Bahrain, Iran, Iraq, Israel, Jordan, Kuwait, Oman, Qatar, Saudi Arabia, Syria, United Arab Emirates, Yemen Arab Republic, and People's Democratic Republic of Yemen.

(which means a large agricultural component) and a low literacy level, often with as few as 10–15 percent of the adult population being able to read and write. These countries are among the candidates for designation as the Fourth or perhaps Fifth World.

Most seriously affected countries. Others that might be candidates are among a group of forty-five countries considered by the United Nations to be the developing countries "most seriously affected" (MSAs) by recent adverse economic conditions, such as high oil prices, inflation, and balance-of-payments deficits.[7] Most of the LLDCs are among the most seriously affected. Also included is a somewhat wider range of African and Asian nations and a few in

at which one currency can be exchanged for the other). Because exchange rates do not account for differences in the purchasing power of currency in different countries, cross-national comparisons of income probably overstate the magnitude of the difference between the world's rich and poor. It has been estimated, for example, that a family living in Ann Arbor, Michigan, would require about $400 a month to live in the same way as a family in Shanghai, whose costs in Yüan would run $150 per month, which is only about $75 at official rates of exchange (Higgins and Higgins, 1979: 283). Despite all of these difficulties, per capita GNP, nevertheless, remains the single best indicator available for making intercountry comparisons, even though it tells us nothing about distributions *within* a society.

7. The balance of payments is a measure of the financial inflows and outflows of a country for a given time period, usually a year.

Latin America. The average 1978 per capita GNP of the most seriously affected developing nations was a mere $303 (Sewell, 1980).

The poverty of the LLDCs and the MSAs stands in stark contrast to the oil-exporting nations of the world, whose price increases of their export products have compounded the problems faced by other developing economies. In 1978 the average per capita income of the eighteen oil-exporting nations stood at $5,043; the average income of the somewhat smaller group of OPEC nations[8] (Organization of Petroleum Exporting Countries) was $5,405. Even among OPEC nations, however, there are great disparities in income. Indonesia and Nigeria are at one end of the spectrum, with 1978 per capita incomes of $360 and $560 respectively, while the United Arab Emirates and Kuwait are at the other end, with incomes of $14,230 and $14,890 respectively, figures that far surpass even the $9,700 income of the average American citizen (Sewell, 1980). In part the differences among OPEC nations reflect not only the high concentration of rich oil deposits in the Middle East, but also the much larger populations of Indonesia and Nigeria compared with those of Middle Eastern oil-exporting countries.

New industrial countries. A fourth important group among the Third World is a set of countries which have realized very rapid growth in their manufacturing sectors and have become important exporters of manufactures. The number of countries in this group, sometimes called the New Industrial Countries (NIC), varies somewhat depending on the criteria used. Brazil, Mexico, South Korea, Taiwan, Singapore, and the British crown colony of Hong Kong are generally included. Argentina, Spain, Portugal, Yugoslavia, Greece, and Turkey are also sometimes included.[9] As a group, the New Industrial Countries are essentially upper-middle-income countries, with annual per capita incomes for most well above $1,000. Moreover, they have experienced substantial increases in their annual per capita incomes, with an average growth rate of roughly 5 percent in real (that is, not inflated) dollars for the 1970–1977 period (*World Bank Atlas*, 1979).

The important point about this growth rate is that it means the economies of the New Industrial Countries have expanded more rapidly than their populations. This is essential if developing na-

8. OPEC consists of Algeria, Ecuador, Gabon, Indonesia, Iran, Iraq, Kuwait, Libya, Nigeria, Qatar, Saudi Arabia, United Arab Emirates, and Venezuela. The eighteen oil-exporting countries include the thirteen OPEC members plus Angola, Bahrain, Brunei, Oman, and Trinidad and Tobago.

9. The World Bank classifies Portugal, Spain, Greece, Turkey, and Yugoslavia as "more advanced Mediterranean countries." Cyprus, Israel, and Malta are also included in this category.

tions are to advance economically and are to provide a better standard of living for their people. Economic expansion is also essential in arresting the overpopulation syndrome. Finally, the figure is also important because it indicates a higher rate of growth in the economies of the New Industrial Countries than that experienced by some of the world's major industrial countries. Consequently, the NIC group has become an important market for the major industrial countries that export capital goods. Moreover, the fact that these countries have industrialized is perhaps the most important characteristic distinguishing them from the rest of the developing world.

The impact of population growth on the economic prospects of developing societies is a crucial factor in understanding the gap between the world's rich and poor. Although developed and developing nations alike have experienced unprecedented economic growth since World War II, developing nations have experienced a somewhat higher growth, in part as a consequence of the lower bases from which they began. The average annual growth rate of developing countries' GNP in the 1960–1973 period, for example, was 5.9 percent, compared with 5 percent among developed nations. But on a per capita basis, the growth of developing countries was only 3.3 percent compared with 4 percent in the developed world (Kegley and Wittkopf, 1979: 114–115). The difference is what is eaten up in much higher rates of population growth of developing nations.   .

The 3.3 percent growth rate figure[10] is, nevertheless, considerable. Yet it conceals wide diversity in the experience and performance of developing countries. David Morawetz describes the diversity:

> On one hand nine countries, with a combined population of 930 million people in 1975, grew at an average annual rate of 4.2 percent or better for the full period [1950–1975], and a second group of nine countries, with 220 million people, grew at between 3 and 4 percent. On the other hand, the large, poor countries of South Asia and many countries in Africa, with a total of some 1.1 billion people, grew in per capita income by less than 2 percent a year between 1950 and 1975. Thus, although it is true that per capita income has roughly trebled for some 33 percent of the people of the developing world during the past twenty-five years, it is also true that for another 40 percent the increase in per capita income has been only one or two dollars. (Morawetz, 1977: 13–14)

Annual increments of one and two dollars in income for many of the world's poor lie at the heart of the fact that the gap between the

10. Morawetz (1977:13), using World Bank data, estimates the per capita growth rates of developing nations, including mainland China, at 3.4 percent for the twenty-five year period 1950–1975, and 3.0 percent if China is excluded.

world's rich and poor is not only vast but widening.[11] This can be readily understood by contemplating the importance of the differences between the base levels at which the world's rich and poor begin. Consider, for example, the difference between a 5 percent income increase for a man earning $1,000 a year and a man earning $10,000 a year. In the first case, the increase is $50, but in the second it is ten times greater, and the absolute difference between the two has widened by $450. Internationally this means that each year's per capita income increase in the United States is equivalent to about a *century's* increase in Bangladesh or India[12] (Morawetz, 1977: 29).

Historically, the widening absolute gap between rich and poor has become most apparent since World War II. One estimate (Brown, 1972: 42) puts the ratio between incomes in the industrializing societies of Western Europe and the rest of the world in 1850 at roughly two to one. By 1950 the gap opened to ten to one, by 1960 to nearly fifteen to one. At present trends, by the end of the century the gap will increase to thirty to one. In slightly different terms, this means the average income of an American of $4,100 in 1970 will increase to $10,000 by the year 2000, while the $90 average income of an Indian will increase to only about $215—a ratio in this particular case of nearly fifty to one (Brown, 1972: 43). More generally, it has been estimated that the 1965 per capita GNP of $145 in the developing nations of the world will increase to only $388 by the century's end, while that of the developed world will increase from $1,729 to $6,126 (Bhagwati, 1972: 28). These stark differences are based on projections that in the long run developed nations will realize higher rates of economic growth than developing nations, while the

11. Although this interpretation of current trends is widely accepted, Caplow (1973) presents an empirically based challenge which contends that on many fronts the poor nations are actually gaining on the rich. But Caplow acknowledges that the gap may be widening nevertheless, concluding: "The rate of progress of a poor country, as measured by percentage changes in its development indicators, generally equals or exceeds the progress of a rich country; but the bases, the 'starting places' for growth of rich and poor nations, differ so greatly that gaps between them tend to increase."

12. Morawetz also points out, however, that a 1 or 2 percent increase in income in Bangladesh or India probably does more to increase economic welfare than a similar increase in the United States. This observation reflects the important concept of *marginal utility*, which suggests that at low income levels the net addition to welfare of a given dollar increment is much greater than at higher income levels. More generally, the law of diminishing marginal utility says that each additional unit of income (or unit of resource) will be used to satisfy a less pressing need than the last unit of income. In other words, people satisfy their most pressing needs first. Because many people in developing societies have not been able to meet many of their pressing needs, a unit increase in income is likely to have a much greater impact on welfare, that is, to have greater marginal utility, than a similar increase in a developed country. See Russett (1978) for evidence consistent with this argument as it relates to life expectancy and infant mortality within and across nations.

latter will continue to experience much higher rates of population growth.

Narrowing the economic gap between rich countries and poor requires that the poor continue to grow economically more rapidly than the rich. Yet only twenty-two developing nations fit this requirement on the basis of their performance from 1960 to 1975. If, as shown in Table 4.2, these rates are assumed to remain constant, only a small proportion of these twenty-two nations has a prospect

Table 4.2
The Gap Between Rich and Poor Nations: Can It Be Closed?*

Country†	GNP per capita, 1975 (1974 U.S. dollars)	Annual growth rate, 1960–1975 (percent)	Number of years until gap closed if 1960–1975 growth rates continue
OECD countries	5,238	3.7	—
Libyan Arab Republic	4,675	11.8	2
Saudi Arabia	2,767	8.6	14
Singapore	2,307	7.6	22
Israel	3,287	5.0	37
Iran	1,321	6.9	45
Hong Kong	1,584	6.3	48
Korea	504	7.3	69
China (Taiwan)	817	6.3	75
Iraq	1,180	4.4	223
Brazil	927	4.2	362
Thailand	319	4.5	365
Tunisia	695	4.2	422
Syrian Arab Republic	604	4.2	451
Lesotho	161	4.5	454
Turkey	793	4.0	675
Togo	245	4.1	807
Panama	977	3.8	1,866
Malawi	137	3.9	1,920
Malaysia	665	3.8	2,293
Papua New Guinea	412	3.8	2,826
China, People's Republic of	320	3.8	2,900
Mauritania	288	3.8	3,224

Source: David Morawetz, *Twenty-Five Years of Economic Development, 1950 to 1975* (Washington, D.C.: World Bank, 1977), p. 29; published for the World Bank by The Johns Hopkins Univ. Press.

*Absolute gap is GNP per capita of the OECD countries ($2,378 in 1950, $5,238 in 1975) less GNP per capita of the individual country.
†All developing countries with population of 1 million or more whose growth rate of per capita income exceeded that of the OECD countries during 1960–1975. OECD stands for the Organization for Economic Cooperation and Development. Its members are Austria, Belgium, Canada, Denmark, Finland, France, Greece, Iceland, Ireland, Italy, Japan, Luxembourg, the Netherlands, New Zealand, Norway, Portugal, Spain, Sweden, Switzerland, Turkey, the United Kingdom, the United States, and West Germany. For purposes of this table, Greece, Portugal, Spain, and Turkey are not considered members of the OECD.

of actually closing the gap within some reasonably distant future. For most the process would take literally thousands of years. Such is not a realistic economic or political goal. As Morawetz notes:

> Fortunately, there are compelling reasons to believe that most developing countries will not place the closing of the gap at the center of their aspirations. First, not all of them regard the resource-wasting life style of the developed countries as an end toward which it is worth striving; at least some seem to prefer to create their own development patterns based on their own resources, needs, and traditions.
>
> Second, when thinking of the per capita income that they would like to attain, most people (and governments) tend to think of the income of a close-by reference group . . . [Most] people in poor countries do not regard the rich foreigners as part of their reference group and hence are not overconcerned with the gap. They are more concerned, it seems with their own internal income distributions and their own place within them. (Morawetz, 1977: 30)

Others may dispute this conclusion, particularly given the ability of modern communications systems to bring the vast international discrepancies in wealth to the attention of the world's most poor. Moreover, as Morawetz notes, elites in developing countries tend to be more concerned with the internation gap in wealth than do poorer people. Since these elites are the ones with whom the governments of rich nations must deal, "the gap" cannot be ignored as an international issue.

Measuring economic development and standards of living. Gross national product, per capita GNP, and their growth rates have been the traditional measures used to assess the progress of economic development. It has become apparent, however, that these measures offer a far too narrow description of the concept of development. The GNP is a measure that may conceal as much as it reveals. For example, despite the fact that developing nations as a whole have realized enormous per capita income gains since World War II, this indicator fails to show that not everyone has enjoyed the fruits of progress. Other factors must therefore be considered in weighing progress toward the reduction of poverty—for example, improving the distribution of income within societies, increasing employment for everyone, and fulfilling basic human needs (Morawetz, 1977). Poverty remains persistent and pervasive, and its meaning in human terms cannot be measured exclusively with facts and figures (see Box 4.1).

The absolute poverty in which literally millions continue to live manifests itself most clearly in the material deprivation so many

Box 4.1
An American Student Discovers the Meaning of the Third World

"I spent the first 24 years of my life in South Carolina. When I left . . . for Colombia [South America], I fully expected Bogota to be like any large U.S. city, only with citizens who spoke Spanish. When I arrived there I found my expectations were wrong. I was not in the U.S., I was on Mars! I was a victim of culture shock. As a personal experience this shock was occasionally funny and sometimes sad. But after all the laughing and the crying were over, it forced me to reevaluate both my life and the society in which I live.

"Colombia is a poor country by American standards. It has a per capita GNP of $550 and a very unequal distribution of income. These were the facts that I knew before I left.

"But to 'know' these things intellectually is much different from experiencing firsthand how they affect people's lives. It is one thing to lecture in air conditioned classrooms about the problems of world poverty. It is quite another to see four-year-old children begging or sleeping in the streets.

"It tore me apart emotionally to see the reality of what I had studied for so long: 'low per capita GNP and maldistribution of income.' What this means in human terms is children with dirty faces who beg for bread money or turn into pickpockets because the principle of private property gets blurred by empty stomachs.

"It means other children whose minds and bodies will never develop fully because they were malnourished as infants. It means cripples who can't even turn to thievery and must beg to stay alive. It means street vendors who sell candy and cigarettes 14 hours a day in order to feed their families.

"It also means well-dressed businessmen and petty bureaucrats who indifferently pass this poverty every day as they seek asylum in their fortified houses to the north of the city.

"It means rich people who prefer not to see the poor, except for their maids and security guards.

"It means foreigners like me who have come to Colombia and spend more in one month than the average Colombian earns in a year.

"It means politicians across the ideological spectrum who are so full of abstract solutions or personal greed that they forget that it is real people they are dealing with.

"Somewhere within the polemics of the politicians and the 'objectivity' of the social scientists, the human being has been lost."

Source: Brian Wallace, extracted from "True Grit South of the Border," OSCEOLA (January 13, 1978), pp. 15–16.

suffer regarding such basics as food, water, housing, health and health care, education, and employment.[13]

Poverty in many developing societies is sustained in part by the persistence of highly unequal distributious of income. Just as the international system is stratified, so domestic societies are also stratified by differentials in income, power, and wealth. It has been estimated, for example, that in the late 1960s perhaps as many as 48 percent of the people living in various Asian, African, and Latin American nations had per capita incomes below $75 annually. For individual countries the proportions are often much higher, such as 59 percent in Ecuador, 71 percent in Burma, and 90 percent in Benin (formerly Dahomey) (Fishlow et al., 1978: 176–178). Widespread poverty therefore often reflects extremely high concentrations of economic wealth in the hands of a few. In Ecuador in 1970, for example, the richest 20 percent of the population is estimated to have controlled nearly 74 percent of the country's national income, compared with 39 percent in the United States (McLaughlin, 1979a: 182). Ecuador may be an extreme case, but it illustrates the problem.

As development strategists shift their attention to the task of meeting basic human needs, the need for alternatives to income measures for assessing the standard of living (particularly the level of physical well-being) in different countries has become especially compelling. In response to this need, the Washington-based Overseas Development Council (ODC), a private research organization, developed a Physical Quality of Life Index (PQLI) which uses various social indicators as a means of assessing progress in meeting basic human needs. PQLI is based on an average life expectancy at age one, infant mortality, and literacy rates. The higher the score, the more favorable the social performance of a country.[14] The Overseas

13. See the essay by Adler-Karlsson in Wriggins and Adler-Karlsson (1978) for a discussion, with supporting data, of these six dimensions of absolute poverty in the world today. Morawetz (1977) also considers various dimensions of poverty and the progress made toward its elimination.

14. "Each of the components [of PQLI] is indexed on a scale of 0 (the most unfavorable performance in 1950) to 100 (the best performance expected by the end of the century). For life expectancy at age one, the most favorable figure expected to be achieved by any country by the year 2000 (77 years) is valued at 100 and the most unfavorable performance in 1950 (38 years in Guinea-Bissau) at 0. Similarly, for infant mortality, the best performance expected by the year 2000 (7 per thousand) is rated 100 and the poorest performance in 1950 (229 per thousand in Gabon) is rated 0. Literacy figures (being percentages) are automatically on a 0 to 100 scale. The composite index, the PQLI, is calculated by averaging the three indexes (life expectancy, infant mortality, and literacy), giving equal weight to each of them. With both the low and the high values stable, movement is toward a fixed rather than a changing target; future improvement or deterioration in social conditions therefore will show up as increases or decreases in PQLI" (McLaughlin, 1979a: 132).

Clearly PQLI is meant as an alternative to per capita GNP as an indicator of well-being. The Overseas Development Council has also developed an alternative to per

Development Council classifies a *developed* country as one which has per capita income of at least $2,000 *and* a high standard of living indicated by a PQLI of 90 or more. A *developing* country is one either with per capita income below $2,000 or a PQLI score of less than 90. Hence, the oil-rich nations of OPEC are developing societies, for despite their often enormous per capita incomes, none achieves a PQLI score of 90.

Table 4.3 lists the PQLI scores and the data on which they are based for several different countries falling into different income groups. Although there tends to be an association between per capita GNP and PQLI (as suggested by the PQLI map of the world shown in Figure 4.2), the important point is that vastly different levels of performance are apparent regardless of the income group into which a particular country falls. Sri Lanka is a particularly striking case. In terms of income, it is among the poorest countries in the world, but its standard of living as measured by PQLI is higher than most upper-middle-income countries. On the other hand, Iraq (a member of OPEC) has a PQLI comparable to the average of low-income countries.

The relatively high PQLI of the People's Republic of China is also noteworthy. It suggests that even in the face of overwhelming numbers of people and low levels of economic well-being, social well-being may nevertheless be attained. Food consumption in China is sometimes used as an illustration of this point.[15] Some experts have concluded that the Chinese people are receiving adequate nutrition, and that few, if any, suffer from the poor nutrition characteristic of so many other developing nations. Moreover, the egalitarian approach of China[16] to income and food distribution has prevented the diversion of food from human to animal consumption, with the result that while the average per capita consumption of food is relatively low, nutritional problems are few. In many other countries average per capita consumption of food is considerably

---

capita growth rates. Known as the Disparity Reduction Rate (DRR), the index measures "the rate at which a country's disparity between performance at any one time and the best expected performance in the year 2000 is being reduced" (McLaughlin, 1979a: 134). See also Grant (1978) for an explication of DRR with considerable comparative data.

15. The development of social indicators such as PQLI has been criticized by some since they rely heavily on quantitative data whose quality are often notoriously poor. Reliable statistics on such basics as nutrition, fertility, and even death rates, for example, are virtually nonexistent for the rural poor in many developing nations. The problem is compounded in the case of China, where the government has traditionally shrouded its domestic situation from external scrutiny.

16. Chinese ideology asserts that hunger is a capitalist problem that can be eradicated only by a socialist solution—equal access by all to available food supplies.

Table 4.3
Economic and Social Indicators of Selected Countries

	Per capita GNP, 1978 ($)	PQLI	Life expectancy at birth (years)	Infant mortality per 1,000 births	Literacy (%)
Low-income Countries	176	41	49	132	35
Bangladesh	90	32	46	153	22
Guinea-Bissau	200	14	39	208	5
India	180	43	50	122	36
Sri Lanka	190	81	68	51	78
Lower-middle-income Countries	454	64	60	75	56
Angola	300	14	39	203	5
China, People's Republic of	400	71	64	56	50–70
Guyana	550	84	68	50	87
Zambia	480	41	46	144	47
Upper-middle-income Countries	1,347	69	61	85	71
Algeria	1,266	51	55	118	44
Cuba	810	92	71	23	96
Iraq	1,860	45	53	104	26
Mexico	1,290	76	65	70	76
Taiwan	1,400	87	71	25	82
High-income Countries	6,300	93	72	21	97
Czechoslovakia	4,720	92	70	20	100
Kuwait	14,890	77	69	39	60
Netherlands	8,390	97	75	10	99
United States	9,700	95	73	14	99

Source: Adapted from John W. Sewell and the Staff of the Overseas Development Council, *The United States and World Development: Agenda 1980* (New York: Praeger, 1980), pp. 152–163.

Note: Countries are grouped into income categories according to the following criteria: Low-income Countries: per capita GNP less than $300; Lower-middle-income: $300–699; Upper-middle-income: $700–1,999; High-income: equal to or greater than $2,000.

higher, but large numbers of people experience malnutrition because of uneven distribution (Schertz, 1977).

The Chinese experience hints at how complex the process of development is. Raising a people's economic and social well-being involves the complex interaction of political, social, economic, and cultural factors, ranging from the level of resource endowment and extent of industrialization to cultural norms regarding family size and the ability and willingness of governments to make diffi-

Figure 4.2
PQLI Map of the World

Notes: Each country's PQLI (Physical Quality of Life Index) is based on an average of life expectancy at age one, infant mortality, and literacy.

The 1978 population of the developed areas of North America, Europe, the Soviet Union, Japan, Australia, and New Zealand (having PQLIs of 90 or above) totals 1,052.6 million. The population of the developing countries of Africa, Asia, Latin America,

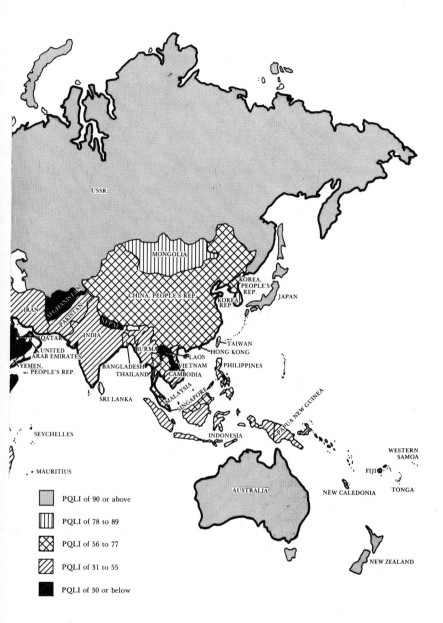

PQLI of 90 or above

PQLI of 78 to 89

PQLI of 56 to 77

PQLI of 31 to 55

PQLI of 30 or below

and parts of Europe and Oceania (having PQLIs of less than 90) totals 3,163.7 million people.

Countries left blank are those for which a PQLI rating is not available.

Source: Martin M. McLaughlin and the Staff of the Overseas Development Council, *The United States and World Development: Agenda 1979* (New York: Praeger, 1979), pp. 154–155.

cult and often politically costly decisions. The relations between rich and poor nations within the framework of the international political and economic system also have a bearing on development.

Impediments to Growth in a Typical Developing Country

We can better understand the multiple dimensions of the political dispute between North and South if we seek to isolate some of the key factors underlying the persistent underdevelopment that is the plight of so many nations of the world today. Hans Singer and Javed Ansari (1977) have identified high rates of population growth, low levels of income, and technological dependence as salient factors intimately linked to a whole range of other considerations.

High population growth. This is easily identified as the single most important factor underlying the widening gap between rich nations and poor. Among other things, higher birthrates mean that developing nations generally have a far larger proportion of young people in their societies than do developed nations. "This means that the poor countries have to devote much more of their resources to the task of raising a new generation of producers, besides providing services of a given standard to an enlarged and rapidly urbanizing population" (Singer and Ansari, 1977).

Low levels of income. This is the principal characteristic that distinguishes the Third World from the First and Second Worlds. Low levels of income create poor economic and social conditions, but low incomes also prevent poorer countries from generating enough economic surplus to make sizable investments in their future economic growth.

> New sectors of modern economic growth thus remain very small, especially in terms of employment, and are often foreign-controlled. The national economy at large remains deprived of new capital infusion. In the poor countries agricultural production accounts for about 40–50 per cent of GNP, while in the rich countries the ratio is 5–10 per cent. Moreover, about three-quarters of the total population of a poor country is engaged in agriculture. (Singer and Ansari, 1977: 49)

It is widely assumed that when so many people are engaged in the agricultural sector many are in fact underemployed, and some perhaps are best classified as unemployed. This means, to use the economist's terms, that labor (which along with land and capital is one of the factors of production) is underutilized. But underutilization is not confined to agriculture. The underutilization of all factors of production "is a central feature of the economy of a poor country" (Singer and Ansari, 1977).

Singer and Ansari suggest that the underutilization of labor is "both the cause and effect of a distortion of the consumption and investment patterns and of high and rising inequalities of income distribution." These contribute to inadeqate investment in education, health, transportation facilities, credit facilities, and so forth. Without this investment in a country's socioeconomic infrastructure, the poor remain poor, and the gap between them and the rich widens.

Technological dependence. Developing countries have not proven able to evolve an indigenous technology appropriate to their own resource endowments. They are dependent upon the richer countries to meet their technological needs. This is especially true of the poorest of the poor, but it is also true of the relatively well-off Third World countries, including the oil-exporting countries, whose underdeveloped socioeconomic infrastructures impede economic growth and change.[17]

The imbalance of technological development may be described thus:

> Almost all world expenditures on science and technology take place inside the richer countries, and research and development are therefore quite naturally directed towards solving *their* problems by methods suited to *their* circumstances and resource endowments. The problems of the poorer countries, however, are not the same; for instance, they need research to design simple products, to develop production for smaller markets, to improve the quality of and to develop new uses for tropical products, and above all to develop production processes which utilize their abundant labour. Instead, emphasis is placed on sophisticated weaponry, space research, atomic research, sophisticated products, production for large high-income markets, and specifically a constant search for processes which save labour by substituting capital or high-order skills.[18] (Singer and Ansari, 1977: 50)

17. See the extensive study, *Appropriate Technologies for Developing Countries,* prepared for the National Academy of Science by Richard S. Eckaus (1977) for an elaboration of some alternatives to technology dependence.

18. The Worldwatch Institute (Norman, 1979) has provided some interesting data on global scientific priorities consistent with the thrust of Singer's and Ansari's arguments. The Institute has noted that worldwide, $150 billion is spent annually on research and development (R & D). About a quarter of this is spent on military R & D, which is about three times the amount spent on developing alternative energy technologies and more than is spent on energy, health, food production, and environmental protection combined. Moreover, only about $30 million is spent annually on research on tropical diseases, maladies that afflict perhaps a billion people in the Third

The causes and especially the consequences of technological dependence are among the principal concerns of Singer and Ansari's study, *Rich and Poor Countries.* A noteworthy result is the widely shared desire among developing nations "to participate in the management of the international economy and to influence the diffusion of technology internationally. . . ." Developing nations are therefore concerned with evolving a strategy for coping with the powerful multinational corporations (MNCs) that have become principal mechanisms for transmitting technological know-how from rich to poor.

Dualism in developing societies. Overall, the social and economic structure of developing societies is characterized by "dualism":

> Most [developing countries] have a large, stagnant, agricultural sector which is linked to the small, modern, large-scale, industrial sector mainly through the supply of resources, both labour and capital, from the former to the latter. The growth of the industrial sector neither initiates a corresponding growth process in the rural sector nor generates sufficient employment to prevent a growing population in the stagnant sectors (Singer and Ansari, 1977).

The reason for dualism in the economic structures of developing societies can be found in their colonial past, when metropolitan powers regarded themselves as the best producers of manufactured goods and their colonies ideally suited to the production of basic foodstuffs and raw materials. This resulted in the absence of "spread effects" in the secondary and tertiary sectors of the colonial economies. Ultimately, rapid population growth overwhelmed the ability of rising incomes in the colonies to produce continued economic growth. (See Higgins and Higgins, 1979: 86–89, for a further elaboration of these ideas.) Yet the hope for a better life in the urban areas has led to a flood of migrants from farm to city, resulting in decrepit urban slums with massive numbers of unemployed seeking work in the small modern industrial sector.[19]

World, but in the United States alone nine times this amount is spent on cancer research. This disparity in medical R & D reflects the concentration of R & D efforts in the developed world. The United States alone accounts for a third of global R & D expenditures, Western Europe and Japan for another third, and the Soviet Union and Eastern Europe for about 30 percent (Norman, 1979:14). This means that less than 5 percent of global R & D expenditures are made in the developing world, where three-quarters of humanity lives. The Worldwatch Institute's report concludes: "As long as the world's R & D capacity remains highly concentrated in the industrial world, the focus will continue to be largely on the problems of the rich countries, and the developing world will remain dependent on imported—and often inappropriate—technology for its economic development" (Norman, 1979).

19. Dualism is perhaps the dominant view of developing nations' economies held by development economists. However, the view is challenged by a group of pri-

The historical pattern of population trends in the industrial world suggests that urbanization and industrialization are associated with *declining* rates of population growth. One reason this pattern is not mirrored in developing societies is that the declines in death rates they have experienced have been much more precipitous than the historical pattern in the industrialized world, resulting more from externally introduced measures to reduce death rates than from the fundamental changes in attitudes toward family size assumed to be associated with urbanization and industrialization. In addition, the industrialization experienced by colonial economies occurred mainly in the areas of basic foodstuffs and raw materials, and as such may not have fundamentally altered the traditional colonial societal patterns. "Hence the checks on family size enforced by the urban industrialization of Europe and the New World operated less effectively in the underdeveloped countries" (Higgins and Higgins, 1979).

Estimates of the number of unemployed in developing nations vary, but the figures all tell essentially the same story of burgeoning numbers of young people entering the labor force far more rapidly than new jobs can be created. The technological dependence of the poor on the rich is related to this dilemma. Because the advanced technology developed in industrialized societies is almost always more capital intensive than labor (that is, employment) intensive, it tends to exacerbate rather than alleviate the plight of the jobless.

The persistence of dualism in the economic structures of developing societies suggests that, even in countries that have emerging

---

marily Third World (specifically Latin American) theorists known as *dependentistas*. Dependency theorists attack the theory of dualism with two major points, explained by Benjamin Higgins and Jean Downing Higgins thus:

1. The concept of dualism, with its division into "modern" and "traditional" sectors, suggests that there are two economic systems operating in (nonsocialist) [developing countries], whereas in fact there is only one; international capitalism, which makes the decision for the whole (nonsocialist) world and determines the outcome in social, economic, and political terms.

2. Whereas standard or "Dualist" economists tend to suggest that the continuing poverty and growing gaps in developing countries reflect failure of developing policies adopted by governments of developing countries, . . . the truth is that the current situation in [developing countries] reflects the *success* of the policies imposed by international capitalism. The persistence of marginal groups of poor workers and peasants in developing countries reflects a consciously planned system, designed to protect profits by keeping peasant incomes and wages down and reserving for capitalists of advanced countries production requiring advanced technology. (Higgins and Higgins, 1979: 100)

Although Singer and Ansari subscribe to the "dualism" characterization, it is clear from their analysis that they also see veracity in the dependency theorists' arguments. Higgins and Higgins (cited above), on the other hand, are critical of the dependency argument, given their analysis of the relationship between the Third World and the capitalist world in terms of trade, foreign investment, and foreign aid.

industrial sectors, the benefits will not be widely shared. In fact, "the industrial sector of the poor countries is really a periphery of the metropolitical industrial economies, critically dependent on them for the technology it uses" (Singer and Ansari, 1977). Benefits will be confined to only those groups in developing societies which are able to link themselves to the rich countries.

> These will become oases of growth surrounded by a desert of stagnation, thus reinforcing other elements of dualism already present in the poorer countries. In this way pockets of growth may develop, but the way leads to polarisation within the poor country, clashing with the objectives of national planning and national integration. This polarisation expresses itself in widening internal income disparities, larger numbers exposed to extreme poverty, and, above all, rising unemployment. (Singer and Ansari, 1977: 37)

The problems faced by developing nations can be characterized as a series of vicious circles, none of which seems capable of being broken because it is so intimately intertwined with a multitude of other intractable problems. That the rich get richer and the poor get poorer seems an inevitable result.

Clearly the plight of developing nations is tied not only to the persistence of their domestic economic and social problems but also to their relationships with the rich nations of the North. We will examine these linkages as seen by the South in detail in chapter seven. Here suffice it to note that developing nations not only depend on the North for technology and manufactured goods, but also for markets in which to sell the raw materials and agricultural products that remain their principal source of the foreign exchange necessary to buy imported goods.

To the extent that the North has become increasingly dependent on the products exported by the South, a system of *inter*dependence between the two has emerged. This provides developing nations with potential bargaining leverage in dealing with the North, as the impact of the OPEC cartel in the world petroleum market has demonstrated. Developing nations generally make poor trading partners with one another, however; instead, they often find themselves as competitors in the Northern market, which undermines Southern unity and reinforces its diversity.

Developing nations tend to trade primarily with the North, while developed nations trade primarily among themselves. Developing nations have therefore generally been price "takers" rather than setters in the international marketplace, "because in the short run the developing countries need the products and services of the developed countries much more than the latter need the output of the former" (Singer and Ansari, 1977). Developing nations have also generally been takers in formulating trade policy and establishing rules of procedure governing international commerce.

The global disparities in income and wealth that divide North and South—and that in turn seem likely to be perpetuated by that division—have produced a highly stratified international political order. In effect, the international system today is hierarchically organized into a kind of class system, with a few top dogs at the pinnacle of the hierarchy and with a far larger number of underdogs forming the base. Understandably Third World nations are not very satisfied with this state of affairs. They have therefore pursued a variety of strategies designed to transform the existing order. Let us examine some of them.

BEYOND DEPENDENCE: THE GOALS OF THIRD WORLD NATIONS

Technological dependence is a critical factor perpetuating the position of the developing nations at the bottom of the world development ladder. Singer and Ansari (1977) argue that "If the technological gap is not overcome the developing countries will remain dependent on the rich economies, and no form of assistance, trade concessions, aid, grants, technical assistance or fortuitous price rises will prove to be of lasting value. International co-operation policies must be devised which serve to remove this fundamental obstacle in the path of development."

Included in this prescription is a list of elements of relations between nations in the context of the North-South conflict, including issues relating to trade, aid, and pricing mechanisms.

A New International Economic Order

Developing nations' policy prescriptions for dealing with these issues came to be known collectively in diplomatic circles during the 1970s as the demand for a New International Economic Order (NIEO), that is, an international economic system radically different from the present one. This demand arises from the relative deprivation Third World nations perceive in their position in the current structure of international economic relations as well as from the persistence of neocolonial and neo-imperial ties between the world's rich and poor. Third World nations see the current system as an instrument of their continued oppression. They would like to be equal to the more advanced countries in the global community in fact, not just in law. The NIEO is viewed as an alternative to the present exploitative system.[20] If the NIEO were implemented as envisioned by the developing nations, the net effect would be a substantial redistribution of income and wealth from rich nations to the poor.

The historical roots of the NIEO can be traced to the 1950s and 1960s, when the Third World, with support from the Second World, began forming a united front for dealing with the industrialized West on international economic issues. These efforts resulted in the first United Nations Conference on Trade and Development (UNCTAD) held in Geneva in 1964. This meeting became the forerunner of several conferences held during the next decade and a half focusing attention on various aspects of the relations between the world's rich nations and its poor.

During the 1964 conference the Group of 77 (sometimes referred to simply as G–77) was formed as a coalition of the world's poor countries to press for concessions from the world's rich. The Group of 77, now numbering over a hundred developing countries, continues to act in that capacity today. UNCTAD has also become a permanent organization within the United Nations family of organizations. Building on the intellectual guidance and aggressive leadership of its first secretary-general, Dr. Raúl Prebisch, UNCTAD has effectively become a spokesman for the world's less fortunate nations.

The issues addressed in the UNCTAD forum (and in other international bodies) have changed over time in response to changing international circumstances. Among the changes of the post-World War II period was the ascendance of three independent centers of industrial power in the North: the United States, Western Europe, and Japan. Because each industrial center has different needs and interests, each has come to respond to the demands of the Third World differently. The United States is essentially a continental power; Western Europe has strong historical ties and cultural bonds with many Third World countries; and Japan, an island nation, is critically dependent on raw-material imports (Burney, 1979). By the time of the fifth meeting of UNCTAD in 1979, the evolving

20. Speaking on behalf of the Third World before the United Nations General Assembly (October, 1979), Cuba's Fidel Castro expressed this view in words commonly used to depict the Third World spirit. He demanded the creation of a "new world order based on justice, on equity, on peace" to replace "the unjust world system that exists today." Under the current system, he said, "wealth is still concentrated in the hands of a few powers" who profit from "exploitation" of the Third World.

patterns associated with these different positions had begun to undermine Northern unity in dealing with the South.

Southern diversity had also become apparent by that time. Different levels of development and differing degrees of economic and political affiliation with the North affected the stakes of individual countries in the outcome of the North-South dialogue.

> Since the early 1970s, for instance, two regional blocs of developing countries—a cluster of countries in South America and the group of countries belonging to the Association of South East Asian Nations—had not only drawn closely together, they had also achieved and sustained rates of economic growth unprecedented in the history of the Third World. The oil-surplus countries in North Africa and West Asia, too, along with some of their neighbors, had achieved a degree of prosperity that was not common in the developing countries. It was the Third World "residual'—the poorest countries, mostly in South Asia and in sub-Saharan Africa—that continued to face the classic problem of underdevelopment. Similarly . . . the Lomé arrangement [discussed in more detail in chapter seven] on trade with the European Community . . . was attractive enough for a number of small African, Caribbean, and Pacific countries to identify their interests with those in Europe. (Burney, 1979: 16)

The net effect of Southern diversity has been to dissipate some of the force behind Third World demands for a New International Economic Order. Yet despite this diversity, and the corresponding variation in the particular issues the Third World may press from time to time, there is little indication the Third World will abandon its drive for a major overhaul of the existing international order.[21]

Political Autonomy

The drive for equality extends beyond economics to politics. Equality of dignity and equality of influence are also at issue.

> Many [Third World] leaders are tired of being ignored, of never being invited to the international high table, or of pressing their views and having them regularly rebuffed. More substantially, many are hostile to the notion that the state system should be organized in its present sharply hierarchical fashion, in which a few with wealth, industrial

---

21. It should be emphasized that Third World goals as expressed by Third World spokesmen are themselves diverse. Efforts by some in the North to characterize Third World demands using "Northern" categories are sometimes criticized by representatives from the South, who see confusion and ethnocentrism in such attempts. For a statement on this matter, see Addo (1981).

and technological strength, and the capability to apply force regularly make decisions that so profoundly affect the conditions and well-being of even distant states. They are coming to insist upon participating in the making of decisions that affect them. (Wriggins, 1978: 39)

Closely related to the drive for equality is the goal of autonomy or independence.

Each state, it is held, should be able to manage its own political and economic affairs without interference from outside: each should be in a position to decide for itself how its resources should be utilized, what policies industrial and agricultural enterprises operating within its borders should follow, and such economic matters as interest rates for loans, rates of exchange, and export subsidies. (Wriggins, 1978: 39)

Just as Third World nations have sought to sever the vestiges of dependency relationships implied by the terms *neocolonialism* and *neo-imperialism*, most have displayed determination to steer clear of the East-West conflict out of fear that one form of domination might simply be replaced by another.

Nonalignment

The nonalignment movement among Third World nations dates from 1955, when twenty-nine Asian and African nations met in Bandung, Indonesia, to devise means of combating colonialism.[22] In 1966, a policy spokesman defined Afghanistan's conception of nonalignment by emphasizing the principle of noninvolvement in the controversies dividing the world: "Afghanistan wishes to be on friendly terms with all countries . . . on the basis of mutual respect. It follows a policy of non-participation in political and military blocs. . . . Our country's observance of the principles of neutrality constitutes the basis for the judgment it passes freely on international issues" (cited in Holsti, 1970).

Obviously this statement was made prior to the internal instability in Afghanistan which arose out of disputes between the pro-Soviet Marxist government and more traditional political forces in the country and which led to the Soviet military intervention in 1979. The statement nevertheless reflects a conception of nonalignment that sees formal association with any alliance as reducing the freedom of a Third World nation. Zambian President Kenneth Kaunda elaborated on the virtues of this orientation in 1964 by ask-

---

22. See Willetts (1978) for an examination of the empirical bases and manifestations of nonalignment.

ing, "What is non-alignment? It is a determination to preserve independence, sovereignty, to respect such independence and sovereignty in other states and to decline to take sides in the major ideological struggles which rend the world. . . . We will not hitch our carriage to any nation's engine and be drawn along their railway line" (cited in Holsti, 1970).

During its early years some of the world's leading political figures were spokesmen of the nonaligned movement. Over time, however, the movement appeared to lose much of its unity and its corresponding political clout as the diversity inherent among Third World nations undermined its cohesiveness. In part, diversity finds expression in the various means Third World nations have adopted in efforts to realize their political objectives, even while they have remained committed in principle to nonalignment. Three exemplary, if competing, means are captured in the terms *revolutionary liberator*, *isolate*, and *ally*.

Revolutionary liberator is a "national role conception" (Holsti, 1970) directed toward the external world. The task of the state adopting the role of revolutionary liberator is "to liberate others or to act as the 'bastion' of revolutionary movements, that is, to provide an area which foreign revolutionary leaders can regard as a source of physical and moral support, as well as an ideological inspirer" (Holsti, 1970). Phases of China's and Algeria's post-World War II foreign policies are examples of this role conception. Others might be found among governing elites who "may find it intolerable to mind their own business when the people in neighboring countries are being systematically oppressed, as in Southern Africa" (Wriggins, 1978).

Elements of the revolutionary liberator role are particularly prevalent among those nations born of a revolutionary experience.[23] In this connection, however, it is interesting to note that the criticism directed against the existing international order by many Third World leaders does not necessarily focus on the exclusivity of the global system but on the manner in which the dispossessed are excluded from a fair share of the global pie. This ambivalence finds expression in the posture Third World revolutionaries sometimes adopt toward international law: law deprives them of the status and rewards possessed by others, but at the same time it guarantees them entrance into the despised system through which they can compete for greater rank and status. The call for the New International Economic Order reflects this penchant for seeing in revolu-

23. It is interesting to note that the United States shares this pattern; inscribed in Latin on the dollar bill is a call for a new order of things for the world: "Novus Ordo Seclorum" (or, translated, "a new order of the ages").

tionary reform the hope for escape from a life of defeat, even while the nation-state remains the dominant form of political organization in the world.

Isolation is another orientation to the predicament of economic underdevelopment and political impotence. Isolationism implies that the way to cope with the external world is by avoiding contact with it. Instead of trying to reform the global structure, isolationism preaches withdrawal from world affairs as the solution.

Isolationism was the dominant foreign policy of the United States during its early history. In the political sphere, isolationism was embodied in George Washington's famous prescription to "steer clear of permanent alliances with any portion of the foreign world." In the economic sphere, Alexander Hamilton urged the use of tariffs to protect infant industries and to promote national development and self-sufficiency.

Until recently, Communist China isolated itself from foreign contact and concentrated its energies on internal development. Burma has also pursued a policy of isolationism. Its leader, General Ne Win, spoke of the fears of foreign involvement of Burma and the country's search for autonomy through self-reliance in words that reflect well the isolationist approach:

> We have got to rely on our own strength in everything. We cannot depend on anybody. We should not try to find fault with anybody. We do not want to quarrel with anyone. . . . Unless we Burmese can learn to run our own country, we will lose it. This kind of aid [bilateral aid to nations in the region] does not help. It cripples. It paralyzes. The recipients never learn to do for themselves. They rely more and more on foreign experts and foreign money. In the end they lose control of their country. (Cited in Holsti, 1970: 270)

Ally is a third orientation some Third World leaders have adopted. The incentives for association with a superpower patron can be particularly compelling. Such ties may produce not only an enhanced sense of national security; they may also result in the promise of foreign aid needed for internal development and perhaps the promise of arms to deal with enemies at home and abroad. Hence, some Third World states may be willing to suffer a partial loss of freedom in return for the material and political compensations offered as an ally of a superpower.

Few Third World nations, however, have chosen to adopt the role of ally. This is understandable, since it runs directly counter to the avowed principles of the nonaligned movement. It is nevertheless true that many developing nations have from time to time chosen to associate themselves with one or the other of the super-powers so closely that their status as nonaligned might be questioned. India, for example, whose prime minister Jawaharlal Nehru was one of the early founders and leading spokesmen of nonalignment, chose in 1971 to conclude a "treaty of peace and friendship" with the Soviet Union (presumably as a counterpoise to India's greatest external threat, China). Cuba, too, has closely intertwined its affairs with the Soviet Union, providing a base for Soviet military personnel in the Western Hemisphere and becoming dependent on huge amounts of Soviet economic aid and credits to sustain its socialist economy.

Most nations of the Western Hemisphere have traditionally been closely associated economically and politically with the United States. Nearly all are members of the Organization of American States (OAS), a post-World War II derivative of the Monroe Doctrine with mutual-security implications.

Other Third World countries have been closely associated with the United States, particularly for purposes of national security. Various Middle Eastern countries that were original members of the nonaligned movement—such as Jordan, Iran, Saudi Arabia, and Egypt—have at one time or another received substantial sums of military aid and perhaps implicit guarantees. Some nations in Asia have been formal treaty partners with the United States in mutual defense arrangements during portions of the postwar period. Included are Pakistan, Thailand, the Philippines, and the Republics of China (Taiwan) and South Korea.

The diversity of opinion within the nonaligned movement was evident at the 1979 Havana summit of nonaligned countries, which was attended by more than 90 nations. As suggested by *Newsweek*, (September 17, 1979), nonaligned countries might be divided into three groups: radicals, conservatives, and independents. Radicals are those generally leaning toward the Soviet Union or China; conservatives are those generally tilting toward the West; and independents are those still committed to the principles of nonalignment in the East-West conflict. Based on this division, only about half of those countries attending the Havana conference could be considered truly nonaligned. The rest would be split about three to two respectively between conservatives and radicals.

Not all Third World nations attended the nonaligned conference. Many Latin American nations did not participate apparently as a way of expressing their dissatisfaction with the Cuban government. The above figures therefore do not wholly reflect the division of the entire Third World among radical, conservative, and truly nonaligned groups. (This should be borne in mind in interpreting the data presented subsequently.)

Because a nation's foreign policy often reflects its internal political circumstances, we can hypothesize that the varying facets of nonalignment stem from different domestic political and economic circumstances. The organization Freedom House has for several years sought to generate comparative assessments of political and civil rights in all countries of the world and to correlate these with types of economic systems (see Gastil, 1980). Examination of these estimates shows some interesting patterns.

For example, none of the eighteen radical nonaligned states was classified (in 1980) by Freedom House as having an "open" political system, that is, one in which political and civil rights, as understood in the Western world, were guaranteed. Each of these eighteen states espoused either socialist economic systems or some combination of socialism and capitalism. Conservative nonaligned states also rarely had open political systems such as constitutional democracies in the Western sense. But they were less likely to have completely closed political systems than the radical nonaligned states. Freedom House classified only one of the radical states as having a partially open political system. Among the twenty-six conservative states, 65 percent were classified as having either open or partially open political systems. Similarly, 40 percent of the conservative nations espoused capitalist economic systems. The remaining 60 percent espoused some combination of socialism and capitalism. None of the conservative nonaligned countries was avowedly socialist.

The truly nonaligned nations have domestic political and economic characteristics that are more similar to the conservative than to the radical countries. Over 60 percent have open or partially open political systems, and nearly all have either capitalist or some combination of capitalist and socialist economic systems. Few are wholly socialist.

Interestingly, the proportion of nonaligned conservative countries in which the military is either in charge of the government or is a dominant force in the society is little different from among the radicals. In fact, there is little appreciable difference among the three groups.

THE PRIMACY OF POLITICS: DOMESTIC OR INTERNATIONAL?

Just as nonalignment is a Third World foreign-policy posture designed to maximize foreign-policy objectives in relation to the East-West dispute, differing interpretations of that posture by Third

World elites appear to reflect the often sharply divergent domestic situations they face. Varying degrees of industrialization and economic development are among these differences. Different cultures and traditions, and varying threats of internal instability arising from religious and ethnic differences must also be weighed—for these, too, are among the numerous dimensions of the relentless diversity that characterize the Third World.

The political elites of Third World countries have diverse perceptions of threats to the physical security or national integrity of their nations. For some the principal threat is internal—a lack of identity with the nation, or the threats of separatism, insurrection, and insurgency. For others, the primary threat is external—a powerful and dynamic neighbor, or one that might become so. If threats are perceived, the incentive for seeking external military assistance is great.

Under such circumstances, the East-West and the North-South conflicts are often not of importance to the governing elites. To be sure, either might be used to solidify support at home. W. Howard Wriggins, the American ambassador to Sri Lanka, observed that: "When David stands up to Goliath, public, bureaucratic, and often military support at home are quickly generated, even if such actions may provoke certain difficulties in foreign political or even economic relations" (Wriggins, 1978). Still, we must entertain the possibility that, for many Third World leaders, foreign policy does not assume primacy. Wriggins maintains that: "Most Third World leaders do not focus their main attention on North-South relations. For them, such issues are often derivative of other goals and preoccupations" (Wriggins, 1978). It is fair to assume, then, that domestic economic and political issues are among the preoccupations of most Third World governing elites.

Having emphasized Third World diversity, it is important to reemphasize its common characteristics and experiences. In varying degrees Third World nations experience poverty, disease, hunger, and a lack of hope. Their societies are vastly dissimilar from the opulent and affluent societies of those nations once—and perhaps still—controlling them. This reality not only defines the current international position of the Third World, but it also conditions Third World efforts to transform the global political order.

The North-South conflict is multifaceted, complex, and potentially explosive. Present and growing discrepancies between rich countries and poor operate as sources of instability and, ultimately perhaps, violence. Two facts—that those most afflicted have had their consciousness raised about the extent of their deprivation and that they have joined together to seek collectively a fundamental restructuring of the globe's political and economic order—guarantee that the North-South conflict will serve as a continuing force for the transformation of world politics. That these same nations are rapidly acquiring the military capabilities to resolve some of their long-standing frustrations adds a new dimension to the conflict and to the urgency of finding and implementing global solutions.

Five

The Rise of Nonstate Actors:
International Organizations
and Multinational Corporations

> The problems which face mankind are now, in the
> main, common to all nations and all areas, and it is
> not possible to resolve them any more by purely
> national, or even regional, responses.
>
> Kurt Waldheim, 1975

> The annual growth rate of IBM . . . at home and
> abroad for the past decade has been sufficiently
> great so that, if it continues uninterrupted for
> another generation, IBM will be the largest single
> economic entity in the world, including the en-
> tities of nation-states.
>
> Robert L. Heilbroner, 1977

Nation-states are the dominant form of political organization in the
world, and their interests, objectives, and capabilities significantly
shape the contours of world politics. But no mapping of the global
political terrain would be complete without locating the role played
by an increasing number of nonstate actors. Transnational political
movements such as the Palestine Liberation Organization; political
parties such as the Social Democrats in the countries of Western
Europe; religious groups such as the Roman Catholic Church; international governmental and nongovernmental organizations like the
United Nations and the International Olympic Committee; and multinational business enterprises such as Exxon and IBM—all have become part of the global topography.

Despite the obvious diversity among these groups, all reflect a
common desire to accomplish their goals by acting transnationally
as well as working within the confines of geographically defined national units. This is obviously the case for the Palestine Liberation
Organization, whose goal is the realization of a national homeland.
But it is also true of the Roman Catholic Church, whose transna-

tional links as well as national hierarchies enable it to spread its religious and moral messages. Even multinational corporations such as IBM and Exxon, whose goals are profit maximization wherever that might best be accomplished, think of themselves as extraterritorial.

This chapter will focus on the historical growth of nonstate actors, the way in which they are used by states to accomplish perceived national interests, and the question of whether these actors have become important agents in their own right, agents beyond the nation-state in the transformation of world politics.

THE GROWTH OF INTERNATIONAL ORGANIZATIONS

There are two principal types of international organizations, those of which governments are members and those comprising private individuals and groups. Neither type is peculiar to the twentieth century. The first modern international intergovernmental organization (IGO), the Central Commission for the Navigation of the Rhine, was established over a century and a half ago by the Congress of Vienna (1815), and the Rosicrucian Order established in 1694 fits contemporary definitions of international nongovernmental organizations (INGOs) (Skjelsbaek, 1971). The number of both types of organizations grew substantially in the half-century prior to World War I, primarily in response to the growth in transnational commerce and communications that accompanied industrialization. On the eve of World War I forty-nine IGOs and over 170 INGOs were in existence (Wallace and Singer, 1970: 272; and *Yearbook of International Organizations, 1978*).

The number of international organizations grew even more sharply after each of the two world wars (see Figure 5.1). In 1940 there were over 80 governmental and close to 500 nongovernmental organizations. By the mid-1970s these numbers had increased to roughly 300 and 2,400 respectively (Wallace and Singer, 1970: 272; Feld, 1979: 258; *Yearbook of International Organizations, 1978*).

Although nearly 90 percent of present international organizations are nongovernmental, the remaining 10 percent are generally more important[1] because nation-states are the principal centers of

---

1. These figures imply that it is easier to identify international organizations than is in fact the case. In principle, IGOs are delimited by a formal set of qualifying characteristics:

> An international governmental organization is an institutional structure created by agreement among two or more sovereign states for the conduct of regular political interactions. IGOs are distinguished from the facilities of traditional diplomacy by their structure and permanence. International governmental organizations have meetings of representatives of the member states at relatively regular intervals, specified procedures for making decisions, and a perma-

Figure 5.1
The Number of International Governmental Organizations, 1815–1976

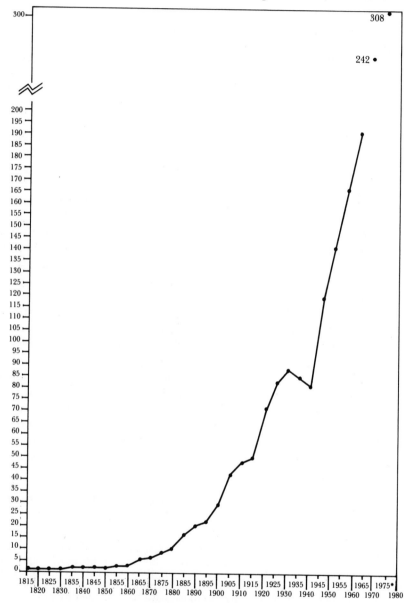

Beginning Year of Each Period

Source: 1815–1960: Michael Wallace and J. David Singer, "Intergovernmental Organization in the Global System, 1915–1964: A Quantitative Description," *International Organization* 24 (Spring 1970), 277; 1970 and 1976: *Yearbook of International Organizations, 1978* (Brussels: Union of International Associations, 1978), n.p.
*Data are for 1976.

authority and legitimacy in the contemporary world. As Jacobson observes:

> Authoritative policies are more frequently made in and applied by governmental than by nongovernmental institutions; consequently in most political systems the former are more important than the latter. But the global system accords even greater importance to governmental institutions than is usually the case. States are the primary focal points of political activity in the modern world, and IGOs presently derive their importance from their character as associations of states. (Jacobson, 1979: 8)

Given this distinction, it is useful to think of INGOs as intersocietal organizations that play a role in facilitating the achievement and maintenance of agreements among governments regarding the elements of international public policy (Jacobson, 1979).

One product of this growth has been the emergence of an incredibly complex network of overlapping national memberships in transnational associations. In 1977, for example, the United States had over 1,200 national representations in international organizations, which was a third more than it had only a decade earlier. A recent study by the Union of International Associations (*Yearbook of International Organizations, 1978*) put the number of national representations of 111 countries in 2,112 international organizations at nearly 55,000. These are truly "networks of interdependence" (Jacobson, 1979) even though they often reflect greater or lesser degrees of conflict as well as cooperation.

These networks span the entire panoply of activities associated with modern societies, from sports and the arts to the social and physical sciences, from law and social welfare to finance, industry, and transportation. In the twentieth century these transnational associations have also come to deal with power politics and national security. Each of the world wars was followed by a concerted attempt to create new international institutions and procedures to

---

nent secretariat or headquarters staff. In some ways IGOs resemble governments, but they are not governments, for the capacity for action continues to rest predominantly with the constituent units, the member states. IGOs can be viewed as permanent networks linking states. (Jacobson, 1979: 8–9)

If, however, the permanence, regularly scheduled meetings, or some other criterion were eased, the number of IGOs in existence would far surpass the roughly 300 cited above (see *Yearbook of International Organizations, 1978*, especially section B, which describes numerous transnational entities that have some characteristics of IGOs). Furthermore, some international organizations have been created by others, and thus do not fit the definition specified above although clearly they are international organizations.

In principle, INGOs are easier to define than IGOs, since the Economic and Social Council (ECOSOC) of the United Nations has followed the practice of granting these organizations consultative status before the council. Again, however, there is reason to believe that the number of INGOs actually in existence is far greater than the number captured by their ECOSOC status.

deal with threats to the peace. The first, the League of Nations, was designed to prevent a recurrence of the catastrophe of 1914–1918 by replacing the concept of the balance of power with the concept of collective security. When collective security failed to restrain states from waging war unilaterally, the League floundered and, by the end of the 1930s, global conflict had broken out again. But planning for a second attempt at peacemaking through an international institution whose purpose was to prevent a similar disaster from occurring began after the onset of World War II. Thus the primary responsibility of the new United Nations organization, which came into existence with the end of World War II in 1945, was the maintenance of international peace and security.

The United Nations is special among the relatively small group of international governmental organizations for several reasons. In principle, the United Nations is a universal membership organization. With the seating of the People's Republic of China and the admission of East and West Germany to the world body in the early 1970s, the United Nations nearly achieved in practice the principle of universality.[2] Also, in carrying out many of its economic and social activities, the United Nations relies heavily on nongovernmental organizations, and hence the line between governmental and nongovernmental functions can become blurred. Examples can be found in the work of the United Nations Children's Fund (UNICEF), the United Nations Fund for Population Activities (UNFPA), and the United Nations University.

The United Nations is a multiple-purpose organization, partly because of its universality of membership. As stated in Article 1 of the United Nations Charter, the purposes of the organization are "to maintain international peace and security"; "to develop friendly relations among nations based on respect for the principle of equal rights and self-determination of peoples"; "to achieve international co-operation in solving international problems of an economic, social, cultural, or humanitarian character, and in promoting and encouraging respect for human rights and for fundamental freedoms for all"; and "to be a centre for harmonizing the actions of nations in the attainment of these common ends." These ideals have carried the United Nations into nearly every corner of the complex network of relations among states. Its conference machinery has become permanent; the organization has provided a mechanism for international conflict management; and it has become involved in a welter of nonsecurity welfare issues in the global arena.

2. North and South Korea are still not members of the United Nations due to the perpetuation of the East-West conflict, which has effectively barred both from membership. Most other states that do not belong, such as Switzerland, are not members by their own choice.

No other IGO can claim the same extensiveness of purpose and membership as the United Nations. In fact, if IGOs are divided along these two dimensions, most are found to be limited-purpose, limited-membership organizations. Using these criteria, one recent study categorized 96 percent of the 289 IGOs existing in 1970 as specific-purpose organizations. Among these, two-thirds were limited-membership, specific-purpose organizations. Only twelve qualified as general-purpose organizations, and only the United Nations approximated universal membership (Jacobson, 1979: 52).

Figure 5.2 provides examples of IGOs classified using criteria analogous to those just described.[3] Clearly there is great variation among the organizations falling into each category, particularly the single-purpose, limited-membership quadrant. The North Atlantic Treaty Organization (NATO), for example, is primarily a military alliance, while others in this category (such as the Nordic Council) are concerned both with conflict resolution and economic cooperation and hence might be regarded as "political" IGOs. In fact, the vast majority of IGOs are concerned with a relatively narrow range of social and economic matters, such as trade integration, common functional services, and other types of economic and social cooperation (Wittkopf, 1972). In this sense IGOs are agents as well as reflections of growing social and economic interdependence.

INGOs are even more difficult to classify than IGOs. The Union

Figure 5.2
A Simple Classification of International Governmental Organizations
Range of Stated Purpose

		Multiple purpose	Single purpose
Geographic scope of membership	Global	United Nations	World Health Organization International Labor Organization
	Inter-regional, regional, sub-regional	Organization of American States Organization of African Unity League of Arab States Association of Southeast Asian Nations	European Economic Community Nordic Council North Atlantic Treaty Organization International Olive Oil Council International North Pacific Fisheries Commission

Source: Adapted from Eugene R. Wittkopf, "A Statistical Classification of International Inter-Governmental Organizations." Paper presented at the Annual Meeting of the International Studies Association, Dallas, Texas, March 15–18, 1972.

3. For an elaboration of the criteria that might be used to classify IGOs, see Angell (1965), Jacobson (1979), Nye (1971), Pentland (1976), Plano and Riggs (1967), Wittkopf (1972), and Jordan (1980).

Table 5.1
International Nongovernmental Organizations, 1909–1976

Category	1909	1954	1956	1958	1960	1962	1964	1966	1968	1970	1972	1976
Bibliography, documentation, press	19	29	26	33	34	41	54	58	69	63	72	77
Religion, ethics	21	79	70	79	87	86	87	93	103	109	112	129
Social sciences, humanistic studies	10	38	57	55	57	57	67	80	90	95	104	133
International relations	12	83	61	71	92	99	106	111	125	127	144	132
Politics	3	12	13	14	17	15	14	15	22	22	27	30
Law, administration	13	31	28	30	37	42	45	48	54	54	58	45
Social welfare	10	52	52	53	56	64	70	76	88	95	104	120
Professions, employers	2	56	67	67	73	76	78	93	105	112	119	132
Trade unions	1	49	48	49	54	54	59	63	70	70	70	67
Economics, finance	3	14	15	16	26	30	33	35	40	45	47	56
Commerce, industry	5	116	123	134	163	160	168	211	233	239	251	273
Agriculture	5	32	27	34	46	55	64	76	83	83	88	105
Transport, travel	5	28	40	43	57	57	63	72	76	82	89	93
Technology	8	34	36	50	60	63	70	83	102	113	133	147
Science	21	81	69	77	83	92	118	137	152	174	184	190
Health, medicine	16	101	100	104	123	133	150	173	214	225	256	306
Education, youth	10	54	56	62	68	71	83	91	105	106	116	134
Arts, literature, radio, cinema, TV	6	41	34	34	57	57	65	70	75	80	80	93
Sport, recreation	6	67	51	55	65	72	76	90	93	99	110	119
Total	176	997	973	1060	1255	1324	1470	1675	1899	1993	2164	2381

Source: *Yearbook of International Organizations, 1978* (Brussels: Union of International Associations, 1978), n.p.

of International Associations (itself an INGO) maintains the most comprehensive, up-to-date information about INGOs. Table 5.1 shows the variety of activities engaged in by INGOs, as well as their growth. These data indicate the greatest growth of INGOs in the postwar period has occurred among those organizations involved in activities of direct concern to governments, namely, economic matters such as industry, commerce, finance, and technology, and not among those concerned with essentially noneconomic matters, such as sports and religious affairs. INGOs are thus likely to have their greatest impact in advanced industrial states (Feld, 1972), such as the United States and the member countries of the European Community, since these are most likely to involve private-interest groups in the national policy-making process.

Not surprisingly, therefore, the membership composition of INGOs tends to weigh more heavily in favor of the Northern industrialized states than of the Southern developing states. Reflecting a characteristic of so many other aspects of international politics, this is also true of national memberships in IGOs (Jacobson, 1979).

Before examining further the impact of international organizations on world politics, we should first ask in what ways states have influenced international organizations. How have they used these instruments, often of their own making, to realize their foreign policy interests and objectives? The historical evolution of the East-West and North-South conflicts as reflected in the United Nations provides insight.

THE UNITED NATIONS: BETWEEN EAST AND WEST, NORTH AND SOUTH

The United Nations as originally conceived was an organization of the victorious allies of World War II. The term itself can be traced to the Atlantic Charter signed by the United States and Great Britain in 1941, in which reference was made to a postwar international organization, and specifically to the Declaration by United Nations signed by twenty-six allied nations in January 1942 (Bennett, 1980).

Given its origins, it is not surprising that "maintenance of international peace and security" headed the list of the new organization's purposes. Primary responsibility for this task was lodged in the Security Council, consisting of eleven members; the council was expanded to fifteen members in 1965, and there has been some pressure for further expansion in order to give Japan and the Federal Republic of Germany permanent membership. The five allied powers principally engaged in the war against Germany and Japan—the United States, the Soviet Union, Britain, France, and China—were made permanent members of the Security Council and given a veto over council actions. This formula reflected the assumption that postwar peace could be maintained only if the great powers, acting in concert, continued to support the principle of collective security. Hence, unanimity was assumed to be essential. Because postwar peace was assumed to depend on the agreement of the great powers, any lack of agreement in the Security Council was viewed as a signal that the ingredient necessary for the resolution of a particular conflict was lacking.

However, the Security Council became quickly ensnarled in the emerging Cold War between the United States and the Soviet Union. Time and again the Soviet Union, unable to mobilize a majority on its side, exercised its veto power to prevent council action on matters with which it disagreed. Thus, what was conceived to be the most important body within the United Nations often became paralyzed, and the new organization's ability to enforce the principle of collective security was severely restricted.

The Security Council is but one of six principal organs established by the United Nations Charter (see Figure 5.3). Among the others, the General Assembly is the only body in which all member states are represented, and all decisions there are made according to majority rule, with no state given a veto. Unlike the Security Council, which was given the power to take action, including the use of force, the General Assembly was only given the power to recommend. But that limited mandate has turned out to be substantial.

Unforeseen by the founders of the United Nations, the power to recommend has made the General Assembly a partner with the Security Council in issues of peace and security and has also made it the primary body responsible for social and economic problems. The scope of this involvement is reflected in the complexity of the United Nations itself. The United Nations today is not one organization, but a conglomerate of countless committees, bureaus, boards, commissions, centers, institutes, offices, and organizations. Some of these are shown in Figure 5.3, but the reality of the United Nations is far less orderly than this diagram suggests.

The proliferation of United Nations bodies and activities reflects the forces underlying the growth of international organizations generally. It also reflects specifically the way states have used the United Nations to accomplish their own objectives. Third World nations, who have combined their growing numbers under the one-state, one-vote rules of the General Assembly, have increasingly fostered United Nations involvement in areas of particular concern to them. But it was not always that way. To many the United Nations was once American-dominated. The reasons underlying the evolution of the United Nations from a Western-dominated political or-

Figure 5.3 The United Nations System

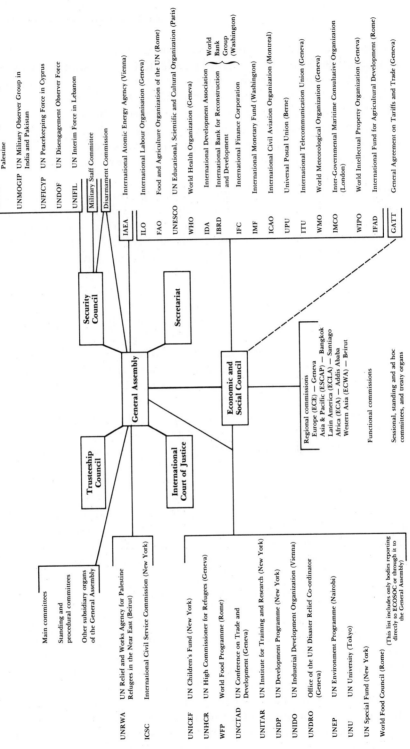

Source: United Nations Office of Public Information.

ganization to a Third World and socialist-bloc-dominated organization are instructive.

Evolving Political Strategies in the Security Council and the General Assembly

In June, 1950, North Korea launched a surprise attack against South Korea. The Security Council was called into session and quickly adopted a resolution supporting the use of force by the United Nations to repel the North Korean onslaught.

Because the Security Council authorized military force against the communist aggression, the defense of South Korea technically became a UN "police action" that bore some resemblance to collective security. Command of the UN forces, however, was exercised by the United States, which also supplied the bulk of the manpower, money, and matériel. It did so because combating the North Korean advance was consistent with the American Cold War objective of containing communism. Consequently, the Korean police action came to be regarded as primarily an American military operation aimed against the Soviet Union and the People's Republic of China and not an instance of effective collective security exercised by the world community (although it is true that many UN members nominally supported the American action).

More importantly, the Korean action was made possible by unique circumstances—the absence of the Soviet Union from the Security Council meeting that voted on the police action because of a protest against the world body's refusal to seat the Chinese Communist government. Had the Soviet Union been in attendance, it surely would have vetoed any UN role in Korea. Prior to 1950 its vetoes had repeatedly frustrated UN efforts to deal with emergent Cold War issues, such as the Berlin blockade and the 1948 coup that brought a communist government to power in Czechoslovakia. In fact, during this period the Soviet Union was the most prolific vetoer in the Security Council. It cast eighty-eight vetoes between 1946 and 1959, and it accounted for 75 percent of the 149 vetoes cast in the first three decades of the UN's existence (Stoessinger, 1977: 6, 22).[4]

The Western powers began to use the veto more frequently when their ability to command a majority in the Security Council diminished. The United States did not register its first veto until 1970,

---

4. The most controversial use of vetoes in the Security Council has been with respect to resolutions regarding peaceful settlement of disputes. Between 1946 and 1979 a total of sixty-one vetoes *in this category* had been exercised. Junn (1980: 30) reports the distribution of responsibility as follows: Soviet Union, 48; United States, 9; United Kingdom, 7; France, 2; China, 1. These numbers do not add up to sixty-one since in some situations two members cast a negative vote.

on the issue of white minority control in Rhodesia and the extension of economic sanctions to South Africa. Since then it has vetoed measures dealing with such issues as the Middle East, Rhodesia, South Africa, the Panama Canal, and the admissions of Vietnam and Angola to the United Nations.

For years the United States prided itself on never having cast a veto in the Security Council. Having now done so on numerous occasions, it is clear that virtue had little to do with the American position—nor was villainy the primary motivation of the Soviet Union's seemingly obstructionist behavior. Rather, the American and Soviet voting behavior reflected the differing parliamentary positions of the superpowers in the United Nations. Until 1960 the Soviet Union was clearly a minority power, the United States a majority power. The veto was virtually the only effective instrument available to the Soviet Union for protecting its national interests, while the United States could assume a more virtuous posture, since it had other devices at its disposal. In this sense the prolific use of the veto by the Soviet Union, often exercised in opposition to proposals put forward by the American-dominated majority, was a reflection, not a cause, of the reasons underlying the seeming inability of the United Nations to command a more central role in postwar international politics.

Recent UN history demonstrates that the United States no longer enjoys majority control, and that the Soviet Union no longer clearly is in a defensive minority position. Between 1961 and 1977 the Soviet Union cast only eighteen of the 110 vetoes it registered between 1946 and 1977. Between 1970 and 1977 alone, the United States cast twenty-one (Riggs, 1978: 529). Thus the two superpowers have come to behave similarly—and in a manner consistent with what the framers of the UN Charter had in mind when they adopted the unanimity principle, namely, that great power agreement was an essential ingredient to the effective maintenance of international peace.

Furthermore, during the early existence of the United Nations, the United States did not have to veto Security Council actions it opposed because it possessed a "hidden veto," an ability to persuade a sufficient majority of other council members to vote negatively so as to avoid the stigma of the United States having to cast the single blocking vote (Stoessinger, 1977). This ability derived from the composition of the Security Council, among whose nine members the United States could easily count upon a pro-Western majority.

The United States enjoyed a similarly commanding position in the General Assembly, where the Soviet Union frequently derided the Americans' "mechanical majority." Figure 5.4 provides evidence of the dominant American position in the assembly. It shows the

Figure 5.4
The Position of the United States and the Soviet Union in the U.N. General Assembly in Relation to Majority Votes, 1946–1975

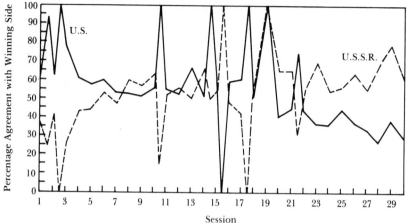

Source: Harold K. Jacobson, *Networks of Interdependence* (New York: Alfred A. Knopf, 1979), p. 115. © 1979 by Alfred A. Knopf, Inc. Reprinted by permission of Alfred A. Knopf, Inc.

percentage of times the United States and the Soviet Union voted with the winning side on roll-call votes in each General Assembly session from 1946 to 1975.

These data do not portray the nuance of behavior underlying United Nations' political processes. For example, they do not reflect the compromises the United States often had to make to garner other nations' support, or, indeed, the resolutions that never came to a vote because that support could not be found (Holmes, 1977).[5] Nor do they reflect different voting patterns on different types of issues. The United States, for example, frequently "found itself at odds with the majority in the General Assembly on issues involving decolonization and economic development much more often than on issues concerning security," Harold Jacobson (1979) has observed.[6] At the same time "the Soviet Union found it easy to vote for

5. It is possible to show, for example, that if votes are weighted by how closely contested they were, on the assumption that minimum winning coalitions are more politically important than overwhelming majorities, then the evidence indicates the United States did not enjoy a commanding position in the General Assembly, even during much of the 1950s. Again, however, this result may reflect, not the absence of political clout, but the unwillingness of the United States to try to influence the outcome of all issues coming before the Assembly. See Wittkopf (1975).

6. See Rowe (1969) for an analysis of the voting success of the United States and the Soviet Union on various categories of issues dealt with by the General Assembly between 1946 and 1966. This study shows that the United States consistently enjoyed greater success on Cold War issues than did the Soviet Union.

the positions on decolonization advocated by the U.N.'s anticolonial majority."

The overall impression is, nonetheless, unmistakable. Until 1960 (the Fifteenth General Assembly), the United States consistently enjoyed a majority position in the General Assembly. Parliamentary successes were also enjoyed between 1960 and 1965 (twentieth session), but since then the United States has been a member of winning coalitions in the General Assembly less often than has the Soviet Union. Furthermore, the American position has noticeably declined over time, while the Soviet position in relation to the majority has improved[7] (see also Wittkopf, 1975).

The dramatic drop in American success in relation to the majority during the Fifteenth General Assembly is noteworthy, for it was then that seventeen new states were admitted to the United Nations, nearly all of them African. Thereafter the United Nations increasingly came to be dominated by the Third World. By the mid-1970s well over half of the nearly 150 members of the organization came from Africa and Asia. In 1945 less than a quarter of the organization's membership came from these two geographic regions (Commission on Transnational Corporations, 1978: 206).

Most of the Third World nations that have joined the United Nations since 1960 have espoused interests and objectives directly related to decolonization and economic development. They did not share the American view that the United Nations was one forum in which to pursue Cold War objectives against the Soviet Union. This did not mean they were necessarily pro-Soviet, for the Soviets, too, had used the United Nations to pursue their Cold War goals. In fact, the increased voting success of the Soviet Union after 1960 was less a consequence of Soviet leadership than of its ability to identify with the political priorities pushed by the new Third World majority. It did mean that the Third World was less than enthusiastic about the uses to which the United States and the Soviet Union sought to put the United Nations. The "mechanical majority" presumed to have been enjoyed by the United States came to an end after 1960.

The impact of these developments on the relative position of the United States and the Soviet Union in the United Nations, and on the United Nations itself, can be illustrated with two cases: the question of seating the People's Republic of China and the struggle between the Security Council and the General Assembly for political control of UN peacekeeping activities.

7. In the period 1971–1974 the United States agreed with the majority 35 percent of the time, while the Soviet's agreement with the majority was nearly 69 percent. These proportions are almost exactly the reverse of what was true in the period 1946–1950 (Riggs, 1978: 525).

The China Question

The "China question" plagued the United Nations for over twenty years—from 1949, when the communists successfully established control over the mainland at the expense of Nationalist Chinese, who retreated to the island of Formosa, until 1971, when the People's Republic of China was finally seated in the world body. The issue was clear: which *government* of China should represent the *state* of China, one of the original members of the United Nations and among the five great powers with a Security Council veto.

An important background to the evolution of this issue is the general question of membership, which the United Nations has persistently confronted. Because the United Nations originated as a coalition of victorious wartime allies, the organization faced for roughly a decade the political question of how those "converted" to the anti-fascist side of peace might be admitted to the club. As the Cold War evolved, both the United States and the Soviet Union approached this issue, not from the viewpoint of who sided with whom during World War II, but rather who sided with whom in the Cold War. Thus the United States assured that Soviet protégés applying for UN membership were denied the necessary Security Council majority, and the Soviet Union used its veto to keep out Western-sponsored applicants. Nearly half of the vetoes cast by the Soviet Union were for this purpose (Stoessinger, 1977).

Finally, in 1955, the United States and the Soviet Union negotiated a compromise that resulted in the admission of sixteen new members to the United Nations. The deal permitted the superpowers to support a politically balanced package of applicants including pro-Eastern, pro-Western, and neutrals to join the United Nations. The agreement opened the floodgates, and, by 1980, the United Nations had more than 150 members, roughly three times the original number.

But mainland China was not part of the 1955 deal. In fact, that matter was the prerogative of the General Assembly, since the issue was not the admission of a new member (an issue subject to veto in the Security Council) but the question of seating a competing government of an existing member state (a matter solely within the jurisdiction of the General Assembly).

The American goal was to prevent the communist government in Peking from being seated at the expense of the Nationalists. The initial American tactic was to avoid direct confrontation. Each year from 1951 to 1960 it proposed that the question be deferred, and year by year it won. Then, in 1961, the United States changed its tactic. Instead of deferring the issue, it proposed that the seating of the

People's Republic of China be considered an "important question." This meant that a two-thirds rather than a simple majority was required. Again, the American proposal prevailed.

Why had the United States changed its game plan? A major reason was the changing composition of the United Nations (see also Stoessinger, 1977). Support for the American position was not easily found among the new members of the United Nations. In fact, in 1960 less than half of the General Assembly cast a vote in favor of the American proposal, while a fifth of the membership abstained (Stoessinger, 1977: 34).

The China issue was debated in the General Assembly for the next decade. While the debate proceeded, important developments were occurring outside the United Nations—a growing split between the Soviet Union and China, the emergence of Soviet-American détente, moves toward rapprochement between the United States and China, and increasing public support within the United States for the admission of the Peking government. In 1971 the United States finally capitulated; the People's Republic of China was seated and the Nationalist government of Taiwan was expelled.

In fact, developments in the General Assembly had proceeded more rapidly than had the change in American policy. In 1970 a majority of the General Assembly voted in favor of seating the People's Republic of China. Only the "important question" strategy barred China's entry. In 1971 Henry A. Kissinger, President Nixon's National Security adviser, undertook his secret trip to China which opened the way for Nixon's famous visit the next year. American policy reflected this changing attitude, with the United States supporting a modified "two Chinas" policy: the Peking regime would be seated in the Security Council, but the government on Taiwan would retain China's seat in the General Assembly. Albania pushed the case for one China—Peking.

> The denouement came on October 25, 1971. After a complicated procedural wrangle, the delegate of Saudi Arabia submitted a motion for postponement that was rejected by a vote of 53 in favor, 56 against, with 9 abstentions. A majority of delegates wanted a showdown right then and there. Since the United States was strongly in favor of postponement, this vote gave an indication of the final outcome. The next vote was crucial: whether the exclusion of the Chiang Kai-shek [Taiwan] regime required a two-thirds vote. Despite intensive last-minute lobbying by the United States, the draft resolution was defeated by a vote of 59 against, 55 in favor, and 15 abstentions. The way was now clear for the Albanian draft [resolution], which was passed by an overwhelming vote of 76 in favor, 35 against, and 17 abstentions. . . . After twenty-two years of diplomatic warfare, the United States had suf-

fered its first dramatic parliamentary defeat. Peking was in, and Taiwan was out. (Stoessinger, 1977: 45)

Over the next decade the United States would suffer other dramatic defeats. In 1974, for example, it was in a distinct minority in opposing the extension by the General Assembly of permanent observer status to the Palestine Liberation Organization. And in 1975 it lost an important battle when the General Assembly went on record branding Zionism "a form of racism and racial discrimination."[8] The vote outraged the American ambassador to the United Nations, Daniel P. Moynihan, and led him to attack the United Nations bitterly. His view is summed up in a phrase he had used shortly before his appointment as American ambassador: "the tyranny of the UN's 'new majority.' "[9] Times had indeed changed![10]

From Uniting for Peace to the Financial Crisis

The political tug-of-war between the Security Council and the General Assembly for political control of UN peacekeeping activities, with the United States and the Soviet Union again principal movers in the contest, also illustrates the impact of member states' foreign policy objectives and actions in the United Nations and the organization's adaptive responses.

Following the return of the Soviet Union to the Security Council in 1950, responsibility for United Nations oversight functions regarding the Korean police action passed to the General Assembly. In an effort to assure the permanence of this arrangement, the United States sponsored the Uniting for Peace Resolution, which granted the assembly the power to meet in emergency session and to adopt collective measures to deal with "threats to the peace, breaches of the peace, and acts of aggression" in the event the Security Council was unable to act because of a veto. The Soviet Union strenuously opposed the measure, because it implied that the United Nations might undertake enforcement measures against the

8. See Stoessinger (1977) for a discussion of the motivations of various states that voted in favor of this resolution.

9. Moynihan's (1975) views of the Third World majority in the United Nations were contained in an article in the March 1975 issue of *Commentary*. Subsequently he wrote a book about his experiences at the United Nations. The title reflected Moynihan's view: *A Dangerous Place* (Moynihan with Weaver, 1978).

10. The erosion of the ability of the United States to work its will in the General Assembly has been matched by a decline in American support of the world body. See Riggs (1978) for evidence of the decline in executive, congressional, and mass public support for the United Nations.

wishes of a great power. But the American position prevailed over-whelmingly.

The first time Uniting for Peace procedures were used following Korea was in 1956, when the General Assembly authorized the United Nations Emergency Force (UNEF) in an effort to restore peace in the Middle East following the eruption of war between Egypt on one side and Israel, Britain, and France on the other. Interestingly, it was not the Soviet Union that cast the negative vote giving rise to the emergency assembly session, but rather Britain and France. Moreover, the General Assembly did not authorize the use of force in the same way it had been used in Korea. Instead, it created a "peacekeeping" force whose functions differed substantially from those implied in the principle of collective security. Collective security requires enforcement measures against an aggressor; peacekeeping implies no punishment, but instead, maintenance of the status quo. In short, both the circumstances and the outcome of this first use of Uniting for Peace were substantially different from what the United States had envisioned only six years earlier.

Emergency special sessions of the General Assembly have been called under the Uniting for Peace provisions only sparingly. A second session was called in 1956 to respond to the Soviet intervention in the Hungarian uprising, but no enforcement procedures were adopted. In 1958 the assembly met to consider developments in Lebanon, where American marines had intervened. In 1960, following a Soviet veto in the Security Council, the assembly took over direction of the United Nations Operation in the Congo (ONUC) which had earlier been authorized by the Security Council. And in 1967 the General Assembly met in emergency session in yet another effort to contain the Middle East conflict. More recently, the General Assembly met in emergency session in December 1979 to consider the Soviet intervention in Afghanistan following a Soviet veto in the Security Council.[11] As in the case of the 1956 Hungarian uprising, no enforcement procedures were authorized in a dispute directly involving one of the two most important members of the Security Council.

The use of Uniting for Peace in 1979 is interesting since some observers of the United Nations had come to regard the "transfer" provisions of the resolution—those moving an issue from the Security Council to the General Assembly—as a dead letter. This conclusion was based on the view that the United Nations Congo operation (1960–1964) had gone too far in opposing the interests of one of the

11. The initiative for an emergency special session was launched by Third World nations. Clearly the United States supported the move, but the fact that it did not have to launch it is reminiscent of the circumstances that led the United States to support the Uniting for Peace procedures in the first place.

superpowers (the Soviet Union, in that case), and that by the mid-1960s the United States had become as apprehensive about the General Assembly as had the Soviet Union in the 1950s. The concern was based on the changing composition of the world body and the corresponding erosion of the ability of the United States to command a majority for positions it espoused. Noteworthy in this regard is that the Uniting for Peace resolution has never resulted in assembly action in quite the same way the United States anticipated when it contemplated the lessons of Korea, namely, the mobilization of collective enforcement against aggressive actions initiated or backed by a great power (see Claude, 1971).

The reality of the American apprehension of the General Assembly was played out in the UN's financial crisis. The Soviet Union did not oppose creation of UNEF by the General Assembly in 1956. But it did refuse to pay for the operation, thus exercising a "financial veto." It also refused four years later to share the costs of the Congo operation. The United States built a compelling legal case that the Soviet Union and others who refused to pay were obliged to assume their share of the costs of these operations. The Soviet Union still refused—because the issue was political, not legal. As Stoessinger (1977) observed, "Never had so many people argued so much about so little money. The financial crisis was in reality a political crisis over the proper role for the United Nations to play in the national policies of its member states, particularly the superpowers. Only secondarily was it a crisis over the costs of UN membership."

The crisis peaked in 1964. The United States threatened to deprive the Soviet Union of its vote in the General Assembly, which, according to Article 19 of the Charter, could be done by majority vote to any state whose obligations to the organization were more than two years in arrears.[12] The Soviet Union threatened to withdraw from the United Nations if this were done, and the United States evaded a showdown.

At that time the United States probably had the votes in the assembly necessary to carry out its threat. But the Soviet threat was more credible and would have been severely damaging to the United Nations. Again the political realities within the United Nations that were a result of the changing composition of its membership—and changes in international allegiances throughout world politics—lurked in the background. The United States may at one time have been willing to allow the General Assembly to exercise political control over United Nations peacekeeping activities, but by the mid-

12. It might be noted that countries other than the Soviet Union were also in arrears on the UN peacekeeping activities, but these states commanded far less attention.

1960s it was less certain that such control would not be detrimental to American interests. This view was thus akin to what the Soviet Union had felt in the 1950s, and especially during the Congo operation in the early 1960s.

In acknowledging the American defeat on the issue of collective financial responsibility for United Nations activities, Ambassador Arthur J. Goldberg added that "the United States reserves the same option to make exception [that is, to withhold support from UN actions with which it disagrees].if, in our view, strong and compelling reasons exist for doing so. There can be no double standard among members of the Organization." The United States thus signaled that it, too, was coming to view the Security Council as the relatively safer haven in which issues of international peace and security should be handled. Since the mid-1960s all questions regarding the financing of UN peacekeeping activities have been handled by the Security Council, where the superpowers can protect their interests with the veto.[13] "The key to superpower behavior in the United Nations is power and influence. Money is a symbol of that power. States will not oppose policies because they refuse to pay for them; they will refuse to pay for them because they oppose them. In this fundamental respect, the two superpowers remain very much alike" (Stoessinger, 1977).

Politics within the Security Council (as well as between it and the General Assembly) have also been affected by the growing majority of Third World nations. The need by the United States to use its veto power in the council indicates that even there its influence is on the wane. The decline in the use of the veto by the Soviet Union also suggests that it has found itself in a relatively more comfortable position on issues that come before the council.

On the most pressing issues regarding world peace, the United States, the Soviet Union, and the other great powers remain the most critical actors in the United Nations. But on other issues which are probably more numerous, Third World nations cannot be ignored. "When the initiative lies with others, the nonaligned still enjoy collectively a negative veto, because no majority of nine can be mustered without them. In the political bargaining process their views must be taken into account even on issues that do not directly interest them" (Riggs, 1978). It seems that the hidden veto once possessed by the United States in the Security Council may have found a new counterpart.

13. The relative increase in the importance of the Security Council within the UN framework is suggested by the number of meetings it holds annually. Between 1946 and 1950 the Security Council held an average of 108 meetings annually. This number declined to less than forty during the 1950s. It rose to about sixty from 1961 to 1975 and then jumped to ninety-three in 1976 and 1977 (Riggs, 1978: 527).

The Third World: From Background to Center Stage

The preceding discussion demonstrates that the superpowers' objectives in the United Nations have been significantly affected by the
increasing number of Third World members. Third World objectives have also been affected by the East-West dispute. In many respects, however, the Third World has been relatively more effective
recently in utilizing the institutional procedures of the United Nations, specifically the General Assembly, to advance its interests
than the superpowers have been in using these same institutional
rules to thwart Third World objectives. For example, the General
Assembly's one-state, one-vote rule enabled the Third World to focus global attention on the issue of colonialism and to effectively
"delegitimize" it as a form of political organization (Claude, 1967).

Economic development has been another principal Third World
objective advanced in the UN forum. In the 1950s the then numer-
ically smaller group of Third World nations pressed for organizational responses to their needs and realized some modest (if less
than hoped for) results. The United Nations Special Fund, for example, was created as a partial response to Third World desires for
substantial United Nations economic development aid.

As their numbers in the United Nations increased in the 1960s,
Third World nations were able to press for economic development
and related issues even more vigorously. Figure 5.5 shows the proportion of the UN membership that the Group of 77, formalized in
1964, comprises. Note that in the early 1960s the group surpassed
the two-thirds mark as a proportion of the total membership. This
means that the Group of 77, if and when it can act as a unit, can pass
any measure it chooses.[14] Figure 5.6 indicates that the G-77 does in
fact manifest considerable unity and has done so increasingly in the
1970s.

Third World interests were reflected in, and were often the
source of, a host of world conferences held during the 1970s. Because these conferences frequently became forums for vituperative

14. Numbers can be translated into General Assembly resolutions, but there are
other ways to exercise influence in the United Nations. Money is the obvious one, and
since the Third World seeks programs that often must be paid for by the United
States and other industrialized nations, the G–77 must exercise caution so as not to
alienate those whose support is critically important to the ultimate realization of
Third World objectives. In this respect the United Nations mirrors in many ways the
structural inequality found elsewhere in world politics. The special status (permanent membership) accorded only five members of the Security Council is the obvious
example, but it holds for other limited-membership organs of the United Nations as
well. See also Jacobsen (1969), Kay (1970a), Keohane (1966 and 1969), Volgy and
Quistgard (1974), Weigert and Riggs (1969), and Wittkopf (1976).

Figure 5.5
The Group of 77 as a Percentage of U.N. Membership*

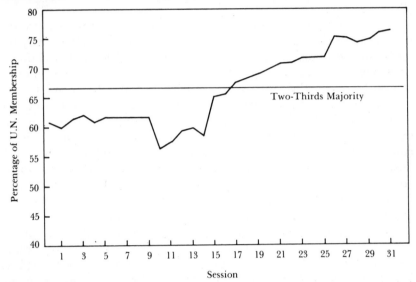

Source: Harold K. Jacobson, *Networks of Interdependence* (New York: Alfred A. Knopf, 1979), p. 118. © 1979 by Alfred A. Knopf, Inc. Reprinted by permission of Alfred A. Knopf, Inc.
*The line represents the percentage of the United Nation's total membership that the future (prior to 1964) or actual (starting in 1964) members of the Group of 77 comprised at each General Assembly session.

exchanges between North and South, their contribution to solving— not just articulating—the global problems the world continues to face have perhaps been minimal. As Bennett points out, the range of ad hoc conferences is, nevertheless, significant: the human environment (1972), the law of the sea (1973), population (1974), food (1974), women (1975), human settlements (1976), water (1977), desertification (1977), disarmament (1978), racism and racial discrimination (1978), technical cooperation among developing countries (1978), technology transfer (1978), agrarian reform and rural development (1979), and science and technology for development (1979). "To review the subjects covered in the world conferences of the 1970s is to list the most vital issues of present world conditions. . . . The conferences represent a beginning in a long and evolving process of keeping within manageable proportions the major problems of humanity. Action plans will have to be revised at later dates, and the evolutionary process will be slow, but momentum has been given to an ongoing set of processes for meeting human demands and aspirations" (Bennett, 1980). In this the United Nations can take some credit.

Figure 5.6
Cohesion of the Group of 77 in Roll Call Votes of the U.N. General Assembly*

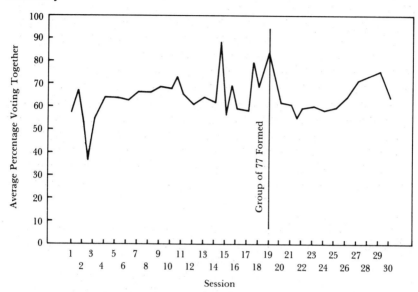

Source: Harold K. Jacobson, *Networks of Interdependence* (New York: Alfred A. Knopf, 1979), p. 119. © 1979 by Alfred A. Knopf, Inc. Reprinted by permission of Alfred A. Knopf, Inc.

*The horizontal line represents the average percentage of the Group of 77 states voting identically at each Assembly session. The nineteenth session, the first after formation of the caucus, was abnormal in that there were only two roll call votes during the session; the usual number is around 150.

Apart from any credit, the pervasiveness of the global ad hoc conference forum is noteworthy. North and South generally disagree on how the United Nations might best create an institutional framework in which to consider the issues that divide them. "[Developing nations] are much more disposed to want development priorities and strategy centrally defined and to want the General Assembly and perhaps the United Nations Conference on Trade and Development (UNCTAD) to review or oversee the rest of the UN system" (Gregg, 1977). These preferences have been played out in the drive of developing nations for universal forums with broad mandates to deal with their desire for a new international order. In contrast, the First World seems to prefer "relatively small, functionally specific forums" generally outside the General Assembly.

From the perspective of the developed Western countries, smaller and more specialized bodies are more likely to involve those states that have a real stake in the outcome of the deliberations and that consequently come prepared for serious and detailed negotiation leading to realistic and concrete results. Large, general-purpose bodies only encourage ill-informed participation by states uninvolved in the issue at hand and thus increase the likelihood of irresponsibly politicizing the agenda. Conversely, the [less-developed countries] realize that their strength comes from their numbers. They therefore want full participation by as many states as possible and consider this an appropriate acknowledgement of the global community's shared stake in the outcome of negotiations on the international order. (Gregg, 1977: 72)

INTERNATIONAL ORGANIZATIONS AND WORLD POLITICS

The political tug-of-war between North and South over the appropriate institutional forums in which to confront their differences is an indication of an important fact—that the United Nations, and international organizations generally, reflect the interests of the nation-states that comprise them. In the words of Inis Claude (1967): "The United Nations has no purposes—and can have none—of its own." But international organizations are also adaptive institutions, capable of adjusting to changing political realities.

It is probably unrealistic to expect too much—or for that matter, too little—from international institutions. International organizations, both governmental and nongovernmental, are important in varying degrees to their individual members. The United Nations in particular probably matters more to Third World nations than to First or Second World nations,[15] but it is important to them as well. In 1980, for example, President Carter suffered severe political damage when a "communications failure" between the White House and the U.S. Mission at the United Nations resulted in a Security Council vote in which the United States, contrary to long-standing policies, condemned Israel for its settlements on the West Bank.

The practice of stronger countries having client states underscores the way states use the United Nations to promote their foreign policy interests. The United Nations has little capacity to rise above the conflicts between states and pursue an independent role in world politics. Various secretaries-general have achieved some degree of autonomy and effectively pursued independent roles in world politics, but such activities are more the exception than the rule. In short, the United Nations is rarely an autonomous international actor, but it has surely shaped the behaviors of states.[16] Indi-

15. For empirical evidence showing greater support for the United Nations among Third World countries, see Rowe (1974b).

16. Finkelstein (1980) challenges the view that IGOs are merely tools of states and forums for the conduct of interstate bargaining. He argues that

IGOs assert independence. . . . They compete for resources and over turf. They behave in ways which are hard to reconcile with the belief that the diplomacy of

viduals who have participated in its affairs may also have had their nationalistic perceptions broadened (Alger, 1965; Riggs, 1977). Because it generally cannot act autonomously, however, the United Nations lacks legitimacy as an independent force in world politics.

The meaning of *autonomy* and *legitimacy* can be illustrated by contrasting the United Nations with the European Community (EC). The latter is made up of three organizations, the European Coal and Steel Community (ECSC, created in 1952), the European Atomic Energy Community (Euratom, 1958), and the European Economic Community (EEC, 1958). The immediate purpose of these institutions, which were first formed by France, West Germany, Italy, Luxembourg, Belgium, and the Netherlands, was promotion of broad economic integration among the six.[17] But some were also hopeful that the institutions might eventually lead to a United States of Europe.

Since 1967 the three communities have shared common organizational structures (see Figure 5.7), the most important of which is the Council of Ministers. As the name implies, the council consists of cabinet ministers drawn from the member states of the European Community. The foreign ministers participate in the council when the most important decisions faced by the European Community are made. In this respect the European Community is little different from the United Nations as an association of nation-states. But the EC also has *supranational* characteristics, that is, the capacity to make decisions binding on its national members without being subject to their individual approval. An important instrumentality in making these decisions is the Commission and its thousands of European technocrats who owe loyalty to the European Community, not to its national constituents. Furthermore, since the mid-1970s the community has enjoyed sources of revenue independent of its member states, and in 1979 the European Parliament began to be chosen by direct election. Previously its members had been chosen by the national parliaments of member states.

None of this means the European Community will automatically become an integrated political entity approximating a United States of Europe, for integration can be halted or even reversed as a consequence of decisions made by nation-states, as the European

member states is the sole determinant of IGO behavior, unless one is prepared to argue also that governments want IGOs to behave that way. . . . IGOs do have purposes of their own. (Finkelstein, 1980: 28)

17. The European Community was expanded to nine members in 1973 with the addition of Denmark, Ireland, and the United Kingdom, and to ten members in 1981 with the addition of Greece. Various other countries have associated status in the EC. Of these, Spain, Portugal, and Turkey are likely eventually to become full members of the EC.

Figure 5.7
The Structure of the European Community

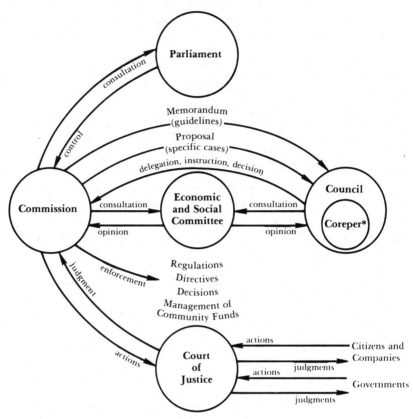

Source: *European Community* (Washington, D.C.: European Community, n.d.), p. 7.
*Committee of Permanent Representatives. COREPER is responsible for doing pre-paratory work for meetings of the Council.

Community's record demonstrates. However, the European Community as an international institution has characteristics that clearly distinguish it from most other international organizations, and in particular from the United Nations. While the United Nations remains almost wholly dependent on its members and therefore does little more than reflect the political reality of the international political system in which it resides, the European Community has a much greater potential capacity independently to shape its regional subsystem, and perhaps the global system as well.

By the mid-1970s fifteen other regional economic schemes had been created in various parts of the world, notably among Third World nations (Jacobson, 1979). Few had achieved anything approaching the same level of economic integration and supranational institution building as Western Europe, however. Although the reasons underlying the generally modest success of such attempts vary, they boil down to the inability of national political leaders to make the kinds of choices that may undermine the very existence of their national political systems. At the same time, these attempts at regional cooperation demonstrate the inability of the countries to solve individually the problems they all face. In this sense, the nation-state seems both ill suited for managing transnational policy problems or for being an agent of organized efforts to do so. The ultimate effect of the collective problem-solving institutions on world politics is therefore problematic. Before probing this matter further, however, let us first examine another transnational manifestation of the transformation of world politics, the multinational enterprise.

THE RISE OF MULTINATIONAL CORPORATIONS: BLESSING OR CURSE?

Investment by individuals of one country in the economic system of another country is not new. Since World War II, however, the volume of direct investment abroad through transnationally organized business enterprises has grown substantially.[18] The term *multinational corporation* (MNC) is popularly used to describe the instrumentality of this transnational phenomenon, which has resulted in the internationalization of production. The impact of this development is suggested by the estimate that by the year 2000 half or more of all industrial production in the world will be accounted for by a relative handful of MNCs (Heilbroner, 1977). And its pace is suggested by the growth of American-based multinational corporations. One study has shown that the number of foreign subsidiaries of 187 United States-based MNCs grew from just over 2,000 in 1950 to nearly 8,000 by 1967, roughly a fourfold increase in less than two decades (Vaupel and Curhan, 1969: 123). This parallels the increase in the number of IGOs and INGOs the world has witnessed since World War II—all three of which have grown more rapidly than the number of nation-states.

The remarkable rise in the overseas activities of businesses whose parent corporations are located elsewhere is one reason why

18. The Commission on Transnational Corporations (1978: 36) reports that direct foreign investment grew from $105 billion in 1967 to $158 billion in 1971 and $287 billion in 1976. The 1976 level represents more than an 80 percent increase above the level existing only five years earlier.

the multinational corporation has commanded attention. Indeed, the term *multinational corporation* often evokes strong emotional responses, suggesting that the MNC has become more than simply the agent of a global system of production. May it have become so powerful and its tentacles so far-reaching that it has undermined the ability of nation-states to control their own fates? Indeed, is it possible that MNCs are undermining the very foundations of the present international system?

The Global Reach and Economic Power of Multinationals

What is a multinational corporation? Definitions differ (see Feld, 1979), but they converge on the notion of a business enterprise organized in one society with activities abroad growing out of direct investment (as opposed to portfolio investment through shareholding). Typically they are hierarchically organized and centrally directed (Jacobson, 1979). Thus "a distinctive characteristic of the transnational organization is its broader-than-national perspective with respect to the pursuit of highly specialized objectives through a central optimizing strategy across national boundaries" (Huntington, 1973).

The initiation of the European Economic Community (EEC) in 1958 gave impetus to this form of business organization. Because the six EEC members anticipated a common external tariff wall around their customs union, it made economic sense for American firms to establish production facilities in Europe. That way they could remain competitive by selling their wares as domestic products rather than foreign imports with their added tariff costs.[19]

Table 5.2 indicates how extensive this form of business organization has become. Nearly 10,400 business firms (based in nineteen First World nations) have at least one foreign affiliate in one or

---

19. The reasons for direct investments overseas are more complex than this simplified explanation suggests. The product-cycle theory is one example. According to this view, overseas expansion is essentially a defensive maneuver designed to forestall foreign competitors and hence to maintain the global competitiveness of domestically based industries. The theory views MNCs as having an edge in the initial stages of developing and producing a new product, and then having to go abroad to protect export markets from foreign competitors that naturally arise as the relevant technology becomes diffused or imitated. In the final phase of the product cycle "production has become sufficiently routinized so that the comparative advantage shifts to relatively low-skilled, low-wage, and labor-intensive economies. This is now the case, for example, in textiles, electronic components, and footwear" (Gilpin, 1975b). See this source and especially Vernon (1971) for an elaboration of the product-cycle theory. Noteworthy is Gilpin's (1975b) conclusion after examining several theories of foreign direct investment: "The primary drive behind the overseas expansion of today's giant corporations is maximization of corporate growth and the suppression of foreign as well as domestic competition."

Table 5.2
Business Firms With One or More Foreign Affiliates by Number of Host Countries and Third World Host Regions, 1977

Location of Parent Firms	Number of Firms with Foreign Affiliates in One or More Developed or Developing Countries	Number of Firms with Foreign Affiliates in Developing Countries				
		Total	In Western Hemisphere only	In Africa only	In Asia only	In More than One of the Three Regions
United States of America	2,783	1,197	522	53	130	492
United Kingdom	1,598	639	97	102	176	264
Germany, Federal Republic of	1,404	316	134	29	57	96
Switzerland	852	109	48	6	11	44
Netherlands	600	104	28	10	18	48
France	564	246	36	125	19	66
Canada	432	121	77	9	12	23
Japan	380	225	46	5	77	97
Belgium	320	90	16	49	2	23
Australia	323	181	11	1	150	19
Italy	249	58	23	9	7	19
Sweden	258	63	27	3	5	28
New Zealand	167	58	2	–	55	1
Denmark	132	22	7	4	4	7
Norway	116	15	4	–	5	6
Spain	79	34	22	4	3	5
Austria	54	11	3	1	3	5
Finland	52	7	4	2	–	2
Portugal	10	6	2	3	1	–
Total	10,373	3,502	1,109	415	737	1,241

Source: Commission on Transnational Corporations, "Supplementary Material on the Issue of Defining Transnational Corporations," U.N. Doc. E/C.10/58, United Nations Economic and Social Council, March 23, 1979, pp. 8, 11.

more host countries.[20] *(Host country* refers to the country in which the operations of a company owned or controlled by a parent firm headquartered in another country are carried on.) The United States, Britain, and West Germany account for over half of these companies, the United States alone for more than a quarter. Although the growth of transnational corporations is a global phenomenon, "the major part of all transnational business is located in the developed areas of North America, Western Europe, and Japan" (Modelski, 1979).

The preference for the First World is implied by the data in Table 5.2. Somewhat less than half of the British and American firms have Third World affiliates, while fewer than a quarter of the German firms have them. The difference between the United States and Britain on one hand, and Germany on the other, reflects differences in their historic patterns of global involvement. Overall, only a third of the more than 10,000 firms referenced in Table 5.2 have affiliates in the Third World.

The dominance of the United States in the network of multinationals is especially apparent from an examination of the economic characteristics of MNCs. In 1976, 54 percent of the 411 industrial firms comprising the Billion Dollar Club (sales of at least $1 billion) were American. The closest competitors to the United States were Japan and Britain, with 12 and 10 percent respectively (Commission on Transnational Corporations, 1979: 14). Among the leading firms were the giants of American industry—Exxon, General Motors, Ford Motor, Texaco, Mobil, Standard Oil of California, Gulf Oil, IBM, General Electric, and International Telephone and Telegraph. But the dominance extends to banking as well. In 1976 Bankamerica Corporation and Citicorp were the two largest banks in the world, with 494 foreign affiliates and combined assets in excess of $135 billion. Japan accounted for twelve of the fifty largest banks in the world while the United States accounted for only ten, but the assets of the American banks outstripped the Japanese, $348 billion to $318 billion (Commission on Transnational Corporations, 1978: 215–216).

The importance of these economic characteristics is illustrated in Table 5.3, which intersperses billion-dollar-or-more firms with nations ranked by the size of their gross national product. The results show that (in 1978) General Motors and Exxon outranked all but twenty-two nation-states. Among the top fifty entries, multina-

---

20. *Transnational* rather than *multinational* is perhaps a more descriptive term for these firms, since many have affiliates in only one host country. Only 54 percent of the 10,373 firms shown in Table 5.2 have affiliates in two or more host countries, and less than 20 percent have affiliates in six or more (Commission on Transnational Corporations, 1979: 8).

tionals account for only nine, but in the next fifty, thirty-two are multinationals.

The spread of their activity and the potency of their economic potential are two important reasons MNCs have commanded so much attention. Furthermore, the attention has been relatively greater on the part of Third World nations, since MNCs are generally more important in developing nations' overall GNP and in their most advanced economic sectors. Third World views of MNCs have also been more charged emotionally, since these predominantly Northern-based economic giants are frequently seen through the nationalistic eyes of the newly independent nations as agents of neocolonialism.

Let us examine briefly three general complaints lodged against multinational corporations: that they have an adverse impact on host nations; that they engage in illegitimate political activity; and that they are beyond national control and thus are undermining the territorial nation-state.

Impact on Host Nations

Multinational corporations have been important transmission belts for the diffusion of technology and managerial know-how across national boundaries. For the home countries of MNCs this movement is often alleged to have occurred at great cost. MNCs are charged with shifting productive facilities abroad to avoid demands of powerful labor unions for higher wages. According to this view, the practice of moving from industrially advanced countries to industrially backward countries, where labor is cheap and unions weak or nonexistent, is the cause of structural unemployment in the advanced countries, because capital is more mobile than labor.

If home countries have incurred costs, have others realized benefits? From one perspective, the movement of capital and production from the First World to the Third has produced net gains for the latter:

> For all the talk (and the reality) of imperialist domination, most of the underdeveloped nations want domestic foreign investment, European and/or American, for a variety of reasons. The multinationals pay higher wages, keep more honest books, pay more taxes, and provide more managerial know-how and training than do local industries. Moreover, they usually provide better social services for their workers, and certainly provide fancy career opportunities for a favored few of the elite. They are, in addition, a main channel through which technology, developed in the West, can filter into the backward nations. To be sure, the corporations typically send home more profits than the

Table 5.3
Countries and Corporations Ranked According to Size of Annual Product, 1978

Rank	Economic Entity	$ (billions)	Rank	Economic Entity	$ (billions)
1	United States	2,117.89	51	Algeria	22.29
2	Soviet Union	965.52	52	Colombia	21.79
3	Japan	836.16	53	Thailand	21.79
4	Germany, West	587.70	54	IBM	21.08
5	France	439.97	55	GENERAL ELECTRIC	19.65
6	China, People's Rep.	424.62	56	Portugal	19.54
7	United Kingdom	281.09	57	Libya	18.96
8	Italy	218.32	58	UNILEVER	18.89
9	Canada	216.09	59	GULF OIL	18.07
10	Brazil	187.19	60	Kuwait	18.04
11	Spain	128.92	61	Pakistan	17.53
12	Poland	128.33	62	CHRYSLER	16.34
13	Netherlands	117.19	63	Egypt	15.52
14	Australia	113.83	64	Israel	15.30
15	India	112.66	65	New Zealand	15.27
16	Germany, East	95.49	66	ITT	15.26
17	Belgium	89.52	67	Chile	15.18
18	Sweden	84.75	68	PHILIPS' GLOEILAMPENFABRIEKEN	15.12
19	Mexico	84.15	69	STANDARD OIL (IND.)	14.96
20	Switzerland	76.05	70	Malaysia	14.54
21	Czechoslovakia	71.32	71	Hong Kong	14.05
22	Saudi Arabia	63.31	72	SIEMENS	13.86
23	GENERAL MOTORS	63.22	73	VOLKSWAGENWERK	13.33
24	EXXON	60.33	74	TOYOTA MOTOR	12.77
25	Austria	52.72	75	RENAULT	12.72
26	Yugoslavia	52.34	76	Morocco	12.61
27	Turkey	51.75			

28	Denmark	50.41	77	ENI	12.57
29	Argentina	50.25	78	Korea, North	12.53
30	Indonesia	48.82	79	FRANCAISE DES PÉTROLES	12.51
31	Nigeria	45.72	80	Peru	12.44
32	ROYAL DUTCH/SHELL GROUP	44.04	81	ATLANTIC RICHFIELD	12.30
33	FORD MOTOR	42.78	82	DAIMIER-BENZ	12.09
34	Korea, South	42.46	83	HOECHST	12.07
35	South Africa	40.94	84	United Arab Emirates	11.44
36	Venezuela	40.71	85	BAYER	11.39
37	Norway	38.50	86	Ireland	11.21
38	Romania	38.17	87	SHELL OIL	11.06
39	Hungary	36.86	88	U.S. STEEL	11.05
40	MOBIL	34.74	89	NESTLÉ	11.00
41	Finland	32.38	90	BASF	10.73
42	Greece	30.53	91	PEUGEOT-CITROËN	10.62
43	TEXACO	28.61	92	E.I. DUPONT de NEMOURS	10.58
44	Bulgaria	28.45	93	MATSUSHITA ELECTRIC INDUSTRIAL	10.02
45	BRITISH PETROLEUM	27.41	94	NISSAN MOTOR	9.75
46	China, Rep. of	23.93	95	NIPPON STEEL	9.52
47	Philippines	23.25	96	WESTERN ELECTRIC	9.52
48	STANDARD OIL OF CALIF	23.23	97	CONTINENTAL OIL	9.46
49	NATIONAL IRANIAN OIL	22.79	98	MITSUBISHI HEAVY INDUSTRIES	9.20
50	Iraq	22.72	99	THYSSEN	9.18
			100	HITACHI	9.15

Source: *World Bank Atlas* (Washington, D.C.: World Bank, 1979), pp. 12 *et passim*; *Fortune*, 100 (August 13, 1979), 208.

capital that they originally introduce into the "host" country; but meanwhile that capital grows, providing jobs, improving productivity, and often contributing to export earnings.[21] (Heilbroner, 1977: 345–346)

From another Third World perspective, however, the costs associated with the multinational firm have been excessive. "The capital, jobs and other benefits they bring to developing economies are recognized, but the terms on which these benefits come are seen as unfair and exploitative and as robbing the new nations of their resources" (Cutler, 1978).

One of the costs is technology dependence. Technology imported from the North impedes local development: what is transferred to the Third World is often not appropriate to the local setting, and the spread effects of industrial activity within developing nations in particular are limited. In addition, because MNCs seek to maximize profits for shareholders, who more often than not reside in the parent state rather than in the host state, capital is not reinvested in the country where production occurs but instead finds its way to someone else's hands. Moreover, the returns are often excessive. In 1965–1968, for example, profit on American direct foreign investment in the First World averaged 7.9 percent, but in the Third World it averaged over 17 percent (Spero, 1977: 198; compare Drucker, 1974).

MNCs benefit in other ways as well. Critics argue that profits represent only a small part of the effective return to parent companies. "A large part of the real return comes from licensing fees and royalties paid by the subsidiary to the parent for the use of technology controlled by the parent" (Spero, 1977). Parent companies admittedly have to absorb the research and development costs of the technology used abroad by others.

> What the critics contend is that subsidiaries in underdeveloped countries pay an unjustifiably high price for technology and bear an unjustifiably high share of the research and development costs. The monopoly control of technology by the multinational corporation enables the parent to exact a monopoly rent from its subsidiaries. And the parent chooses to use that power to charge inordinately high fees and royal-

21. Underdeveloped nations themselves have begun to spawn multinational firms. *Fortune* magazine's 1978 list of the 500 largest industrial corporations outside the United States showed 34 companies headquartered in the developing world, a figure 48 percent higher than the previous year (Heenan and Keegan, 1979: 102). Thus

> the multinational corporation, long regarded by its opponents as the unique instrument of capitalist oppression against the impoverished world, could prove to be the tool by which the impoverished world builds prosperity. . . . Third World multinationalism, only yesterday an apparent contradiction in terms, is now a serious force in the development process. (Heenan and Keegan, 1979: 109)

ties to disguise high profits and avoid local taxes on those profits. (Spero, 1977: 198)

The "transfer" pricing mechanism is another device used by multinationals that can effectively increase their profits while minimizing their tax burdens. The raw, semiprocessed, or finished materials produced by a parent's subsidiaries located in different countries are in effect traded among the subsidiaries. Since the same company is sitting on both sides of the transaction, the sales or "transfer" prices of these import-export transactions can be manipulated so as to benefit the parent firm.

> Some firms do this as objectively as they can, without regard to tax considerations. But there are also some who exercise this discretion so as to minimize their global taxes and maximize their after-tax earnings. Since tax rates vary around the world, they accomplish this by recording profits in jurisdictions where taxes are relatively low. (Cutler, 1978: 11)

The net effect is increased capital flow from South to North. Poverty is said to be the primary product (Müller, 1973–1974).

In sum, the multinational corporation, while conferring some benefits on host states, may do so only at great cost.[22] Critics of the MNC argue, in fact, that the MNC has had a negative effect on developing nations' growth prospects. Joan Edelman Spero has conveniently summarized the arguments of the critics:

> Multinational corporations often create highly developed enclaves which do not contribute to the development of the larger economy. These enclaves use capital-intensive technology which employs few local citizens; acquire supplies from abroad, not locally; use transfer prices and technology agreements to avoid taxes; and send earnings back home. In welfare terms the benefits of the enclave accrue to the home country and to a small part of the host population allied with the corporation. (Spero, 1977: 199)

Politics and Multinational Corporations

The charges often lodged against multinational corporations are not confined to the adverse effects they allegedly exert on Third World

22. The economic consequences of the activities of multinational corporations are not, of course, altogether discernible. The effects show country-by-country variations and assessments do not point to consensus. Charles Kindleberger (1969), for instance, contends that despite the monopolistic and exploitative tendencies of MNCs, multinationals in the aggregate have, paradoxically, expanded competition and enhanced world economic efficiency.

development prospects. They also extend to the involvement of MNCs in local political affairs.

Perhaps the most notorious instance of a multinational corporation's intervention in the politics of a host state occurred in Chile in the early 1970s. There, International Telephone and Telegraph (ITT) attempted to protect its interests in the profitable Chiltelco telephone company by preventing Salvador Allende, a Marxist, from being elected president and then exercising political power effectively. ITT's efforts to undermine Allende included giving monetary support to his political opponents and attempting to induce the American government to launch a program designed to disrupt the Chilean economy once Allende was elected.

Multinationals have also used bribery to influence key foreign officials. The extent of such activity by American firms was unearthed in the aftermath of the Watergate scandal in the United States in the early 1970s. The Securities and Exchange Commission and later a congressional inquiry disclosed improper foreign payments totaling more than $100 million made by 100 American firms (Cutler, 1978: 18).

The Chilean ITT case and the bribery scandals of the 1970s suggest that MNCs have a capacity to undertake their own private foreign policies. The efforts probably less often involve direct political action or bribery than they do legitimate lobbying of the host government's legislators and advertising "to influence the climate of ideas" (Nye, 1974). Regardless of the particular form, however, such private political activity "contravenes the traditional assumption of world politics that governments deal with governments and that citizens or corporations affect governments of other countries indirectly through policies they press upon their own government. But . . . citizens and corporations are also affecting the governments and politics of other countries by dealing with them directly, quite apart from the activities of their home governments" (Nye, 1974). Such transnational activity may not be unique to MNCs, but the global reach and potential economic power of MNCs give added significance to their activities.

In addition to direct political roles, multinationals indirectly serve as instruments through which national governments pursue their objectives. The United States, for example, has sought to use the foreign affiliates of American-based multinationals to extend into other jurisdictions its policies regarding trade embargoes against other nations (Nye, 1974). Similarly, the governments of the Organization of Petroleum Exporting Countries effectively used the multinational oil companies in 1973–1974 to achieve OPEC's goal of using oil as a political weapon against the West. Multinationals have also been used to enhance American intelligence-gathering capabilities in other societies. In these cases it almost seems that the multinational corporation is the captive of governments.

On the other hand, multinational corporations often lobby their home governments for policies that back the MNCs in disputes with host governments. The Hickenlooper amendment, which stipulates that American foreign aid will be cut off from any country that nationalizes American overseas investments without just compensation, is an example of home-state support of multinationals' overseas activities. More generally, multinational corporations facilitated creation of the liberal multilateral trading system supported as a policy objective by the United States since World War II, and multinationals in turn have helped shape the specific policies regarding trade and taxes that contributed to the realization of that goal. In this sense, MNCs may help governments decide what their objectives are.

Controlling Multinational Corporations

It is clear that multinationals have become important actors in world politics in the sense that decisions critical to nation-states are now made by entities over which those nations may not have control. This, in fact, and not the question of expatriated earnings, is the heart of the question of ownership or control of MNCs so central to Third World perceptions of these corporate giants. "Most host governments believe that foreign owners will subordinate the interests of the host nation to their own international interests and that they will be less amenable than local owners to the host government's views" (Cutler, 1978). But the question of control is not confined to the Third World, for the international interests of multinational firms are not necessarily more compatible with the interests of home governments than with those of the hosts.

The potential long-run importance of multinational corporations for the transforming world political order is vividly depicted by Richard J. Barnet and Ronald E. Müller:

> The global corporation is the most powerful human organization yet devised for colonizing the future. By scanning the entire planet for opportunities, by shifting its resources from industry to industry and country to country, and by keeping its overriding goal simple—worldwide profit maximization—it has become an institution of unique power. The World Managers are the first to have developed a plausible model for the future that is global. They exploit the advantages of mobility while workers and governments are still tied to particular terri-

tories. For this reason, the corporate visionaries are far ahead of the rest of the world in making claims on the future. In making business decisions today they are creating a politics for the next generation. (Barnet and Müller, 1974: 363)

Whether the "corporate visionaries" will succeed in creating a better, more humane, and just world is questioned. "For some, the global corporation holds the promise of lifting mankind out of poverty and bringing the good life to everyone. For others, these corporations have become a law unto themselves; they are miniempires which exploit all for the benefit of a few" (Gilpin, 1975b).

Those who view the MNC favorably see national competitiveness giving way to a supranational world order in which welfare issues will be of more importance than narrow ideological or security contests. Because the MNC knows no national boundaries, and because its interests are disrupted by national aggressiveness and militarism, the MNC from this perspective is characterized as a "peacemonger" (Ewing, 1974).

Those more negatively disposed toward MNCs maintain that because of their desire for political stability in order to realize maximum profits, they will often deal with repressive political regimes and "powerfully oppose the kinds of revolutionary upheavals that in many backward areas are probably the essential precondition for a genuine modernization" (Heilbroner, 1977). Furthermore, multinationals may be the agents of a worldwide spread of economic benefits, but the distribution of these benefits is not even. Hence, multinationals perpetuate and deepen global inequality. And because they threaten national autonomy, *all* countries are challenged by the rise of independent, transnationally organized corporations.

> According to this view, the diminution of the role of the nation-state would signal a new feudalism rather than healthy progress. Kings and corporate barons will engage in conflicts and coalitions, but the serfs of the world will suffer. The real global divisions will not be among nations, but between a world city knit together by transnational elites and the diverse but intense parochialisms of the world countryside. The decline of the nation-state would not be a sign of health but a sign of disaster: "a sound international order cannot be built on the wreckage of nation-states." The nation-state provides the internal order and sense of political community that underlie democratic institutions, and there is little prospect that our political norms can be adapted to keep pace with the evolution of powerful and autonomous transnational corporations playing an increasingly political role. (Nye, 1974: 167)

Optimists and pessimists may differ in their evaluations of the ultimate consequences of the rise of multinational corporations,[23] but they share the view that if nation-states are to manage these corporate giants they will have to devise new transnational institutions of their own capable of controlling a phenomenon that presently operates outside national and international legal and political jurisdictions.

NONSTATE ACTORS AND THE TRANSFORMATION OF WORLD POLITICS.

Because multinational corporations challenge the nation-state, they also challenge the very foundations of the contemporary global system. But states will not wither away easily.[24] Conflict between them and MNCs is therefore to be expected. As Robert Heilbroner (1977) has observed, "what we seem to be witnessing . . . is a conflict between two modes of organizing human affairs—a 'vertical' mode that finds its ultimate expression in the pan-national flows of production of the giant international corporation, and a 'horizontal' mode expressed in the jealously guarded boundaries of the nation-state."

In the meantime, the rise of multinational corporations and the prodigious growth in other types of nonstate actors challenge the traditional state-centric theory of international politics, which holds that nation-states are the primary actors on the world political stage. Because the state has "purposes and power," it "is the basic unit of action; its main agents are the diplomat and soldier. The interplay of governmental politics yields the pattern of behavior that students of international politics attempt to understand and that practitioners attempt to adjust or to control" (Nye and Keohane, 1971; see also Mansbach et al., 1976).

Clearly such a view no longer adequately depicts the complexity of world politics. An adequate conceptualization of contemporary world politics must acknowledge the existence not only of government-to-government interactions, but also the influence that nonstate actors exert on a government's ability to formulate public policy and on the ties that exist between nonstate actors directly. Thus,

23. For elaborations on the prospective significance of multinationals, see Barnet and Müller (1974), Bergsten et al. (1978), Ewing (1974), Heilbroner (1977), Nye (1974), Vernon (1971), and the essays in Ball (1975) and Modelski (1979).

24. See Cutler (1978) for a discussion of current efforts to regulate multinational corporations.

nonstate actors—IGOs, INGOs, and MNCs—help to build and broaden the foreign policy agendas of national decision makers by serving as transmission belts through which one nation's policies become sensitive to another's (Keohane and Nye, 1975). At the same time, some nonstate actors are capable of pursuing their interests largely outside the direct control of nation-states while at the same time frequently involving governments in particular problems as a result of their activities[25] (Nye and Keohane, 1971).

These reflections invite the conclusion that

> There has developed on the global level an interconnected and intensified . . . complex of relationships, usually described as interdependence, in which demands are articulated and processed through formal as well as informal channels, governmental as well as non-governmental organizations, national as well as international and supranational institutions. These processes of interaction are interdependent—that is to say they are a system—and they perform a variety of functions, most prominently those of welfare and security. They are the structures through which governments perform a variety of functions; they are the way in which state and society seek to arrange their domestic and foreign environment. (Hanrieder, 1978: 1278)

The transformation of world politics is being played out in these complex, interdependent relationships among diverse national and transnational actors. This by no means indicates that the nation-state is dead, however. Governments still retain the capacity to influence, indeed to shape, transnational interactions. It is not accidental that supranationalism (as in Western Europe) has been confined largely to economic interactions, and that matters of national security are confined largely to government-to-government interactions.

Thus it is important not to exaggerate the importance of nonstate actors and their impact on nation-states. Nation-states retain a (near) monopoly on the use of coercive force in the international system. The majority of new international governmental organizations founded in the 150-year period since the Congress of Vienna (1815) were established *following* the most warlike periods, but there is almost no association between the number of IGOs in the international system and the incidence of interstate war during the

---

25. An example of the often relative autonomy of nonstate actors was provided by the international response to the American effort to organize a worldwide boycott of the 1980 Summer Olympics in Moscow. For the American policy position, it was important that West Germany and Japan were among those who decided not to participate. However, several national Olympic committees voted to participate even though their governments had favored a boycott. Included among them were the national Olympic committees in Britain, France, Italy, and Australia.

150-year period[26] (Singer and Wallace, 1970). The nation-state cannot be lightly dismissed, therefore; it still molds the activities of nonstate actors more than its behavior is molded by them. Hence it would be premature to abandon the focus on the nation-state in international politics, just as it is inadequate to regard the state as the only relevant actor or the sole determinant of its fate.

26. Because this conclusion contradicts other findings regarding IGO involvement in conflict management, perhaps it should be asked whether the data and analysis from which it derives might be interpreted differently. The conclusion is based on the assumption that there should be an association between the amount of war and organization within closely constrained time periods (five years). If, however, the data are arranged into twenty-five rather than five-year periods (which is perhaps a reasonable length in which to expect institutional developments to have an impact on the international system), then ". . . the data would appear to support the argument that as the number of IGOs has grown, the amount of violence in the global system has decreased." (Jacobson, 1979: 214, n. 1)

Part III

THE INTERPLAY OF
TRANSNATIONAL POLICY ISSUES

Six

The Transformation of the
International Political Economy:
Perspectives from the First World

> The changes now in train in the international economy are far from new; they are counter-international in part; they are political as well as economic; and they are anything but orderly. They are happening nonetheless.
>
> Fred Hirsch, 1976

> The paradox of an interdependent world economy is that it creates sources of insecurity and competition. The very dependence of one state on another and the necessity for access to external markets and sources of raw materials cause anxieties and suspicions that exacerbate international relations.
>
> Robert Gilpin, 1975

Transnational economic issues are one of the most important factors transforming world politics. Economic issues have become the source of some of the most heated political controversies of the contemporary world. The confrontationist "high politics" of great power struggles are often rooted in the quiet world of "low politics" —the world of economic policy making.

The undercurrents of "low politics" are powerful. They pull the struggle for national security and for political power into new shapes both by constraining the use of political power and by influencing how and when such power may be used. For these reasons the transformation of world politics cannot be understood without also understanding the transformation occurring in the international economic system.

The potential of economic factors as determinants of political circumstances is illustrated by the dramatic increase in international trade the world has experienced over the past quarter-century. At the start of the 1980s world exports were valued at over a trillion dollars annually, more than four times greater than a decade earlier. World exports now account for roughly 15 percent of all nations' combined gross national products. This proportion is double what it was only ten years earlier.

This trend portends a fundamental transformation—emergence of an interdependent global economic system. *Interdependence* is a term that is now widely used to draw attention to the increasingly interlocked natures of the economies of the nations of the world. Because the extent of interdependence between particular nations varies greatly, some analysts (such as Waltz, 1970 and 1979) have questioned whether it is appropriate to regard the world today as more interdependent than in previous periods.[1] But if we think of interdependence as *mutual sensitivity* and *mutual vulnerability* (Keohane and Nye, 1977), from a global perspective there is little question that the economic fate of nation-states has today become intertwined at unprecedented levels. When the *internal* welfare of nations is seen as being increasingly interlocked, the dependence of one country on another is made all the more apparent. For many states, interdependence means the inability to control their own fate.

The external economic environment affects countries whether they like it or not. High interest rates in one country lead to high interest rates in others. Recession at home becomes recession abroad. Inflation is felt everywhere. Its control rests with no single country, but with many. National decision makers may abhor these facts, as may the citizens they govern, but in many important respects nations are increasingly unable to control or even ignore them. The world energy situation provides an obvious example: the uneven distribution of world energy consumption compared with production has necessitated massive transfers of both petroleum and cash across national borders. Another example of interdependence is found in the pressure on the world's food and mineral resources that has resulted from the unprecedented increases in population.

The linkages between the United States and the rest of the world illustrate how important transnational economic ties have become. As described by an American policy maker, "Nearly 10 million American jobs depend on our exports. Two-thirds of our imports are raw materials that we do not or cannot readily produce.

---

1. Part of the difficulty arises out of the multiple meanings of *interdependence*. For a sampling of empirical studies using quantitative indicators to assess trends in various aspects of global interdependence, see Katzenstein (1975), Krasner (1976), Rosecrance et al. (1977), and Rosecrance and Stein (1973).

One out of three dollars of U.S. corporate profits is derived from international activities" (Christopher, 1978: 1).

Rising interdependence has raised important questions about the problems that have long affected world politics. The balance of fiscal power now seems as important to national security and the quality of life as does the balance of military power. The confluence of military, political, and social factors has tended to merge and confuse issues. As one American policy maker observed, "The outward surge of American corporate enterprise at its present magnitude has a powerful impact on a broad spectrum of policy issues . . . [and it has become] difficult to know where business ends and foreign policy, political and economic, begins" (Samuels, 1970).

The increasing importance of global economic conditions has influenced political relations among nations and, indeed, has stimulated transformations in world politics generally. The term *political economy* highlights the intersection of politics and economics, which have assumed increasingly tight linkages as the world has grown more interdependent economically.

It is in the intersection of politics and economics that some of the most significant controversies in world politics find dramatic expression. The contests between rich and poor, North and South, supplier and producer, metropole and colony, and advantaged and disadvantaged are all crucially affected by the interplay of political and economic forces. Political economy has become important because politics (the exercise of power) determines economics (how things of value are distributed). "Economics is when I have it; politics is when you want it" (Hirsch, 1976). Under conditions of scarcity, the two become inseparably joined.

The conditions in the global political economy have even called into question the suitability of conventional institutions through which countries interact, including the nation-state itself. One eminent international economist has speculated that "The nation-state is just about through as an economic unit. . . . The world is too small. It. . . [does] not permit the sovereign independence of the nation-state in economic affairs" (Kindleberger, 1969). Changes within the global political economy thus challenge the entire texture of world politics.

The purpose of this chapter and the next is to explore the sources of these developments and to assess their implications. Discussion will focus on four interrelated aspects of the international political economy: (1) the international monetary system; (2) the system of international trade as conducted among the industrialized nations of the First World, and (3) between them and the developing nations of the Third World; and (4) the economic linkages between the First World and the planned economies of the Second World.

THE TRANSFORMATION OF THE
INTERNATIONAL MONETARY SYSTEM

Nation-states came into being as the principal actors in world politics in part to further the capacity of their people to acquire desired economic goods, to enhance the general economic welfare, and to protect what was obtained (including the political status achieved as a consequence of past economic success).

States have organized themselves for these purposes quite differently. Some have developed what can be thought of as "open" economic systems. Open systems in principle allow the "invisible hand" of the marketplace to determine the flow of economic transactions within and across the state's borders. For that reason such countries usually have what are called "market" economies. At the opposite end of this spectrum are "closed" systems. Because closed systems rely on government intervention to regulate and manage the economy, they are also called "centrally planned" or "command" economies. Taxes, wage and price controls, monetary regulations, tariffs, and other policy instruments are used in closed systems to inhibit competitive market forces as determinants of economic transactions.

"Open" and "closed" are useful conventions for classifying differences between economic systems. But they are relative terms. No economy is completely open or closed. Every system has, to a greater or lesser extent, ingredients of both types.[2]

Where a nation falls along the open-closed continuum is important in undertanding how it might adjust imbalances in its economic transactions with the rest of the world. For many states, trade is the most important international economic transaction. A deficit in their *balance of trade* would result from an imbalance between exports and imports, from more being purchased abroad than is sold. The *balance of payments* is a more inclusive summary statement of a state's financial transactions with the rest of the world. The

2. In fact, all national economies are relatively closed; none is a completely unregulated, laissez-faire, free-enterprise economy. The tendency of government authorities to intervene in their economies may be partly a consequence of the growing dependence of states on one another for the goods necessary for economic well-being, including such critical commodities as oil. Cameron (1978) argues that increased collectivism at home is a consequence of vulnerability to international economic forces. This conclusion raises the question of whether increased international interdependence will necessarily lead to a further concentration of economic as well as political power in the hands of national governments.

balance-of-payments figure includes, for example, items not included in trade, such as foreign-aid transfers and the repatriation of income by citizens employed abroad who send their paychecks home.

> The process of adjusting international income to international expenses is straightforward for countries with closed economies. For example, they can simply reduce or increase their imports of certain commodities by fiat. Countries with relatively open economies can do the same—impose import restrictions or capital controls—but that has the effect of making their economies significantly less open. Nations committed to maintaining the openness of their economies have two major means to make adjustments—changing the level of domestic economic activity or changing the exchange rate of their currency [the rate at which one nation's currency can be converted into another]. Both of these techniques of adjustment leave the market unimpaired, but each can have a major impact on the fabric of social life. If, for example, a country has a balance-of-payments deficit, either lowering the level of economic activity—deflating—or lowering the exchange rate—devaluation—is designed to reduce the country's international expenditures while increasing its international revenues. However, deflating the economy means putting people out of work and applying downward pressure on real wage levels. Similarly, an effective devaluation will also reduce real wage levels. In short, these adjustment techniques work by affecting the level of employment and the level of income. (Block, 1977: 2)

Regardless of whether a country's economic system is relatively open or closed, the process of adjusting its international economic transactions has important domestic consequences. This fact helps explain why states are sensitive to the way international commercial relations are organized and conducted.

In principle, and in conformity with the notion of sovereignty, economic relations between states are voluntary. They are cooperative exchanges that nations enter into freely for mutual benefit. Indeed, the *raison d'être* of foreign trade is that it provides advantages to both parties engaged in the exchange. According to the principle of *comparative advantage*, all nations will benefit *if* each specializes in producing what it can best produce (those things in which it has relative advantages) and *if* it buys from others the things *they* are better equipped to produce. When trade is unfettered by nonmarket forces or politically imposed barriers, all nations benefit. This simple conclusion—that the net gain in welfare to most countries is greater as a consequence of their trade with one another—constitutes the fundamental assumption of classic (liberal) international trade theory.

The actual operation of the international economic system is, of course, far more complicated. Nations routinely interfere with free trade, whether in pursuit of self-advantage or out of fear of victimization. Political considerations thus interrupt the free flow of goods across national boundaries. And because states are not equal economically (some are endowed with greater resources and productive capacities than others), the state of the international economy is shaped by political motives among unequals. Such motives include the search for self-benefit instead of mutual benefit, for self-advantage at the expense of others. Competition among countries in the international economic hierarchy, and not just cooperation among them, is evident. Among the reasons that some nations prefer relatively open economic systems and others relatively closed ones is the desire of all to control the way international economic transactions affect national conditions; different paths to the same goal are selected, based on differences in national circumstances and different vulnerabilities to exploitation.

The variation evident in national postures toward international economic issues undoubtedly stems as well from the relative positions in which countries find themselves in the international pecking order. Rules governing international commerce (like rules governing international politics) often evolve according to the wishes of the stronger players. Historically, these have been the advanced capitalist societies of the Western industrialized world, notably Britain in the nineteenth century and the United States in the twentieth. The more powerful states have habitually used military superiority and economic advantage to exercise leverage over others.

> This leverage is generally used to create an international order with a high degree of openness so that capitalists from the strongest economy will be able to take advantage of opportunities for profit in other countries. In short, a world order in which the flow of goods and capital is determined largely by market forces will maximize the advantages for the country with the highest level of technical development and with the most enterprising and strongest firms. (Block, 1977: 3)

More powerful capitalist states prefer open systems because their relatively greater control of technology, capital, and raw materials provides them greater opportunities to reap the advantages of a system that operates according to the principle of comparative advantage. At the same time that the more powerful states have special advantages, however, they also have special responsibilities. They must assure that nations facing balance-of-payments deficits will be able to obtain the credits necessary to finance their deficits. If the powerful states cannot do this, they are likely to move toward more closed economies domestically, which would undermine the open international system otherwise advantageous to them (Block, 1977). Generally, powerful states must make certain that the liquidity (the reserve assets held by states for purposes of settling their international accounts) in the system is sufficient for purposes of carrying on international financial transactions. In short, those states with the greatest ability to influence the system also have the greatest responsibility to assure its effective operation.

The ability of the more powerful states to manage the international economic system can change. In the twentieth century, America assumed the managerial role played by the British in the nineteenth century. This shift, particularly obvious by the end of World War II, reflected the changed pecking order of the powerful in world politics. If such a shift occurred once, perhaps it might occur again. Indeed, most observers agree that the international political economy is undergoing a profound transformation. The nature and source of this transition can be better appreciated by an examination of the role of the United States in the management of international economic relations in the post-World War II period and the challenges that have been mounted against that role. Focus on the international monetary system is crucial, for, as Charles P. Kindleberger (1977b) has observed, it is here that occurred "the primary unraveling of the American dominance, hegemony, or leadership in the world economic system."

The Role of the United States in Managing the International Monetary System

Planning among the World War II allies for the postwar world began even as the allies continued their military struggle against the Axis powers. Any number of lessons had been drawn from the experiences of the interwar years, particularly the great depression of the 1930s. A principal lesson was that the United States could not remain aloof from world affairs, as it had sought to do after World War I. As a result, the United States played an active leadership role in molding the various rules and institutions that were to govern international relations in the post-World War II world.

In the economic sphere the rules and institutions came to be known as the Bretton Woods system, named for the New Hampshire conference site where the agreements were negotiated. As envisioned in the Bretton Woods agreements of 1944, these rules and institutions would lead to a postwar international monetary system characterized by stability, predictability, and orderly growth. Governments would have primary responsibility for enforcing the rules and otherwise making the system work effectively. They would be assisted by the International Monetary Fund (IMF), created at Bretton Woods as a formal mechanism to assist states in dealing with such matters as maintaining equilibrium in the balance of payments and stability in their exchange rates with one another. The International Bank for Reconstruction and Development (IBRD), now known popularly as the World Bank, was also designed as a vehicle to facilitate recovery from the war, although its role has since expanded to include promoting economic development in the Third World.

The postwar economic structure rested on three important political bases: "the concentration of power in a small number of states, the existence of a cluster of important interests shared by those states, and the presence of a dominant power willing and able to assume a leadership role"[3] (Spero, 1977).

Power was concentrated in the hands of the developed countries of Western Europe and North America. Neither Japan nor the Third World posed an effective challenge to Western dominance, and the communist states of Eastern Europe and the Soviet Union effectively removed themselves (or were removed) from the rest of the international economy as they concentrated on internal development and construction of their own socialist system of international economic relationships. The concentration of power thus minimized the number of states whose agreement was necessary in order to make the system operate effectively.

Effective operation of the system was facilitated by the interests shared among these states, including a preference for an open economic system combined with a commitment to limited government intervention, if this proved necessary. The onset of the Cold War was a powerful force cementing Western cohesion on economic issues. Because the West saw itself faced with a common external enemy, economic cooperation came to be perceived as necessary, not only for prosperity, but also for national security. This perception contributed to a willingness to share economic burdens. It was also an important catalyst to the assumption of leadership by only one state and to the acceptance of that leadership role by others. The leader was, of course, the United States.

America's role until the 1960s. Although the International Monetary Fund and the World Bank have become important instruments for effective operation of the international economic system, in the im-

---

3. The subsequent discussion of the international monetary system draws on this source.

mediate postwar period they proved insufficient for the task of managing postwar economic recovery. These institutions were simply given too little authority and too few financial resources to cope with the enormous economic devastation suffered by Western Europe during the war. The United States stepped into the breach.

The United States dollar became the key to America's managerial role. Backed by a vigorous and healthy economy, a fixed relationship between gold and the dollar (that is, $35 per ounce of gold), and a commitment by the government to exchange gold for dollars at any time (known as dollar "convertibility"), the dollar became as good as gold. In fact, it was preferable to gold as the liquid investment for other countries' balance-of-payments surpluses and savings. Dollars earned interest, which gold did not; they did not entail storage and insurance costs; and they were needed to buy imports necessary for survival and postwar reconstruction.

Thus the postwar economic system was not simply a modified gold standard system; it was a dollar-based system. Dollars became a major component of the international reserves used by national monetary authorities in other countries, and of the "working balances" used by private banks, corporations, and individuals for purposes of international trade and capital transactions. Moreover, the dollar became a "parallel currency," that is, it was universally accepted as the "currency against which every other country sold or redeemed its own national currency in the exchange markets" (Triffin, 1978–1979). In order to maintain the value of their currencies, central banks in other countries either bought or sold their own currencies, using the U.S. dollar to raise or depress the currencies' value. Such intervention was often necessary, since, under the Bretton Woods agreements, states were committed to keeping fluctuations in their exchange rates within very narrow limits. Bretton Woods, in other words, was based on a system of fixed exchange rates (as opposed to floating rates, where only market forces determine currency values).

A central problem of the immediate postwar years was how to get American dollars into the hands of those who needed them most. One mechanism was the Marshall Plan, which provided Western European nations with resources to buy the American goods necessary to rebuild their war-torn economies. Eventually $17 billion in Marshall Plan assistance flowed to Western Europe.

International liquidity in the form of dollars was also provided by the deliberate American encouragement of deficits in its own balance of payments, through massive outflows of foreign aid and expenditures to maintain the burgeoning American overseas military commitments. In addition to providing international liquidity, the

United States supported European and Japanese trade competitiveness and condoned certain forms of protectionism (such as Japanese restrictions against products imported from the United States) and discrimination against the dollar (such as the European Payments Union, a multilateral European group which promoted intra-European trade at the expense of trade with the United States). These short-run costs were incurred on the basis of the assumption that in the long run, a rejuvenated Europe and Japan would provide widening markets for American exports. The perceived political benefits of strengthening the Western world against the threat of communism were also considerable.

"The system worked well. Europe and Japan recovered and then expanded. The American economy prospered in spite of or partly because of the dollar outflow which led to the purchase of American goods and services" (Spero, 1977). Furthermore, the "top currency" role of the dollar facilitated the globalist foreign policy posture the United States assumed in the postwar years (Strange, 1971). Other nations were more than happy to hold dollars as a reserve currency, even without convertibility into gold. The foreign economic and military aid programs of the United States overseas were made possible by acceptance of the dollar as the means of paying for them. Business interests could readily expand abroad because American foreign investments were often considered desirable, and American tourist dollars could be spent with few restrictions. In effect, the United States operated as the world's banker. Others were required to balance their financial inflows and outflows. In contrast, the United States enjoyed the advantages of operating internationally without the constraints of limited finances. The political and economic importance of the United States also meant that developments within the nation had significant implications for the monetary affairs of other nations. Through the pervasive dollar, the United States came to exert influence on the political and economic affairs of most other nations (Blake and Walters, 1976).

Yet there were costs. Just as the United States was able to exert influence over others, it became sensitive to what was happening elsewhere. Massive private investments overseas, perceived to be linked to domestic prosperity, created concern in the United States about "nationalization" of American overseas enterprises and of American holdings by foreign governments. The vast number of dollars held by others also made the American domestic economy vulnerable to financial shocks abroad. Decision makers therefore sought to insulate the American economy from these shocks, but the task was made more difficult because some tools available to others were proscribed by the status of the dollar as a reserve currency. Devaluation of the dollar, for example, would adversely affect political friends and military allies who had chosen to hold large amounts of American currency and was an action unlikely to be taken in an environment characterized by hostility toward and competition with the Soviet bloc.

In 1959, Robert Triffin (then an American government official) suggested that the dollar-based international monetary system was inherently not viable. Triffin explained in his own words what became known as the "Triffin dilemma":

> I forecast that (a) if the United States corrected its persistent deficits, the growth of world reserves could not be fed adequately by gold production at $35 an ounce; but that (b) if our deficits continued, our foreign liabilities would far exceed our ability to convert them into gold upon demand, and bring about a gold and dollar crisis. (Triffin, 1978–1979: 272)

Eventually both of Triffin's predictions proved accurate: a means of feeding world reserves other than through dollar-linked gold had to be found; and the number of foreign-held dollars came to far outstrip the ability of the United States to convert them into gold. The latter circumstance led the United States to sever the link between the dollar and gold.

The demise of American dominance, 1960–1971. By as early as 1960 it was apparent that the "top currency" status of the dollar was on the wane. Thereafter, the dollar-based international monetary system unilaterally managed by the United States became a multilaterally managed system under American leadership. Several factors help to explain the dollar's declining position.

If a dollar shortage was the problem in the immediate postwar years, by the 1960s a glut became the problem. The willingness of others to hold the dollar as a reserve currency eroded. Indeed, the costs of overseas military activities, foreign economic and military aid, and massive private investments produced increasing balance-of-payments deficits, which earlier had been encouraged but later ran out of control. Furthermore, American gold holdings in relation to the growing number of foreign-held dollars declined precipitously. Given these circumstances, the possibility that the United States might devalue the dollar led to a loss of confidence by others and hence an unwillingness to continue to hold dollars as reserve currency. The French under the leadership of Charles de Gaulle even went so far as to insist on exchanging dollars for gold.

At the same time that a dollar glut came to characterize the international liquidity situation, massive transnational movements of capital came to reflect increasing monetary interdependence. The internationalization of banking, the internationalization of production via multinational corporations, and the development of a Eurocurrency market[4] outside direct state control were all stimulants to interdependence. An increasingly complex relationship between economic policies engineered in one country and their effects on another was the result. This dependence of one state on another promoted efforts to protect the value of states' currencies from attack by speculators. A mechanism evolved for swapping the currency of one nation for claims held by another. Known as the Basel Agreement, it was designed to cope with the various foreign exchange crises that punctuated the 1960s, particularly those affecting the British pound. Various mechanisms to ease the strain of a run on American gold stocks were also devised since such a run could undermine confidence in the dollar and hence the system as a whole.[5] Finally, a form of "paper gold" known as Special Drawing Rights (SDRs) was created in the IMF to facilitate the growth of international liquidity by means other than increasing the outflow of dollars.

Although the United States was the chief proponent as well as supporter of the various management techniques devised during the 1960s, none proved sufficient to counter the crises that began to afflict the dollar in the late 1960s and early 1970s. Following devaluation of the British pound in late 1967 and the resulting massive speculation against the dollar in the form of gold purchases, the United States began to act unilaterally to protect the dollar.

> In March 1968, the United States simply announced that it would no longer support the price of gold at $35 an ounce in the free market. From that point on, there would be a two-tier gold market, with official transactions at $35 an ounce and the free market allowed to reach its own level. This amounted to renunciation of a U.S. obligation under the Bretton Woods Agreement. It stopped short, however, of a unilateral U.S. refusal to redeem all dollars held by foreign central banks for gold. (Block, 1977: 194)

The two-tier gold market eased the pressure on the United States to protect the dollar. It did not end speculation against the dollar, however. Instead, it shifted the burden for controlling the ef-

---

4. Eurocurrencies are dollars and other currencies held in Europe as bank deposits and lent and borrowed outside the country of origin.

5. See Block (1977) for examination of the evolution of United States international monetary policy during this period, which included capital controls at home in addition to the other devices already mentioned.

fects of speculation to others. Selling dollars for other currencies became, under the new arrangement, the only way to speculate against the dollar. To maintain their currencies' exchange rates, foreign central banks were compelled to absorb as many dollars as speculators made available for sale.

The unwillingness of others (including possibly monetary authorities in other countries) to hold American dollars was grounded in the changing international political system as well as the changing economic system. By the 1960s the European and Japanese recovery from World War II was complete, which meant that American monetary dominance and the privileged position of the dollar were no longer palatable. In a sense, however, the rejuvenated economies were still subject to the wishes of the wealthy United States. To them this may have been perceived as a loss of sovereignty.

The Europeans and Japanese especially came to resent the prerogatives the United States derived from its position as the world's banker and from its ability to determine the level of international liquidity through its balance-of-payments deficits. Not only did these prerogatives affect the economies of Europe and Japan, they also gave the United States the ability to make foreign expenditures for political purposes that came to be less and less acceptable to others.

Among the political pursuits with which many European nations disagreed was the Vietnam War. And among the economic conditions which they came to share was inflation, which in the United States was stimulated by the Johnson administration's unwillingness to raise taxes to finance either the Great Society domestic programs or the Vietnam conflict. In this sense Europe was "forced" to pay for another country's foreign policy adventures, about which they had fundamental reservations.

The evolving relationship between the United States and the Soviet Union reflected in détente also had an impact on the Western-based economic system. The decline in fear of, and hostility toward, the Soviet Union as an external threat carried with it a decline in the willingness of others to accede to American leadership. The changing international political environment thus combined with the changing international economic environment to militate against continued American hegemony in international monetary matters.

The United States domestic economic situation also began to erode its leadership position, particularly as inflation contributed to a relative loss in competitiveness of American goods overseas. Historically, the United States had enjoyed favorable balances of trade. This was important, since the favorable trade balances were used to offset the unfavorable payments balances, which by the end of the 1960s had become chronic. The favorable trade situation itself eroded by 1971, however, when for the first time in the twentieth century the United States suffered a trade deficit of $2 billion. The situation worsened in 1972, when the deficit reached $6.2 billion. The political response to this situation was perhaps predictable. Cries by industrial, labor, and agricultural interests, which already had begun to adopt protectionist positions regarding trade policy (designed to insulate the domestic economy from foreign competition), became even more shrill.

The reasons for the inability of the United States to control its balance-of-payments deficits are many and varied, including an unwillingness to pull back from the costly, globalist foreign policy posture the nation had assumed since World War II and a lag in modernization of its economic productive facilities, growing out of the decision of American-based multinational firms to build branch plants abroad rather than new facilities at home. These ideas are elaborated by Fred L. Block, whose revisionist analysis of the roots of the American payments deficits concludes thus:

> The exercise of American political and military power on a global basis has been designed to gain foreign acceptance of an international monetary order that institutionalizes an open world economy, giving maximum opportunities to American businessmen. It would be absurd for the United States to abandon its global ambitions simply to live within the rules of an international monetary order that was shaped for the purpose of achieving these ambitions. So it is hardly surprising that the United States continued to pursue its global ambitions despite the increasing strains on the international monetary order. The fundamental contradiction was that the United States had created an international monetary order that worked only when American political and economic dominance in the capitalist world was absolute. That absolute dominance disappeared as a result of the reconstruction of Western Europe and Japan, on the one hand, and the accumulated domestic costs of the global extension of U.S. power, on the other. With the fading of the absolute dominance, the international monetary order began to crumble. The U.S. deficit was simply the most dramatic symptom of the terminal disease that plagued the postwar international monetary order. (Block, 1977: 163)

Whatever the fundamental causes of its payments deficits, part of the blame for the newly emergent trade deficit was laid at the doorstep of America's major trading partners. Japan and West Germany in particular were criticized as having undervalued currencies (that is, their currencies did not accurately reflect the cost of Japanese and German goods within those countries). This made their goods attractive internationally (and to the American consumer), which in turn enabled these countries to generate balance-of-payments surpluses. Again, regardless of the particular reasons, there was little question that the position of the United States in international trade was deteriorating. Although the value of American exports had increased tremendously during the postwar years, the nation's share of total world exports declined from 16.7 percent in 1955 to 11.7 percent in 1971 and an estimated 11.3 percent in 1976. (In contrast, the European Community increased its share from just over 30 percent in 1955 to 41 percent in 1971 and 39 percent in 1976; and Japan increased its share from 2.1 percent in 1955 to 6.4 percent in 1971 and 6.6 percent in 1976.)

Faced with these factors, President Nixon in August 1971 inaugurated what was termed a New Economic Policy. Wage and price controls were imposed at home, the convertibility of dollars into gold was suspended, and a surcharge of 10 percent was levied on all imports as a way of forcing America's trading partners into a revaluation of their currencies. Eventually the dollar was devalued by some 18 percent (effected by increasing the price of an ounce of gold), and in December 1971 the currencies of other nations were adjusted to better reflect their real values. A system of free-floating currency values emerged, one where currency values are determined by market forces rather than governmental regulations. Together, these actions had the effect of suspending the 1944 Bretton Woods agreements under which the international monetary system had operated for nearly three decades.

The actions of the United States in 1971 came as a shock to other members of the international monetary system. The actions represented a new stridency in America's approach to international economic matters that perhaps reflected the simultaneous perception of Americans of their dependence on the rest of the world and their realization that the United States alone could no longer determine the course of international monetary matters. Thus the political bases on which the Bretton Woods system had been built lay in ruins. American leadership was no longer accepted willingly by others nor exercised willingly by the United States. Power had come to be more widely dispersed among the states making up the system, and the shared interests that once bound them together had dissipated.

International Monetary Disorder: The 1970s and Beyond

Formal negotiations on reform of the international monetary system were begun in the summer of 1972. Before anything could be decided, however, the world economy suffered yet another shock—a massive increase in the price of oil effected by the Organization of Petroleum Exporting Countries shortly after the 1973 Yom Kippur War in the Middle East. The impact of the price rise on the oil-import costs of consuming nations was dramatic. The cost of American oil imports skyrocketed from less than $8 billion in 1973 to over $24 billion the following year. For other Western industrialized nations the increase in costs was even more severe, moving from $22.2 billion in 1973 to $61 billion in 1974. And the import costs of the non-oil-producing countries of the Third World moved from $6 billion in 1973 to $16 billion in 1974, or from 9 percent of their export earnings to 20 percent (*International Economic Report of the President, 1976*: 5)

The global economic impact of these skyrocketing costs was equally substantial: worldwide inflation and worldwide recession now occurred simultaneously, and, as Figure 6.1 demonstrates, substantial dislocations occurred in the balance-of-payments positions of many nations as billions of "petrodollars" flowed to the oil-producing states. Thus a major new problem arose in the international monetary field—how to recycle "petrodollars" from oil producers to oil consumers.

Although some observers had predicted that the magnitude of the recycling problem would lead to the imminent collapse of the international economic order, recycling did occur despite obstacles. In addition to the IMF, the World Bank, and individual nations, private banks in the capitalist world proved particularly effective in managing the flow of funds. In the process, however, the debt burden of many nations, particularly in the Third World, assumed ominous proportions.[6] Thus the problem of recycling has persisted, and it was given another jolt by the oil price increases announced by OPEC members in 1979 and 1980.

Although the world entered a recessionary period following OPEC's actions in 1973–1974, worldwide inflation persisted. *Stagflation*—the term coined to describe a stagnant economy characterized by a coincidence of rising unemployment and high inflation—entered the lexicon of economic discussions.[7]

6. The fear is that the burden of servicing the debt will outstrip the developing nations' capacity, particularly if their debt-service payments grow more rapidly than their export earnings. Unfortunately, it is difficult to determine the precise magnitude of this debt. Estimates vary in part because of the difficulty of measuring the value of private loans not guaranteed by the public sector, and hence loans that are beyond those normally reported to and by government agencies. The World Bank (*World Development Report, 1979*: 29), reports that the outstanding debt of low- and middle-income countries in 1977 was $258 billion, a figure that presumably refers to public debt only. See also McLaughlin (1979a).

7. The advent of world "stagflation," for example, provoked Roy Jenkins, president of the European Common Market's executive commission, to warn that "We face no less than the breakup of the established economic and social order on which postwar Europe has been built. If we don't change our ways while there is still time—and 1980 could be the last opportunity—our society will risk dislocation and eventual collapse" (*Los Angeles Times*, March 23, 1980).

Figure 6.1
Current Account Balances, by Groups of Countries, 1973–1979

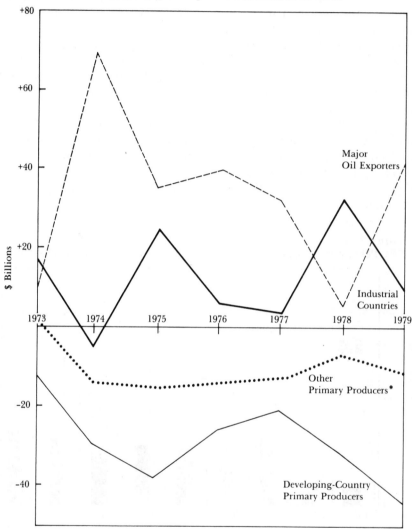

Source: John W. Sewell and the Staff of the Overseas Development Council, *The United States and World Development: Agenda 1980* (New York: Praeger, 1980). International Monetary Fund staff projection.

*Australia, Finland, Greece, Iceland, Ireland, Malta, New Zealand, Portugal, Romania, South Africa, Spain, Turkey, and Yugoslavia.

Note: Centrally planned economies are not included.

The persistence of global inflation is illustrated in Figure 6.2, which charts petroleum prices from 1972 through mid-1979. Although oil prices continued to climb from 1974 to 1979, it is noteworthy that in real terms (constant, noninflated dollars) oil in 1978 was actually less expensive than in 1974. Not until the official posted price of OPEC oil moved above the $20 per barrel mark in 1979 did the real return to OPEC increase. The differences between the current and constant dollar cost of petroleum is, of course, inflation. This means that, despite the enormous increases in the numbers of dollars OPEC nations earned between 1974 and 1979, the dollars were not worth any more in terms of the goods and services they could buy than they were in 1974. Even with the continued upward spiral of petroleum prices since mid-1979, illustrated in Figure 6.3, it is doubtful that the real return to OPEC increased substantially.[8]

Figure 6.2
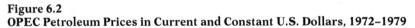
OPEC Petroleum Prices in Current and Constant U.S. Dollars, 1972–1979

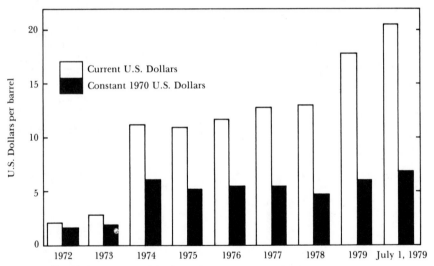

Source: *World Development Report, 1979* (New York: Oxford University Press for the World Bank, 1979), p. 11.

Note: The prices shown are average prices for each year. They refer to petroleum exports by the Organization of Petroleum Exporting Countries, and are based on estimates of realized export prices and government sales prices, weighted by countries' shares in total output. Realized and government sale prices are f.o.b. loading ports in OPEC countries. The prices in constant US dollars have been deflated using the Index of International Prices, which is an index of the c.i.f. prices of manufactured goods exported by industrialized countries to all destinations. The prices shown for 1979 are estimates based on information available as of July 1, 1979.

8. See Ecklund (1980) for an examination of the impact of spiraling inflation and the declining value of the dollar on the real price of oil.

Figure 6.3
World Price of Oil, 1979–1980

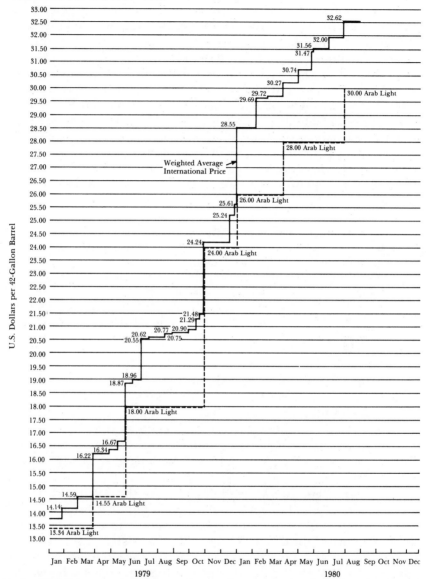

Source: U.S. Department of Energy, Energy Information Administration, "Weekly Petroleum Status Report" (October 3, 1980), p. 40.

Note: Internationally traded oil only. Arab Light refers to Benchmark Crude, which is used by OPEC to set official sales price.

Although the cost of oil increased for everyone, its impact on the United States was particularly severe because of the role of the American dollar in international economic affairs. American dependence on foreign sources of oil began to grow dramatically at precisely the time that the per-barrel cost of oil first shot upward. Massive amounts of dollars were therefore spent overseas, expenditures that topped $40 billion for petroleum and petroleum products in 1977 and then soared to a record $56 billion in 1979[9] (see Figure 6.4). Overall, foreign-dollar claims against the United States (U.S. government indebtedness and banks' liabilities to foreigners) roughly doubled between 1969 and 1972, and then doubled again by 1977, moving from $78 billion (in 1969) to $373 billion (in 1977). International reserves also doubled twice during this period, moving from $79 billion in 1969 to $159 billion in 1972 and $319 billion at the end of 1977.

> Taken together, official and private dollar and Eurodollar holdings [stood] . . . well in excess of $700 billion. . . . This fantastic increase in international liquidity was well on its way before the suspension of the convertibility of the dollar [into gold] in August 1971, the generalized adoption of floating [exchange] rates in March 1973, and the fivefold increase in oil prices in the fall of that year. It has continued since then, however, at an unabated pace, and is undoubtedly the biggest factor in triggering the worst global inflation in history. (Triffin, 1978–1979: 273)

The massive influx of dollars into the international monetary system requires that someone be willing to hold them. The decline in the value of the dollar during the 1970s suggests that the dollar is no longer sought. Figure 6.4 charts the declining value of the dollar in relation to the German mark and the Swiss franc, two national currencies that showed particular strength against the dollar during this period.

The coincidence of the declining value of the dollar and the rising cost of foreign-oil imports illustrated in Figure 6.4 suggests that America's seemingly insatiable energy appetite is an important underlying cause of the decline of the dollar. Persistent inflation in the United States—itself fed by rising fuel costs, the cumulative costs of past wars and present defense expenditures, and federal budgetary increases in the public sector generally—is also a factor. Ironically, the decline in the value of the dollar internationally may also feed domestic inflation as the dollar cost of foreign-produced goods in-

9. If imports of mineral fuels, lubricants, and related products are added to the somewhat narrower import category of petroleum and petroleum products, total American import costs were $44.5 billion and $60.1 billion in 1977 and 1979 respectively.

Figure 6.4
United States Petroleum Import Costs and the Value of the United States Dollar, 1970–1979

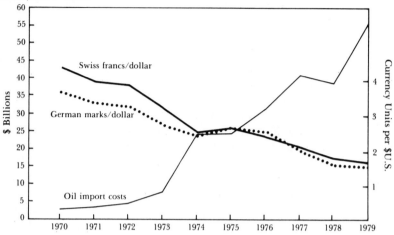

Source: Petroleum import costs for 1970–1976, U.S. Department of Commerce, *Business Statistics, 1977* (Washington, D.C.: Government Printing Office, 1978), p. 115; for 1977, U.S. Department of Commerce, *Survey of Current Business*, 59 (November 1979), S–20; for 1978–1979, U.S. Department of Commerce, *Survey of Current Business*, 60 (March 1980), S–20. Currency units per dollar, United Nations, *Monthly Bulletin of Statistics*, 34 (April 1980), 222–224.
Note: National currency units per dollar are based on midpoint exchange rates for the end of the period shown.

creases. The importance of this fact is heightened by the growing proportion of imports in America's national product. In the decade ending in 1978, American imports as a proportion of GNP more than doubled, moving from 3.9 percent in 1969 to 8.1 percent in 1978. Since total American imports in 1978 were $172 billion, it is clear that the impact of foreign goods on domestic prices is likely to be significant.[10]

From the perspective of foreign countries, the persistent economic problems of the United States erode their willingness to hold dollars, which, of course, contributes to even further decline in the value of the dollar. As Triffin observes,

> the continued overflow of dollars abroad has piled up an enormous indebtedness (often called "overhang") of foreign dollar balances . . . which private holders are more and more tempted to unload on the

10. The inflationary impact of more costly foreign goods may be compounded by domestic producers, who, faced with reduced competition, may increase their own prices to maximize their profits. Similarly, workers may seek to increase their wages to maintain their real incomes in the face of rising costs of foreign-produced goods. But domestic price and wage inflation eat up the positive effects of American trade and payments balances that derive from the greater competitiveness abroad of American goods since the devaluation of the dollar.

market, and which central banks are absorbing, more and more reluctantly, to slow down the depreciation of the dollar vis-à-vis their own
currencies, and the consequent damaging impact on their own trade,
production, and employment. (Triffin, 1978-1979: 274)

The persistence of United States balance-of-payments deficits combined with the accumulation of foreign indebtedness "explains the
gloomy view of foreigners—and of many Americans—about the future of [the] once mighty dollar."

But designing an alternative international monetary system to
the one built on the once mighty dollar has proved difficult and elusive. Financial ministers and even heads of state met from time to
time during the 1970s in efforts to deal with the recurrent problems
facing the international monetary system. The IMF has provided a
forum for continuing efforts at reform, and it has developed a special $10 billion fund, known (by the name of a former managing
director of the fund) as the Witteveen facility, to be parceled out to
nations facing particularly heavy trade deficits. Discussion has also
focused on the possibility of creating within the IMF a "dollar substitution account" that would enable nations to trade unwanted dollars for IMF-backed funds rather than dumping them on the open
market. Nevertheless, nothing comparable to the agreements forging the Bretton Woods system over three decades ago has yet been
put in place. The inability of states to reach agreement is perhaps itself a reflection of growing interdependence—states are no longer
certain how to maximize their interests in a global context while
simultaneously minimizing the domestic economic and political
costs of foreign entanglements.

In the meantime, various states and groups of states have
moved toward reducing the role of the dollar in international economic affairs. The revolutionary government that assumed power
in Iran in 1979, for example, proposed that oil be paid for in currencies other than the dollar. Oil-producing nations typically price
their oil in dollars, which they must either invest or swap for other
currencies. If oil were priced in something other than dollars, the
value of the dollar could decline precipitously and the price of
America's imported oil go even higher.[11] If the role of the dollar diminished, the ability of the United States to pursue some of its foreign policy objectives might be curtailed.

11. Since oil is not only priced in dollars but also typically paid for with dollars,
the declining value of the dollar reduces the cost of oil to countries whose currencies
have appreciated, since the same amount of foreign currencies (such as yen, marks,
or francs) translates into larger numbers of dollars than when the dollar was "worth
more." See Ecklund (1980) for supporting data.

A less radical alternative that might ease pressure on the dollar without unduly affecting the United States would be to exchange dollars for a "basket" of key currencies that would be more stable than the dollar alone. Some combination of German marks, Swiss francs, and Japanese yen, for example, together with the dollar, could serve this purpose.

Still, many observers see the current worldwide energy picture as a critical factor underlying the present international monetary disorder as well as the prospects for reform. Following the 1979 oil-price spiral, the future did not appear auspicious:

> The most immediate peril of the soaring price of oil is that the industrial world and the majority of developing countries are confronted with the specter of chronic, global stagflation. Money sent overseas to pay for oil cannot be spent or invested at home, and this forces national monetary authorities to create more money to make up for what is being lost. In 1979, the U.S. will pay $65 billion for its oil imports, and by 1981 that could easily top $80 billion. The result for the U.S. and for much of the rest of the world is serious inflation and—with OPEC pricing its oil ahead of the global inflation rate—an inflation with no end.
>
> In fact, oil price rises now account for 25% to 50% of total inflation around the world. . . . National economic policies having proved ineffectual over the longer run, the OPEC effort to push oil prices ahead of world inflation threatens to become a deadly spiral that an occasional recession will slow but never really kill. Governments that try to fight the inevitable inflation that higher oil prices bring will find themselves curbing economic growth and raising unemployment, moves that could force them out of office. And nations that have to import their oil are faced with enormous balance-of-payments deficits that only heavy borrowing and fierce attempts to export can alleviate. (*Business Week*, November 19, 1979: 176–177).

Faced with the prospect of soaring costs and declining standards of living worldwide, the system of floating exchange rates that replaced Bretton Woods in the early 1970s has become less and less acceptable to some countries. In theory, a system of freely floating exchange rates ought to adjust the payments balances of countries either in surplus or in deficit. In practice, the almost daily fluctuations in the rate at which one currency can be exchanged for another is a source of instability and unpredictability. Not surprisingly, therefore, the system of floating exchange rates was never completely free of government intervention (and hence has been called the "dirty float"). Yet, as indicated earlier, the willingness of governments to continue to enter foreign exchange markets and to sell their own currencies to support the dollar became increasingly less acceptable because of the adverse effects on their own well-being.

In partial response to this situation the European Community in 1979 launched the European Monetary System (EMS), whose purpose is to stabilize the currency values of the member nations of the European Community against one another and against the dollar. The European Monetary System is projected to include eventually a European Monetary Fund and the creation of a common reserve asset called the European Currency Unit (ECU), which "could reduce Europe's historical dependence on the dollar and the monetary policy of the United States by offering Community members (and perhaps eventually other countries) an attractive alternative asset for reserve, and possibly even transaction, purposes" (Cohen, 1979).

Whether the European Monetary System can succeed in its ambitious goals remains to be seen.[12] Minimally, the goals suggest an attempt by a regional subsystem to introduce order into the recent international monetary chaos. To this extent it is testimony to nations' dissatisfaction with the current disarray. Beyond dissatisfaction, the EMS may be progenitor of a new international monetary system based on regionalism rather than internationalism. According to this view (see Novak, 1979, for an elaboration; see also Preeg, 1976), until the turn of the century international economic affairs will be marked by American dominance in the Western Hemisphere, European Community dominance in Western Europe and in those areas of Africa and the Caribbean linked by treaty to the European Community, and Japanese dominance in the Far East and Southeast Asia. The currency dominant in each sphere would be backed by political, and perhaps military, dominance of the hegemonic power. Each of the three power centers would seek to maximize harmony within its own area while protecting itself from inroads of the other two powers. At the same time, each center in this trilateral, regional structure might seek closer ties with Eastern Europe, the Soviet Union, and China in order to maximize its economic advantages.

Whether such a regionalized international economic system will emerge in a manner consistent with this picture, and whether out of that system a new, truly global system might again reemerge, is problematic. The image, nevertheless, suggests how pervasive

12. See Cohen (1979) for a skeptical view of the prospects for success. Arguments supporting the desirability of success from the viewpoint of the United States are advanced in Triffin (1978–1979).

transition in the current structure of international monetary affairs has become. If one of the lessons of the 1930s underlying the Bretton Woods system was the necessity of American participation in world affairs, perhaps another is that international peace may also be at stake as national decision makers pursue the task of repairing the disarray of the present international monetary order (Spero, 1977).

Thus the international monetary system is currently in a troubled and ambiguous state. Its future shape is unclear, its prospects for adaptive reform and revitalization uncertain. Unfortunately, the path to the creation of a stable future for international monetary arrangements is partially obstructed by the connection of that system politically with other global factors. Most directly linked to the issues of international monetary adjustment are the evolving dimensions of international trade relationships.

THE TRANSFORMATION OF THE INTERNATIONAL TRADE SYSTEM

The recurrent crises in the international monetary system and the seeming intractability of world energy issues overshadow the entire structure of international economic and political affairs. Moreover, just as these forces point to the possible emergence of a trilateral regional system of monetary arrangements, already these forces have induced states to compete more intensely in overseas markets to obtain the foreign exchange necessary to pay for imports, principally oil. Growth in protectionist sentiment has paralleled the intense competition for export markets as different countries and groups of countries seek to insulate themselves from foreign incursions and to shield themselves from reliance on external developments.[13] Such beggar-thy-neighbor strategies cannot work for every country, however; not every country can run a balance-of-trade surplus. As in the case of balances of payments, when one country is in a surplus position, another must experience a deficit.

Increased protectionism can lead to lower trade growth globally and nationally. Such a development can be particularly troublesome for countries incurring substantial oil-import debts. The burden of servicing debt is generally measured by the ratio of interest payments and amortization to exports. A figure of 10 to 15 percent is not disturbing, but "by the end of 1975, the debt-service ratios of

13. Mechanisms available for implementing protectionist strategies are discussed below.

some countries were approaching 40 percent, and a few reached as high as 60 percent" (Kindleberger, 1977a: 85). To generate the often staggering numbers of dollars such percentages represent,[14] an increase in export earnings is critical. Growing protectionism associated with increased export competition may mean the markets simply will not materialize. The effects on those holding the loans, particularly private banks in the Western world, could be catastrophic, but the impact would extend far beyond them.

Beyond the immediate problem of debts, growing protectionism entails a move away from the open or liberal multilateral trading system that has been nurtured during much of the post-World War II period (a system according to classical international trade theory in which none lose and most benefit). The forces currently militating against a liberal multilateral trading system can be better understood by examining the historical evolution of that system since World War II.

America's Leadership Role: From the 1940s to the 1970s

The importance of the United States to the international trade system derives from the combination of the size of its economy and the magnitude of its production sold abroad. In 1977, for example, American exports equaled 6 percent of its gross national product. This contrasts sharply with many other countries in the world who are relatively more "involved" in the world economy. Japan's exports-to-GNP ratio in the same year, for example, was 13 percent, West Germany's 24 percent, Britain's 25 percent, the Netherlands' 45 percent, Taiwan's 48 percent, and Liberia's 65 percent. Despite these higher ratios, however, only West Germany's exports rivaled in value the more than $121 billion of United States production sold abroad. In fact, the ranking among these seven countries in terms of the exports-to-GNP ratio is exactly the opposite of the countries' ranking in terms of the size of their economies. The gross national product of the United States in 1977 was nearly four times that of West Germany and many hundreds of times greater than that of Liberia. Generally, therefore, the American economy and United States policies relating to foreign economic matters are much more

14. McLaughlin (1979: 239) puts the debt service of 83 developing nations on $170 billion in external public debt in 1975 at $13.96 billion. This represents a debt-service ratio (payments as a percentage of exports) of 8.8 percent. Since 1975, however, it appears that the debt-service burden has become more pronounced. *Business Week* (November 19, 1979: 182) reports that "debt service payments have raced ahead of exports in 75% of all oil-importing countries from 1973 to 1978. . . . In fact, debt grew 2½ times faster than exports in more than half of these countries."

important to other nations than their economies and policies are to the United States, despite the relative decline in American economic dominance. As U.S. trade representative Reuben Askew (May 25, 1980) put it, "True, we are no longer the single, pre-eminent economic power in the world. But we are still the strongest."

The importance of the United States to the world economy was even more pronounced in the immediate postwar period. Today the United States accounts for roughly a quarter of the world's total GNP; in 1947 it accounted for half of all world production. It is not surprising, therefore, that the United States became the dominant voice in matters of trade as well as monetary affairs.

The liberal trading system that the United States promoted, like the position it took toward international monetary matters, was once again informed by the lessons the 1930s seemed to suggest. The beggar-thy-neighbor policies associated with the intense economic nationalism of the interwar period were viewed as a major contributing cause of the worldwide economic catastrophe of the 1930s, a catastrophe which ultimately ended in global warfare. In the postwar period, priority was assigned to removal of barriers to trade, particularly tariffs, whose purpose as an instrument of international economic policy is "to alter the structure of production by expanding the output of the protected goods" (Kindleberger, 1977a).

Management responsibilities for the postwar economic system as envisaged during World War II were to be entrusted to an International Trade Organization (ITO), which was to seek lower restrictions on trade and set rules of commerce. It was hoped that the ITO together with the IMF and World Bank could assist in avoiding repetition of the international economic breakdown that followed World War I. But ITO was stillborn.

The United States was the prime mover behind all three of these specialized international agencies. ITO failed when the liberal trading system envisioned in the Havana Charter was so watered down by demands from other countries for exemptions from the generalized rules that the United States government deemed the document worthless. In its place, the United States sponsored the General Agreement on Tariffs and Trade (GATT). In a sense, GATT, which is now an established international agency, became the cornerstone of the liberalized trading scheme originally embodied in the ITO.

The *most-favored-nation* (MFN) principle became the mortar of efforts to promote free and unfettered international trade. According to this principle the tariff preferences granted to one nation must be granted to all other nations exporting the same product. In other words (and in contrast to what the term seems to imply), the principle seeks elimination of preferential treatment and discrimination in the granting of trade concessions; every nation is to be treated the same as the most favored one, provided, of course, that the trading partners have previously agreed to grant one another MFN status.

Under the aegis of GATT and the most-favored-nation principle, a series of multilateral trade negotiations aimed at tariff reductions with broad national participation were undertaken. The seventh and most recent of these sessions was the Tokyo Round of Multilateral Trade Negotiations (MTN), so named since the basis for the negotiations was established in Tokyo in 1973. The MTN were brought to successful conclusion in Geneva in 1979 after nearly five years of bargaining.

Prior to the Tokyo Round, the last major international effort to reduce tariff rates was the Kennedy Round of negotiations, which actually took place during the Johnson administration (1964–1967). This was the high point of postwar momentum toward a liberalized trading system. Particular progress was made in reducing tariffs on industrial goods. And in this, as well as all prior multilateral trading conferences, the United States was the principal mover. As "leadership" implies, the United States was willing to accept fewer immediate benefits than its trading partners in anticipation of the longer-term benefits of freer international trade. In effect, the United States was the locomotive of expanding production and trade worldwide. By stimulating its own growth, the United States was an attractive market for the exports of others, and the outflow of United States dollars stimulated the economic growth of other nations in the "American train." Evidence supporting the wisdom of this strategy, particularly the association between tariff reductions and export growth, is provided in Figure 6.5. The average duty levied on imports to the United States was reduced by more than half between the late 1940s and the early 1960s. Correspondingly, world exports nearly tripled during this period.

The lack of progress during the Kennedy Round in reducing tariff barriers on agricultural products, and subsequent disagreements over this issue, began to raise doubts among American policy makers about the wisdom of America's expansionary policies. The immediate challenge was posed in 1966 in the Common Agricultural Policy (CAP) instituted by the European Economic Community (EEC). Toward others, CAP was a protectionist tariff wall designed to maintain politically acceptable but artificially high prices for farm products produced within the EEC. The effect was to curtail American agricultural exports to the EEC, which by the 1960s had become a principal trading partner of the United States.

Figure 6.5
Trends in Trade and Tariffs, 1928–1978

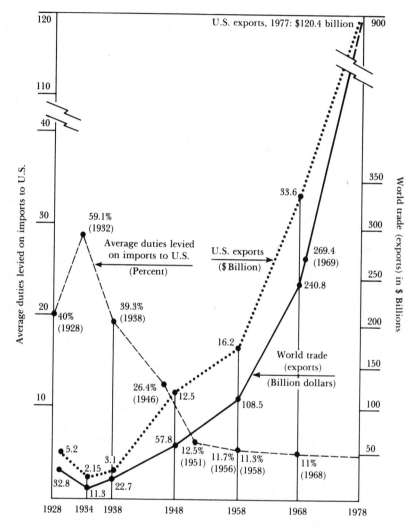

Source: *The Trade Debate* (Washington, D.C.: U.S. Department of State, 1978), p. 6.
Note: U.S. Export totals include military grant-aid and foreign merchandise.

Concern in the United States about the challenge of an economically revitalized and politically united Europe was among the factors that marked a change in the postwar multilateral trade system.
Other factors that began to erode the foundations of the liberalized
trading system included the extension by the European Community

of preferential trade treatment to nations in Africa, the Mediterranean, and the Caribbean; the expansion of the Common Market from six members to nine in 1973; the extension of associate status to others; and the feeling by many Wesfern nations that Japan continued to pursue highly protectionist trade policies in contrast to the liberalized trading scheme the others were seeking to create (Spero, 1977). Generally, the forces undermining the trade structure were much the same as those which undermined the international monetary system. The collapse of that system itself contributed to the lack of forward movement on trade matters.

In much the same way that the monetary disorder of the 1970s reflected the inability of the Bretton Woods system to master the international economic forces that had been unleashed, the erosion of the liberalized trading system of the 1950s and 1960s reflected the inability of GATT and the most-favored-nation principle to keep pace with new developments.

> GATT was formed to promote free-market competition among a maximum number of countries under a relatively few simple rules: nondiscrimination (the United States must treat Japanese and European products equally, for example); no barriers to imports other than declining tariffs; and no protection of faltering industries from import competition except through temporary measures taken publicly in emergency cases. These were rules for a simpler era, when trade was a fraction of its present volume, tariffs were the main trade barrier, a few Western countries dominated international trade and postwar optimism for international free enterprise was high—at least in the United States, which was the pre-eminent economic superpower.
>
> Although by the 1970s all of these circumstances had changed drastically, the GATT rules remained substantially the same and, as a result, were widely ignored. Without viable international rules, trade relations quickly revert to the law of the jungle. (Graham, 1979: 52)

The Demise of American Leadership: The 1970s and Beyond

The political necessity of maintaining product prices above their economically justifiable levels, illustrated by the European Community's agricultural policies, reflects an important underpinning of protectionist logic, namely, that protectionism often appeals to powerful domestic political interests which perceive the costs of free trade as greater than its benefits. The *infant industry* argument is perhaps the best-known rationale employed against free trade. According to this argument, tariffs or other forms of protection are necessary so as to nurture young industries until they can mature and until their ultimate lower-cost production enables them to compete effectively in the world marketplace.

The infant industries argument is articulated most commonly in Third World countries, for whom the absence of protection from more efficient Western firms prohibits realization of domestic industrialization goals. Among developed countries the argument against free trade is more commonly rationalized by the perceived need for protection from cheap foreign labor, or perhaps from more technologically sophisticated producers.

The techniques affording protection through nontariff mechanisms vary. *Import quotas*, for example, specify the quantity of a particular product that can be imported from abroad; they can have the same effects as tariffs by restricting imports, raising domestic prices, cutting consumption, and encouraging production (Kindleberger, 1977a). In the late 1950s, the United States established import quotas on oil, arguing that quotas were necessary to protect the nation's security. The economic effect was that the government, rather than the marketplace, determined how much would be imported and by whom. Sugar is another commodity the United States has subjected on occasion to quotas in pursuit of its foreign policy objectives, particularly in the Caribbean (see Krasner, 1978). The effect of quotas is to protect domestic producers regardless of their efficiency relative to foreign producers. Often this means the consumer either pays higher prices or must settle for commodities inferior to those that could otherwise be obtained from abroad.

Export quotas also impose barriers to free trade. Export and import quotas are similar, but the two differ in that import quotas are unilateral instruments of policy, while export quotas are imposed pursuant to negotiated agreements between producers and consumers. The United States has utilized export quotas to induce Japan, Hong Kong, South Korea, and Taiwan to limit their sale of textiles in the United States (Kindleberger, 1977a). *Orderly market arrangements* is a term sometimes used to describe these American-initiated instruments of protection.

Import and export quotas are two examples of a class of trade restrictions known as *nontariff barriers* (NTBs). NTBs have become more important forms of protection than tariffs (in the area of industrial products, at least, tariffs are now relatively unimportant inhibitions against the free flow of goods and services across national boundaries). Some types of NTBs have become particularly ubiquitous with the rise of the welfare state. As advanced industrial societies seek to ensure the welfare of their citizens through numerous and often extremely complex government regulations regarding health and safety, foreign-produced goods frequently cannot compete. Examples are the emission-control and safety standards imposed on the auto industry by the United States government to reduce air pollution and the risk of serious injury. When initiated, these standards, although meeting domestic needs, put burdens on certain foreign auto producers.

Health and safety standards have come to be regarded as necessary and legitimate forms of government regulation. They have no necessary bearing on international trade, but if they are imposed to limit external competition, and only secondarily, if at all, to safeguard domestic welfare, then they become legitimate objects of attack by free-trade advocates. The problem lies in the difficulty of distinguishing legitimate NTBs from regulations designed primarily to limit foreign competition. The difficulty is illustrated by the French and British, who "strongly suspect that U.S. noise regulations restricting the supersonic Concorde passenger plane are, at basis, an attempt to repress competition in the aircraft industry after the U.S. decision not to produce the Boeing SST" (Kindleberger, 1977a).

The range and variety of NTBs are extensive.[15] Just as health and safety regulations may be designed legitimately to protect a nation's citizens, the variety of measures often taken to limit foreign imports in contravention of what liberal trade theory would otherwise see as mutually beneficial to all—a liberal multilateral trade regime—is often deemed justified. Even though the goods produced by one country may be superior in quality and cheaper in price than those produced in another country, the latter country may still use import quotas, export quotas, and other nontariff barriers to keep the superior, less-expensive, foreign-produced goods out. It will do this if it perceives the superior performance of the foreign goods as resulting, not from purely market forces, but from government subsidies granted to the export industries in the producing country. Such subsidies reflect a *neomercantilist* posture, a term that specifically refers to "a policy whereby a state seeks to maintain a balance-of-trade surplus by reducing imports, stimulating home production, and promoting exports" (Blake and Walters, 1976). Generally, neomercantilism refers to state intervention in economic affairs for purposes of enhancing the state's economic fortunes.[16] Japan is frequently described as a neomercantilist power, having achieved tremendous export growth in the postwar years as a consequence of an intimate government-business alliance.[17] Hence, some would

15. Most governments, for example, give preference in letting contracts for government work to domestic producers. Although such preferences may make eminently good sense politically, they effectively inhibit foreign competition. Tax structures can also have an important effect on industries' competitive postures.

16. Recall the discussion of mercantilism in chapter four.

17. *Dumping* is one device allegedly used by Japan to accomplish its neomercantilist objectives. Dumping means selling products abroad at prices below those in the exporter's own domestic market.

argue, it is appropriate that countermercantilist policies should be adopted against such a country. The protectionist urge is not the exclusive preserve of any one state or group of states. It is a reminder of the political foundations of policies that might otherwise seem purely economic in origin.

The case for protection is often compelling. Free trade may promise benefits to all, but the costs to particular domestic groups confronting adverse economic circumstances as a result of free trade are often substantial. To workers standing in an unemployment line because the factory in which they worked was forced to close because it could no longer compete with foreign producers, the fact that other consumers are able to buy a cheaper product is little consolation. Business and labor alike are therefore prone to argue for protection. Because they are politically powerful, they frequently get protection. Foreign economic policy, in these circumstances, is motivated by domestic political considerations.

The Multilateral Trade Negotiations conducted in Geneva between 1975 and 1979 were initiated against the background of monetary instability, surging oil prices, "stagflation"—and a growing incidence of neomercantilist and nontariff challenges to the liberal trading system the United States and others had espoused and promoted for decades. Lowering tariffs on industrial commodities remained a concern in the Tokyo Round of negotiations, but increased emphasis was placed on reducing barriers to the free flow of agricultural products. The question of how to deal with nontarifff barriers also assumed new importance. Thus the Tokyo MTN not only took place in an atmosphere of increased international interdependence; the negotiations were also significantly colored by it.

Developments in the United States were a prelude to the Geneva meetings of 1975–1979. Because the United States had exercised a leadership role in trade matters during the Bretton Woods era just as it had in monetary affairs, it is not surprising that domestic developments in the United States stimulated new departures in international trade policies.

The Kennedy Round was founded on the Trade Expansion Act of 1962, passed by the United States Congress in an effort to improve the competitive trade position of the United States in relation to the European Economic Community. The president's authority to negotiate trade matters under the Trade Expansion Act expired with the end of the Kennedy Round. Thereafter, Presidents Johnson and Nixon fought a rearguard action against the rising protectionist forces that bombarded Congress with trade-restriction demands. The reasons for the waning of support for a multilateral free-trade system were related to the many factors already discussed: "specific threats to particular industries, general and increasing weakness of the American economy, the worsening of the U.S. balance of trade, and the feeling that the protectionist policies of the EEC and Japan were a source of U.S. problems" (Spero, 1977). The shifting constellation of political forces within the Western world and between it and the communist world was also important. The consequence was a loss of American leadership within the system.

Nixon's New Economic Policy, announced in August 1971, not only had the effect of suspending the Bretton Woods agreements under which the international monetary system had operated for a quarter of a century but was also a serious blow to the multilateral free-trade scheme.

> From the viewpoint of U.S. foreign trade, the policy was an assault on domestic economic problems, on the Congress, and on the other members of the Western economic system. It sought to deal with domestic sources of trade and monetary deterioration through wage and price controls and measures to encourage a rise in productivity. It sought to placate a protectionist Congress by an extremely aggressive stance toward American economic partners. And it sought to deal with those partners by imposing a 10 percent surcharge on dutiable imports and by demanding a realignment of currencies to reestablish the American balance-of-trade equilibrium. (Spero, 1977: 81)

Despite Nixon's almost bellicose approach to monetary and trade matters, the world was spared a spiral of retaliatory, protectionist trade measures such as the 1930s had witnessed. Whether the MTN will prevent a resurgence of protectionism is more problematic, however, for the forces underlying such sentiments are pervasive.

What did the Tokyo MTN accomplish? The negotiations themselves and the final agreements were a reflection of the sensitivity of countries to the reality of international interdependence, the response to interdependence that protectionism implies, and the challenge to American leadership that both interdependence and protectionism have mounted.[18] As Stephen D. Krasner observes:

18. New international rules were elaborated to deal with subsidies and countervailing duties, dumping, government purchasing, product stands, custom valuation and licensing, agriculture, aircraft, and developing nations. Graham (1979) provides a useful, brief discussion of the new rules in each of these areas. He concludes that "the Tokyo Round agreements effectively replace the GATT rules. While remaining on the books, the old rules will be largely ignored when they conflict with new agreements. The GATT rules, for example, require that all imports from all sources be treated equally. The Tokyo Round agreements by contrast, condone discrimination by stipulating that only signatory countries are to enjoy the benefits" (Graham, 1979: 56–57). As we note in chapter seven, departure from GATT's rules regarding nondiscrimination among trading partners is an issue of particular importance to Third World countries.

The outcome of the Tokyo Round does not accord with any general principle. In some areas the agreements closely conform with liberal ideals of increasing trade, enhancing the autonomy of the market, and upholding nondiscrimination. In other areas the agreements fail to expand trade, legitimate state intervention, and endorse discriminatory practices. The underlying rationale for this outcome was not general principle but particularistic interests. In areas where there are not significant import-competing industries or where there are crosscutting cleavages within sectors, steps were taken which move the international trading system closer to the liberal ideal. In areas where import-competing industries dominate national political decisions, the MTN agreements endorse existing discriminatory and restrictive practices. (Krasner, 1979: 524–525)

Whether a trade regime[19] that combines such seemingly incompatible objectives as liberalism and protectionism can survive might be questioned. What seems beyond question is the inability of the United States to exercise the same kind of leadership, and absorb the same kinds of costs, as it once did. Against this background, the prospects of the world economy will depend on the ability of the countries of the world to devise and coordinate their policies in order to serve everyone's interest in freer trade. The threats to trade are vividly summarized in the words of Reuben Askew (May 25, 1980), who noted that recent events

> have inspired apocalyptic predictions for an international trade war. While such predictions are increasingly frequent, I do not anticipate a trade war or anything resembling one. My counterparts among our major trading partners share this view. We are willing to work together to resolve our predictable trade disputes.
>
> This, of course, is our objective in the United States. We seek a world in which trading nations can compete more freely and more fairly for more open markets. We know that we will not achieve this ambition by resorting to the autarky of protectionist trade barriers. Yet, protectionist pressures abound in our ailing world economy. According to our latest estimates, about two-thirds of world trade is still managed by governments either through tariffs or through non-tariff trade barriers. The free flow of world trade remains largely an ideal. How do we avoid confrontations over trade that no one wants?

The future undoubtedly hinges in part on how that question is answered.

19. A regime is "a set of rules, norms or institutional expectations that govern a social system" (Hopkins and Puchala, 1978).

Seven

The Transformation of the International Political Economy: Second and Third World Perspectives

The years immediately ahead will reveal whether the will exists to meet head-on the problems faced by a quarter of the human race. The task is to help raise the productivity of hundreds of millions of people who, by their own efforts alone, are unable to break out of the grip of absolute poverty. If we fail, the world faces a perilous era.

Robert S. McNamara, 1979

My guess is that, in spite of all kinds of controversies which are going on, and if we avoid war . . . in the decade ahead . . . things will move in the direction of greater integration of the Communist-governed countries into the world economy.

Willy Brandt, 1978

The international monetary and multilateral trading systems that evolved during the postwar decades did so primarily under the aegis of the Western industrialized nations whose interests and objectives they served. For reasons of their own as well as antipathy to the West, the Soviet Union and its Eastern European allies created an economic order with only minimal linkages with the First World. Developing nations on the periphery of the First World were also outside the privileged circle, yet the perpetuation of colonial economic linkages into the era of political independence intertwined the Third World with Western systems over which they had little control. Many Third World nations thus viewed the existing economic structure as one that was inimical to their interests and a means of preserving their underdog status. The end of colonial domination—from their perspective—merely ushered in a period of more subtle and devious exploitation.

To cope with their desperate economic situation, developing nations have called for creation of a new international economic order. The debate—or lack of it—over creation of a new order has been an issue largely between the First and Third Worlds. The communist countries have formed political alliances with one side or the other from time to time, and on a variety of issues, as political advantage seemed to dictate. But in part because of their own relative lack of economic ties with the South (as well as the West), and in part because they believe they bear no responsibility for the consequences of colonialism suffered by the Third World, the Second World has not been an intimate participant in some of the most recent contentious economic debates between North and South (except, perhaps, as a critical observer, and, on occasion, as meddler when those issues have provided opportunities to be exploited to the advantage of the Second World).

The Second World has become more intimately linked to the First World, however. The economic problems associated with the planned or command economies of the socialist world have forced the Soviet Union and its allies to seek greater contacts with the West to realize their own domestic economic objectives. The West has shown receptivity to these overtures for political as much as economic reasons. Whether the market economies of the West can effectively manage their relations with the command economies of the East is, however, uncertain. The aggressive entry of the Soviet Union into the Western trading system, and the modest success it has realized in competing for the purchase of goods within the capitalist international marketplace, constitute new elements in the international economic system, elements whose long-term consequences remain to be seen.[1] Whether the economic ties between East and West nurtured during the 1970s will survive the demise of détente also remains to be seen.

NORTH-SOUTH RELATIONS: CONFRONTATION, DIALOGUE, OR STALEMATE?

The historical roots of the developing nations' demands for a new order can be traced to the 1964 United Nations Conference on Trade and Development (UNCTAD), where a number of nations banded to-

---

1. The international monetary order remains effectively a preserve of the First World, although the transformation in the effective operation of that system has certainly been affected by demands and expectations emanating from outside this charmed circle.

gether to form the Group of 77 as a coalition of the world's poor to press for concessions from the rich. The G–77 effectively joined the nonaligned movement during the 1973 Algiers summit of non-aligned nations when issues relating to economic as well as political "liberation" came to the fore. Algeria, then chairman of the non-aligned countries, led the call for what became the Sixth Special Session of the United Nations General Assembly, held in the spring of 1974. Using their superior numbers, the Group of 77 secured passage of the Declaration on the Establishment of a New International Economic Order.[2] Significantly, both the declaration and the special session coincided with the worldwide energy and food crises of the early and mid-1970s. These crises, as one observer put it, " 'united' the rich North and the poor South in a new partnership of economic misery" (Kim, 1979).

The Declaration on the Establishment of a New International Economic Order drew attention in particular to the principle of sovereign control of natural resources and of economic activity. A program of action spelled out specific measures relating to trade, international credit, capital flows, and economic rights. Later in 1974 the General Assembly, again reflecting the voting majority commanded by the developing nations, adopted the Charter of Economic Rights and Duties of States. The charter reasserted the sovereign right of national control over internal wealth and resources. Foreign investment, foreign ownership of property, activities of transnational corporations, and the right of states to join primary-commodities-producers' associations were additional points.[3]

Other issues were broached at subsequent regular meetings and special sessions of the General Assembly and at the United Nations Conference on Trade and Development. Included in the discussions were the topics of debt relief for developing nations through cancellation or rescheduling, commodity price stabilization, compensa-

2. Rothstein (1979) notes that the article *the* is attached to the phrase "New International Economic Order" by developing nations, while *a* is used by those, principally developed countries, who see only a reformed world order.

3. Significantly, developing nations have not challenged the state system itself, only the way it presently functions. Thus the choice of the word *international* rather than *global* or *world*, is significant. "The growing assertiveness of the developing countries cannot be found to herald the beginning of a new world," observed Robert W. Tucker:

> What we find in the demands of the developing countries is not a challenge to the essential structure of the international system but a challenge to the distribution of wealth and power within this system. It is not the state system per se that is condemned, but the manner in which the system operated in the past and presumably continues to operate even today. It is primarily through the state that the historically oppressed and disadvantaged nations seek to mount a successful challenge to what governing elites of developing countries view as persisting unjust inequalities. (Tucker, 1980: 471)

tory financing mechanisms to stabilize export earnings, and price indexation which would tie the prices developing nations receive for the goods they export to the capital goods they import from the North (Jacobson, 1979). The summary of principal issues in the five UNCTAD conferences held during the 1960s and 1970s shown in Box 7.1 illustrates both the background and evolution of some of the specific Third World demands.

Because UNCTAD has effectively become a spokesman for the world's poor, it has been a central stage on which the North-South conflict has been played. But developing nations pressed the issues noted above in a variety of other international forums as well, including the IMF, the World Bank, the Third United Nations Law of the Sea Conference, and the ad hoc Conference on International Economic Cooperation (CIEC), which met in Paris for roughly eighteen months between the end of 1975 and mid-1977.[4]

Not surprisingly, developed countries did not accede willingly to Third World demands and have actively resisted those regarded as most threatening or costly. But neither were they able to redirect those demands in the direction they preferred. The CIEC was to have been the progenitor of a forum outside UNCTAD for a continuing North-South dialogue. It ended in failure.

If the failure of the CIEC dashed Northern hopes for a non-UNCTAD forum for a continuing North-South dialogue, the South has also experienced frustration in many forums on many issues. The Multilateral Trade Negotiations concluded in Geneva in 1979 are a case in point.

In principle, developing nations won an important concession at Geneva: extension of the principle of nonreciprocity, thus permitting developed nations to grant trade preferences to developing nations without violating GATT's rules regarding most-favored-nation nondiscrimination. This enabled developed nations to extend even further to the Third World the preferential trade treatment embodied in the Generalized System of Preferences (GSP) which most First World nations had granted developing nations during the past decades. Such preferential treatment is a significant departure from the nondiscrimination principle dominant throughout the Bretton Woods period.

The practical effects of the GSP on the main issues of Third World concern were nevertheless minimal. This fact, combined with developing nations' perception that the MTN unduly catered to the interests of Europe, Japan, and the United States, explains why

4. One study (Hart, 1978) concludes that NIEO negotiations were conducted in seventy-six regional and global forums between April 1973 and June 1977 alone. The number would be even larger if meetings held in subsequent years could be counted.

Box 7.1   The Evolving Stages of UNCTAD

UNCTAD I, Geneva 1964

• The creation of a forum to attract attention to issues supporting the developing countries, not covered by existing institutions.
• The formalization of the Group of 77 and beginning of discussion on a few issues such as terms of trade, resource gap, and Generalized System of Preferences (GSP).

UNCTAD II, New Delhi 1968

• Between 1964 and 1968 the UNCTAD secretariat focused more seriously but still sporadically on GSP, the needs of the developing countries for assistance, terms of trade, technology transfer, and selected development policies.
• The Conference led the OECD to initiate work on a scheme of preferences.
• Dr. Raúl Prebisch retired in 1969 as the Secretary-General of the UNCTAD.

UNCTAD III, Santiago 1972

• Unlike the Geneva and New Delhi meetings, where these issues were considered separately, UNCTAD III saw discussion on interrelationships between trade, money, finance, and development at a technical level.
• Initiation of an effort by Mr. Robert McNamara, President of the World Bank, to mobilize global support for the poor, suggesting ways to integrate the bottom 40 percent of the population in the development process.

UNCTAD IV, Nairobi 1976

• Stocktaking of progress in various forums (CIEC, GATT) on decisions taken at the Sixth and Seventh Special Sessions of the UN General Assembly in 1974 and 1975, respectively, particularly in the light of the oil price increase, monetary instability, recession, inflation, increased balance of payments gap of the non-oil developing countries, decline in commodity prices, and the uncertainty that the minimum development needs in many developing countries would be met.
• Main emphasis on commodities (Integrated Programme for Commodities—Common Fund) and to a lesser degree on external debt.
• Resolution on a Common Fund symbolized G-77 unity.

UNCTAD V, Manila 1979

• Emphasis on trade and financial flows aspects of the relationships between developed and developing countries.
• Emphasis on growing interdependence between different parts of the world economy.
• Efforts to bring socialist countries into the dialogue on economic issues.
• Emphasis on trade liberalization and concern about expanding protectionism.

Source: Mahmud A. Burney, "A Recognition of Interdependence: UNCTAD V," *Finance and Development* 16 (September 1979): 18.

most Third World nations did not accede readily to the MTN accords. Their reluctance in the face of what otherwise was heralded as a concession to their needs reflects an impatience with principle, a restless concern for immediate specific benefits.

The restiveness stems from the lack of progress that Third World nations have experienced on so many of the items of contention between the North and the South. The impediments to change on each of the numerous and complex NIEO demands are many. Understanding the Third World perceptions from which these demands emanate is important.

The background to these perceptions is, of course, provided by the enormous inequities between North and South discussed in chapter four. The Third World contains about three-fourths of the world's population, but it accounts for only about one-fifth of the world's combined gross national products. Furthermore, the disparities between the world's rich and poor have grown, and the gulf is projected to widen still further in the future. The present division of the world between an overpopulated and often poverty- and hunger-stricken Southern Hemisphere and an affluent, consumption-oriented North is thus likely to persist. Many Third World leaders perceive these stark realities as the product of a system so structured as to systematically assure perpetuation of international inequality. In particular, they find four items in their relationships with the North particularly irksome. W. Arthur Lewis, the Nobel Prize-winning economist, has summarized them thus:

> First, the division of the world into exporters of primary products and exporters of manufactures.
> Second, the adverse factoral terms of trade for the products of the developing countries.
> Third, the dependence of the developing countries on the developed for finance.
> Fourth, the dependence of the developing countries on the developed for their engine of growth. (Lewis, 1978: 3)

Roger D. Hansen, a distinguished observer of the political economy of North-South relations, has summarized Third World perceptions in the form of five general propositions:

- Efforts at international trade liberalization through the instrument of the General Agreement on Tariffs and Trade (GATT) had been singularly biased in favor of products of interest to developed-country exporters, and the developing countries had therefore gained little from the six rounds of tariff-cutting negotiations that took place between 1947 and 1967. [Furthermore, rising protectionist sentiment in the North] seemed all too likely to neutralize a considerable portion of the potential benefits of the Tokyo Round.

- The volume and value of foreign aid flowing from North to South have been unjustifiably low whether measured by "absorptive capacity" of funds in Southern development projects or by proclaimed Northern commitments to assist Southern development efforts.
- The North had systematically rejected—or stalled for lengthy periods of time before accepting in altered form—a wide variety of Southern proposals to increase the availability to the South of scarce foreign exchange needed in the development process.
- Northern multinational corporations have in general restricted their potential contribution to the Southern development process in countless ways. Among the most obvious and widespread have been (a) the limitation on tax liabilities through certain patterns of transfer pricing, (b) the limitations on job creation through the use of capital-intensive production methods and artificial limitations on exports, (c) the exaction of monopoly rents on the corporations' technology, and other, less generalized, forms of corporate behavior. In addition, these companies have on occasions interfered in internal politics of host countries, with or without the support of their home governments. Finally, they and their home governments have been able to limit . . . international capital flows to host governments in situations involving serious corporation-host government conflict.
- The terms of trade have moved consistently against the typical developing-country export basket, and they have done so for reasons that are related structurally to the operations of the Bretton Woods system. (Hansen, 1979: 48–50)

Other Southern perspectives on North-South relations could be noted, such as the "collective" or "Southern self-reliance" perspective, which sees Southern self-help and political unity as major Third World goals.[5] Another is the basic human-needs perspective discussed in chapter four.

It is important to emphasize that the foregoing summary of Southern perceptions is neither universally shared within the Third World nor "an *analytical assessment* of major Southern complaints about present international economic structures and processes, but rather a developing-country *feeling* about the *equity aspects* of North-South economic relations which has grown over the past two

---

5. Political unity designed to enhance Southern bargaining strength in dealing with the North was linked to the premise that OPEC would provide political support to developing nations in international forums and financial support in building other producers' associations. Although OPEC political support was forthcoming, its money was not. "Unless the OPEC countries reverse their thinking and contribute substantially to such a strategy, [the Southern self-reliance] perspective will most probably never amount to more than a rhetorical adjunct to the global inequity perspective" (Hansen, 1979).

decades" (Hansen, 1979). Nevertheless, despite important differences within the orientations and experiences of the nations of the South, there appears to be veracity to many Southern complaints about past injustices and their roots.

Regarding the charge against GATT, for example, Hansen notes that "few economists have disputed this perception, and most attempts to measure the extent of the problem have suggested that Northern levels of protection (through quota restrictions, health and safety regulations, nominal and effective tariff structures, variable levies, internal taxes and price supports, etc.) were costing the South several billion dollars per year in forgone export earnings during the mid-1960s, the most significant portion stemming from agricultural protectionism" (Hansen, 1979). Some Third World complaints against Northern-based transnational corporations are rooted in demonstrated fact (see Moran, 1975).

What about the charges regarding the terms of trade,[6] proposals to increase the availability of scarce foreign exchange, and foreign aid? Are they reasonable?

The Terms of Trade

Trade-related issues are at the core of many Third World demands. The structure of trade relationships between many developed and developing nations evolved during the age of imperialism, when colonies existed for the presumed benefit of the colonizers[7] (Boulding, 1978). Frequently this meant that the colonies were sources of primary products, such as agricultural commodities and mineral resources, and markets for the finished manufactured goods produced in the metropole.[8] This pattern persists today as a general description of the structure of trade ties between developed and developing nations. In 1976, developing countries as a whole relied upon primary products (including fuels) for 81 percent of their export earnings (the money necessary to buy goods from abroad). Developed countries, in contrast, relied on primary products for only 23 percent of their earnings, with manufactured products accounting for nearly 76 percent (see Table 7.1).

6. *Terms of trade* refers to the relative value of goods exported compared with goods imported.

7. See Boulding and Mukerjee (1972) for evidence that the acquisition of colonial empires *did not* benefit the imperialist powers economically.

8. From alternative perspectives in economics, it is problematic whether the agriculturally oriented and technologically underdeveloped societies might not have occupied this role even in the absence of colonialism.

Table 7.1
Composition of World Exports and Imports, by Groups of Countries, 1976
(percentages)

	Developed Market Economies	Developing Market Economies	Centrally Planned Economies	World
	Exports			
Primary Products	**22.9**	**81.2**	**37.0**	**39.2**
Food, beverages, and tobacco	10.8	13.5	9.4	11.3
Crude materials (excluding fuels); oils and fats	7.1	8.7	8.8	7.7
Mineral fuels and related materials	5.0	59.0	18.8	20.2
Manufactured Products	**75.7**	**18.5**	**56.5**	**59.2**
Chemicals	9.4	1.4	4.8	6.9
Machinery and transport equipment	37.7	3.7	29.3	28.2
Other manufactured goods	23.6	13.4	22.4	24.1
Miscellaneous	**1.4**	**0.3**	**6.5**	**1.6**
Total	**100.0**	**100.0**	**100.0**	**100.0**
	Imports*			
Primary Products	**42.3**	**31.0**	**30.6**	**39.2**
Food, beverages, and tobacco	11.3	10.4	13.5	11.3
Crude materials (excluding fuels); oils and fats	8.5	4.7	7.8	7.7
Mineral fuels and related materials	22.5	15.9	9.3	20.2
Manufactured Products	**56.3**	**65.9**	**66.3**	**59.2**
Chemicals	6.8	7.4	6.5	6.9
Machinery and transport equipment	24.5	37.0	34.1	28.2
Other manufactured goods	25.0	21.5	25.7	24.1
Miscellaneous	**1.4**	**3.1**	**3.1**	**1.6**
Total	**100.0**	**100.0**	**100.0**	**100.0**

Source: Martin M. McLaughlin and the Staff of the Overseas Development Council, *The United States and World Development: Agenda 1979* (New York: Praeger, 1979), p. 207. Based on United Nations data.

*World import figures include certain imports which, because their regions of destination could not be determined, are not otherwise included in the import figures in this table.

Note: Data do not include trade among the centrally planned economies of Asia, the exports of Rhodesia, or the trade between the Federal Republic of Germany and the German Democratic Republic.

Another important characteristic of production patterns in developing nations is that these countries often depend for foreign exchange earnings upon a single primary product, such as petroleum or other mineral resources, or agricultural products, such as coffee or tea. In fact, in the 1975–1977 period, only fifteen primary commodities[9] accounted for nearly two-thirds of the exports of developing nations (Sewell, 1980: 188). Figure 7.1 illustrates for a selected group of thirty-four developing nations the often excessive dependence of Third World nations on a limited range of primary products for foreign exchange earnings.

The terms-of-trade argument between North and South captures the significance of developing nations' dependence on a narrow range of primary product exports. Developing nations believe that the prices they receive for their exports vary erratically in the short run and deteriorate persuasively in the long run, whereas the prices of the manufactured goods that they import increase steadily.

Evidence supporting this proposition is readily available (see Prebisch, 1964; Hansen, 1976: 178; Pirages, 1978: 239; and Rosen and Jones, 1980: 170). However, the sharp upturn of world commodity prices in 1973–1974 led some observers to conclude that the terms of trade were moving in *favor* of developing nations (a point that incidentally underscores the importance of the base year against which comparisons are made). The purchasing power of developing nations' exports in fact increased by nearly 20 percent between 1970 and 1975, but the bulk of this was accounted for by the rise in petroleum prices. Excluding petroleum exporters and the group of seven developing countries known as "fast-growing exporters of manufactures," the purchasing power of the remaining developing nations' exports actually declined by 5 percent between 1970 and 1975. And for the poorest Third World countries they declined by nearly 25 percent (Sewell, 1977: 209).

Nonetheless, analysts still differ on the question of whether the terms of trade of developing nations have deteriorated and, more importantly, on the causes of the alleged deterioration.[10] Third World demands, however, are influenced by perceptions. As Rothstein notes (1979), "Many economists doubt that there has been a secular decline in the terms of trade for commodities, but what is

9. Petroleum, sugar, coffee, copper, timber, cotton, rubber, iron ore, cocoa, phosphate rock, tin, maize, rice, tobacco, and tea. The principal Third World exporters of these products are shown in Table 9.3.

10. Streeten (1974) provides a useful discussion of the terms-of-trade debate. See also Blake and Walters (1976) and Singer and Ansari (1977). A critical view of the debate is provided by Higgins and Higgins (1979).

Figure 7.1   Developing Country Dependence on Primary Products for Foreign Exchange Earnings

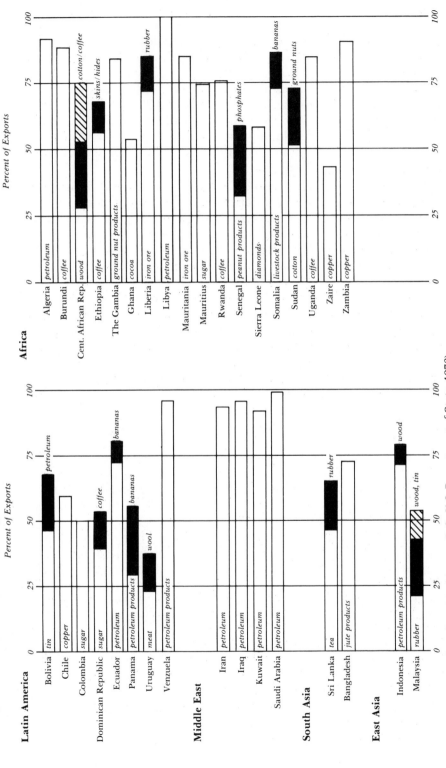

Source: *The Trade Debate* (Washington, D.C.: U.S. Department of State, 1978).

believed or assumed—taken on faith—is more important here than analytical argument."

Among these perceptions is the belief that the terms of trade have deteriorated due to the structural characteristics of the international economic order. The argument runs as follows:

> Technological innovation is the most important factor that perpetuates old patterns of economic domination. In a relatively unmanaged market, natural resources flow toward those countries in which the greatest amount of value can be obtained from them. The technologically developed countries use natural resources to produce a wider variety of more sophisticated products more cheaply than can the less developed countries. The less developed countries, then, are locked into an established international economic system that does not benefit them to the degree that it does the industrial countries. (Pirages, 1978: 55–56)

Furthermore, the natural appeal for the high-technology, labor-saving devices produced in the North is reinforced by worldwide advertising campaigns designed to create and sustain demands for them. The high cost of production for such goods becomes institutionalized through the wage and fringe-benefit programs fixed by powerful labor unions in negotiations with giant corporations. "Wage cuts during periods of diminished demand for products have been extremely rare. When price cutting by industries in 'nouveau riche' countries such as Japan or Taiwan has an impact on industrial economies, 'orderly marketing agreements' are used to curb the importation of cheaper products" (Pirages, 1978). The ability to limit economic competition is enhanced by the concentration of economic activity in fewer and fewer numbers of corporate conglomerates.

Developing nations face an industrial world with inherent as well as contrived competitive advantages. They also lack the ability to become more competitive themselves. In fact, they compete among themselves to sell commodities to the North at prices set by the North rather than by the exporting nations. Organized labor is unable to effect higher prices for raw materials "because there are alternative sources of supplies for most raw materials, the extraction of these raw materials is energy—rather than labor— intensive, and the supply of labor in relation to demand for it is overwhelming in most less developed countries"[11] (Pirages, 1978). In a system where those with the most money determine prices, Third World na-

---

11. W. Arthur Lewis (1978) argues that unproductive agricultural labor is a particularly compelling cause of developing nations' continuing underdevelopment.

tions find themselves unable to determine the terms of trade for their products.

Faced with such circumstances, it is not surprising that diversification of export industries, rather than continued dependence on a few primary products, is a preferred goal of many developing nations. Generally, developing nations place high value on the goal of industrialization and on developing import-substitution industries in particular (that is, building industries to produce the goods otherwise purchased overseas, such as gasoline, pesticides, or other refined petroleum products). Gaining access to the markets of developed nations is a corresponding goal. Foreign aid has been a favored Northern instrument for meeting Southern demands for development assistance. But "trade, not aid" has been the plea of many developing nations, who feel that they have been systematically denied access to markets in developed countries through both tariff and nontariff barriers. The goal reflects two facts: "(a) the overwhelming importance of the Western market economies for the developing countries as sources of export earnings; and (b) the importance of the manufactured goods sector as a source of expansion"[12] (Singer and Ansari, 1977). It is in this context that developing nations have sought preferential trade treatment (as opposed to most-favored-nation treatment) so as to build up diversified export industries capable of competing on equal terms with those of developed economies. The Generalized System of Preferences adopted by most First World countries is a partial response to this plea.[13]

Whether developing nations as a whole will succeed in their ambitious industrialization goals, and whether in particular this will reduce their "structural dependence" on the North, is problematic. Developing nations remain critically dependent on the industrial world for technology. Unless this dependence is lessened, even im-

---

12. Manufacturers have become the fastest-growing export sector of developing countries as a whole (although not for all of them equally, as chapter four's discussion of the new industrial countries makes clear). Excluding oil exports, manufactures accounted for 33 percent of the exports of the developing nations in 1975, a figure projected to grow to more than 50 percent by 1985 (Lewis, 1978: 36). It is not surprising, therefore, that "to several [less-developed countries] the abolition of restrictions on manufactured imports is much more important than anything that can happen in the commodities area" (Lewis, 1978).

13. But the slowness in coming and the limits of the GSP are germane to Southern perceptions regarding the grudging acceptance by the North of Southern proposals to increase the availability of foreign exchange:

The South requests a system of generalized tariff preferences (GSP) to increase its capacity to export manufactured goods to the North in 1964; in 1974 the U.S. Congress finally adopts legislation granting the President the power to implement a scheme that bears only a pale resemblance to the program requested a decade earlier. (Hansen, 1979: 149)

port-substitution industrialization is unlikely to mitigate the structural dependence of the South on the North.

> Import substitution shifts the geographical location of manufacturing plants, but continued technological dependence will ensure that the real terms of trade continue to go against the poor countries—except for short-run periods where effective producer cartels raise the prices of scarce commodities—and in favor of the rich countries from which the required intermediate inputs flow.[14] (Singer and Ansari, 1977: 39)

This observation suggests that the principle of comparative advantage on which liberal trade theory is based is not entirely neutral. According to this principle, no one loses from free trade. But factor endowments (such as land, labor, and capital) are not so distributed that all gain from a system of free and unfettered international trade. Some may be systematically denied benefits, others enjoy special privileges as a result of the contributions made by the less fortunate to those already well endowed. In other words, the international division of labor implied by the principle of comparative advantage reinforces the advantages of some, while making permanent the dependencies of others. Inequalities are thus perpetuated, with unequal distributions of technological capabilities a critical factor. The perceived need among many developing nations to create a new order founded on something other than liberal precepts[15] derives from their raised consciousness about the way in which the

14. Elsewhere in their study of rich and poor nations Singer and Ansari argue that

> The deterioration of the terms of trade of primary products in relations to manufactured commodities really concealed, during the 1950s and 1960s, a deterioration of the terms of trade of the poor countries in all their dealings with the rich countries. Clearly, the latter relationship between types of *countries* is more significant than the former relationship between types of *products*. (Singer and Ansari, 1977: 36)

Rothstein, drawing on the work of Streeten (1974), makes an analogous point.

> Poverty causes bad terms of trade, not vice versa, because the poor countries cannot move easily into better exports and have bad records wit the quality of exports (doing worse than the rich countries even with the same exports). This implies that the terms of trade for *countries* (the [less-developed countries]) may decline, but not for commodities per se. (Rothstein 1979: 77, n.32)

See also the discussion of historical cycles in the terms of trade for agricultural products in Lewis (1978). A critical argument of Lewis's study is that the terms of trade have moved against the products of tropical countries due to their surplus labor and underproductive agricultural sectors:

> The terms of trade are bad only for tropical products, whether agricultural or industrial, and are bad because the market pays tropical unskilled labor, whatever it may be producing, a wage that is based on an unlimited reservoir of low-productivity food producers. (Lewis, 1978: 37)

15. Higgins and Higgins (1979) suggest that the problem is one of assisting developing nations in "shifting from yesterday's colonial structure to today's comparative

existing economic order operates—advantageously to a few and disadvantageously to the many.

Price Stabilization

Reversing the alleged deterioration in their terms of trade with the North is a long-term objective of Third World nations. An immediate short-run goal, however, is the reduction of fluctuations in the prices they receive for their commodities. This has led some Third World nations to advocate the formation of producers' cartels modeled after the Organization of Petroleum Exporting Countries for purposes of extracting monopoly controlled returns on exports, for price indexation (that is, for linking the prices developing nations receive for exports to the prices they must pay for imports), and for negotiated agreements to regulate trade in their major commodity exports.

Little significant progress has been made on any of these aims. In the face of stiff opposition from the industrialized world, the quest for price indexation has been quietly laid aside. OPEC remains the premier example of an effective producers' cartel (in part because energy is so vital to the industrialized nations, thus making them vulnerable to foreign suppliers), but its success has not been emulated in other commodity markets. In fact the success of OPEC may not be reproducible given the obstacles to political unity among other commodity suppliers and the relative invulnerability of the North to interruptions in supplies of most raw materials. It is only in the area of commodity trade, specifically price stabilization, that the South has made some headway toward realization of its goals, but progress has been so modest as to lend credence to Third World perceptions about the unwillingness of the North to help the South overcome its dependence on the North.

Commodity trade is important in North-South relations because most developing nations derive the bulk of their export earnings from commodity exports. It is also important because about 80 percent of Third World commodity exports are consumed by the First World (Rothstein, 1979: 40). Exports to the Second World are insignificant, and domestic consumption within producing nations is very low. "Consequently, the developing countries may suffer severely—and proportionately more than their developed trading partners—from instabilities in commodity trade, and they normally lack the resources and the flexibility to diversify or to save in the

advantage." This requires abandoning "liberalized trade" in the old sense of laissez-faire and supplementing it with policies (such as preferential trade treatment) that will permit industrial firms in developing nations to compete effectively with firms in advanced countries.

good years in order to cushion the bad" (Rothstein, 1979). Further-more, given the existing distribution of economic power in the world, "it is the rich countries which determine the terms, because in the short run the developing countries need the products and services of the developed countries much more than the latter need the output of the former" (Singer and Ansari, 1977). (Petroleum is, of course, a significant exception.) Developing nations have thus gener-ally been price "takers" rather than setters in the international mar-ketplace; they have also generally been takers in formulating trade policy and establishing rules of procedure governing international commerce.

The attempt to create a new commodity order was a principal objective of the Group of 77 and UNCTAD during much of the 1970s. The issue came to the fore during the UNCTAD IV meeting in Nai-robi, Kenya, in 1976, when the G–77 secured adoption of the pro-posed Integrated Programme for Commodities (IPC) as one of its major goals.

The European Community provided what might in some re-spects be interpreted as the intellectual inspiration for UNCTAD's proposal for an integrated commodity program (Hart, 1978). In 1975 the EC concluded an agreement with forty-six African, Caribbean, and Pacific nations (the so-called ACP nations), mostly former col-onies of Europeans; this agreement has been viewed by some (such as Higgins and Higgins, 1979) as a genuine attempt to respond to the demands of the Group of 77, or at least to the demands of former colonies of the member-states of the European Community. The agreement, known as the Lomé Convention, granted the ACP nations preferential trade access to the European market without the re-quirement of reciprocity for the EC nations. It also increased the amount of foreign aid available to the ACP countries while giving them a voice in the management of aid projects. With respect to ex-port earnings, the Lomé agreement created a scheme known as STABEX—a compensatory financing mechanism designed to stabi-lize ACP export earnings in the event they fall short of their average over the four preceding years.[16] STABEX was described shortly after its inception as "ground-breaking" and "politically genuinely significant"[17] (Gruhn, 1976).

16. The second Lomé Convention was initialed in 1979. Covering fifty-seven ACP nations, it contained a new scheme called MINEX designed to provide mineral pro-ducers the same benefits that STABEX earlier granted producers of other com-modities, primarily tropical products. See Shonfield (1980).

17. See Gruhn (1976) and Bywater (1975) for further discussions of the Lomé Convention. For a critical evaluation that views the Lomé Convention as a step toward the regionalization of the international economic system, see Novak (1979). Noting that most ACP nations are African and that in return for its concessions the EC won preferential access to ACP raw materials, Novak (1979) concludes that "This

Had the Integrated Programme of Commodities been approved as originally conceived, it, too, could have been described as ground-breaking and genuinely significant. It was envisioned originally to have covered eighteen products[18] and to have consisted of five elements:

> creation of buffer stocks for about 10 storable commodities, financing of the buffer-stock operation through a "common fund" to which both producers and consumers would be expected to contribute, improved and expanded export-earnings stabilization, long-term supply and purchase agreements, and expansion of processing in less developed producing nations. (McCulloch and Piñera, 1979: 156)

Thus conceived, the Integrated Programme was indeed revolutionary.

> The IPC reflected an effort by UNCTAD and the Group of 77 to establish an entirely new pattern of decision making in one very important part of the international economy. What was being sought, at least initially, was in some ways unprecedented: a new level and degree of international decision making and international management, the imposition of common principles and a central financing (and presumably supervising) institution, and joint support for a major redistribution of benefits and a new ordering principle for at least part of the trade and aid system. This was extraordinarily ambitious. . . . (Rothstein, 1979: 56)

Attention focused eventually on the Common Fund and the proposal for buffer stocks. The Group of 77 pushed for a $6 billion fund and a significant voice in its management. Developed nations opposed both the amount, most of which they would have to finance, and the management proposals, which were heavily weighted in favor of the South.

What finally emerged was a far cry from the ambitious original goals.[19] After two years of negotiation, an agreement was reached in

---

reciprocal trade pact . . . effectively excluded Asia, Latin America, and North America from African trade preferences. The EEC thus established with Africa a special and important geoeconomic and geopolitical relationship."

18. Bananas, bauxite, cocoa, coffee, copper, cotton, hard fibers, iron ore, jute, manganese, meat, phosphates, rubber, sugar, tea, tropical timber, tin, and vegetable oils.

19. See Rothstein (1979) and Schechter (1979) for examinations of objectives and the evolution of strategies regarding the Integrated Programme and the Common Fund in particular.

1979 to create a $750 million arrangement consisting of two "windows." One, with an initial endowment of $400 million, would serve as a kind of bank to assist individual commodity organizations in purchasing buffer stocks of raw materials. The second, a $350 million window, would essentially operate as an international aid organization designed to help poorer developing nations expand, diversify, and market their commodity exports. This scheme is much closer to what most industrialized nations wanted than what the Group of 77 and the UNCTAD secretariat had sought. "The responsibility for maintaining price stabilization will remain with the individual commodity agreements, with no intervention from the Common Fund. As a result, the new institution is not expected to create substantial economic benefits for the developing countries" *(The Inter Dependent,* May 1979). Moreover, the voting arrangements for the Common Fund envisioned at the time of the agreement gave the industrialized world substantial political clout. In short, the new commodity fund could perhaps be viewed as a political victory, but it seems unlikely to have the profound impact on commodity trade once sought by advocates of the New International Economic Order.

Foreign Aid

Another aspect of the Southern complaint finds expression in the charge that "the volume and value of foreign aid flowing from North to South have been unjustifiably low" (Hansen, 1979). Certainly, by some empirical standards, the volume of aid has been substantial. The United States alone has granted over $150 billion in aid since the end of World War II. Other developed nations have since joined in the effort, and various international institutions have channeled significant amounts of resources to the Third World—institutions such as the World Bank, the United Nations, the Inter-American, Asian, and African Development banks, the European Community, and various OPEC and Arab institutions. Collectively, the total volume of bilateral and multilateral resources flowing to developing countries in the mid-1970s was roughly $20 billion annually. Tens of billions more could be added if private resource transfers are counted, including private investments, loans, and credits, and grants by private voluntary agencies.

Historically, the United States has been the most prominent aid donor, with official development assistance ranging from $3 billion to over $4 billion annually over the past two decades. Beginning in the 1960s other Western nations began to contribute significant amounts of aid. These nations together with the United States make up the Development Assistance Committee (DAC) of the Organization for Economic Cooperation and Development (OECD).[20] In 1978 the DAC accounted for $18.2 billion, or 80 percent, of the worldwide development assistance flowing to developing nations and multilateral institutions (see Table 7.2). Communist-country aid has been much less significant in volume. Little more than three-quarters of a billion dollars of communist aid was granted in 1978, representing less than 4 percent of total worldwide flows.

OPEC nations comprise a significant new addition to the world's list of aid donors. In 1977 OPEC's $5.8 billion in aid topped United States bilateral aid flows and represented over a quarter of worldwide development assistance. (Note from Table 7.2, however, that both the volume and relative proportion of OPEC aid decreased sharply in 1978.)

Against this background, what is the basis for the have-nots' charge that the volume and value of aid have been insignificant and inadequate? Any number of yardsticks can be used to measure the extent to which aid allocations have fallen short of what developing nations perceive their needs to be and donors' abilities to meet those needs. The generally agreed-upon standard for measuring the burden of aid has been donors' GNP, and the often-enunciated target is to transfer resources equivalent to 0.7 percent of GNP. As Table 7.2 indicates, OPEC nations have far exceeded this target, but DAC donors and particularly communist countries are far short of it. And the trend has been downward rather than upward. This is particularly true for the United States, as Figure 7.2 demonstrates. Between 1965 and 1978 United States development assistance as a proportion of its GNP declined by more than half—plummeting from 0.49 percent in 1965 to 0.23 percent in 1978. The United States now ranks near the bottom of the list of DAC donors in terms of the proportion of its production that it allocates to foreign aid.

The rapid decline in the relative volume of American aid reflects a failure to increase aid commensurately with either real increases in GNP or inflation. The consequence has been a sharp decline in the purchasing power of the aid that is granted. Although the annual net flow of official United States development assistance increased by $1.9 billion (or 66 percent) between 1961 and 1978, when inflation is taken into account the value of American aid actually decreased by 24 percent—falling from $2.9 billion in 1961 to $2.2 billion in 1978 in constant 1961 dollars (Sewell, 1980: 233). These trends are charted in Figure 7.3. Developing nations have experienced tremendous population increases since 1961, and most

20. DAC members are Australia, Austria, Belgium, Canada, Denmark, Finland, France, West Germany, Italy, Japan, the Netherlands, New Zealand, Norway, Sweden, Switzerland, the United Kingdom, and the United States.

Table 7.2
Net Official Development Assistance and Total Net Flow of Resources to Developing Countries and Multilateral Institutions, by Groups of Countries, 1973, 1975, and 1977-1978

	Amount ($ millions)				As Percentage of Total				As Percentage of GNP			
	1973	1975	1977	1978	1973	1975	1977	1978	1973	1975	1977	1978
Net ODA Flows												
DAC Countries	9,351*	13,585	14,696	18,204	79.4	68.4	68.9	80.1	0.30	0.35	0.31	0.32
OPEC Countries	1,308	5,512	5,845	3,701	11.1	27.8	27.4	16.3	1.41	2.70	1.96	1.11
CPE Countries†	1,120	750	778	825	9.5	3.8	3.7	3.6	0.09	0.05	0.04	0.04
Total	**11,779**	**19,847**	**21,319**	**22,730**	**100.0**	**100.0**	**100.0**	**100.0**	—	—	—	—
Total Official and Private Flows												
DAC Countries	24,628	40,378	50,725	69,695	89.3	81.8	85.7	91.8	0.79	1.05	1.08	1.23
OPEC Countries	1,740	8,164	7,591	5,294	6.3	16.5	12.8	7.0	1.88	4.01	2.54	1.58
CPE Countries	1,220	840	890	920	4.4	1.7	1.5	1.2	0.10	0.06	—	—
Total	**27,588**	**49,382**	**59,206**	**75,909**	**100.0**	**100.0**	**100.0**	**100.0**	—	—	—	—

Source: John W. Sewell and the Staff of the Overseas Development Council, *The United States and World Development: Agenda 1980* (New York: Praeger, 1980). Based on Organization for Economic Cooperation and Development data.

*Not including aid to Portugal.
†Net ODA (official development assistance) flows from the centrally planned economies of the U.S.S.R., Eastern Europe, and the People's Republic of China are OECD secretariat estimates. CPE (centrally planned economies) figures do not include aid to centrally planned developing countries.

Figure 7.2
United States Official Development Assistance in Comparison with All Other DAC Countries, 1965–1978 (as percentage of GNP)

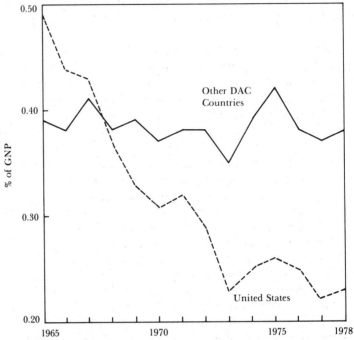

Source: John W. Sewell and the Staff of the Overseas Development Council, *The United States and World Development: Agenda 1980* (New York: Praeger, 1980). Based on Organization for Economic Cooperation and Development data.
Notes: Finland and New Zealand not included until 1970. Portugal not included after 1972.
U.S. ODA (official development assistance) amounted to 2.79 per cent of GNP at the beginning of the Marshall Plan in 1949. Between 1949 and 1952, US ODA averaged 9.4 per cent of U.S. federal expenditures. By 1977, this figure had dropped to 1.1 per cent of federal expenditures.

aid donors have "tied" their aid to purchases in the donor country[21] (even though the donor country may not be the lowest-cost producer of the goods developing nations need). When these two facts are added to the picture, it becomes clear that the per capita volume of foreign aid among Third World countries is small and its value shrinking.

A final indication of the relative insignificance of foreign aid is gleaned from comparisons between aid and other expenditures.

21. *Tying* means that aid recipients are required to spend their aid dollars to purchase goods produced in the donor country. C. Fred Bergsten (1973: 104) argues that "tying alone reduces the real value of aid by 10 to 30 percent below its nominal value." It should also be clear that tying aid to the products of donor countries effectively makes aid a subsidy for the domestic producers of those products.

Figure 7.3
Current Value and Real Values of United States Official Development Assistance, 1961–1978

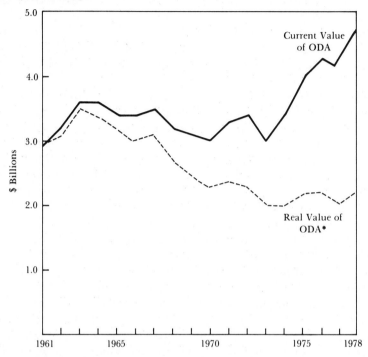

Source: Martin M. McLaughlin and the Staff of the Overseas Development Council, *The United States and World Development: Agenda 1979* (New York: Praeger, 1979), p. 257. Based on Organization for Cooperation and Development data.
*In constant 1961 dollars. 1976 and 1977 figures are estimates.
Note: The "real value" of ODA (official development assistance) is calculated by adjusting for inflation and/or changes in currency values; it reflects the problem of being able to buy fewer and fewer goods for the same or even more U.S. dollars.

Global military expenditures, for example, are nearly twenty times greater than official government-to-government economic aid flows. The disparity is even greater in the United States. Furthermore, Americans in 1977 spent nearly four times as much on tobacco products and nearly seven times as much on alcoholic beverages as their government spent on official development assistance (McLaughlin, 1979a: 256).

Beyond criticisms of the volume and value of aid, developing nations are often critical of the political strings attached to foreign aid grants and loans. For example, the United States, like many other donors, has used its foreign aid for purposes of wooing friends and potential allies (especially in its competition with the Soviet Union).

Such a practice may no longer be as blatant as it once was, but the United States continues to concentrate its aid in countries where it perceives maximum political payoff.[22] As C. Fred Bergsten observed before becoming a member of the Carter administration, "The United States regards developing countries both large and small . . . solely as pawns on the chessboard of global power politics. Rewards go only to the shrinking list of explicit collaborators" (Bergsten, 1973).

The United States' behavior is not exceptional. OPEC has sprinkled its lavish resources among a relatively small group of nations. In 1976, for example, more than 60 percent of its aid was allocated to Arab countries, with much of the rest spread among Asian and African nations with sizable Muslim populations (McLaughlin, 1979a: 261). Britain and France have also over the years given much of their aid to their former colonies. Some observers have even suggested that foreign aid is often a tool used by the North to perpetuate neocolonial and neo-imperial ties,[23] thus further subordinating the weak and poor while contributing to the welfare of those already strong and rich. Ironically, however, many Third World countries seem unable to live without foreign aid, even though they may be unhappy about living with it.

Among other things, the flow of aid in the form of loans has contributed to the debt-burden problem that has become so acute for some developing nations. As interest and amortization payments on prior loans mount, new loans are necessary not for the purpose of augmenting economic development but simply to keep going. The search for relief from this seemingly self-perpetuating burden of foreign aid is reflected in the NIEO drive for debt rescheduling (changing the payment dates) or cancellation. Developed nations have responded to this concern only haltingly and selectively, however.

In the meantime, developing nations continue to require external assistance, a need that is likely to persist for some time. It seems probable that the burdens of this dependence will be eased and the developing nations able to assume greater autonomous responsibility for managing their own affairs only if the drive for a new economic order is somehow able to move forward in a manner consistent with Third World objectives.

22. In fiscal year 1977 Egypt, Israel, Portugal, Syria, and Jordan received nearly all of the $1.8 billion in American aid known as "security supporting assistance." Bangladesh, Indonesia, India, Pakistan, and the Philippines joined these other five nations as the principal recipients of American economic assistance. Collectively, the ten accounted for 46 percent of American economic aid in fiscal 1977 (McLaughlin, 1979a: 258).

23. See Hayter's *Aid as Imperialism* (1971) for one such interpretation.

THE EVOLUTION OF EAST-WEST ECONOMIC LINKAGES

"In foreign economic relations, politics and economics, diplomacy and commerce, industrial production and trade are woven together. Consequently, the approach to them and the management of them must be integrated, tying into one knot . . . our political and economic interests." This observation by Soviet President Leonid Brezhnev (cited in Huntington, 1978) underscores the extent to which politics and economics in command or planned economies are often intertwined inextricably. In the postwar period, governments in Western nations have increasingly intervened in their economies to manage economic conditions. The resurgence of neomercantilist philosophies and policies is a manifestation of the interventionist strategies of many governments with regard to the international economic system. Yet there is an important difference between the planned economies of the Soviet Union and Eastern Europe and the market economies of the First World. In the latter, prices play an important role in encouraging production and regulating the distribution of goods and services. In planned economies, production and distribution decisions are made by the government.

This difference between planned and market economies has an important bearing on commercial relations between them. "For the West, the underlying rule would still be that any trade can take place unless a government prevents it; while for members of COMECON [Council for Mutual Economic Assistance, that is, the intergovernmental organization that coordinates economic policy among the Soviet Union and certain East European countries], and especially for the U.S.S.R., the rule would be that no trade takes place unless the state initiates it" (Vernon, 1979). Differing perceptions of the way gains are realized from international commercial transactions flow from this fundamental distinction. "The Soviet system is based on the proposition that social gain is maximized by the state's commands. The American system, like the system of most Western countries, is fashioned on the proposition that as individuals pursue their private gain, the benefits for the country will exceed its costs, yielding a social gain" (Vernon, 1979).

The ideological distinctions between the capitalist West and the socialist East concerning the role of government in economic affairs have remained constant throughout the post-World War II period. The nature and volume of East-West commercial interactions, however, have not. The evolution and expansion of economic ties between the First and Second Worlds can best be attributed to changing perceptions of the costs and benefits such ties produce. Not surprisingly, this evolution closely parallels the seven periods used to describe the evolution of the Cold War in chapter three: (1) wary friendship (1945–1946); (2) mutual antagonism and belligerence (1946–1952); (3) rhetorical hostility and behavioral accommodation (1953–1962); (5) competitive cooperation (1963–1968); (6) détente (1969–1978); and (7) "contestation" (1979–?).

From Wary Friendship to Mutual Antagonism

During World War II, Western planners anticipated the participation of the Soviet Union in the postwar international economic system, just as they originally anticipated Soviet cooperation in maintaining the postwar political order. Although economic ties between the Soviet Union and the West prior to the war had not been extensive, the war itself, through American lend-lease assistance, had led to closer links. Moreover, the Soviet Union had participated in the Bretton Woods negotiations.

There was little question in the West that Eastern Europe would be an active partner in the postwar economic system. Trade between Eastern and Western Europe had been extensive before the war, and even as late as 1947 it was assumed that these ties would eventually be reestablished (Spero, 1977).

But 1947 was a critical year in the evolving political struggle between East and West, for it was then that President Truman effectively committed the United States to an anticommunist foreign policy. In June 1947 Secretary of State George Marshall outlined an American commitment to aid in the economic recovery of Europe. The European Recovery Program, as the Marshall Plan was formally called, was put in place the following year. Although its immediate objectives were couched primarily in economic terms (see Block, 1977), the Marshall Plan, too, became a political weapon in the evolving anti-Soviet orientation of the United States.

In devising the Marshall Plan, American policy makers considered the possibility that Eastern Europe and perhaps the Soviet Union itself might actively participate in the recovery program (see Jones, 1964). Whether they were ever serious contenders for Marshall Plan assistance can be doubted, however.[24] The program was formulated in such a way that the Soviet Union would have had to divulge information about its internal conditions and to permit Western involvement in its reconstruction efforts. The Soviets were unlikely to accept such conditions, which could be seen as threats to their sovereign autonomy. Moreover, much of the debate in Con-

24. Immediately after the announcement of the Marshall Plan, the Kremlin established the Communist Information Bureau (Cominform) to facilitate supervision of policy coordination in Eastern Europe.

gress over the plan was framed in terms of "stopping the onslaught of communism" (see Berkowitz, Bock, and Fuccillo, 1977). This was certainly not the kind of rhetoric that would endear the recovery program to Soviet policy makers. In any event, the Soviet Union rejected the offer of American aid and also refused to permit Poland and Czechoslovakia, both of whom had been offered Marshall Plan assistance, to accept it (Spero, 1977).

Following formation of the Organization for European Economic Cooperation (OEEC)[25] as the European instrumentality for receiving and coordinating American economic assistance, the Soviet Union in 1949 created the Council for Mutual Economic Assistance (CMEA or Comecon) "to reinforce Eastern economic cooperation in isolation from the West" (Spero, 1977). Comecon was designed to carry out what was known at the time as the Molotov Plan for the economic integration of Eastern Europe.[26]

Under Soviet hegemony the nations of Comecon became remarkably inward-looking. In 1938 over two-thirds of East European exports went to Western Europe; only 10 percent went to the Soviet Union or other Eastern countries. By 1953 these proportions were nearly reversed: 64 percent of Eastern exports were traded among the Eastern European countries and the Soviet Union; less than 15 percent went to Western Europe, and only a trickle found their way to the Western Hemisphere (Spero, 1977: 249). More importantly, the Soviet Union was able to use its superior political and military capabilities to force its weaker neighbors to pursue economic policies clearly advantageous to the Soviet Union. Thus the Soviets not only created an international economic system isolated from the West but used that system to augment their own capabilities to carry on political and military competition with the West.

The West did little to inhibit the economic isolation of the East. In fact, under American leadership, economic ties between the socialist and capitalist worlds were actively discouraged. The United States was particularly sensitive to trade in so-called strategic goods, items that might bolster Soviet military capabilities and thus threaten Western security. Accordingly, the United States sought to embargo the sale of strategic goods to the Soviet Union and its communist allies, and it sponsored the Coordinating Committee (Cocom) as a mechanism for inducing its own allies to join in a unified embargo effort.

25. The OEEC was reconstituted in 1960 as the Organization for Economic Cooperation and Development (OECD).

26. The Eastern European members of Comecon are Bulgaria, Czechoslovakia, the German Democratic Republic, Hungary, Poland, Romania, and the Soviet Union. Albania was expelled as a member following the split between China and the Soviet Union. Since 1962 membership in Comecon was made available to non-European countries, and Outer Mongolia and Cuba are its two non-European members.

Although a measure of agreement was reached, the United States was never able to elicit from its allies comparable enthusiasm for the use of economic instruments for prosecuting the Cold War.

> For the United States, the strategic embargo was intended to impair not only Eastern military strength but Eastern political and economic power as well. The U.S. embargo therefore was directed at military capability in its largest sense, that is, at non-military goods which would enhance economic performance and development as well as at military goods. On the other hand, because the Europeans and Japanese had a greater economic stake in trade with the East than the United States, they tended to feel that a broad embargo would simply encourage greater Eastern solidarity without hindering military and political capability. Thus they advocated a more limited definition of strategic goods, namely, those with direct military implications. As a result of allied resistance, the international list was always less comprehensive than the U.S. control list. (Spero, 1977: 250)

The United States also placed more restrictions on the granting of financial resources to the communist countries than did its allies, and in 1951, during the Korean War, it moved to strip the Soviet Union and other communist countries of any trade preferences. Thus the East was denied markets for its own products as well as access to Western goods and finances (see Spero, 1977, for details). Economics joined hands with politics in creating and conducting the Cold War.

Toward Competitive Cooperation

Relations between East and West began to change toward the end of the 1950s, roughly coinciding with the ascension to power of Nikita Khrushchev in the Soviet Union in the mid-1950s and the formation of the European Economic Community in Western Europe in 1958. Hostility persisted, to be sure, but elements of polycentrism as well as accommodating initiatives began to appear in both the East and the West. At least in the economic sphere, some thawing of the Cold War was in the offing.

Khrushchev sought to rejuvenate the moribund CMEA as an instrument for the promotion of intra-Comecon trade. Greater policy coordination, standardization of industrial products, emphasis on long-term trade agreements, establishment of an international bank for socialist countries, and increased specialization and division of labor among Comecon countries were sought as accompaniments to the expansion of trade. The results, however, were disappointing because of the persistence of a previous bias toward economic self-sufficiency, a scarcity of goods, and the poor quality of those goods available (Korbonski, 1973). These factors, combined with the growing demand of their economies, led the communist countries to increase substantially their trade with the noncommunist world. "In time, member states [of Comecon] were openly urged to acquire modern technology in the West instead of trying to develop it at home in order to accelerate the process of development" (Korbonski, 1973). Western Europe was a willing participant in the expansion of trade, and between 1958 and 1971 the value of trade between the CMEA and the EEC increased fivefold (Kuhlman, 1976).

Access to Western technology led to an increased interest on the part of the East Europeans in more trade with the West. Eventually, the Soviet Union itself began to seek greater trade ties with the capitalist world. This desire for trade exists even today and is a result of the nature of the command economies of socialist states. For managers in planned economies the primary incentive is to meet quantitative production goals and not to make *qualitative* improvements in the goods produced. Research and development also tend to be separated from applications in the productive mainstream of the economy (Spero, 1977). Thus economic efficiency (greater productivity) is difficult to achieve, and the dampening of overall economic growth is a recurrent if unintended consequence.[27]

During the 1960s growing demand within socialist countries for consumer goods and the continued inability of the Soviet agricultural system to meet its production goals also contributed to an increased interest in greater trade with the West. In 1964, Khrushchev made the Soviet Union's first major purchase of Western grain. The combination of production, consumer, and agricultural demands in the East and general receptiveness in the West led to a $6.4 billion increase in East-West trade between 1960 and 1968[28] (Nove, 1978: 16; and Figure 7.4 in this book).

Nevertheless, as long as the Cold War continued, East-West trade remained unimportant, both as a percentage of world trade and as a per-

27. Yergin (1977) has also suggested that the division of economic activity toward the Soviet Union has had a detrimental effect on technological change: "Within the Comecon bloc, the trend appears to be that the Soviet Union has pulled down the level of production of what were more advanced countries, such as Czechoslovakia."

28. Although East-West trade grew significantly during the 1960s, there apparently is a point beyond which the Soviet Union will not permit a major realignment of East-West relations, particularly if it should come through liberalization of domestic politics that challenge the supremacy of the Soviet form of communism. The Soviet Union demonstrated this in 1968 when, with other Warsaw Pact nations, it intervened militarily in Czechoslovakia to terminate the Czech experiment in domestic liberalism. The Brezhnev Doctrine, enunciated following the intervention, asserts the right of the Soviet Union to intervene militarily in the domestic politics of any socialist state threatened by internal revolt or "imperialism."

centage of the total trade of East and West. Although both East and West Europe favored greater commerce and took steps in that direction, the United States and the Soviet Union continued, for political reasons, to reject any major change in East-West economic relations. The large self-sufficient economies of the superpowers enabled them to be less influenced by the potential economic advantages of interaction than their smaller and more trade-oriented partners and more influenced by overriding political and security concerns. . . . Not until the late 1960s and early 1970s . . . did the policies of the superpowers change. Political tensions decreased, and forces encouraging East-West economic interaction were able to come into play. (Spero, 1977: 253)

From Détente to "Contestation"

Détente became the official policy of both the United States and the Soviet Union with the inauguration of President Nixon in January 1969. A shift in trade relations between the superpowers occurred both as a symptom of and a spur to détente.

Two interrelated political factors affected the Soviet desire for increased commercial ties. The first was the growing tension between the Soviet Union and China. This conflict placed a premium on the Soviets establishing relatively stable relations with the West, a stability that trade might facilitate. The second factor was a growing Soviet perception, even without Soviet rivalry with China, of the desirability of reducing tensions with the United States, presumably as a way of reducing the threat of war and the cost of armaments. Moreover, the drive for economic advancement was motivated by the Soviet desire "as a superpower . . . to fly its flag in the entire world's economy, not merely that of its own bloc" (Yergin, 1977).

To fly its flag the Soviet Union had to move from the "extensive" mode of economic development ("growth based upon increases in the labor force and the capital stock") to an "intensive" mode ("growth resulting from improved technology leading to higher productivity") (Yergin, 1977). Accordingly, the Soviets' desire for increased commercial ties between East and West was motivated by a third concern, one primarily economic. Access to Western technology and the credits necessary to buy it were sought as means to rejuvenate the sluggish Soviet economy, and grain imports were necessary to supplement shortfalls in Soviet agricultural production.[29]

American interests in expanded commerical ties, on the other hand, were principally political—they would contribute to what

29. See Holsti (1979) for an examination of alternative explanations of the continuing weakness of the Soviet agricultural system.

Secretary of State Henry A. Kissinger described as a "vested interest in mutual restraint" on the part of the superpowers and give the Soviets "a stake in international equilibrium." What the Soviets wanted from détente (of which expanded commercial intercourse was only one element) was therefore consistent with what the United States wanted, namely, "a scheme to moderate the Soviet world revolutionary thrust by increasing Soviet dependence on stable relationships with the United States and other Western nations" (Brown, 1977). This was the logic upon which Kissinger's "linkage" strategy for the containment of Soviet influence and expansionism was predicated.

There were potential commercial advantages for the United States as well, however. Over time the willingness of other industrialized nations to restrict trade with the communist world had waned, with the result that they were capturing the major share of communist trade with the West.[30] This is shown in Figure 7.4, which illustrates the growth in East-West trade between 1968 and 1977 together with the small United States proportion of the total volume.

Perhaps the high point of détente was achieved at the 1972 Moscow summit when the two Cold War antagonists initialed the first Strategic Arms Limitation Talks (SALT) agreement. SALT was certainly the cornerstone of détente, but expanded East-West trade was part of the mortar. A joint commercial commission was established at the summit, whose purpose was to pave the way for the granting of most-favored-nation (MFN) status to the Soviet Union and the extension of U.S. government-backed credits to the Soviet regime.

The Nixon administration also expressed interest in selling greater quantities of American grain to the Soviet Union. During the Moscow summit Nixon commented several times to Brezhnev and Premier Alexei Kosygin that grain sales to the Soviet Union would have a beneficial impact on American public opinion, symbolizing to the American public the tangible rewards of the waning of the Cold War and the advent of détente (Kissinger, 1979). At the time the Soviet leadership expressed little interest in a formal response to the proposal. But shortly thereafter the American government negotiated an agreement providing the Soviet Union with $750 million in credits with which to buy American agricultural products.

Unknown to the administration at the time, the Soviet Union was facing a catastrophic crop failure. The Soviets desperately needed American grain. Hence, they quietly set about putting to-

---

30. In 1976, for example, other Western industrialized nations captured 29 percent of communist trade, while the United States share was only 2.5 percent (U.S. Department of Commerce, 1978: v). The corresponding percentages in 1977 were 25 and 1.7 respectively (U.S. Department of Commerce, 1979: v).

Figure 7.4
East-West Trade and U.S. Share

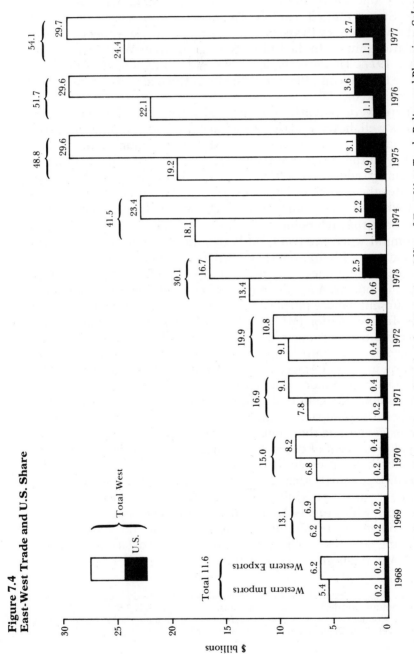

Source: U.S. Department of Commerce, Industry and Trade Administration, Office of East-West Trade Policy and Planning, *Selected Trade and Economic Data of the Centrally Planned Economies* (Washington, D.C.: Government Printing Office, June 1979), p. 4.
Note: East = Bulgaria, Czechoslovakia, East Germany, Hungary, Poland, Romania, U.S.S.R. and People's Republic of China. West = Austria, Belgium, Canada, Denmark, West Germany, France, Italy, Japan, Luxembourg, Netherlands, Norway, Sweden, Switzerland, Great Britain and U.S.

gether one of the largest commercial transactions in history, a transaction that led to a sharp increase in the world price of grain. Thus, what was to have produced a positive impact on American public opinion turned into a blunder, casting a shadow over the entire question of expanded East-West trade. Kissinger recounts the effects of the Soviet grain deal in his memoirs:

> [The Soviets] gave us a lesson in the handicaps a market economy has in negotiating with a state trading enterprise. Each of our grain companies, trying to steal a march on its competitors, sold the largest amount possible and kept its sale utterly secret, even from the US government. Not for several weeks did we realize that the Soviets had, by a series of separate transactions, bought up nearly one billion dollar's worth of grain in one year—nearly our entire stored surplus. And we had subsidized the deals at a time when the Soviet Union quite literally had no other choice than to buy our grain at market prices or face mass starvation. . . .
>
> At first the sale was hailed as a political masterstroke. It led to the usual maneuvering as to who should get credit. . . . Soon, however, no one wanted any credit; the grain sale rapidly became a political scandal; Nixon was accused of selling at bargain rates to our adversaries and driving up the price to American consumers. (Kissinger, 1979: 1270)

Eventually an agreement providing for more orderly entry of the Soviet Union into the American grain market was negotiated, but the political damage wrought by "The Great American Grain Robbery" was substantial. "The sale turned from a step toward détente and a boost to the U.S. economy into a political threat to the policy of détente and an economic debacle" (Spero, 1977).

Even more damaging was the fate of most-favored-nation status and increased credits for the Soviet Union. Most-favored-nation treatment was to have been granted by the U.S. Trade Act of 1974, which provides MFN status for the Soviet Union and other communist countries in fulfillment of the 1972 Trade Agreement between the United States and the Soviet Union. But a congressional amendment (known as the Jackson-Vanik amendment) made MFN contingent upon liberalization of communist policies relating to Jewish emigration. Evidence suggests that the Soviet Union did tacitly agree to permit freer emigration of Soviet Jews, but in January 1975 it rejected these conditions, labeling them a violation of the 1972 Trade Agreement (which had called for an unconditional elimination of discriminatory trade restrictions and the principle of noninterference in domestic affairs). Other members of Comecon quickly followed suit and rejected the conditions imposed by the U.S. Congress.

Denial of MFN was a slap in the Soviet face, for it "symbolized [the Soviet Union's] exclusion from the international economic system, whereas the restoration of most-favored-nation status symbolized the end of Western discrimination" (Spero, 1977). The slap became a black eye when the United States played the "China card" and granted the People's Republic of China, the Soviet Union's principal communist rival, most-favored-nation status in early 1980.

More significant than symbolic was the issue of U.S. government-backed credits. Because Soviet and Eastern European currencies are not convertible (that is, they are subject to government controls and therefore not easily exchanged for Western currencies), and because the exports from which they earn hard (Western) currencies have been relatively limited, communist economies generally have lacked the foreign exchange necessary to buy the goods from the West that they desire. During the 1970s this situation changed as a consequence of heavy borrowing from the West. By 1978 Eastern debt to the West was in excess of $50 billion (Portes, 1978; see also Portes, 1977; and Nove, 1978), up from only a few billion dollars at the beginning of the decade. Much of this debt was owed to private lenders, but a continued dramatic increase seems unlikely in the absence of either sharply increased export earnings by the Comecon nations or the extension of government-backed credits by the West, particularly the United States.[31]

The issue of American credits to the Soviet Union evolved in a manner similar to the most-favored-nation question. In late 1974 the Stevenson amendment to the U.S. Export-Import Bank authorization bill limited American credits to the Soviet Union to $300 million over a four-year period.[32] Congressional action appears to have been motivated by a desire to assert legislative control over the activities

31. Comecon countries typically seek to balance their trade on a bilateral basis, rather than multilaterally. Thus the Soviet Union will seek to balance its trade with each of the Eastern European nations rather than with all of them collectively, as is the case in the Western miltilateral trading system. Consistent with this strategy, barter trades with the West can be used to circumvent the constaints of limited availability of hard currencies.

These swaps take a number of different forms. One consists of straight barter of specific quantities of goods, such as American soft drinks for Russian vodka; another more generalized form allows the Western partner to choose from a shipping list; a third consists of barter that pays off the Western partner with future output from a specified plant—so-called compensation deals. (Vernon, 1979: 1042)

Compensation deals are potentially attractive as a means through which Western firms might gain access to the Soviet Union's extensive reserves of raw materials, including oil and natural gas. In return for "pay-backs" in raw materials, the Soviet Union gains Western technology, equipment, and managerial skills.

32. During a fifteen-month period in 1973–1974, the Export-Import Bank extended $469 million in credits for sixteen projects that also received an equal amount of private backing (Huntington, 1978: 77).

of the Export-Import Bank as well as concern growing out of the 1972 grain deal and the abuses unveiled by the Watergate scandal. The impact on expanding East-West trade was devastating.

> It now appears that the Stevenson Amendment was the decisive reason that the Soviets refused to put the trade agreement into effect. From their point of view, such an action was rational. For the most part, the need for most-favored-nation status was (and is) primarily theoretical. Credits, on the other hand, were of immediate importance and utility. If trade were to expand substantially, credits were required. But the Stevenson Amendment said, in effect, that after having made an important concession [regarding the emigration of Soviet Jews], the Soviets would be eligible for less in credits over the subsequent four years than had already been received over the previous two, before they had made any concession! It looked very much as though the Congress were putting a ceiling over trade rather than a floor under it. (Yergin, 1977: 532)

Upon assuming office the Carter administration committed itself to the policy of détente and apparently to the principle of normalizing East-West commercial relations. But in the face of congressional constraints East-West trade stagnated in the second half of the 1970s.

Furthermore, the Carter administration was also committed to a worldwide campaign on behalf of human rights, apparently in part due to the perceived need to devise a cause around which a new domestic consensus regarding America's world role might be built. In the context of Soviet-American relations, this often led to sharp American attacks on the Soviet Union's human-rights policies. It also led to arguments that the United States ought to use its commercial relations with the Soviets, and particularly the Soviets' desire to acquire high technology goods from the United States, as leverage to realize American foreign policy objectives in the human-rights area. Voices could be heard urging the administration to use whatever instruments were at its disposal to counter continued high levels of military spending by the Soviet Union, its overseas military build-up and arms transfers to the Third World, and its backing of Cuban intervention in Angola, Ethiopia, and elsewhere in Africa. As argued by Samuel P. Huntington, a one-time member of the Carter administration's National Security Council staff:

> To be meaningful, détente must be comprehensive and reciprocal. One superpower cannot expect to invoke its spirit only in situations in which it serves that power's interests. If the Soviets, for example, continue to employ military means, including those of their allies, to expand their influence in Africa and elsewhere, the United States and its

allies will eventually have no choice but to begin to close the door of economic détente. Economic detente and military adventurism cannot go hand-in-hand for long. At some point the Soviets will have to make a choice.[33] (Huntington, 1978: 69)

President Carter emphasized the theme of "choice" in an address at the U.S. Naval Academy in 1978, and he also hinted at the fragility of continued Soviet-American cooperation when he warned that "to be a basis for widening the scope of cooperation . . . détente must be . . . truly reciprocal. . . . [But] to the Soviet Union, détente seems to mean a continuing struggle for political advantage and increased influence. . . . The Soviet Union can choose either confrontation or cooperation. The United States is adequately prepared to meet either choice." Shortly thereafter the president moved to influence Soviet thinking. As a reprisal for the trials of Soviet human rights dissidents, Carter imposed new controls on the sale of oil technology to the Soviet Union, and he canceled the sale of a computer to the Soviet news agency *Tass* that was to have been used at the 1980 Summer Olympics in Moscow. Little more than a year later, additional punitive measures were instituted: a partial grain embargo and further restrictions on American exports following the Soviet military intervention in Afghanistan in late 1979. The commercial ties that a decade earlier had been both a spur to détente and a reflection of it became the victim as well as the instrument of sharply increased Soviet-American rivalry.[34] Détente had faded, and in its place a phase of superpower "contestation" had arisen.[35] A

33. Huntington (1978) specifically argued that the United States government should seek to translate the technological superiority of American capitalism into an instrument to influence Soviet decision-making: "if war is too important to be left to the generals, surely commerce is, in this context, too salient to be left to bankers and businessmen." For alternative views on the issue of transferring American technology to the Soviet Union, see Holzman and Portes (1978), Kiser (1978), Mountain (1978), Klitgaard (1978), all in the same issue of *Foreign Policy* in which the Huntington article appears, and Vernon (1979).

34. In part as a consequence of the decision of the U.S. government to restrict commercial ties with the Soviet Union, the value of Soviet-American trade in the first six months of 1980 was only half of what it had been in the comparable period of 1979. (U.S. Department of Commerce, 1980: 4)

35. Yergin (1977) persuasively argues that there are two basic images of the Soviet Union operating within the Washington policy-making community. One sees the Soviet Union "as a revolutionary state, single-mindedly geared to expansion. . . . For those who hold this view, détente is not merely a fraud, but a danger, a relaxation less of tension than of the American guard, so enabling the Soviet Union to take advantage of American goodwill." This is the image that was dominant during the height of the Cold War. In contrast, the image dominant during the early 1970s "views the Soviet Union less as a world revolutionary state than as a conventional great power. While obviously possessing vast military strengths and not lacking in imperialist drives, it is still a cautious power, concerned with protecting what it has, and with much to

heated East-West political struggle had resumed, and there was risk of a possible uncontrolled arms race. The basis for mutually advantageous trade relationships was also jeopardized if not demolished. The deteriorating political relationship between the two superpowers illustrated once again that East-West economic collaboration and political/military confrontation are incompatible—the later must recede before the former can advance meaningfully. Hence whether the economic exchanges between East and West which had been so painstakingly cultivated during the 1970s can be restored will depend largely on whether the Soviets and Americans can resolve the political and military issues that divide them.

Somewhat ironically, the latest phase of Soviet-American hostility has opened the door for the expansion of economic détente between the United States and the People's Republic of China. Should the trade agreements reached between China and the United States in 1980 continue to grow, their magnitude could transform significantly the complexion of world economic relationships. That development would undoubtedly have profound effects not only on subsequent political and military relationships between the Chinese and American trade partners, but would also diminish substantially the Soviet Union's sense of security and increase further its sense of isolation. Whether the prospects for world peace and prosperity would be enhanced poses a troublesome question for the future.

THE FIRST, SECOND, AND THIRD WORLDS IN THE 1980s

The ebb and flow of East-West commercial interactions during the 1970s is an indication of how fragile and subject to political considerations these ties are. The critical question for the 1980s is how relations between the United States and both the Soviet Union and the People's Republic of China will evolve. A major lesson of the 1970s is that the state of political relations will more readily shape economic affairs between East and West than the latter will affect the former,

gain from stability" (Yergin, 1977). These images in turn lead to quite different views of Soviet-American trade. The first sees "trade [as] one of the major items of transport on the 'one-way street.' " For those subscribing to the second image, "trade is one of the major means of encouraging a détente, establishing mutually advantageous relations, and strengthening the Soviet stake in international stability." Finally, Yergin argues that the image of the Soviet Union dominant at any particular time is critically related to Soviet behavior—if Soviet behavior reflects adventurism, this strengthens the political hand of those subscribing to the Cold War image; if an effort to reduce tensions is more apparent, this bodes well for those subscribing to the détente image. Commercial interactions between the United States and the Soviet Union will be affected accordingly. Developments in American policy as the 1970s ended and the decade of the 1980s commenced suggested that the Cold War image may once more be emerging dominant in American policy-making circles.

especially in the short-run (a point examined in some detail in Portes, 1978).

Continued Soviet hegemony in Eastern Europe will enable the Soviet Union to impose its will regarding East-West commercial interactions on its Eastern European allies more easily than the United States will be able to get its allies in Western Europe to share its fears and support its policies. The difficulty the Carter administration experienced in getting its NATO partners to boycott the 1980 Moscow Olympics in retaliation over the Soviet invasion of Afghanistan is illustrative. More significantly, perhaps, trade between East and West is generally more important to the superpowers' European allies than it is to the superpowers themselves. Continued trade in the European context may therefore give rise to powerful domestic lobbies in Europe supporting its perpetuation. Such a development could contribute to the weakening of ties between the United States and Europe and could lead to the development of the regional economic systems.

At this stage in history, economic "interdependence" between East and West exists primarily in the area of the East's hard currency debt to the West (see Portes, 1977). Should intra-European trade continue to increase, however, it is conceivable that, at least within the European context, "interdependence" might become an appropriate description for a much wider range of economic interactions. Such a development is potentially significant to the Third World, for its implies that the Second World would come to identify its interests more clearly with the First World on issues comprising North-South relations (see Portes, 1978).

The Second World as a whole thus far has established only modest economic ties with the Third World. Those that do exist appear dictated more by political expediency than by such liberal economic principles as comparative advantage.[36] Should ties between East and West become more closeknit, the polarization between North and South may become more pronounced.

Polarized or not, the demands of the South for some kind of fundamental restructuring of the international economic order are un-

36. At the end of the 1970s the Soviet Union was the largest producer of oil in the world. It is also the principal supplier of oil to Eastern Europe. There are projections, however, that the Comecon, too, will shortly come to be dependent on oil imports from the Third World. Given these projections, Portes (1978) makes the interesting point that Eastern Europe in particular might take advantage of its comparative technological sophistication in arms production to secure oil from the Third World: "For the East, the economic basis for this trade [arms exports] is at least as strong as the strategic and political rationale, since military equipment represents the Eastern comparative advantage *par excellence:* the only type of machinery in which the East can claim a rough technical parity with the West, and even superior quality or performance for cost in some areas" (Portes, 1978).

likely to abate or their stridency to diminish. The demands may be muted from time to time, and the diversity inherent within the Third World may permit separate bargains to be struck between the North and factions within the South on certain issues. But the perception of the Third World that the present structure of the international economic order preserves its dependent and unequal position in the international hierarchy is likely to fuel for some time demands for a radical transformation of the international division of labor, the structure of world industry, and the global trading system.

Assuming Soviet-American rivalry can be contained, integrating the economies of the First and Second Worlds into an orderly global economic system requires the development of new rules of procedure, and perhaps new institutions, that will be able to cope effectively with relations between market and command economies (Spero, 1977). The persistent inability of First World nations to devise means for coping effectively with their own economic affairs attests to the difficulty that merging First and Second World affairs will encounter, while the threat to Soviet hegemony in Eastern Europe that greater ties between East and West imply may cause the Soviets to proceed cautiously.

Even more problematic is how Third World demands and aspirations might be satisfied and properly managed. If the contentious rhetoric surrounding the North-South debate persists and the global inequality on which it is based continues, is it reasonable to expect the North to submit voluntarily to the demands of the South? Or is it more reasonable to expect the North to submit to Southern demands out of self-interest—borne of the realization that Northern well-being is a function of Southern health, and in particular the South's ability to buy what the North sells? Or further, is the most likely prospect Northern acquiescence to Southern demands due to growing Northern dependence on what the South already controls?

"We are going to create a new world order in which deprived people will not always be deprived, and oppressors will not always be oppressors," declared President Abolhassan Bani Sadr of Iran in the aftermath of the Islamic revolution of 1978–1979. That declaration—and the sentiment animating it—is likely to be heard increasingly in a world of widening income disparities, rising aspirations, limited prospects for economic growth, resource scarcities, and unabated population expansion.

Eight

The Population-Food Equation: Global Trends in Population Growth and Food Supplies

> If one postulates that the human race began with a single pair of parents, the population has had to double only 31 times to reach its present huge total.
>
> Robert S. McNamara, 1977

> For the first time since the beginning of the Industrial Revolution, there are signs that continuously expanding human demands are overriding the capacity of new technology to offset the constraints inherent in the natural systems and resources on which humanity depends.
>
> Lester R. Brown, 1979

The importance of population factors in global political relations cannot be underestimated. Because the nature of politics is determined to a substantial degree by the unequal distribution of valued resources in the global environment, how people are distributed *within* that environment and how they organize themselves to facilitate the quest for the necessities of life profoundly shape the nature of world political interactions. Similarly, changes in the distribution of people and in the resources they seek affect not only how people live, and if they *are* to live, but also the kinds of rites, rituals, and institutions that evolve from efforts to acquire scarce resources. These changes thus serve as catalysts in the transformation of the world's political system.

At few times in history have the number of people and their distribution in the world had more far-reaching global political implications than today. This is because at no previous time has the world had so many new inhabitants being added so rapidly to its population. The over four billion people who now occupy the globe constitute a significant proportion of all the people who have ever lived, and the proportion promises to grow even further as tens of thousands of new faces are added daily. In fact, if present population trends are projected ahead eight centuries, ours will be a standing-room-only planet, with land surface of only one square foot per person.

No one can seriously contemplate such a world. Nor are the other images that have been conjured up to shock the public consciousness realistic portraits of the future.[1] What they do tell us is that the pressures of population growth pose a serious threat to the human condition, one unprecedented in scale. The relevant questions, therefore, are, "At what level will the world's population be stabilized?" and "How will that stability be achieved?" The answers have important implications for world politics.

Surprisingly, however, observers of international relations have until recently usually given only passing attention to the political implications of population dynamics, even though some have argued that "the pressure of population is the most influential single factor in shaping the future of the human species" (Lerche and Said, 1979). Perhaps the population explosion with all its associated consequences has not attracted the same attention as other events because it has been so silent. As one observer noted:

> We are witnessing a landing of three billion persons on this planet. They come by day, by night, one by one, two by two, or three by three . . . they are landing everywhere, particularly in the developing countries. If they would land from the planet Mars, it would make great news in the newspaper. But they land from this planet and remain unnoticed. (Bernard Chatel, cited in Cleveland, 1976: 62)

The most immediate and obvious consequence of the silent explosion is the pressure it exerts on food supplies. But hunger is only one of the problems currently associated with, if not caused by, population pressures. Other areas of policy that may be affected by population growth include those dealing with literacy, oceanic fisheries, natural recreation areas, pollution, inflation, environmental illnesses, housing, climate change, overgrazing, overcrowding, income distribution, urbanization, deforestation, minerals, health

---

1. For example, Fremlin (1964) suggests that contemporary population trends projected nine centuries hence would see a world with more than 60 billion people, with housing requirements necessitating the construction of a single 2,000-story building girding the entire planet.

services, water, unemployment, endangered species, energy, political conflict, and individual freedom (Brown, McGrath, and Stokes, 1976).

The range of issues touched by population pressures today may be symbolic of the reality of tomorrow—a world with resources insufficient to sustain adequately an overpopulated planet. The capacity of existing national and international political and social institutions to cope with such a world will be severely tested.

This glimpse of a possible future is not meant to cast a shadow. Instead, it is intended to underscore the necessity of better understanding the interplay of population dynamics and resource consumption in today's world.

TRENDS IN WORLD POPULATION GROWTH

The rapid growth of world population today is described by a simple mathematical principle articulated in 1798 by the Reverend Thomas Malthus, namely, that population grows geometrically or exponentially (1 to 2, 2 to 4, 4 to 8, and so forth) rather than arithmetically (1 to 2, 2 to 3, 3 to 4).[2] When population increases in such an accelerating fashion, the compound effect can be staggering. Consider, for example, the consequences resulting from the simple individual decision of whether to have two children or three. If parents decide to have three children, and if each of their children and their children's children make the same decision, by the third generation thirty-nine people would have been born—three in the first, nine in the second, and twenty-seven in the third. If, however, the initial decision had been to have two children instead of three, and if each child made the same choice, over three generations only sixteen people would have been born (two in the first, four in the second, and eight in the third). Projecting these same patterns to whole societies, the cumulative consequences can be enormous. For example, the population of the United States in 1968 was 200 million. Assuming two-child families, the population would grow to 300 million by the year 2015. However, if we assume three-child families, 300 million will be reached before the turn of the century and the population will have doubled to over 400 million by 2015. Ex-

2. Thomas R. Malthus' thesis is stated alternately in his own words: "I think, I may fairly make two postulata. First, that food is necessary to the existence of man. Secondly, that the passion between the sexes is necessary, and will remain nearly in its present state. Assuming, then, my postulata as granted, I say, that the power of population is indefinitely greater than the power of the earth to produce subsistence for man. Population, where unchecked, increases in geometric ratio. Subsistence only increases in an arithmetical ratio. . . . ."

tending these same projections over a century, the population of the United States in 2068 would exceed 800 million if three-child families were the rule, but would remain well under 400 million with two-child families.

The rate of world population growth today is not only a function of aggregate birth or fertility rates. It is also a consequence of sharply lower death rates in many areas of the world that have been the result of advances in medical science, agricultural productivity, public sanitation, and technology. The paradox posed by sharply reduced death rates is that this favorable development has contributed to an accelerating rate of population growth—a population explosion.

The explosive proportions of today's population growth are illustrated in Figure 8.1, which indicates that it took from the beginning of time until the early 1800s for world population to reach one billion people. Due to substantial declines in death rates, world population reached two billion about 100 years later, in 1930. Since then, additional billions have been added even more rapidly: three billion was reached by 1960, and four billion was reached in 1975. If present growth rates persist, the world will add another 80 million

Figure 8.1
The Growth of World Population Since the Beginning of the Industrial Era

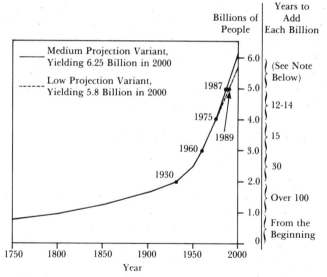

Source: U.S. Department of State, "World Population: The Silent Explosion—Part I," *Department of State Bulletin* 78 (October 1978), 46. Based on United Nations data.

Note: The number of years it will take to add the fifth and subsequent billions will depend primarily on the pace of fertility declines, and to a lesser extent mortality trends, in developing countries.

every year, reaching the 6 billion figure in the year 2000 and well beyond that in succeeding decades.

How rapidly the world adds billions to its number is predicted by its growth rate. Worldwide, the rate of population growth is believed to have peaked at about 2 percent in the early 1970s, and to have declined to 1.8–1.9 percent by 1977 (U.S. Department of State, 1978c: 45).[3] One way to contemplate how sensitive world population growth is to even such small incremental rates of change is to consider how long it will take the population to double given a particular growth rate. Just as money deposited in a savings bank will grow more rapidly if interest is paid not only on the original investment but also on interest payments, population increases are a function not only of increases in the original number of people but also of those increases accruing from past population growth. Thus a population growing at a 1 percent rate will double in 69 years, whereas a population growing at a 2 percent rate will double in only 35 years.[4] The actual pace of future population expansion is, of course, problematic. But whatever the ultimate rate of growth, trends are apparent and the consequences inevitable; it is not a question of *whether* the world will become more crowded, but of *how crowded* it will become. We can better understand why this result is inevitable if we go beyond the simple arithmetic of population growth.

POPULATION DYNAMICS: NATIONAL AND REGIONAL VARIATIONS IN POPULATION GROWTH

Population growth rates are a function of the number of births and deaths per year. In the United States, there were 14.7 births per 1,000 population and 8.9 deaths per 1,000 in 1976 (Haupt and Kane, 1978: 17, 26). The difference between these two figures, converted to a percentage, indicates that the rate of natural population increase (the rate of growth due to the excess of births over deaths) in the United States in 1976 was 0.58 percent. This is an annual rate typical of industrialized nations today. Hence, the difference between the U.S. rate of 0.58 percent as a typical industrialized nation and the

3. The Population Reference Bureau (Haupt and Kane, 1978: 45) puts the world population growth rate in 1978 at 1.7 percent. At this rate, the world will still add over 70 million people a year, but less than the 80 million cited above. See McNamara (1977) for data on population growth rates in different historical periods.

4. This is merely another more general way of illustrating the point that population grows exponentially rather than arithmetically. A quick way to calculate the impact of differenct growth rates on doubling time is to divide 69 by the percentage of growth. Thus a population growing at 1 percent will double in sixty-nine years, but a population growing at 3 percent will double in twenty-three years.

world population growth rate of 1.8–1.9 percent is largely a function of the population explosion in the Third World.

The effect of migrant labor.   Technically, the rate of natural increase is not the same as the growth rate, since the latter takes account of net migration patterns, while the former does not. The growing importance of cross-national migration as a factor in the population equation cannot be overemphasized. The migration of workers seeking employment beyond their country of citizenship has become a growing, worldwide phenomenon. Migrant labor—both legal and illegal—is often welcomed by the host country because migrant wages are typically low and the country accepting migrants pays little if anything for their health, education, and welfare needs. Some countries, moreover, encourage people to emigrate as a way of reducing unemployment at home, and because migrants can be counted on to return considerable portions of their income to their needy families in their home country. At times, labor migration has been widespread. An undetermined but large number of Mexicans have crossed the border into the United States in search of jobs. Millions of migrant workers have also emigrated from southern Europe and the Middle East to northwestern Europe: "At the height of the 'guest worker' era [the mid-1970s], one of every seven manual laborers in Germany and in Britain was a migrant, and one out of four in France, in Switzerland, and in Belgium" (Barnet, 1980b: 56). These patterns—as well as their political and economic impact upon relations among nations, including the contribution made to the further transnationalization of the globe—need to be considered in any assessment of global population and resource trends. (See Barnet, 1980b, for a thoughtful discussion of this aspect of world politics.)

Factors influencing birth rates and fertility rates.   The greatest increases in population recently have occurred in the developing world, where the medical and agricultural revolutions have most dramatically affected the incidence of death; they have been least great in the developed world, where births and deaths have nearly stabilized. The obvious inference is that those nations whose economies are least able to support a standard of living above the poverty level are also those with the greatest increase in the number of people for whom to care. The dramatic differences in the growth rates of developed and developing nations virtually assure that this pattern will persist into the future. It has been estimated that the 3 billion people who inhabited the Third World in 1975 will have grown to 5 billion by the year 2000, while the comparable increase among developed nations will be only from 1 billion to 1.3 billion (U.S. Department of State, 1978c: 47). These projections are shown graphically in Figure 8.2, which also illustrates the already sharp discrepancies between the populations of the North and the South.

Birth rates measure the number of births in a society for every 1,000 people. The fertility rate—the number of live births per 1,000 women between age fifteen to forty-four years in a given year—is a more refined measure, since it relates more directly to the age-sex group that has the highest probability of giving birth. In developing nations, high levels of fertility derive from a variety of sources. Entrenched religious norms often sanction and encourage parenting, prescribing the bearing of children, particularly male offspring, as both a duty and a path to a rewarding afterlife. In addition, cultural traditions in many societies ascribe prestige and social status to women according to the number of children they bear. But most importantly, perhaps, high fertility rates are affected by economic factors. For example, large families may be a source of "social security" for parents who live in societies where there are no public programs to provide for the elderly. Under such conditions, parents usually try to have as many children as possible so that they can be cared for in their old age. Where the infant mortality rate is high, the incentives for creating many offspring are even greater—the more children produced, the higher the probability that some will survive. In some countries of the developing world, in fact, half of all deaths occur before the age of five (U.S. Department of State, 1978b: 5). Thus the logic underlying high fertility rates is often most compelling where poverty in all its manifestations is most widespread; the tragedy is that such high rates often reinforce the persistence of poverty, and vice versa.

High fertility rates in the developing world can also be perpetuated by government policies. Although most Third World countries now have some kind of national population program, there remains a residue in the thinking of Third World governing elites that a large population somehow confers upon a country status and influence in world politics—perhaps because a large population is a prerequisite for a large army. Indeed, some Third World nations regard population and birth control programs as a conspiracy of the rich against the poor, as yet another neo-imperialist effort by the industrialized nations to preserve their position in the international pecking order and to deprive the developing nations of the manpower thought to be essential for industrialization and militarization.

The momentum factor. All of these factors reinforce the persistence of high fertility rates in many areas of the world. But even more important in understanding the population explosion in the Third

Figure 8.2
The Population Explosion (Where the People Are Likely to Be in the Year 2000)

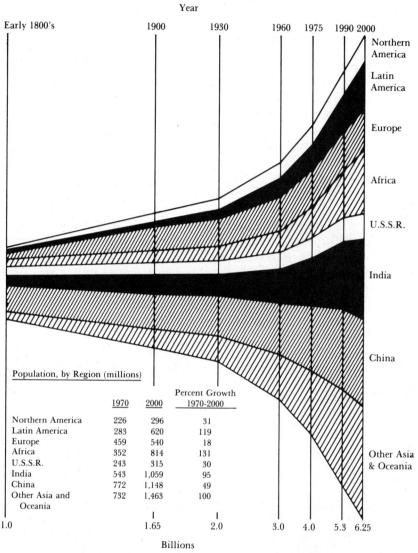

Year

			1900	1930	1960	1975	1990 2000	
Early 1800's

Northern America

Latin America

Europe

Africa

U.S.S.R.

India

China

Population, by Region (millions)

	1970	2000	Percent Growth 1970-2000
Northern America	226	296	31
Latin America	283	620	119
Europe	459	540	18
Africa	352	814	131
U.S.S.R.	243	315	30
India	543	1,059	95
China	772	1,148	49
Other Asia and Oceania	732	1,463	100

Other Asia & Oceania

1.0	1.65	2.0	3.0	4.0	5.3 6.25

Billions

Source: U.S. Department of State, "World Population: The Silent Explosion—Part I," *Department of State Bulletin* 78 (October 1978), 48. Based on United Nations data.

World (which is a result of high, but declining, birth rates, and rapidly falling death rates) is the "momentum" factor, "which might be likened to the momentum of a speeding passenger train that cannot be brought to an immediate stop even with the full application of the brakes"(Population Reference Bureau, 1976). Population momentum is especially great in societies with high proportions of young people. In these societies families are formed and babies produced at a rate faster than older persons die. This process will continue until the age structures shift toward equal numbers of people in each age group.

Consider, for example, the three age and sex population profiles shown in Figure 8.3. Mexico's profile shows an "expansive" population, because each new age group or cohort contains more people than the one before it. By way of contrast, the United States has a "constrictive" profile, since recent cohorts have been smaller than preceding ones. Sweden's profile is of a "stationary" population, since it has roughly equal numbers of people in each cohort.

While most nations of the developed world have moved in the direction of Sweden's "zero-population growth" profile, developing nations generally mirror the Mexican pattern. An immediate consequence is that developing societies have very large proportions of dependent children (less than fifteen years old), usually in the range of 40–45 percent of their total population compared with 25 percent in the developed world. In other words, there is only about one working-age adult for each child under fifteen in the Third World compared with nearly three working-age adults in the developed countries (U.S. Department of State, 1978c: 47). Such a large propor-

Figure 8.3
Population Pyramids: Three General Profiles of Age and Sex Composition

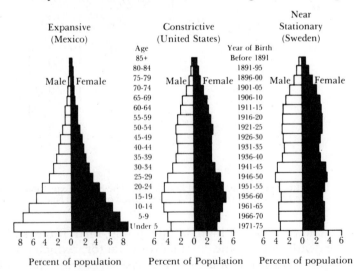

Source: Arthur Haupt and Thomas Kane, *Population Handbook* (Washington, D.C.: Population Reference Bureau, 1978), p. 14.

tion of dependent children places a heavy burden on public services (for example, the educational system) and encourages immediate consumption of economic resources rather than their reinvestment to promote future economic growth. As these same children become of working age, they also contribute to the enormous unemployment and underemployment problems that developing nations typically face. Yet a country whose population grows faster than its economy cannot absorb increasingly large numbers of working-age people into the productive mainstream of society. Indeed, the resources required are enormous. The government of Egypt has estimated that on the average it costs 7,000 Egyptian pounds ($10,000) to create a new job. It has also been estimated that 922 million additional workers will be added in the developing world between 1970 and 2000. Based on these figures (and ignoring inflation), the developing world will require the expenditure of $9.22 trillion just to absorb the *increases* in the numbers of their working-age people.[5]

The rapid growth of already massive urban areas is a related syndrome. It has been estimated that by 1990 at least a dozen Third World cities will have populations in excess of 9 million people. In many instances the estimated rates of growth and the sheer numbers involved are astounding. Lagos, Nigeria, a city of 800,000 in 1960, will be a city of 9.4 million in 2000; Cairo, with 5.7 million inhabitants in 1970, will grow to 16.4 million by the year 2000; and Mexico City, with 10.9 million inhabitants in 1975, will become a massive urban center of nearly 32 million people. Already many urban areas are better termed agglomerations than cities,

> with extensive shantytowns in which living conditions are deplorable; agglomerations where people, other than the urban elite and middle classes are without adequate water, sanitation, health, education, and other social services; where people are often living five or six in a room, acutely aware of the great disparity in wealth and poverty about them. All this contributes to alienation and frustration on a massive scale. (U. S. Department of State, 1978b: 3)[6]

5. Developed nations must also cope with a dependency problem as a result of their population profiles, namely, caring for a proportionately larger number of older people.

> However, the developed countries were able to build their economies, partly through the contributions of the now elderly, before this burden became major. The problems it presents are arousing increasing concern in the developed countries but are less critical than those imposed on the developing countries by their heavily youth-biased age structures. (U.S. Department of State, 1978c: 47)

6. Urbanization is also related to the pressures on needed social services associated with rapid population growth, because urban development requires more investment in infrastructure than does rural development.

> Urban housing is more expensive than rural housing. The proportion of urban children for whom schooling is provided is always much higher. . . . The town

The sheer momentum of population growth in the Third World which is associated with such deplorable conditions is also intimately linked to the age profiles of developing nations. Because each cohort is typically larger than the one before it, the number of young men and women entering their reproductive years will also grow. Figure 8.4 demonstrates the importance of this momentum by projecting a larger proportion of prospectively fertile age groups in the developing world. It also demonstrates how vastly different the population growth of the developed and developing worlds is likely to be, which is, of course, partly a consequence of the vastly different age structures of the populations comprising the two worlds. The predictable consequence will be the rapid emergence of a world in which only a tiny fraction of its population will reside in developed countries.

Figure 8.4
Population by Age and Sex (1975 and 2000)

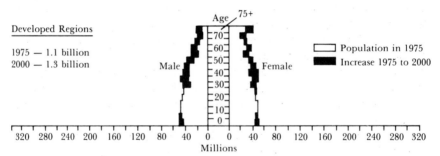

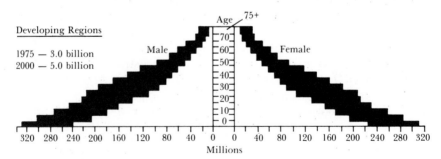

Source: U.S. Department of State, "World Population: The Silent Explosion—Part I," *Department of State Bulletin* 78 (October 1978), 47. Based on U.S. Bureau of the Census data.

---

has to mobilize its own hospital service, piped water supplies, bus transportation. In all these respects the towns require more per head in terms of quantity than rural areas.... (Lewis, 1978: 39–40)

W. Arthur Lewis also notes that urbanization fosters the dependence of developing countries on the North for their capital needs (Lewis, 1978).

Stemming the tide of an ever expanding population implies that the Third World must move toward a replacement-level rate of fertility, as many industrialized nations have already done. Replacement is measured by the net reproduction rate (NRR), which is the average number of daughters born to a woman who survive to childbearing age given prevailing levels of fertility and mortality. An NRR of 1.0 is the exact replacement level, since at this level each generation of mothers is having exactly enough daughters to replace that generation in the population. In societies where the death rate among females prior to the end of the reproductive age is high, replacement-level fertility requires a NRR greater than 1.0. As death rates fall, proportionately fewer births are required.

Today, some two dozen countries in the developed world are at or below replacement-level fertility. In the United States, the NRR in 1975 was 0.83, and the total fertility rate (the total number of children born, not just daughters) dipped below 1.8 births per woman (Haupt and Kane, 1978: 20, 22). Both of these figures are below replacement-level fertility.[7] Yet the population of the United States continues to grow, with over a million more births than deaths each year (Haupt and Kane, 1978: 23). This is a dramatic example of population momentum at work.

In general, population growth will continue for as much as fifty to seventy years after replacement-level fertility is achieved. This startling fact underscores the urgency of grappling with the population problem, "for every decade of delay in achieving an NRR of 1—replacement level—the world's peak population will be some 15% greater . . ." (U.S. Department of State, 1978c: 49).

The case of Mexico dramatizes the impact of such momentum on a particular developing country. In 1970, the population of Mexico stood at 51 million. Of this number, 46 percent were under the age of 15, 65 percent under the age of 25, and the NRR was estimated at 2.7 (U.S. Department of State, 1978c: 49). If the fertility rate in Mexico were to decline to the replacement level by the turn of the century, Mexico's population would eventually stabilize at 174 million, or roughly three and a half times its present size. But if the fertility rate were not to reach the replacement level until 2020–2025, Mexico's population would not stop growing until it reached 269 million, which is over five times its present size (U.S. Department of State, 1978c: 49).

7. In the United States, a total fertility rate of 2.12 is considered replacement level. The number is slightly higher than two (the number of children sufficient to exactly replace both parents) because slightly more males than females are born, and because not all children survive to childbearing age (Haupt and Kane, 1978). In the developing world, total fertility rates must be greater than 2.12 in order to achieve replacement level, much as the NRR must be greater than 1.0, due to higher mortality rates.

The implications of population momentum for the world as a whole are illustrated in Figure 8.5. If current trends in fertility continue, it appears the world might reach the goal of replacement-level fertility around the year 2020 (McNamara, 1977: 31). Some seventy years later this would lead to a steady-state population something in excess of 11 billion people. If replacement-level fertility were not reached by this time, of course, the world's ultimate population size would be much greater. Conversely, if replacement-level fertility could be reached earlier, the impact would be equally substantial. As Robert S. McNamara, president of the World Bank, has observed, "if the date at which replacement-level fertility is reached could be advanced from 2020 to 2000 . . . the ultimate population would be approximately 3 billion less, a number equivalent to 75 percent of today's world total. This reveals in startling terms the hidden penalties of failing to act, and act immediately, to reduce fertility" (McNamara, 1977: 32).

The obvious question, then, is how can replacement-level fertility be achieved?

Figure 8.5
Momentum of World Population Growth

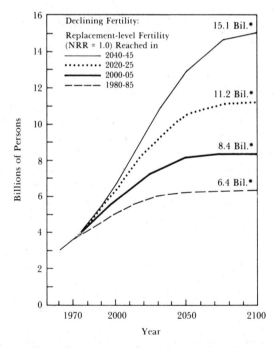

Source: U.S. Department of State, "World Population: The Silent Explosion—Part I," *Department of State Bulletin* 78 (October 1978), 50.
*Stabilization level.

The Demographic Transition Theory

The drop in the worldwide population growth rate that occurred in the 1965–1975 decade coincided with the introduction of national population and family planning programs in many areas of the developing world.[8] By the end of the 1970s nearly all of the developing nations of the world had initiated some kind of national population program, and some of the most impressive declines in birth rates have been registered in those nations which have instituted programs to reduce fertility (see U.S. Department of State, 1978b). Assistance in developing such programs has been provided by many developed nations through their foreign aid programs, by international organizations such as the UN Fund for Population Activities, and by nongovernmental organizations such as the International Planned Parenthood Federation. Clearly, then, it would appear that one way to cope with the global nature of the population problem is through concerted national and international efforts.[9]

However, many of the developing nations which registered the most impressive gains during the 1970s in controlling population growth rates had not only instituted vigorous national population programs but had also made measurable social and economic progress over a number of years. Their experience is thus consistent with the move toward a steady-state population in most developed countries, which may be explained by what is known as the *demographic transition theory.*

This theory seeks to explain the transition that Europe and later North America experienced between 1750 and 1930, when a condition of high birth rates combined with high death rates was replaced by a condition of low birth rates and low death rates. The transition was initiated when death rates began to fall, presumably as a result of economic and social development, and especially because of rising standards of living and improved controls over disease. In such circumstances, the potential for substantial population growth was, of course, great. But then birth rates also began to decline, and during this phase population growth slowed. Such declines are assumed to occur because economic growth alters attitudes toward family size. In preindustrial society, children are economic bonuses. As industrialization proceeds, they become economic burdens.[10] They inhibit social mobility and capital accumula-

8. There is also evidence of sporadic rises in death rates in some poorer developing nations associated in part with food shortages. See Brown (1978) for details.

9. See U.S. Department of State (1978a; 1978b) and McNamara (1977) for discussions of various policies designed to cope with the population problem.

10. In the United States, for example, the cost of raising and educating a child was estimated in the mid-1970s to be nearly $70,000 (Brown, 1979: 28).

tion. The transition from large to small families, with the associated decline in fertility, is therefore usually assumed to arise in industrial and urban settings. This final stage in the demographic transition was achieved when both birth and death rates reached very low levels. With fertility levels near the replacement level, the result was a very low rate of population growth, if any at all. The panel on the left in Figure 8.6 depicts the demographic transition experienced by most nations in the developed world.

By contrast, the panel on the right in Figure 8.6 makes clear that the developing nations have not yet experienced rapidly falling birth rates following the extraordinarily rapid increase in life expectancy that occurred after World War II. In fact, the precipitous decline in death rates has largely been the result of more effective

Figure 8.6
The Demographic Transition in Developed and Developing Countries

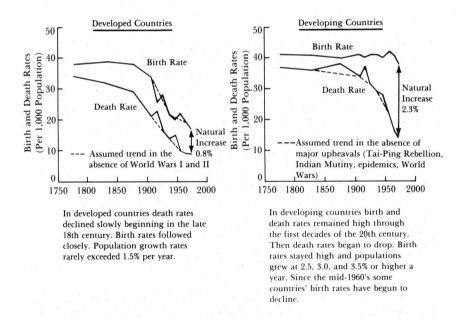

In developed countries death rates declined slowly beginning in the late 18th century. Birth rates followed closely. Population growth rates rarely exceeded 1.5% per year.

In developing countries birth and death rates remained high through the first decades of the 20th century. Then death rates began to drop. Birth rates stayed high and populations grew at 2.5, 3.0, and 3.5% or higher a year. Since the mid-1960's some countries' birth rates have begun to decline.

Source: U.S. Department of State, "World Population: The Silent Explosion—Part I," *Department of State Bulletin* 78 (October 1978), 52. Based on United Nations data.

In developed countries death rates declined slowly beginning in the late 18th century. Birth rates followed closely. Population growth rates rarely exceeded 1.5% per year.

In developing countries birth and death rates remained high through the first decades of the 20th century. Then death began to drop. Birth rates stayed high and populations grew at 2.5, 3.0, and 3.5% or higher a year. Since the mid-1960's some countries' birth rates have begun to decline.

"death-control" measures introduced by the outside world.[11] The decline in developing nations' death rates thus differs sharply from the long-term, slow declines that Europe and North America experienced. They have been the result of externally introduced and rapid environmental changes rather than the fundamental and evolutionary changes that affect a nation's policies, institutions, or ways of life (Ehrlich, Ehrlich, and Holdren, 1977). In particular, developing nations have failed to experience the more or less automatic decline in fertility rates that follows the decline in the rate of mortality that, according to the demographic transition theory, is assumed to be associated with economic development.

If one accepts this line of reasoning the policy implications for developing nations are clear (see also Harkavy, 1975). If declining fertility follows more or less *automatically* from improvements in the standard of living, the appropriate approach to the population problem is to attack *first* the problems of economic and social development that inhibit improvements in the quality of life. The population problem will then take care of itself. The slogan "development is the best contraceptive" reflects this view, which was widely shared by Third World delegates attending the 1974 World Population Conference. It is a view generally consistent with the European experience, where industrialization and the wealth it promoted coincided with rapid declines in fertility rates.

Recent research has raised questions about the proposition that development is the best pill. Reexamination of nineteenth-century European data by Princeton University's Office of Population Research has shown substantial variations in the timing, pace, and presumed causes of changes in fertility and mortality levels:

> Fertility declines often preceded or coincided with mortality declines, instead of following them; . . . regional variations in fertility appeared most closely related to cultural and linguistic rather than developmental factors; and . . . overall, fertility levels and trends bore no clear relation to development. Fertility declines occurred in provinces that were rural, very poor, not well educated, and subject to high infant mortality. Nationwide, fertility began to fall in peasant, Catholic France nearly a century earlier than in England, though it was England that was the leader in the Industrial Revolution. (U.S. Department of State, 1978c: 53)

11. Sri Lanka (formerly Ceylon) is frequently cited as an example of the effects of public-health measures on the death rates of developing nations. Malaria and malaria-related diseases were a major cause of historically high death rates in Sri Lanka, which in 1945 stood at 22 per 1,000. In 1946 the insecticide DDT was introduced in an effort to eradicate the mosquitoes that carry malaria. In a single year the death rate dropped 34 percent, and by 1955 it had declined to about half the 1945 level (Ehrlich, Ehrlich, and Holdren, 1977: 197).

These empirical analyses place many of the central arguments of the demographic transition theory in question. But even if the essential outlines of the theory are accepted (that economic development is the engine propelling declines in both mortality and fertility), arguments can be advanced to suggest that the situation in the developing world today is significantly different from what Europe faced at the time of its economic development. One difference already has been noted, namely, the much steeper decline in mortality experienced by developing nations compared with Europe. Another difference is that developing nations generally started out in the post-World War II period with much higher birth rates (due mainly to earlier and more widespread marriage) than Europe experienced at the onset of its demographic transition. The average birth rate in the developing world between 1950 and 1955 has been estimated at 42.1 per 1,000; by contrast, Europe's birth rate at the onset of the Industrial Revolution is estimated to have been 30–35 per 1,000 population (U.S. Department of State, 1978c: 53). Finally, the combinaion of rapid declines in death rates and persistently high birth rates has led to population growth rates "two or three times as high as those experienced during Europe's period of most rapid population growth." Rates of increase as high as 3 percent a year or higher are not unheard of in the developing world; in Denmark, by contrast, the rate of natural increase never exceeded 1.5 percent (U.S. Department of State, 1978c: 53). In short, "the totally unprecedented disequilibrium between birth and death rates in the developing countries since the end of World War II is the reason for the massive burgeoning of world population" (U.S. Department of State, 1978c).

Given this disequilibrium, it is not surprising that many nations of the developed world have sought a more direct attack on the population problem than the one implied by the "development is the best contraceptive" perspective. Thus, during the 1974 World Population Conference in Bucharest, Romania, various proposals were articulated. Some advocated general economic and social development as a path to population control. Others countered that economic development alone is not enough, that rising gross national products will have little or no effect in the absence of a redistribution of wealth so that the benefits of modernization are spread to those most needing them. Extending this logic, still others observed that population control is a political as well as economic problem that necessitates reforms at home in order for the welfare of individual families to be improved, and that nothing less than income redistribution assuring equality and benefits to all is required for fertility reduction. Still others proposed more conventional methods, advancing the view that control of the birth rate itself could substantially address the problem and contribute to subsequent development.

Not surprisingly, the final document coming out of the Bucharest conference reflected elements of both the developing and developed nations' approaches to the population problem. The conference also endorsed the principle of respect for "the right of persons to determine in a free, informed, and responsible manner the number and spacing of their children." While this phrase was part of a larger endorsement of the concept of family planning, it also reflected the notion that parenthood and families are intensely personal phenomena over which some people may object to governmental control, even cajoling. This is perhaps even more true of international efforts to deal with population growth. A persistent theme voiced by many developing nations at the World Population Conference as well as in previous policy rhetoric was that people remain one of their most valuable resources. The efforts of more advanced states to get developing nations to control their population growth were seen as yet another attempt to perpetuate the underdevelopment of the Third World.

In this connection, it is pertinent to note that many developed nations have no overall national population programs of their own. The belief that there are "too many people" has meaning only in relation to something else, such as food and renewable and nonrenewable resources. Measured against any of these yardsticks, it is not the less developed nations of the Third World that consume most; instead, it is the more advanced industrialized societies. Indeed, it is this observation that forces consideration of the role played by political and nonpolitical factors in determining the availability or nonavailability of food and other resources.

POPULATION GROWTH AND FOOD SUPPLIES

Three-quarters of the world's inhabitants live in developing nations; only a quarter live in developed nations. But compared with the Third World, people living in the developed world both produce and consume more of the world's food supply; they have higher nutritional levels; they control more of the food supplies that enter into the international marketplace; and they show every sign of continuing to place substantial demands on the capacity of the world to produce adequate supplies of food in the future.

The Transformation of the World Food Situation

The gloomiest of Thomas Malthus's predictions made nearly two centuries ago was that the world's population would eventually outstrip its capacity to produce enough food to sustain its growing numbers. This prediction was based on what Malthus regarded as the simple mathematical fact that population grows exponentially whereas agricultural output grows only arithmetically. What Malthus did not foresee was that agricultural output would also grow at an increasing rate, largely as a consequence of technological innovations.

Increases in world food output have been particularly impressive since World War II. In the twenty-five years from 1950 to 1975, world grain harvests nearly doubled, moving from 685 million tons to 1.35 billion tons (Brown, 1978: 129). For people living in the developed world, this has meant a substantial increase in their per capita food consumption. In the decade and a half ending in 1979, for example, the food production of developed nations increased over 40 percent, resulting in an increase in per capita food consumption of roughly 23 percent. In the developing world, by way of contrast, the average amount of food consumed per person increased by only 6 percent during this same period, despite the fact that total food production increased by 58 percent[12] (see Figure 8.7). The reason for these striking differences, of course, is population growth, and in particular the much higher growth rates of developing nations. In fact, the unprecedented increase in world food production between 1950 and 1975 has been more than matched by equally unprecedented population increases; while food production nearly doubled during this period, the world's population increased by almost two-thirds (Brown, 1978: 129).

The Green Revolution. Little more than a decade ago, it looked as though the world's food problems might be moving toward solution largely as a consequence of the "Green Revolution"—the introduction of new high-yield strains of wheat and rice in such countries as

12. It is important to emphasize that averages such as these mask important differences among countries. For example, the United Nations Food and Agriculture Organization has estimated that food production in Most Seriously Affected (MSAs) developing nations declined from a growth rate of 3.2 percent in 1961–1970 to 2.1 percent in 1970–1976, with the result that per capita production actually decreased by .4 percent. It has also noted that the per capita decline in food production was more than three times this rate among African nations, and that the number of developing nations with population growth rates higher than food production growth rates rose from 56 in the 1960s to 69 in the 1970s (Food and Agriculture Organization, 1977: 4, 6).

Figure 8.7
Indexes of Total Food Production and Per Capita Food Production in Developed and Developing Countries, 1955–1979 (1961–1965 = 100)

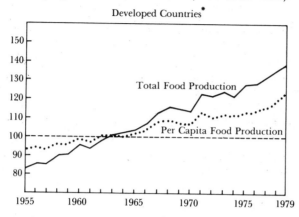

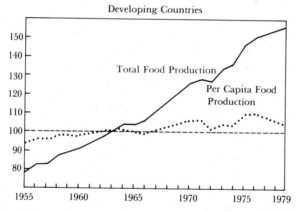

Source: John W. Sewell and the Staff of the Overseas Development Council, *The United States and World Development: Agenda 1980* (New York: Praeger, 1980). Based on U.S. Agency for International Development and U.S. Department of Agriculture data.

Notes: Data for 1979 are preliminary. Centrally planned economies are not included. Data do not include non-food commodities such as coffee, fibers, or rubber.

*United States, Canada, Europe, Japan, Australia, New Zealand, and South Africa.

Mexico, the Philippines, India, Pakistan, and (now) Bangledesh. The Philippines and India even moved toward self-sufficiency in these grains, a feat of significant proportions. In fact, the remarkable accomplishments of the Green Revolution in developing nations, made possible by the transfer of high-energy agricultural technology from Western nations, were outstripped by Western and communist nations. Grain production in developing nations increased by an average of 180 million tons from 1948 to 1952 and 1971 to 1975 through a combination of increasing per-acre yields and increasing numbers of acres under cultivation.[13] Developed nations, on the other hand, increased production by 203 million tons solely through increasing yields, not by placing additional lands into production (Schertz, 1977:17).

Regardless of these differences, the generally optimistic world food picture changed dramatically in the early 1970s. Food production between 1971 and 1972 declined, but worldwide demand increased through a combination of population growth in developing nations and rising affluence in developed nations. Then a series of weather-induced calamities in China, the Soviet Union, Africa, and the subcontinent of Asia shifted the world food situation to the crisis point as world food reserves in 1974 reached their lowest point in twenty years. As shown in Table 8.1, world grain reserves, defined in terms of the equivalent number of days of world grain consumption, dropped from ninety-three days in 1969–1970 to only thirty-seven days in 1973–1974. This drop in reserves occurred *despite* the return to production of American cropland that had been previously idled as a way of coping with chronic overproduction by the American farmer. This cropland had effectively provided the world a cushion against agricultural disasters elsewhere. But since 1974 the cushion has been eliminated, and, as the data in Table 8.1 indicate, world food reserves still have not been rebuilt to their pre-1974 levels.[14] Thus, while the crisis atmosphere of 1974 has dissipated, the need to grapple with the issue of world food security has not.

Fish consumption. Another element that colored the world food picture in the early 1970s was a dramatic change in the growth pattern of the world's supply of fish. Fish had become an important ingredient in the world food supply, with the annual fish catch roughly equivalent to an average of forty pounds per person annually (well above the world's equivalent yield of beef),[15] thereby making an important contribution to the world's protein consumption

13. There were domestic costs, however. The Green Revolution tends to favor relatively more progressive farmers to the detriment of the most impoverished elements in agrarian societies.

14. In late 1977, however, the American government once more moved to create incentives for American farmers to take some of their cropland out of production in order to maintain farm incomes in the face of domestic grain surpluses.

15. The world's production of beef peaked in 1976 at twenty-six pounds per person, declining in 1979 to twenty-four pounds per person (*New York Times,* February 5, 1980: C2).

Table 8.1
Indicators of World Food Security, 1960–1978
(million metric tons and days)

	Reserve Stocks of Grain*	Grain Equivalent of Idled U.S. Cropland	Total World Reserves	Reserves as Days of Annual Grain Consumption
		(million metric tons)		
1960–1961	168	68	236	103
1961–1962	180	81	261	112
1962–1963	154	70	224	93
1963–1964	157	70	227	94
1964–1965	152	71	223	88
1965–1966	155	78	233	88
1966–1967	130	51	181	68
1967–1968	157	61	218	79
1968–1969	175	73	248	87
1969–1970	208	71	279	93
1970–1971	193	41	234	76
1971–1972	155	78	233	73
1972–1973	172	24	196	60
1973–1974	127	0	127	37
1974–1975	132	0	132	40
1975–1976	123	0	123	37
1976–1977	126	0	126	36
1977–1978†	151	0	151	43

Source: Martin M. McLaughlin and the Staff of the Overseas Development Council, *The United States and World Development: Agenda 1979* (New York: Praeger, 1979), p. 189. Based on U.S. Department of Agriculture data as compiled by the Worldwatch Institute.

*Based on carry-over stocks of grain at the beginning of the crop year in individual countries for year shown.
†Preliminary estimate.

(Brown, 1974: 147). Between 1950 and 1970 the world fish catch increased steadily at an average annual rate of 5 percent, far in excess of population growth during this same period (Brown, 1978: 18). Then, in 1970, after reaching an annual catch level of 70 million tons, the trends were abruptly reversed, and the world catch of fish stabilized at 65–70 million tons annually (Brown, 1978: 18). With population growth continuing, the net result has been a decline in per capita fish consumption: fish from the world's fisheries peaked at 43 pounds per person in 1970, but totaled in 1979 only 36 pounds (*New York Times*, February 5, 1980: C1).

Overfishing is among the prominent reasons for the deterioration of the world fish catch. The fish harvest in many areas of the world may have reached its maximum sustainable yield. In fact, it has been estimated that "Catches of most of the thirty-odd leading species of table-grade fish may now exceed maximum sustainable levels; in other words, the species' regenerative capacities cannot sustain even the levels of the present catch"[16] (Brown, 1978: 22).

In large measure overfishing is related to the increased use of technology-intensive fishing methods by some countries, notably the Soviet Union and Japan, for whom fish have become an important dietary element. As the world's fish catch stabilizes, and perhaps declines, those who have become dependent on oceanic resources for food are likely to turn to other sources, thereby intensifying the pressures on land-based food sources. Lester R. Brown, president of the Worldwatch Institute and an expert on global resources, has observed that "Deprived of oceanic sources of protein, they [the Soviet Union and Japan] will likely have to offset declines by importing more feedgrains and soybeans to expand indigenous poultry and livestock production. Taking such a tack will place additional pressures on exportable grain supplies, but the only alternative is belt-tightening" (Brown, 1978).

Food, Population, and Wealth

The transformation of the world food situation from one of relative surplus at low prices to relative scarcity at high prices in the early 1970s culminated in a world food crisis. The reason for this sharp turn was not simply crop failures; it was also the decision of the Soviet Union to enter world grain markets in an unprecedented way to make up for shortfalls previously absorbed by the Soviet economy. This set the stage for the purchase of huge amounts of American grain in 1972. The Soviets quietly set up contracts to purchase 28 million tons of grain—most from the United States—in the largest commercial transaction in history (Brown, 1974). Total Soviet purchases in 1972 and 1973 increased nearly fourfold over the previous two years, a fact which contributed significantly to the rise in de-

---

16. One of the consequences of overfishing is that states have sought to extend their sovereign jurisdiction far beyond their coastal waterways so as to protect "their" resources from encroachment by others. In 1977, for example, the United States extended its fishing zone to 200 miles in order to protect the relatively less efficient American fishing industry from the Soviets and Japanese. More generally, the concept of a 200-mile exclusive economic zone in the high seas surrounding coastal states has received widespread support in the Third United Nations Conference on the Law of the Sea. This concept can be explained in part by the desire of states with less highly developed technologies to protect what they regard as theirs from encroachment by others currently possessing the capacity for exploitation. Fish are only one of the resources at issue here; but to many developing nations, particularly those in Latin America, they are a very important and valuable resource.

mand for food supplies elsewhere in the world. Japan and Western Europe also contributed to the rising demand by substantially increasing their import requirements over previous years.

The massive increase in the price of oil between 1973 and 1974 exacerbated the world food problem by increasing the cost of fuel and fertilizer used in agricultural production. The combined impact of this set of factors was a 300 percent increase in the price of grain in the face of what worldwide was only a 3 percent shortfall in grain production (Sewell, 1979: 60–61). The result was that "rising food prices added as much to . . . global inflation as did rising petroleum costs" (Sewell, 1979).

Rising prices can have a particularly severe impact on poorer families, who (following the principle known in microeconomics as Engel's Law) typically spend a much greater percentage of their budget on food than higher income groups. Conversely, the capacity to acquire more food is a function of *effective demand*—that is, possession of the income necessary to buy more food. Many people in the developing countries simply are not capable of registering an effective demand for food, because they do not have the purchasing power necessary to secure an adequate diet. Nor are they likely to obtain such income in the future. At the time of the 1974 World Food Conference, the UN Food and Agriculture Organization (FAO) estimated that 460 million people in the developing world suffer from malnutrition.[17] It has also been estimated that this number will continue to grow since those suffering from malnutrition are likely to be among those in society with the fewest economic resources. As the FAO put it:

> Even if the increase in the *effective demand* for food in developing . . . economies could be met by a combination of increases in domestic production, food aid and commercial imports, the number of people suffering from severe protein-energy malnutrition would not fall, but would continue to rise from 460 million (excluding China) in 1969–74 to about 750 million in 1985. . . . Malnutrition cannot be removed unless the need for food is backed by the requisite purchasing power, and increasing food production does not necessarily increase the purchasing power of malnourished people. (Food and Agriculture Organization, n.d.: 12)

17. Malnutrition refers to a deficiency in the quality of food eaten, that is, in its protein, vitamin, and mineral content. It is often difficult to distinguish malnutrition from undernutrition, which implies a deficiency in the *quantity* of food eaten measured in terms of calories. Hence, the term *protein-energy malnutrition* is sometimes used to refer to both undernutrition and malnutrition (Food and Agriculture Organization, n.d.).

This dire picture underscores the extent to which access to food is a function of wealth.[18] The FAO estimates that the per capita daily food supply in the developed world in terms of calories is 32 percent above daily requirements, but in the developing world the daily supply is insufficient to meet requirements in almost every region of the world except Latin America (Food and Agriculture Organization, 1977: 16). Even more striking are differences in the daily per capita supply of protein: for developing nations as a whole, their supply of protein was only 58 percent of that in developed countries (Food and Agriculture Organization, 1977: 17). This difference is intimately related to the much higher rate of protein consumption derived from animals in the developed world compared with animal protein consumption in the developing world. This in turn helps explain why rising affluence has placed increasing pressure on world food supplies.[19]

One of the characteristics of economic and social development is that people climb the "food ladder" as well. This accounted for a substantial portion of the rise in the per capita food consumption in developed nations during the 1960s and 1970s. Grain consumption patterns demonstrate this fact:

> In the poorer countries, the average person can get only about 180 kilograms of grain per year—about a pound per day. With so little to go around, nearly all grain must be consumed directly if minimal energy needs are to be met. But as incomes rise, so do grain consumption levels. In the wealthier industrial societies such as the United States and the Soviet Union, the average person consumes four-fifths of a ton of grain per year. Of this, only 90 to 140 kilograms is eaten directly as bread, pastries, and breakfast cereals; most is consumed indirectly as meat, milk, and eggs.
>
> In effect, wealth enables individuals to move up the biological food chain. Thus, the average Russian or American uses roughly four times the land, water, and fertilizer used by an Indian, a Colombian, or a Nigerian. (Brown, 1978: 134)

18. The picture is made even more disconcerting when the consequences of malnutrition are considered. Malnourishment—particularly in the form of protein deficiency in infancy—can lead to permanent brain damage, as well as retard normal growth and invite debilitating disease. The physical problems persist, often after the food deficiency is corrected; permanently disabled people are left to then propagate still another generation of malnourished and disabled children. The obstacles to personal and national development presented by this vicious circle are overwhelming.

19. The Food and Agriculture Organization (n.d.: 14) estimates that population growth accounts for 70 percent of the increase in the demand for food in the developing countries, but only 55 percent in the developed countries. Rising incomes account for the remaining portions. See also Schertz (1977: 20) for a breakdown of changes in cereal consumption attributable to population and income changes in various world areas.

The importance of the consumption of food in developed nations is underscored by the fact that while these nations comprise about a quarter of the world's population, they consume nearly 40 percent of its food supply. And the importance of their indirect consumption of grain is revealed by the fact that "450 million tons of cereals, about a third of world production, are fed to livestock in these countries—this exceeds the total human consumption of cereals in India and China combined" (Food and Agriculture Organization, n.d.: 15). These statistics underscore the reality of a world in which people of some societies starve while people in others spend heavily for weight reduction. The disparity in the food consumption patterns of the rich and the poor is dramatized by the fact that in 1973 the amount of money spent on cat and dog food in the United States was greater than the gross national product of each of seventy-four member-states of the United Nations (Finlay and Hovet, 1974: 104).

These same considerations have an important bearing on the evolving structure of international trade in food. Who gets what food, and at what cost, is a function of more than differences in consumption patterns. It is also related to differences in productive capacity and the unequal distribution of effective demand (that is, the political control over resources) in the global arena.

CHARACTERISTICS OF INTERNATIONAL FOOD TRADE

The developed world consumes two-thirds of the world's cereal imports, leaving only a third for the more populous developing world.[20] The largest cereal-importing nations are also in the North. Japan, the United Kingdom, and Italy are the three largest cereal importers. Together with West Germany, they account for more than 40 percent of all cereal imports, although their combined population is just over 7 percent of the world's population (Food and Agriculture Organization, n.d.: 15). For the most part, the United States and Canada have become the principal source of these commodities, especially the former (despite the fact that the American farmer

20. Cereals are particularly important because they account for over one-half of total energy supplies of food (Food and Agriculture Organization, 1977: 6). Moreover, the sharp fluctuation in the world food situation in the early 1970s was caused mainly by changes in the production of this group of commodities, a fact which attests to their importance in the structure of international trade in food. Three cereals—wheat, rice, and corn—make up nearly half of all cereal production in the world, with a number of minor grains (oats, rye, barley, millet, and soybeans) making up the remainder (Pirages, 1978: 82). Of the three most important cereals, wheat and corn are the principal export products; although rice is central to the diet of perhaps half the world's population, it is not exported in large quantities (Pirages, 1978: 81–82).

comprises only a minuscule proportion of the world's agricultural work force).[21]

The North American Breadbasket

Worldwide dependence on the "North American breadbasket"[22] is a post-World War II development. The region was not even the principal source of grain exports prior to that time, being outstripped by Latin America. Also noteworthy is that Western Europe was the only food-deficit region prior to the war; all others were net exporters of food (Brown, 1978).

This picture has changed dramatically in the past thirty years. Nearly every world region except North America and Oceania has become a net importer of food. "Literally scores of countries have become food importers since World War II, but *not one new country has emerged as a significant cereal exporter during this period*" (Brown, 1978). Today, only five nations are significant food exporters—the United States, Canada, Australia, New Zealand, and Argentina. Of these, the United States and Canada are clearly the most important. They accounted for 66 percent of world grain exports in 1979–1980 (see Table 8.2). In addition, the United States has been the principal exporter of other agricultural products, particularly soybeans, an important source of protein. In the period 1972–1974, U.S. soybean exports comprised more than four-fifths of the world total (Seevers, 1978: 731).

Of the many reasons for the development of the unprecedented near monopoly of the world's exportable grains now exercised by North America, Lester Brown cites population growth and agricultural mismanagement, particularly in developing nations, as primary.[23] He describes the impact of population growth in particularly compelling terms:

> As recently as 1950, North America and Latin America had roughly equal populations—163 and 168 million, respectively. But while North

21. In the early to mid-1970s, the United States accounted for 42 percent of world wheat exports and 63 percent of world corn exports (Pirages, 1978: 82).

22. This phrase is from Brown (1978).

23. Brown also notes that "most national food deficits exist because the surpluses produced in the countryside are no longer sufficient to feed the swelling urban population." Citing the 10 percent increase in the number of urban dwellers between 1950 and 1975, he concludes: "In effect, this record rate of urbanization was made possible by North American food surpluses" (Brown, 1978: 137). The continuing pressure of urbanization on global food supplies is suggested by the U.S. government's *The Global 2000 Report to the President* (1980b: 242), which projects the urban population in developing nations will increase by 1.2 billion people between 1975 and the year 2000.

Table 8.2
World Net Grain Trade by Groups of Countries and by Regions
(million metric tons)

	1969/70-1971/72 Average	1977/78	1978/79	1979/80
Developed Market Economies	**26.4**	**74.8**	**79.5**	**104.5**
North America	54.1	104.7	107.9	129.0
Western Europe	−24.2	−20.7	−15.1	−17.0
Australia and New Zealand	10.9	13.4	9.7	15.9
Japan	−14.4	−22.6	−23.0	−23.4
Centrally Planned Economies	**−13.3**	**−34.1**	**−34.1**	**−56.6**
People's Republic of China	−5.4	−7.4	−9.7	−8.5
U.S.S.R. and Eastern Europe	7.9	−26.7	−24.4	−48.1
Developing Countries	**−19.7**	**−32.9**	**−36.7**	**−42.8**
Africa and Middle East	−8.1	−17.0	−16.9	−20.6
Asia	−11.5	−14.3	−14.7	−15.5
Latin America	−0.1	−1.6	−5.1	−6.7
Other	**−1.4**	**−1.7**	**−1.8**	**−2.1**
Total Interregional Exports*	**65.0**	**118.1**	**117.6**	**144.9**
Total World Exports*	**105.1**	**166.0**	**172.7**	**194.3**

Source: John W. Sewell and the Staff of the Overseas Development Council, *The United States and World Development: Agenda 1980* (New York: Praeger, 1980), p. 180. Based on U.S. Department of Agriculture data.

*Interregional exports includes only those grain exports which move from one region to another; world exports includes all exports of grain whether intra- or inter-regional.

Note: The world grains that are traded include wheat and wheat flour, milled rice, and coarse grains (corn, barley, rye, oats, and sorghum). Net exports are on a July to June year.

America's population growth has slowed markedly since the late fifties, Latin America's has increased explosively. Several larger countries such as Brazil, Mexico, Venezuela, and Peru have population growth rates of 3 percent or more per year. If the North American population of 1950 had expanded at 3 percent per year, it would now be 341 million instead of 236 million. Eating at current food-consumption levels, those additional 105 million people would absorb virtually all exportable supplies, leaving North America struggling to feed itself. (Brown, 1978: 136)

To a considerable extent, however, the dependence of most of the world on North America for food is also related to wealth. Western Europe and Japan in particular do not rely on external sources to supply their own *traditional* primary consumption of grain. Instead, they rely on external sources to improve the variety and protein content of their diets. As a practical matter this means importing feed grains for animals. As one analyst observed:

> The European Community imports from the United States almost 60 percent of its protein requirements for animal feed, with additional imports from Canada and Australia. Japan imports nearly 80 percent of its feed requirements. Considering the importance of relatively affluent nations in Europe and Japan as grain importers, and the fact that Soviet and Eastern Europe purchases reflect attempts to provide more meat for citizens' diets, it becomes clear that the thrust of most international grain transfers is to expand and sustain the diets of comparatively wealthy societies. (Christensen, 1978: 758)

The impact exerted by wealth on international food transfers is not confined to developed nations. For many nations in the developing world, agricultural products are a primary means of earning the foreign exchange needed to buy capital equipment or other goods from abroad. Frequently these export products are dietary supplements for people in wealthier countries.

> This has a number of important consequences. First, many export products such as sugar, tea, coffee, cocoa and sisal, have limited nutritional value, and hence cannot be directly "diverted" from the international marketplace to meet pressing domestic needs. Second, there are limited internal markets for most traditional export crops, and larger domestic markets are unlikely to develop until income increases. To the extent that internal markets develop, they are most likely to reflect the tastes of the wealthier portions of the domestic population. Such patterns of export agriculture can easily lead to a sharp and direct trade-off between foreign exchange earnings . . . and the production of basic foodstuffs. (Christensen, 1978: 758–759)

In short, differences in income levels both internally and internationally help explain the anomaly that it often makes more economic sense for developing nations to produce food products for export rather than for domestic consumption, despite the fact that many of their own poor (who lack effective purchasing power) may suffer from undernutrition or malnutrition.[24] The differences in in-

24. Conversely, the changing structure of world demand for and supply of food has made it economical for *developed* nations to produce for export primary products instead of manufactures. The shift may become particularly significant for the United States, which finds itself for the first time in a hundred years selling abroad more agricultural goods than manufactured goods and high-technology products.

come levels also suggest that the present structure of international trade in foodstuffs is likely to persist.

But whether the North American breadbasket will be able to supply the increasing demand for food that population growth and rising incomes are likely to generate is problematic. Projected increases in the demand for food are shown in Table 8.3. By 1990, developed nations are expected to increase their demand for grains by nearly a third (from 617 million tons in 1970 to 847 million in 1990). This is equivalent to about 90 percent of current United States production (Sewell, 1979: 64–65). Well over 80 percent of this projected increase will be for feed grains, not direct food consumption. During the same period, developing nations (market and centrally planned economies combined) are expected to increase their demand for grains by more than 470 million tons, an increase more than double current American production. Roughly two-thirds of this increase is for direct food consumption.

The ability of the North American breadbasket to meet this demand using current agricultural techniques would require massive new amounts of energy, fertilizer, and water. Assuming that this is possible, food-producing and consuming countries alike probably would share sharp increases in the prices of food. But not only would the price of food escalate dramatically. With increases in the number of mouths to feed, demand would also increase. Under conditions of scarcity, economics and politics would undoubtedly determine who would get fed, and they undoubtedly, would be those who have the income or influence to compete successfully. The result would be some agonizing decisions. For instance, it is inconceivable that any American president would risk supplying foreigners ahead of those who elected him to office. Hence the world's leading supplier of food might well decide to meet its own needs while the world's majority risk starvation.

The picture is made even more unpleasant when the consumption habits of Americans are recalled. When compared with those living on subsistence incomes and food supplies, the effects of the American population on global welfare defy comprehension. Consider the magnitude of that consumption associated with the addition of each new American:

> Every 7½ seconds a new American is born. He is a disarming little thing, but he begins to scream loudly in a voice that can be heard for seventy years. He is screaming for 26,000,000 tons of water, 21,000 gallons of gasoline, 10,150 pounds of meat, 28,000 pounds of milk and cream, 9,000 pounds of wheat, and great storehouses of all other foods, drinks, and tobacco. These are the lifetime demands on his country and its economy. (Rienow and Rienow, 1967: 3)

Table 8.3
Annual Grain Consumption, by Main Types of Uses and Groups of Countries, 1970–1990 (million metric tons and kilograms)

	Actual Consumption 1970	Projected Demand 1985	1990
Developed Countries			
	(million metric tons)		
Food	160.9	164.1	164.6
Feed	371.5	522.7	565.7
Other uses	84.9	109.5	116.4
Total	617.3	796.3	846.7
	(kilograms)		
Per Capita	576	649	663
Developing Market Economies			
	(million metric tons)		
Food	303.7	474.5	547.2
Feed	35.6	78.6	101.9
Other uses	46.4	75.4	88.5
Total	385.7	628.5	737.6
	(kilograms)		
Per Capita	220	240	246
Developing Centrally Planned Economies*			
	(million metric tons)		
Food	164.1	215.2	225.3
Feed	15.3	48.7	61.4
Other uses	24.6	36.0	39.1
Total	204.0	299.9	325.8
	(kilograms)		
Per Capita	257	298	304
World Total			
	(million metric tons)		
	1,207.0	1,724.7	1,910.1

Source: Martin M. McLaughlin and the Staff of the Overseas Development Council, *The United States and World Development: Agenda 1979* (New York: Praeger, 1979), p. 188. Based on data from the Food and Agriculture Organization of the United Nations.

*Albania, the People's Republic of China, Mongolia, the Democratic Republic of Korea (North Korea), Romania, and the Socialist Republic of Vietnam.

Constraints on Increasing Food Production

The solution of supplying adequate food to the world is constrained by the ability of current techniques to continue producing the dra-

matic increases in yields that have been realized in the past, even if the future seems to require them. In particular, the returns on ever-expanding amounts of fertilizer—which more than any other factor contributed to the doubling of world grain production between 1950 and the mid-1970s—appear to be diminishing. During the 1950s, grain production increased by ten million tons for every additional million tons of fertilizer used; by the 1960s the return had declined to between seven and eight million tons of additional grain; and by the 1970s the return had declined even further, to less than six million tons of grain (Brown, 1978: 165).

Because most of the developing world has not yet experienced the dramatic productivity increases associated with technology-intensive agriculture, it is here that many analysts look when seeking an answer to the question of how the world's growing billions will be fed. Ultimately there may be biological constraints in the form of limited water supplies and arable land that will inhibit limitless growth in food production (see Brown, 1978, and Pirages, 1978, for discussions of these constraints; and Eckholm, 1976, for a wide-ranging discussion of the effects of environmental degradation on food production systems). In the course of the next couple of decades, or so, however, the constraints appear to be of a different sort. As Wassily Leontief put it in his United Nations study, *The Future of the World Economy,*

> The most pressing problem of feeding the rapidly increasing population of the developing regions can be solved by bringing under cultivation large areas of currently unexploited arable land and by doubling and trebling land productivity. Both tasks are technically feasible but are contingent on drastic measures of public policy favourable to such development and on social and institutional changes in the developing countries. (Leontief et al., 1977: 11)

Or, as Lester Brown (1978) observed, "Whether the world can expand food production is not at issue. How much it will cost to do so and how the cost will relate to the purchasing power of the world's poor are the real questions."[25] These observations suggest that if,

25. Cost is an issue that warrants emphasis. Pirages (1978: 97) notes, for example, that the average American spends more than $600 per year for food produced and distributed using energy-intensive technologies. This is more than the average per capita income in many developing nations. He has also noted the demands on world energy supplies that would result if American production techniques were adopted worldwide:

It is estimated that for every American 336 gallons of gasoline per year is used just for food production, transportation, and processing. Assuming that petroleum would be the energy source for world agriculture, using 336 gallons of gasoline per person for agricultural purposes would use up known world petroleum

and how, the problems raised by the ominous trends of rising population and diminishing food supplies are addressed will depend upon the kind of political as well as human response the world makes.[26]

Providing Sufficient Food: The International Response

Recognition of the important role of developing nations in ensuring adequate world food supplies was made in the summer of 1979, when the United Nations convened a World Conference on Agrarian Reform and Rural Development. Although many developing nations attending the conference appear not to have made the strong commitment to land-reform measures necessary to overcome the non-technical obstacles to increased agricultural productivity, the conference itself was perhaps a symbolic recognition of the truly global dimensions of the world food situation.

Equally symbolic was the 1974 World Food Conference in Rome, described by Sayed A. Marei, the secretary-general of the conference, as "an historic advance toward political solutions of the world food problem." The conference, called at a time when the most dire of Thomas Malthus's warnings appeared to be coming true, addressed itself to three main objectives: stepping up food aid in the short run, establishing food reserves as insurance against future shortfalls as an interim measure, and increasing agricultural productivity in the long run. Two new world bodies were established by the conference: a World Food Council, whose purpose is to be the highest United Nations organ on food policy; and a $1 billion International Fund for Agricultural Development (IFAD), whose purpose is to serve as an international lending institution for promoting agricultural development.[27]

---

reserves in only twelve years—just to meet these agricultural needs. The green revolution represents the export of high-energy American agriculture to the less developed world. To the extent that it is successfully exported, the world energy dilemma will be increased by added energy requirements.

26. The political constraints are local as well as international. In the absence of effective demand among the local inhabitants comprising the poorest of the poor in developing nations, governmental intervention becomes necessary to assure adequate food supplies should they become available through, say, external aid as in the case of Cambodia (Kampuchea) in the late 1970s. Such governmental encouragement is inhibited, however, by the absence of marketing and transportation systems generally characteristic among Third World nations. The presence of other often pervasive forces, such as corruption among local officials, complicates the problem immeasurably.

27. IFAD was created at the initiative of Saudi Arabia and is unique among international financial institutions in that its governing board is composed of equal numbers of members from Western industrialized nations, from OPEC nations, and from developing nations. In this way no single group can dominate the organization, which is the first institution in which OPEC contributions have been made on the same scale as Western donor-countries' contributions.

Some progress has been made on the several fronts defined at the 1974 conference. For example, one obstacle to increased agricultural production discussed at that time was the shortage of increasingly expensive petroleum-based fertilizers. To deal with this situation, the Food and Agriculture Organization has organized a "fertilizer pool" designed to help countries in need and to provide funds necessary to augment fertilizer production.[28] The United Nations Industrial Development Organization (UNIDO) has also helped to identify fertilizer needs and has assisted in the goal of increasing world production, particularly in the developing world.

But many obstacles to assuring world food security today and in the future remain. Five years after pledging themselves to the achievement of that goal, the nations attending the conference still had not resolved the practical difficulties of building up and managing a system of nationally held grain reserves.[29] Nor had many other goals set in Rome in 1974 been realized. As the World Food Council noted following its fourth annual meeting in 1978, "the low rate of increase in food production in the food-deficit developing countries reflects the failure of the international community to achieve the high priority for those objectives called for by the World Food Conference. . . ."

> It expressed its concern about slow progress in mobilizing external resources, adjusting the agricultural sector in food-deficit countries to encourage food production, achieving a higher priority for nutrition, overcoming constraints to food production and distribution, achieving greater support by multilateral and bilateral donors to increase the supply of agricultural inputs, and carrying out agrarian and scoio-economic reforms. (McLaughlin, 1979b: 99)

This list of slow-progress items underscores the breadth and complexity of the issues the world faces as it marches toward a twenty-first-century world of over six billion people. Once more, then, the desirability of curbing population growth as a way of eas-

28. In 1970 the FAO estimated that the total cost of production of fertilizers in the developing world in 1990 would come to roughly $15.2 billion (Food and Agriculture Organization, n.d.: 23). Since this estimate was made prior to the oil-price hikes the world has experienced since 1973–1974, it is no doubt much too conservative an estimate of actual cost; but it nevertheless provides some sense of the order of magnitude that this single dimension of the food productivity question entails.

29. See McLaughlin (1979a) for a discussion of some of the relevant issues. This continuing series by the Overseas Development Council, published annually as *The United States and World Development: Agenda,* is an excellent source for many of the details related to food and other international development issues. Global projections of population growth, food production, and resource consumption, including projections regarding fertilizer use, can be found in *The Global 2000 Report to the President* (1980a and 1980b).

ing pressures on food supplies recommends itself—as does a change in the dietary habits of the world's wealthy.

Pending these changes, the North American breadbasket promises to continue playing a dominant role in the world food picture. Not only does the United States in particular serve as the principal source of commercial food sales in the world, it is also the principal source of "food aid," having distributed some $26.7 billion worth of food on concessional terms between 1960 and 1977 (McLaughlin, 1979a: 191). The genesis of this program goes back to 1954, when Public Law 480 (the Food for Peace act) was passed by Congress in part as a way of disposing of burdensome food surpluses generated by the extraordinarily productive and sophisticated American farm technology.[30]

Not surprisingly, the Food for Peace program has served as an important vehicle for the pursuit of American foreign policy objectives, which as a practical matter means that food aid has often been channeled to those countries in which the United States has a political interest. But Congress has also amended Public Law 480 from time to time to assure that Most Seriously Affected developing nations (MSAs) receive food aid, and that countries with particularly low per capita incomes receive assistance. More recently, in 1977 Congress attached a human-rights provision to the law to prohibit assistance going to countries that consistently violate "recognized human rights." (There is an irony here in that, to many nations in the world, there is no more basic a human right than the right to food. This view is, however, antithetical to the typical Western view of human rights as essentially political rather than economic in nature.)

Whatever its intended purposes, both the willingness and ability of the United States to sustain its food-aid program is contingent upon a host of domestic political and economic considerations as well as the availability of agricultural commodities. During the food-crisis years of the early 1970s, for example, U.S. food-aid shipments were only about a fourth of what they had been during the mid-1960s. Moreover, during the 1974 World Food Conference the United States delayed commitment of additional food aid at a time when literally millions of the world's poorest people were confronting starvation, a move that proved to be one of the most divisive issues of the conference. Eventually the United States did pledge additional food aid but, since 1974 Public Law 480, shipments have stabilized at about 5 percent of total American agricultural exports—a sharp decline from the 1970 figure of 16 percent, or the 1960 figure of 25 percent (McLaughlin, 1979a: 191).

30. Several of the essays in Brown and Shue (1977) deal with various aspects of United States food-aid programs.

Apart from the particulars of the 1974 incident,[31] the American reaction indicated the willingness of powerful states in trying times to use resources at their disposal to secure bargaining advantages in their relations with other states, and to assure maintenance of their standards of living at home. It also suggests that, when push comes to shove, politics tend to dominate economic and welfare considerations, with narrowly defined perceptions of self-interest often the dominant guidelines.

Should another food crisis occur, food-exporting states will necessarily have to assume the role of crisis managers. That necessity grows out of the unprecedented dependence of the world—rich and poor alike—on the North American breadbasket, which has placed nearly everyone in a vulnerable position. Minimally, the food supplies of a large part of the world have become dependent on the persistence of favorable weather conditions in North America.[32] Should disaster strike there, the shock waves would indeed be global. Generally, present global trends in consumption and production of food suggest that the days of relative food surplus at low prices may be permanently gone, that relative food scarcity at high prices will persist. Lester Brown describes the situation and its possible consequences:

> The international community must at least prepare for the possibility that the food scramble of recent years may not be temporary. Most of the slack appears to have gone out of the world food economy, leaving the entire world in a vulnerable position. Consequently, the U.S. and Canadian governments could someday find themselves in the uncomfortable position of having to decide who would and would not get North America's extra food in time of scarcity. In effect, the two governments would be operating a global food-rationing program. Although they have not consciously sought this responsibility, they must now reckon with it. (Brown, 1978: 138).

How might Canada and the United States choose? The "lifeboat" and "triage" analogies are advanced by neo-Malthusians as alternatives for dealing with food scarcity.[33] Both analogies assume

31. Among them is the fact that, during the World Food Conference, the U.S. Congress was debating the issue of how much food aid should be used for strictly political purposes, and how much for humanitarian purposes. See Pirages (1978) for a brief discussion of this event in the context of food as a basic human right.

32. Some analysts believe that weather conditions during the twentieth century have been unusually favorable. See Ehrlich, Ehrlich, and Holdren (1977) for a discussion of this matter.

33. These analogies were popularized by Hardin (1974) and Paddock and Paddock (1967) respectively. The term *triage* refers to World War I battlefield experience, when surgeons were forced to choose whom to treat from among overwhelming numbers of wounded soldiers. For critiques of the analogies, see Gordon (1979), Howe and Sewell (1975), and Soroos (1977).

that, by subsidizing countries incapable of becoming viable, scarce resources are being diverted from those countries that do have a chance of surviving, thereby threatening the entire human enterprise. The rich who are manning the lifeboat must therefore choose among the millions at "sea" who are struggling to climb aboard the lifeboat—for not all can be saved without all being swamped. The triage analogy reaches essentially the same conclusion. Following the battlefield argument, nations are to be separated into three groups: those that need no help, those that are beyond help, and those that will survive only with intensive care. The policy prescribes that resources ought to be concentrated on the third group.

Determining who will live and who will be left to starve is an uncomfortable predicament. Proponents of lifeboat logic nevertheless challenge the morality of encouraging continuing population growth through provision of food and medicine that prevents people from dying. If population growth will ultimately be held in check by starvation and disease in any event, then the appropriate question from this perspective is "At what level should starvation and disease take hold?" If the population level in a particular country is 200 million instead of 100 million, and if 4 million deaths occur annually per 100 million, 8 million deaths rather than 4 million represent a quantum jump in human misery of questionable morality.

In spite of its disarming logic, to many observers the policy prescription flowing from the lifeboat analogy is morally repugnant. Furthermore, the prescription assumes that resources are inadequate to feed everyone. In the long run this may be true—although there is still considerable room for increasing global food production, particularly in many food-deficit nations of the Third World—but in the short run it is not. To provide the world's nearly 500 million malnourished people with an adequate diet would require only about 12 million additional tons of cereals. "This is only about 1 percent of world consumption, about 30 percent of what the United States feeds its livestock, and less than half of the grain directly and indirectly lost each year through food waste by American families" (Howe and Sewell, 1975: 61). Thus the problem is not simply one of shortage; to a substantial extent it is a matter of distribution.

The critical fallacy of the lifeboat and triage analogies is the assumption they make that, if somehow a few nations can be cut adrift, the problems they represent will go away. This is unlikely.

> The untreated battlefield soldiers and the drowning swimmers repulsed from the lifeboat simply disappeared from the scene, but nations and peoples do not die in that manner. If massive famine were to occur in South Asia, tens of millions of individuals might die; but In-

dia, Pakistan, and Bangladesh would remain with hundreds of millions of survivors, just as the Chinese people remain after centuries of periodic famines. The attitude of the survivors toward American and Canadian authorities who had decided to "screen them out" would not be hard to imagine. (Gordon, 1979: 77)

GLOBAL CARRYING CAPACITY: HOW MANY IS TOO MANY?

If the lifeboat logic holds any water at all, it is perhaps most accurate to conceive of the entire globe as the lifeboat in which all of humanity will either remain afloat or sink together. This conclusion is reinforced by the fact that the *carrying capacity* of the global system—the maximum number of human beings or other life forms that the earth's delicate ecosystem can support—is certainly finite. Technological innovations and man's continuing ability to alter the environment make precise determination of the earth's ultimate carrying capacity difficult. But the evidence of finiteness is already undeniable.

The pressures exerted on the global carrying capacity by population growth are particularly evident (see Box 8.1). The advanced industrial societies of the North are largely responsible for this fact as they seek through industrialization and agricultural development to improve their already high standards of living. "When population growth occurs in societies where wealth and technology have led to high production and consumption lifestyles, the added demand on energy supplies, fisheries, foreign products, minerals, natural recreation areas, and water is inordinately large" (U.S. Department of State, 1978b).

The ecological pressures of population growth are apparent in the environmental degradation experienced in many Third World nations as well, where already impoverished but growing millions cut down more forests for fuel and clear more land for food.

Vast areas of Africa, South and Southeast Asia, the Middle East, and Latin America have been crippled by slash-and-burn agriculture, overcropping, overgrazing, and consequent wind and water erosion. Millions of acres of forest have been sacrificed to the ever-growing need for cropland, firewood, and timber. Deprived of water-holding cover, millions of tons of virtually irreplaceable topsoil have been washed into the sea. The Sahel, Nepal, Haiti, Java, and many other regions have been described as ecological disaster areas. But the population pressures which caused the damage remain, with ever-growing numbers attempting to subsist from ever-depleting natural resources. (U.S. Department of State, 1978b: 3)

Box 8.1   The Impact of Population Pressures on the Global Carrying Capacity

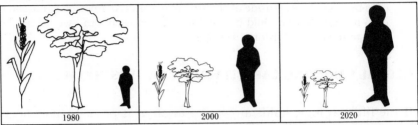

| 1980 | 2000 | 2020 |

Living resources essential for human survival and sustainable development are increasingly being destroyed or depleted. At the same time human demand for those resources is growing fast. The problem is illustrated above. If current rates of land degradation continue, close to one third of the world's arable land (symbolized by the stalk of grain) will be destroyed in the next 20 years. Similarly, by the end of this century (at present rates of clearance), the remaining area of unlogged productive tropical forest will be halved. During this period the world population is expected to increase by almost half—from just over 4,000 million to just under 6,000 million. The predicament caused by growing numbers of people demanding scarcer resources is exacerbated by the disproportionately high consumption rates of developed countries (illustrated below).

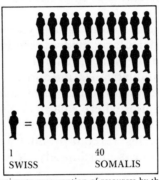

1
SWISS

40
SOMALIS

Disproportionate consumption of resources by the affluent.
One Swiss consumes as much as 40 Somalis.

Source: *Development Forum* 8 (March 1980): 9.

Worldwide, the evidence of environmental stress is manifold. As summarized by officials in the U.S. Department of State, environmental stress and degradation manifest themselves thus:

- Most fundamentally, [in] the destruction of vegetation cover, the source of man's food and oxygen;
- The decline, since 1970, in the world fishing catch, due largely to overfishing and pollution of spawning beds;
- Rapid depletion of oil and gas reserves;
- Similarly rapid depletion of metals resources;
- Overcrowding and impairment of national parks, wildlife preserves, city parks, beaches, and other natural recreational areas;

- Destruction of animal and plant wildlife by farming, timbering, urbanization, pesticide and fertilizer poisoning, and hunting;
- Environmental illnesses (notably emphysema, stroke, parasitic infections, heart disease, and cancer) caused by the introduction of new chemicals into the ecosystem, by air and water pollution, and by crowding;
- Water shortages due to the massive water requirements of modern agriculture, industry, and consumer living; depletion of underground water supplies; pollution of lakes and rivers; and exhaustion of promising water catchment and irrigation sites; and
- Damaging rainfall and temperature pattern changes brought on by carbon dioxide in the atmosphere from wood and fossil fuels, dust from urban and agricultural activity, and the thermal effects of waste heat and economic activity. (U.S. Department of State, 1978b: 3-4)

If this kind of damage and its associated ills are the product of a world of over four billion people, what might we expect in a world of six, ten, or twelve billion?

Nine

The Energy Tangle
and Resource Power

Whoever controls world resources controls the
world in a way that mere occupation of territory
cannot match.

Richard J. Barnet, 1980

We must assume that the period available to us
for transition from an oil-based economy to one
founded substantially on new energy resources
will probably not exceed 20 to 25 years.

Walter J. Levy, 1978

People in the world's rich nations eat a disproportionately large
share of the world's foodstuffs. They also consume a disproportionate share of its energy. But the rich nations are not the primary
sources of the energy resources that enter the international marketplace. Instead, they have become increasingly dependent on a small
number of developing nations to supply the increments in their
seemingly insatiable energy appetites. These facts underlie the crisis atmosphere pervading the continuing worldwide energy crunch.

Knowledge of the immediate effects of the energy situation and
the perceived need to do something about it have become so widespread as to obscure how recent a global policy problem energy
really is. It was not until the winter of 1973–1974, when the Arab
members of the Organization of Petroleum Exporting Countries
sharply increased the price of oil and simultaneously cut their production, that the global dimensions of the energy problem came into
focus. Prior to that time energy had been relatively cheap and available in seemingly limitless quantities, especially in the United
States. But since 1973 energy has been dear and in relatively short
supply. Projections to the year 2000 suggest this situation will not
change, at least concerning fossil fuels (petroleum, natural gas, and
coal), which are precisely the fuels on which the world has come to
depend to an extraordinary degree (e.g., see *The Global 2000 Report
to the President*, 1980a). The energy situation will thus continue to

propel transformations in the global political system—perhaps to revolutionize it.

PATTERNS OF ENERGY PRODUCTION AND CONSUMPTION: PAST AND PRESENT

The enormous gap between the energy consumed in developed and developing nations is illustrated in Figure 9.1. The rate of per capita energy use in the North is ten times that of the South. Even more striking are variations in the energy use in different world regions (see Figure 9.2). As Ruth Leger Sivard, director of the nonprofit research organization World Priorities, points out, the difference between the lowest average energy consumption by region (South Asia) and the highest (North America) "is a gap typical of the extremes in economic conditions in the modern world; energy consumption per capita in North America is fifty times as large as in South Asia" (Sivard, 1979a: 10).

Figure 9.1
Per Capita Energy* Consumption (metric tons)

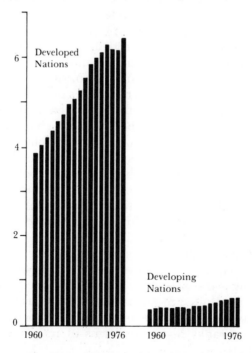

Source: Ruth Leger Sivard, *World Energy Survey* (Leesburg, Va.: World Priorities, 1979), p. 10. Copyright © World Priorities, Leesburg, Va. 22075, U.S.A.
*Includes fuelwood.

Figure 9.2
Regional Comparisons, per Capita GNP and Energy* Consumption, 1976

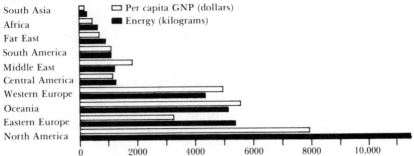

Source: Ruth Leger Sivard, *World Energy Survey* (Leesburg, Va.: World Priorities, 1979), p. 11. Copyright © World Priorities, Leesburg, Va. 22075, U.S.A.
*Includes fuelwood.

Figures 9.1 and 9.2 indicate how closely energy consumption is associated with the production of goods and services as measured by GNP. In 1976, for example, per capita energy consumption in developing nations was only 10 percent as much as in the developed world. The average income per capita of developing countries was only 9 percent as high (Sivard, 1979a: 11).

In a sense, these differentials reflect the extent to which energy has been substituted for labor in the industrial societies of the North. In industrial production, in transportation, and in the distribution of goods and services, intensive uses of energy have become the hallmark of the modern industrial society. Not surprisingly, therefore, developing nations of the South, which have not yet experienced the full extent of mechanization that is characteristic of industrial societies, see higher rates of energy use as the key to more rapid economic development and better standards of living.

There are differences in the energy consumption associated with given levels of economic output for different countries, however. Yugoslavia and Portugal, for example, have about the same per capita incomes, but Yugoslavia uses twice as much energy per capita as Portugal; India uses more energy per capita than Sri Lanka, but has an appreciably lower per capita GNP (Sivard, 1979a: 11). Most striking is the difference among developed nations, particularly between the United States and other industrial societies. The United States uses almost twice as much energy per capita as Sweden, but Sweden ranks higher in terms of its per capita income (Sivard, 1979a: 11).

Several reasons account for the high level of energy usage in the United States. Historically, energy has been abundant and cheap in the United States, a fact that has perhaps encouraged development of wasteful energy practices. Americans' personal habits are also important, particularly the preference for private automobiles as the principal mode of transportation. It has been estimated that transportation accounts for 55 percent of all petroleum used in the United States (roughly 10 million barrels per day of a total of 18.3 million barrels per day in 1977), of which the automobile accounts for 85 percent[1] (*Newsweek*, July 16, 1979: 33). In other words, the automobile accounts for something over 8.5 million barrels of petroleum consumed per day in the United States—which is almost exactly the amount the United States imported from abroad in 1977 (*World Oil*, August 15, 1978: 48).

Clearly such an enormous level of consumption, which increasingly has been met by importing petroleum from abroad, has an important bearing on the entire world energy picture—a fact about which European nations are particularly sensitive. The argument is that Europeans effectively subsidize American oil consumption by being forced to pay higher energy costs than would hold if the United States were to curb its energy appetite (see Stobaugh and Yergin, 1980, for a brief discussion of the European view of American energy policies, or lack thereof).

Historical Trends in Fossil Fuel Usage

Rapid increases in the rate of energy usage are primarily a post-World War II phenomenon. In 1950, for example, world energy consumption was 2.5 billion tons of coal-equivalent energy, and world population stood at 2.5 billion people. Although population increased rapidly during the next quarter-century, energy use increased even more rapidly. By 1976 the world's 4.2 billion people were consuming 8.3 billion tons of coal-equivalent energy, nearly double the rate of only a few decades earlier (Sivard, 1979a: 6–7). (Note in Figure 9.1 that the greatest increase in per capita consumption occurred in the developed world.) This rapid increase was closely tied to the unprecedented level of economic growth that the world experienced in the postwar era. During the period from 1950 to 1973, the world economy expanded at a rate of 4 percent annually, an expansion spurred by the 7 percent growth in world oil output during this period (Brown, 1979: 17). On a per capita basis, this meant that the amount of oil available increased from an average of 1.5 barrels per person in 1930 to over 5.3 barrels in 1973 (Brown, 1979: 18). (One barrel of oil equals 42 U.S. gallons.)

1. It should be noted that the population density in the United States is substantially less than in other industrial societies, notably in Western Europe.

This dramatic rise in oil production has made oil and, somewhat less so, natural gas the principal sources of commercial energy in the world today.[2] Their widespread use is of relatively recent origin, however, having grown most rapidly since 1950.

Historical patterns of energy consumption in the United States illustrate the transition to oil and gas dependence. Little more than a century ago fuelwood was the principal energy source in the United States. As the mechanical revolution altered the nature of transportation, of work, and of leisure, coal began to replace fuelwood. At the beginning of the twentieth century, coal had become the dominant source of energy worldwide; by 1913 coal accounted for 75 percent of the world's energy consumption (Sivard, 1979a: 7).

The shift from coal to oil and natural gas was spurred by new technological developments, particularly the internal combustion engine. Because the United States was well endowed with petroleum resources, it "moved ahead more rapidly than the rest of the world in the development of oil-based technologies, in particular the automotive and petrochemical industries. By the late 1940s, oil was the principal fuel used in the United States" (Sivard, 1979a: 7).

The massive worldwide shift from coal to oil in residential, transportation, and industrial sectors occurred somewhat later than in the United States. As shown in Figure 9.3, oil accounted for less than a third of world energy production in 1950. But by 1965 it equaled coal production and in the next decade oil rapidly outstripped coal as the principal energy source. Everywhere the reasons were the same. Energy derived from oil and gas was cleaner and less expensive than coal. (Coal had also been inexpensive but effective labor demands for higher wages and more costly safety standards had increased its relative cost.) From the end of the Korean War until the early 1970s, oil prices actually declined worldwide compared to the prices of other commodities, with natural gas prices showing a similar decline in the United States, where it was more extensively developed than in other parts of the world (Willrich, 1975). These price trends are documented in Figure 9.4, which compares the export price of oil with the weighted average prices of other major commodities and of manufactured goods. The picture is clear: until the abrupt and unprecedented skyrocketing of prices effected by OPEC in the early 1970s, oil was relatively inexpensive. It therefore made good economic sense to use it in large quantities. This development makes understandable the fact that by the 1980s, the world was using "thirty thousand gallons of petroleum every

---

2. Fuelwood and charcoal are important noncommercial energy sources in developing nations and account for 90 percent of their world production (Sivard, 1979a: 10).

Figure 9.3
World Production of Primary Energy (billion metric tons of coal equivalent)

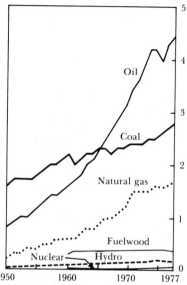

Source: Ruth Leger Sivard, *World Energy Survey* (Leesburg, Va.: World Priorities, 1979), p. 7. Copyright © World Priorities, Leesburg, Va. 22075, U.S.A.

Figure 9.4
Export Price of Oil and Average Prices for Commodities and for Manufactures (indexes, 1955 = 100)

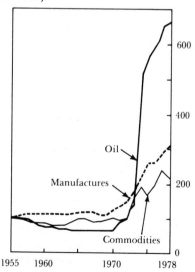

Source: Ruth Leger Sivard, *World Energy Survey* (Leesburg, Va.: World Priorities, 1979), p. 9. Copyright © World Priorities, Leesburg, Va. 22075, U.S.A.

second," and why at that time "about ten thousand gallons a second [were] consumed in the United States" (Barnet, 1980a: 47).

The Rise of OPEC: Consumers, Producers, and the Multinational Oil Companies

The chief actors propelling the worldwide shift from coal to oil were eight multinational corporations known as "the majors"—Exxon, Gulf, Mobil, Standard Oil of California, Texaco (all American-based), British Petroleum, Royal Dutch Shell, and Compagnie Française des Pétroles. In the mid-1970s these eight firms (the first seven of which are often referred to as the "seven sisters") controlled nearly two-thirds of world oil production (Abrahamsson, 1975: 80). In addition, as vertically integrated firms they controlled major segments of the transportation, refining, and marketing aspects of the oil industry as well.

The majors were largely unfettered in their search for, production, and marketing of low-cost oil. Concessions from nations in such oil-rich areas as the Middle East were easy to obtain. The communist countries were virtually the only ones from which the majors were barred. It was essentially a buyer's market, which meant that the majors had to control production output so as to avoid glut and chronic oversupply. They did this by keeping other competitors, known as "independents," out of the international oil system, by engaging in joint ventures and otherwise cooperating among themselves to restrict supply, and by avoiding price competition (Spero, 1977). The oil companies were thus able to manage the price of oil at a level profitable for themselves even while the price of oil relative to other commodities declined.

An abundant supply of oil at low prices facilitated the rapid recovery of Western Europe and Japan from World War II and encouraged consumers to adopt energy-intensive technologies, such as the private automobile. The overall result was an enormous growth in the worldwide demand for and consumption of energy.

To sustain high growth rates, continual development of new oil deposits was required. But because the real cost of oil did not increase commensurately with the cost of other commodities, goods, and services, the incentives for developing petroleum reserves outside the Middle East waned. And incentives for developing new technologies for alternative energy sources, such as coal, were virtually nonexistent. This meant that when OPEC increased the price of oil fourfold in the winter of 1973–1974, oil consumers had no recourse but to absorb the costs because of the absence of energy alternatives. As Mason Willrich comments:

A declining price is socially desirable if it reflects an abundance of a natural resource. But such a price trend can be very costly in the long run if it fails to anticipate resource scarcity or reflect environmental and social costs. In a properly functioning market, therefore, the economic rent on a non-renewable natural resource tends to rise rather steadily so that higher-cost alternatives will be available when the cheaper resource is exhausted. (Willrich, 1975: 31)

In addition to increasing global demand, another factor that facilitated OPEC's success was the growing dependence of much of the world on Middle Eastern oil. By 1977, as shown by the regional breakdowns in Table 9.1, the Middle East accounted for nearly 36 percent of world oil supplies but less than 3 percent of its demand. The importance of particular countries in the Middle East is even more striking: in 1977 only two countries, Iran and Saudi Arabia, accounted for nearly a quarter of the entire world s production of oil.[3]

The excess of Middle Eastern oil supply over demand is used to make up the shortfall created by the noncommunist nations of the industrial world. The import dependence of Japan and Western Europe is especially noteworthy. Together they account for over 30 percent of the world demand for oil but produce less than 3 percent domestically. The result is an 18-million-barrel-per-day dependence on foreign sources of oil. American dependence on foreign sources is somewhat less in barrels per day, but the aggregate level of American consumption—30.1 percent of all the oil consumed in the entire world—is extraordinary. Moreover, as domestic supplies of American oil continue to be depleted, American import dependence will grow with a corresponding pressure on OPEC's productive capacity.[4]

Other factors besides the absence of energy alternatives and worldwide dependence on Middle Eastern oil were necessary to OPEC's success. Among them was the effective wresting of control

3. Iranian oil production dropped dramatically following the 1979 Iranian revolution. The impact of this turn of events on world oil supplies illustrated how closely demand and *available* supplies have come to be balanced, a point we will consider in more detail below. (In a normally functioning market, supply and demand tend to balance one another. This is not necessarily true in the short run, however. Nor in the case of oil is it necessarily true in the long run. The intervention of OPEC into the market may impede the effective functioning of market forces that would otherwise cause supply and demand to move toward equilibrium.)

4. At the time of the OPEC price hikes in 1973–1974, the United States depended on foreign sources of oil for only 17 percent of its total energy needs, and only 4 percent was provided by Arab oil. In contrast, Western European nations in the European Community depended on foreign sources of oil for 60 percent of their total energy needs, 42 percent provided by Arab oil alone, and Japan depended on foreign sources of oil for 78 percent of its total energy supplies, 34 percent provided by Arab oil (*International Economic Report of the President*, 1975: 8).

Table 9.1
World Petroleum Demand and Supply by Regions, 1977 (thousands of barrels daily)

Region	Domestic demand (consumption)	Domestic supply			Excess supply over demand	Excess demand over supply	Percent of World	
		Crude oil	NGL	Total			Domestic demand	Domestic supply
United States	18,325	8,179	1,617	9,796	—	8,529	30.1	15.66
Canada	1,664	1,222	309	1,531	—	133	2.7	2.45
Latin America	3,990	4,506	238	4,744	754	—	6.5	7.59
Western Europe	14,235	1,262	85	1,347	—	12,888	23.4	2.15
East Europe & Soviet Union	10,087	11,407	215	11,622	1,535	—	16.6	18.58
Africa	1,165	6,211	140	6,351	5,186	—	2.0	10.15
Middle East	1,570	22,131	335	22,466	20,896	—	2.6	35.92
Japan	5,015	12	—	12	—	5,003	8.2	0.02
Australia & New Zealand	795	442	56	498	—	297	1.3	0.80
China	1,465	1,807	N.A.	1,807	342	—	2.4	2.89
Other Asia & Oceania	2,590	2,332	35	2,367	—	223	4.2	3.79
World Total	60,901	59,511	3,030	62,541	1,640	—	100.0	100.00

Source: *World Oil* 187 (August 15, 1978), 48.

of production and pricing policies from the multinational oil companies by the governments making up OPEC. This occurred over a period of several years as the bargaining advantages enjoyed by the multinationals vis-à-vis the host governments of producing countries deteriorated. The shift from multinational control of oil to government-to-government determination is made evident by the fact that the major oil companies' share of world oil traffic had fallen by 1980 to 43 percent, whereas six years earlier 80 percent of the oil traded in the global market was handled by them (*Newsweek*, Jan. 21, 1980: 72).

The typical arrangement under which Middle Eastern nations granted concessions to the majors gave these countries a return in royalties per barrel. This had the effect of linking the producing countries' income directly to the volume of production (Abrahamsson, 1975). As long as production was high and the volume growing, there was little problem with this arrangement. But since the majors used production controls to avoid oversupply, the potential for adverse effects on producing countries themselves was high. Thus, as early as 1949, Middle Eastern nations began renegotiating the terms of their concessionary agreements with the oil companies. Following a price reduction by Exxon in August 1960, which had the effect of offsetting some of the gains made by producing countries under their new profit-sharing agreements, OPEC was formed. Its purpose was to prevent decreases in prices and income.

> As stated in the first resolution of OPEC, and more explicitly in the June 1968 resolution, there are three main objectives of the organization: first, to obtain stable and, if possible, higher oil revenues for its members; second, . . . to obtain higher prices for its oil; and third, to obtain a greater measure of control over production in its member states. (Abrahamsson, 1975: 81)

At the time OPEC was formed few observers foresaw the power it would eventually wield. By comparison with the 1970s, gains made by the organization in the 1960s were in fact modest, but not insignificant. In particular, OPEC succeeded in maintaining the posted price of oil (the official price used to calculate their revenues) at the same time that the market price fell. "The result was that, during the sixties, host producing states received larger per-barrel revenues at corporate expense" (Wilkins, 1976). By the 1970s, however, the bargaining strength of the producing states had so increased that they were able to take control of oil prices and production policies. They also were able, for the first time, to assert their right to participate in ownership of oil-producing ventures in their own countries, which amounted to nationalization through negotiation with the oil companies rather than expropriation.[5]

One factor that eroded the bargaining power of the major oil companies was the increase in the number of independents in the field. In 1952 the "seven sisters" produced 90 percent of the crude oil outside North America and the communist world; by 1968 this percentage had declined to little more than three-quarters (Wilkins, 1976: 162). Production was not the only segment of the industry where the dominance of the "seven sisters" was affected. "In every part of the oil industry—concession areas, proven reserves, production, refining capacity, tanker capacity, and product marketing— the percentage held by the top seven companies declined in the fifties and sixties" (Wilkins, 1976).

On the other hand, the bargaining power of producing states was enhanced in the early 1970s as the market price of oil began to rise in response to increasing demand and limited supplies.[6] One result was an increase in the amount of money that producing states earned.[7] This was important, for "monetary reserves meant that the important oil producers could afford the short-term loss of earnings that might result from an embargo or production reduction carried out in an effort to increase the price of oil or to seek other concessions from the [oil] companies and the consuming states" (Spero, 1977).

The catalyst to the OPEC price hikes and production moves of 1973–1974 was provided by Libya. Following a coup in September 1969 which brought to power a radical government headed by Colonel Muammar Qaddafi, Libya was able to effect production re-

5. Wilkins (1976) provides a useful summary of the evolution of host government ownership of the oil investments in producing states. On the significance of these developments, she observes that

> these actions seemed to herald basic changes in the industry: The old concessions would be replaced by host government participation; the companies would no longer own their producing properties in the major exporting countries; production levels would be set by governments; security of crude-oil supplies would be endangered; prices, unpredictable. The multinationals were now to be buyers of oil. (Wilkins, 1976: 174)

Wilkins also points out, however, that host governments would remain dependent on the multinationals for needed technical aid in exploration and production.

6. "Supplies were curtailed owing to nationalizations (in Algeria, Iraq, and Libya), the spread of host-country production cutbacks (in Libya and Kuwait), the May, 1970, closing of the pipeline from the Saudi Arabian fields to the eastern Mediterranean as a result of a bulldozer severing the line, and the American government's inaction, which had halted the development of American off-shore resources and the Alaskan pipeline" (Wilkins, 1976).

7. The total official reserves of the major oil-producing states increased from $2.9 billion to $5.2 billion between 1964 and 1970 and to $8.2 billion in 1971 (Spero, 1977: 220).

ductions and subsequent price increases for its oil. Several factors contributed to Libya's success, including the high proportion of Western European oil imports that came from Libya and the fact that Occidental Petroleum, an American independent, had substantial stakes in Libyan oil and thus was vulnerable to government pressures. The fact that Occidental was an independent also prevented a common policy by the majors in dealing with Libya (see also Penrose, 1976, for a fuller discussion of Libya's bargaining advantages). But the important point is what the other oil-producing states learned from the Libyan experience.

> It revealed the vulnerability of the companies and the unwillingness of the Western consumers to take forceful action in support of the companies. It also led to a major conceptual change in the minds of oil producers by demonstrating that government revenues could be raised not only by increasing exports but also or instead by increasing price. (Spero, 1977: 223)

OPEC's assertiveness on the issues of prices, production, and participation continued in the wake of the Libyan confrontation with the oil companies. For the Arab members of OPEC, the possibility of using oil as a political weapon to affect the outcome of the unsettled Arab-Israeli dispute was a related issue of considerable concern. The common desire of the Arab countries to defeat Israel was in fact one of the key elements cementing cohesion among the Arab members of OPEC (specifically cohesion within OAPEC, the Organization of Arab Petroleum Exporting Countries). "The need to be unequivocal in their commitment was made stronger because the various pan-Arab and Palestinian organizations, straddling national boundaries, could threaten existing state regimes that failed to show the appropriate degree of enthusiasm for the cause" (Vernon, 1976). When the Yom Kippur War broke out between Israel and the Arabs on October 6, 1973, the stage for using the oil weapon was set.

Less than two weeks after the outbreak of the war, the OPEC oil ministers seized the right unilaterally to determine prices, and the Arab producing countries decided to reduce production levels. Between October 16, 1973, and January 1, 1974, OPEC raised the price of oil from $3.01 per barrel to $11.65. This more than quadrupled the pre-October price of $2.59. Previously, prices had been determined through negotiations with the oil companies. Now, the companies learned of the governments' October increases from the newspapers (Wilkins, 1976). Control over prices and production thus shifted unequivocally from the oil companies to the host governments.

Arab members of OPEC sought to accomplish their political goals regarding the Arab-Israeli dispute by cutting back oil production and by imposing an embargo on exports to consuming countries considered too pro-Israeli. The embargo was specifically targeted against the United States and the Netherlands, whereas the oil curtailment was more general in scope. Eventually both of these tactics were set aside—but not before the American Secretary of State Henry Kissinger issued a thinly veiled threat that the United States might use military force to assure the continued flow of oil to the "free world,"[8] and not before the American government facilitated the disengagement of Arab and Israeli forces and a partial return of Arab territory occupied by Israel during the June war of 1967. But the price hikes remained.

The obvious lesson to be learned from the events of 1973–1974 is that the oil weapon, having been used once, can be used again. The inability of the major multinational oil companies to control the international oil system as they had done for decades was also an important lesson. During the crisis, in fact, the oil companies responded "with the conditioned reflexes of entrepreneurs minimizing their risks at the margin." As Raymond Vernon, an expert on multinational corporations, observed: "The patterns of oil distribution in the crisis, dictated by the principles of greatest prudence and least pain, were curiously non-national. Anyone looking for confirmation of the view that it paid a country to have an oil company based within its own jurisdiction would have found scant support for such a hypothesis in this brief episode in the oil industry's history" (Vernon, 1976). The fact that the major oil companies enjoyed record earnings while losing their administrative control of oil production lends support to the accuracy of this thesis.

A final important lesson of 1973–1974 was that even the United States had become vulnerable to economic pressures exerted by foreign powers. This is an essential factor in understanding the rise of OPEC as a significant international actor. There seems to be widespread agreement among observers (see Lenczowski, 1976) that the shift from a buyer's market to a seller's market and the change in the position of the major oil companies vis-à-vis producers and inde-

8. The statement made by Kissinger that attracted perhaps the most attention was during an interview with *Business Week* (January 13, 1975) where, in response to a question as to whether the government had considered military action to deal with OPEC, and in particular the question of oil prices, Kissinger replied:

A very dangerous course. We should have learned from Vietnam that it is easier to get into a war than to get out of it. I am not saying that there's no circumstance where we would not use force. But it is one thing to use it in the case of a dispute over price; it's another where there is some actual strangulation of the industrialized world.

pendents significantly altered the global energy picture in the 1970s. Another major factor was the movement away from relative self-sufficiency in oil production that the United States had traditionally enjoyed.

Untangling the Energy Situation: The Role of the United States

Historically, the United States has been a major producer as well as consumer of energy, particularly oil. In 1938, for example, the United States accounted for nearly two-thirds of world crude oil production, and over 70 percent of production in the noncommunist world (Darmstadter and Landsberg, 1976: 33). Even as recently as 1960, American production accounted for over a third of world production and nearly 40 percent of production among noncommunist nations. By 1973, however, these proportions had slipped to 17 and 20 percent, respectively. The changing position of the United States in world oil production is documented in Table 9.2.

As can be seen from these data, American oil production began to decline in the early 1970s. With rising domestic demand, the need for America to import from abroad became apparent. Importantly, the need became substantial at the time of OPEC's oil price hikes of 1973–1974. Prior to that time, although showing a sharply rising trend, American imports of oil as a proportion of consumption had remained within manageable boundaries, hovering around 20 percent in the mid-1960s. By 1973, however, imports accounted for over a third of American consumption (Darmstadter and Landsberg, 1976: 31). The United States, like much of the rest of the world, had become vulnerable to the economic and political pressures of foreign powers.

Growing American dependence on imported oil helped create the conditions that made the OPEC price hikes and production controls of 1973–1974 possible. Several factors contributed to this increased dependence, including: "accelerated demand for energy in the aggregate; a dramatic falling off of reserve additions of oil and natural gas; severe constraints, largely for environmental reasons, on the use of coal; lags in the scheduled completion of nuclear power plants; and protracted delays in oil and gas leasing" (Darmstadter and Landsberg, 1976).

Growing demand for oil was at the core of the problem. Demand for oil in turn was related to price, which, as noted earlier, actually declined relative to other commodities from the 1950s to the 1970s. Hence, there was little incentive for, or public interest in, conservation measures.

Table 9.2
World Crude Oil Production, 1960–1978 (bpd = barrels per day)

Major Areas and Selected Countries	1960		1970		1973		1975		1976		1977		1978 (est.)	
	1,000 bpd	Per cent	1,000 bpd	Per cent	1,000 bpd	Per cent	1,000 bpd	Per cent	1,000 bpd	Per cent	1,000 bpd	Per cent	1,000 bpd	Per cent
North America	7,845	37.3	11,373	25.1	11,452	20.5	10,550	19.9	10,389	17.9	10,546	17.6	11,232	18.5
United States	7,055	33.5	9,648	21.3	9,189	16.5	8,370	15.8	8,154	14.0	8,244	13.8	8,701	14.3
Canada	519	2.5	1,305	2.9	1,798	3.2	1,460	2.7	1,339	2.3	1,321	2.2	1,324	2.2
Mexico	271	1.3	420	.9	465	.8	720	1.4	897	1.5	981	1.6	1,207	2.0
Central and South America	3,470	16.5	4,758	10.5	4,666	8.4	3,585	6.7	3,553	6.1	3,530	5.9	3,548	5.8
Venezuela†	2,854	13.6	3,703	8.2	3,364	6.0	2,345	4.4	2,301	4.0	2,238	3.7	2,166	3.6
Ecuador†	7	*	5	*	204	.4	160	.3	187	.3	183	.3	202	.3
Other	609	2.9	1,050	2.3	1,098	2.0	1,080	2.0	1,065	1.8	1,109	1.8	1,180	1.9
Western Europe	289	1.4	375	.8	370	.7	550	1.0	776	1.3	1,260	2.1	1,679	2.8
United Kingdom	2	*	2	*	2	*	20	*	244	.4	744	1.2	1,082	1.8
Norway	0	0	0	0	32	.1	190	.4	279	.5	279	.5	356	.6
Other	287	1.4	373	.8	336	.6	340	.6	253	.4	237	.4	241	.4
Africa	289	1.4	5,982	13.2	5,902	10.6	4,990	9.4	5,849	10.1	6,236	10.4	6,120	10.1
Algeria†	185	.9	976	2.2	1,070	1.9	960	1.8	1,052	1.8	1,123	1.9	1,225	2.0
Libya†	0	0	3,321	7.3	2,187	3.9	1,480	2.8	1,929	3.3	2,064	3.4	1,993	3.3
Nigeria†	18	.1	1,090	2.4	2,053	3.7	1,795	3.4	2,071	3.6	2,097	3.5	1,910	3.1
Gabon†	—	—	110	.2	150	.3	225	.4	225	.4	222	.4	225	.4
Other	86	.4	485	1.1	442	.8	530	1.0	572	1.0	730	1.2	767	1.3
Asia-Pacific	554	2.6	1,340	3.0	2,272	4.1	2,215	4.2	2,528	4.4	2,787	4.6	2,843	4.7
Indonesia†	419	2.0	855	1.9	1,339	2.4	1,305	2.5	1,508	2.6	1,685	2.8	1,637	2.7
Other	135	.6	485	1.1	933	1.7	910	1.7	1,020	1.8	1,102	1.8	1,206	2.0
Middle East	5,269	25.1	13,937	30.7	21,158	38.0	19,590	36.9	22,235	38.3	22,430	37.4	21,603	35.6
Saudi Arabia†	1,319	6.3	3,798	8.4	7,607	13.7	7,075	13.3	8,367	14.4	9,014	15.0	8,530	14.1
Kuwait†	1,696	8.1	2,983	6.6	3,024	5.4	2,085	3.9	1,918	3.3	1,783	3.0	1,865	3.1
Iran†	1,057	5.0	3,831	8.4	5,861	10.5	5,350	10.1	5,940	10.2	5,699	9.5	5,207	8.6
Iraq†	969	4.6	1,563	3.4	1,964	3.5	2,260	4.3	2,442	4.2	2,493	4.1	2,629	4.3
Abu Dhabi‡	0	—	691	1.5	1,298	2.3	1,370	2.6	1,952	3.4	1,999	3.3	1,832	3.0
Qatar†	173	.8	367	.8	570	1.0	440	.8	498	.9	445	.7	484	.8
Other	55	.3	704	1.6	834	1.5	1,010	1.9	1,138	2.0	997	1.7	1,056	1.7
Total Non-Communist	17,716	84.3	37,765	83.3	45,820	82.3	41,695	78.5	45,331	78.1	46,789	78.0	47,025	77.5
Communist World§	3,310	15.7	7,610	16.7	9,865	17.7	11,650	21.9	12,728	21.9	13,213	22.0	13,683	22.5
Soviet Union	2,960	14.1	7,049	15.5	8,420	15.1	9,630	18.1	NA	—	10,934	18.2	11,215	18.5
Other	350	1.6	561	1.2	1,445	2.6	2,020	3.8	NA	—	2,279	3.8	2,468	4.1
Total World	21,026	100.0	45,375	100.0	55,685	100.0	53,120	100.0	58,059	100.0	60,002	100.0	60,708	100.0

Source: Congressional Quarterly, *The Middle East* (Washington, D.C.: Congressional Quarterly, 1979), p. 75.

*Production or percentage of production is negligible. †Member of Organization of Petroleum Exporting Countries. ‡Figures for 1976, 1977 and 1978 include all United Arab Emirate countries. §Includes Soviet Union and other Warsaw Pact nations, China, Cuba and Yugoslavia.

Increased demand for gasoline was particularly acute. Between 1960 and 1965, gasoline consumption grew at an annual rate of 2.8 percent; thereafter it accelerated to more than twice that rate. But if consumption patterns had remained at their 1960–1965 levels, the lower growth rate for gasoline "would have 'freed' another 630,000 barrels of oil per day in 1972—another 4 percent of American oil consumption, or 13 percent of oil imports"[9] (Darmstadter and Landsberg, 1976: 28).

On the supply side, however, American domestic oil production was not keeping pace with trends in consumption. United States reserves as a proportion of total world reserves steadily declined, and new additions failed to keep pace with discoveries elsewhere, particularly the Middle East and North Africa (Darmstadter and Landsberg, 1976). These developments had the effect of removing surplus American productive capacity, thus making the United States increasingly dependent on (and vulnerable to) foreign sources of supply. Western Europe and Japan had lived with knowledge of such dependence for some time. "But for the United States, previously confident that its own excess productive capacity could be deployed in times of crisis . . . , the increased reliance on imports signified an unexpected turn of events. . . . It was a new and sobering situation" (Darmstadter and Landsberg, 1976).

The failure of American productive capability to keep pace with developments in other areas of the world reflected the preference of the oil industry for overseas investments, where the rate of return was much greater. This shift is shown in the historical data in Table 9.2, which documents the extent to which current world production of oil has come to be concentrated in the hands of relatively few developing nations.[10] The fact that these nations are largely in the politically volatile Middle East is a source of added concern.

There is little reason to believe, however, that American dependence on external sources of oil will be reduced substantially in

9. Decreased auto efficiency due to the introduction of pollution control devices is among the factors often cited to explain the rise in American gasoline consumption. But other factors associated wth American preferences regarding the automobile were also important, including

steadily increasing car weight, large engine size, rapid spread of air conditioning, and other extras that lessened fuel efficiency. Failure of annual mileage per vehicle to decline, as had been anticipated by some as a result of more two- and three-car families, is still another. (Darmstadter and Landsberg, 1976: 28)

10. "In 1950 developing nations as a whole produced only 18 percent of the world's commercial energy. By 1977 they accounted for over 40 percent of a greatly enlarged global total, and appeared to be on their way to producing the major share of world supplies. Between 1950 and 1977 developing nations' production of energy jumped from 429 million tons (coal equivalent) to 3,800 million tons" (Sivard, 1979a: 8). In terms of oil alone, the nations of OPEC accounted for over half of the world's total production (in 1977).

the near future. In concert with other industrial nations, the Carter administration pledged in 1979 not to increase American oil imports through 1985 beyond their 1977 level, and it sought to develop a massive national energy program relying on conservation incentives and the development of alternative energy sources to ensure that dependence on foreign oil would be reduced in the future.

Faced with rapidly rising import costs, the United States did manage to reduce its imports from the 1977 figure of 8.81 million barrels per day to 8.28 million barrels a day in 1979 (U.S. Department of Energy, 1980b: 14). Experts, nevertheless, seem unconvinced about the long term. Based on a six-year study of energy undertaken at Harvard University, for example, Robert Stobaugh and Daniel Yergin project that American import requirements will increase from the nearly 9 million barrels per day in the 1970s to 14 million a day by the late 1980s. The likely cost *increase* would be $60 billion annually (in 1978 dollars)[11] (Stobaugh and Yergin, 1979: 840), or double the roughly $60 billion the United States paid for oil imports in 1979.

Beyond the economic impact of high and increasing oil import costs, including inflationary pressures and adverse effects on the American balance of payments, American dependence on foreign sources of oil also raises important questions regarding national security.

OIL AND NATIONAL SECURITY

Will oil-importing nations permit oil exporters to reduce the flow of oil to the point where it adversely affects the economic and perhaps political well-being of importers? What steps might importers take to assure the supply of oil to their petroleum-dependent societies?

These questions are most relevant to the advanced industrial societies of the North, which not only depend on oil to an extraordinary degree but which also possess the military might that could be perceived as the means to assure their continued economic and po-

---

11. These projections assume oil will cost between $30 and $35 per barrel, a level which reflects price increases due to inflation as well as "abnormal" increases associated with the pressures on production a 14 million barrel-per-day American dependence would create. What they appear not to reflect, however, are the increases which may result from "abnormal" political developments, such as internal instability in oil-producing countries. The average price of oil traded internationally shot up from less than $14 dollars per barrel in January 1979 to nearly $30 per barrel a year later—a more than 100 percent increase in a single year. In part, this reflected scheduled OPEC price increases (Figure 6.3). But it also reflected the impact of supply shortages created by the Iranian oil cutback following its revolution in the spring of 1979.

litical survival. That U.S. foreign policy makers might contemplate the use of military force to guarantee American oil imports is suggested by the statements made by senior foreign policy officials at the time of 1973–1974 OPEC price squeeze.[12] Also indicative of this thinking is the Carter administration's emphasis on development of a rapid-deployment military force with skills peculiarly suited for intervention in the Persian Gulf area, presumably to counter any Soviet adventures in the region.

The reasons that such extreme actions are even considered are clear: no other issue in an interdependent world—not population, not food, not a score of others that might be mentioned—touches so directly on the primary raison d'être of the nation-state—national security. In the final analysis, the energy crisis of the winter of 1973–1974 was not a crisis because of the long lines of motorists behind often empty gasoline pumps. Nor were the price increases in gasoline and other petroleum products alone sufficient to produce a crisis atmosphere. Instead, the crisis was born of the stark realization that petroleum touched the very nerve center of the industrial nation. "The oil crisis in 1973–74," observes Mason Willrich (1975), "posed by far the most traumatic challenge to economic interdependence in the post-World War II period. [For it] . . . drove home the point that the lifeblood of their [oil-dependent] national economies was under foreign control."[13]

The point was reinforced again in 1979 in the wake of the Iranian revolution. Supply shortages occurred following production cutbacks by the new Iranian government, particularly in the United States, for which Iran had become a major supplier of oil. The announcement by OPEC at that time of another round of sharp increases in prices compounded the problem and contributed to further awareness of the new levels of dependency and vulnerability.

The Iranian situation was particularly troublesome for the United States. For several years prior to the Iranian revolution, the United States had pumped billions of dollars worth of sophisticated military equipment into Iran, apparently in part out of conviction that the government of Shah Muhammad Reza Pahlavi would use Iranian military might to protect the oil-rich Persian Gulf area from outside, namely Soviet, interference, thus assuring a continual flow

12. See Knorr (1976) for a critical evaluation of the limits of both military and economic power in the context of the energy situation.

13. One of the interesting sidelights of the need to recycle "petrodollars" is that many of these dollars have been reinvested in Western nations. In the United States this led to concern that American businesses and property were coming to be owned by foreigners, with the result that several American states passed or began considering laws designed to restrict foreign ownership.

of Persian Gulf oil to the West. Similar motivations were behind the massive American arms shipments sent to Saudi Arabia. The revolutionary government that came to power in Iran in 1979, however, was resolutely anti-American. Thus, with Iran removed from the ranks of pro-Western nations in the region, Saudi Arabia's position as a politically Western-oriented oil supplier gained added significance. The importance of Saudi Arabia is underscored by the fact that it is the largest producer in OPEC, accounting for the bulk of OPEC production and reserves. Stobaugh and Yergin observe (1979: 838): "Two facts summarize the world oil picture as it is: the Organization of Petroleum Exporting Countries dominates the international petroleum market; and Saudi Arabia dominates OPEC."

The issue of Saudi Arabian security became not simply one of assuring Saudi Arabia's ability to protect its vital oil fields, but also of averting a repeat of the internal political disruptions that Iran had experienced. But in response to the question of "How stable is the country on which the world has become so dependent?" the cautious observer has reason for concern. Stobaugh and Yergin described the situation in early 1979 thus:

> Too little is known about internal relations in Saudi Arabia to make any solid predictions. What is obvious, however, is that a pre-modern social structure, based upon kinship, has been catapulted into the modern age. No one, not even members of the royal family, can guess how successfully the present system will adjust to the new world—or for how long. No one who has assimilated the lessons of Iran can confidently assess what the corrosive effects of instant wealth will be, and how suddenly they will bubble to the surface. And Saudi Arabia is surrounded by rivals and enemies—Iran, not only unstable but with a rising influence of Shi'a [Shiite] Islam, antithetic to the Sunni Islam of Saudi Arabia; South Yemen, with a Marxist government aided by Cuban and Soviet military elements; Iraq, with a Soviet military presence. Thus, at the very least, the United States and the other Western countries are depending on a regime in a highly unstable environment to provide the leading part of their imported oil and to stabilize the world oil market.[14] (Stobaugh and Yergin, 1979: 839)

The continuing Arab-Israeli conflict is an additional complicating factor that cannot be ignored in assessments of these relationships. At the same time that the United States is a staunch supporter

14. The seizure of the Grand Mosque in Mecca in late 1979 by hundreds of militants led Stobaugh and Yergin to speculate that this

> may well prove in retrospect, to have been the single most important development relevant to energy in 1979. For it seemed to say—and this, no doubt, was an intention of its perpetrators—that the great stabilizer of the world oil market is itself not stable. That such a conspiracy could go undetected is deeply disturbing. (Stobaugh and Yergin, 1980: 577)

of Israel, Saudi Arabia is staunchly pro-Arab and has financed Arab efforts to establish a homeland for the Palestinian people on territory now occupied by Israel. The situation is further complicated by the political and military backing that the Soviet Union has accorded the more radical Arab states and the Palestine Liberation Organization. Thus oil, a symbol of the North-South conflict, has become intimately linked with the East-West conflict. And both overlay a potentially explosive regional conflict in one of the world's most politically volatile regions.

The geopolitical and geostrategic dimensions of the oil situation extend beyond the immediate boundaries of the Middle East. Assuring the supply of oil requires not only access at the wellhead but also secure supply routes to refiners and consumers.[15] The most important of these routes is from the Persian Gulf area to the Cape of Good Hope at the tip of Africa, and from there to Europe and North America.

The importance of this particular route has grown over time. In 1965 the bulk of crude oil going to Europe traveled through the Suez Canal. A decade later the canal was relatively unimportant as a sea lane because of its closing during the 1967 Arab-Israeli War (it was reopened in 1975) and because of the development of supertankers too large to pass through the canal. The African route is now far more important. These changes are shown in the maps in Figures 9.5 and 9.6, which illustrate the major oil sea lines of communication in the Southern seas as seen from a Southern perspective.

Another factor revealed in these maps is the dramatic shift in the character of the Western and Soviet military presences between 1965 and 1976. In 1965 Western nations had a military presence in the Persian Gulf area, the Arabian Peninsula, the Horn of Africa, southern Africa, and West Africa. The Soviet Union had virtually no presence in any of these areas. By the mid-1970s, however, the situation had virtually reversed itself, with Soviet facilities widely dispersed and Western facilities substantially contracted.

Gaining access to foreign territory for military purposes is something that can change rapidly in very short periods of time, particularly in the Third World, as both the United States and the Soviet Union have learned. Thus there is nothing immutable about these patterns of overseas military build-ups. Neither should we draw the inference that the Soviet Union is seeking to establish its influence along the oil sea lanes with a view toward interdicting them in order to exert political pressure on the West. Such a conclu-

15. It is interesting to note that at the beginning of 1980 Canada, the United States, and Western Europe accounted for more than half of the world's crude oil refining capacity. The Middle East, in contrast, accounted for less than 5 percent (U.S. Department of Energy, 1980a: 20–21).

Figure 9.5
The Southern Seas: Oil Sea Lines of Communication and Western and Soviet Military Facilities, 1965

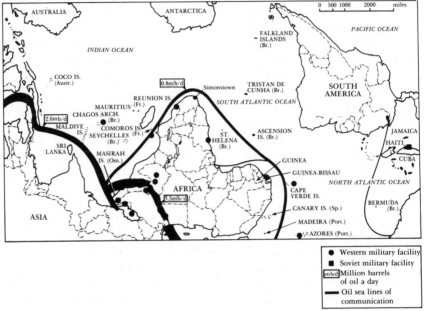

Source: Geoffrey Kemp, "The New Strategic Map," *Survival*, 19 (March/April, 1977), 51. Published by the International Institute for Strategic Studies, London.

Figure 9.6
The Southern Seas: Oil Sea Lines of Communication and Western and Soviet Military Facilities, 1976

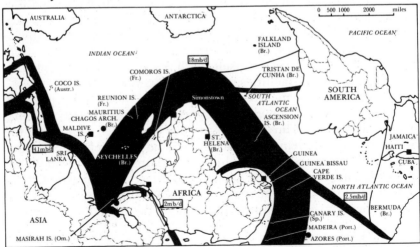

Source: Geoffrey Kemp, "The New Strategic Map," *Survival*, 19 (March/April, 1977), 51. Published by the International Institute for Strategic Studies, London.

sion may be tempting, but this scant evidence is by no means conclusive. Moreover, it is dangerous to infer intentions from opportunities or capabilities.

We can say with more certainty that the Soviet Union will likely play a more important role in the global energy picture of the future than it has in the past. Note from Table 9.2 that the largest producer of oil at the end of the 1970s was not Saudi Arabia or any other member of OPEC; it was the Soviet Union. The Soviet Union is also a net exporter of oil, despite the fact that its domestic consumption is high (see Table 9.1). Many of these exports go to communist countries in Eastern Europe, where they have played a part in the more general pattern of economic linkages among Comecon nations. Communist countries as a group have also exported about a million barrels of oil a day to Western nations.

Whether the Soviet Union will be able to retain its enviable status as an oil-exporting nation is questionable. In 1977 the Central Intelligence Agency (CIA) released a report predicting that Soviet productive capacity would peak in the early 1980s (at 11 to 12 million barrels a day) and then decline sharply. It also predicted that by 1985 the Soviet Union and Eastern Europe would be required to import "a minimum" of 3.5 million barrels a day, with import requirements perhaps going as high as 4.5 million barrels (Central Intelligence Agency, 1977: 13). Should these predictions prove correct (the Soviet government has refuted the CIA's projections[16]), the net effect would not only be a reduction of Soviet oil supplies to Eastern Europe and the West but also an inducement for the Soviet Union to compete for OPEC oil for its own use.

PATTERNS OF ENERGY PRODUCTION AND CONSUMPTION: THE FUTURE

Will OPEC produce more as worldwide dependence on its resources grows? How long will its resources last? What alternatives to fossil fuels exist now or might become feasible in the future? Each of these questions is intimately related to the world's energy future.

The Role of OPEC

The ability of OPEC to maintain the political cohesion necessary for effective management of the international oil market is by no means

16. The Soviet refutation stems from national pride and a reluctance to admit vulnerabilities, as well as expectations about the ability of the Soviets to extract and transport oil from known Siberian deposits at a rate greater than they had hitherto managed.

assured. Wide divergences in members' foreign-policy interests and objectives exist, particularly with respect to the question of Israel.[17] The members are also geographically dispersed with widely disparate sociocultural systems, vastly different population sizes and levels of income, and a kaleidoscope of internal and external problems and priorities. Moreover, by the 1980s OPEC had come to appear less a politically cohesive organization than a collection of states motivated simply by economic gain. OPEC's seeming inability to coordinate the price at which its members sell oil (other than the minimum charged) illustrates the point. By late 1979, for example, 25 percent of OPEC oil was sold at a price higher than the official contract prices (Stobaugh and Yergin, 1980: 576). The cartel has, nevertheless, endured for some time now, and in the process of enduring its members have learned valuable habits of collaboration and compromise. It seems reasonable to assume, therefore, that OPEC will remain a potent factor in the global energy future.

Certainly the resources of the OPEC members assure that they, individually if not collectively, will remain a dominant factor. In 1978 OPEC accounted for nearly half of the world's oil production. It also accounted at the beginning of the 1980s for more than two-thirds of proven world reserves of crude oil. Only three countries (Iran, Kuwait, and Saudi Arabia) accounted for over 45 percent of world reserves, and Saudi Arabia alone accounted for more than 25 percent (U.S. Department of Energy, 1980a: 20–21). This guarantees that Saudi Arabia will continue to play a pivotal role in the world oil picture into the foreseeable future. As Stobaugh and Yergin (1979) point out, "[Saudi Arabia] carries the brunt of adjustment within OPEC, at various times closing the valve to keep prices from falling, and opening the valve to keep prices from rising." The impact of such decisions extends far beyond pricing.[18]

But will OPEC produce more oil as worldwide dependence on its resources grows? At least two factors are important in assessing this question, one technical, the other political.

17. See Lenczowski (1976) for a discussion of the policies and priorities of various OPEC members in the context of the 1973–1974 oil crisis. The war that erupted in 1980 between Iran and Iraq, both feuding members of OPEC, is symptomatic of the often sharp differences among the cartel's members.

18. Saudi Arabia "opened the valve" in the summer of 1979 by increasing its oil production one million barrels a day to ease supply shortages caused by the Iranian production cutback. The move was widely interpreted as an inducement to the government in Washington to adopt a more pro-Arab posture in its efforts to secure a comprehensive Middle Eastern peace settlement.

The Nigerian government also brandished the "oil weapon" in 1979 when it nationalized British Petroleum. In explaining its action Nigeria accused the oil company of shipping British North Sea oil to the white minority regime in South Africa,

From a technical point of view, world demand for OPEC oil may simply outstrip the cartel's productive capacity. The CIA's 1977 study of the international energy outlook to 1985 projected this will happen by roughly 1983. Walter J. Levy, on the other hand, argues that OPEC's current productive capacity is sufficient to meet the demand for its oil likely to exist in 1985 (Levy, 1978–1979). This projection assumes, however, that non-OPEC oil-producing developing nations will significantly increase their production above current levels, and that communist nations will make no demands on OPEC's resources. Levy also points out that if assumptions about the growth in demand for oil prove incorrect, "a precarious balance indeed between energy demand and available supply" could develop.

Political decisions by OPEC nations may seriously affect the long-term balance between supply and demand.[19] Take, for example, the impact of rising prices. According to the laws of supply and demand, rising prices normally encourage production while discouraging consumption. But in the case of oil, rising prices may actually discourage production. "In countries with limited capital needs," as Lester Brown (1979) points out, "a higher price satisfies these needs with a lower volume of exports."

Brown points out that inflation also discourages production: "Uncertainty about the future value of money, particularly the dollar, provides a logical reason for oil-producing countries to keep as much of their wealth as possible in the form of oil underground." Erosion of the value of the dollar (associated with inflation in the American economy as well as other factors) is especially troublesome since the value of oil is stated in terms of dollars.[20] Even if OPEC members decided not to leave their resources underground,

---

but some observers suggested the real target was the British government, which at that time was considering lifting its economic sanctions against Zimbabwe (Rhodesia).

A third example is perhaps provided by the $2-per-barrel price hike announced by Saudi Arabia in May 1980. The increase came shortly after the American Public Broadcasting System showed a film entitled *Death of a Princess*, regarded by the Saudi regime as an unfair portrayal of Saudi society and Islamic law. Some news commentators therefore interpreted the price increase as a reprisal against the United States for its refusal to block public viewing of the film.

19. Thiel (1979) suggests that "political" limits reduce OPEC's production by 5 to 10 percent below technically feasible levels. He estimates OPEC's capacity will be 44 million barrels a day by 1985, a level that would be reduced by "political" considerations to the more likely range of 39.5–42 million barrels a day. For alternative projections of world demand for oil compared to OPEC's production capacity, see *The Global 2000 Report to the President* (1980b).

20. Devaluation of the U.S. dollar in the early and mid-1970's was one of the factors disrupting agreements on the price of oil reached by host producing states and the multinational oil companies.

upward spiraling prices for oil are necessary in an inflationary environment for OPEC members simply to stay even.

Another factor that may encourage production limits is disappointment with the progress and prospects of economic development plans that OPEC members have already experienced. Political turmoil aside, if a developing, oil-producing country is experiencing slow progress in building a non-oil-based economy, it may be preferable to prolong the period during which high oil revenues will be earned. The oil-rich nations have discovered there are limits to their "absorptive capacity," that is, to the ability of their economies to absorb new monies to be spent on industrialization and other forms of modernization. Hence the incentives for acquiring new capital through the sale of additional oil are reduced. In fact, the greatest incentive may be to leave oil underground so it can be extracted later—and at higher prices—to promote subsequent growth.

The situation is complicated by the fact that nothing may adequately replace the resources and riches oil producers now enjoy. Walter J. Levy underscores the problem:

> We must expect that sooner or later many producing countries will seriously question the value of much of their development program in terms of its potential contribution to their economic progress, political stability, employment, budgetary receipts, and foreign exchange income. Many of them will painfully realize that their industrial efforts could not possibly begin to replace the government and foreign exchange revenues that they have become accustomed to receiving from their oil production, nor provide them with a prosperous non-oil based economy. (Levy, 1978–1979: 294)

More poignant, perhaps, is the observation that "the odds at this time are that when the oil revenues begin to peter out, a number of the OPEC countries will find themselves not too much better off than before—like Spain, after it had been inundated by gold and silver from its Latin American empire in the late sixteenth and early seventeenth centuries" (Levy, 1978–1979: 294).

All of these factors suggest that oil exporters may decide to reduce production as current rates of extraction begin to exceed discoveries of new reserves. This is what Lester Brown calls a "depletion psychology."

> Countries will be forced to reckon with the day when their oil reserves are exhausted. The problem this poses for the exporters is far greater than merely substituting new energy sources for petroleum. They will also have to adjust to the loss of a major source of revenue. At some point, the urge to postpone the day when the wells go dry could be-

come compelling. This fear of using up the last of an irreplaceable resource is a subtle factor, not easily measured, but just as the changing
market psychology led to a dramatic oil price increase in late 1973, so
the emergence of a depletion psychology could markedly reduce oil
production. (Brown, 1979: 21)

Psychological responses to these circumstances aside, the oil
producers might well conclude that a reduction in production is
economically rational, according to classic principles of capitalism.

Fossil Fuel Reserves

Oil today accounts for nearly half of the world's commercial energy
production (see Figure 9.3). Coal and natural gas account for 30 percent and 19 percent respectively, with nuclear power and hydropower making up the rest (Sivard, 1979a: 7). Of these commercial energy sources, hydropower is the only one that depends on renewable
resources. Fossil fuels are not renewable. Once they are spent, they
are gone forever. This fact underlies the possibility of an OPEC "depletion psychology" as well as the more ominous specter that the
world's nonrenewable energy resources may soon be consumed.

Estimates of the world's reserves of fossil fuels are imprecise
and often vary considerably from one source to the next. Yet all
agree that coal is vastly more abundant than either oil or gas. In the
United States, for example, where domestic energy resources have
always been abundant, conservative estimates now indicate that the
amount of crude oil available will run out before 1990[21] and gas reserves will be depleted shortly thereafter. The reserves of coal, however, would last for over six centuries. (A useful discussion of global
energy resources can be found in the Ford Foundation-sponsored
study *Energy: The Next Twenty Years*, Landsberg et al., 1979; see
also *The Global 2000 Report to the President*, 1980a and 1980b.)

Similar disparities characterize the worldwide distribution of
proven and estimated reserves of coal, oil, and natural gas. As depicted in Figure 9.7, the amount of coal that is ultimately available
is probably more than 10,000 billion metric tons, while estimated
reserves of oil and gas are less than 40 percent of this amount (Sivard, 1979a: 8). (Figure 9.7 depicts only *estimated* energy resources,
not precise amounts.) This also means that the resources currently
in shortest supply are the ones being depleted most rapidly. The
comparative production data in Figure 9.7 show that the amount of
coal used is only a fraction of available resources. By contrast, "in

21. Oil depletion began when the first drop was extracted from the earth. This is
a reminder that many of the resources of the ecosphere are finite and nonrenewable.

the 1950–1977 period, production of natural gas was equivalent to one-third of the world's existing reserves, while production of oil was close to one-half of what are now judged to be the remaining reserves of this fuel" (Sivard, 1979a: 8).

How long will available reserves of oil and gas last? Simple arithmetic suggests the answer—not long. In the case of oil, for example, the U.S. Department of Energy (1980a) estimates that in 1978 average daily production of oil was roughly 60 million barrels while proven world reserves of crude oil stood at 641.6 billion barrels. Assuming current production is consumed (not stockpiled), this means that at current rates, proven reserves of oil will be complete-

Figure 9.7
Estimated World Resources, Reserves, and Past Production of Fossil Fuels (billion metric tons of coal equivalent)

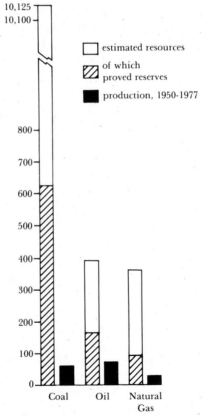

Source: Ruth Leger Sivard, *World Energy Survey* (Leesburg, Va.: World Priorities, 1979), p. 8. Copyright © World Priorities, Leesburg, Va. 22075, U.S.A.

ly used up in little more than 10,000 days—or shortly after the turn of the century.[22]

Any number of factors might interrupt this timetable, including the discovery of new reserves, developments in alternative energy technologies, and variations in the rate of conservation and consumption. Following the quadrupling of oil prices by the OPEC cartel in 1973–1974, for example, the world entered a recession, which had the effect of dampening the demand for oil. The ratio of energy consumption to growth in the production of goods and services in industrial societies–the so-called energy coefficient—also proved to be substantially smaller following 1974 than previously.[23] Supply shortages were relieved as earlier discoveries of oil in Alaska and the North Sea were put into production, and new finds of apparently massive proportions in Mexico have become known. At the same time, however, public concern about nuclear power has dramatically altered projections about the role this energy source might play in meeting future needs.

All of these factors illustrate the difficulties associated with projections about our energy future. Nevertheless, virtually every available estimate of future energy requirements projects that demand, particularly for oil, will be more in the future—not less—than it is now.

In the noncommunist world, for example, oil consumption has been projected to increase from 51 million barrels a day in 1977 to 62 million barrels a day in 1985 (Levy, 1978–1979: 288; see also Arad et al., 1979, and *The Global 2000 Report to the President*, 1980a and 1980b). This is a conservative estimate that assumes full utilization of all non-oil-based energy resources. It is also based on the assumption that oil consumption will increase only 2.5 percent a year, compared with much higher rates of growth prior to the 1973–1974 oil

---

22. *World Oil* (August 15, 1979: 64) estimates natural gas reserves at 2,369 trillion cubic feet. Unfortunately, it provides no daily production from which projections of the ultimate availability of gas might be calculated. However, as indicated later, estimates of proven and ultimately recoverable reserves of natural gas indicate gas in the United States will remain a viable energy source for at least half a century. Even more optimistically, the World Energy Conference held in Istanbul in 1977 predicted that the amount of ultimately recoverable reserves were sufficient, at current consumption rates, to last the world almost another century (Barnet, 1980a: 53). See also Levy (1978–1979) for a more detailed discussion of various projections of world oil reserves and when they might be consumed.

23. Energy use generally tends to be highest in earlier stages of industrial development and to decline as the economy becomes more service oriented and as more efficient forms of energy, such as electricity, are consumed. The decline in the energy coefficient also suggests a more efficient use of energy, perhaps reflecting the impact of conservation efforts.

price hikes. This latter projection is based not only on a lower energy coefficient in the 1977 to 1985 period compared with earlier years, but also on the assumption that economic growth will proceed at a much slower pace than historical post-World War II rates. (Levy, 1978–1979: 280, assumes an energy coefficient of 0.81 between 1977 and 1985 compared with 1.13 between 1965 and 1973. He also assumes an economic growth rate of 3.6 percent annually from 1977 to 1985. This figure contrasts with the 4.7 percent rate achieved from 1965 to 1973 [Levy, 1978–1979: 289].)

The importance of specifying these assumptions is to point out that if any one of them should prove to be wrong—if economic growth proceeds more rapidly, or if energy should be used less efficiently—the pressures of demand for oil on existing supplies would be great. At the very least, there still would be upward pressures on the price of oil, with adverse economic consequences.

> In cruder but all-too-plausible terms, consuming nations would be bidding against each other not only in terms of price, but also in terms of political actions. Some would have to accept a severe reduction in the supply of oil that would be available at prices they could afford to pay. All would suffer individually, and the strain on the cohesion of key Western allied nations could be very grave indeed, not to mention the friction between rich and poor countries. (Levy, 1978–1979: 289–290)

Alternative Energy Sources

If world population grows to 6 billion or more people by the year 2000, and if world oil production tapers off to, say, an annual growth rate of one percent as a consequence of such factors as inflation, rising oil prices, and the perceived need to stretch dwindling reserves, the per capita availability of oil will be sharply lower in two decades than it is now.[24] These projections are charted in Figure

24. John W. Sewell of the Overseas Development Council points out that few projections of future energy demand explicitly consider the impact that alternative development patterns in less developed nations will have on the world oil economy. Most assume that "people living in rural areas of developing countries will not switch from traditional energy sources to petroleum at rates faster than those that have occurred historically." Sewell questions this assumption on two grounds:

> First, the vast majority of people in the developing countries are still using noncommercial sources of energy for most of their activities; that is, they rely on wood, dung, crop residues, and human and animal power for almost all the energy they consume. Any satisfactory degree of development, however, requires a sharp increase in the developing countries' use of inanimate sources of energy. Second, population pressure is reducing the per capita availability of noncommercial sources of energy through deforestation and soil erosion. As a result of these two factors, there will be increased demand for all types of energy—particularly oil—by the developing countries. (Sewell, 1979: 67)

9.8, which suggests that the post-World War II era can be divided into three relatively distinct periods in terms of per capita oil production: "from 1950 to 1973, when oil production per person climbed rapidly, reaching a new high every year; from 1973 to 1978, when it was static; and from 1978 to 2000, when it will be declining, perhaps by as much as one third" (Brown, 1979).

The accuracy of this projection of future oil supplies is less important than the overall message it conveys: the era of abundant (and inexpensive) oil is gone. The consequences for the future may be profound. The unprecedented economic growth of the world economy prior to 1973 was associated with unparalleled increases in oil production, while the period of essentially static oil output from 1973 to 1978 was associated with severe stresses on the international economic order. "If the transition in oil production per person from rapid growth to stagnation contributed to the economic stresses of recent years, what will a further transition to declining oil production per person lead to?" (Brown, 1979).

Declining oil supplies will not lead to declining energy supplies if economically and politically viable energy alternatives are found and utilized. In addition to increased reliance on coal and natural gas, greater use of nuclear and hydropower could ease the transition to a non-oil-based energy system. Oil derived from unconventional sources such as tar sands and shale could also become economically viable, and renewable forms of energy might also become feasible, such as solar, tidal, and wind power, geothermal energy, and bioconversion.

Figure 9.8
World Oil Production per Capita, 1950–1978, with Projections to 2000

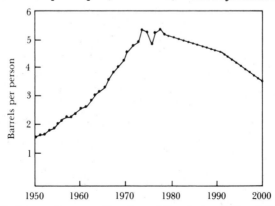

Source: Lester R. Brown, *Resource Trends and Population Policy: A Time for Reassessment* (Washington, D.C.: Worldwatch Institute, 1979), p. 24.

In the short term (five to ten years), however, neither unconventional nor renewable energy sources are likely to play a major role.[25] Coal, natural gas, and nuclear power are therefore likely to figure prominently as alternatives to oil. But each is beset with a range of economic, technical, and political uncertainties.

Coal. The world's most abundant energy resource is coal (see Figure 9.7). But the feasibility of greatly expanding its use as an alternative to oil is circumscribed by the environmental hazards it poses.

> These [hazards] go further than the health risks and degradation of the land associated with coal mining. Coal burning pours sulphur dioxide pollutants into the air which have a pervasive long-term effect on vegetation, fish and animal life, people, and even structures. Coal also shares with oil and gas the problems associated with carbon dioxide (CO_2) build-up. The burning of fossil fuels is believed largely responsible for a 10 percent increase in CO_2 in the atmosphere in the past century.
>
> The global consequences of CO_2 are not fully understood but there is concern that its accumulation in the atmosphere, as use of fossil fuels continues to grow without adequate environmental controls, may have a "greenhouse effect," causing irreversible and dangerous changes in the world climate. Severe climatic damage could turn fertile lands into deserts, or melt the polar ice cap, raising the global sea level 15 to 25 feet. (Sivard, 1979a: 19)

Such social costs or "externalities" associated with a more widespread use of coal are difficult to measure, but they lay the basis for sustained political opposition to this energy source.

Natural Gas. Natural gas is cleaner and more convenient to use than either oil or coal, and estimates of proven and ultimately recoverable reserves indicate it is a viable source of increased energy at least for the next half century (Sivard, 1979a). Unlike coal, however, "on a regional basis potential production [of natural gas] is very unevenly distributed as compared with demand, and the global development of the potential for rapid growth in consumption is dependent on export trade. Storage and transportation present problems which have not yet been resolved" (Sivard, 1979a).

25. Stobaugh and Yergin (1979) are more optimistic about the potential role of solar power, at least in the United States. They and Sivard (1979a) provide useful discussions of the technical, economic, and political factors associated with alternative energy strategies. A somewhat more technical discussion can be found in Ehrlich, Ehrlich, and Holdren (1977).

The largest market for natural gas is in the United States, where in the mid-1970s nearly half of all the amount used worldwide was consumed (Willrich, 1975: 40). However, development of new natural gas reserves in the United States has not kept pace with consumption, and reserves of gas, which dropped 10 percent in the decade following 1967, were estimated in 1978 to be able to sustain only ten years of consumption (based on the 1978 rate of 20 trillion cubic feet, the equivalent of nine million barrels a day of oil) (Stobaugh and Yergin, 1979: 847). *World Oil* (August 15, 1979: 64) puts the United States proportion of proven reserves of gas (in 1978) at only 8.5 percent of the world total. Historically the United States has met virtually all of its need for gas from domestic sources. Clearly this seems likely to change, with the United States becoming dependent on foreign sources for yet another essential energy need.

The Soviet Union is the world's second largest consumer of natural gas. It is also an important producer but, unlike the United States, it has vast reserves of the resource—over a third of proven world reserves (*World Oil*, August 15, 1979: 64). The Middle East and North Africa also have important reserves of gas. That they are not presently being used efficiently is made evident by the fact that much of the gas associated with the production of oil is simply flared. In Saudi Arabia alone, the amount being flared was at one time the equivalent of one-sixth to one quarter of U.S. consumption (Willrich, 1975: 41).

The problem is getting gas from the wellhead to consumers. Assuming environmental constraints can be overcome, pipelines are the preferred method of transport. But they are expensive and massive engineering projects, such as the projected 4,800-mile system linking Alaska to the continental United States or the projected 2,500-mile pipeline from the Soviet Union to West Germany. Liquefied natural gas is an alternative, perhaps the only one for transhipment from the Middle East to North America or the growing Western European and Japanese markets.

More than $30 billion has already been invested in liquefied natural gas projects (Sivard, 1979a: 21), and the United States already imports a modest amount of liquefied natural gas from Algeria. Serious disagreements exist among experts as to the safety of liquefied natural gas, however. As Sivard (1979a) points out, because liquefaction of gas permits a 1/600th reduction of its volume, "[a] tank of [liquefied natural gas] contains 600 times as much energy as the same size tank of natural gas. If it should spill, it would vaporize and become highly inflammable and explosive. In a densely populated area, such an accident could result in catastrophe." Concern for safety has combined with cost considerations and sensitivity to de-

pendence on OPEC sources to constrain development of new liquefied natural gas projects, at least in the United States (Stobaugh and
Yergin, 1979).

Nuclear Energy. Among known technologies, nuclear energy is seen
by many as the leading alternative to dependence on fossil fuels. Already nuclear power accounts for one percent of worldwide energy
usage and six percent of its electrical requirements (Sivard, 1979a:
21). Some project that by the year 2020 nuclear power could account
for a third of the world's energy needs. This assumes, however, that
conditions will be favorable to its continued development. At present, at least, they are not.

The accident at the Three Mile Island nuclear power plant in
Pennsylvania in 1979 sent shock waves throughout the nuclear industry and the world. Skeptics who had questioned the safety of
nuclear energy seemed to be vindicated. Catastrophe was averted,
but even without the threatened meltdown of the reactor core, the
accident resulted in a larger release of radioactive contamination
than ever previously experienced by the American commercial nuclear industry.

The consequences of Three Mile Island are likely to include a
slowdown in the deployment of nuclear power. In the aftermath of
the Pennsylvania accident, Sweden, Italy, and Switzerland announced a reassessment of their nuclear programs, and opponents
of nuclear power in such widely dispersed countries as France,
West Germany, Taiwan, and Brazil had their political hand
strengthened (Dunn, 1979). The Three Mile Island incident will thus
likely further restrict what had already become a slowdown in the
deployment of civilian nuclear energy facilities; even before the accident, the total nuclear power capacity in the world by the year
2000 had been estimated at only 1,000 gigawatts (1 gigawatt = 1 billion watts), less than half the amount projected only a few years
earlier (Dunn, 1979: 75).

Another possibility growing out of the Three Mile Island accident is that safety standards will be augmented, thus adding to already sharply rising costs of producing energy from nuclear power.
The question of whether it is less expensive to generate electricity
from coal or nuclear power has become a major point of controversy in the United States, the world's technological leader in nuclear power; yet calculating the costs of either coal or nuclear
power, particularly when externalities are considered, is virtually
impossible (Stobaugh and Yergin, 1979). In any event, cost is another factor that has led to sharply lower estimates of the role that
nuclear power will play in the future.

Among the other controversies affecting the potential of nuclear power is the issue of waste disposal. Spent fuel from nuclear-generating facilities must be removed periodically. It is then "cooled" in water to remove some of the most intense radioactivity before being reprocessed, a procedure that removes still useful uranium and plutonium from other waste materials.

No safe procedure for handling nuclear waste—some of which remains dangerous for hundreds of thousands of years—has yet been devised. In the meantime, large quantities of nuclear waste have been building up, much of it as a result of weapons production. In the case of nuclear-generating facilities in the United States, spent fuels have been piling up in specially designed storage facilities, many of which will be filled by 1985 (Stobaugh and Yergin, 1979). The problem is compounded by the lack of reprocessing facilities. Stobaugh and Yergin explain:

> In the 1960s and early 1970s, government and industry planners assumed that the spent fuel would be reprocessed, to recover still-usable fissionable material from useless and dangerous waste materials, as soon as enough reactors were in operation to support the large-scale facilities for economical reprocessing. Both the government and the nuclear industry postponed important technical decisions about the treatment and disposal of the waste materials pending the start of large-scale reprocessing. (Stobaugh and Yergin, 1979: 854)

But in response to the fear that nuclear know-how would proliferate to countries that did not possess such capabilities, both the Ford and Carter administrations placed a moratorium on development of reprocessing facilities and on the so-called breeder reactor, a reactor that generates fuel faster than it consumes it in its own chain reaction. The Carter administration subsequently called for international agreement "to defer all commercial reprocessing of spent fuel, to renounce the recycling of plutonium as fuel, and to slow commercialization of the fast breeder reactor . . ." (Dunn, 1979). Although these goals have not been fully achieved, some progress in developing international standards among nuclear suppliers to prevent proliferation has been realized (for details, see Dunn, 1979; Brenner, 1979; and Nye, 1979). The range of energy security and proliferation problems associated with nuclear decision making was addressed in a multilateral forum known as the International Nuclear Fuel Cycle Evaluation (INFCE). Launched by President Carter in 1977, the two-year study was undertaken by several international agencies and sixty-six states.

The nuclear proliferation issue is essentially one of national security: nuclear-generating facilities produce weapons-grade material, specifically highly enriched uranium and plutonium. Neither of these materials, which can be used to create a nuclear explosive device, is used commercially as fuel in the current generation of nuclear power reactors.[26] Yet at current and projected rates of production the amount of such material created will eventually make available enough weapons-grade material to place within reach the construction of tens of thousands of nuclear bombs every year, not only by additional nations but also by terrorist groups. Preventing the spread of nuclear weapons is therefore intimately tied to the development of safeguards in the commercial nuclear industry.

Analysts do not fully agree on how readily weapons-grade materials produced by commercial generating facilities can actually be converted into bombs (compare the views in Wohlstetter, 1976–1977, and Betts, 1977). However, the drive of many nations to acquire a nuclear capability for essentially political or perhaps even national security purposes vastly complicates the question of how to maximize the use of nuclear power in an oil-dependent world while simultaneously minimizing its threat to human survival.

An argument can also be made that merely possessing the capability to explode a nuclear device is not equivalent to possessing a militarily meaningful nuclear force. Joseph S. Nye, Jr., a Harvard political scientist who chaired President Carter's interagency committee on nonproliferation from 1977 to 1979, makes the point:

> [T]here are many steps after a first nuclear test. A single crude explosive device does not bring entry into a militarily meaningful nuclear club. (Indeed, that cliché should be avoided.) While the rate of proliferation refers to the politically symbolic event of a first explosion, the degree of proliferation refers to the size, military quality, and deliverability of a country's nuclear arsenal. The difference between a single crude device and a modern nuclear arsenal is as stark as the difference between having one small apple and having an orchard. In short, nonproliferation does not end with the next bang. (Nye, 1979: 104)

The complexity of the question is further compounded by the apparent vulnerability of nuclear facilities to attacks by terrorists or saboteurs. Such attacks might be carried out for essentially polit-

---

26. Commercial generating facilities generally use natural uranium, in which the fissile isotope U-235 occurs in low concentrations (less than 1 percent), or slightly enriched uranium (3 to 4 percent). Nuclear weapons, by way of contrast, require highly enriched uranium, which, at present, can be produced by only a few states.

Plutonium is a man-made element produced as a byproduct of uranium-burning reactors. If separated from spent fuel by chemical reprocessing, it can be used to produce additional electrical generating capacity. However, only about ten kilograms of plutonium are needed to make a nuclear weapon (U.S. Arms Control and Disarmament Agency, 1979a: 23).

ical purposes. (Dunn, 1979, reports, for example, that "in April 1979 the core of a French research reactor to be fueled with weapon grade uranium and scheduled to be shipped to Iraq was sabotaged— allegedly by Israel.") Yet the radioactive contamination that might result could threaten far more than the intended political targets.

The proliferation issue also runs directly counter to the interests of many developing nations, for whom nuclear power remains an attractive and viable mechanism for rapidly increasing their energy production as they aspire to realize their economic development objectives. Developing nations have in fact rarely shown concern for the issue of reactor safety, apparently because the risks do not outweigh what are seen as the considerable advantages of sharply increased energy production (Cooper, 1978). Developing nations will therefore continue to press existing nuclear power for reactors and the fuel to keep them going. According to one estimate, made before the Three Mile Island incident, twenty of the thirty-four countries expected to have nuclear plants in operation or under construction by 1985 will be in the Third World (Cooper, 1978: 127). Moreover, because the nuclear export business is potentially very lucrative, nuclear suppliers can be expected to take advantage of foreign sales—if only to help earn the foreign exchange necessary to offset the rising costs of imported oil.

Symbolic of these many forces was the $8 billion nuclear deal concluded between West Germany and Brazil in 1975 (for details, see Gall, 1976). Among other things, the German-Brazilian package signaled that the United States no longer had a monopoly over civilian nuclear technology, and it demonstrated that other nuclear suppliers (France as well as West Germany) may be willing to provide all elements of the nuclear fuel cycle, including enrichment and reprocessing facilities (Falk, 1978).[27] Determining precisely what these developments portend for the security aspects of nuclear technology questions is difficult.[28] They do suggest, however, that while the nuclear industry may now be crippled, it remains very much alive. The linkage between the growth of civilian nuclear power and the proliferation of nuclear weapons is nearly impossible to sever, the INFCE report concluded. But the final report also rejected the Carter administration's call for a moratorium on commercial re-

27. In June 1977, however, West Germany suspended the export of reprocessing plants (Nye, 1979). Guidelines were also drawn up subsequent to 1975 to ensure that commercial competition among nuclear suppliers does not undermine nonproliferation safeguards.

28. See Kegley, Raymond, and Skinner (1980) for a cross-national empirical study suggesting the close linkage between the transnational commerce in uranium fuels, the diffusion of nuclear energy technology, and the enhanced probability of nuclear weapons dispersion.

processing of nuclear fuel; rejected, therefore, was the view that denying the latest nuclear technology to consumer nations was the best way to prevent nuclear weapons dispersion. The validity of that proposition can now only be tested by time.

This brief perusal of short-term alternatives to energy derived from oil is perhaps more disheartening than encouraging. Among other things it demonstrates that the energy issue is in fact a complex interplay of technical, economic, environmental, and national and international political issues. Finding a solution to the energy problem therefore requires a frontal attack on a multitude of well-entrenched forces, not the least of which is the standard of living to which much of the developed world has become accustomed or to which others aspire. Mustering the political will to make the frontal attack may prove the most formidable task. Yet the need is clear. As Denis Hayes states in his book on the transition to a postpetroleum world, "Most energy policy is still framed as though it were addressing a problem that our grandchildren will inherit. But the energy crisis is *our* crisis. Oil and natural gas are our principal means of bridging today and tomorrow, and we are burning our bridges" (Hayes, 1977).

IS OIL PECULIAR?

Just as oil and gas are bridges between today and tomorrow, OPEC is the link between an essential source of commercial energy and its ultimate destination. The cartel's success in manipulating the global oil system stems from the fact that oil is in high demand but is unevenly distributed throughout the world. Are there other commodities with these same characteristics? Are other OPECs therefore possible? Might they, too, become vehicles used by developing nations to enhance their economic and ultimately their political bargaining strength in dealing with the North?

The data displayed in Table 9.3 seem to support the proposition that Third World nations already hold substantial commodity power. Note, for example, that in the 1975–1977 period, developing (market economy) countries accounted for 97 percent of the world's exports of cocoa, 96 percent of its exports of rubber, and 83 percent of its exports of tin. Yet none of these commodities has effectively come under monopoly control the same way oil has—despite the fact that producers' associations have been formed in many of these commodity markets.[29] Apparently something other than, or in addition to, controlling world exports or instituting cooperative arrangements accounts for the rise of powerful cartels.

In one of the several studies sponsored by the Council on Foreign Relations as part of its 1980s project, Ruth W. Arad and Uzi B. Arad (1979) argue that three sets of conditions are necessary for translating control over the supply of a natural resource into effective political power: *scarcity* ("the global, physical availability of the raw material in question, relative to other natural resources as well as possible substitutes"); *distribution* ("the political and economic character of the market for the specific raw material, its existence in reserve form among the consuming nations, and its pattern of consumption"); and *essentiality* ("the intrinsic importance of the raw material . . . either in security or in economic terms"). After surveying the applicability of these prerequisites for a range of nonrenewable natural resources, the Arads conclude that "only one resource appears to meet all three criteria: petroleum."

"Effective political power" in the Arads' study means the use of resource power for realizing political returns, not simply economic or commerical benefits. The use of such resource power was exemplified in 1973–1974 when the Arab members of OPEC used production controls and a selective embargo against the United States and the Netherlands in an effort to change these two countries' pro-Israeli policies. The Arads' conclusion suggests that few if any other resources are likely to be used in a similar way.

A variety of studies have been made of the possibilities of other resource markets becoming cartelized; most agree that oil is unique.[30] A peculiar combination of economic and political conditions seems to support effective cartelization of international commodity markets. Insight into these conditions is gained by a brief comparison of the petroleum market and OPEC's experience with other commodity markets. In doing so it is important to distinguish between nonrenewable resources, such as oil and nonfuel minerals,

29. Historical examples of producers' associations or producer-consumer agreements include the International Council of Copper Exporting Countries (CIEP), the Union of Banana Exporting Countries (UPEB), the International Bauxite Association (IBA), the Cocoa Producers Alliance (COPAL), the International Tin Agreement (ITA), the International Sugar Agreement (ISA), the International Coffee Agreement, the International Cocoa Agreement, and the International Wheat Council.

30. Among them are Arad and Arad (1979), Krasner (1974), Pirages (1978), Smart (1976), Spero (1977), Stern and Tims (1976), and Varon and Takeuchi (1974). Other studies relevant to this topic are Choucri (1972), Connelly and Perlman (1975), Schneider (1976), Winberg (1979), and Wu (1973).

Table 9.3
Major Primary Commodity Exports of Developing Market Economies, 1978 and 1975–1977 Average ($ millions and percentages)

Major Exports*	Developing market economy exports, 1978 ($ millions)	Developing market economy exports, 1975–1977 average ($ millions)	(as percentage of world exports of commodity†)	Major Suppliers, 1975–1977, with percentage of world exports supplied by each	
Petroleum	136,823‡	122,360	90	Saudi Arabia, 24% Iraq, 7%	Iran, 15% Nigeria, 6%
Coffee	10,179	7,637	92	Brazil, 21% Ivory Coast, 7%	Colombia, 13% El Salvador, 5%
Sugar	5,128	4,067	47	Brazil, 7% Dominican Republic, 4%	Philippines, 6% India, 4%
Copper	3,695‡	3,427	57	Chile, 19% Zaire, 10%	Zambia, 14% Peru, 4%
Timber	3,254‡	2,796	25	Malaysia, 7% Ivory Coast, 3%	Indonesia, 7% Philippines, 2%
Cotton	2,813	2,346	46	Egypt, 9% Syria, 3%	Sudan, 6% Mexico, 3%
Iron Ore	2,071‡	2,179	40	Brazil, 17% India, 5%	Liberia, 6% Venezuela, 4%
Rubber	2,544‡	2,143	96	Malaysia, 52% Thailand, 11%	Indonesia, 22% Sri Lanka, 5%
Cocoa	3,483	1,954	97	Ghana, 26% Ivory Coast, 15%	Nigeria, 19% Brazil, 14%

Tin	1,560‡	1,251	83	Malaysia, 40% Thailand, 11%	Bolivia, 15% Indonesia, 11%
Rice	1,320	1,177	42	Thailand, 16% Burma, 4%	Pakistan, 9% Egypt, 2%
Phosphate Rock	940‡	1,137	63	Morocco, 34% Togo, 4%	Kiribati,§ 7% Senegal, 4%
Tea	1,303	1,014	79	India, 26% Kenya, 8%	Sri Lanka, 25% Indonesia, 6%
Tobacco	1,403	913	32	Brazil, 6% India, 4%	Zimbabwe, 5% South Korea, 3%
Maize	876	893	13	Argentina, 7% Brazil, 2%	Thailand, 3%

Source: John W. Sewell and the Staff of the Overseas Development Council, *The United States and World Development: Agenda 1980* (New York: Praeger, 1980), pp. 188–189. Based on data from the Food and Agriculture Organization and the World Bank.

*Ranked by average value of exports in 1975–1977 period.
†World exports of commodities (on which these percentages are based) include the Soviet Union and Eastern European countries.
‡1977 figure.
§Includes Nauru, Christmas Is., and Ocean Is.

Notes: Exports are f.o.b. (free on board) values.
Unless otherwise indicated, the data do not include the exports of the Asian centrally planned economies, Cuba, Hong Kong, or Singapore.
The fifteen major primary commodities listed above constituted 67 per cent of total developing-market-economy exports in the 1975–1977 period.
The fifteen major developing-market-economy exporters in the 1975–1977 period were Saudi Arabia, Iran, Brazil, Nigeria, Kuwait, Venezuela, Iraq, Indonesia, Libya, South Korea, Taiwan, Malaysia, India, Algeria, and Argentina.

and renewable resources, such as agricultural products, particularly foodstuffs. This distinction is useful since the prospects for effective producers' cartels are likely to be much greater for nonrenewable than for renewable resources.

Economic Factors

The two fundamental market conditions necessary for effective monopoly power are (1) a lack of responsiveness to prices by consumers; and (2) a lack of responsiveness in the supply of a commodity growing out of increases in its price. These two conditions are known technically as price inelasticity of demand and supply.

Price Inelasticity. If the *demand* for a commodity is price-inelastic, this means the amount consumed will change little even if its price increases substantially. Price inelasticity of demand is essential to a producer's cartel whose goal is to maximize the amount of foreign exchange it earns from its product. If demand is price-elastic, the total amount of money earned by producers will be less at the new, higher price than at the old, lower price due to reduced consumption. But if demand is price-inelastic, total revenues will be greater at the higher prices.

Price inelasticity of *supply* operates in much the same way. If supplies are price-inelastic, this means that new producers will not (or cannot) enter the market to take advantage of the higher rates of return associated with higher prices. If new producers do enter the market, which means supply is price-elastic, the increased supply would likely drive prices back down, making the foreign exchange earned no greater and perhaps even less than before prices were increased. Even if prices do not go back to previous levels, the reduced market share individual producers would control would reduce their monetary receipts. Clearly, then, price inelasticity of supply is also essential to effective producers' cartels.

There is little question that in the case of oil both demand and supply conditions favored OPEC's success. The important role that oil had come to occupy in the world energy picture was reflected in the near absence of any change in global demand following the fourfold increase in the price of oil in the winter of 1973–1974 (Smart, 1976). On the supply side, the long lead time required to develop new petroleum sources (demonstrated by the time required to bring the Alaskan and North Sea finds into production) combined with the absence of energy alternatives (including domestically produced oil) to preclude movement away from dependence on OPEC oil. Furthermore, petroleum is relatively difficult to stockpile in massive amounts, thereby undercutting the availability of another potential tool that might have been used by consumers to ride out short-term supply shortages caused by OPEC production controls.

Do similar conditions apply to other basic commodities, particularly nonfuel minerals? At least in the short run, the answer appears to be yes. With respect to price elasticity, for example, it appears

> that only the producers of natural rubber, citrus fruits, bananas, natural fibers, and possibly tin, confront market conditions that would make export controls self-defeating. The demand for other raw materials is not very responsive to price. Like oil exporters, most other producers face a demand structure that would make it possible for them to increase their foreign exchange earnings if they could effectively cooperate. (Krasner, 1974: 73)

Even in the "medium term," supplies of most commodities are price-inelastic, at least to the point that collusion among producers would not be detrimental to them.

> Large investments and lead times of several years are needed to bring new supplies of most minerals to the market. Crops can be grown efficiently only in certain climatic and soil conditions, and some, such as coffee, require four to five years before new plantings bear fruit. The benefits of collusion in other raw materials, as well as in petroleum, would not immediately be dispelled by new output. (Krasner, 1974: 74)

From a longer-term perspective, however, the possibilities of reaping benefits from higher commodity prices are considerably more problematic. Bension Varon and Kenji Takeuchi (1974), writing in the immediate aftermath of OPEC's fourfold price increases in 1973–1974, attempted to determine the transferability of that experience to nine other major minerals[31] traded internationally. They found that demand is considerably more price-elastic for other minerals than for oil. This would therefore undermine the benefits accruing to producers from cooperative actions designed to increase their revenues.

> Calculations based on historic experience for tin, aluminum and copper, for example, suggest strongly that in the long run the drop in demand more than offsets any price increase, so that the total return to

31. Iron ore, bauxite, copper, manganese ore, lead, nickel, phosphate rock, zinc, and tin. In the early 1970s these nine minerals accounted for 85 percent of the estimated value of all nonfuel mineral production in the world (Varon and Takeuchi, 1974: 498).

the producers eventually becomes less than before the price change. Although the econometric measurement of price elasticities is a tricky process leading to differing estimates of individual cases, there is little disagreement on the broad point about short-term and long-term price elasticity. (Varon and Takeuchi, 1974: 505–506)

Three factors not operative in the short run but potentially available in the long run explain these differences, with implications for supply as well as demand: stockpiles, recycling, and substitutes.

Stockpiles. Oil is not easily stockpiled. Many other commodities are, particularly nonfuel minerals. The United States, for example, has maintained since 1939 large "strategic stockpiles" of certain minerals. Such inventories are designed, in principle, to give the United States a cushion against the actions of foreign producers. Furthermore, the way these stockpiles are managed can affect world prices, as they have historically in the case of tin and, somewhat less so, manganese and zinc (Varon and Takeuchi, 1974).

Recycling. This is another long-term possibility. Recovering metal from scrap material is already feasible in many minerals industries. Augmenting existing recycling capacity may take time, and the resultant product may well be more expensive. But the important point is that in many cases minerals are not completely used up when they are consumed. Oil is.

Substitution. This is a third long-term possibility for undercutting nonfuel producers' cartels. If aluminum becomes too expensive for making cans, tin can be substituted. If tin becomes too expensive, glass or plastic might be used. To be sure, even oil has its substitutes. Coal, hydropower, and nuclear energy are already available alternatives for generating electricity. Certain forms of alcohol can be used to fuel cars, and even synthetic lubricants can be produced. "But oil nevertheless enjoys extraordinary advantages in relation to other minerals because it performs so many functions better than any substitute can at a remotely comparable price. None of the metals can claim this high resistance to rational substitution over such a range of functions" (Smart, 1976). At least in the long run, then, market conditions for the nonfuel minerals are considerably more favorable to consumers than in the case of oil. Varon and Takeuchi conclude, "In short, the infrastructure for weathering a crisis at manageable cost within tolerable time is more sophisticated in this sector [metals] than in the oil sector" (Varon and Takeuchi, 1974).

To political elites in developing countries, however, the long run may not be relevant. Since one of their principal political goals is staying in power, the important fact is likely to be that market forces in the short run for fuel and nonfuel commodities will be similar. Understanding OPEC's peculiar success therefore requires an examination of political as well as economic factors.

The Intersection of Politics and Economics in Commodity Markets

An unequal distribution of world production and consumption of basic commodities is intimately related to the prospects of successful producers' cartels. There is nothing particularly political about this characteristic, but the implications stemming from it are.

By the 1970s Western Europe and Japan were already highly dependent on foreign sources of oil, and the United States became so increasingly as it moved toward the 1980s. As U.S. import dependence grew, the importance of OPEC oil increased, not just to the United States and those already dependent on foreign suppliers, but to the world as a whole.

Do analogous levels of dependence on foreign sources apply to other commodity markets? Again, the answer appears to be yes. The United States, for example, imports over half of its consumption of such basic minerals as manganese, cobalt, bauxite and alumina, chromium, tin, nickel, potassium, gold, zinc, and mercury (*Mining and Minerals Policy, 1979*, 1979: 54–55). And the United States is not unique in this respect. As shown in Table 9.4, other First World countries are even more dependent on foreign sources of certain industrial raw materials than is the United States.[32]

This does not necessarily mean that the First World is dependent on the Third World for the minerals it imports, however. Canada is a principal source on which the United States relies for many of its mineral imports. Similarly, other developed nations are often important sources of mineral products that enter world trade. Australia (together with Jamaica) is an important producer of bauxite and alumina; South Africa is an important source of manganese, chromium, platinum, and gold; the Soviet Union is an important producer of these same four minerals. In fact, the major exporters of most minerals in the world today generally include developed as well as developing countries. An examination of the distribution of world mineral reserves indicates this situation is unlikely to change

---

32. Pirages (1978) notes that dependency statistics such as those displayed in Table 9.4 should be used cautiously since, for a number of reasons, they can be misinterpreted. One reason is that the data often change sharply from one year to the next. The data in Table 9.4 indicate the United States was a net exporter of copper in 1975, but the U.S. Department of the Interior reported in 1979 (*Mining and Minerals Policy, 1979*, 1979: 55) that the United States imported 19 percent of the copper it consumed in 1978. See also *The Global 2000 Report to the President* (1980b) for global supply and demand projections for nonfuel minerals.

Table 9.4
Dependence of Non-communist Industrialized Nations on Selected Imported Industrial Raw Material, 1975 (imports as a percent of consumption)

	United States	European Community	Japan
Aluminum (ore and metal)	84	75	100
Chromium	91	98	98
Cobalt	98	98	98
Copper	*	98	90
Iron (ore and metal)	29	55	99
Lead	11	85	73
Manganese	98	99	88
Natural rubber	100	100	100
Nickel	72	100	100
Phosphates	*	100	100
Tin	84	93	97
Tungsten	55	100	100
Zinc	61	70	53

Source: *International Economic Report of the President, 1977* (Washington, D.C.: Government Printing Office, 1977), p. 187.

*Net exporter.

in the future[33] (Arad and Arad, 1979). Effective producers' cartels are much less likely to emerge when the principal producers share widely divergent levels of development.[34] Producers' associations consisting of such politically antagonistic states as South Africa and the Soviet Union are even more unlikely.

The Arads (1979: 43) conclude that on the basis of developing nations' shares of world trade only three commodity markets (other than petroleum) could currently be said to be under the control of Third World countries—tin, bauxite, and, to a lesser degree, copper. In each case the number of producers involved is relatively small. This parallels OPEC's experience. But none of these markets enjoys the same degree of financial power that OPEC nations had amassed by the time they experimented in converting resource power into political power.

33. In the long run, deep-sea mining may prove an important source of minerals, thus further undermining the ability of developing nations to control the flow of minerals in the world marketplace. Especially important are the potato-sized concentrations of minerals known as manganese nodules. These nodules contain a wide variety of metallic components. Copper, nickel, cobalt, and manganese are the ores of principal commercial interest.

34. Bauxite may prove to be an exception. See Spero (1977) for an account of efforts to create a bauxite producers' association. Spero also includes case studies of similar efforts in the copper and banana markets.

The massive amounts of foreign exchange that OPEC nations held by the early 1970s were important to the cartel's success since that foreign exchange minimized the economic risks that individual nations faced. Short-term economic losses incurred as a result of production controls could be endured in an effort to secure long-term gains. The fact that Saudi Arabia and Kuwait were willing to exercise a leadership role by bearing the brunt of production reductions also contributed to the ability of all producers to maintain the new, higher oil prices (Spero, 1977).

Similar conditions do not characterize the developing nations that are producers of tin (Malaysia, Indonesia, Bolivia, and Thailand), bauxite (Jamaica, Guyana, and Surinam), and copper (Zambia, Chile, Peru, and Zaire). None enjoys a level of international reserves sufficient to permit short-term economic losses in hopes of realizing long-term gains.[35] Moreover, many have large populations and are currently engaged in expensive development projects whose financing is heavily dependent on the foreign exchange that tin, bauxite, or copper earn. In short, many of the same developing nations on which the North depend for mineral supplies are themselves export-dependent (Arad and Arad, 1979). This seriously undermines their ability to translate resource power into political power without running the risk of doing substantial economic (and hence potentially political) damage to themselves. Oil is peculiar in this respect, since it is the only commodity on which the North is disproportionately dependent that developing nations "enjoy [to] a tremendous advantage due to their significantly lower degree of export-dependence" (Arad and Arad, 1979).

Furthermore, it is important to recall that oil is more resistent to substitution by other products than most nonfuel minerals. Perhaps no other mineral is as essential to security and economic well-being in the long run as oil. In the short run, however, severe dislocations might occur if the supply of various resources to consumers is cut off. Iron ore, copper, and aluminum stand out as more essential or critical than most materials other than oil (Arad and Arad, 1979). Of these, only copper and aluminum (bauxite) are traded internationally by developing nations in large volumes. The implication, then, is that most nonfuel minerals traded internationally do not enjoy the same degree of essentiality as oil, even in the short run.

35. For comparative purposes, it is interesting to note that in December 1977 Saudi Arabia had over $30 billion in international reserves. Of the eleven producers of tin, bauxite, and copper listed here, Malaysia was the country with the largest reserves, but they amounted to less than 10 percent of the Saudi Arabian level. For most producers the level of reserves was only a fraction of that enjoyed by Saudi Arabia (McLaughlin, 1979a: 156–165).

But the most important factor distinguishing the OPEC nations (particularly the most important ones, the Arabs) from the other commodity-producing developing nations is one that is overtly political—the sense of shared values that transformed OPEC from simply another commodity-producer's association into an effective and cohesive political force. The shared value was antipathy toward Israel combined with a common desire among the most important members of OPEC to use the oil weapon to affect the outcome of the long-standing and bitter Middle East conflict. In this respect it is important to recall that OPEC's political moves of 1973–1974 (as opposed to its economic actions), namely, the production controls and selective embargo, were initiated by members of the Organization of Arab Petroleum Exporting Countries. This does not suggest, however, that even the Arab members of OPEC are completely united in their outlook; nor is it meant to suggest that OPEC as a whole can remain united (the move away from price ceilings toward price floors reflects the lack of unity). Nevertheless, no other producers' association currently operating and none on the horizon is likely to be galvanized into political action by political impulses comparable to those that once mobilized the Arab members of OPEC. This is the key factor underlying oil's peculiarity.

Another political factor related to OPEC's success should also be mentioned: the compliance of the major oil companies with OPEC's action. Consumers, through their governments, offered no particular resistance to OPEC. This does not distinguish oil from other situations (Krasner, 1974); but the fact that the major oil companies offered no resistance does. In other commodity markets, including cocoa, coffee, and bananas, for example, the multinational corporations involved had offered various types of resistance to host government efforts to control the markets (Krasner, 1974; Spero, 1977). "In dealing with the oil companies, OPEC's members hit mush and, following Lenin's dictum, pushed on. The benefits petroleum-exporting states have derived from their association with multinational corporations surpasses those bestowed on any other group of Third World exporters. Tacit assistance from multinational corporations . . . distinguishes the oil market from that of other raw materials" (Krasner, 1974).

Oil is peculiar. Its peculiarity derives fundamentally from the presence of political forces underlying OPEC's success that seem unlikely to be found in other commodity markets either now or in the foreseeable future. But even if the political factors were present, the underlying economic realities of most commodity markets severely limit the possibility that other Third World nations will be able to emulate OPEC's success in translating resource power into political power.

Bushels vs. Barrels: Food as a Political Counter to Petroleum

In grappling with the question of whether OPEC's success might be repeated by other developing states with other commodities, we have purposefully concentrated attention on nonagricultural commodities. The reason for making this distinction is quite simple but very important: "mineral reserves not extracted today remain, in principle, to be extracted in the future, but crops not harvested, or harvested and destroyed, are lost, with all of their value, forever" (Smart, 1976). In short, agricultural investments will be lost unless production is maintained. This fundamental fact alone seems to distinguish international commodity markets in renewable and nonrenewable resources.[36]

Despite this general obstacle to effective cartelization of agricultural commodity markets, the suggestion is frequently made that world food producers—specifically grain producers, especially those in the North, whose products comprise a significant share of international trade in foodstuffs—control the production and price of their products so as to counteract the monopoly power of the OPEC cartel. In other words, bushels of grain could be traded by the North for barrels of oil. Is this feasible? Can the North use agricultural cartels to retaliate against certain developing countries?

At first glance the answer appears to be yes; agricultural products could be effectively used by developed nations as a weapon against OPEC. Unlike other agricultural commodities, investments in grain can be preserved even if current production is not marketed, because grains can be stored. Furthermore, the world trade in grain is controlled by a few major producers: today the only significant grain exporters in the world are the United States, Canada, Australia, New Zealand, and Argentina. Of these, the United States and Canada are clearly the most important, accounting for between a half and two-thirds of total world grain trade in recent years. These facts appear to undermine the heterogeneity characteristic of other commodity-producing countries. Because the world's grain producers already share important political characteristics, some of the political obstacles to effective producer cooperation inherent among other commodity producers do not seem relevant.[37]

36. Smart (1976) also points out that "in the case of most renewable resources . . . the possibilities of rapid substitution are so considerable, and the general price elasticities of demand and alternative supply so large, that effective cartelization by producers, except as a limited response to falling prices, is implausible."

37. It is also interesting to note that world grain trade is controlled by a relatively small number of multinational firms. The behavior of the multinational oil companies during the 1973–1974 crisis makes it uncertain whether this is a blessing or a curse. But in principle, at least, the fact that a small number of firms are largely re-

Obviously there are some complications, however. If it were so easy to trade bushels for barrels, the United States would long ago have coupled its advantages in agricultural production with its otherwise enormous political, economic, and military strength to "force" OPEC into submission.

To understand why the United States has not done what otherwise seems so obvious and easy, we need only note some of the other characteristics of the world trade in grain. Recall in particular that most consumers of North American grain are other developed-market economies, with the Second World an important consumer from time to time. If the United States and Canada manipulated world grain prices to a level comparable to one bushel equals one barrel, the consequences would extend far beyond the intended victims.[38] Among the victims would be the North American consumer. Whether political elites in the United States and Canada would be either willing or able to withstand the domestic political consequences of such action is doubtful.

Other unintended victims of artificially high grain prices would include those developing nations whose people already suffer the simultaneous consequences of malnutrition and ineffective demand for food due to inadequate purchasing power. Also important to note is that many of these same countries already suffer from the extraordinarily sharp oil price rises the world has experienced in the past decade. But if world food prices were to increase in an effort to counteract OPEC's prices, OPEC would probably increase the price of oil in return. For OPEC not only has the ability to pay for whatever food it wants at whatever price grain producers might find politically palatable given the other considerations we have noted (the World Bank estimates that OPEC's cash surplus may reach $120 billion in 1980 alone); OPEC also has the ability to retaliate with discriminatory countermeasures of its own.

Finally, in considering the effects of any increases in world grain prices, we should note that among those affected would be the developing countries identified as the New Industrial Countries (NIC)—those who have shown some capability to move beyond the persistent absence of economic development so characteristic of the Third World as a whole. Many of these countries have provided rap-

---

sponsible for the world grain trade should make it easier to use food to promote political objectives. See Dan Morgan's *Merchants of Grain* (1979) for an account of the operations of five of the world's principal grain firms—Cargill, Continental, Louis Dreyfus, Bunge, and André.

38. This assumes, of course, that others would still buy grain at such inflated prices. Robert S. Bergland, President Carter's secretary of agriculture, once wryly commented, "There's not much market for wheat costing $18 a bushel."

idly expanding markets for American agricultural products.[39] This growth reflects the sensitivity of world food demand to rising incomes. Since this growth at least suggests the possibility that the world's poor may become better off, would it be either wise or ethical to increase prices beyond their reach?[40]

All of these factors add up to a characterization of the bushels for barrels argument as a "dirty bomb." It would hurt far more than its intended victims. It would hurt the world's poorest countries, and in particular the poorest people within them. It would hurt consumers in producing countries themselves. It would hurt the citizens in those countries the United States and Canada have counted among their most important political and military allies since World War II. It might hurt the domestic agribusiness in the major producing countries by curtailing sales to some developing countries who are increasingly able to pay for food imports. It conceivably could curtail even further sales to the Second World. Should this happen, the prospects for renewed efforts to relax tensions between traditionally antagonistic political and military rivals might fall victim to the dirty bomb (for reasons other than the overtly political ones that motivated the Carter administration to curtail grain exports to the Soviet Union following the Soviet intervention in Afghanistan).

Dirty or not, would the bomb "get" OPEC? Unlikely. That OPEC has the resources to buy whatever food it wants at almost any price has already been noted. Across-the-board price hikes in food are therefore unlikely to work. And if they will not work, it is certain that price hikes targeted solely at OPEC would be ineffective. If OPEC were selected for discriminatory treatment, only a small diversion of food destined for other consumers would be necessary to undercut the discriminatory pricing system. There is little doubt that others would be willing to make such diversions for purposes of realizing other gains. "Even OPEC countries have concluded that discrimination among customers in oil sales is difficult and probably ultimately ineffective because of this problem of diversion" (Cooper, 1979).

The inapplicability of selective food-price increases is especially apparent if we compare OPEC's food dependence with the rest of

39. In the 1978–1979 crop year, nonoil-producing developing nations had a net import of 42 million tons of grain, a 50 percent increase over their purchases from abroad as little as two years earlier (*New York Times*, July 4, 1979).

40. It is important to emphasize, however, that merely increasing exports to developing nations does not ensure that the poorest income groups in those societies are reaping any benefit. Note also that increased imports by these nations imply that they are unable to meet domestic demand for food out of domestic production. The result once more is to increase pressures on the North American breadbasket.

the world's dependence on OPEC's oil. "Whereas industrialized countries import 85 percent of OPEC oil and the United States alone imports 17 percent, OPEC countries all together import only 14 percent of world trade in wheat" (Cooper, 1979: 2). Under such circumstances the probability that someone would divert foodstuffs to OPEC nations is high.

There is another important technical difference—perhaps the most important one—between the international oil and food markets. World oil exports make up 60 percent of total oil production. By contrast, the corresponding ratio for wheat is only 16 percent (Cooper, 1979: 3). This means there is considerably more latitude in the world for increasing the amount of foodstuffs that enter the international marketplace than there is in the case of oil. Although most countries in the world are net importers of food, they nevertheless produce much additional food at home. They may be willing to divert some of that production to export in a contrived food market so as to realize the available economic or political benefits. Moreover, there is considerably greater flexibility for increasing world food production than world oil production, particularly if the price is right (high). Under such circumstances, OPEC would have no difficulty getting all the food it wanted. Thus, as an American undersecretary of state concluded, "our dominance in world wheat exports gives us virtually no leverage over OPEC, even if we thought it would do some good" (Cooper, 1979).

RESOURCE POWER AND THE FUTURE

As developing nations continue to press for some kind of basic restructuring of the existing international economic order, and as the North finds it expedient to accommodate at least some of those demands, it is possible that governments will successfully exert greater control over international economic matters. Because economic issues are usually closely tied to political matters, the possibility must be entertained that resource power will increasingly be used as a vehicle for realizing political objectives.

In this connection it is relevant to emphasize that the control Northern nations already exercise over so many facets of international politics and economics underlies the desire of the Third World to use whatever it has at its disposal in order to improve its bargaining leverage and relative position with the North. This same control also means, of course, that the North already has considerable leverage over the South, and the North has shown itself adept at using its advantages for political purposes. Considerations of political influence as well as resource power thus remain central to an understanding of global politics. Nevertheless, uncertainty and an anticipation of the unexpected also seem to have become necessary elements in understanding how the world political system is being transformed from today's future into tomorrow's present.

Part IV

THE INTERPLAY OF
ARMS AND VIOLENCE

Ten

The Quest for National Security: Trends in Military Capabilities

> In the name of national security, all things can be threatened. All risks can be taken. All sacrifices can be demanded. . . . Those who decide on national-security policy do not appear to recognize the radical changes that have taken place . . . throughout the world over the last few decades.
>
> Richard J. Barnet, 1979

> Ours is a new era, one which calls for a new kind of courage. For the first time in the history of mankind, one generation literally has the power to destroy the past, the present, and the future; the power to bring time to an end.
>
> Hubert H. Humphrey, 1963

All nations seem to want many of the same things—security, the preservation of cherished national traditions and distinct ways of life, sovereign freedom, status, and wealth. The dilemma for world politics is that these values often can be gained only at the expense of other nations.

This simple formula for looking at the global system finds expression most clearly in the relative military might of nations. All nations are not equal. Some have more than others—more strength, more wealth, more respect and status. And they seek to preserve that position, just as others struggle to overturn it, for all countries cherish national advantage; none willingly accepts subordination.

PURCHASING MILITARY POWER: TRENDS IN MILITARY SPENDING

A good indicator of people's values, we are sometimes told, is how they spend their money. If governments are no exception to this rule, then how governments allocate their revenues reveals something about their value priorities and the threats to those values. Examination of the national budgets of governments reveals an unmistakable pattern: all countries value security and search for it through outlays of national revenues for arms. They spend money to obtain security because of the conviction that the acquisition of weapons will make them safe.

Not only is the commitment to purchase military protection nearly universal; in many countries it also is growing dramatically, as more and more nations spend substantial and often increasing proportions of their income for arms and armies. Globally, the aggregate outlays of revenues for weapons since the midpoint of this century have exceeded $4 trillion ($4,000,000,000,000!) and continue to rise at a current annual rate (1977) of nearly $434 billion (U.S. Arms Control and Disarmament Agency, 1979b: 1). Another way of stating this fact is to note that the world spends over a million dollars a minute on arms. Moreover, the amount of money spent annually on arms and armies has risen almost constantly, with only intermittent periods of modest reductions. Even when stated in constant prices these facts persist, for military spending has increased at a rate *faster* than the rise in prices[1] (Sivard, 1977a, 1977b, 1979b).

Social and Economic Effects of Military Spending

The money devoted to military spending affects in significant ways how the earth's more than 4 billion people live. The revenue spent on military hardware and personnel is revenue that cannot be spent to meet the fundamental human needs of a starving, illiterate, and disease-ridden planet. Military preparedness commands relatively more resources than other problems requiring resources for their solution. Sivard (1977a, 1977b, 1979b) summarizes comparative indicators by noting:

- The world's military budget equals the annual income of 1.8 billion people in the thirty-six poorest nations.
- Through public budgets, the world community carries more insurance against deliberate military attack than against illness, disease, and all natural disasters. The world's arms budget is nearly double the world's expenditure on public health care.
- The world's budget for military research is more than four times the size of its budget for energy research.
- World military expenditures per year average $12,330 per soldier; public expenditures for education average $219 per school-age child.

1. The $4,200 billion that has been spent on military programs since 1960 would be valued at $6,600 billion in 1979 prices (Sivard, 1979b: 6).

- The developed nations spend 20 times more for their military programs than for economic assistance to the poorer countries.
- In two days the world spends on arms the equivalent of a year's budget for the United Nations and its specialized agencies.
- Three hours of military spending in the world equal a year's expenditures for international peacekeeping forces.
- In pounds per person, the world has more explosive power than food.

These comparisons suggest that most countries are more concerned with protecting their citizens from foreign attack through arms expenditures than they are with enhancing their citizens' welfare through social, educational, and health expenditures. Because increasing proportions of national incomes are devoted to war and defense against war, the level of resources available to cope with social problems is necessarily diminished. While it cannot be assumed safely that money not spent for defense *would* be spent for present and future human needs, the possibility that global military spending contributes to global poverty, and to the violence which such poverty can breed, is worth considering. Global military spending cannot be said to directly *cause* a decline in the standard of living of the earth's population, but military spending and world poverty appear to be intimately linked.

These inferences are corroborated at the national level—high rates of military spending appear to entail social and economic costs. Comparatively speaking, nations which spend the most on arms do not do as well as others in providing for their people. Consider how the United States and Soviet Union, first in military spending, ranked (in 1977) among all nations across various social indicators—in infant mortality, 17th (United States) and 34th (Soviet Union); in teacher per school-age population, 12th and 23rd; in physicians per population, 21st and 1st; in population per hospital bed, 31st and 7th; and, in life expectancy, 7th and 29th (Sivard, 1979b: 28–29). These rankings lead to the conclusion that "When the rate of military spending is high, social well-being lags. . . . The ten biggest military spenders make a relatively poor showing in social indicators" (Sivard, 1977a). The rankings suggest that when *security* is defined in the broadest sense of the term—security in the expectation that one will live a full life—then security is *not* being purchased by the acquisition of arms. The hypothesis that a trade-off exists between military spending and social welfare was articulated by President Jimmy Carter, who said that "When you spend money for defense, you don't spend it on education or health or other services or goods. And I think the shift away from weapons toward peaceful goods and services in the long run is favorable for world peace, and also you get more jobs per dollar spent. . . ."

Figure 10.1 shows that the rich nations, particularly the United States and the Soviet Union, spend by far the most for military preparedness. Throughout nearly the entire 1963–1977 period, these two superpowers have accounted for two of every three dollars spent for arms in the world. Next in order are China, West Germany, Britain, and France, which account for approximately another 15 percent of the world's total. Hence, the top six spenders account for four-fifths of all military expenditures in the world.

Although historically the rich nations have been the most prone to allocate their budgets to the acquisition of arms, with military expenditures usually rising in periods of peace as well as war, the desire to arm is becoming increasingly widespread. In fact, one of the major ways in which the global arena is being transformed is in the extent to which poorer nations have been mimicking the budgetary

Figure 10.1
World Military Expenditures, 1968–1977 (billions of constant 1976 dollars)

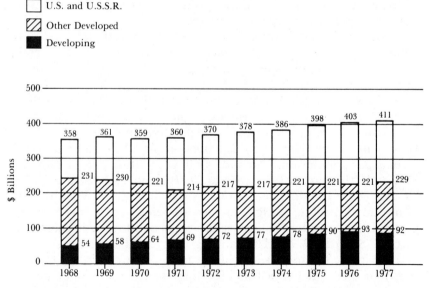

Source: U.S. Arms Control and Disarmament Agency, *World Military Expenditures and Arms Transfers 1968–1977* (Washington, D.C.: Government Printing Office, 1979), pp. 1, 61, 65.

Note: World military expenditures in 1977, which in constant dollars amounted to $411.3 billion, were $433.9 billion in current dollars.

habits of the rich nations by allocating increasing proportions of their limited national treasuries for the weapons of war.[2] But between 1967 and 1975 developing nations accounted for an increasing share of total, world military expenditures, growing from 15 to 23 percent. This increasing proportion suggests that those who can least afford weapons have been most prone to make the greatest sacrifice to obtain them.

Measuring Military Spending

The sum of money spent is one basic indicator of military expenditures. Another, perhaps more meaningful index, is the *relative burden* that military spending represents. Typically, this is calculated as the proportion of the gross national product accounted for by military spending. In 1977 total world military expenditures accounted for 5.7 percent of the sum of the world's GNPs (U.S. Arms Control and Disarmament Agency, 1979b: 4). This entails an appreciable decline from 1968 levels, which stood at 7.2 percent. The pattern shows military expenditures as a percent of all GNPs declining steadily from 1968 to 1973, rising briefly from 1974 to 1975, and then continuing downward since 1976 (U.S. Arms Control and Disarmament Agency, 1979b: 4).

Global trends in the relative burden of military spending are largely the result of changes in the developed countries. To gain insight into national differences, it is useful to compare the variations in the military burden among different states. Table 10.1 displays this pattern by grouping the nations of the world by share of GNP devoted to military expenditures on the vertical axis and by GNP per capita on the horizontal axis. The data again show that the most burdened militarily are the least developed economically. Collectively, these figures point to a relative increase in the developing countries' burden in comparison to developed countries: "The military share of GNP in developing countries in 1977 surpassed that in developed countries, reversing their relative positions a decade before. In 1977 the military share of GNP was 5.6 percent for developed countries and 5.9 percent for developing countries; 7.4 percent and 6.1 percent were the respective figures in 1968" (U.S. Arms Control and Disarmament Agency, 1979b: 4).

2. The growth of developing countries' military expenditures slowed in 1976, however, and, "In 1977, for the first time in the decade, constant dollar military expenditures of developing countries as a whole declined slightly (1 percent)" (U.S. Arms Control and Disarmament Agency, 1979b: 2). This decline was offset by increases in developed countries, where military spending rose 2.9 percent in 1977.

Table 10.1
Relative Burden of Military Expenditures, 1977

Military expenditures as % of GNP	GNP per capita				
	Less than $200	$200–499	$500–999	$1000–3000	More than $3000
More than 10%		Egypt	North Korea Syria	Oman Israel Iraq Iran Bulgaria	United Arab Emirates Saudi Arabia Soviet Union
5–10%	Somalia Cape Verde Pakistan	China Yemen Mauritania Congo	Jordan Peru South Korea	Taiwan Poland Singapore Hungary Turkey South Africa Romania	Kuwait East Germany Czechoslovakia United States
2–4.99%	Chad Tanzania Ethiopia Mali Burma India Mozambique Upper Volta Afghanistan Burundi	Rhodesia Sudan Indonesia Thailand Uganda Philippines Zambia Madagascar Kenya Togo	Morocco Malaysia Nigeria Guyana Bolivia	Yugoslavia Greece Portugal Algeria Uruguay Argentina	United Kingdom Bahrain France Netherlands West Germany Sweden Belgium Norway Spain Italy Australia Denmark Switzerland Canada

1–1.99%	Malawi Zaire Rwanda Bangladesh Nepal Sierra Leone	Cent. Afr. Rep. Honduras Senegal Papua New Guinea Cameroon Benin Haiti	Nicaragua Ecuador Tunisia Dom. Rep. Ivory Coast Paraguay El Salvador	Venezuela Cyprus Ireland Brazil	New Zealand Finland Libya Austria Luxembourg
Less than 1%	Niger Sri Lanka Gambia	Liberia Ghana Botswana	Guatemala Colombia Swaziland Mauritius	Jamaica Mexico Panama Malta Fiji Trinidad & Tobago Barbados Costa Rica Surinam	Japan Gabon Iceland

Source: U.S. Arms Control and Disarmament Agency, *World Military Expenditures and Arms Transfers 1968–1977* (Washington, D.C.: Government Printing Office, 1979), p. 4.

Note: Within each cell, countries are ranked according to military expenditures as percent of GNP.

ACQUIRING MILITARY POWER: TRENDS IN MILITARY CAPABILITIES

Global trends in military spending have generated changes in the kind of international environment in which the nations of the world reside. Each nation's pervasive fear of others, combined with its spending for national security, has led to a world populated by nations possessing more and more weapons of ever more destructiveness.

Modern Weapons Technology

The technology associated with modern weapons has radically transformed the nature of warfare. In World War II, the largest "blockbuster" bombs were believed to deliver a power of 10 tons of TNT; the atomic bomb that the United States dropped on Hiroshima in the waning days of World War II had the power of over 12,000 tons of TNT; today the Soviet Union possesses a nuclear bomb with the explosive force of 57 megatons of TNT (57 million tons). It is obvious that the use of such weapons in large numbers would threaten the destruction, not only of entire cities and countries, but possibly, when radiation effects are considered, of the entire population of the globe (see U.S. Office of Technology Assessment, 1979). The possibility of total destruction which today's weapons pose to civilization was vividly captured by Albert Einstein's famous remark that he did not know what the weapons of a third world war would be, but that in a fourth world war they would be "sticks and stones."

That more bucks lead to the purchase of more bombs with more bang is an unmistakable trend. That the increasing explosive force that dollars have purchased has rendered our age an age of overkill is a cliché substantiated by the facts. The current nuclear arsenals of the two superpowers, the United States and the Soviet Union, make the lethal characteristics of the present strategic atmosphere clear. The warheads on one U.S. Trident-type submarine are capable of destroying 167 cities in the Soviet Union; a single U.S. bomber can deliver a force level equal to 10,000,000 tons of TNT, which is almost twice the tonnage delivered by all participants in World War II. The combined nuclear inventories of the two superpowers, with explosive power equivalent to 1,300,000 Hiroshima-sized bombs, are able to destroy every city on earth seven times over. Moreover, refinements in military technology enable the superpowers to deliver these weapons within a few hundred feet of targets as far away as 9,000 miles in a matter of minutes.

The world, in short, has been transformed by the changes in military capabilities that military spending has purchased. Today's weapons are increasingly destructive, deadly, and accurate. As Figure 10.2 demonstrates, the first generation of bombs (like the single device that reduced Hiroshima to rubble) had a destructive area of three square miles, and the delivery systems available then limited the destruction to a single target. The U.S. MX missile, if deployed, would be capable of destroying an area seventy-eight times as extensive, and devastate ten targets at once. (The reason for this is because missile systems may be "MIRVed"—in which case each multiple, independently targetable vehicle carried by a ballistic missile can be directed to a separate target.) Moreover, the explosive power of contemporary nuclear weapons is incomparably more lethal than the one which killed roughly 100,000 people at Hiroshima. (Approximately the same number subsequently perished from radiation poisoning, burns, and other injuries.) As *Washington Post* correspondent Richard Harwood notes,

> Our young pilots today . . . could fly over Leningrad some morning and with a single bomb, exploded at 3,000 feet, kill perhaps 900,000 people and seriously injure another 1,225,000. It would create winds of a velocity of 470 miles an hour—far greater than any hurricane. These winds would hurl people through the air at high speeds smashing them into buildings. Air pressures from the explosion would strike houses with the force of 180 tons. All that from one bomb. It would have a yield of 1 million tons of TNT.[3] (Harwood, 1979: 1)

The systems for delivering these weapons have become more diversified; they include, not only airplanes, but submarines that launch missiles from beneath the ocean's surface and land-based missiles. And technological improvements enable adversaries to target their weapons with increasingly pinpoint precision.[4]

3. Estimates of the number of people who would perish in the event of a nuclear clash vary (see chapter eleven, especially Figure 11.2). The U.S. Arms Control and Disarmament Agency calculates that attacks limited to military and industrial targets would produce immediate U.S. fatalities from 105 to 130 million and Soviet fatalities of 80 to 95 million (*The Defense Monitor*, February 1979: 2).

4. Improvements in the accuracy of intercontinental missiles led Sivard to observe that as the United States and Soviet Union

> approach the bull's eye, making the ICBM itself increasingly vulnerable to destruction, the competition has begun to move to a new phase in the nuclear race: mobile basing designed to make the ICBMs harder to find in a nuclear war. An attacker will have to use many more missiles to destroy them. In event of war, the area in which they are hidden will become a desolate moon-scape, a huge radioactive sponge. (Sivard, 1979b: 12)

Figure 10.2
Number of Targets that Can Be Attacked and Area that Can Be Destroyed by Different U.S. Strategic Weapon Systems

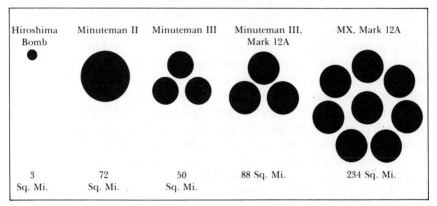

Source: *The Defense Monitor* (September–October, 1978), p. 3.

To these changes in the global environment must be added the fact that the nuclear arsenals of the superpowers continue to grow. When World War II came to an end, there was but one atomic bomb that had been produced still in existence. By 1979 the United States had stockpiled 9,200 *strategic* nuclear weapons (weapons designed for use against an adversary's homeland) and the Soviet Union had 5,000. In addition, the two superpowers possess tens of thousands of *tactical* nuclear weapons whose combined explosive power alone has been estimated at roughly 50,000 times the amount of explosive power unleashed on Hiroshima in August 1945[5] (Stockholm International Peace Research Institute, 1976). (Tactical nuclear weapons are generally smaller in size and yield than strategic weapons and are designed for direct support of combat operations.) The present rate of growth in nuclear weaponry is an average of three additional bombs a day.[6]

The fact that these arsenals are backed up by a diverse set of different types of conventional and bacteriological weapons demonstrates that the increased militarization of the world continues unabated at many levels. We should not underestimate the sophistication and deadliness of these nonnuclear weapons. Among them

5. The exact number of tactical nuclear weapons remains a closely guarded secret. *The Defense Monitor* (February 1979) estimates that "the United States has as many as 30,000 nuclear weapons (including about 20,000 tactical weapons) and the Soviet Union has about 20,000 nuclear weapons."

6. These estimates are discussed in the following sources: Sivard (1976, 1977a, 1977b); TRB (1978); Finlay and Hovet (1975); and The Disarm Education Fund (1978).

are "supersonic bombers that travel 1,100 miles per hour at cruising altitude, chemical fireballs of near-nuclear strength, cluster bombs containing 600 bomblets each, ultra-rapid fire guns, smart bombs guided by TV and laser beams, and fully maneuverable, unmanned aircraft controlled from the ground" (Sivard, 1976: 11). These weapons consume over four-fifths of the world's military budgets. "Although the term overkill is usually not applied to these weapons . . . their potential for indiscriminate destruction of civilian populations" suggests that "the destructive capabilities of conventional and nuclear weapons now overlap" (Sivard, 1977b).

The Proliferation Problem

The quest for weapons of almost unimaginable destructive capability has not been confined to the two superpowers. The balance of terror has been exacerbated by the decision of others to develop nuclear weapons of their own, decisions which have produced the so-called proliferation problem. *Proliferation* refers to the probability that more and more nations will seek to become members of the "nuclear club."[7] The assumption is that the decision of one nation to develop nuclear capability will prompt others to take that step. The result will be, it is feared, a global environment populated by many states possessing nuclear weapons, with an enhanced probability that one or more of them would choose to use the weapons.

The fact that American acquisition of nuclear capabilities was followed by the Soviet Union, Great Britain, France, China, and India supports the view that further proliferation is likely if not inevitable.[8] Estimates vary, but most observers acknowledge that many other states have the resources to develop nuclear weapons—and that they may be inclined to do so in the future. In part this view was reinforced by India's successful nuclear explosion in May 1974, which demonstrated that states with civilian (peaceful) nuclear energy programs could simultaneously and surreptitiously pursue a weapons capability. The U.S. Energy Research and Development Administration (cited in *The Defense Monitor*, February, 1979) has estimated that by 1987 thirty different countries could have the capabil-

7. The addition of new nuclear states is commonly referred to as the Nth country problem. The increase in the number of states possessing nuclear weapons is called "horizontal" proliferation, in contrast to increases in the capabilities of an existing nuclear state. The latter is often referred to as "vertical" proliferation.

8. Although there has not been any public admission by the Israeli government that it possesses nuclear weapons, many reporters and intelligence analysts believe that the Dimona reactor in the Negev desert has produced sufficient plutonium for approximately twenty 15-kiloton bombs.

ity to produce nuclear weapons.[9] Whether any of them will choose to do so is a matter of conjecture. The varied postures that states have taken toward the Nuclear Non-Proliferation Treaty (see chapter twelve) suggest, however, that we are likely to witness an increase in the number of states possessing nuclear weapons as the 1980s unfold. The use of nuclear power for electrical generation reinforces this prognosis (see Kegley, Raymond, and Skinner, 1980). As President Carter observed, "We know that by the year 2000 nuclear power reactors could be producing enough plutonium to make tens of thousands of bombs every year."

Even more disturbing, perhaps, is what appears to be the accessibility of nuclear know-how.[10] During 1978–1979 Pakistan apparently made a successful end run around the technology-export controls of the United States and several Western European governments when it quietly bought all the basic parts—allegedly with funds supplied by the radical government of Libya—necessary for a uranium-enrichment plant. Should Pakistan choose to convert its uranium-enrichment laboratory into a bomb-producing facility,[11] it is probable this would touch off a nuclear arms race between India and Pakistan, two traditional enemies in an already volatile area of the world. The feared chain reaction that would induce other nations to engage in the nuclear game might then be set off.

Weapons Acquisitions at the Second Tier

If but a handful of nations have hitherto refrained from the temptation to join the nuclear club, many clearly have not refrained from joining a colossal race to obtain more and more conventional weapons. That many developing nations are devoting substantial portions of their national resources to the acquisition of arms, often outstripping the efforts of industrialized nations, has already been noted. The result is that the weapons of war are no longer concen-

9. The list is as follows: Argentina, Austria, Belgium, Brazil, Canada, Republic of China, Czechoslovakia, Denmark, Egypt, Finland, East Germany, West Germany, Iran, Israel, Italy, Japan, Mexico, Netherlands, Norway, Pakistan, Poland, Portugal, Romania, South Africa, South Korea, Spain, Sweden, Switzerland, Turkey, and Yugoslavia.

10. In testimony before a Senate Government Affairs subcommittee headed by Sen. John Glenn in 1978, a Harvard University economics major, Dimitri A. Rotow, gave an "extensive and detailed exposition" of how to make an atomic bomb, in order to demonstrate how easy it is to build these dangerous weapons. According to one witness, a former Atomic Energy Commission bomb designer, Rotow's statement was convincing in showing that "the average person can understand how these are built. . . . Building a car from the ground up is vastly more complicated than building a nuclear bomb."

11. By early 1980 some observers were suggesting that Pakistan would test a nuclear device before the end of 1982. See Smith and Bhatia (1980) for an assessment.

trated in selected geographical areas of the world. The nearly universal drive for military power has led to the diffusion of arms and large standing armies throughout the world.[12]

Variations in military spending in Third World regions are summarized in Figure 10.3. The data show that the most rapid spending increases occurred in the Middle East, but Africa and Latin America, both of which spent considerably less in 1968 than nations in the Middle East or East Asia, have shown substantial increases in military expenditures.[13] But there has been a relative stabilization of military spending since 1975 which is evident in all Third World regions, with the exception, perhaps, of Africa in 1977.

The Size of Armed Forces

Spending on weapons is only one clue to military power. Another is the number of men and women in the armed forces of national gov-

Figure 10.3
Military Expenditures in Third World Regions, 1968–1977 (billions of constant 1976 dollars)

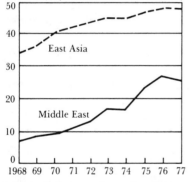
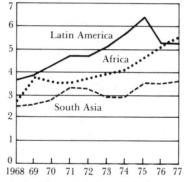

Source: U.S. Arms Control and Disarmament Agency, *World Military Expenditures and Arms Transfers 1968–1977* (Washington, D.C.: Government Printing Office, 1979), pp. 2–3.

12. As Waltz (1975) describes it, "states imitate the military innovations contrived by the country of greatest capability and ingenuity. And so the weapons of major contenders, and even their strategies, begin to look much the same all over the world."

13. "Data indicate that 53 countries—about one-third of the nations of the world —spent more, in real terms, for military purposes in 1976 than in any of the preceding nine years. Almost one-half of these countries are in Africa (16) or Latin America (9). The pattern is even more pronounced with respect to size of armed forces. Of the 42 countries with armed forces larger in 1976 than in any of the preceding nine years, 17 were in Africa and 9 in Latin America. Conversely, only 4 or 5 countries in the Near East or East Asia reached new highs for either of these variables" (U.S. Arms Control and Disarmament Agency, 1978b: 7).

ernments. Worldwide, military personnel have grown steadily in the past twenty years, from 18.6 million soldiers in 1960 to over 23 million by 1976 (Sivard, 1976: 6). This represents nearly a 20 percent increase.[14] Equally revealing is that "all of this build-up has been concentrated in the developing countries, where the growth of forces has exceeded both the rapid growth of population and the development of an industrial base. In the developing countries, on average, there are now four soldiers in the regular forces to ten workers in manufacturing industry" (Sivard, 1976: 7). This compares with a ratio of one to ten in developed countries. In 1960, 47 percent of the world's regular armed forces were employed by developing nations; by 1974, 56 percent were in the armed forces of developing nations. Between 1960 and 1978 the regular military in developing countries increased 64 percent, "accounting for virtually all of the rise in military manpower [worldwide] during the period" (Sivard, 1979b: 8).

For relatively poor nations to subsidize the growth of their military establishments at such rates constitutes a considerable financial burden. But when the costs of equipping such armies with weapons are added, the sacrifice becomes enormous. Indeed, it raises the question of how countries with underdeveloped industrial bases are able to produce the weapons that soldiers are presumably trained to use, particularly since the manufacture of those weapons requires sophisticated technologies. Part of the answer rests with the use made by developing nations of military personnel as nation-building instruments for nonmilitary purposes. But a major part of the answer is that the great powers either give or sell them arms.

Changing Patterns and Problems of Arms Transfers. The magnitude of present-day international trafficking in arms is captured by information on the dollar value of arms transfers. The world's trade in conventional arms increased by more than 7 percent in constant dollars between 1976 and 1977, reaching $16.7 billion in constant 1976 dollars; that is 1.6 percent of the world's total trade (U.S. Arms Control and Disarmament Agency, 1979b: 7). This represents an increase of about 90 percent in the value of arms imports in the decade 1968–1977, during which time the accumulated dollar value of arms transfers surpassed the $104 billion mark (U.S. Arms Control and Disarmament Agency, 1979b: 113). The reason for this growth rests

14. The U.S. Arms Control and Disarmament Agency (1979b: 6) estimates that worldwide the number of men and women in the armed forces in 1977 was 26.3 million, which is an 11 percent increase over the 1967 figure. It also notes, however, that this is not an increase relative to the world's population or relative to such social indicators as numbers of teachers and physicians.

not only in the fact that more arms are being transferred but also that their technological sophistication is greater and more costly.

The magnitude of contemporary arms transfers is further portrayed by the data in Table 10.2, which show the number of different types of weapons transferred by the four principal suppliers from 1973 to 1977.[15] These data underscore the extent to which technologically sophisticated military weapons have been dispersed from a relative handful of nations to nearly all.

Important to recognize in this regard is the extent to which developing nations have become the recipients of arms transfers. In the early 1960s, when data on arms transfers first began to be collected, the industrialized world (principally NATO and Warsaw Pact countries) accounted for over half of world arms imports. But by 1976, the *developing* world accounted for 78 percent of all arms purchases (Sivard, 1977b: 10). Figure 10.4, which shows the distribution of arms transfers by supplying countries and recipient regions in 1967 and 1977, demonstrates the nature of this shift over the most recent decade for which data are available.[16]

Particularly noteworthy is the sharp increase in arms imports by nations in the Middle East. This increase coincided with two other developments. One was the decision of the United States, clearly the world's leading arms supplier,[17] to shift from military assistance in the form of grants to other countries to outright sales of weapons. Historically, the vast proportion of U.S. arms transfers

15. In 1977, five countries supplied 85 percent of the world's arms exports (see Figure 10.4 below).

16. Note that the developing world itself has become a growing source of arms exports.

The developing nations are no longer an insignificant source of arms in world trade, and their contribution is growing. Of the 24 countries that exported more arms in 1976 than in any of the preceding 9 years, even after adjustment for inflation, more than half are classified as developing. Two each are in Latin America (Brazil and Cuba) and the Near East (Israel and the [People's Democratic Republic of Yemen]); four are in Africa (Morocco, Nigeria, Somalia, and Uganda); and five are in East Asia (North Korea, Republic of Korea, Singapore, Taiwan, and Vietnam). The remaining three are European (Greece, Spain, and Yugoslavia). (U.S. Arms Control and Disarmament Agency, 1978: 8–9)

(The reader is cautioned that the classification of developed and developing nations implied above is not the same as that used in constructing Figure 10.4.)

17. It has been estimated that from 1961 through 1977, the United States sent arms "worth perhaps $71 billion to 161 countries" (TRB, 1978: 2). It is this volume of activity that led Jimmy Carter during the 1976 presidential campaign to label the United States "the world's leading supplier of the weapons of war." The United States increased its arms exports by an annual rate of 6 percent over the 1968–1977 decade; over the 1973–1977 period, "U.S. arms exports of $21.6 billion were slightly larger than U.S. economic aid of $18.9 billion" (U.S. Arms Control and Disarmament Agency, 1979b: 10).

Table 10.2
American, British, French, and Soviet Weapons Exports to the Third World, 1973–1977

	Africa				East Asia and Oceania				Latin America			
	U.S.	U.S.S.R.	U.K.	France	U.S.	U.S.S.R.	U.K.	France	U.S.	U.S.S.R.	U.K.	France
Tanks, self-propelled guns, artillery	152	2,610	75	175	4,062	650	30	10	593	550	—	190
Armored personnel carriers/armored cars	86	1,950	30	550	1,202	190	20	—	650	40	—	110
Surface combatants	—	20	10	40	119	112	—	—	64	10	30	5
Submarines	—	1	—	—	2	—	—	—	16	—	5	—
Supersonic aircraft	8	460	—	90	361	30	—	—	18	80	10	60
Subsonic aircraft	—	80	5	5	333	—	20	—	186	5	20	—
Helicopters	9	70	—	90	819	60	—	30	86	40	—	50
Missiles	—	7,300	200	240	192	—	40	—	—	170	—	30

	Middle East				South Asia				Total, all suppliers, all regions
	U.S.	U.S.S.R.	U.K.	France	U.S.	U.S.S.R.	U.K.	France	
Tanks, self-propelled guns, artillery	3,630	6,060	940	340	30	570	—	—	20,667
Armored personnel carriers/armored cars	5,044	2,980	40	460	122	350	—	25	13,849
Surface combatants	29	22	75	—	2	3	6	—	547
Submarines	—	—	3	—	—	4	—	—	31
Supersonic aircraft	609	880	5	120	—	220	—	30	2,981
Subsonic aircraft	274	200	5	—	—	40	—	—	1,173
Helicopters	288	200	30	200	—	40	10	180	2,202
Missiles	4,267	6,400	250	—	—	1,000	130	—	20,219

Source: Adapted from U.S. Arms Control and Disarmament Agency, *World Military Expenditures and Arms Transfers 1968–1977* (Washington, D.C.: U.S. Arms Control and Disarmament Agency, 1979), pp. 160–165.

Note: Data exclude Soviet exports to North Vietnam and U.S. exports to South Vietnam provided out of funds appropriated to the military organizations in the Defense Department, and weapons exports to Albania, Greece, Malta, Spain, Turkey, and Yugoslavia.

Figure 10.4
**Arms Transfers by Supplying Countries and Recipient Regions, 1967 and
1977**

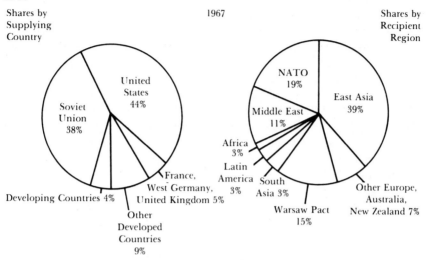

Shares by Supplying Country — 1967

United States 44%
Soviet Union 38%
Developing Countries 4%
France, West Germany, United Kingdom 5%
Other Developed Countries 9%

Shares by Recipient Region — 1967

NATO 19%
East Asia 39%
Middle East 11%
Africa 3%
Latin America 3%
South Asia 3%
Warsaw Pact 15%
Other Europe, Australia, New Zealand 7%

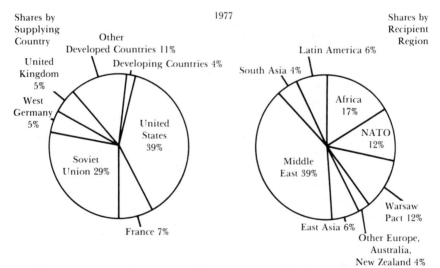

Shares by Supplying Country — 1977

Other Developed Countries 11%
Developing Countries 4%
United Kingdom 5%
West Germany 5%
United States 39%
Soviet Union 29%
France 7%

Shares by Recipient Region — 1977

Latin America 6%
South Asia 4%
Africa 17%
NATO 12%
Middle East 39%
Warsaw Pact 12%
East Asia 6%
Other Europe, Australia, New Zealand 4%

Source: 1967 adapted from U.S. Arms Control and Disarmament Agency, *World Military Expenditures and Arms Transfers 1967–1976* (Washington, D.C.: Government Printing Office, 1978), pp. 115–156; 1977 from U.S. Arms Control and Disarmament Agency, *World Military Expenditures and Arms Transfers 1968–1977* (Washington, D.C.: Government Printing Office, 1979), pp. 8, 10.

Note: 1967 figures based on constant 1975 dollars.

were in the form of grants, aid, and credits. These were justified on grounds that such give-aways would augment the capabilities of American allies to resist Soviet initiatives in the Cold War competition between the two superpowers. The shift toward arms sales as an alternative to grant assistance began in earnest during the first Nixon administration and in particular after enunciation of the so-called Nixon Doctrine. Among other things, the Nixon Doctrine emphasized the necessity of developing nations assuming a greater share of their own defense burden (and, by implication, the United States less). Arms sales, as opposed to grants, were assumed to be consistent with this outlook.

The second factor giving rise to the influx of Middle Eastern arms imports was the OPEC oil price increase in 1973–1974. This enabled many Middle Eastern nations to pay for the military hardware they sought (either for themselves or for others they chose to subsidize). As Donald Rumsfeld, secretary of defense under President Gerald R. Ford, put it in describing the oil-producing, arms consuming nations, "Most of these customers are ready to pay cash; they ask no gifts of the U.S."

Cash can become an important economic rationale for foreign military sales, especially for a country like the United States, which has experienced persistent balance-of-payments deficits. Moreover, since other nations need cash too (to pay for oil imports, for example), the competition for revenue can itself become a rationale for continuing what many regard as the unsavory business of trafficking in arms.

To many critics, another factor which explains why the great powers, their own supremacy unchallenged, should choose to arm others is the sheer magnitude of the arms export business. Because the sale of weapons constitutes big business, the companies in the business comprise a powerful domestic lobby for the continuation of arms transfers abroad. That arms manufacturing is, by its very nature, an expensive proposition, is a contributing factor as well. One way to reduce the per-unit cost of a particular weapons system, therefore, is to produce weapons for foreign consumption as well as for the immediate security needs of the producing state.

The arms race between the superpowers has generated such an accelerating technology in the development of weapons systems that many weapons are obsolete by the time they reach the production stage or shortly thereafter. What, then, should be done with the weapons? How might the investment in their development be recovered? A tempting answer, it appears, is to sell obsolete weapons to developing countries who will buy them. What cannot be sold can be given away in the form of foreign assistance in the hope that such a gift will buy the loyal political friendship of the recipient.

In fact, the search for allies in a politically fragmented world has been an important reason underlying the willingness of great powers to sell arms. Allies have been armed as a way of enlisting their aid in maintaining a worldwide strategic balance. They have also been encouraged by the superpowers to provide for their own defense with the arms provided them. The existence of a nation that refuses to engage enthusiastically in this nearly universal form of behavior (such as Japan) has been known to offend the superpowers who so feverishly spend their national income for arms—especially when the deviant nation experiences exceptional economic growth at the same time that it refuses to spend vast sums of money on arms.

Whether the arming of other nations has accomplished all the intended foreign policy objectives of the superpowers is open to dispute. For example, one of the propositions on which the United States and the Soviet Union seem to have based their policies is that peace can be maintained by spreading arms to strategically pivotal recipients. Yet because many of the recipients of arms, by purchase and aid, are Third World nations where the incidence of interstate conflict and domestic political instability is very high, it is not surprising to find that many instances of regional violence have occurred in precisely those countries which have armed themselves the most. Moreover, the United States has been found to have armed *both* sides in several Third World conflicts, such as in the Indo-Pakistani clash, and so have the Soviets on occasion. (See Simpson, 1967, for some other American examples.)

Arms sales and aid have been questioned on ethical grounds by those who value democracy and the growth of democratic institutions in the world. It has been observed, for instance, that in the mid-1970s the majority of the eighty-five states purchasing American arms were authoritarian regimes that prohibited political dissent (*The Defense Monitor*, February, 1978: 2). There is also evidence to suggest that American arms assistance to developing countries has contributed to the strength of military dictatorships among recipient nations (Rowe, 1974a).

From the viewpoint of recipient nations, however, the reasons for seeking weapons are not hard to identify. They hope to attain prestige in the world's pecking order. Among certain developing nations in particular, the drive to acquire arms from the advanced nations is also related to their desire to obtain military tools to deal with internal opposition. Expanding military capability has also been married with nationalism in the minds of many Third World leaders, who appear to cling to the traditional assumption that military power is a prerequisite for dealing with political problems. Finally, some developing countries have been willing to pay an extraordinary price for arms because they feel threatened by countries on their borders, countries which themselves may be in the process of arming.

Weapons Production in Developing Nations. The dramatic militarization of the globe has been augmented by the increasing willingness and capacity of developing nations to enter into their own weapons production programs. It has been said that "those nations who can, manufacture [arms], and those who cannot, purchase" (Stanley and Pearton, 1972). As Peleg (1980) has shown, increasing numbers of developing nations are producing their own arms rather than buying them from others, even though that production is often more costly initially than importing would be. This development reduces considerably the capacity to reverse the global armament race.

Although many Third World nations have used a variety of mechanisms to increase substantially their military capabilities (thus mimicking the habits of their military superiors) none rivals the military might of the two superpowers. Hence, the ability of the United States and the Soviet Union to manage strategic nuclear weapons systems has been, and promises to remain, a salient characteristic of global politics. For this reason, the evolution of the superpowers' strategic doctrines deserves special attention.

NUCLEAR WEAPONS AND FOREIGN POLICY: THE SOVIET-AMERICAN CASE

The dropping of the atomic bomb in the closing days of World War II is the most important event distinguishing prewar from postwar international politics. In the blinding flash of a single weapon and the shadow of its mushroom cloud, the international arena was transformed from a "balance of power" system to one more akin to a "balance of terror." Ever since, a central policy question facing nations has been what to do *with* atomic (and later thermonuclear) weapons and what to do *about* them: (1) should they be used and, if so, how? and (2) how can their use by others be prevented? Indeed, no country from 1945 to the present has failed to appreciate the dangers (or, to some, the opportunities) which such weapons of mass destruction have posed to nations and the world at large.

Although the existence of incredible weapons of mass destruction has been a constant throughout the postwar period, the United States and the Soviet Union have assumed varying postures toward their use. For analytic convenience, their policy postures can be broken into two periods: the era of American monopoly or superiority in strategic weapons beginning in 1945 and the subsequent period (roughly since 1960) when the United States no longer stood alone in its capacity to annihilate another nation without fear of its own destruction.

Views of Nuclear Power During the Period of American Superiority

A review of United States policies since 1945 suggests that when nations enjoy military superiority vis-à-vis their principal adversaries, they tend to think of strategic weapons as instruments in diplomatic bargaining, that is, as tools to be used for the political purpose of molding others' behavior. The concept of "compellence" (Schelling, 1966) describes the American view of nuclear weapons during the period of American nuclear superiority. *Compellence* suggests that nuclear weapons were to be used as instruments of influence, as instruments for getting others to do what they might not otherwise do.[18] At the height of the Cold War, the United States repeatedly sought to gain bargaining leverage by conveying the impression that it was willing to use nuclear weapons against the Soviet Union. Political victories could be won through intimidation, it was felt. Symptomatic of this thinking was Secretary of State John Foster Dulles's practice of what he termed *brinkmanship*—the strategy of backing adversaries into the corner and taking them to the brink of war by threatening them with nuclear destruction.[19]

From a position of strength, U.S. threats of *massive retaliation* against Soviet population and industrial centers were deemed an appropriate way of deriving from the possession of superior destructive force the realization of American foreign policy objectives. This strategy was labeled *countervalue* because it proposed to target American weapons on objects the Soviets would most value, industrial and population centers, and thereby maximize the bargaining leverage of the United States. The alternative is a *counterforce* strategy, in which destructive capability is targeted against the enemy's military forces and weapons rather than its industrial and population centers.

From the perspective of the Soviet Union, the doctrine of massive retaliation was threatening and potentially destabilizing. The Soviet response was twofold. Following Nikita Khrushchev's assumption of power, *peaceful coexistence* came to dominate Soviet rhetoric. Essentially peaceful coexistence became a recipe for continuation of Soviet-American rivalry with the assumption that com-

18. See Singer (1963) for an analogous discussion of this concept which distinguishes between persuasion and dissuasion as strategic goals in internation bargaining.

19. Dulles's practice of this strategy was more rhetorical than real. For elaboration, see chapter three and Kegley and Wittkopf (1979). It is important to consider as well the important differences between Dulles's rhetoric and the policies of the Truman and Eisenhower administrations in general.

munism's inevitable victory over capitalism could be won without the necessity of armed conflict. Perhaps it reflected a perception by the Soviets that, in the event of war, they would be annihilated while the United States would survive. In any event, the subsequent Soviet response to the threat of massive retaliation was to continue to build its own nuclear force and to develop sophisticated means of delivering nuclear weapons against the United States. The successful launching of the world's first space satellite (Sputnik) in 1957, which proved as well the Soviet capability to deliver a nuclear warhead, demonstrated the technological advances the Soviet Union had made since breaking the American monopoly of atomic weapons in 1949.

Views of Nuclear Power Since the Waning of American Superiority

American strategic superiority eroded steadily during the 1950s and thereafter. In the course of the shift toward parity or equality in the Soviet-American strategic balance, the assumption that weapons of mass destruction could actually be used began to be challenged. Awareness of the unacceptability of using nuclear bombs as forward weapons was associated with doctrinal shifts away from strategies of compellence and confrontation. The idea that nuclear weapons could be employed in diplomatic bargaining was dealt perhaps a death blow by the nearly suicidal Cuban missile crisis of 1962.[20] Since that time, nuclear weapons have served the purpose primarily of deterring aggression. *Deterrence* entails reliance on the possession of strategic capabilities to prevent others from attacking. This doctrinal shift was important. It marked the end of a period in which leaders perceived weapons as useful for coercive purposes and the beginning of another in which weapons of mass destruction have been used defensively by threatening to impose unacceptably high costs on an adversary manifesting aggressive behavior.

Ironically, this more cautious concept relating to the use of nuclear arsenals has served to stimulate the arms race rather than inhibit it. For a deterrent strategy rests on the ability of a country to deliver without question unacceptable damage on any opponent. To

---

20. This is not to suggest that nuclear threats have permanently disappeared from the dialogue of superpower bargaining. They still intermittently reappear, either implicitly or explicitly, such as during the 1973 Middle East War, and again during the 1979–1980 crises associated with the Iranian hostage episode and the Soviet intervention into Afghanistan. There are, moreover, some strategists within both the United States and the Soviet Union who continue to advocate nuclear blackmail for political goals. The prevailing view since 1962, however, has been that nuclear weapons cannot successfully be used to compel an adversary into doing something he would not otherwise do.

ensure a capacity to inflict such high costs, a "second-strike capability" is necessary. The concept of second-strike capability implies that a country must be able to withstand an initial strike by an adversary in order to be able to retaliate with a devastating second blow. In this way the adversary will be assured of destruction, thus deterring the initial preemptive attack.

At the present time the United States and the Soviet Union enjoy approximate balance or equivalence in their strategic levels. Both maintain relatively invulnerable second-strike capabilities. This development has led to a situation in which each power has deterred the other from a direct attack upon itself. Thus deterrence has produced an uneasy but nonetheless continuing period of peace between the superpowers. The lesson has not been lost on the leaders of either. In fact, *mutual deterrence* based on the principle of *mutual assured destruction* (MAD) has come to characterize superpower relations today. The term *balance of terror* accurately describes the essential military stalemate between the superpowers, for mutual deterrence is based on the military potential for, and psychological expectations of, widespread death and destruction for both combatants in the event of a nuclear exchange. Peace, in short, is presumed to be the product of mutual vulnerability. As Robert Oppenheimer pointed out in drawing a famous analogy, the superpowers have become like two scorpions in a bottle—if one attacks the other, it must do so at the price of its own destruction.

The relative mutual invulnerability of the superpowers' retaliatory forces led the United States during the Nixon administration to opt for a strategy of "sufficiency," meaning that assured destruction was to be maintained, but no longer would the United States seek to retain superiority in relation to the Soviet Union. At the same time, given that relative equivalence or parity existed in the strategic capabilities of the superpowers, an effort was made to keep the Soviet Union from attaining superiority over the United States. This emergent balance in the strategic arsenals of the two superpowers laid the basis for the SALT talks (Strategic Arms Limitation Talks),[21] which can be interpreted as an effort by both sides to prevent collapse of the fragile balance of terror that underpins mutual assured destruction. The SALT negotiations attempted to guarantee each superpower's second-strike capacity by preventing either from developing the kinds of weapons that could be used to destroy an opponent without fear of retaliation. Although the pur-

21. This is not to imply that the basis for SALT was rooted exclusively in these developments in the strategic-force-level ratio of the two superpowers. The roots of SALT can also be traced to other political and diplomatic factors that predated the Nixon administration.

suit of this shared goal has not been without difficulties, both super-powers have thus far managed to achieve that goal. An unstable peace has resulted, and the learning of a modicum of trust between the rivals may have resulted.

The evolution of Soviet-American military competition suggests several general patterns: that arms races are propelled by mutual fears; that national security is perceived to be enhanced by the ac-quisition of arms; that each partner to the competition is extraordi-narily sensitive to advances in military capabilities by the other; and that sensitivity to military advances derives from the fear that they might undermine the fragile strategic balance, thereby making one partner vulnerable to attack by the other.

To any characterization of Soviet-American military competi-tion should also be added the tendency of each to pursue an arms race and arms control simultaneously, the propensity of each to seek peace while preparing for war, and the inclination of each to assume that national security can be purchased, and that the price of national security is never too high (even though neither super-power possesses enough money ever to buy enough security).

The major product of these assumptions has, for the most part, been a self-perpetuating arms race. To a remarkable degree, the So-viets and Americans have responded to each others' strategic ac-tions in *reciprocal* terms. Initiatives taken by one party provoked similar countermeasures by the other. Each superpower has per-ceived its own actions as merely the response to the other's initia-tives. The result is a classic action-and-reaction syndrome. Box 10.1 documents the syndrome by tracing the dynamics of the Soviet-American nuclear competition. What is striking is the extent to which the strategic choices of each nation predict the subsequent choices of the other; the result has been convergence in the super-powers' strategic levels and in their policies for dealing with them. There is some irony, perhaps, in the fact that the two superpowers, as a consequence of their strategic competition, maintain awesome military arsenals and espouse policy positions that are very much alike.

The steps taken in the superpowers' continuing strategic dia-logue during 1980 provide the most recent instance of this pattern. The Carter administration announced a shift from its traditional countervalue strategy toward a posture resembling the Soviets' counterforce strategy. For the first time, Carter declared, American nuclear missiles would be targeted more toward military facilities, command posts, and political centers, and less on Soviet cities. To some, the policy change signaled the American desire to keep a pre-sumably equally restrained opponent from targeting American pop-

Box 10.1

Action ⇄ **Reaction**
in the Nuclear Competition

The dynamics of the nuclear arms race ensure that development of a new weapons system by one power will in a relatively brief period be followed by a comparable achievement by the other. Both powers have had "firsts." Neither has stayed ahead for long. The US generally has a technological lead of several years, but the futility of the race for short-term advantage is demonstrated by a chronology of developments to date.

US 1945   atomic bomb   1949 USSR
The nuclear age began with the explosion of a US A-bomb of 12.5 kilotons (equivalent to 12,500 tons of TNT) over Hiroshima, Japan. The single bomb, which destroyed the city, introduced to the world a concentrated explosive force of unprecedented power. Within four years, the USSR conducted its first atomic test.

US 1948   intercontinental bomber   1955 USSR
By 1948, the US had begun to replace the propeller planes of World War II with long-range jets. The first planes developed for strategic (intercontinental) bombing required refueling to reach another continent. In 1955, the US began deployment of the all-jet intercontinental bomber, and the USSR soon followed suit.

US 1954   hydrogen bomb   1955 USSR
The H-Bomb multiplied the explosive force of the A-bomb 1,000 times. The first US thermonuclear bomb had a yield equivalent to 15,000,000 tons of TNT; a year later the USSR tested a bomb in the million-ton range.

USSR 1957   intercontinental ballistic missile (ICBM)   1958 US
Following intensive development by both nuclear powers, a land-based missile to carry nuclear warheads intercontinental distances was successfully flight-tested by the USSR in 1957, and by the US a year later. By 1962 both nations had ICBMs with a range of 6,000 miles, each missile able to carry a payload equivalent to 5–10,000,000 tons of TNT.

USSR 1957   man-made satellite in orbit   1958 US
Sputnik I by the USSR initiated a space race which quickly took on military functions; the first US satellite was launched into orbit the following year. Through 1979 more than half the superpowers' satellites have been military: for surveillance, targeting, etc.

US 1960 submarine-launched ballistic missile (SLBM) 1968 USSR
A nuclear-powered submarine which could fire long-range missiles from a submerged position was the third means of strategic delivery. The US produced the nuclear-powered Polaris, with missiles with a range of 1,200 nautical miles. Eight years later the USSR had comparable nuclear subs.

Continued

Box 10.1   *(continued)*

US 1966   multiple warhead (MIRV)   1968 USSR

Multiheaded missiles increased the number of targets a missile could hit. US MIRVed missiles carried three warheads, each with sixteen times the explosive force of the Hiroshima bomb. The USSR had them two years later.

USSR 1968   anti-ballistic missile (ABM)   1972 US

The USSR deployed 64 defensive missiles around Moscow. The US began construction of the Safeguard system in 1969 and had one site completed when a treaty restricting ABMs was signed in 1972. Generally judged militarily ineffective, ABMs were restricted to one site in each country in 1974. Subsequently the US site was closed.

US 1970   multiple independently-targeted   1975 USSR
                       warhead (MIRV)

Further development of multiple warheads enabled one missile to hit three to ten individually selected targets as far apart as 100 miles. The USSR began to flight-test MIRVs three years after the US put them in service; in 1976 the USSR deployed the six-headed SS-19.

US 198?   new long-range cruise missile   198? USSR

Adaptable to launching from air, sea, and land, a new generation of long-range missiles is under development. The cruise missile is small, relatively inexpensive, highly accurate, with the unique advantage of very low trajectory. Following the contours of the earth, and flying under radar, it will be able to destroy its target without warning. The US is in the lead in this technology.

Source: Ruth Leger Sivard, *World Military and Social Expenditures 1979* (Leesburg, Va.: World Priorities, 1979), p. 13. Copyright © World Priorities, Leesburg, Va. 22075, U.S.A.

ulation centers. But to others—including the Soviets—the shift was seen as an attempt by the United States to ensure an American first-strike capability. Reacting with alarm as though the American aim was more warlike than peaceful, Soviet leaders began pleading for additional arms-control negotiations.

To be militarily invulnerable, to contain an escalating and costly arms race, to remain prepared to meet any military challenge, to maintain an invincible deterrent capability, and to preserve peace—these are the primary goals of *both* competing superpowers. To see one's nation as the best hope for peace and the strongest voice for restraint is characteristic of the self-image of *both* countries.[22]

22. All of these assumptions can be found in President Carter's "National Security Goals" speech (February 18, 1980), which claimed that "It is important that everyone understands that every action that I have taken is peaceful and is designed to preserve peace." It is important to emphasize that the same thinking is equally evident in Soviet statements as well.

It is questionable, of course, whether the assumptions inherent in the Soviet-American strategic dialogue are warranted. Have they produced the goals both have set for themselves? To be sure, as President Eisenhower once noted, the view is compelling that "Until war is eliminated from international relations, unpreparedness for it is well nigh as criminal as war itself." But, nonetheless, has the logical outcome of this view—a nuclear arms race—been the intention of its participants? Indeed, has the security of either the United States or the Soviet Union been enhanced? Or, as a result of the nuclear competition, have the superpowers instead actually imperiled their security? The answers to these troublesome questions are not altogether clear.

THE SIGNIFICANCE OF MILITARY POWER IN CONTEMPORARY WORLD POLITICS

The search for national security through the acquisition of arms is understandable in a world where states perceive themselves ultimately responsible for their own self-defense. The beliefs are pervasive that peace is a product of strength and that security can be obtained by the possession of as much or more firepower than one's enemies have. The fears engendered by visions of nuclear devastation and by the cognizance of a nation's vulnerability to physical destruction also contribute to the belief that devastation might be avoided by the attainment of a sufficient deterrent capacity. Defense planners often base their plans on "worst-case" analyses, which frequently result in the perceived need for even further military preparation in order to avoid fulfillment of these nightmares. The urge to arm is further stimulated by the ubiquitous influence of defense planners in the policy-making process of most countries. The policies proposed by defense planners have also an uncanny, if understandable, habit of reflecting military thinking, and foreign policy decision makers have a penchant for adopting the vocabulary and concepts of their military advisers.

In many countries of the world the belief that military capability will lead to national security is reinforced by the existence of powerful lobbies representing those in industry and government whose jobs are contingent upon the continuation of the arms race. The urge to arm also finds support in the attitudes of the many citizens who have a tendency to equate patriotism with military might.

The reasons for the rapid global militarization are many, but more significant, perhaps, are the consequences of this militarization. Have not the internal structures of nations, the kinds of foreign policies they pursue, and the nature of military power itself changed as a result of this diffusion of military power throughout the globe? If so, should we not consider the possibility that the meaning of military might has been transformed by the dispersion of increasingly destructive armaments?

The Domestic Consequences of Global Militarization

One way to consider the effects of global militarization is to examine the nature of the regimes governing the countries of the world. The global system is made up of many states led by authoritarian governments, often military dictatorships. Correspondingly, the number of states controlled by democratic political processes remains small. It is plausible that the reason for this entrenchment of nondemocratic regimes is in part a result of the domination of military establishments, especially in the developing countries, where the military often constitute the most highly organized and visible symbols of nationhood.

The global arms race may also have adversely affected world economic growth. Military expenditures may diminish the rate at which wealth is accumulated in countries that allocate significant portions of their budgets to defense. Growth rates of arming nations may be retarded because military expenditures fail to generate new capital, for military investment does not lead to additional growth and income by spilling over through multiplier effects to other sectors of the economy. Building a new missile is a one-time expenditure that does not stimulate subsequent economic benefits. Unlike the allocation of money for the construction of a tractor, a highway, or a hospital, it fails to create additional capital that catalytically produces new jobs or facilitates the further expansion of the economy.

For much the same reason that military spending may depress economic growth rates, it may also contribute to inflationary pressures. The reason is rather simple. Although the workers producing a new missile are paid for their labors, they not only are producing goods which fail to generate additional growth and income (capital goods), they also are not contributing to an expansion of the goods available for consumption in the marketplace. They have more money, but they have not contributed to expansion of the number of refrigerators, television sets, or other consumer goods they might wish to purchase. Hence, more dollars are chasing the same stock of goods, which is one of the classic conditions conducive to inflation.

The drain of military spending on economic growth is especially evident in advanced, industrial societies. It is often said that military spending is beneficial to a nation's economy because it creates jobs that, in the absence of that spending, would not exist. But that argument can be refuted by evidence. A report released by Senator Edward M. Kennedy (1977), for instance, found that for every increase of $1 billion in the military budget in the United States, 11,600 *fewer* jobs were created than would have been by a $1 billion infusion into the nonmilitary sector. Some jobs apparently are *lost* as the military budget climbs. And growth rates may also be diminished by the burden which military spending exerts on depletion of raw materials which often are in short supply. For example, "in peacetime the Department of Defense consumes one-half as much jet fuel as that used by all U.S. commercial airlines" (Sivard, 1977b: 5).

It may be questionable to assume the existence of a direct causal linkage between military expenditure increases and retarded economic growth rates, rising unemployment, reduced productivity, balance-of-payments deficits, and the like. But if a causal connection is dubious in the short run (where military spending *can* mean new jobs, for example), in the long run it can be compelling. As Barnet (1979) has observed, "Mounting evidence appears to confirm what common sense would suggest: A country which, year after year, spends more than $100 billion annually to support a bureaucracy of four million people who produce nothing, and which buys hundreds of thousands of machines that make nothing, is not on the road to prosperity." Indeed, as Sivard (1979b) summarizes, "no analytical studies . . . have yet established a positive link between military expenditures and economic development in the broad sense. There is, in fact, a growing body of evidence pointing to retarding effects through inflation, diversion of investment, use of scarce materials, misuse of human capital. . . ." Nowhere, perhaps, is the negative impact of military spending on economic growth more exemplary than in the Soviet Union. In 1977, the Soviet Union was allocating over $132 billion in support of its military (including the largest standing army in the world, consisting of 4.7 million soldiers in uniform). Its reward for this investment is less than enticing: "Recent figures show the Soviet economy grew in 1979 at 2 percent as against a planned 4.3 percent, and industrial productivity 2.4 against 4.7 percent, with productivity in agriculture and transport falling" (Rothschild, 1980: 33). Most inquiries thus suggest that few nations benefit economically from investments in military goods and services, at least in the long term.

Does Military Spending Guarantee National Security?

Is it possible that massive military spending may, paradoxically, undermine the strength and resources of a nation? No less a sober policy maker (himself an experienced military careerist) than former President Dwight D. Eisenhower was provoked years ago to ask just such a question; he concluded:

> There is no way in which a country can satisfy the craving for absolute security—but it can easily bankrupt itself, morally and economically, in attempting to reach that illusory goal through arms alone. The Military Establishment, not productive of itself, necessarily must feed on the energy, productivity, and brainpower of the country, and if it takes too much, our total strength declines. (Quoted in *The Defense Monitor*, September–October 1977, p. 5)

Eisenhower's ideas are worth considering in any definition of national security. As Norman Cousins, an American diplomatic representative and former editor of the *Saturday Review*, has stated (March 18, 1979), "The security of the American people depends not on the pursuit of force, but on the control of force. Although spending money is a form of security to a country, massive military budgets are destroying both the United States and the Soviet Union."

Beyond the economic costs, has the dispersion of military capabilities, especially since the advent of nuclear weapons, increased the vulnerability of most nation-states, making them less rather than more secure? Today nearly all states are characterized as "conditionally viable" (Boulding, 1962), because they are dependent upon other states for their survival. Even the superpowers can be readily penetrated and instantly destroyed, and they in turn have the capacity to destroy many others as well. The destructiveness of weapons and their dispersion, then, have led ironically to a decrease in the security and independence of all.

Changes in Foreign Policy Objectives

As a consequence of the creation and dispersion of increasingly destructive weapons systems, some of the traditional objectives of foreign policy have been transformed by necessity. The first change has been a marked decline in the willingness of the states with the largest arsenals to use force in pursuit of many of their foreign policy objectives. For them, the most lethal of military tools (strategic weapons) have become too dangerous to use against others to achieve national goals. In an age of overkill, their use could invite national extinction. Thus, a long-standing tradition in world politics—that force can be employed as a method of last resort to achieve objectives against an adversary—may have eroded.

This is not to suggest that "limited" force—or even the threat of force—may not sometimes be used in the pursuit of political objectives, especially by less-developed countries; but among the most-armed, the superpowers, the pursuit of national interests by brute force has been markedly rare. Particularly since the Cuban missile crisis in 1962, both the United States and the Soviet Union have been noticeably reluctant to threaten the use of force against each other in order to get their way. They have instead maintained their strategic arsenals for the primary purpose of deterring aggression (which testifies to the persistent fear they have of each other, and to the lingering distrust of their adversary's inclination to violate this pattern of restraint).

It is important to emphasize that the reluctance to threaten the use of force applies to the superpowers' relations with one another, but not necessarily to their relations with other nations. American willingness to use force in pursuit of its foreign-policy objectives was made dramatically clear in Vietnam. Moreover, both superpowers have been prone to flex their military muscles by using or threatening to use force to influence the outcome of conflicts in which they themselves are often not the principal antagonists. It would also be premature to conclude that the day of superpower threatening superpower is over for good. Recall Jimmy Carter's warning in his State of the Union address (1980) at the height of the Iran and Afghanistan crises: "An attempt by any outside force to gain control of the Persian Gulf region will be regarded as an assault on the vital interests of the United States of America, and such an assault will be repelled by any means necessary, including military force."

A second possible impact of the militarization of the globe on traditional foreign policy pursuits may be the gradual demise of the quest for territorial acquisition. The goal of territorial expansion per se no longer appears to constitute an objective of at least most of the industrialized countries. As one astute observer put it, "major territorial disputes have virtually disappeared from relations among the highly modernized states" (Morse, 1976). (The same is not true, however, among the less modern or developing portions of the world.) More accurately, recent world history has been the history of the cession of territory, not its acquisition.[23] The liquidation of the colonial system was not an accident. It occurred by choice. The choice was made because the costs associated with controlling lands and peoples exceeded the benefits. Colonies proved to be un-

23. This is not to suggest, however, that territorial ambitions have disappeared, or that occupation of foreign territory by another state does not on occasion occur (witness the Soviet intervention in Afghanistan in 1979). It is merely to raise the question whether hegemonial aspirations of great powers have given way to the pursuit of *influence* in foreign countries. If so, the distinction marks an important turning point in the policy goals of great powers, and ushers into being a different kind of international system from those that predate the present one.

profitable. Moreover, colonial empires failed to enhance the security of states possessing them, as technology rendered meaningless the protection traditionally provided by the buffer of territory. At the same time that territorial imperialism may be waning, however, neo-imperialism—the economic penetration and domination of foreign markets—remains very much a pervasive element of contemporary world politics.

What Does "Power" Mean? Even though the threatened use of force and territorial ambitions may have abated as nations acquire more and more armaments, we must examine some of the assumptions on which policy makers seem to base their decisions. Foremost is the question "what is power?" Perhaps the *central* concept in international relations, the term *power* remains, nevertheless, highly ambiguous. One definition sees power as the ability of one actor to get another actor to do what it might otherwise not do—to exercise influence over another.

Such a conception acknowledges that power is a political phenomenon. Power entails the ability to coerce, to get what one wants through manipulation (which is perhaps why politics—as the exercise of influence—is often regarded as "dirty"). Indeed, political power is self-consciously manipulative. To say that nations pursue power is to say that they seek the ability to control others and thereby obtain control over their own destiny. This conception argues that power is, by definition, necessarily relational—a state can only have power over some other actor, and it has power only to the extent that it can get its way with that actor. Because power is the capacity of a state to achieve its goals with respect to some actor, it can only be measured by examining relations between nations and answering the question: who will dominate and who will be subservient?[24]

This conventional view of power has led many theorists to consider the necessary elements that enable states to achieve their goals—that is, to attempt to isolate the factors that contribute to national power. It has generally been thought that many factors may contribute to the ability of a state to achieve its goals vis-à-vis others, and that these factors, or some combination of them, can be ranked in such a way as to devise a composite index of the power potential of countries (see Cline, 1975; Ferris, 1973). Power potential is thus a measure of a country's total capabilities. It should be possi-

---

24. For excellent reviews of the semantic and operational issues pertaining to the definition of power, see Holsti (1977) and Waltz (1979).

ble, then, to rank the nations of the world according to their relative power. Such rankings would reveal the power or dominance hierarchy of the system, differentiating the strong from the weak, the great from the nongreat.

Military force is obviously a crucial ingredient in calculating power ratios. This stems from the long-cherished belief that the capacity to destroy leads to the capacity to influence. But power has also been believed to stem from relative national differences in societies' population size, geographical location, economic resources and raw materials, technological capacities, national character, ideology, forms of government, levels of economic development, educational levels, national morale, and the like.[25] However, there is no consensus on how these factors can most meaningfully be weighed, or what their relative importance should be in making comparisons across nations. All observers agree that nations are not equal in their capacity to influence others. The power capabilities of some greatly exceed those of others. But agreement on a list of the most powerful nations, let alone a ranking of the nations in terms of their power capabilities, is itself lacking.

Part of the difficulty of arriving at a definition of what constitutes power—and what factors contribute most to it—is that the potential impact of many of these contributing factors is subjective rather than concrete. To a considerable degree, power ratios are products, not of objective measurements, but of how those concrete factors are *perceived*. Thus, a political confrontation between two actors is likely to be influenced not only by actual but also by perceived strength. And not only must capabilities be perceived; threats to use them must be *credible*—a nation must believe that its opponent can and will use its strength to influence the outcome of a conflict. Possession of a weapon does not increase a nation's power if an adversary believes that it will not be used.

We have noted that those with the greatest nuclear arsenals do not necessarily get their way in political conflicts. This fact is even more evident if one examines the relations between strong and weak nations as measured by their relative military capabilities. Weaker states have often gotten their way politically against their military superiors. A Vietnam that was weak in the conventional military sense succeeded against a vastly more militarized France, and, later, America, in getting what it wanted, despite the weapons preponderance of its adversaries. An armada of missiles and bombers

25. See Coplin and Kegley (1975) for a comparative inventory and critique of factors that are assumed to contribute to the power potential of nations.

capable of inflicting horrendous destruction did not enable the United States to prevent the emergence of a communist government in Cuba, only 90 miles from its shores. Similarly, vastly superior military power did not prevent seizure of the USS *Pueblo* by North Korea in 1968 or the incarceration of American diplomatic personnel by Iran a decade later. The seeming inability of the Soviet Union to influence the course of events in Afghanistan without using military force also suggests that the malaise of military power is not peculiar to the United States. In these and other important instances, so-called second- and third-rate military powers appear at times to have exerted more influence over the superpowers than the superpowers have over them. In fact, at times those nations most prepared militarily seem to have the least influence diplomatically (see Holsti, 1977). One of the major lessons of contemporary world politics, in short, is that the power to destroy is *not* the power to control. If ever military capabilities were a significant contributing part of national power, that contribution appears to have declined, perhaps irreversibly. "Real power—the ability to affect others—seems in fact more widely dispersed than perhaps at any time in the world's history" (Bundy, 1977).

A related lesson of recent years is that influence derives from sources that may be more potent than military might, in particular, economic power (for further discussion, see Hoffmann, 1975; Keohane and Nye, 1973 and 1977; Morse, 1976; Caporaso and Ward, 1979). Economic capacity, trade and investment strategies, and the distribution of relative monetary strength may in the long run be more influential than the distribution of arms and armies. In part the continuing importance of the United States in the postwar international system derives as much from its economic strength as from its military might. But the same holds true for other nations. This was glaringly evident in 1973–1974, when the oil-producing nations were able to bring the militarily superior nations of the Western world to their knees.

The nature of military capabilities has so changed that military inferiority may not necessarily be a liability (see Schelling, 1966). Historically it has been shown that those who have been the least armed have also been the least likely to be attacked (see Richardson, 1960a). Conversely, the acquisition of arms may invite attack because weapons elicit fear and aggression in others (see Berkowitz and LePage, 1970). But the incentives for attacking a nation that is defenseless are not overwhelming. Here, some theorists have argued that what you prepare for is what you get, and that enemies are most dangerous when they are provoked—and nothing is more provocative than the maintenance of a sophisticated system of delivering destruction. In this age some of those countries which have spent the least for weapons—such as Japan or Austria—may ironically be more secure than their heavily-armed counterparts. Relevant in this context is the warning once made by President John F. Kennedy: in the event of another total war, regardless how it might begin, the superpowers would ultimately become targets of destruction.

Some critics of the present world condition have questioned whether the logic that sustains contemporary circumstances might not be challenged. These observers have called for a revolution in the way the problem of national security has been approached. They note that unarmed or defenseless countries would be able (especially in the absence of a meaningful foreign threat) to practice a flexibility in their foreign policies which their armed neighbors cannot. They would be freed from the responsibilities which the possession of (military) power confers. Unarmed nations would not have to manage that capability or to devote their time and energies to controlling its use; moreover, they would be freed to concentrate their energies on the development of their economies. While such countries would have to live in the constant shadow of others' missiles, they could nonetheless live in the comfort that those missiles are not directed at them. Although disarmed nations may have more actual political troubles, they are likely to have fewer imaginary ones, so this reasoning holds. They could also live in the knowledge that the absense of a military capability would not preclude them from exercising influence by other means.

But these are speculative, even utopian, thoughts. It would be premature to declare the advent of an age in which the meek have inherited the earth. The notion persists that arms will make nations secure and powerful, and the quest for arms continues unabated. Although the global arena may be undergoing a fundamental transformation as a result of the declining utility of military capabilities (in part because the dispersion of increasingly destructive weapons throughout the globe has made them increasingly difficult to use), the quest for power and security through military capabilities persists, nevertheless. Nations continue to negotiate in the language of military power. Armed forces of the world continue to maintain a symbiotic relationship—the existence of armed forces in one country necessitates and rationalizes their creation and maintenance in others. That the international system, at least in the foreseeable future, will become an even more militarized one, can be predicted without fear of being embarrassed by subsequent developments.

What will be the consequences of this dominant trend in international society for the kind of environment in which states and their citizens live? Is human history becoming, as H. G. Wells long ago prophesied it would, more and more a race between self-restraint and survival?

Eleven

War and Other Forms of Violent Conflict in World Politics

> In the past, war has been accepted as the ultimate arbiter of disputes among nations. But in the nuclear era we can no longer think of war as merely a continuation of diplomacy by other means. Nuclear war cannot be measured by the archaic standards of victory or defeat.
>
> Jimmy Carter, 1979

> In this age . . . there can be no losers in peace and no victors in war.
>
> Lyndon B. Johnson, 1963

If global politics are to be understood, the problem of war must be confronted. War has been condemned as a method for resolving human conflict but defended as a necessary instrument of justice. Nations have come into being through it and have disappeared because of it. War has been ceaselessly debated, but it has been relied on as the ultimate means of self-preservation. Yet, today, as never before, it poses a danger to the survival of the human race.

It is understandable that an institution regarded as "sanctioned massacres" (Kelman, 1973), as an industry whose product is death, evokes a response of anxiety and makes us want to turn away in terror. Nonetheless, throughout history, war has operated as a catalyst of change in the relations of nations. War, as a dominant and persistent characteristic of international politics, must be examined. "It is not enough . . . to shudder over pictures of bloated bodies floating up on a beach, or of maggoted corpses piled up like cordwood. All the poetic fervor in the world against war will not abolish war if men do not understand how wars begin and how peace must be made" (Norman Cousins, cited in McNeil, 1965).

TRENDS IN INTERNATIONAL VIOLENCE

Daily papers and television news programs are constant reminders that we live in an age of violence. They attest to human ingenuity in devising new modes of aggressiveness and to the seemingly habitual reliance on force as a method of resolving political conflicts. Preparing for and making war looks like the major preoccupation of the world. It has been estimated, for instance, that in the 1945–1978 period "there were no more than twenty-six days . . . in which there was no war somewhere in the world; . . . on any given day . . . there is an average of twelve wars going on somewhere in the world" (Sampson, 1978: 60).

It has been hypothesized by Norman Cousins (cited in Beer, 1974: 7) that since 3600 B.C. there have been over 14,500 major and minor wars which have taken the lives of over 3.5 billion people. Another study recorded 14,531 wars over 5,560 years of history, which translates into an average of over 2.5 wars a year (Grieves, 1977: 7). Other, less speculative, accounts support this estimate.[1] Wright (1942) documented 278 wars from 1480 to 1940; Richardson (1960b), looking at the period between 1820 and 1949, identified over 300 wars; and Pitirim Sorokin (1937), perusing human history from approximately 1100 through 1925, records 862 wars. In the process he found that his native Russia had experienced over a thousand-year span only one quarter of a century without war.

Each of these compilations, like others, points toward a grim characteristic of world politics: the recurrent willingness of people to fight makes warfare a common attribute of global relations. William James's (1968) suggestion that "history is a bath of blood" may be hyperbole, but the repetitive incidence of warfare between and within nations supports the interpretation.

To better understand warfare and its meaning in the contemporary world, we must first attempt to define and measure it more precisely. Has warfare increased or decreased in frequency and magnitude over the years? Are transformations in violence in the international system occurring to such an extent that the nature and function of war are changing? Indeed, is warfare in the contempo-

---

1. Estimates vary, depending on the criteria used to define war. Kende (1971), for example, identified 97 "local wars" in the 1945–1965 period, most of which were essentially intranational wars of one sort or another. In comparison, Azar's (1973: 2) inventory of "wars, domestic upheavals, and large-scale hostilities" in the 1945–1970 period identified some 559 instances of such violence; Luard's (1968: 62–64) list of "external wars" involving sovereign states included 9 such wars between 1940 and 1965, and 62 between 1865 and 1965; Sivard (1979b: 9) lists over 120 hostilities between 1955 and 1979.

rary international system different from the warfare of fifty or a hundred years ago?

While no one would deny that there has been fighting around the globe throughout recorded history, few seem able to agree on a precise definition of a war. For example, legal definitions—according to traditional international law, which assumes that armed conflict becomes a war when it is *declared*—are of little help. By such definitions, there have been *no* wars since 1945. There is also no agreement concerning the number and kind of participants and the number of casualties that must be involved before fighting that results in death is considered "war." But such criteria are necessary if the phenomenon of war is to be defined. Some rules are needed to distinguish between "war" and other forms of international conflict.

Conflict and War

War cannot be considered mere conflict. Conflict entails, at a minimum, the existence of two or more parties who perceive differences between or among them and who are committed to resolving those differences to their own satisfaction. Conflict may be seen as an intrinsic product of communication and contact between peoples; when groups interact, some conflict is inevitable. As an essential part of all social interaction, therefore, conflict should not necessarily be regarded as either infrequent or an anomaly.

Nor should conflict necessarily be regarded as undesirable. Conflict performs many positive functions (such as enhancing social solidarity, clarifying values, stimulating growth, and promoting learning) which, if managed, are constructive to human progress. Coser (1956), for instance, observes that close contact leads to both friendship and enmity, for cooperation may produce conflict, and that conflict, paradoxically, may promote cooperation.

But when conflicts between nations are not managed successfully, the potential for violence as a method of resolution arises. Clausewitz's dictum that war is merely an extension of diplomacy by other means underscores the fact that force is but one mechanism through which nations may seek to achieve their political objectives. But it is the deadliest way. War means that diplomacy failed, that persuasion did not work, and that bargaining was unsuccessful. War is, in this sense, as Clausewitz stated, "a form of communication between nations," albeit an extreme form.

Intrinsic to this definition is the notion that war entails the use of organized military force against an adversary to achieve political objectives. This definition leads to the conclusion that necessary conditions for interstate war are (1) the existence of independent political units, (2) the existence of conflict (actual or perceived) among them, and (3) the employment of armed force by at least one unit that results in significant numbers of deaths to members of the opposing national unit. (A civil war entails conflict and death within a nation but not between nations.)

War: Some Empirical Evidence

Perhaps the most rigorous scientific effort to explore the historical incidence of war according to this conception is the Correlates of War Project, headed by Professors J. David Singer and Melvin Small. Small and Singer (1979) have identified 105 wars in the 1815–1977 period, defined as sustained military conflicts involving at least two states (one of whom must be a sovereign nation) which resulted in at least 1,000 battle deaths. (And see Singer and Small, 1972, for statistical details.)

By examining the distribution of these wars over time, it is possible to arrive at some conclusions about the extent to which war has undergone change. For analytic purposes, the world system can be broken into seven historical periods which conform to what many scholars and policy makers conventionally regard as major transition points in contemporary history (see Figure 11.1). Absent from the data are World War I (1914–1918) and World War II (1939–1945), which involved nearly the entire world in violent conflict. But these periods should be kept in mind in attempting to observe historical shifts, so that the impact which world conflagration can exert on subsequent trends is not forgotten.

In interpreting Figure 11.1 it is important to note that each period does not span the same number of years. Moreover, inferences about changes in the incidence of war should take cognizance of the fact that the number of sovereign nations comprising the international system has steadily increased (from 29 in 1815 to 149 in 1977).[2] This is important because the number of wars can be hypothesized to be a function of the number of actors—the number of opportunities for contact among them will increase as the number of nations increases, and such contact is likely to generate increased occasions for conflict and war.[3]

2. The average number of nation-states for each period shown in Figure 11.1 is as follows: 1816–1849, 29; 1850–1870, 39; 1871–1890, 34; 1891–1914, 42; 1919–1939, 64; 1946–1965, 95; and 1966–1977, 135.

3. To make temporal comparisons more meaningful, Small and Singer (1979) have "normalized" the data with common denominators: annual averages (or wars per year) and averages of the number of wars begun per period per system member. This facilitates inference by partially controlling for variations in both the size of the global system and in the lengths of the period. The reader is encouraged to review those indicators to pursue their interpretation.

Figure 11.1
Frequency of Wars Begun in Seven Historical Periods, 1816–1977

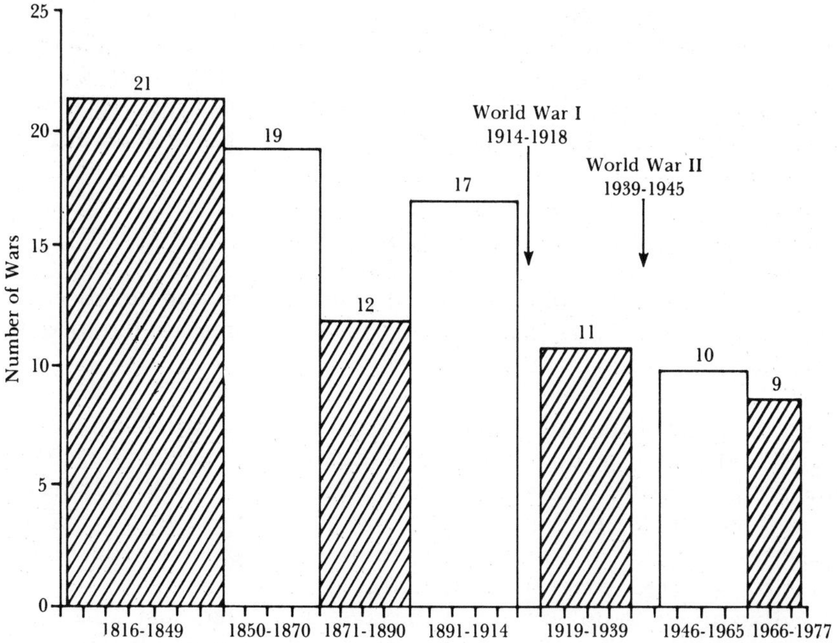

Source: Adapted from Melvin Small and J. David Singer, "Conflict in the International System, 1816–1977: Historical Trends and Policy Futures," in Charles W. Kegley, Jr., and Patrick J. McGowan (eds.), *Challenges to America* (Beverly Hills: Sage, 1979), p. 95.

Figure 11.1 shows what was suspected: war has been a recurrent phenomenon. But the frequency of war has not been consistent; instead, the pattern is one of fluctuation. A linear trend in the incidence of war is not apparent.[4] None of the periods attests to man's ability to control internation violence throughout the globe. Note, however, that the frequency of wars declines (from twenty-one to nine) as we move from the first through the last period. There appears, if anything, to be perhaps a modest downward trend in the outbreak of wars between nations.

Small and Singer (1979) found that while there has not been a decline in the average number of wars initiated per year, there has been a decline in the amount of war each nation experiences. That is, war appears to be becoming less general—most nations are managing to reduce the number of wars in which they become involved.

4. This finding is supported by Richardson's (1960b) data and is reinforced by K.J. Holsti's (1966) empirical study, which found no significant variation across time in the incidence of war: in the 1919–1939 period, 27 instances of military force were found, as compared to 25 in the 1945–1965 period. Subsequently Holsti (1977) identified in addition eleven instances of armed conflict in the 1965–1975 period.

But because some nations continue to experience war with repetitious frequency, the overall picture for the international system as a whole is one in which the outbreak of war looks persistent despite the recent modest decline. Perhaps the safest conclusion that can be drawn is that "no significant trend upward or downward is manifest over the past 150 years" in the number of wars occurring (Singer and Small, 1972). This conclusion is amenable to several interpretations.

Alternate Pespectives on the Causes of War

The initiation of war often has been likened to contagious disease. Hence some observers have argued that war is best understood as an epidemic caused by many viruses.

Does violence breed violence? The adage "violence breeds violence" reflects this idea, as do many diplomatic histories which allege that the seeds of future wars are found in past wars. World War II (as an outgrowth of World War I) and the recurrent wars in the Middle East (essentially the same battle being fought over decades) have been interpreted from this perspective.

Existing data do not permit the conclusion that past wars have *caused* subsequent wars. But the impression provided by the data tends to support the proposition in the sense that the frequency of past wars tends to be correlated with the incidence of wars in a following period.[5] This finding conforms to the well-known view of history that, "Other things being equal, the more frequently things have happened in the past, the more sure you can be they will happen in the future" (Horst, 1963).

Is war inevitable? Many people believe that war is inevitable, including a surprising number of those who have considered it a constructive force.[6] Those subscribing to the belief in war's inevitability have often taken their ammunition from the fact that historically war has been so recurrent.

Could it be this is a kind of self-fulfilling prophecy? Expecting war and violence, people prepare for it, and then discover that their actions promote the very conditions which make war most likely. Consider the reflection of Sir Frederick Maurice: "I went into the

5. Care should be exercised in placing confidence in conclusions derived from correlational analysis. No association or correlation between two variables, no matter how reliable, constitutes proof that one is the cause of the other.

6. See Nef (1968) for a trenchant critique of the idea that war promotes human progress.

British Army believing that if you want peace you must prepare for war. I believe now that if you prepare thoroughly for war you will get it" (cited in Eddy and Page, 1924).

This causal factor notwithstanding, evidence fails to support the thesis of war's inevitability. That history has been replete with wars does not, as some have argued (see Stockton, 1932), necessarily mean that we will always have them in the future. Preoccupation with violence may blind us to an important fact, namely, that war is the exception, rather than the rule, as a mode of international intercourse. Most nations historically have experienced more peaceful than bellicose interactions with others.

Indeed, anthropologists have demonstrated that war is not a universal institution (Mead, 1968; Etzioni, 1968; Sumner, 1968; Kluckhohn, 1944). There are societies that do not know war. Even some nations have been relatively immune to war for prolonged periods (Switzerland and Sweden). What this suggests is that war is not necessarily inevitable and that peace may be possible. It also suggests that mankind is not doomed to a historical determinism which denies free will, that nature has a purpose, and that human behavior is not a victim of historical forces beyond man's ability to control or modify. Moreover, there is evidence to indicate that the outbreak of war has stabilized and may even be declining moderately. When it is recalled that the decline has occurred despite the dramatic increase in the number of nations in recent decades, it would appear that the possibility that a nation will escape the war experience is improving. This temporal variation, making war less—not more—likely for most nations, hardly enhances confidence in theories of war's inevitability.

Is war rooted in human nature? Some have argued that war is inevitable because man's essentially evil nature dooms him to express that nature in violent behavior. For instance, Sigmund Freud (1968) and Konrad Lorenz (1963) contend that aggression is innate, stemming from man's physiology and genetic programming. Noting that Homo sapiens is the most deadly of the species, ethologists (those who study animal behavior in order to better understand human behavior) have similarly argued that man is one of the few species who routinely kills his own kind by practicing "intra-specific" aggression such as war. Most other species only kill other species, except in the most unusual circumstances (cannibalism in certain tropical fishes is one exception).

Most social scientists have challenged these theories on empirical and logical grounds. If warfare is an inevitable impulse deriving from human nature, critics have asked, then how can the relatively infrequent occurrence of war be explained? If aggression is an inherent part of human nature, a biological necessity, presumably all humans should express this genetically determined form of behavior.

Many social scientists have concluded that war is a learned trait, that it is a part of our cultural and environmental—not biological—heritage.[7] Aggression is a propensity acquired early in life as a result of socialization and learning; therefore, according to this perspective, a conditioned response to conflict for which substitutes can be found and learned. The fact that many societies have learned to manage conflicts without war suggests that human nature can express itself in a variety of ways; and it suggests that violence is not necessarily an inborn drive or trait that makes war inevitable.

Because foreign policies are generally made by collectivities rather than by single individuals (hence under circumstances that circumscribe individual discretion), the way human nature finds expression is constrained by the social-psychological factors typically associated with group decision making. For these reasons most observers have rejected the once prevalent belief that violence derives from an innate aggressiveness in human nature. Violence may derive from conditions, but not from human drives. As Gurr (1970) puts it, "The capacity, but not the need, for violence appears to be biologically entrenched in men."

Are there cycles of war and peace? If war is recurrent but not necessarily inevitable, how might variations in the amount of war over time be explained? The absence of a clear trend in the frequency of war does not discount the possibility that nations engage in war periodically (though not continually), and that therefore the incidence of war might rise and fall over long stretches of time as latent enmities between nations erupt into violence. Here yet another theoretical interpretation of the evidence suggests itself: that social processes are at work in the world political system which create cycles in the incidence of war. According to this perspective, world history is governed by cycles of war and peace, in which the frequency of war in the global system oscillates rhythmically between peaks and valleys (see Modelski, 1978). The image is one of world history guided by an all-powerful invisible hand built into the system's structure (or derived from divine origin) which causes evolutionary patterns to manifest themselves.

There may be deterministic overtones in such theories, but they have an intuitive appeal. It seems plausible that a war experience

---

7. The debate over the nature/nurture question will probably never be resolved. For a review of the debate as it pertains to international relations, see Nelson (1974).

produces aftereffects which may last for generations. Presumably, therefore, a nation experiencing war will exhaust itself and extinguish its enthusiasm for another war, but only for a time. This idea has been labeled the "war weariness" hypothesis (Blainey, 1973). Italian historian Luigi da Porto's reasoning is an example of one version: "Peace brings riches; riches bring pride; pride brings anger; anger brings war; war brings poverty; poverty brings humanity; humanity brings peace; peace, as I have said, brings riches and so the world's affairs go round" (cited in Blainey, 1973). The implication is that it takes time to move through these stages, which explains why there may be alterations between periods of enthusiasm for war and of weariness of war.

Arnold J. Toynbee's *A Study of History* (1947) is a classic illustration of the view that history oscillates between periods of war and periods of peace, with the cycle taking over a century. Tests of this proposition have led to conflicting results, however. Wright (1942) suggested that if periods of war do exist, they can best be described as comprising intervals of peace lasting about fifty years between major outbreaks of war. Richardson (1960a) and Sorokin (1937) interpreted their data to entail cycles of over 200 years from peak to peak, and Dewey (1964) estimated a 177-year cycle to be operative. And, looking at the proposition that "periods of high violence in the system will be followed by a decrease in the level of violence" (and, conversely, that "periods of low systemic violence will be followed by an increase in violence"), Denton and Phillips (1971) measured the amount of war under way rather than the number of wars begun and concluded that peaks in international violence occur every twenty to thirty years.

The evidence in Figure 11.1 suggests that if a cycle in the worldwide incidence of war is present,[8] it probably is closer to a twenty-year duration. But the evidence does not permit a safe inference about the existence of war cycles. If there are periods of violence and of peace in global relations, they are difficult to discern from the data. The pattern revealed is best described cautiously as "a fluctuating pattern, perhaps suggesting a mild periodicity" or "a very crude periodicity"[9] (Small and Singer, 1979).

From several theoretical standpoints, therefore, statements regarding the extent to which warfare in the global system is undergoing transformation might be questioned. The evidence presented here does not (headlines notwithstanding) support the notion that

8. For further discussion of cycles in international history, see Klingberg (1979).

9. Interestingly, Small and Singer (1972) report that "no cyclical patterns are apparent when we examine the military experiences of the individual nations which participated in several wars."

the number of wars is increasing. Wars appear, instead, to be stable in number, and may even be declining. There is, furthermore, little evidence to justify the proposition that war is necessarily inevitable. But there is likewise little to support the utopian dream that a warless world is just around the corner.

But if radical transformation in the incidence of war is not to be expected, war's character may nevertheless be undergoing fundamental change. This possibility can be examined by shifting focus from the frequency of war to the severity of war. That shift might prove profitable in understanding the changing nature of warfare in the contemporary world.

THE CHANGING CHARACTER OF VIOLENCE IN INTERNATIONAL POLITICS

If the good news is that wars may not be increasing in frequency, the bad news is that wars are becoming more deadly. One of the clearest long-term trends in the global system is a dramatic increase in the intensity and severity of war. The destructiveness of war can be measured by the most important statistic: the toll of human life. It has been estimated that "less than 2 million people died in wars between 1820 and 1863. From 1864 to 1907 about 4.5 million died" (Russett, 1965: 12–13). World War I claimed the lives of 8.5 million soldiers, whereas 15 million troops and over 65 million civilians (over 3 percent of the world's population at the time) died during World War II. Since World War II, it has been estimated that wars have claimed the lives of 25 million human beings (Sampson, 1978: 61).

The fact documented by these statistics is that since 1820 warfare has taken more and more life, both absolutely and relative to population size. The overall trend in casualties was spiraling most rapidly prior to World War II. Sorokin (1937) notes, for instance, that the casualty rate in Europe for the first quarter of this century exceeded the "total casualties for all the preceding centuries taken together." More apocalyptically, Russett (1965: 12–13) has noted that death from war has increased tenfold every fifty years, and comments that "If this growth rate . . . were to continue, wars by around the end of this century would kill the equivalent of the present population of the globe." Thus a significant aspect of the overall casualty rates is that they have risen in conjunction with technological developments, a factor that will be considered shortly.

As overall casualty rates have gone up, increasingly these costs have been borne by civilians and noncombatants; the casualty rates of the soldiers doing the fighting have actually gone down. This is partly because civilian populations have increasingly become the target of weapons of destruction, as in the use of aerial bombardment.

Nuclear Weapons and the Probability of War

The introduction of nuclear weapons creates new dangers that may exacerbate this trend. Today's nuclear weapons are far more destructive than those used against Japan during World War II. Consequently the prospect of waging even what is sometimes called a "limited" nuclear war with today's weapons is too horrible to contemplate. Indeed, it is conceivable that in the event of a nuclear holocaust, life as we know it would cease. President Kennedy's warning that "a full-scale nuclear exchange lasting less than 60 minutes . . . could wipe out more than 300,000,000 Americans, Europeans, and Russians" (cited in Van Dyke, 1966: 364) is today much too modest an estimate when the destructive power of present weapons is considered. President Carter's national security council staff estimated that the toll in lives in the United States and the Soviet Union alone would approach this level. The catastrophic proportions of such destruction are illustrated in Figure 11.2, which shows that the expected death toll of a nuclear war would be nearly nine times greater than the number of deaths suffered by Soviets and Americans in previous wars. And these figures do not include tens of millions more who would suffer the ravaging effects of radiation. Studies of the immediate and delayed effects of nuclear war (see Lewis, 1979, and Box 11.1) picture a postnuclear environment that is repugnant to contemplate.

How has the increasing destructiveness of modern weapons changed the nature of contemporary warfare? Indications of change are easy to detect. Small and Singer (1979) note, for instance, that the length of wars steadily increased between 1815 and World War II, but began a dramatic decline thereafter. Wars since 1945 have simply been shorter. Similarly, the average number of nation-participants in major wars (which had been rising steadily since 1815) has declined sharply since World War II. Wars are also more geographically confined. In fact, wars today are increasingly local wars involving small countries using conventional weapons. Fatalities from war have also decreased substantially since 1945, which constitutes a reversal of the 1820 to 1945 trend toward increasing casualties (see Small and Singer, 1979, for supporting data). When the modest erosion in the incidence of major wars since 1945 is added to this picture, an unmistakable impression results: warfare appears to be

Figure 11.2
Estimated Soviet and American Deaths in a Nuclear War

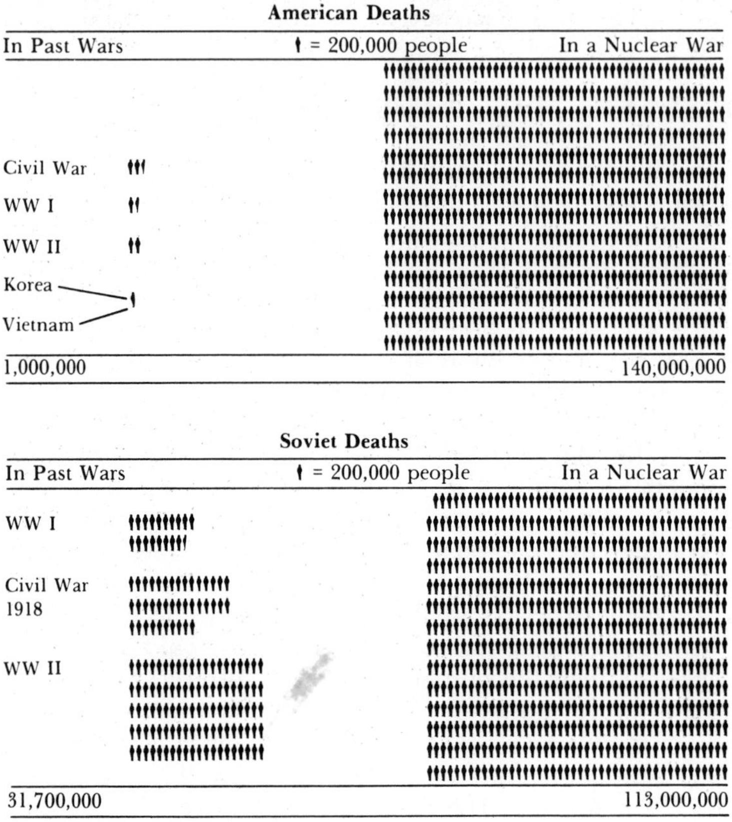

American Deaths

In Past Wars	♦ = 200,000 people	In a Nuclear War
		†††
		†††
		†††
		†††
Civil War †††		†††
WW I ††		†††
WW II ††		†††
Korea ⟍		†††
Vietnam ⟋ †		†††
1,000,000		140,000,000

Soviet Deaths

In Past Wars	♦ = 200,000 people	In a Nuclear War
WW I †††††††††† ††††††††		†††
Civil War †††††††††††††† 1918 †††††††††††††† ††††††††††		†††
WW II †††††††††††††††††† †††††††††††††††††† †††††††††††††††††† †††††††††††††††††† ††††††††††††††††††		†††
31,700,000		113,000,000

Source: *The Defense Monitor* (February 1979), p. 8. Estimates provided by the U.S. National Security Council.

undergoing a substantial transformation in the present international system.

Paradoxically, the world's most powerful nations often appear the most constrained to use their military strength, since the destructiveness of modern weapons seems to have reduced their practical utility. This thesis was articulated by Winston Churchill in 1953, when he inquired if weapons might breed restraint. He confessed he had on occasion

the odd thought that the annihilating character of [nuclear weapons] may bring an utterly unforeseeable security to mankind. . . . It may be that when the advance of destructive weapons enables everyone to kill anybody else no one will want to kill anyone at all.

Box 11.1   Two Views of the Aftermath of a Nuclear Attack

A Physicians' View

Medical "disaster planning" for a nuclear war is meaningless. . . . There is no possible effective medical response. Most hospitals would be destroyed, most medical personnel dead or injured, most supplies unavailable. Most "survivors" would die. . . .

A 20-megaton nuclear bomb . . . would create a fireball 1½ miles in diameter, with temperatures of 20 million to 30 million degrees Fahrenheit. . . . All living things would be vaporized within a radius of "ground zero." Six miles from this point, all persons would be instantly killed by a huge silent heat flash traveling at the speed of light. . . . Within a 10-mile radius, the blast wave would slow to 180 mph. In that area, winds and fires would probably kill 50 percent of the population, and injure another 40 percent. . . . Within 20 miles of the center, 50 percent of the inhabitants would be killed or injured by the thermal radiation and blast pressures, and tens of thousands would suffer severe burn injuries. . . .*

A Chemist's View

Policymakers underestimate the full impact of a nuclear attack on the United States because they focus on isolated factors, such as casualty figures from the blast and radiation.

Long after the attack, survivors would suffer doubt, fear, demoralization, guilt, disorientation, apathy, and antipathy toward authorities. . . . Among those who lived, a high rate of abnormal behavior, ranging from the non-functional to the antisocial, can be anticipated.

With the psychological stresses and severe shortages of resources, even the simplest requirements of survival will become major tasks. The destruction of urban centers would have a ripple effect throughout the country, with a crippling impact on food and fuel supplies, medical services, and labor and productive capacity. In fuel supplies alone, 98 percent of the petroleum refining capacity would be destroyed. . . . The food supply also would be hard-hit because of a concentration of food processing facilities. . . .†

---

*Physicians for Social Responsibility, "The Medical Consequences of Nuclear War," as reported by the Associated Press (March 8, 1980).
†Dr. Arthur Katz, in a study prepared for the Senate Banking Committee by a team of researchers at the Massachusetts Institute of Technology, as reported by the Associated Press (March 29, 1979).

Again in 1955 Churchill speculated:

> After a certain point has passed, it may be said, the worse things get the better. . . . Then it may be that we shall, by a process of sublime irony, have reached a stage in this story where safety will be the sturdy child of terror, and survival the twin brother of annihilation. (Cited in Van Dyke, 1966: 378)

This predicament provides a potent explanation for the decline since 1945 in war involving major powers. In fact, general war between great powers has not occurred in the past 35 years (although wars by proxy, such as China's and the Soviet Union's support for opposing sides in the 1977–1978 Vietnam-Cambodia conflict, have been chronic). It was perhaps the incredible costs and risks of fighting which led President Nixon to say, in the context of the Vietnam War, that "I seriously doubt that we will ever have another war. This is probably the very last one." The sentiment has been shared by others. Writing "On the Obsolescence of War," Weltman (1974) has noted, for instance, that "violence as an instrument of foreign policy has increasingly become highly inefficient, if not counterproductive."

Although the possibility of nuclear war certainly lingers, and although the superpowers continue to stockpile the weapons of war, it can be questioned if warfare is the intended purpose. The goals may have changed from winning in war to deterring an adversary from initiating it: "each player wants not so much to win as to avoid loss" (Copeland, 1969). This development, to the extent that it is more than a transitory phase, signals a relatively new development in international politics.

A rival explanation for the world's ability thus far to avoid nuclear war is also worth contemplating. This is the pessimistic view that humankind has escaped nuclear devastation largely by sheer luck. By the laws of probability, so this reasoning goes, the longer nuclear arsenals continue to exist, the likelihood that human miscalculation will inevitably trigger a nuclear exchange approaches certainty. According to probability theory, in other words, any event that can possibly happen will happen; the question is not if, but when. From this perspective, deterrence is inherently unstable—it cannot be perpetual. That the odds are not good for avoiding nuclear holocaust for a prolonged period is rather compelling, inasmuch as the risk of error, miscalculation, or accident, is great. Moreover, the limits to rationality under conditions of stress, the obstacles to effective interstate communication, the risks associated with competitive confrontations—all enhance the potential dangers.

These apocalyptic thoughts suggest that the destructiveness of nuclear weapons will lead, not to their nonuse, but rather to annihilation—later if not sooner. At best, nuclear weapons produce a precarious stability in the absence of real security, because the weapons possess the capacity to permanently destroy both stability and security. The ostensible peace among the superpowers since 1945 may, indeed, be the product of luck rather than a *pax atomica*. The idea that holding ever more powerful weapons will make nations ever more safe may thus be questioned.

Which Nations Are Prone to War?

In his inspection of war in previous periods, Wright concluded (1942) that new nations are more prone to initiate wars than are mature states. Part of the reason for this is that newly independent nations tend to go through a period of intense nationalistic feelings, and the kind of nationalism pervasive today has tended to serve as a catalyst to war.[10]

It is noteworthy, in addition, that the type of political system of a country has little bearing on the likelihood that a nation will become a participant in war. Historically, democracies have been involved in war as frequently as have autocracies (Wright, 1942). Inspection of the participants in wars since 1945 suggests that this pattern continues today. This casts considerable doubt on the proposition that "making the world safe for democracy" would produce peace; indeed, history has not been kind to the theory that democratic states are peaceful states. Democracies have entered war much too frequently to place much confidence in their ability to extinguish the penchant for violence. Alexis de Tocqueville has suggested, instead, that not only is democracy not a safeguard against war, but that democracies, once engaged in war, tend to be the most vicious and unrestrained. Presumably the arousal of mass involvements and hatreds in democratic societies accounts for this feature, as George F. Kennan (1951) has observed.

Closely associated with nationalism is another national attribute related to the probability of war involvement: level of economic development. Wright (1942) found that advanced, industrialized societies with relatively high standards of living tend to be satisfied, status-quo states, and therefore the least prone to initiate a war which could risk the loss of that valued status. (There are, of course, many exceptions to this general tendency, such as Germany in 1939.) On the other hand, historically the most warlike states have been the poorer states (again, with important exceptions such as the United States in Vietnam in the 1960s and 1970s, and the Soviet Union in Afghanistan in 1979–1980). At least insofar as the geo-

---

10. Nationalism entails a sense of loyalty and devotion to a nation, an attitude of national consciousness exalting one nation above all others and placing primary emphasis on the promotion of its culture and interests as opposed to those of other nations or supranational groups. Kenneth Boulding has commented (cited in Nelson, 1974) on the violence-provoking consequences of this disposition by noting that nationalism is "the only religion that still demands human sacrifice."

graphic locus of war is concerned, this pattern seems to persist today. Sivard (1979b: 8) reports, for instance, that of "more than 120 armed conflicts between 1955 and the early part of 1979, all but six occurred in developing nations."

Several hypotheses have been proposed to explain this tendency. Some have argued, for example, that poor societies are internally unstable and that instability breeds war. This position views high levels of domestic conflict as promoting high levels of foreign conflict, as government officials attempt to divert attention from domestic ills. A variant of this idea contends that aggression is primarily a response to frustration, and that poor societies, being frustrated in their ability to satisfy their quests, are more war-prone. This notion helps explain war in the Third World as an attack on problems of self-esteem through attack on foreign enemies. We attack what we fear or envy.

Alternatively, war in the developing world may be seen as an effort to rectify perceived status discrepancies, wherein the nation initiating the war is seen as acting to reduce the difference between its ascribed and achieved status. Other explanations of war in preindustrial societies include the hypothesis that such wars are stimulated by the desire of less-developed nations to sever their dependency relationships with advanced nations, and especially with their former colonial masters, whose exploitative policies are seen as undermining their ability to grow economically. The Algerian and Indochinese wars are often cited as cases in point.

But before we conclude that poverty breeds war, it is important to note that those nations *most* impoverished are also among the least war-prone. (Exceptions to the general pattern abound, such as Bangladesh, Ethiopia, Somalia, Uganda, and Cambodia.) The most plausible explanation of the infrequency of conventional war in some of the poorest of the poor countries is that although they share all the frustrations and deprivations which might be expected to find expression through war, they are inhibited from venting their frustrations because they do not have the military or economic resources to sustain its costs. Thus the poorest nations share in common one attribute with the wealthiest: the infrequency with which they engage in war. Neither can afford to wage war, but for quite different reasons.

This pattern certainly does not mean that the poorest nations will always remain peaceful. Indeed, if the past is a guide to the future, then impoverished nations which experience a degree of development will be those most likely to participate in future wars, as economic growth and the rising expectations it often brings lead to outbursts of aggressiveness (Choucri and North, 1975).

The dispersion of the weapons of war throughout the Third World also exacerbates the problem of war. The future may well witness the specter of a peaceful developed world in the midst of a violent less-developed world. Western Europe, during its period of transition from relative poverty to the apex of development, experienced periods of extreme violence. Wright estimates that the major European states were at war about 65 percent of the time in the sixteenth and seventeenth centuries (Van Dyke, 1966: 359). Violence decreased only as European nations moved significantly up the ladder of development in later centuries.[11] If Third World nations advance economically so as to follow the European pattern, the world probably will be an even less peaceful place for some time into the future.

NEW MODES OF VIOLENCE IN INTERNATIONAL POLITICS

The present global system is highly stratified. The widespread use of such terms as *superpower, major power,* or—less flatteringly —*banana republic* is a reminder that the society of nations is by no means classless (Wallace, 1971). The hierarchical structure of the system encourages states to compete with each other for power and to struggle for status. Moreover, many of the resources for which nations compete are finite and scarce. The result is that nations frequently engage in conflict in order to compete for these resources. In addition to war itself, three other types of conflict characterize the transformed global arena, as a consequence, in part, of this competition: crises, civil wars, and terrorism.

Crises

It is a cliché that we live in an age of crisis. Former President Dwight D. Eisenhower, for instance, reflected in his memoirs that he could not "remember a day that has not brought its major or minor crisis" (cited in Hermann, 1972).

But the relationship between international *crisis* and international *violence* is not obvious (Brecher, 1977). Certainly a correlate of crisis is an increase in the amount and intensity of hostile messages between conflicting parties (Zinnes, Zinnes, and McClure, 1972). But crises may perhaps best be regarded as something less than international violence or war, even though more hostile and

11. Beer (1974: 28) similarly notes that over a third of the major wars occurring in the world since 3600 B.C. took place in Europe. The vast majority of these were initiated when the European states were adjusting to economic growth; the preceding prolonged period of economic stagnation was also a period of relative peace.

risky than most routine forms of communication. Milburn (1972) appropriately observes that the Chinese word for crisis means both threat and opportunity.

Because of the risks and costs of contemporary war, crisis may best be seen as a hostile form of competitive bargaining in interstate conflicts, performing the function that war often traditionally played, namely, forcing an enemy to comply with one's wishes.

> Their . . . function is to resolve without violence, or with only minimal violence, those conflicts that are too severe to be settled by ordinary diplomacy and that in earlier times would have been settled by war. Perhaps former Defense Secretary McNamara had something like this in mind when he said: "There is no longer any such thing as strategy, only crisis management." Churchill's famous aphorism "Peace is the sturdy child of terror" may require elaboration: Crisis is the big brother who mediates between the child and the parent. (Snyder and Diesing, 1977: 455–456)

The superpowers have been particularly prone to become involved in crises in the post-World War II period. In part, we can hypothesize, this was because of the willingness of the United States and the Soviet Union to flex their military muscles. According to a Brookings Institution study (Blechman and Kaplan, 1978), the United States and the Soviet Union have been especially prone to the use or threat of force to achieve their foreign policy objectives, often in internal conflicts in other nations. According to this study, "gunboat diplomacy" was practiced 215 times by the United States (an average of 7.2 incidents per year over a thirty-year period); in contrast, there were 115 recorded instances of Soviet attempts to use or threaten force to achieve foreign political objectives.

As coercive mechanisms, crises are, of course, fraught with peril. By their very nature they are provocative situations which take hostilities to the verge of war. Such threatening conditions in the past have often triggered war itself.[12] But nations appear willing to play the risky game of crisis politics, nevertheless. Implicit in their willingness, perhaps, is the assumption that crises can be effectively managed because, as rational actors, nations will ultimately avoid the final step to war. This assumption is a premise upon

---

12. As "anticipations of approaching harm that trigger feelings of stress," international *threats* are regarded as preliminary to (antecedents of) conditions of overt behavior of states (crises) and of war. For a review of the literature dealing with conceptions of threat, threat perceptions, threat agendas, and the like, see McGowan and Kegley (1980).

which much of American strategic thinking has been based (Schelling, 1960 and 1966).[13]

To contend that crises may be substitutes for war is to beg the question of what a crisis is. Unfortunately few observers seem able to agree on its meaning—despite the frequency with which the term is used. But Hermann's (1972) definition is a guide. He contends that "a crisis is a situation that (1) threatens the high-priority goals of the decision-making unit, (2) restricts the amount of time available for response before the decision is transformed, and (3) surprises the members of the decision-making unit by its occurrence." These attributes are, indeed, features of some of the most conspicuous crises of our age, such as the Cuban missile crisis, the Berlin blockade, and the Formosan Straits crisis. Each involved elements of surprise, threat, and time pressure. Each also involved the risk of war. In each, a sense of urgency precipitated by unanticipated maneuvers by others was involved. But all failed to spill over into military hostilities.[14]

The frequency of international crises provides a crude measure of global tension. In practice, global tensions often translate into situations where one state confronts another with a military threat. Such threatening displays take a variety of forms, ranging from mobilizations to deployments, from border crossings to displays of arms and seizures. They entail both martial words and deeds short of war. Small and Singer (1979) have inventoried all such confrontations short of war involving at least one major power since 1816. Figure 11.3 displays the frequencies of these crises in the seven-period chronology.

The evidence in Figure 11.3 demonstrates the historically chronic nature of military confrontations. From the perspective of changes over time, however, the message is ambiguous. But it does suggest several conclusions: (1) the number of military confronta-

13. The assumption may be dubious. Ole R. Holsti (1972) sardonically notes: "There is scant evidence that along with more lethal weapons we have evolved leaders more capable of coping with stress." For critiques which emphasize the tendency for crises to escalate because of time pressures, inadequate information, fear and anxiety, and personal stress which normally attends crisis situations, see Green (1966); Rapoport (1964); Kahn (1965); and Verba (1961).

14. According to this conception, crises which culminate in violence cease to be crises and become wars. Examples of wars which were preceded by crises include World War I; Bay of Pigs, Cuba (1961); Tibet (1959); Goa (1961); Suez (1956); Kashmir (1948); the Dominican Republic (1965); and Hungary (1956), among others. Conversely, some situations popularly termed crises in fact do not meet these conceptual tests. The global energy situation is an example. Surely the situation involves "threat," but neither "surprise" nor, somewhat less so, "time pressure," can be appropriately used to describe the global energy predicament.

Figure 11.3
Proportion of Military Confrontations Involving at Least One Major Power in Seven Historical Periods, 1816–1977

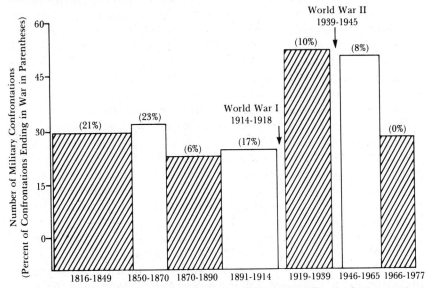

Source: Adapted from Melvin Small and J. David Singer, "Conflict in the International System, 1816–1977: Historical Trends and Policy Futures," in Charles W. Kegley, Jr., and Patrick J. McGowan (eds.), *Challenges to America* (Beverly Hills: Sage, 1979), p. 98.

tions has been fairly stable over time, (2) the average number of crises per year has risen in the twentieth century compared to the nineteenth, and (3) there is a modestly increasing trend in the incidence of military confrontations since 1816. More importantly, the data are consistent with Ole R. Holsti's (1972) proposition that (4) crises often escalate into war—a consistently large proportion of crises eventually culminate in war. But (5) this correlation between the incidence of crisis and the subsequent incidence of war declines in the twentieth century. That is, crises are less prone to result in war in the present century. As previously suggested, a plausible explanation for this might be found in the inhibiting influence of deadly weapons. The evidence lends support to the theory that the costs of warfare have curtailed its frequency. Many crises arise, but most have been managed successfully (especially since 1965).

Abolfathi, Hayes, and Hayes (1979) are among other analysts who have corroborated these findings.[15] Their study shows that 307

15. For empirical comparative research on these phenomena, see Hopple, Rossa, and Wilkenfeld (1980) and Mahoney and Clayberg (1980). The latter study provides an illuminating investigation of the Soviet image of crises and threats, as well as trend data about the incidence of Soviet threat perception between 1946 and 1975.

crises occurred between 1946 and 1976. The distribution is fairly stable across time, but the 1966–1976 period has been slightly less crisis-prone than the earlier periods. The average number of crises per year in the 1966–1976 period was 8.1, whereas the 1956–1976 annual average was 10.3. Part of the decline from the earlier period may be due to abatement of the Cold War and the shifting power configurations that occurred during the 1960s and 1970s. This evidence also indicates that the percentage of crises involving large powers has declined. The finding fits well with the previous interpretation that military confrontation has increasingly been perceived as a risky game by the superpowers. In contrast, crises between smaller powers continue unabated, steadily accounting for 10 to 15 percent of the total number of incidents. This suggests that the less-armed nations remain crisis-prone, and that, relatively speaking, the temptation to test adversaries' intentions with military threats is an option only the less-powerful are unable to resist—or able to afford.

Civil Wars

Still another form of violence in global politics entails wars within nations—civil wars. Luard (1968) speculates that civil wars "have become perhaps the most common of all types of international military activity" and estimates they are almost twice as common in the post-World War II period as in the period between the world wars.

Not only are civil wars commonplace nowadays; they are also lethal. Taylor and Hudson (1972: 110–115) attribute over one million deaths to domestic violence between 1948 and 1967. Gurr (1970: 3) notes that "ten of the world's thirteen most deadly conflicts in the past 160 years have been civil wars and rebellions; since 1945 violent attempts to overthrow governments have been more common than national elections."[16]

Small and Singer (1979), examining only instances of civil wars resulting in at least 1,000 battle deaths per year, found exactly 98 civil wars in the 161 years following 1816. (See Table 11.1.)

Clearly civil war is not an exclusively modern phenomenon. However, the frequency of civil war does indicate that some periods have been relatively more immune to civil violence than others. In fact, the incidence of civil war appears to conform to a periodic cycle, with periods of frequent civil-war activity followed by periods of inactivity. But rather than theorizing that a periodic cycle deter-

16. Blackburn et al. (1973) identified 552 internal wars in the period between 1946–1970 alone and found a general but steady rise in the incidence of these violent wars since 1962.

Table 11.1
Frequency and Severity of Civil Wars, 1816–1977

Period	Number of Civil Wars Begun	Number of Civil Wars Begun per Nation	Battle Deaths per Year	Battle Deaths per Year per Nation	Percentage of Civil Wars Inter-nationalized
1816–1849	12	.41	2,828	97.5	25
1850–1870	15	.38	135,650	3,478.2	7
1871–1890	6	.18	2,200	64.7	0
1891–1914	17	.40	15,498	392.6	18
1919–1939	11	.17	46,100	720.3	18
1946–1965	26	.27	107,920	1,136.0	27
1966–1977	11	.08	133,250	987.0	18

Source: Adapted from Melvin Small and J. David Singer, "Conflict in the International System, 1816–1977: Historical Trends and Policy Futures," in Charles W. Kegley, Jr., and Patrick J. McGowan (eds.), *Challenges to America* (Beverly Hills: Sage, 1979), pp. 100, 101.

mines the pattern, it is more plausible to link these periodic swings to structural changes occurring in the international environment. The relatively high levels of civil war exhibited in the 1850–1870 and 1891–1914 periods might be attributed to the effects of imperialism, industrialization, mass ideology, and nationalism, for example, whereas the frequency of civil war in the 1946–1965 period can be linked confidently to the break-up of the European colonial empires.

Also noteworthy are the indicators Small and Singer provide of the severity of civil wars. The number of lives lost in civil violence has remained high throughout the 161-year span but shows an alarming growth especially since World War II. Small and Singer note an ominous indicator of this trend: "13 of the first 15 most severe civil wars were fought in the twentieth century, [and] eight of those 13 were fought since 1946" (Small and Singer, 1979: 101–102). Some of the most deadly civil wars, in short, are the most recent.

Civil war and revolution have simultaneously been defended as instruments of justice and condemned as the immoral acceptance of violent change (Paynton and Blackey, 1971). They entail ingredients of both. The American, Russian, and Chinese revolutions all employed violence but were rationalized as necessary to realize aspirations for social change. In fact, most civil wars and revolutions have been savage in their destructiveness, a property that appears to be a characteristic of internal wars.

Civil wars stem from a variety of causes, from a wide range of intellectual, economic, social-structural, political, and evolutionary variables (Eckstein, 1972). And, as Gurr (1970) has shown, internal violence derives in part from man's reaction to the frustrations of his social and political environment.

Many observers (see Olsen, 1971) have explained the pervasiveness of internal violence in terms of the destabilization caused by rapid growth. Civil violence seems to occur in countries where conditions are improving because modernization generates expectations that can often not be satisfied. Governments, in other words, are often unable to keep pace with rising expectations (Gurr, 1970). "Economic modernization leads to political instability rather than political stability," according to Henry A. Kissinger.

What are the international consequences of civil wars? The trend toward increasing severity of internal wars suggests the possibility that civil wars lead to interstate wars—wars between sovereign states. The reasoning behind this inference is that great powers have global interests and are concerned with fostering the growth of friendly governments in other countries and preventing hostile governments from coming to power. Consequently great powers are prone to intervene militarily in civil wars to protect what they perceive to be their political interests in a politically fragmented world.[17] Outside powers, therefore, intervene to help maintain existing governments, to overthrow them, or to prevent what is perceived to be an unstable foreign situation from deteriorating into a development seen as inimical to the great power.

Participants in civil wars are also often tempted to invite external support for their cause. In an intensely fought civil struggle, foreign assistance may be the margin between defeat and victory; hence the search for assistance is frequently intense. Intervention then often breeds further intervention: "where one outside power or alliance becomes involved in a dispute of this kind, another almost invariably becomes so in due course" (Luard, 1968).

A similar interpretation can be inferred from the evidence in Table 11.1. A consistently high percentage of civil wars has become internationalized through military intervention by an external actor. Typically, as inferred from this span of 161 years, nearly one in five civil wars ultimately becomes an interstate war. Thus periods of high civil violence may also tend to be periods of high interstate violence. While that correlation does not prove the direction of causation, the evidence suggests that civil wars promote international wars, and not vice versa. Some of America's more recent foreign in-

17. Little (1975) concludes that military intervention in civil wars has been an almost exclusively major-power phenomenon. Looking at fifty cases of intervention over two centuries, Little finds that the chance of great-power intervention is about 15 percent.

volvements, for example, began as U.S. responses to internal wars (Lebanon, the Dominican Republic, Korea, and Vietnam); and Soviet interventions have also occurred in countries undergoing violent internal disruptions (Hungary, Ethiopia, and Afghanistan). As *The Defense Monitor* (November 1979: 2) observed, in 1979 foreign combat troops were actively engaged in over 20 percent of the 37 domestic rebellions occurring at that time.

A consideration of the international consequences of civil wars would not be complete without attention to another proposition: the hypothesis that civil unrest promotes external aggression, not by provoking great power intervention, but rather because, under conditions of civil disturbance, political leaders try to mitigate internal disorder by diverting people's attention toward foreign adversaries. The assumption is that national cohesion rises in the face of external threat. From this perspective, then, civil violence is seen as breeding foreign conflict and war.

This hypothesis has a rich folklore as well as an intuitive appeal. At least since Thucydides, it has been part of the conventional wisdom that conflict at home is related to conflict abroad, and that leaders wage the latter in order to resolve the former. Machiavelli, for instance, advised the Prince to undertake foreign wars whenever turmoil within the state became too great. More recently, Hermann Goering advocated the same idea in Nazi Germany by contending: "Voice or no voice, the people can always be brought to do the bidding of the leaders. That is easy. All you have to do is tell them they are being attacked and denounce the pacifists for lack of patriotism" (cited in Gilbert, 1950). Before he became an American secretary of state, John Foster Dulles (1939) expressed a similar sentiment: "The easiest and quickest cure of internal dissension is to portray danger from abroad. Thus group authorities find it convenient always to keep alive among the group members a feeling that their nation is in danger from one or another of the nation-villians with which it is surrounded."

Implicit in this view is the notion that external war results in increased domestic support of political leaders. Morris (1969) forcefully summarizes this view:

> To put it cynically, one could say that nothing helps a leader like a good war. It gives him his only chance of being a tyrant and being loved for it at the same time. He can introduce the most ruthless forms of control and send thousands of his followers to their deaths and still be hailed as a great protector. Nothing ties tighter the in-group bonds than an out-group threat.

Whether war in fact solves internal problems and whether political leaders actually initiate wars in order to deal with domestic violence are empirical questions. Fortunately, the proposition that domestic violence is a precondition to, and precipitant cause of, international war has been subjected to rigorous scientific testing. The findings, moreover, have been consistent. Empirical studies by Cattell (1949), Rummel (1963), and Tanter (1966), among others, have repeatedly failed to show a substantial connection between a country's level of domestic instability and its external aggression. In short, an otherwise plausible theory fails to be supported by the evidence. (See Stein, 1976, and Scolnick, 1974, for a review of this literature.)

We can be somewhat relieved to find that civil disturbance, in general, does not lead to foreign belligerency. But the important qualification—that under some circumstances the relationship between domestic violence and foreign conflict may hold—should be considered. There are examples in both authoritarian and democratic political systems of domestic conflicts that have led to foreign aggressiveness (Zinnes and Wilkenfeld, 1971). Internal stress has also led to foreign belligerence in some African nations (Collins, 1973). Moreover, in highly militarized societies, reductions in civil strife have been associated with increases in foreign belligerence (Kegley, Richardson, and Richter, 1978).

But for most nations, perhaps, the most compelling reason for the absence of a direct linkage between civil unrest and foreign aggressiveness is that "When domestic conflict becomes extremely intense it would seem more reasonable to argue that there is a greater likelihood that a state will retreat from its foreign engagements in order to handle the situation at home" (Zinnes and Wilkenfeld, 1971). Foreign aggressiveness in fact may be a function of internal solidarity in militarized societies, because only in such societies can a state's energies be freed from domestic demands in order to focus attention on the resolution of international problems. A militarized society is not so likely to be intimidated by the prospect of escalating international antagonisms; and such societies alone have the resources to deal either alternately or concomitantly with both civil and foreign wars (Kegley, Richardson, and Richter, 1978). Given the increasing militarization of the nations of the world, these findings suggest that the linkage between aggression at home and abroad may well increase in the future.

Terrorism

Our television and newspapers tell of the growing incidence of yet another alarming kind of violence that is transforming the global system: international terrorism. Almost daily the media report the kidnappings and at times murder of diplomats and of government and corporation leaders, bombings, sabotage, and the taking of hostages. While the instruments of terror are varied and the motivations of the terrorists diverse, all terrorist activity is meant to achieve political objectives. Moreover, terrorism often has a uniquely international character (see Mickolas, 1976; Sloan and Kearney, 1978; Pierre, 1976). Although some terrorist activities begin and end in a single country, a large proportion transcends national borders. Terrorism is thus a form of political violence that is primarily global in scope.

Although terrorism did not originate in the contemporary era, it does seem to be a distinctive disorder of the modern world (Fromkin, 1977). "Terrorism has grown from an esoteric aspect of aggression and violence to a predominant means for international and intranational conflict resolution" (Blair and Brewer, 1977). It arises so frequently perhaps because it is a strategy which even the weak can employ. Modern technology may have contributed inadvertently to its apparent increasing incidence, for a crucial part of the terrorists' strength derives from the instant access that television provides as a medium of communication in which to publicize their grievances. The ability to bring the terrorist act into the global spotlight by securing publicity is a catalyst to the fear which the act is intended to generate. And part of what makes terrorism so terrifying is the message that anyone can become its victim.

The prevalence of international terrorism in today's world is abundantly clear. Estimates of the incidence of international terrorist activities vary somewhat (see Pierre, 1976; Sloan and Kearney, 1978). But all surveys indicate that nonterritorially based terrorism has become a ubiquitious feature of world politics. Recent trends are depicted in Figure 11.4 and Table 11.2.

The figures are not comforting. They suggest that terrorism, as a recurrent form of violence in international politics, shows only a modest recent decline despite international efforts to bring it under control. And not reassuringly, there is no decrease in casualties (or injuries) resulting from terrorist acts in this period. The 3,336 terrorist acts reported accounted for the killing of 2,689 people and the wounding of 5,955 more; "these attacks caused more deaths . . . in 1979 than during any previous year since . . . 1968. . . . One fourth of all attacks between 1968 and 1979 resulted in casualties" (U.S. Central Intelligence Agency, 1980: iv, 1).

As the data in Table 11.2 suggest, international terrorists employ a variety of methods in pursuit of their objectives. Nearly one-half (47.6 percent) of all efforts entailed the use of explosive bombings in the 1968–1979 period, although many other kinds of techniques have found persistent use. In general, many terrorist

Figure 11.4
International Terrorist Incidents, 1968–1979

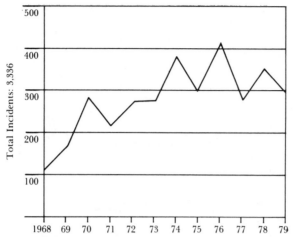

Source: U.S. Central Intelligence Agency, National Foreign Assessment Center, "International Terrorism in 1979" (Washington, D.C.: Director of Public Affairs, Central Intelligence Agency, April 1980), p. 1.

methods are *not* intended to cause casualties; but the trend toward incidents aimed at that end—most notably assassination attempts—has increased (U.S. Central Intelligence Agency, 1980).

Regional breakdowns indicate that international terrorism is largely a phenomenon of the industrialized countries. Nearly half of all incidents in 1979 occurred in Western Europe. Throughout the 1968–1979 period, 38 percent of all incidents were reported in Western Europe, followed in frequency by Latin America (25.8 percent), the Middle East and North Africa (15.9 percent), and North America (11.4 percent). When the geographical distribution of terrorist incidents is inspected over time, the regional trends suggest that international terrorism, like a virus, is spreading. (See the Central Intelligence Agency 1980 report, especially p. 14.) This raises the possibility that a demonstration effect may be operative, wherein the success of some acts of terrorism encourage others to engage in similar acts. In this sense, international terrorism may be a contagious phenomenon.

When considering *where* international terrorism occurs one must also examine the stated objectives of terrorists. One clear pattern is revealed in the tendency for "officials and businessmen—and especially individuals who are symbols of Western power and wealth—[to be] the primary targets" (Central Intelligence Agency, 1980: 1). This suggests that international terrorism is largely an at-

Table 11.2
Geographic Distribution of International Terrorist Incidents, 1968–1979

Method	North America	Latin America	Western Europe	U.S.S.R./ Eastern Europe	Sub-Saharan Africa	Middle East/North Africa	Asia	Oceania	Trans-regional	Total
Kidnaping	3	144	25	0	40	34	15	2	0	263
Barricade-hostage	6	19	24	0	2	19	3	0	0	73
Letter bombing	15	9	100	0	14	7	37	0	4	186
Incendiary bombing	30	72	256	3	4	53	34	4	0	456
Explosive bombing	214	403	641	8	12	250	48	12	0	1,552
Armed attack	3	37	38	1	23	62	24	0	0	188
Hijacking*	6	23	19	1	7	28	16	0	0	100
Assassination	17	62	94	0	20	38	14	1	0	246
Theft, break-in	3	45	14	0	0	14	2	0	0	78
Sniping	12	32	9	1	1	13	3	0	0	71
Other actions†	9	15	47	1	1	13	1	0	0	87
Total	318	861	1,267	15	124	531	197	19	4	3,336

Source: U.S. Central Intelligence Agency, National Foreign Assessment Center, "International Terrorism in 1979" (Washington, D.C.: Director of Public Affairs, Central Intelligence Agency, April 1980), p. 15.

*Includes hijackings by means of air, sea, or land transport, but excludes numerous nonterrorist hijackings.
†Includes occupation of facilities without hostage seizure, shootouts with police, and sabotage.

tack on the advantaged by the disadvantaged, and that it takes place where representatives of the wealthy and powerful live.

A corollary to this idea is the overwhelming tendency for terrorist groups to be based in ethnic minority movements (like the Basques in Spain). International terrorism thrives among peoples whose major complaint is that they lack a country. And it occurs most often in the industrialized world, where discrepancies in income are often severe and where minority groups are sometimes deprived of the political rights and freedoms enjoyed by the majority. In these locations and circumstances, rural guerrilla warfare is not a possible route to self-assertion. But terrorist tactics are.

The likely sources of terrorist activity underscore the fact that terrorism is not perceived to be a disease by all (except by the victims). One man's terrorist may, to another, be a liberator.

Like warfare, terrorism has been both condemned as a repugnant form of violence and defended by some as a necessary instrument of justice. The many trends in world politics portending increasing scarcities of resources and disparities of wealth indicate that, should present trends continue, international terrorism is likely to persist.

We might conclude by considering another gloomy possibility: the threat posed by the advent of *nuclear* terrorism. That terrorists may have access to nuclear weapons is a cause for alarm, for the global environment is favorable to such terrorist operations (Beres, 1978). The hundreds of nuclear facilities dispersed throughout the globe provide ample opportunities for terrorists to acquire these methods of destruction and to employ them for their political purposes. Beres (1978) does not reassure us that the chances of this happening are remote when he reports that "there already have been at least 175 instances of violence or threats of violence against U.S. nuclear facilities since 1969"; that, according to one study, "possibly even one person working alone . . . could, within several weeks, design and build a crude fission bomb"; and that "U.S. Army Special Forces exercises have shown that nuclear weapons storage areas can be penetrated successfully without detection despite guards, fences, and sensors." The fact that terrorists are known for their willingness to take extreme risks, to die for their causes, suggests that nuclear weapons in their hands presents new dangers of mass violence.

Nor can reassurance be found if one examines the toll on human life directly attributable to acts of international terrorism. Jenkins (1978: 117) reports the number of fatalities in incidents of interstate terrorism increased nearly 700 percent in the 1968–1977 decade. That this trend in world politics is likely to continue is a distinct possibility. Jenkins concludes:

Table 11.3
The Global Spread of Refugees, 1979

Destination	Region or Country of Origin	Number of Refugees
North and South America		
Argentina	Europe, Latin America	35,000
Brazil	Latin America	35,000
Canada	Europe, Latin America, Asia	42,000
Chile	Europe	3,000
Colombia	Latin America	1,500
Costa Rica	Latin America	9,000
Cuba	Latin America	2,500
Honduras	Nicaragua	10,000
Mexico	Latin America	3,000
Paraguay	Europe, Latin America	1,500
Peru	Europe, Chile	1,100
United States	Europe, Latin America, Asia	734,000
Europe		
Austria	Europe, Latin America, Asia	20,000
Belgium	Europe, Latin America, Asia	17,000
Denmark	Europe, Latin America, Asia	1,800
France	Europe, Latin America, Asia	140,000
Greece	Europe	2,600
Italy	Europe, Latin America, Asia	12,000
Netherlands	Europe, Latin America, Asia	8,000
Norway	Europe, Latin America, Asia	6,000
Portugal	Africa, Latin America	7,500
Romania	Chile	1,000
Spain	Latin America, Africa, Europe	15,000
Sweden	Europe, Latin America, Asia	20,000
Switzerland	Europe, Latin America, Asia	30,000
Turkey	Europe, Asia	1,100
United Kingdom	Europe, Latin America, Asia	150,000
West Germany	Europe, Latin America, Asia	120,000
Yugoslavia	Europe	2,000

The use of terrorist tactics will persist as a mode of political expression, of gaining international attention, and of achieving limited political goals. Although no terrorists have achieved their stated long-range goals, and in that sense have failed, their use of terrorist tactics has won them publicity and occasional concessions. Their tactical successes probably will suffice to preclude the abandonment of terrorist tactics. (Jenkins, 1978: 115)

THE HUMAN TRAGEDY OF VIOLENT CONFLICT

The preceding review of trends in the incidence and severity of a variety of forms of violent conflict suggests little reason for optimism

Table 11.3
The Global Spread of Refugees, 1979 (continued)

Destination	Region or Country of Origin	Number of Refugees
Africa		
Algeria	Africa, Latin America	52,000
Angola	Zaire, Namibia	180,000
Botswana	Zimbabwe, Angola, Namibia	19,000
Burundi	Rwanda	50,000
Djibouti	Ethiopia	20,000
Egypt	Europe, Asia, Africa	5,000
Ethiopia	Sudan	11,000
Gabon	Equatorial Guinea	60,000
Kenya	Uganda, Ethiopia	6,000
Morocco	Europe, Africa	500
Mozambique	Zimbabwe	100,000
Rwanda	Burundi	7,500
Senegal	Africa	5,000
Somalia	Ethiopia	500,000
Sudan	Ethiopia, Zaire	250,000
Yemen Arab Republic	P.D.R. of Yemen	15,000
Zaire	Angola, Burundi, Rwanda	530,000
Zambia	Zimbabwe, Angola, Namibia	70,000
Asia, Oceania		
Australia	Europe, Latin America, Asia	304,000
Malaysia	Philippines, Cambodia, Vietnam	140,000
New Zealand	Europe, Latin America, Asia	10,000
Thailand	Laos, Cambodia	140,000
Vietnam	Cambodia	140,000

Source: Adapted from United Nations High Commission for Refugees,
Spring 1979, pp. 6–7.

or reassurance. The record seems to indicate that violence within
and among nations remains a tenaciously entrenched characteristic
of world politics.

This simple conclusion masks the tragic human consequences
of violence. Violence translates into individuals and families fleeing
from one country in hopes of finding refuge, and perhaps a better
life, in another country. The global dimensions of the refugee problem are suggested in Table 11.3, which lists as of 1979 the countries
in which over 4 million human beings have sought asylum. The magnitude of the refugee problem is, in fact, much greater than even
this staggering figure. To this number must be added 1.75 million
Palestinian refugees in the Middle East and tens of thousands of
displaced persons—50,000 in Burma, 200,000 in Cyprus, 500,000 in
Ethiopia, 700,000 in Lebanon, 450,000 in Laos, and 3.5 million in
Vietnam (United Nations High Commission for Refugees, Spring
1979)—and nearly 100,000 Cuban émigres. Religious preference, the

color of one's skin, the expression of political dissent—these are some of the factors that often create refugees. But war, whether intranational or international, remains a paramount cause.

Destruction of the environment is another tragic consequence of violence. Modern warfare has not only uprooted tens of thousands of people; it has also destroyed their homes, desecrated their forests and farmlands, and disrupted their urban centers.

President Kennedy's prediction in 1963 that "mankind must put an end to war or war will put an end to mankind" has taken on new meaning in a world characterized by interdependence and worldwide dispersion of highly destructive weapons. Could it be that a world so ingenious in perpetrating violence will also learn that war and violence are too costly, too dysfunctional to persist?

Twelve

Power Balances, Arms Control, and World Peace

> Peace, n. In international affairs, a period of cheating between two periods of fighting.
>
> Ambrose Bierce, 1925

> [The burdens of "armed peace" are either] slow destruction in the consequence of expenditure . . . for war, or swift destruction in the event of war.
>
> Jean de Bloch, 1898

In an era when an increasing number of nations possess the capacity to destroy other nations, and perhaps extinguish the human species, the control of interstate violence may be said to be *the* preeminent problem of contemporary life. Unfortunately, proposed solutions to the problem of war are overly abundant, perhaps to an unmanageable degree. Implicit in most is the assumption that cures for violence can be found in the causes of war, that if the roots of war can be found, statesmen will be able to preserve peace simply by eliminating the sources of war. But efforts to inventory the causes of war (see Blainey, 1973; Pruitt and Snyder, 1969; Waltz, 1954) invariably conclude that the list of factors noted is selective and partial.[1] This may be because of the fact that, in principle, anything may be suspected of being related to war in some way.

But perhaps the analytic tradition which assumes that "understanding why wars occur is a necessary preliminary to the develop-

---

1. Such efforts usually attempt to identify the principal theories of the causes of war. For example, Rosen and Jones (1980) list twelve causes of war: power asymmetries, nationalism-irredentism, international social Darwinism, communications failure and mutual misperception, arms races, the promotion of internal integration through external conflict, instinctive aggression (cultural propensities of violence) and war-peace cycles, economic and scientific stimulation, military-industrial complexes, relative deprivation, population limitation, and conflict resolution. Similarly, Couloumbis and Wolfe (1978) posit that war is caused by systemic failure, human aggression, great-power imperialism, economic rivalry, elite and popular fatalism, political conspiracy, and general movements of history.

ment of an effective operational theory for avoiding them" (Snyder, 1969) is *not* the most advantageous approach. Instead, might we profit by asking not what the causes of war are, but rather, what the sources or conditions are that lead to *peace*? If peace is defined as the absence of war, then presumably consideration of the conditions under which peace prevails might clarify ways in which war might be avoided. The search of scholars and statesmen for an answer to the problem of war

> . . . has usually been based upon the assumption that when there is war, something must be causing it. It could, however, be that there is something absent which permits war to break out. Such an absent factor could never be discovered by focusing attention on the war situation. The search must be extended to include factors possibly safeguarding peace. The causes of war may then be found to lie in faulty conditions of peace. (Levi, 1974b: 200)

Following this reasoning, we shall inquire here about the military factors which, hypothetically, may be assumed to contribute to the control of international violence. What conditions inhibit the outbreak of war? What factors, if absent, undermine the prospects for global peace?

Two basic ideas about how international peace might be created and how international violence might be controlled focus on *military force* as a central ingredient, arguing, first, that peace is a product of power balancing power, and, second, that peace can be achieved through arms control and disarmament.

THE BALANCE OF POWER

It is often assumed that the frequent recourse to war among nations stems from the nature and structure of the global system. The international political system makes security dear and peace precarious by granting states sovereign status and encouraging them to jealously guard their own autonomy. Moreover, the system is highly stratified; power, wealth, and resources are not evenly distributed. Because these scarce elements are highly valued, states are often intensely motivated to compete with one another for them. In the course of this competition, each state is encouraged to seek, above all else, its own national self-interest, the perpetuation of its own survival, and the promotion of its relative power position. Under such conditions, the system resembles a primitive, anarchic arrangement which places responsibility for the preservation of peace on each individual state which must rely on its own devices to maintain its own security. It is little wonder that the international political system is so often seen as conforming to Hobbes's notion of "a war of all against all," a dynamic of perpetual conflict and struggle.

At least since Thucydides's reflections on how a state might best preserve itself in ancient Greece, statesmen and scholars have wrestled with the problem of maintaining the independence of nations and at the same time curtailing war. Many believe that the anarchical nature of the system is, and will remain, a permanent feature of international life. Restructuring the international environment—and the insecurity and violence it breeds—is not, therefore, a viable strategy for peace. Instead, the basic "realities" of the system must be acknowledged.[2] Peace can come not by reforming the system which promotes violence but by managing it in such a way as to restrain the incidence and severity of warfare.

How might such a disorderly and unstable system be effectively managed? A traditional approach has been to tie the survival of states and the maintenance of peace to the functioning of a system of military balances. What is meant by this concept, broadly captured in the phrase, "balance of power"? Is it grounded in reality or illusion?

The term *balance of power* is highly ambiguous and has been used in a variety of ways.[3] But one of its many meanings refers to the basic idea that peace will result when the power of states—defined in this instance primarily in military terms—is distributed in such a way that no one state would be strong enough to pose a meaningful threat to the other states. Should one state, or a collection of states, obtain enough power to constitute a threat to the others, those threatened would unite out of self-interest and form a defensive alliance to restore the balance and maintain the status quo. The equilibrium or balancing of power that would result from such collusion among the threatened states would be sufficient to prevent the would-be attacker from pursuing its expansionist goals. Peace would thus be produced from the equilibrium that results from the balancing of contending factions.

The theoretical corollaries of the balance-of-power approach to world peace are many. Foremost is the notion that the goodwill and conciliatory motivations of other nations cannot be relied upon. All nations are seen as driven exclusively by self-interest, and all are perceived to define those interests in terms of power and the cease-

2. Reflecting this view, Morgenthau's (1973) treatise remains the authoritative application of realist thinking in international politics.

3. For instance, Haas (1953a and 1953b) identifies at least eight mutually exclusive definitions of the concept. Other critics identifying multiple uses of the concept include Claude (1962), Wight (1968), and Bueno de Mesquita (1975b).

less quest for it.[4] Each state can therefore be expected to attempt to expand its power until it is checked by a countervailing power. Thus all are locked into a perpetual struggle for power as each attempts to enhance its position relative to other states.

Implicit in this prescription is the belief that the acquisition of military capabilities enhances the prospects of a state avoiding war. Classic balance-of-power theory is predicated on the notion that weakness leads to war, that vulnerability invites attack from power-lusting aggressors. Hence we encounter again the idea that the best way to preserve peace is to prepare for war. When all nations are seen as driven by expansionistic power drives, this kind of response is not hard to understand. When imperialistic aggression is assumed to be the normal (indeed, proper) goal of competitive states, then the belief follows that one should strengthen one's own military capability as a means of protection against the hegemonial aspirations of potential adversaries; the hegemony is not to be shared. This reasoning invariably leads to an acceptance of arms and arms races and the quest for military superiority. Indeed, balance-of-power theory is predicated on an acceptance of war as an inevitable and necessary tool of foreign policy in international politics. In addition, the maintenance of the sovereign independence of individual states is a paramount value; and sovereign independence may be preserved by war. A state is entitled to resort to force whenever its preservation is threatened (see Gulick, 1955).

The assumptions of balance-of-power theory appear on the surface dubious at best. The theory sounds like a recipe for pure conflict, not peace. But proponents of the theory as it was practiced in seventeenth-, eighteenth-, and nineteenth-century European international politics were not mad. They assumed that a system founded on suspicion, antagonism, fear, and competition could produce peace. The mechanism believed to translate these presumably violence-promoting features into international stability was alliance.

Alliance Politics

Coalitions were believed to be formed out of self-interest in an almost mechanistic fashion to protect any state threatened or under attack by a potential adversary. But the process was seldom automatic. In practice, one among the powers favoring the status quo

4. This perspective denies that it is in the self-interest of states to enhance the welfare of others. Mutual aid is not acknowledged as rewarding, only competition and struggle. The balance-of-power view is also incompatible with the related idea of collective security discussed in more detail subsequently.

typically had to assume the lead in building a coalition among the other powers by convincing them of the potential threats they faced. Counteralliances were expected to form, nevertheless, because states would not tolerate aggression because the aggressor might ultimately turn, with enhanced capabilities, against those sitting on the sidelines. Thus, rational calculations of power would encourage coalitions approximately equal in power.[5] And since alliances were highly flexible and nonpermanent, they could shift readily so as to maintain an even distribution of power.

Alliances in the classical European balance-of-power system were not based on friendships or loyalties, but on interests and capabilities. The principle of "no permanent ties, only permanent interests" lubricated the dynamics of alliance politics, and thereby made a balance, an equilibrium, more probable. Ironically, through such competitive jockeying for power, nations seeking advantages by attempting to increase their power were driven to form coalitions which ultimately prevented any nation from achieving dominance. In principle, then, coalition politics would produce a stalemate. The system would be policed by competition. Critical in policing the system was the balancer—a role often played by Great Britain in the eighteenth and nineteenth century, when it threw its support toward one or another alliance system to assure that no one achieved preponderance. And, supposedly, the search for preponderance would produce not war but a peace founded on parity.

Alliance competition, however, could not achieve equilibrium automatically, but only if certain "rules" of behavior were followed. Morton Kaplan's (1975) study of the classic balance of power suggests some "essential rules" necessary if this approach to peace is to succeed. His inspection of the historical operation of the balance-of-power system indicated that a balance preserving peace would result if, and only if, nations behaved according to the following rules:

> (1) increase capabilities but negotiate rather than fight; (2) fight rather than fail to increase capabilities; (3) stop fighting rather than eliminate an essential actor; (4) oppose any coalition or single actor which tends to assume a position of predominance within the system; (5) constrain actors who subscribe to supranational organizational principles; and (6) permit defeated or constrained essential national actors to re-enter the system as acceptable role partners. (Kaplan, 1975: 259)

5. According to the so-called size principle, rational actors will tend to form coalitions sufficient in size to ensure victory and no larger; hence political coalitions tend to be roughly equal in size, it is presumed. See Riker (1962) for a discussion, with applications to international coalitions in the context of balance-of-power theory.

Under these rules, competition is appropriate. Power is to be sought, not disdained. Force and war are approved as means to obtain power. The independence of each national unit is cherished; to preserve one's own autonomy, the autonomy of others is supported out of self-interest. Efforts to subvert national independence through international organization or world government are to be restrained. Competition leads to the equalization of weapons capabilities among the major competitors. The fear bred by the pursuit of force encourages states to form alliances to enhance their power base and to prevent adversaries from attacking. Defensive alliances emerge to counter nations with preponderant capabilities, and states intervene in conflicts by allying with the weaker side. Alliances dissolve when the threat of aggression diminishes; they are never permanent. And because today's adversary may be tomorrow's friend, defeated aggressors are treated with moderation and never annihilated or otherwise removed from the system.

These postulates of the balance-of-power approach to peace assume that peace will be produced by having power distributed through the dynamics of alliance politics. As such, this proposal for dealing with the problem of war is a solution which preserves the problem, for warfare is not abolished. It serves rather as a way for measuring national power and as a means for changing the distribution of power.

It has often been noted that the successful operation of a balance of power presupposes not only that nations will act according to the rules of the system but also that the essential prerequisites for the approach be present.[6] States must seek to maintain a balance through rational pursuit of their self-interest guided by possession of sufficient and accurate information. But there must also be (1) a sufficiently large number of independent states to make alliance formation and dissolution readily possible; (2) a system limited to a geographically confined area of the globe; (3) freedom of action for the central decision makers of the states in the system; (4) relative equality in the capabilities of states; (5) a common political culture in which the rules of the game are recognized and respected; (6) a modicum of homogeneity of the nations in the system; (7) a weapons technology which inhibits quick mobilization for war, prevents the pursuit of prolonged wars, and reduces the prospects of wars of annihilation; and (8) the absence of supranational institutions capable of determining the policies states pursue.

6. Analyses of the conditions necessary for power balances to form remain inconclusive. Waltz (1979) provides a useful review and critique of the conventional reasoning associated with this topic and posits that "balance-of-power politics prevail whenever two, and only two, requirements are met: that the order be anarchic and that it be populated by units wishing to survive."

It is questionable whether these conditions exist in the contemporary global system. Because of technological requirements, among other things, alliances (such as NATO and the Warsaw Pact) are today relatively binding, precluding adjustments of the power distribution through shifts in the composition of coalitions. The global system is now universalized, comprising not a handful of states but over 160. The freedom of the decision makers responsible for making foreign policies is, more often than not, constrained substantially by domestic factors. The system is politically and culturally fragmented. And the capabilities of states are not evenly matched; furthermore, the destructiveness of contemporary weapons systems has changed the balance-of-power concept in operation in Europe from the seventeenth to the nineteenth century compared to the world in the twentieth century. Power cannot be aggregated when the possession of nuclear weapons gives any one possessor the capacity to annihilate at will. And transnational institutions and quasipermanent ties reduce the flexibility necessary for a balance of power to effectively maintain the peace.

The Eurocentric system that existed from the mid-seventeenth century until World War I, and perhaps through World War II, is generally regarded as the heyday of balance-of-power politics. But even in that era the proposition that peace would result from the pursuit of military preponderance was not without its critics. War may have been relatively limited in scope, duration, and severity during that alleged "golden age of diplomacy," but the restraints on the incidence of interstate violence may have been the result more of technological, cultural, and geographical conditions than of the constraints exerted by an equilibrium of forces. As Dehio (1962) argues, the classical European balance of power was always precarious at best. The regularity with which wars broke out in Europe during this period (when the fundamental prerequisites of the balance were extant) attests to the failure of the balance-of-power mechanism to preserve peace. While it might be argued that the balance of power may, at times, have prolonged the length of peacetime between wars, and possibly limited the extent of wars once they occurred, it is questionable that a balancing of power has ever been able to keep the peace in the long run.

Equally dubious is the assumption that relative strength leads to peace. Rather, it has been shown that preparation for war and the acquisition of relative superiority over an adversary may actually invite attack: in five of nine wars involving great powers in the 150 years between the Congress of Vienna (1815) and the mid-1950s, the nations which were attacked were appreciably stronger militarily than those initiating the war (Singer and Small, 1975: 233). (World War I, the Russo-Japanese War, and the Korean Wars are examples.)

Surprisingly, and running counter to the logic of balance-of-power theorizing, "major power wars are often initiated by nations which are relatively inferior, but gaining vis-a-vis the leaders" (Singer and Small, 1975). This empirical regularity hardly speaks well for the hypothesis that seeking military advantages over others deters aggression. Instead, the growth of a state's military power may so terrify its adversaries that a pre-emptive strike is presumed necessary.

It was perhaps World War I that more than anything else helped discredit balance-of-power politics. The catastrophic proportions of that conflict caused many to view the balance-of-power mechanism as a *cause* of war instead of as a vehicle for peace. Indeed, the arms races, the secret treaties, and the entangling commitments that were connected with balance-of-power politics prior to the outbreak of the war were all seen as having contributed to the conflict. This anti-balance-of-power position was articulated most vehemently by President Woodrow Wilson. Wilson and other idealists hoped to supercede the balance of power as a method of preserving peace by replacing it with the principle of *collective security*. The League of Nations embodied that principle, under the assumption that peaceful nations, acting in concert, could collectively deter—and, if necessary, counteract—aggression. The shift in perspective was profound. In contrast to the rules of the balance of power, collective security theory proposed: (1) to retaliate against *any* aggressive act or attempt to establish hegemony—not just those acts which threatened the global system as a collectivity;[7] (2) to involve the coordinated participation of *all* member states—not just a sufficient number to stop the aggressor; and (3) to create an international organization to identify acts of aggression and to organize a military response to such acts—not just to let individual states make such decisions from their individual sovereign perspectives.

Unfortunately, the mechanism of collective security also failed to work. Japanese aggression against Manchuria in 1931 and China proper in 1937 and Italy's invasion of Ethiopia in 1935 were widely condemned, but no resistance was organized in response. There was also no collective response to counter German aggression against Czechoslovakia in 1938. Collective security failed to prevent World War II and, like the balance of power, became a discredited theory. The security of individual states could not be protected in a system of anarchy.

In the post-World War II era, balance-of-power thinking has re-emerged in some quarters. Theorists and statesmen such as former Secretary of State Henry Kissinger have sought to restore a version

---

7. The central assumption of collective security is that *any* war threatens the entire system.

of the balance concept as the only "realistic" approach to security given the conditions in which all states exist. The effort is a reaffirmation of the belief that national self-reliance is the only trustworthy safeguard of security in an unstable world and of the traditional assumptions that peace can only come through strength and that a potential aggressor must be confronted with a preponderance of power if it is to be successfully deterred. Richard Nixon's words echoed an approach to peace which has many historical precedents when he argued, "We must remember the only time in the history of the world that we have had any extended period of peace is when there has been a balance of power . . . it will be a safer world . . . if we have a strong, healthy United States, Europe, Soviet Union, China, Japan, each balancing the other. . . ."

The reasons for the persistence of balance-of-power theorizing rest on a number of assumptions about the nature of world politics in our age. Two deserve special attention: that alliances deter war and that systemic polarization leads to war.

Do Alliances Deter War?

As has been observed, in both classical balance-of-power theorizing and in the precepts underlying post-World War II efforts to create some notion of global equilibrium or balance, alliances have been thought to be fundamental. Alliances are assumed to be the trigger which makes the balance work by throwing antagonistic coalitions into opposition in such a way that neither is able to obtain superiority over the other. Alliances are believed to create balances precisely because they *aggregate* power.

Presumably what makes two nations join in a defensive alliance is mutual fear of a third party; the alignment can help each nation offset the power of the adversary, either by adding an ally's power to its own or by denying the addition of that power to the enemy (Fedder, 1968). The assumption is that by combining or aggregating power, the probability of avoiding war with a potential aggressor is increased.[8] It is this assumption that leads proponents of the balance mechanism to recommend it as a solution to the problem of war.

How valid is this assumption? Is international order a product of alliance formation, as some contend (Osgood, 1968; Liska, 1968)? Does the formation of alliances which combine the power of two or more states enhance their security?

---

8. And, of course (and consistent with balance-of-power theory), alliances also tend to be formed *after* war erupts, to redress the new threat to the balance and to restore the *status quo ante bellum* (the condition that existed prior to the outbreak of war).

If the assumption of the theory is correct, then historical periods in which alliance levels are high should also be periods in which wars were less frequent. Studies have shown that during the nineteenth century, higher levels of alliance aggregation were associated with the absence of war (Singer and Small, 1968). However, in the twentieth century, Singer and Small find that this hypothesis no longer holds: when alliance levels are high, the international system is more war-prone. It is true that the incidence of war involving advanced industrialized societies such as the NATO and Warsaw Pact members has been rare since World War II. But overall this statistic renders questionable the balance-of-power approach to peace. The decline of the flexibility of today's alliance systems, the development of rigid enmities between certain states (such as the United States and the Soviet Union), and the ideological colorations and bureaucratization of most alliance systems may serve to undermine their stabilizing capacity. So, too, the destructiveness of today's weapons systems may be seen as eroding the balancing function traditionally performed by alliance formation.

Regardless of the reasons, nations which join alliances are the ones most likely to experience war (Singer and Small, 1969 and 1975). The marked preference of many Third World nations for non-alignment in great-power disputes may represent a policy resting on enlightened awareness of today's realities and on astute self-interest. But then again, quite obviously many governments (especially those entrenched in either the Eastern or Western bloc arrangements and other industrialized countries choosing to live under the Soviet or American nuclear umbrella) still see in alliance a form of protection and means of avoiding war.

Postwar Models of International Systems

There are different ways in which power may be distributed among the states comprising the international system. Some of these possible power configurations are merely hypothetical, having no historical counterparts (see Kaplan, 1957 and 1975). But in those configurations which are believed to have existed, the military capabilities of the actors range from highly concentrated on the one end of the continuum, to highly dispersed on the other. Hypothetical examples of the former might be empire or world government, while the approximate equality of the independent nations comprising the classical European state system after 1648 is an example of the latter.

The structure of the global distribution of power has undergone fundamental transformation since World War II. Most nations were devastated by the war,[9] a situation which left the United States in a clearly superior position, its economy accounting for half the GNP of the nations of the world. And of course the United States was the only nation in possession of an awesome new weapon, the atomic bomb. The demonstration that the United States was willing to use that instrument created a psychological global environment wherein it had unprecedented capability to exercise influence and get its way. That fact means we can describe the immediate postwar environment, however temporarily, as a *unipolar* power configuration. Power was concentrated in the hands of one dominant actor.

The period was short-lived, however, The recovery of the Soviet economy, the growth of its military capabilities and its maintenance of a large standing army, accompanied by the onset of Soviet-American rivalry, transformed the structure of the system. The Soviets cracked the American monopoly of atomic weapons in 1949 and exploded a thermonuclear device in 1953, less than a year after the United States. These developments led to a *bipolar* distribution of power. Power was concentrated in the hands of the two superpowers, and their competition colored all other dimensions of political life on the planet. Symptomatic of the bipolar structure was the creation of opposing alliance systems, which were born in part out of the pressure that the superpowers exerted to attract allies, and in part out of the tendency of less-powerful nations to look to one or the other of the superpowers for protection in what was perceived to be an intensely hostile international environment.

The concept of two *poles* is especially apt in this context because a pole is a fit metaphor for a magnet—it both repels and attracts (Nogee, 1975). The formation of the North Atlantic Treaty Organization (NATO), linking the United States to the defense of Western Europe, and the Warsaw Pact, linking the Soviet Union in a formal alliance to its Eastern European satellites, were manifestations of this emerging polar power structure. Correspondingly, each superpower's allies gave it forward bases from which to carry on the competition. The competition was punctuated by recurrent confrontations and crises that marked the concern of the superpowers for power and security in an atmosphere pervaded by mutual suspicion.

The bipolar distribution of power itself contributed to the crisis-ridden postwar atmosphere. By grouping the nation-members of

9. Consider the position of the Soviet Union at that time. Its industrial, agricultural, and transportation systems had either been destroyed or severely damaged. An estimated 20 million Soviets had lost their lives; the ratio of Soviet to American war deaths was about seventy to one.

the system into two blocs, each led by a superpower, the bipolar structure bred insecurity among all actors (Spanier, 1975). The balance was constantly at stake. Each bloc leader feared that its adversary would attain hegemony. In such a system, every move, however defensive, was interpreted as an attempt to achieve preponderant status. What one side gained was seen as a loss for the other. Utmost importance was therefore attached to recruiting new friends and allies, while fear that an old ally might desert the fold was ever present. Thus there was little room for compromise in the bipolar world. Every maneuver appeared a new initiative toward world conquest; hence, every act of hostility was to be met by a retaliatory act of hostility. Endemic to the struggle was the notion that peace was impossible, that the most that could be hoped for was a momentary pause in overt hostilities based on a mutual respect for the territorial status quo.

To a significant extent the cause of the competition between the United States and the Soviet Union in the postwar period was simply the concentration of power in the hands of the two superpowers. Like it or not, each posed the only realistic military threat to the other. To be sure, ideological and related differences reinforced the perception of threat each felt from the other, but the concentration of power in two poles (two states) was the principal source of the threat. Consequently, the alliance configurations (NATO and the Warsaw Pact) which so often came to be seen as synonymous with bipolarity were in fact little more than *reflections of* (rather than causes of) Soviet-American military dominance. "Alliances and blocs are types of *relations* between states in the system that are influenced by the prevailing structure," observe Snyder and Diesing (1977), "but do not constitute that structure. Thus the rough equality between the two alliances prior to 1914 did not make the system bipolar, nor did the loosening of the U.S. and Soviet blocs during the 1960s and early 1970s make that system multipolar." Instead, the structure of the system is determined by the degree to which power is concentrated in the hands of *states*.

The fact that the major Cold War coalitions associated with bipolarity did begin to disintegrate in the 1960s and early 1970s is indicative of the shift in the power configuration which occurred during that period (especially in the changes in perceptions that followed the Cuban missile crisis of 1962). As bipolarity deteriorated, what has been described as a bipolycentric system (Spanier, 1975) began to replace it. *Bipolycentrism* is a concept recognizing the continued military superiority of the United States and the Soviet Union, and the continued reliance, at least ultimately, of the alliance partners on their respective superpower patrons for security. At the same time, the new system allows considerable room for maneuver on the part of weaker alliance partners; hence the suffix *polycentric*, connoting the possibility of many centers of power and diverse relationships among the nations subordinate to the superpowers, such as those that have been nurtured between the United States and Romania, on the one hand, and those between France and the Soviet Union, on the other. At the same time, the secondary powers are assumed to use these ties, as well as others established across alliance boundaries by the secondary powers themselves (such as between Poland and West Germany), to enhance their bargaining position within their own alliance. While the superpowers remain dominant militarily, diplomatically there is much greater fluidity in the actual foreign-policy behavior of alliance partners than is true in a strictly bipolar system. And new foreign policy roles (other than simply "aligned" or "nonaligned" status) are created for actors in this less rigid system.

Rapid technological innovation in the major weapons systems of the superpowers was one of the principal catalysts of change in the polarity structure of the international system. In particular, the advent of technologically sophisticated intercontinental ballistic missiles (ICBMs) eroded the necessity of forward-base areas for purposes of striking at the heart of the adversary, thereby diminishing the drive to create and maintain tight, cohesive alliance systems composed of reliable partners.

In addition, the deterioration of alliance groupings was accelerated by the narrowing of the difference between Soviet and American military capabilities. European members of NATO in particular began to question whether the United States would, indeed, trade New York City for Paris or Bonn. Under what conditions might Washington or Moscow be willing to risk a nuclear holocaust, it was asked. The uncertainty aroused by such questioning led to the further fragmentation of the global power distribution. Other nations decided to protect themselves by developing their own nuclear capabilities, and many centers of power began to emerge. Power, in short, became increasingly diffused, and the old alliance structures began to disintegrate as fears of aggression and territorial expansion abated.

How the present world distribution of power can most accurately be described is difficult to determine.[10] The decline of East-

10. The ambiguity of the present system is one reason why definitive description is difficult. It is also difficult because analyses of this question are colored by different assumptions about the importance of emergent global trends. Nogee illustrates

West tension in Europe (Goldmann, 1973; Goldmann and Lagerkranz, 1977), the emergence of Japan and the European Community as significant and powerful new actors, the rise of China and its open conflict with the Soviet Union—all are ingredients of a transforming international political system. These trends make a multipolar system (approximating the structural characteristics of the classical European balance of power) a potential model for describing emerging political realities. Yet, although one might envision (as former Secretary of State Kissinger was on occasion prone to do) a multipolar system in which the United States, Soviet Union, Japan, China, and a united Europe were the major actors, the equilibrating mechanisms of the classical balance of power are of doubtful relevance to the contemporary world. The classical system was maintained by the willingness of the major actors to enter into alliances with anyone (ideology did not matter) and to use war as an instrument of policy.[11] The argument that these conditions apply to present-day international politics is doubtful. Even if one could plausibly envision a relative equilibrium of military capabilities between the United States, the Soviet Union, China, Japan, and a united Europe by the year 2000, the destructiveness of modern weapons, which seems more likely to increase than abate by that time, makes it difficult to imagine a re-emergent balance-of-power system with operating characteristics analogous to the classical European state system.

The ongoing ideological conflict between the Soviet Union and China makes it particularly difficult to use multipolarity as a concept applicable to present-day international politics. Instead, *triangular politics* appears a far more fitting term to describe the Chinese in the world power equation and evolving structure of the international system.

Tripolarity[12] connotes a system comprising three nations with relatively equal power potential vis-à-vis one another as defined by their economic and military capabilities, especially in the area of nuclear weapons capability. But that description does not apply to

---

the difficulty by noting the many terms employed to designate the current international structure:

> bimodal, bipolar, loose bipolar, very loose bipolar, tight bipolar, bi-multipolar, bipolycentric, complex conglomerate, détente system, diffuse bloc, discontinuity model, heterosymmetrical bipolarity, multipolar, multihierarchical, multibloc, pentapolar, polycentric, oligopolistic, tripolar, and three-tiered multidimensional system within a bipolar setting. (Nogee, 1975: 1197)

11. But then war was typically limited in duration, in extensiveness in terms of population and industrial centers, and in devastation, a "requirement" imposed by technology.

12. The following brief summary is based on Yalem (1972) and especially Spanier (1975), who prefer to describe triangular arrangement as tripolar.

present-day strategic realities. Objectively, China cannot be defined as the power rival, militarily, of either the United States or the Soviet Union, although diplomatically China's role has assumed increasing importance. Nor is it likely to achieve such capability quickly. But as the Chinese continue to develop nuclear weapons and a capacity to deliver them, at least in Asia, they may transform the power distributions which have heretofore dominated world politics. Deterrence under such conditions would have to be directed not simply at one actor, but two, and in particular toward preventing a military attack by two against one.

Indeed, preventing two against one would appear to be the key element defining foreign policy behavior in a nuclear tripolar system. Foreign policy behavior in a tripolar world would thus be based on a rational calculation of interest and power in which ideology is a peripheral consideration. "As a broad generalization, it can probably be hypothesized that, *whereas in a bipolar system the great fear of each power is becoming militarily inferior lest the opponent achieve military superiority and a dominance that may not be reversible, in a tripolar system the fear of each pole is diplomatic isolation*" (Spanier, 1975, emphasis in original).

Restraints on behavior in such a system derive from the fear that if a nuclear exchange involving only two of the actors were to occur, the combatants would probably be so severely devastated that the noninvolved actor would emerge "the victor"—even if the noncombatant were initially the weakest of the three, such as China.[13] Restraints also derive from fear of becoming permanently isolated. A tripolar system would encourage, in principle, two actors coalescing against one, particularly if the third appears unduly aggressive or interferes in the sphere of influence of another (such as China's sphere in Asia, the Soviet Union's sphere in Eastern Europe, or the American sphere in the North Atlantic and the Western Hemisphere). Nonaggressiveness and noninterference therefore appear compatible with the interests of all, and become more rather than less probable under the conditions of nuclear tripolarity.

Tripolarity, however, does not currently exist. In the present system, possession of a second-strike nuclear capacity and the means to deliver it is a precondition for a power to be considered a "pole." China, which does not possess such a capacity, cannot therefore be said to comprise a third pole. But tripolarity may come into

13. John Culver (a former member of the U.S. Senate Armed Services Committee) reported in March 1979: "President Brezhnev told Senator Kennedy recently that he was convinced that even one nuclear bomb dropped by either of the superpowers would result in a general nuclear exchange—not only for our two nations but for the entire world. If one goes, they all go, he said."

existence as China further develops its nuclear arsenal. Press reports in May 1980 indicated that China had successfully tested a long-range missile capable of striking Moscow or the West Coast of the United States. China may therefore subsequently develop sufficient weapons capabilities to be considered a pole in a tripolar arrangement. As for most other dimensions of military and economic capabilities, however, China is likely to remain far less powerful than either the United States or the Soviet Union for some time. Thus it is more accurate to employ the triangular concept to describe the important elements that have characterized American, Soviet, and Chinese behavior toward one another during the past several years. The concept helps explain Chinese apprehensiveness of Soviet-American détente; it provides insight into Soviet concerns about Sino-American rapprochement; and it makes the American support of polycentric tendencies in the communist camp generally (and fear of Russo-Chinese fence-mending in particular) understandable. It also explains the manifest caution exhibited by all three central actors.

Do Power Concentrations Promote or Inhibit War?

The debate over the distribution of power and the probability of war has been vigorous, and the issue remains unresolved.[14] The conventional view has argued that an excessive concentration of military power in a single state is a condition inviting war, especially among great powers. In other words, peace occurs most frequently when power is evenly distributed among states (Hinsley, 1963). But others, noting the *pax Romana, pax Britannica,* and *pax Americana* of previous historical periods, contend that peace may depend, instead, upon the existence of a preponderance or an imbalance of power (Organski, 1968).

But these extremes of the power-dispersion, power-concentration continuum are rare and not pertinent to today's international system. In between we find proponents of two contending models of power and alliance configurations—the bipolar and multipolar structures—both of which have historical counterparts. Which of these arrangements, it is asked, best enhances the prospects for a viable system of power balancing power?

Many have argued that, by its very nature, a polarized system concentrating power in two competing blocs will lead to war. The hardening of alliances, it is reasoned, invariably leads to a struggle

14. For discussions of the idea that the frequency of interstate violence is related to the nature of the international environment, see Volgy (1974); Rosenau (1980); Harf, Hoovler, and James (1974); and Kegley and McGowan (1979).

for dominance. The situation entails a crisis-prone environment of pure competition, in which the threat of war is ever present. By definition, a bipolar world is one in which each bloc attempts to attain superior military capability. Constraints on the recourse to violence (especially the possible intervention of third parties to restore the balance) are lacking, since the balancer role is absent. Similarly, a bipolar world may be violence-prone because the confidence and certainty of decision makers is greatest in a system where the outcome of aggressive behavior is readily calculated, as is true when only one adversary's power needs to be considered rather than that of many (Deutsch and Singer, 1975).

Conversely, multipolar systems are regarded by these same theorists as more stable, in part because the existence of more autonomous actors gives rise to more potential alliances that can be formed to counterbalance a would-be aggressor. Shifting alliances can only occur when there are a number of independent actors or power centers; a relatively large number of actors is essential to the operation of a balance.[15] Moreover, since in a multipolar system there is contact among more nations,[16] the relative amount of information-processing time that can be allocated by decision makers to any one of them will decrease, with the result that a kind of uncertainty is generated that breeds caution (Deutsch and Singer, 1975). In such a system, policy is more flexible because of the need for adjustments in the relations between nations. As a consequence, wars are believed to be less likely.

But arguments have also been advanced to defend bipolarity as a means of maintaining peace. For instance, Waltz (1971) has argued that a bipolar world like the one that emerged in the 1950s is a stable world because it encourages states to use caution and assume greater responsibility for their actions in world affairs. Ironically, despite the potential for mutual hostility and destruction, stability may result from these conditions in part because superpower stalemate and mutual antagonism give less-developed nations more room to maneuver, thus promoting more overall flexibility in the system. Peace may be produced, in short, when conditions reach the brink of war. Under such conditions, central actors control minor conflicts and prevent them from erupting into a war that would destroy the world. It is also assumed that uncertainty keeps the leaders of nations alert and stimulates the pursuit of information which,

15. Kaplan (1957) assumes that a stable balance-of-power system requires the existence of at least five powerful states or blocs of states.

16. The concept of interaction opportunities refers to the fact that, as the number of autonomous actors increases, the probability that more actors will develop relationships with an expanding number of other actors also increases.

in turn, diminishes the amount of misperception and miscalculation about the intentions of rivals. This interpretation is reinforced by the argument that "the division of all nations into two camps raises the costs of war to such a high level that all but the most fundamental conflicts are resolved without resort to violence" (Bueno de Mesquita, 1975a).

That deductive theorizing can lead to contradictory but equally plausible conclusions should not be surprising. But the question of the relationship between polarities and global stability is, after all, empirical as well as theoretical. Which theory, when confronted with evidence, has the most to recommend it?

The evidence is mixed. Waltz's (1971) argument that a bipolar world is more stable than a multipolar one finds partial (albeit impressionistic) support in the fact that in the bipolar environment of the 1950s, when the threat of war was endemic, major war did not occur. During the height of the Cold War, the superpowers threatened to go to the brink many times. But war between major states did not actually occur. This suggests that the perpetual competition of the bipolar world might, paradoxically, have produced caution and restraint rather than recklessness and violence.

Systematic quantitative studies of the association between polarities and global stability suggest that the probability of war is *not* related to the number of poles in the system, but that as the number of poles increases, the wars which erupt are likely to be longer (Bueno de Mesquita, 1975a).[17] These results may be explained by yet another empirically grounded finding, namely, that periods in which the polarity of the international system undergoes rapid change are also the periods most prone to violence and war. That is, eras in which there is dynamic structural change may be the least stable. Extending this perspective, it has been determined that, in the current century, "as polarization rises, so does war" (Singer and Small, 1975).

Rosecrance (1966) has also suggested that the global system will be least stable under two conditions: either very high or very low polarization, and he has presented evidence consistent with this interpretation. Investigating the same hypothesis, Singer and Small (1975) concurred: "By and large, when the system has been either very diffuse or highly polarized, interstate war has increased." Thus, in general, increases in the extent to which power is concentrated in the hands of a few actors makes for a more war-prone system. Likewise, extensive dispersions of power throughout the system (lack of effective supervision by two or three giants) increase

17. For a statistical study which finds, instead, that wars are less frequent but more prolonged in bipolar than in multipolar systems, see Haas (1970).

the probability of war. *Changes* in the dispersion and concentration of power may also produce war.

This implies for the present transforming international system that swift change in the structure of the global system would likely increase greatly the probability of war. But, historically, polarity structures have seldom undergone rapid alterations. The gradual shift since 1945 from a unipolar to a bipolar structure, followed in turn by the emergence of a bipolycentric system and possibly the ultimate advent of a tripolar world, indicates that the reemergence of either an extremely polarized (unipolar) or extremely diffused (multibloc) structure is not likely in the near future. This relative lack of polarity variation should have a stablizing effect.

Such a conclusion should not lead to the assumption that the present global system is conducive to the successful operation of a balance-of-power mechanism similar to that which operated in previous centuries. The conditions which in the past facilitated an equilibrium capable of keeping the peace are no longer in existence. Hence we must continue to live in a world in which stability is precarious at best. The search for peace through a balance of power remains, as ever, elusive. The world in which the balance of power was believed capable of preserving peace is gone, perhaps forever, for "only if the possibility of nuclear war were eliminated might a multipolar balance of power function" (Wright, cited in Nogee, 1975). Because of the destructiveness of today's conventional weapons, it is doubtful that a balance of power could function even if the unlikely possibility of eliminating nuclear weapons were achieved. Claude's (1962) suggestion—that our world has become increasingly less suitable for the operation of a balance-of-power system, in combination with the realization that continued systemic polarization and rapid change, if unabated, reduce the probability of peace—indicates that if war is to be controlled, other solutions should be considered.

DISARMAMENT AND ARMS CONTROL

The ideas that force can be used to prevent the use of force by others and that peace can be produced by balancing power with power and by distributing it appropriately are the most popular traditional approaches to the control of interstate war. But the repeated failure of states to make those ideas work, coupled with the capacity of today's weapons to annihilate humanity, have led statesmen and scholars to propose other solutions to the problem of war. One such proposal is to do away with the instruments of violence themselves. This approach constitutes a frontal attack on the theory that power can be balanced with power in that it proposes to do away with power itself. The idea has a long history, which can be traced to the Biblical prescription that nations beat their swords into plowshares. The realities of the contemporary international system underscore why such an idea should gain particular currency today.

A reading of history might easily lead to the conclusion that the weapons of nations contribute in some way to the frequency of war. A number of reasons can be cited for this linkage. Arms are designed for use in conflict. A nation which arms is signaling to others the importance it attaches to the means of war, and possibly unveiling its aggressive designs. If others perceive such potentially aggressive moves as being directed toward them, they may be induced to arm or perhaps launch a preemptive counterstrike. Furthermore, the possession of arms, some believe, often creates the temptation to use them.

On the other hand, nations without weapons cannot initiate wars. Nor are they always the most likely targets of aggression from their armed neighbors (although they are not freed from the fear of that possibility). Instead, could it be that, as the Bible suggests, those who live by the sword tend to die by the sword? In the contemporary period, this adage translates into the observation that each new increment of military power may give the world that much less security.

The incentives for controlling arms have increased greatly since the horrors of Hiroshima and Nagasaki. The threats which nuclear weapons pose to the stability and survival of the international system were lucidly expressed by President Kennedy in a 1961 address to the General Assembly of the United Nations:

> Today, every inhabitant of this planet must contemplate the day when this planet may no longer be habitable. Every man, woman and child lives under a nuclear sword of Damocles, hanging by the slenderest of threads, capable of being cut at any moment by accident or miscalculation or by madness. The weapons of war must be abolished before they abolish us.
>
> Men no longer debate whether armaments are a symptom or a cause of tension. The mere existence of modern weapons—ten million times more powerful than any that the world has ever seen, and only minutes away from any target on earth—is a source of horror, and discord and distrust. Men no longer maintain that disarmament must await the settlement of all disputes—for disarmament must be a part of any permanent settlement. And men may no longer pretend that the quest for disarmament is a sign of weakness—for in a spiraling arms

race, a nation's security may well be shrinking even as its arms increase.

These words capture vividly the fragility of the global system. They underscore the threat of national catastrophe which weapons pose to all. They conjure up the image of Armageddon and predict death under a mushroom cloud unless a reduction in the world's military arsenals is achieved. The vision portrayed challenges the conventional wisdom that arms produce security. Indeed, the right to arm is itself questioned.

Although the idea that war can be controlled by removing the instruments of warfare is not new,[18] even if it has taken on a new urgency today, one of the few constants in the changing international system has been the repetition with which disarmament has been simultaneously proposed but ignored in practice. Governments have rarely disarmed.[19] To speak of disarmament, then, is to speak of an idea largely devoid of empirical referents. Disarmament proposals—and there have been many, especially *after* wars—have seldom been implemented. To be sure, some nations occasionally have decreased their armaments levels. But these instances have often been temporary and involuntary—disarmament imposed by coercion on the vanquished by the victors in a war, as when the Allied powers attempted permanently to disarm a defeated Germany after World War I. Even less frequent have been instances of unilateral disarmament, wherein individual nations have voluntarily reduced their arms levels, or of policies of explicit arms restraint such as those carried out by the Japanese since 1945.[20] Hence disarmament

18. Examples of disarmament proposals include those made by the czar of Russia in 1816; by Premier Nikita Khrushchev of the Soviet Union in 1959; by France in 1831, 1867, and 1869; by Great Britain in 1870; by Italy in 1877; and, multilaterally, in the Hague peace conferences of 1899 and 1907, the League of Nations' World Disarmament Conference of 1933, and rather continuously by the United Nations since 1946 but especially in the U.N. Special Session on Disarmament in 1978.

19. There have been exceptions. The Chinese states in 600 B.C. formed a disarmament league that produced a peaceful century for the league's members (Puchala, 1973); and the Great Lakes were made a disarmed area in 1818.

20. Note the Japanese insistence on not rearming (despite pressure from the United States that they "begin to act like a great power" and that they "should assume responsibilities") has not lead to a reduction of Japan's sense of security. (This position was due, in part, because the Japanese felt that they could count on the United States to provide for Japan's security.) On the contrary, by choosing not to compete militarily, it can be argued that Japan has been able to compete more successfully economically. The Japanese experience suggests that political power can derive from economic power, and that military power can be a liability of sorts. It is noteworthy, however, that pressure is mounting in Japan for increases in military spending far in excess of the rate (approximately 1 percent of GNP) that was maintained in the 1946–1980 period.

may be, as John F. Kennedy suggested, an idea whose time has come, but nevertheless it remains an idea that has rarely been practiced. But the theory does have, on the face of it, a compelling logic. If war is defined as the use of force to settle interstate differences, then war could not occur in the absence of the instruments of force.

Disarmament (the reduction of armaments, if not their abolition) may be usefully distinguished from a related concept, *arms control*. The latter term is generally used to refer to cooperative agreements between states designed to regulate arms levels either by limiting their growth or by placing restrictions on how they might be used. Arms control is less ambitious than disarmament, since it seeks not to eliminate weapons but to regulate their use or moderate the pace at which they are developed. The objectives of arms control are therefore more modest. The fact that arms control sets limitations (compared to the goal of total disarmament) perhaps explains why efforts to control arms have been more successful than have efforts to disarm and why the control of arms is a foreign policy goal of many nations. It also helps explain one of the major paradoxes of world politics—the simultaneous pursuit of an arms race and arms control.

Historical examples of arms control efforts can be found as early as 1139, when the Second Lateran Council prohibited the use of crossbows in fighting. More recent examples include the 1907 Hague Conference's prohibition against firing projectiles from balloons and the agreement among the United States, Britain, Japan, France, and Italy at the Washington Naval Conferences (1921–1922) adjusting the relative tonnage of their fleets. An unsuccessful example is found in the 1921 League of Nations effort to realize an arms production moratorium, a proposal which culminated in 1933 in the League of Nations abortive World Disarmament Conference.

The post-World War II period has witnessed a variety of arms-control proposals. The Baruch Plan (1946) called for the creation of a United Nations Atomic Development Authority which would have placed nuclear energy under international control. The proposal was never implemented. American and Soviet scientists also have met informally since 1957 at the so-called Pugwash Conferences to discuss problems regarding the control of nuclear weapons. President Eisenhower made his "open skies" proposal for inspection by air of Soviet and American territory, but that proposal, offered at the Geneva summit conference of 1955, failed to culminate in an agreement. So, too, did the Rapacki Plan of 1957, which would have prevented the deployment of nuclear weapons in Central Europe. Postwar efforts have not been without their successes, however. As

Table 12.1 shows, eight major multilateral arms control agreements were reached in the 1961–1978 period.

Controlling Nuclear Arms

Particularly conspicuous in any chronicle of successful arms control achievements have been those agreements reached between the United States and the Soviet Union and between them and other nations as a result of the superpowers' efforts. The incentives for the superpowers to seek to control their arms are, of course, enormous. As noted in the previous chapter, a nuclear war between the superpowers would likely result in the death of over 250 million Soviet and American citizens. While it might be possible to contemplate such a level of destruction intellectually, it would surely be the product of moral bankruptcy. McGeorge Bundy, former national security adviser to President Kennedy, has addressed the gap between the thinkable and the politically tolerable.

> There is an enormous gulf between what political leaders really think about nuclear weapons and what is assumed in complex calculations of relative "advantage" in simulated strategic warfare. Think-tank analysts can set levels of "acceptable" damage well up in the hundreds of millions of lives. They can assume that the loss of a dozen cities is somehow a real choice for sane men. In the real world of real political leaders—whether here [in the United States] or in the Soviet Union—a decision that would bring even one hydrogen bomb on one city of one's own country would be recognized in advance as a catastrophic blunder; ten bombs on ten cities would be a disaster beyond history;

Table 12.1
Multilateral Arms Control Agreements, 1961–1978

Agreement	Date Entered into Force	Number of Countries Party to Agreement
Antarctic Treaty	6/23/1961	20
Partial Test Ban Treaty	10/10/1963	111
Outer Space Treaty	10/10/1967	80
Treaty Prohibiting Nuclear Weapons in Latin America	4/22/1968	22
Nuclear Nonproliferation Treaty	3/5/1970	111
Seabeds Arms Control Treaty	5/8/1972	68
Biological Weapons Convention	3/26/1975	87
Environmental Modification Convention	10/5/1978	27

Source: *World Armaments and Disarmament: SIPRI Yearbook* (London: Taylor & Francis, 1980), pp. 443–447.

and a hundred bombs on one hundred cities are unthinkable. Yet this unthinkable level of human incineration is the least that could be expected by either side in response to any first strike in the next ten years, no matter what happens to weapons systems in the meantime. (cited in *The Defense Monitor*, February 1979)

Given this situation, Soviet and American arms control efforts have understandably focused on ways to minimize the threat of nuclear war. Their products are documented in Table 12.2, which lists the bilateral arms control agreements reached between the United States and the Soviet Union in the post-1960 period. To these might be added an indeterminate number of tacit understandings about the level and use of weapons that the two powers seem to have

Table 12.2
Bilateral Arms Control Agreements Between the United States and the Soviet Union as of December 1979

Agreement	Date Signed	Date Entered In Force
"Hot Line" Agreement*	6/20/1963	6/20/1963
Improved "Hot Line" Agreement	9/30/1971	9/30/1971
Nuclear Accidents Agreement	9/30/1971	9/30/1971
ABM Treaty	5/26/1972	10/3/1972
Interim Agreement on Offensive Strategic Arms	5/26/1972	10/3/1972
Standing Consultative Commission for SALT	12/21/1972	12/21/1972
Basic Principles of Negotiations on the Further Limitation of Strategic Offensive Arms	6/21/1973	6/21/1973
Threshold Test Ban Treaty with Protocol	7/3/1974	(not in force as of 12/31/1979)
Protocol to the ABM Treaty	7/3/1974	5/24/1976
Treaty on the Limitation of Underground Explosions for Peaceful Purposes	5/28/1976	(not in force as of 12/31/1979)
Convention on the Prohibition of Military or Any Other Hostile Use of Environmental Modification Techniques	5/18/1977	(not in force as of 12/31/1979)
Treaty on the Limitation of Strategic Offensive Arms	6/18/1979	(not in force as of 12/31/1979)
Protocol to the Treaty on the Limitation of Strategic Offensive Arms	6/18/1979	(not in force as of 12/31/1979)

Source: U.S. Arms Control and Disarmament Agency, *Arms Control 1978* (Washington, D.C.: Government Printing Office, 1979), p. 75; *World Armaments and Disarmament: SIPRI Yearbook 1980* (London: Taylor & Francis, 1980), pp. 469–478.

*In the aftermath of the Cuban missile crisis in 1962, the "hot line" was installed to facilitate direct communication between the White House and the Kremlin in the event of a similar future crisis.

agreed to, understandings which have not achieved the status of formal treaties but which the two superpowers have nonetheless observed. In this category, for example, might be included the superpowers' commitment to refrain from the nondefensive use of their nuclear arsenals, as indicated by President Carter's pledge that the United States would not be the first country to use nuclear weapons in war and President Brezhnev's promise in 1980 that Soviet nuclear weapons would never be used against a nonnuclear country.

Most notable of the arms control agreements reached by the superpowers are the two so-called SALT (Strategic Arms Limitation Talks) agreements. SALT I, signed in 1972, consisted of (1) a treaty which restricted the deployment of antiballistic missile defense systems by the United States and the Soviet Union to equal and very low levels, and (2) a five-year interim accord on strategic offensive arms, which restricted the number of ICBM (intercontinental ballistic missiles) and SLBM (submarine-launched ballistic missiles) launchers each side was permitted to have. The SALT II agreement of 1979 substantially revised the quantitative restrictions of SALT I and began as well to place certain qualitative constraints on the superpowers' strategic arsenals.

The essentials of SALT II, although perhaps the most extensive and complicated arms control agreement ever negotiated, are nevertheless quite simple. First, the agreement called for placing an overall ceiling of 2,400 (to be reduced to 2,250 by the end of 1981) on the number of ICBM launchers, SLBM launchers, heavy bombers, and ASBMs (air-to-surface ballistic missiles with ranges over 600 kilometers) each side is permitted to maintain. Within this overall ceiling, several subceilings specified additional restrictions on particular types of nuclear systems. As illustrated in Figure 12.1, the first subceiling limited each superpower to 1,320 launchers equipped with MIRVs (multiple independently targetable reentry vehicles) plus heavy bombers equipped with long-range cruise missiles. The second subceiling limited the total number of launchers of MIRVed ballistic missiles to 1,200, and the third subceiling restricted each nation to the deployment of no more than 820 MIRVed ICBMs.

In addition to these numerical limits, SALT II placed other constraints on the superpowers. For example, the accord banned construction of additional fixed ICBM launchers and increased in the number of fixed heavy ICBM launchers. It also limited the number of warheads permitted on ICBMs and ASBMs to ten, and the number permitted on SLBMs to fourteen. This constraint, unlike any in SALT I, would have the effect of inhibiting qualitative improvements in the payload delivery capabilities of the superpowers' missiles. At the time of the signing of SALT II, the U.S. State Depart-

Figure 12.1
SALT II Allotment of Strategic Nuclear Delivery Vehicles

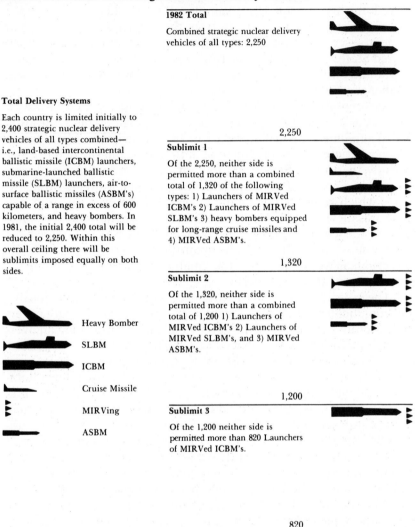

1982 Total

Combined strategic nuclear delivery
vehicles of all types: 2,250

Total Delivery Systems

Each country is limited initially to
2,400 strategic nuclear delivery
vehicles of all types combined—
i.e., land-based intercontinental
ballistic missile (ICBM) launchers,
submarine-launched ballistic
missile (SLBM) launchers, air-to-
surface ballistic missiles (ASBM's)
capable of a range in excess of 600
kilometers, and heavy bombers. In
1981, the initial 2,400 total will be
reduced to 2,250. Within this
overall ceiling there will be
sublimits imposed equally on both
sides.

Heavy Bomber

SLBM

ICBM

Cruise Missile

MIRVing

ASBM

2,250

Sublimit 1

Of the 2,250, neither side is
permitted more than a combined
total of 1,320 of the following
types: 1) Launchers of MIRVed
ICBM's 2) Launchers of MIRVed
SLBM's 3) heavy bombers equipped
for long-range cruise missiles and
4) MIRVed ASBM's.

1,320

Sublimit 2

Of the 1,320, neither side is
permitted more than a combined
total of 1,200 1) Launchers of
MIRVed ICBM's 2) Launchers of
MIRVed SLBM's, and 3) MIRVed
ASBM's.

1,200

Sublimit 3

Of the 1,200 neither side is
permitted more than 820 Launchers
of MIRVed ICBM's.

820

Source: U.S. Department of State, *The Strategic Arms Limitation Talks*, Bureau of
Public Affairs, Special Report 46 (Revised), May 1979, p. 7.

ment estimated that the total number of strategic nuclear weapons
possessed by the United States and the Soviet Union would be perhaps as many as 8,500 fewer by 1985 than the two sides would have
possessed in the absence of SALT II (see Figure 12.2). The number of
strategic nuclear delivery vehicles would also be somewhat smaller
than otherwise anticipated, which as a practical matter means that

the Soviet Union would not be permitted to deploy as many delivery vehicles as American defense planners believe it otherwise would deploy.

But the difficulty of obtaining arms control agreements is illustrated by the problems the SALT II agreement encountered. The treaty had not yet been considered by the U.S. Senate at the time of the U.S. presidential election of November, 1980. The victor, the Republican candidate Ronald Reagan, had campaigned for office on a platform that opposed the terms of the SALT II agreement. Hence the obstacles to formal ratification of this treaty remained formidable, although the absence of ratification did not necessarily indicate that both sides would be unwilling eventually to subscribe to its basic terms.

This list of achievements in arms control is rather impressive, suggesting that limitations on the number and destructiveness of weapons have been, and remain, possible. But the accomplishments mask many of the failures and camouflage the lack of meaningful controls of armaments in many other areas. Indeed, these accomplishments might even serve to *promote*, rather than eradicate, the dangers posed by contemporary weapons. Critics have noted, for instance, that arms control agreements may provide a false sense of security by encouraging us to think that the arms race is being meaningfully controlled when, in actuality, it is not. "If we believe that our arms are safely controlled, we may cease our efforts to work for disarmament or for whatever will bring an end to the problem of war" (Ziegler, 1977).

One indicator of this possibility is the unabated development and testing of nuclear weapons. The six nuclear states are known to have made 1,221 nuclear explosions between 1945 and 1979: India, 1; China, 25; United Kingdom, 30; France, 86; the Soviet Union, 426; and the United States, 653 (*World Armaments and Disarmament*, 1980: xxxii). This pace was *not* slowed by the partial test ban treaty of 1963, because it only proscribed atmospheric and underwater testing, not underground explosions.[21] In fact, 60 percent of these explosions have taken place since the 1963 partial test ban treaty (*World Armaments and Disarmament*, 1980: xxxii).

Since nations seem to persist in the notion that security derives from arms accumulation, and that the benefits of arms restraints are limited, it may be argued that they have preserved those cherished notions by only controlling those armaments which they had little intention of, or incentive for, developing. The "threat" system

21. Neither France nor China is a party to the partial test-ban treaty. China has conducted atmospheric testing of nuclear weapons, but since 1974 France has conducted all its nuclear explosions underground.

Figure 12.2
Soviet and American Strategic Nuclear Delivery Vehicles, 1979 and 1985
(launchers)

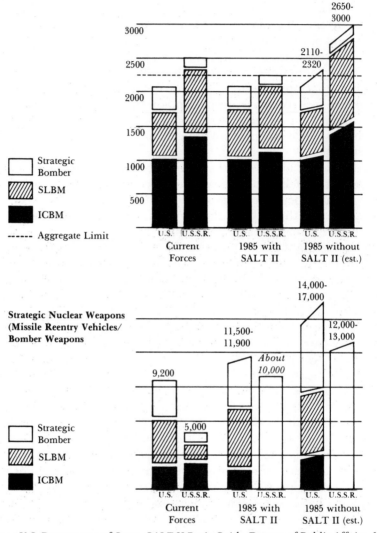

Source: U.S. Department of State, *SALT II Basic Guide*, Bureau of Public Affairs, May 1979, p. 7.

of armaments was not seriously challenged, for instance, by the abolition of nuclear weapons from Antarctica or Latin America,[22] where

22. Latin America was made a nuclear-free zone in the 1967 Treaty of Tlatelolco. However, neither Brazil nor Argentina, the only two countries in the area with nuclear potential and aspirations, has (as of mid-1980) fully agreed to the provisions of the treaty.

the temptations for their deployment were not great. But where the leading nations have perceived their vital interests to be at stake, they have been less than willing to moderate their penchant to accumulate ever more deadly weapons systems. The cynic might argue that arms control has been largely a fraud devised to disguise the continuation of preparations for war, or even a conspiracy conducted (cooperatively) by the great powers to spread complacency in the public mind and thereby preserve the unquenchable thirsts of their military establishments for more money and arms.

More realistic, perhaps, may be the charge that arms control accomplishments rarely impose meaningful restrictions, and that, rather than imposing caps on arms races, they merely stabilize, legitimize, and provide orderly rules for the continuation of the races. The SALT agreements, for example, were widely perceived as significant pauses in the extraordinarily expensive Soviet-American arms race, and they were presented to the American and Soviet publics as important steps toward the control of arms. Yet some critics have questioned whether they accomplished either task. Noteworthy, for example, is that during the five years covered by the SALT I agreement (1972–1977), the combined military spending of the two superpowers exceeded $1 trillion. This is a rate of spending greater than that of the quarter century between the end of World War II and the signing of the SALT I agreement, when total military spending was $2.3 trillion. This works out to about 9 percent of the total United States GNP produced since the end of the war, and about a quarter of that of the Soviet Union. If this rate of spending were projected to the year 2000, the aggregate defense costs of the United States and the Soviet Union would at that time stand in excess of $5 trillion. Now, however, even with the signing of two strategic arms agreements—and even if the effects of inflation are controlled—this projection appears likely to be much too modest. The SALT agreements, in short, fail to promise a reduction in the military spending propensities of either superpower. "I want to dispel any idea that SALT is going to mean any reduction in the strategic budget," proclaimed General David C. Jones, chairman of the U.S. Joint Chiefs of Staff (July 26, 1978).

Also revealing is what the SALT agreements failed to restrict. SALT I, for example, froze the number of strategic launchers in operation or in the process of construction at the time of the agreement, but it failed to cover strategic bombers or to prevent the kinds of qualitative improvements that can make quantitative thresholds meaningless. One such improvement was in the number of strategic warheads a single missile could launch against an enemy (MIRVs). And in fact the number of independently targetable warheads deployed on missiles by the superpowers in 1977 was four times greater than when the SALT talks began—even though SALT I froze the number of delivery vehicles at the superpowers' disposal. Perhaps this is the kind of situation Herbert Scoville, Jr., a former deputy director of the Central Intelligence Agency, had in mind when he noted at the time of the signing of SALT I: "Arms control negotiations are rapidly becoming the best excuse for escalating rather than toning down the arms race" (cited in Barnet, 1977).

SALT II, as noted earlier, contained provisions which may inhibit some qualitative improvements in nuclear weapons technology. However, the agreement specifically permitted each side to test and deploy one new "light" ICBM system. This allowed the United States to proceed with development of a new, mobile land-based missile system, which, significantly, the Carter administration announced it was going to develop even *before* SALT II had been signed. Known as the MX, the new missile system was initially projected to cost more than $30 billion. Estimates have increased progressively since then.

It is the pattern revealed in these developments that led one former American policy maker, Leslie H. Gelb (1979), to conclude that "Arms control has essentially failed. Three decades of U.S.-Soviet negotiations to limit arms competition have done little more than to codify the arms race."

Impediments to Effective Arms Control

Why have arms controls been so ineffective, and why have agreements to control the size and dispersion of weapons been so modest? The incentives for the creation of meaningful arms control would seem to be many, and mutually beneficial to all. Significant controls of the weapons of war would save money, reduce tension and the dangers of war, symbolize an expression of the desire for détente, reduce health hazards, reduce the destructiveness of war, erode the potential of one achieving a power advantage over others with the corresponding threat of provoking a preemptive counterattack, and achieve a propaganda advantage for those advocating peace (Van Dyke, 1966). To these might be added moral satisfaction and the opportunity to live in a global environment free of the fear of instant obliteration.

But arms are not being controlled in today's international system, and the reasons for the continued reliance on military preparedness as a path to peace are many. They stem from the fear that is endemic to the international system as it is now structured. Most nations are reluctant to engage in arms limitations in an atmosphere where trust of their adversaries is lacking, and trust is unlikely to be cultivated as long as those adversaries remain armed with threatening weapons. Hence nations find themselves caught in a vicious circle of fear and insecurity: others' arms provoke fear, fear stimulates the desire to arm for defense, armament in turn encourages the enemy to increase its arms, and so it goes in a never ending spiral. The chain is difficult to break, and efforts to do so have failed whenever the underlying fear has persisted.

This fear helps explain the self-defeating posture nations assume in negotiating arms control agreements. "The military establishments on both sides subscribe to the same two basic principles: (1) 'Don't negotiate when you are behind. Why accept a permanent position of number two?' and (2) 'Don't negotiate when you are ahead. Why accept a freeze in an area of military competition when the other side has not kept up with you?' " (Barnet, 1977). The result of this syndrome is clear: when fearful nations abide by the axiom that they should never negotiate out of fear, and that they should never negotiate from a position of weakness, then they are left with no option but to refuse to negotiate. It is little wonder that meaningful agreements have been so hard to achieve. Arms bargaining is a game of give and take, but all participants typically want to take much and give little because security is dear and fear is strong. The process is described by a former United States arms negotiator thus: "U.S. negotiators are almost invariably given instructions, in effect, to close all of the other side's loopholes but to keep their own open. Nor surprisingly, Soviet instructions seem similar. Thus, the talks begin to grind exceedingly fine and slow" (Gelb, 1979).

The problems of arriving at meaningful arms control agreements are compounded by other obstacles. A precondition to agreement is the perception of the achievement of secure *mutual* deterrence (Smoke, 1975), but such power configurations are seldom perceived. Stable arms-control ratios are also particularly difficult to achieve in an era of rapid technological innovation. Technology can on the one hand make obsolete weapons systems which have been banned yet at the same time can encourage states to make qualitative refinements of their existing weapons systems. The possibilities of such innovations exacerbate the excessive difficulties of comparing the relative military strengths of parties to an agreement. "What are equivalent weapons?" is a question on which few observers (even within a given country) are able to agree. And of course achieving agreement on ratios of strength constitutes, as Henry Kissinger often remarked, a political problem of considerable magnitude, not just a technical one. Orchestrating arms negotiations to keep them in balance with political negotiations in other areas, and convincing various publics and pressure groups that the benefits of an agreement outweigh the costs, require considerable skill and energy.[23]

Equally troublesome is the difficulty of separating the control of weapons from other issues. Nowhere is this more evident than in the Soviet-American dialogue, where the evolution of arms talks have been inextricably tied to the vicissitudes of the Soviet-American competition in other areas (Gelb, 1979).

In fact, policy makers have often sought to link these issues. Ronald Reagan, in his successful 1980 campaign for the presidency, stated:

> I don't think you simply sit down at the table with the Soviet Union to discuss arms limitation, but you discuss the whole attitude—as to whether we're going to have a world at peace or whether we're simply going to talk about weaponry and not bring up these other . . . subjects. In other words, I believe in linkage.

Arms control and detente are symbiotic—the former assists the development of the latter, and the latter fosters the former. Deterioration of East-West relations in nonmilitary areas can therefore jeopardize prospects for arms control,[24] and an escalating arms race reduces considerably the probability of improved Soviet-American political relationships. As Henry A. Kissinger once observed,

> An unconstrained arms race in the strategic field will over any period of time be inconsistent with improved political relationships. . . . Sustaining the build-up requires exhortations by both sides that in time may prove incompatible with restrained international conduct. The

23. Many people benefit financially from the perpetuation of arms races and become lobbyists against arms agreements because they can lose their jobs by an abatement of military spending. Groups exist in all societies whose influence is tied to the continuation of the arms race. For literature exploring the effects of military- industrial complexes, see Rosen (1973) and the series of articles on "The Military Industrial Complex: USSR/USA" in the *Journal of International Affairs* (1972).

24. For instance, presumably in partial reaction to the Soviet invasion of Afghanistan, President Carter announced (March 16, 1980) that the United States might renounce the Strategic Arms Treaty (SALT II) even if Moscow continued to abide by its terms. He stated that his administration might at some point determine that the agreement was no longer in the nation's interest, "in which case I would notify the Soviet Union that the terms of the treaty are no longer binding." He elaborated, saying "Ordinarily, when a treaty is signed between the heads of two nations, the presumption is that the treaty will be honored on both sides after some further development. One further development that would cause me to renounce the treaty would be . . . to determine an interest of our nation that might cause such a rejection, in which case I would notify the Soviet Union that the terms of the treaty were no longer binding" (*New York Times*, March 16, 1980, p. A1). For this and other reasons, Reagan had expressed his desire to suspend some of the principle terms of the SALT II agreement and to renegotiate others.

very fact of a strategic arms race has a high potential for feeding attitudes of hostility and suspicion on both sides, transforming the fears of those who demand more weapons into self-fulfilling prophecies.

The linkage between arms control and the overall climate of opinion in which the two superpowers must act would suggest that the inability of the two states to reach accommodation in areas not directly related to arms control will nonetheless constitute an obstacle to the negotiation of meaningful arms control agreements.

Perhaps the obstacles to the control of arms are insurmountable. The idea that a disarmed world would be a more secure world does not have the force of history behind it, whereas the idea that military preparedness produces security does. It may be that peace via disarmament and arms control is, as critics have charged, a utopian dream.[25]

Alternatively, it may be that the control of arms is a practical necessity, even though the international milieu is not conducive to the quest of that goal.[26] Problems which cannot be solved are seldom raised. It may be that the ability of states to sucessfully control their proclivity to arm has been realized so infrequently because it is only the symptom of problems not yet capable of being solved. It can be argued that arms control rests on the prior ability of nations to settle their political disputes successfully, something they have not always done. Managing political conflicts without violence may be the key to arms control. For arms, after all, may be less causes of war than they are symptoms of political tension. Arms may be the fruits, not the seeds, of war: "Men do not fight because they have arms. They have arms because [they are afraid and] they deem it necessary to fight" (Morgenthau, 1967). From this perspective, controlling arms is contingent upon the removal of fears that affect the political contests of nations.

The belief that armament reductions would enhance the prospects of peace is a theory for the control of violence that has not as yet been meaningfully implemented. Thus, because we have no actual contemporary experience of politics among nations in a disarmed world, we have no way of knowing whether a disarmed world would indeed be a peaceful world. A disarmed world might actually have *more* political troubles, even if it would have fewer military expressions of them.

25. Other critics have noted that arms control efforts are doomed to failure, not because the proposal to control arms is idealistic, but because it does not go far enough. "Arms control does not solve the basic problem of armaments. States still have them, and if they have them, they can use them" (Ziegler, 1977).

26. See Sibley (1963) for a statement which argues for both the necessity and possibility of unilateral disarmament.

Thirteen

International Law, International Organization, and World Peace

In the conflict of arms, laws must be silent.

Hugo Grotius, 1625

Everything that is done in international affairs must be done from the viewpoint of whether it will advance or hinder the establishment of world government.

Albert Einstein, 1946

Two central paths to international peace and stability have been pursued since antiquity. The first entails essentially *military* solutions to the problem of war. A second path seeks avoidance of war through *political* solutions. The logic underlying this orientation is that war is symptomatic of the failure of politics. As the eminent political philosopher Emil Brunner put it in 1947, in reaction to the dominant view of war as expressed by Clausewitz, "the claim that war is the *ultima ratio* of politics is simply a superstition."

INTERNATIONAL LAW AND WORLD ORDER

Legal procedures provide one potential source for the peaceful control of interstate conflict, but their contribution has often been questioned. Some students of jurisprudence have viewed the international legal order as deficient, even nonexistent (Tung, 1968). Others have considered it meaningless. Because one normally thinks that a legal order is created for—among other reasons—the basic purpose of deterring violence, and because legal orders are evaluated in terms of their ability to effectively control violence (Falk, 1968), the recurrence of war has led some to conclude that international law is simply "irrelevant" to the regulation of armed conflict between nations (see Hoffmann, 1971). Still others have character-ized international law as "weak and defenseless," hopelessly "vague," "in its infancy," and debilitated by "the virtual absence of a reliable, powerful, impartial enforcement machinery" (see Fried, 1971).

Such skepticism runs counter to the way most of us have been conditioned to think of law. By tradition, law is widely perceived to be a useful method of settling disputes. There is intuitive appeal in the notion that conflicts can be resolved by recourse to a court of law, and the expectation that legal approaches can be employed to redress grievances is deeply instilled in Western philosophic tradi-tions.[1]

Skepticism regarding the role of law in international politics and interstate war often seems warranted. But before concluding that law has no place in controlling global conflict, it is first neces-sary to examine the major attributes of the international legal order as revealed in both the legacy of doctrinal tradition and actual state practice.

The Nature of the International Legal Order

International law is generally considered to be the body of rules that governs the conduct of states in their relations with one an-other.[2] Why this conception should predominate stems from the his-torical origins of the international legal system, which are conven-tionally (but imprecisely) traced to the 1648 Treaties of Westphalia, which created the so-called Western state system. Perhaps it would be more accurate to say that the system of international law did not take its present shape until the Congress of Vienna (1815) at the end of the Napoleonic wars (Parry, 1968).

1. The belief that each unwelcome form of behavior could be eliminated or re-duced in frequency by making it illegal was considered by a former French foreign minister, Aristide Briand, to be a peculiarly American outlook. Warfare was seen as part of this orientation. For instance, in 1918 the American Salmon O. Levinson ar-gued against the fact in his day that war was legally defined as "a contest between na-tions under the sanction of international law," contending that "In dealing with any other form of evil one's first impulse is to have the legislature or congress pass a law making the practice illegal and criminal. If that is the way to deal with ordinary grievances, why not take the beaten path with the greatest of all wrongs? We want not 'laws of war' but 'laws against war' as we have laws against murder and bur-glary" (cited in Russell, 1936). The same idea finds expression in the Japanese consti-tution.

2. This definition avoids the controversy created by those traditional interpreta-tions of law as "commands" from a sovereign authority which restrain actors from behaving in a particular manner, for, as shall be seen, the international system lacks a central, law-giving authority.

Present international law derives from precedents found in the evolutionary development of the international political system itself (Hoffmann, 1961; Falk, 1962 and 1970). The conception of international law which the global community now accepts rests on these political foundations, which in turn find expression in the *corpus juris gentium* (the body of the law of nations) that has grown considerably over the past three centuries. A selective inventory of some of the basic legal principles relevant to the control of war illustrates the nature of this general body of rules commonly recognized.[3]

No principle of international law is more important than the doctrine of state *sovereignty*. This cardinal concept recognizes a privileged status for states among all transnational actors in the global arena. State sovereignty means that no authority is legally above the state in the global hierarchy except the authority which the state voluntarily confers on organizations which it creates.

Nearly every tenet of international law supports and elaborates the concept of sovereignty. For instance, state sovereignty justifies the principle of the *equality* of states. Equality stipulates not the fiction that all states are equal in military power, resources, or size, but instead that each is entitled equally to full respect by other states and full protection of the legal rules which the system acknowledges. As a corollary, all states are awarded the right of independence which guarantees them autonomy in their internal affairs and external relations, under the logic that the independence of each state presumes that of all others.

Furthermore, international law stipulates that states not interfere in the internal affairs of other states: the *noninterference* principle forms the basis for states' duty of *nonintervention*, that is, the duty to refrain from uninvited involvement in activities within another state's borders. This classic norm has eroded considerably in recent decades; states have violated it increasingly as the world has become more interdependent and as their capabilities to pursue complex foreign policy goals have become more varied. Nonetheless, the rule of noninterference is consistent with the prescribed right of every state to exercise *jurisdiction* over only its own *territory*: each state is granted control over practically all things on, under, or above its bounded territory. (There are exceptions to which states have agreed and which have been codified in international law: for example, immunity for diplomatic envoys of other nations

---

3. Reviews of the rules of international law are numerous, lengthy, and complicated. See Gould (1957); Bishop (1962); Coplin (1966); Von Glahn (1976); Akehurst (1970); Brownlie (1973); and Sorensen (1968) for treatments of the subject. The discussion here follows the interpretation of Sorensen.

while those officials represent their country in another country, occupy embassies abroad, and so forth.)[4]

Additional principles safeguard the state. Because the state is under the legal influence of no superior power, sovereignty is absolute—states are the only legitimate subjects of international law. Individuals and transnational institutions (although of increasing concern to international law) do not have sovereign rights—they have gained standing because states see benefits in making them subjects of international law for limited purposes.

In practice, sovereignty gives the state freedom of choice with respect to every aspect of its internal life. The theory of domestic jurisdiction permits a state to establish whatever laws it wishes for its own citizens, including the rules for determining the conditions under which individuals can acquire citizenship.[5] It can create whatever type of political system or form of government it desires, irrespective of the acceptability of that type of government to other states. It also has sovereign freedom to regulate—or not to regulate—economic transactions within its boundaries. And it is empowered to require those living on its soil to fight for the state's survival.

Because statehood encompasses many legal prerogatives, it is not surprising that states seek to preserve an international legal system while at the same time other political entities would strive for the same rights within that system. In fact, many principles in the body of international law articulate rules for acquiring statehood, and hence entry into the established legal system. The Montevideo Convention of 1933 on the Rights and Duties of States summarizes the major components of statehood. A political entity aspiring to statehood must possess a permanent population, a defined territory, and a government capable of both ruling its citizens (claiming legitimacy) and entering into formal relations with other states. Other rules exist for determining how and when these conditions are satisfied. Essentially, the acquisition of statehood is dependent upon a political entity receiving recognition from other states. Thus

4. It was the violation of this principle by Iran when American diplomats were incarcerated in 1979 that distinguished that situation from other hostage-takings or acts of terrorism. As the World Court put it in its May 1980 ruling in favor of the United States, "This case is unique and of very particular gravity because here it is not only private individuals or groups that have disregarded and set at naught the inviolability of a foreign embassy, but the Government of the receiving state itself."

5. Different conventions regarding the acquisition of *nationality* are practiced by states. Two principles generally have been selected to confer nationality—*jus soli* (citizenship is determined by the state on whose territory the birth took place) or *jus sanguinis* (nationality is acquired by birth from descent from a parent of a national). In some states a combination of these two principles is found.

international law holds that certification of whether a state exists rests in the hands of other states; that is, preexisting states are entitled to extend *diplomatic recognition* to another entity.[6] When extended, this enables the recognizing state to enter into formal relations with the entity being recognized (again, according to a series of regulations defining rights and duties). Because recognition is a voluntary political act, *nonrecognition* is a legally institutionalized form of public insult toward a government aspiring to statehood—a form of sanction against an unwanted regime.

In the present global system no significant land mass remains *terra nullius* (territory belonging legally to no one). Because nearly all the earth's surface (except the oceans) is now within some state's sovereign control,[7] no areas remain for colonization, and the birth of a new state must necessarily be at the expense of an existing one. Hence, recognition of a new state almost always entails recognition of a new government's control over a particular piece of territory.

Associated with sovereignty are numerous international rules for the orderly conduct of interstate relations. Sovereign states have almost unlimited rights to do as they please in their foreign relations with other states. Indeed, in foreign policy "international law permits a complete freedom of action" (Parry, 1968) and contends that the preservation of sovereignty is the states' primary foreign policy objective. The doctrine of neutrality enables states to avoid taking sides in disputes between other contending parties. On the other hand, doctrines of current international law stipulate that states negotiate their disputes and even spell out rules for the conduct of negotiations. However, international law does not obligate nations to reach agreement or resolve their dispute peacefully.

States are free to enter into treaty arrangements with other states. Again a large body of rules specifies how treaties are to be activated and interpreted.[8] International law contends that treaties

6. A distinction between two types of recognition is sometimes made. *De facto* recognition is provisional and capable of being withdrawn in the event the recognized government is superseded by another; it does not carry with it the exchange of diplomatic representatives or other legal benefits and responsibilities. The government which is recognized *de jure*, on the other hand, obtains full legal and diplomatic privileges from the granting state. The distinction underscores the fact that recognition is a political tool of international law, implying approval or disapproval of a government. Recognition of a government may, of course, be withdrawn at any time according to the procedural rules for severing diplomatic relations.

7. Antarctica is an exception to this generalization. The Antarctic Treaty, put into force with the support of the superpowers in 1961, places this territory outside the jurisdiction of any state and thereby precludes its conquest by any one. Antarctica is administered jointly by a number of states, including the United States and the Soviet Union.

8. The law of treaties comprises by far the largest proportion of the law of nations. Treaties have a law-making function, and the precedents they establish contrib-

voluntarily entered into are binding (*pacta sunt servanda*). But it also reserves the right of states to abrogate treaties previously agreed to by reference to the escape clause known as *rebus sic stantibus*—the principle that a treaty is binding only as long as there is no vital change from the circumstances as they existed when the treaty was concluded, and that parties to the treaty have the right to determine when those changes occur.[9]

The right of self-defense in international law reinforces the ability of the state to do whatever it deems necessary to safeguard its sovereign rights. This does not preclude states from enhancing their own welfare at the expense of others. Nor is the use of force prohibited; indeed, the doctrine of *military necessity* justifies the taking of "protective" military measures to guard paramount interests. From this it is a short step to the traditional *jus ad bellum* (the right to resort to war) and to the claim that states have an unlimited right to make war. Indeed, the legal justification for belligerency "in defense of the system's rules" (Kelsen, 1945) enjoys a long history in international law. When national interests were perceived to demand it (especially prior to World War II), states were legally free to engage in a variety of forceful self-help measures, including going to war.

Historically, international law has also identified forcible procedures short of war for redress of grievances. Acts such as military occupations, blockades, embargoes, and boycotts are included in this category, as are reprisals, retorsions, invasions, shows of strength, and mobilizations as forms of retaliation.

Jus belli (the law of war) comprises a significant proportion of the body of laws among nations, providing rules for declaring, conducting, and terminating war, as well as prohibiting certain kinds of war. In all these matters, international law reserves for the state the right to judge the propriety of its own actions, even while it acknowledges that other states may judge those acts as violations of the law.[10] As the eminent publicist J. L. Brierly (1944) concluded, international law thus creates a system wherein states are "legally

---

ute to rule creation for the signatory parties. The number and diversity of treaties have grown rapidly as states have negotiated understandings among themselves in response to new problems. Peter H. Rohn's "United Nations Treaty Project" quantitatively maps these trends. See Rohn (1968 and 1970) for a description of this project. Data from it are reported in *Treaty Profiles* (Rohn, 1976) and the five-volume *World Treaty Index* (Rohn, 1974).

9. For an illustration of the enduring diplomatic use of *rebus sic stantibus* logic, see the example in the context of the SALT treaties p. 414, note 24.

10. Other statements of the legal acceptance of nondefensive acts of self-help include Wheaton's (1846) view that "every state has a right to resort to force" and Bishop's (1962) view that international law is not violated "when a state resorted to war for any reason it felt proper."

bound to respect each other's independence and other rights, and yet free to attack each other at will."

Does International Law Constitute an International Legal Order?

Collectively, sovereignty and the legal principles derived from it lend fundamental shape to the international political system and the behavior of states in that system (DeVisscher, 1957). Indeed, international law reinforces a state-centric view of world politics. The global condition is thus legally dependent on what central governments elect to do with each other and to their own populations.[11]

The legal system produced by the principles of international law is regarded as structurally defective by many theorists. Absent at the international level are formal institutions (resembling those within states) capable of performing the essential functions that all legal systems must allegedly perform. Critics make the following points.

First, every legal system must *make* its rules through recognized procedures, but in world politics a legislative body capable of laying down the law does not exist. Rules are made only when states willingly observe them or articulate them in the treaties to which they voluntarily subscribe. No systematic legislative method exists to amend or revoke them. Noteworthy in this respect are the provisions of Article 38 (section 1) of the Statute of the International Court of Justice, generally accepted as the authoritative statement on the sources of international law. It states that international law derives from (1) custom, (2) international treaties and agreements, (3) national and international court decisions, (4) the writings of legal authorities and specialists, and (5) the "general principles" of law recognized since the Roman Empire as part of "natural law" and "right reason" and perceived as inherent in the legal systems of

11. In this context, public international law is said to take precedence over all national laws—municipal law (law within the state) is subservient to it. On first appearance, this conveys the impression that international law constrains meaningfully what governments can do within their borders. But this is not the case, because the international law that takes precedence over national law stipulates as an operating premise that all sovereign governments are empowered to regulate their internal conditions according to their own preferences, with few meaningful restrictions. International law, in short, does not limit the state's freedom of action toward its own citizens; it liberates the state to act domestically as it pleases. It is this absence of constraint on state action that explains why governments so eagerly voice support for international law. Democracies, dictatorships, totalitarian governments, rich and poor countries—all are enthusiastic supporters of this system. It gives each of these governments nearly unconstrained power internally and assures each entry into a system designed to protect government independence. States therefore accept the precedence of international law over national law because the former confirms the power of the latter.

all states. The absence of any reference to a world parliament or congress reflects the lack of global legislative mechanisms.

Second, every legal system must *interpret* the rules enacted, but in world politics no authoritative judicial body is empowered to identify the rules created, record the substantive precepts reached, specify when and how the rules apply, and identify instances of violation. Instead, each state is responsible for performing these tasks itself according to its own definition and concept of justice. The World Court (International Court of Justice) does not have the power to perform these functions without the consent of states. Furthermore, the use of the court is not required and compliance with its verdicts is not mandatory in the absence of efforts by the international community to seek UN Security Council enforcement of a World Court ruling.

Finally, every legal system must *execute* the law, but in world politics no executive body is capable of enforcing the rules. There is, obviously, no world government. The enforcement function is performed through the self-help procedures of each state, whereby compliance is voluntary and retaliatory sanctions are exercised by one state against another if and when the former perceives the latter to have violated the former's rights. The whole system rests, therefore, on the willingness of states to abide by the rules to which they have consented, on the capacity of each state to enforce the norms of behavior it values, and on every state's ability to exercise self-restraint.

In sum, international law rests on a consensual foundation—states are accountable only to the regulations to which they freely choose to abide. This creates a self-help legal system: the rules governing interactions between states are made by the states themselves (not by a higher authority). Each state can determine what the rules are, when they apply, and when and how they should be enforced. They make their own laws (see Onuf, 1980). Given this conception, nearly anything becomes permissible as long as it is justified as enhancing self-preservation of the state, which is the highest value in the system.

Can a system ostensibly designed to control the behavior of states do so when "in the last analysis, . . . the states are still above the law" (Hoffmann, 1971)? When everyone is above the law, can anyone be outside of it? Can there be any real outlaws in a global arena organized on this basis? These questions have led legal theorists to ask whether international law is really law (see Coplin, 1966). To the skepticism derived from observation of the principles of conduct states have assigned themselves can be added still other attributes that render the efficiency of the international legal order suspect. Nine of the more conspicuous of these alleged structural defects, emanating from a system that subjects states to no regulative authority above them, follow.[12]

1. International law cannot make credible its claim for universality. A valid legal system must represent norms shared by those it governs. The existence of community values is usually seen as a minimal requirement for the formation of a legal system, according to the precept of Roman law *ubi societas, ibi jus* (where there is society, there is law). The international order is culturally heterogeneous and lacks a common-value consensus (Bozeman, 1960 and 1971). Instead of an integrated community of nations, "diverse systems of public order" exist throughout the global system (McDougal and Lasswell, 1959).

2. International law denies participation in the creation of rules to a substantial proportion of the members of the global system. International law still reflects the legal preferences of the European actors present when its basic rules were created. Most states (particularly those in the Third World) do not share the worldview expressed in Western culture and resent inheritance of rules and procedures for norm maintenance outside their own traditions—rules which are perceived to be inimical to their own needs and supportive of the interests of prosperous countries, such as principles of recognition and the former legitimation of colonialism. Northrup (1952) observes, for instance, that Asian culture emphasizes accommodation and compromise, rather than Western adversarial judicial procedures.

3. International law perpetuates competition among states and justifies the pursuit of national advantage. Indeed, international law is said to legitimize the drive for preponderance rather than to restrain it. Hence, international law contributes not only to cooperation but also to conflict (Lissitzyn, 1963). Self-help, the operative principle of international law, does not control power; it is instead a concession to power.

4. International law is subservient to national expediency rather than to conceptions of morality or justice. As in the context of any

12. Evaluations of the adequacy or inadequacy of international legal institutions depend on the legal school or paradigmatic perspective from which the assessment is made. International legal scholarship is itself divided into contending analytic orientations (e.g., positivists, naturalists, realists, neorealists, sociologists of law, "eclectics," etc.), each of which is somewhat incompatible with the others. For reviews and assessments of these legal traditions and their implications, see Coplin (1969), Nussbaum (1961), and Gould (1957).

legal system, the legal thing to do is not necessarily the moral thing to do. Is it moral, for instance, for some to starve while others live in comparative opulence, even if legal rules support this kind of gross inequality? By worshiping the unbridled autonomy of sovereign independence, international law follows the "iron law of politics"—that legal obligations must yield to the national interest (Morgenthau, 1973). It is said that this kind of concession must ultimately undermine respect for legal norms, for legal systems are partially justified and ultimately command respect and allegiance through their capacity to distribute justice equitably. But a system that makes power politics the master of international law, instead of placing legal controls on power politics, can be regarded as deficient (Kaplan and Katzenbach, 1961).

5. International law is an instrument of the powerful for oppression of the weak. In a voluntary consent system, the rules to which the powerful willingly agree are usually those that serve their interests—and these tend to preserve the existing hierarchy, to perpetuate the privileges of the powerful, and to further the discrepancy between the dominant and the subordinate. International law is perceived to preserve the prerogatives of the haves and to deny realization of the aspirations of the have-nots (see Friedheim, 1965). (It might be noted, however, that some rules protect the right of expropriations.)

6. In many areas, international law is little more than a justification of existing practices. When a particular behavior pattern becomes widespread, it tends to become legally obligatory. Rules *of* behavior are over time defined as rules *for* behavior (Hoffmann, 1971). Like laws in primitive societies that are created in the absence of formal government, this tendency explains why custom is an important source of international law. Kelsen's contention that states ought to behave as they have customarily behaved (see Onuf, 1980) and Hoebel's (1961) dictum that "what the most do, others should do" reflect this perspective in *positivist* international legal theory.[13] Most analysts operating from positivist theory assert that, if a type of behavior, such as war, occurs frequently, then it ought to be legally

13. The importance of custom as a source of international law is central to the so-called *positivist* school of thought. Positivists stress the consensual basis of legal norms and therefore see the practices of states as the greatest source from which laws are derived. In the absence of formal machinery for the creation of rules at the international level, positivist theories turn to customary rules for evidence of what the law is, positivists turn to foreign policy pronouncements of leaders, repeated usage in conventions voluntarily acquiesced in by states, general practice (by an overwhelmingly large number of states), judicial decisions of national and international tribunals, and legal principles stated in UN resolutions.

approved. The dependence of rules on custom means that international law is shaped more by the policies of states and the attitudes of their leaders than by law. The pace of change in legal norms is necessarily exceedingly slow. International law's capacity to legislate new rules is diminished—law changes after behavioral patterns change, not before. Why international law operates less as an agent of system transformation than as a force for the preservation of the status quo is explained by this characteristic.

7. It is difficult to determine what constitutes international law. This follows naturally from the customary basis of international law. Relatively little international law has been codified. Often what has been codified deals with the relatively trivial or agreed-upon norms so hopelessly vague (such as "treaties ought to be fulfilled in good faith") that their impact on behavior is minimal. And in many important areas of conduct, international law remains silent.

8. International law does not have an assured mechanism for identifying transgressions. In the absence of a centralized institutional authority, it is difficult definitively to identify what a sovereign state is forbidden to do to gain redress for alleged norm violations. Everything is therefore permissible (Falk, 1970), and international law imposes few meaningful restraints on state behavior.

9. Ambiguity and lack of central institutions encourage the use of international law for propaganda purposes.[14] When states alone can define the rules and interpret them, almost any policy action can be rationalized by citing one or another of the many vague and contradictory existing legal precedents as a justification. This permits international law to operate as a foreign policy tool, a symbol of rectitude, instead of as a guide to conduct. The malleability of international law for policy purposes led Wright (1953) to note that most states characteristically use international law to get what they can and to justify what they have obtained.

14. This perspective reflects the so-called realist or policy-science approach to international law. Policy scientists suggest that inquiry about international law be guided by how policy makers in the real world think about and use international law when they make decisions. Their central "realistic" conclusion is that most foreign policy makers know little about international legal norms and care even less. In making their decisions, statesmen tend to ask not "What is the legal thing to do?" but instead "What will advance the interests of the state?" Only secondarily, if ever, do they concern themselves with the legal implications of their actions. When they do think legally, this orientation contends, statesmen use international law after the fact to excuse legally the option exercised and to package it for public consumption in legal rhetoric. See Lasswell and McDougal (1966–1967) for an explication of the policy-science perspective.

Other problems with and deficiencies in contemporary international law could be added to this list. But these nine are sufficient to demonstrate the fundamental inadequacies generally perceived to afflict the international legal order. International law does not police the actions of states toward one another. States retain the power to define for themselves what the law is. International law is most developed and consistently followed in those domains remote from states' security interests, such as international commerce, treatment of diplomats, transnational communication, and the like. It is relatively primitive in those areas most immediately relevant to states' sovereignty. The paradox that the subjects of international law are above it prevents law from restraining behavior in the heated arena of high politics. It is here that nations are least inclined to agree. When national survival or welfare is perceived to be at stake, self-restraint ceases to control behavior. Legal agreements are likely to govern only those disputes perceived as essentially noncontroversial.

The characteristics of international law suggest why it is regarded by traditionalists as obsolete, why it is understood by modernists as premature (Wright, 1955), and why so many realists regard it as a meaningless contribution to world peace.

The Functions and Relevance of International Law: Some Qualifications

International law may be fraught with deficiencies, but the proposition that it is irrelevant can be challenged on both theoretical and empirical grounds. It is clear that states themselves do not deem international law irrelevant. In fact, they attach much importance to it and expend considerable energies and monies to affect it. All are decidedly interested in revising it in ways that serve their purpose, or in maintaining and strengthening those rules already in operation that enhance their own interests. The animated attention given by states to renegotiate the "law of the seas" is testimony to this belief. And every state officially supports the concept of international law. All promise to observe international law and to enforce it. "If international law were as meaningless as some of the more extreme 'realistic' theorists suggest," George Quester (1971b) observes, "reasonable men would not spend so much time haggling and fighting over its interpretation."

An important reason why nations value international law is because their political interests are served by a legal system that promotes a common understanding of the rules of the game. Law helps to shape expectations, and common rules enhance predictability in international affairs. This reduces potential chaos and uncertainty, and thereby facilitates planning. In the event of a crisis, for instance, norms of conduct contribute to negotiation by eliminating the need to decide upon a procedure for deciding—and this is no small service. International law also provides a medium for precise communication between states (Falk, 1968) and a mechanism for the dissemination of information. It is an "institutional device for communicating to the policy makers of various states a consensus on the nature of the international system" (Coplin, 1975). Such communication helps contribute to the formation of a shared global political culture. The consensus which international norms express is imperfect, reflecting what Coplin (1966) calls an "immature political culture," because the system's members agree on certain general values at the same time that they fail to recognize the implications of these values for their own behavior. Thus, while the cultural characteristics of world politics are of secondary importance in explaining state behavior (Levi, 1974b), they are still important.

All of these functions serve every member of the system, and the benefits they confer explain why international law receives states' support. World politics would undoubtedly be worse off in the absence of this system, however inchoate and primitive it might be.

It is nonetheless tempting to assume that the lack of a hierarchically superior body renders international law useless for its most critical functions. That assumption stems from cognizance of the fact that international law's alleged deficiencies lie not with the laws but with their creators—the states. The assumption also stems from the tendency to compare the international legal order with the highly centralized systems of nation-states. But the comparison is of limited utility. The differences hide important similarities and obscure the really important comparative question: which type of legal order is more effective? Comparison invites the specious conclusion that the presence of a formal legal structure (a centralized, vertical system of law) is automatically superior to the decentralized, self-help, horizontal counterpart of international law.

This conclusion is not sustainable. The absence of an assured procedure for the identification of a violation of international law and the absence of an authority monopolizing the instruments of violence to enforce these rules do *not* mean that states choose to exercise their sovereign freedoms without restraint or to routinely disobey prevailing customs and rituals. A voluntary compliance system need not be normless, with a high incidence of disrespect for rules. Disobedience is statistically rare. States *do* police themselves. They *do* comply with existing laws, even though they do not have to. The anarchy observed in world politics is actually an ordered anarchy (Bull, 1977; Luard, 1976).

Why is this so? Self-restraint often works because even the most powerful states see its benefits. International reputations are important. So is integrity. An enlightened view of a state's long-term self-interests recommends voluntary accommodation with others, compliance with agreements, and deference to legal obligations. A preference for order over disorder is also rooted in self-interest. Those who ignore international law or who break customary norms may pay prohibitive costs for the exercise of their ability to do as they please: other nations thereafter may be reluctant to enter into agreements with them and reprisals and retaliation are risked. Rule breakers face criticism from abroad and perhaps at home. Law provides for sanctions to be taken for indiscretion; in fact, procedures for ostracizing those who break the rules and for punishing them economically and politically (if not necessarily militarily) are provided. Hence only the most ambitious or desperate state is prone to disregard international rules.[15]

Unorganized legal systems, moreover, do not have to be violent or even rule-less (Masters, 1969; Falk, 1968; Kaplan and Katzenbach, 1961). Even in a system in which actors are above the law, and reliable coercive sanctions are absent, other types of self-help measures may operate effectively. As Michael Barkun (1968) notes, law is possible "without sanctions," that is, without the kinds of institutionalized sanctioning processes and procedures for punishment of rule violation typically found in domestic legal systems.

Conversely, the mere presence of formal institutions for rule enforcement is no guarantee of rule compliance. Indeed, no legal system is capable of deterring all its members from disregarding or breaking existing laws. Thus it is a mistake to expect any legal system, including the international legal system, to prevent all criminal behavior or to insist that any violation of the law proves the inadequacy of the legal structure. That asks too much of law. It places a burden on international law that no system can fulfill. Hence, every instance of the breakdown of international law should not be inter-

15. The counterpart to this view of law in domestic legal systems is found in the way national governments are controlled by law. The "command theory of law" associated with the legal philosopher John Austin suggests that law works because it is backed by superior force. But in dealing with national governments, domestic law in fact "is backed up by less force than is international law" (Fisher, 1969). Yet governments routinely comply with domestic law because the political costs of failing to do so outweigh the gains realized from breaking the law (see Fisher, 1969, for an elaboration). Thus the president of the United States routinely complies with decisions of the Supreme Court even if they run counter to what the president wants—*and even though the president (executive branch) is in charge of the force presumed to make law work*. The obvious example was President Nixon's compliance with the Supreme Court's edict (1974) that he surrender tape recordings that were sought as evidence by the House Judiciary Committee in its impeachment proceedings against Nixon in the Watergate scandal.

preted as confirmation of general international lawlessness any more than a single murder in a domestic system should be regarded as indicating the absence of law. Similarly, neither the presence nor absence of the regulation of the use of force in settling disputes between nations is a precondition for the existence of international law. Indeed, may not the "deficient" international legal system in fact be performing its central job—the prevention of violence between societies—more effectively than the allegedly sophisticated systems found within societies? All legal systems are strained under conditions of crisis, and few, when tested severely, are able to contain violence. As many people may have died from civil wars as have perished from wars between sovereign states.[16] By this bloody criterion, perhaps international law is not doing such a poor job after all. Maybe the usual criteria by which legal systems are evaluated are dubious. Perhaps we should be less concerned with structure, with institutional machinery, and more with performance. If so, the proposition that international law is irrelevant to the containment of violence hardly seems warranted.

In the context of world politics international law also contributes to the regulation of the routinized, everyday, relatively peaceful transactions constantly occurring across national borders. As contacts between nations have grown more frequent, the need for rules to manage these transactions has grown. International law has responded well to that need. Although the development and application of international rules remains somewhat primitive, the *content* of these emergent rules is often sophisticated. It is in the areas of international commerce, trade, mail, tourism, and migration (to name but a few) that the growth of international litigation has been most dramatic. Compliance with regulations in these areas has been consistent; thus, mutually beneficial collaborative experiences may generate expectations for their continuation. The ascendance of new kinds of nonstate actors has also created a need for new laws to regulate their internal administration as well as their intercourse with one another and with the nations with whom

16. Symptomatic of trends underway in world politics is the growth of "the international law of internal war" in response to this increasingly transnational problem. According to classic international law, revolution within a society was permissible, and rules were provided for its conduct (the most important being the prohibition of external intervention into another state's internal insurrection). This conception has receded. States routinely intervene in others' domestic conflicts (the United States in Vietnam, the Soviet Union in Afghanistan) because they perceive their welfare to be involved in what happens outside their own territorial jurisdiction. Internal war today is everybody's external problem. International law is changing to reflect and control this new condition. See Falk (1968) for a penetrating discussion.

they come into contact.[17] Here again international law has responded, and the formation of norms has been rapid and extensive.

Law and Peace

As useful as these functions of international law might be, and as promising as the prospects for the further development of a regime of world law might ultimately become, the skeptic, nevertheless, might counter by noting that these contributions fail to address the most destructive of all behavior—war. Does not international law provide for war by making rules for it? Is the most vital function of law, the prevention of violence, therefore not performed?

Several responses to this criticism can be made. First, international law as presently conceived is not intended to preserve peace among nation-states. Prohibitions against recourse to war have appeared in the past and will undoubtedly appear in the future, but international law is not designed to enforce such strictures. Since international law is not designed to constrain interstate violence, it has *not* broken down simply because war has broken out.

Second, instead of doing away with war, international law preserves it as a sanction against the breaking of rules. Thus war is a device of last resort to punish aggressors and thereby maintain the system's legal framework.

Third, it is also accurate to characterize international law as an institutional *substitute* for war. That is, legal mechanisms exist that enable states to resolve their conflicts before they erupt into open hostilities. In this sense, legal procedures can be considered alternatives to war, if not deterrents to it, since in theory they may make recourse to violence unnecessary and thereby preserve peace.

Included among the legal means of conflict resolution are procedures for registering protests, expressing denials, making accusations, withdrawing ambassadors, and articulating threats, all in the context of the laws of negotiation. Similarly, international law has clear rules regarding the use of mediation (where a third party proposes a nonbinding solution to a controversy between two other states);[18] good offices (when a third party offers a location for dis-

17. The expansion of the number and competencies of international organizations has stimulated the growth of international law and invigorated it in the process. Resolutions of the UN General Assembly perform a "law-making" function, for instance, and these rules strengthen further the legal ties that bind states together. Noteworthy is the legislation that has emerged through this mechanism in the areas of decolonization, the New International Economic Order, and apartheid.

18. A prominent example was President Jimmy Carter's mediation efforts at the Camp David meeting between the leaders of Egypt and Israel in 1978.

cussions among disputants but does not participate in the actual negotiations); and conciliation (when a third party assists both sides but does not offer any solution). Two more powerful techniques for the settlement of interstate disputes are arbitration (where a third party gives a binding decision through an ad hoc forum) and adjudication (where a third party offers a binding decision through an institutionalized tribunal, such as a court). All of these mechanisms are based on the expectation that pacific means can resolve controversies.

The historical record provides modest support for the view that states are able successfully to resolve their differences short of war. Of eighty-six interstate conflicts between 1919 and 1975, for instance, K. J. Holsti (1977: 487) found 153 attempts by the contending parties to negotiate, mediate, or adjudicate their differences (note that one conflict may entail several types of settlement attempts). Sixty-five of these attempts were successful. In other words, 42 percent of the time, states between 1919 and 1975 have been able to resolve their differences by resort to one or more pacific settlement procedures. This proportion is by no means overwhelming and may be interpreted more with concern than applause. But it also seems likely that, if legal procedures had not been available, at least some of these sixty-five cases would likely have resulted in settlement by force. In this sense, at least, law has made a positive contribution to peace.[19]

This is not to suggest that international adjudicative machinery is well developed or functionally effective, however. Nowhere is this more evident than with the World Court, presumably created as the highest court on earth. Between 1946 and 1970, "only twenty-nine Judgments in contentious cases and thirteen Advisory opinions have been handed down. For that matter, only forty contentious cases were filed with the Court during its first twenty-four years of operation" (White, 1974: 262). Moreover, the court's jurisdiction is not compulsory. It has no enforcement power. That power rests with the UN Security Council. Although all members of the United Nations are members of the court, by 1970 only forty-eight had affirmed their willingness automatically to accept the court's jurisdiction in conflicts involving them. The United States, for example, defines its position in the so-called Connally amendment (a reservation attached to the statute of the World Court by the U. S. Senate),

---

19. See also Butterworth (1976) for data and documentation sustaining this general pattern of peaceful modes of conflict management. For evidence on the statistical relationship between the use of arbitration and the frequency of war, see Raymond (1978 and 1980) and Stuyt (1972).

which reserves for the United States the determination of which conflicts it will submit to the Court.

Most judicial settlements of conflicts between transnational actors in fact take place in the *domestic* courts of one of the contestants, rather than in international or supranational tribunals.[20] Here there is strong evidence of compliance with decisions reached, although some manifestations of ethnocentrism and partiality are evident as well. For instance, Nagel (1969: 159–160) reports that the United States wins 85 percent of its court cases when they are settled under American domestic law, but only 25 percent of its cases when the domestic law of another country is primarily applicable. When international law and custom provide the basis for court decisions, however, the United States wins 56 percent of the cases it submits for adjudication.

Against this background, it is important to demonstrate that international law has shown a capacity to change in response to changing global conditions. Some of the changes have affected the world climate of opinion regarding international politics and war.

Consider the changing attitudes concerning the permissibility of war. There has been a gradual but steady decline in the international community's tolerance of war as well as a rejection of the absolute right of states to employ force to achieve their foreign policy objectives. Even the classic concept of the so-called *just war* (that the state can judge when its use of force in self-defense is justified) is increasingly criticized; revisions, restrictions, and refinements of this precept are more frequently evident (see Walzer, 1977).

A departure in prevailing attitudes toward war[21] was initiated at the Hague conferences of 1899 and 1907, which devised rules for limiting violence in war. Of course World War I revealed that rules of warfare could neither contain destruction nor reduce its scope. In fact, they may have contributed, inadvertently, to the level of destruction, for the rules of international law at that time constituted a recipe for devastation.

However, in the aftermath of World War I, and in response to the abhorrence of it, a decisive step was taken with the signing of the Covenant of the League of Nations. Articles 11 to 17 of the covenant stipulated that in no case could a state resort to war until three

20. See Falk (1964) and Lillich (1972) for a discussion of the role of domestic courts in the international legal process.

21. Examination of classic international law regarding interstate violence reveals a clear fact: "the fundamental conceptions of international law can best be understood if it is assumed that they maintain and support the rule of force" (Keeton and Schwarzenber, cited in Falk, 1962).

months after a judicial determination by the League had elapsed. But the most important signal of the transformation of international values occurred in 1928 with the signing of the Treaty Providing for the Renunciation of War as an Instrument of National Policy. Known as the Kellogg-Briand Pact (officially the Pact of Paris) this treaty (signed by sixty-two states by 1939) for the first time prohibited recourse to the use of force as an instrument of national policy. This orientation was reaffirmed in the 1933 Anti-War Treaty of Rio de Janeiro and in the Nuremberg War Crimes hearings at the end of World War II, both of which spoke of war as "the supreme international crime." And the United Nations Charter reflected the now prevailing view of warfare by unequivocally outlawing war and the threat of war in pursuit of national political objectives.

One survey (Kegley, 1980) of the contents of major international legal texts from 1810 to the present demonstrates the dramatic extent of this transformation.[22] (See Figure 13.1.) Clearly a radically changed international environment has emerged:

> The willingness of nations to subscribe, even in principle, to the renunciation of their rights to use (except in self-defense) force is a significant step, an expression of willingness to move in one direction rather than the other, and a disclosure of consensus on the most important aspect of political order in world affairs. (Falk, 1965: 233–234)

Although it is difficult to demonstrate that this change has any influence on the behavior of particular states (Wright, 1953), it demonstrates the capacity of international law for change. And any change in the rules of international behavior may in turn modify how policy makers think when they contemplate the use of force.[23] Henceforth, world politics must be conducted in an atmosphere where resort to violence is generally regarded as unacceptable. When war is no longer licensed by international law, and when the global system itself has abrogated *jus ad bellum* (the right to make

22. This evidence, which measures quantitatively temporal changes in attitudes about the perceived legality of war in the international community, is derived from the Transnational Rules Indicators Project (TRIP), which is concerned with normative change across many dimensions of international law (see Kegley, 1975; and Raymond, 1977 and 1980).

23. There are many reasons for this historic transformation in the values of the international community. It is tempting to speculate that the most important is growing awareness of the horrors of modern warfare, that the perceived legitimacy of war has declined in association with each incremental increase in the magnitude and brutality of war. But this does not suggest that the rejection of war has necessarily been related to changes in the incidence of war. Statistically, the frequency of war has not varied with the growth of its legal prohibition. Instead, the rejection of the use of force has declined in proportion to increases in the violence of modern warfare more than the frequency of its occurrence.

Figure 13.1
The Legal Prohibition of War, 1815–1980 •

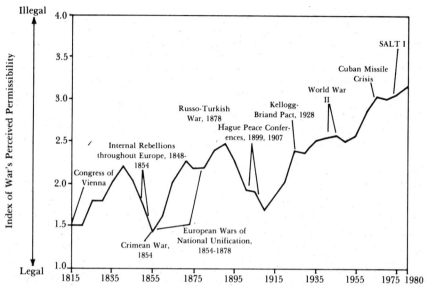

Source: Transnational Rules Indicators Project (Kegley, 1975, 1980).

war), then *animus belligerandi* (the intention to make war) becomes a crime. Those who desire to make war, regardless of the worthiness of their cause, thus become criminals. That may be an important psychological restraint and a not unimportant contribution. (Political realists, however, would undoubtedly disagree, arguing that aggressive leaders will not be restrained by any delegitimation of violence.)

Alongside this growing consensus on the prohibition of war is the growth of law regulating the methods that may be used in war —*jus in bello* (war's means).[24] While the cynic may conclude that this component of the law of nations comprises little more than instructions for killing, the restrictions that international law places on the weapons that can be used and the conditions under which fighting is permissible mitigate the extent to which wars produce death. The objections voiced in international law to the use of poi-

24. The most dramatic evidence of this development was the conclusion in 1977 of the four-year Geneva Conference on Humanitarian Law attended by more than 100 nations. Two protocols were adopted, the first of which added twenty-eight new rules to the one principle governing internal wars since the 1949 Geneva Conventions, the second providing new instruments for "Red Cross law" stipulating regulations for the treatment of noncombatants and prisoners of war. Characteristically, North-South issues dominated much of the conference, crosscutting East-West differences about the rules of warfare.

son gas as a military weapon, or prohibitions against biological and chemical warfare, move world politics in the direction of civility and away from barbarism.

So, too, do rules for the treatment of prisoners and the wounded. The rule of noncombatant immunity, prohibiting direct attack on civilians; the rule of proportionality, requiring that the damage inflicted not be more than that necessary for victory; and the rules of combat limiting the amount and kind of damage that soldiers and their commanders may impose on targets—all limit somewhat the suffering caused by modern warfare. (To this hopeful observation the cynic might reply that rules which make war less destructive also help to make it more frequent.)

Most significant for contemporary world politics is the emerging consensus proscribing the first use of nuclear weapons. Although this tacit rule of international law is not enforceable, it is instructive that not one of the states capable of breaking it has done so since the United States used an atomic bomb against Japan in 1945. Admittedly, there is tragic irony in the fact that this rule, if ever broken, may destroy the very foundations of civilization as they are presently known. But this should not blind us to the significance of normative restraints on states' behaviors.

Finally, international law helps to preserve world peace by enhancing the prospect for crisis management. International rules of the game impinge upon the behaviors of states by structuring how disputes are perceived, providing rituals for their management, and presenting obstacles to their escalation.

> In the most primitive sense international law posits boundaries upon conflict. These boundaries function as limits upon the means available to states in contention with one another. . . . Among the most essential boundary rules the following may be mentioned: 1. No concerted use of military force across international boundaries for unspecified objectives; 2. No use of nuclear weapons to influence outcomes . . . ; 3. No overt military intervention . . . within a state belonging to a rival superpower's bloc or sphere of influence; 4. No extension of the scope of overt violence associated with an internal war. . . across an international frontier; 5. No insistence upon victory in a violent encounter. . . . (Falk, 1970: 52–53)

As these norms of restraint become increasingly entrenched, they enhance the role that legal understandings, however tacit, can play in moderating future conduct. Even the most skeptical of theorists must acknowledge that the global context of relations among nations benefits from the emergence of legal rules as a growing force in world politics.

Various reform movements designed to strengthen legal approaches to peace have arisen. The World Peace Through World Law movement, for instance, predicates its approach on the belief that the present international legal order is, as ever, inadequately structured to prevent war and preserve peace.[25] That orientation sees substantial reform of existing international legal institutions as a necessary precondition to the establishment of world peace, consistent with the view that, to transform the incidence of interstate violence, not only norm change but also legal change must occur. But the prospects are dim that international law will develop into world law—at least until the international political system makes the transition from an unorganized collectivity of independent units to an organized community, or, as John F. Kennedy expressed it, until "a beachhead of cooperation may push back the jungle of suspicion," and the world will "join in creating . . . not a new balance of power, but a new world of law, where the strong are just and the weak secure and the peace preserved." That conclusion leads naturally to a consideration of the role that international organizations have played in the maintenance of global peace.

INTERNATIONAL ORGANIZATION AND WORLD ORDER

The growth of international organizations designed to protect their members from the threat of war has been persistent, particularly in the twentieth century. To understand this political approach to peace the theoretical underpinnings that motivate the formation of international institutions presumably devoted to world order must be understood.

The United Nations and the Preservation of Peace

As in the case of its predecessor the League of Nations, the primary mission of the United Nations, as its charter states, is to keep the peace. The stipulation that membership is open to all "peace loving" countries reaffirms this purpose, as does the charter's requirement that members "settle their international disputes by peaceful means in such a manner that international peace and security, and justice, are not endangered." Members, moreover, are pledged to "refrain in their international relations from the threat or use of force against the territorial integrity or political independence of any state."

25. This movement is extensive, and has created a voluminous literature that continues to grow. Clark and Sohn (1966) remains the definitive introduction to the premises of this approach to peace.

Collective security is generally regarded as the cornerstone of the UN's role in keeping international peace. Ideally, collective security stands as a counterpart to the balance of power as a mechanism for maintaining peace among nations. While the balance-of-power concept assumes that each nation, acting in its own self-interest for its individual protection, will form coalitions offsetting others and that the resulting equilibrium will assure international peace and stability, collective security is fundamentally a shared approach to peace. It asks that each state take responsibility for every other state's security. Joint action against any transgressor is to be undertaken; *all* are to act in concert to check the expansionistic drives of any. The superior power of the entire community is presumed sufficient to deter any aggression from occurring in the first place, or, failing that, to defeat any potential violator of the peace. Being united, the global community possesses the capacity to overawe any aggressor.

Although the principle of collective security was considered one of the main tenets of the League of Nations, the history of the interwar years makes clear that its implementation was not successful. The League's inability to muster a collective response to the Italian invasion of Ethiopia and the Japanese invasion of Manchuria signaled the collapse of collective security, as did the expansionist policies of Nazi Germany. Germany under Adolf Hitler was the most potent threat to the existing order. It repudiated one element after another of the Versailles peace treaty that formally concluded World War I, and it undertook territorial aggrandizement in Europe. As it did so, the League of Nations and the Western democracies in particular proved incapable of stemming the Nazi onslaught. Then—in 1938 at Munich, Germany—Great Britain and France agreed to German annexation of a large part of Czechoslovakia in return for what British Prime Minister Neville Chamberlain called "peace in our time."

The appeasement at Munich was nothing more than that. On September 1, 1939, Germany attacked Poland. Shortly thereafter Britain and France declared war on Germany. The shaping of a new world order had begun with the onset of World War II.

There are many reasons for the failure of the League of Nations to put collective security into practice. In the aftermath of its failure, some critics noted sadly the perhaps illusory expectations upon which the design was built, for many of the preconditions necessary to an effective system of collective security were absent. Among them was the absence of the United States, which refused to join the organization President Woodrow Wilson had so vigorously supported. A sense of membership in a common international society was missing, and the idea of collective measures was resisted by the great powers, who feared that the collectivity might use its strength against them. The tendency to give lip service to the value of general peace but to organize resistance only to those violations deemed threatening to one's own security; the fear of inequities in sharing the risks and costs involved in an organized response; and the problem of objectively defining an instance of aggression and obtaining concurrence on that aggression as "unjust"—also contributed to the undermining of the collective security system. In the final analysis, states rejected collective security because they feared it would involve them in war unnecessarily and thereby, paradoxically, broaden rather than constrain war.

Furthermore, as a principle, collective security is one that is designed essentially to preserve existing interstate power hierarchies. This feature runs counter to the interests and aspirations of the majority at the bottom of the pyramid. The central fallacy of the theory of collective security was that it expected a state's desire to see other states protected to be as strong as its desire to protect itself. This assumption has seldom been sustained. The result was that collective security was stillborn. The League of Nations never managed to put it into practice.

The architects of the United Nations were painfully aware of this experience and the lessons it suggested. As a consequence, it can be argued that the United Nations rejected a restoration of the collective security concept, at least in full-fledged support of the principles that encompassed it (see Claude, 1962 and 1971). Instead, the United Nations was structured in a manner that partially restored the balance of power as a framework for the maintenance of peace.

The United Nations Charter is replete with evidence that nation-states are to remain the fundamental units of world politics with their sovereign rights unimpaired. The principle of collective security was *not* implemented, for at the very least that concept leaves to an international organization the determination of when states are to use force for the collective good. The three central organs of the United Nations—the Security Council, the General Assembly, and the Secretariat—in themselves do not possess real authority to deal with war and threats of war. A collective response to external aggression is contingent upon the willingness of the individual states that are UN members to agree on a response. This is most evident in the Security Council, where a veto by any of the five permanent members can block a resolution or enforcement action designed to cope with threats to international peace. Similarly, the General Assembly is severely restricted in its capacity to mount collective action in response to international crises, for it can only make recommendations for peacekeeping initiatives. And the secretary-general and the working staff of the Secretariat are confined by the charter to the role of alerting the Security Council to any situation considered a threat to world peace and of providing administrative support for peacekeeping operations that the Security Council initiates. In practice, these restrictions have meant that peacekeeping operations tend to occur only with the consent of the disputing states.

In short, sovereignty reigns supreme. The United Nations is a concession to the independence of states; it was not designed to supersede them by placing supranational controls on national initiatives. Inis Claude summarizes the manner in which the principle of collective security was largely bypassed in the United Nations Charter:

> In the final analysis, the San Francisco Conference must be described as having repudiated the doctrine of collective security as the foundation for a general, universally applicable system for the management of power in international relations. The doctrine was given ideological lip service, and a scheme was contrived for making it effective in cases of relatively minor importance. But the new organization reflected the conviction that the concept of collective security has no realistic relevance to the problems posed by conflict among the major powers. (Claude, 1962: 164–165)

Does this realization render the United Nations seriously flawed as an instrument for realizing its primary purpose—preserving world peace? To be sure, yes; but only to a degree. The structural deficiencies built into the United Nations resemble and replicate those evident in world politics, rather than providing a meaningful substitute for them. But the United Nations is more than a mere debating society, a forum for discussion of world problems. It is also more than an institutionalized arena for the conduct of power politics among its members. Although the United Nations has fallen short of the ideals envisioned by its founders (principally because of the absence of cooperation between at least two of the five permanent members of the Security Council), it has nevertheless made important contributions to the management of global conflicts. Like any adaptive institution, it has responded to changing international circumstances and the advent of new kinds of threat to the peace, thus mirroring transformations occurring in world politics generally. For instance, the Third World push for the New International Economic Order has been forcefully articulated in UN forums in part because of the Third World's advantage from the rule of one state, one vote.

The conflict between the United States and the Soviet Union that erupted almost simultaneously with the UN's founding prevented the organization from pursuing an institutional approach to world peace according to the precepts of collective security. The Korean police action provided a glimmer of hope, but that brief interlude in global responsibility for world peace was so colored by unusual circumstances that it was never a harbinger of things to come; nor, indeed, was it a true collective security operation. Other efforts to preserve peace were undertaken in the uncertain formative period of the United Nations (see Table 13.1), but for the most part the experiences revealed the weaknesses of the United Nations system for the maintenance of international peace and security.

The real innovation occurred in 1956, when the General Assembly, acting under the Uniting for Peace resolution, created the first United Nations Emergency Force (UNEF) and charged the secretary-general with primary responsibility for its operation. The principles surrounding UNEF were quite different from the principle of collective security. The latter emphasized checking aggression through collective enforcement. UNEF, by contrast, emphasized noncoercive activities aimed at reestablishing and maintaining peaceful international intercourse. In particular, UNEF was designed to forestall the competitive intrusion of the superpowers into a potentially explosive situation. Similar principles guided the creation of the United Nations Operation in the Congo (ONUC, 1960) and the United Nations Force in Cyprus (UNFICYP, 1964). It is noteworthy that neither Soviet nor American military contingents were assigned to these forces.[26]

Secretary-General Dag Hammarskjöld (1953–1961) articulated the principles surrounding *preventive diplomacy*, a term that has since become virtually synonymous with UN peacekeeping, in his annual report to the General Assembly in 1960:

> Preventive diplomacy . . . is of special significance in cases where the original conflict may be said either to be the result of, or to imply risks for, the creation of a power vacuum between the main blocs. Preventive action in such cases must in the first place aim at filling the vacuum so that it will not provoke action from any of the major parties, the initiative for which might be taken for preventive purposes but

(text continues, p. 446)

26. UNEF-II, created in the aftermath of the 1973 Yom Kippur War, included a contingent from Poland, the first time a Warsaw Pact member has been included in a UN peacekeeping operation.

Table 13.1
United Nations Peacekeeping Operations: A 35-Year Box Score

Name	Location	Dates	Size	Assignment and Results	Contributing Countries*
UNTSO (UN Truce Supervision Organization)	Armistice or cease-fire zones between Israel and Arab neighbors, chiefly Egypt and Syria	1948 to present	30 to 567 officer observers	Observe and report on compliance with armistice agreements (1949–1956) and cease-fire arrangements (1956, 1967, 1973); cooperate with UNEF and UNDOF (see below).	Afghanistan, Argentina, Australia, Austria, Belgium, Burma, Canada, Ceylon, Chile, Denmark, Ecuador, Finland, France, India, Indonesia, Ireland, Italy, Nepal, Netherlands, New Zealand, Norway, Peru, Portugal, Soviet Union, Sweden, Thailand, Uruguay
UNMOGIP (UN Military Observer Group in India and Pakistan)	Kashmir cease-fire zone	1949 to present	30 to 65 officer observers	Help fix cease-fire line; report on compliance with cease-fire agreement.	Australia, Belgium, Canada, Chile, Denmark, Ecuador, Finland, Italy, Mexico, New Zealand, Norway, Sweden, Uruguay, United States
UNEF-I (first UN Emergency Force)	Israel-Egypt border and entrance to Gulf of Aqaba (Sharm el-Sheik)	1956 to 1967	Up to 6,000 troops	Supervise 1956 cease-fire and withdrawal of British, French and Israeli forces; patrol border and Sharm el-Sheik; oversee compliance with armistice. Dismissed by Egypt, May 1967; 6-Day War followed.	Brazil, Canada, Colombia, Denmark, Finland, India, Indonesia, Norway, Sweden, Yugoslavia

Operation	Location	Dates	Strength	Function	Participating countries
UNOGIL (UN Observation Group in Lebanon)	Lebanon near Syrian frontier	June to December 1958	Up to 214 officer observers	Investigate Lebanese charges of infiltration from Syria. Terminated after "Arab solution," approved by General Assembly, calmed situation.	Afghanistan, Argentina, Burma, Canada, Ceylon, Chile, Denmark, Ecuador, Finland, India, Indonesia, Ireland, Italy, Nepal, Netherlands, New Zealand, Norway, Peru, Portugal, Sweden, Thailand
ONUC (Opération des Nations Unies au Congo)	Various places in Congo-Leopoldville (now called Zaïre)	1960 to 1964	Up to 20,000 troops; included fighter aircraft	Help new government keep order, prevent secessionist attempt; remove or neutralize Belgian, Soviet, and other intervention attempts. Katanga secession attempt ended early 1963; other civil conflict continued but ONUC withdrew 1964.	Argentina, Austria, Brazil, Canada, Denmark, Ecuador, Egypt, Ethiopia, Ghana, Guinea, India, Indonesia, Ireland, Italy, Liberia, Malaya, Mali, Morocco, Netherlands, Nigeria, Norway, Pakistan, Sierra Leone, Sudan, Tunisia
UNTEA (UN Temporary Executive Authority)	West Irian (West New Guinea)	1962 to 1963	21 officer observers; security force of up to 1,600 troops	Observer group until cessation of Dutch-Indonesian hostilities; security force to keep order during transitional UN administration. Terminated upon planned transfer of sovereignty to Indonesia, May 1963.	Brazil, Canada, Ceylon, India, Ireland, Nigeria, Sweden

Table 13.1
United Nations Peacekeeping Operations: A 35-Year Box Score (continued)

Name	Location	Dates	Size	Assignment and Results	Contributing Countries*
UNYOM (UN Yemen Observation Mission)	Yemen-Saudi Arabia border region	1963 to 1964	Up to 25 officer observers plus air reconnaissance	Observe and report on compliance with UAR-Saudi Arabia agreement to end intervention in Yemen civil war. Unsuccessful; terminated Sept. 1964 although conflict continued until 1968.	Australia, Austria, Canada, Denmark, Ghana, India, Netherlands, Norway, Pakistan, Sweden, United States
UNFICYP (UN Force in Cyprus)	Key conflict points between Greek and Turk Cypriot communities	1964 to present	Up to 7,000 troops	Help prevent new communal fighting. Failing negotiated settlement by parties (Cyprus, Greece, Turkey), force remains. Helped protect civilians during new fighting after Turkish invasion, 1974.	Australia, Austria, Canada, Denmark, Finland, Ireland, New Zealand, Sweden, United Kingdom
UNIPOM (UN India-Pakistan Observation Mission)	India-West Pakistan frontier (Rann of Kutch)	1965 to 1966	90 to 100 officer observers	Observe cease-fire and mutual withdrawal in area of 1965 fighting. Terminated after withdrawal following Tashkent Agreement.	Brazil, Burma, Canada, Ceylon, Chile, Denmark, Ethiopia, Finland, Ireland, Italy, Nepal, Netherlands, New Zealand, Nigeria, Norway, Sweden, Venezuela

Name	Location	Dates	Troops	Mission	Countries
UNEF-II (second UN Emergency Force)	Suez Canal and Sinai Peninsula (Egypt-Israel DMZ)	1973 to 1979	Up to 7,000 troops	Observe and facilitate Israeli-Egyptian ceasefire disengagement in Suez sector; patrol DMZ in Sinai and verify compliance with disengagement agreement.	Austria, Canada, Finland, Ghana, Indonesia, Ireland, Panama, Peru, Poland, Senegal, Sweden
UNDOF (UN Disengagement Observer Force)	Golan Heights (Syria-Israel DMZ)	1974 to present	1,289 military observer troops	Observe compliance with Israel-Syria disengagement agreement.	Austria, Canada, Finland, Peru, Poland
UNIFIL (UN Interim Force in Lebanon)	Southern Lebanon and Lebanese/Israeli border	1978 to present	6,000 troops	Confirm withdrawal of Israeli troops from Southern Lebanon, restore Lebanese security, ensure the return of authority to government of Lebanon.	Australia, Fiji, Finland, France, Ghana, Indonesia, Iran, Ireland, Italy, Nepal, Netherlands, Nigeria, Norway, Senegal, Sweden

Sources: Adapted from *The Inter Dependent*, special issue entitled "UN 30," July–August 1975, Vol. II, No. 7. © 1975 United Nations Association of the United States of America, Inc. *UN Monthly Chronicle* 15 (April, June, August, and October 1978); *World Armaments and Disarmaments: SIPRI Yearbook 1980* (London: Taylor & Francis, 1980), p. 480; United Nations, Department of Public Information, "Current United Nations Peace-Keeping Operations and Observer Missions," n.d., pp. 1–4.

*Includes only countries contributing military personnel in significant numbers. Does not include countries furnishing transportation, supplies, etc., of which the United States has been most important in major operations.

might in turn lead to counter-action from the other side. The ways in which a vacuum can be filled by the United Nations so as to forestall such initiatives differ from case to case, but they all have this in common: temporarily . . . the United Nations enters the picture on the basis of its noncommitment to any power bloc, so as to provide to the extent possible a guarantee in relation to all parties against initiatives from others. (Hammarskjöld, 1965: 402)

The development of preventive diplomacy came about because of the changing international political environment, particularly the Cold War competition between the United States and the Soviet Union, the threat that that competition posed for the entire world because of the destructiveness of modern weapons, and the increase in the number of Third World nations whose interests and objectives are not necessarily the same as those of the superpowers (Claude, 1967 and 1971).

What to one state is impartial UN intervention into a conflict is not, however, necessarily impartiality to another. The Soviet Union turned against the UN's Congo operation when it came to see the organization as pursuing policies that were inimical to Soviet interests. The Soviets pressed their opposition in various ways, most visibly in their refusal to support the principle of collective financial responsibility for the peacekeeping operation. The Congo experience proved in the long run to have a debilitating impact on the ability of the United Nations to deal with other conflicts. Significantly, it was almost a full decade after the UN force went to Cyprus before the United Nations launched another major peacekeeping operation. The UN force assigned to the Sinai peninsula in 1973 (UNEF-II) was agreed upon only after the policy of détente, to which the United States and the Soviet Union were committed, had been severely threatened by the eruption of war in the Middle East. Furthermore, control of the force was placed firmly in the hands of the Security Council, thus reaffirming the primacy of the great powers in matters of international peace and security.

The assertion of Security Council authority undermined the ability of the secretary-general to pursue an independent role in world politics. Preventive diplomacy as defined by Hammarskjöld reflected the secretary-general's frustration with the UN's legal structure, particularly the inability of the Security Council to perform adequately its central purpose, maintaining peace. Given the charter's constraints, Hammarskjöld sought to redefine and expand the constitutional authority granted his office to undertake actions on behalf of the world community. More than his predecessor, Trygve Lie of Norway, Hammarskjöld saw his role as an active participant in the management of crises. Consequently, Hammarskjöld enlarged the responsibilities of the executive organ of the United Nations by using his "good offices" to moderate international disputes before they escalated into war, by mediating conflicts between contending parties, and by strengthening the UN's administrative support for peacekeeping operations. The 1956 UNEF-I operation and later the Congo force were only the most visible and ambitious manifestations of Hammarskjöld's preventive diplomacy efforts.

Hammarskjöld's successor, U Thant of Burma, pursued a much less activist role. Responding to increasing pressure from both the United States and the Soviet Union, U Thant's efforts concentrated on the management of crises identified by the Security Council or the General Assembly rather than by the secretary-general. This approach to the use of the United Nations was more akin to the emphasis existing in the 1950s, which stressed crisis response rather than crisis prevention. The shift reflected the basic reality upon which the United Nations is built—that its effectiveness depends ultimately upon the willingness of the great powers to take concerted actions to deter violence. Accordingly, U Thant adopted a low profile on security issues and instead sought to act as a world spokesman on issues relating to the emerging North-South confrontation, and in particular as an advocate for principles of justice, stability, and equality.

Kurt Waldheim, who took over the post of secretary-general in 1972, continued U Thant's policy. He sought to resolve interstate disputes (as exemplified by his efforts to obtain release of the American hostages seized in Iran in 1979). But he also remained sensitive to the constraints imposed by the charter on his office, and on the United Nations generally, and by the political realities that the United Nations more often mirrors than shapes.

Increasingly, the mission of the United Nations has been directed toward "rear door" approaches to the challenge of creating a warless world—to the need to alleviate the conditions of poverty, inequality, frustration, and despair that characterize the daily lives of so many millions in the world. In this sense, the United Nations is addressing some of the presumed causes of war rather than its symptoms (the failure of political solutions and the consequent recourse to violence as a final arbiter of grievances). But whether in this domain the United Nations is any better equipped for the enormous task is questionable indeed. With a meager annual budget of $2.5 billion (no larger than the budget of the City of Los Angeles) and a mere 44,000 civil servants scattered around the world, the United Nations is a small sponge in the global sea of problems of unprecedented proportions. But its search for solutions constitutes a step along the path toward a more secure world, inasmuch as the United

Nations' nonsecurity functions may ultimately make important differences in the kind of global environment in which nations operate.

In some respects this cautious conclusion must also be used in any evaluation of the UN's future role in managing security issues. There is little doubt that prior UN peacekeeping activities have made positive contributions to the control of violence. But the range of instances where it has been intimately associated is exceedingly small. One recent study of over 100 international wars and crises since World War II concluded that "less than 20% . . . elicited UN resolutions calling for a halt to a threat or act of force, and in only about a half of these has the Organization met with 'success'—namely, compliance by the parties *soon* after the UN directive" (Finlayson and Zacher, 1980).

The concept of preventive diplomacy seems to imply that the United Nations can be especially effective in dealing with conflicts among nonaligned nations in the Third World. On the basis of the UN's historical record, it seems more accurate to suggest that the United Nations will become involved when a nonaligned state is threatened by another aligned with one or the other of the superpowers; "in those cases where nonaligned states aggressed against or threatened aligned ones . . . , UN involvement has seldom gone beyond the debate stage" (Finlayson and Zacher, 1980). The number of Third World conflicts that qualify for active United Nations involvement appears, therefore, to be severely restricted.

Finally, it should be noted that even when the United Nations has become involved in international disputes, its *peacekeeping* record has been substantially more distinguished than its *peacemaking* achievements. In most cases of UN intervention, the underlying causes of conflict have either remained, or they have been removed by forces external to the organization itself. By no means does this denigrate the violence-preventing achievements of the organization. Despite its weaknesses, the United Nations may be what John F. Kennedy labeled "our last best hope in an age where the instruments of war have far outpaced the instruments of peace." But it does raise the question of whether, by succeeding more in peacekeeping than in peacemaking, a UN presence postpones ultimate political solutions by muting the urgency of political compromise.

Regional International Organization as an Approach to Peace

If the United Nations reflects the lack of shared community values and a common purpose characteristic of the global environment, perhaps regional organizations of states that already share some interests and cultural traditions offer better prospects for dealing politically with the problem of war.[27]

One piece of evidence consistent with the view that regionalism may be the path to peace is found in the fact that while both *universal* and *regional* IGOs (international governmental organizations) have increased in number in response to rising international interdependence and the perceived need to confront mutual problems through collective problem-solving mechanisms, the proportionate growth of regional IGOs has substantially exceeded that of the universal IGOs.

The North Atlantic Treaty Organization (NATO) and the Warsaw Pact (WTO) are the best-known examples of regional security organizations. Others include the ANZUS pact (Australia, New Zealand, and the United States) and the now defunct Southeast Asia Treaty Organization (SEATO). Regional organizations with somewhat broader political mandates in terms of their agendas and perceived competencies include the Organization of American States (OAS), the League of Arab States, the Organization of African Unity (OAU), the Nordic Council, and the Association of Southeast Asian Nations (ASEAN).

The possibility of regional organizations was anticipated in Article 51 of the United Nations Charter, which provides that "Nothing in the present Charter shall impair the inherent right of individual or collective self-defense if an armed attack occurs against a Member of the United Nations, until the Security Council has taken the measures necessary to maintain international peace and security."

The contribution of regional organizations to world peace has, nevertheless, been open to dispute. NATO and the other mutual-security arrangements that the United States built in the 1950s were a direct consequence of the American government's disappointment with the United Nations. These organizations were created under the rubric of Article 51 and frequently described as instruments of "collective security." But they are not. They are regional alliance systems designed to promote "collective self-defense" in the face of a common external enemy.

> Collective security properly refers to a global or regional system in which *all* member countries insure each other against *every* member; no state is singled out in advance as the enemy, and each might be an aggressor in the future. Alliances, however, usually come into exist-

27. The literature on regional organizations is substantial. See Falk and Mendlovitz (1973); Nye (1968 and 1971); Russett (1967); Myrdal (1955); and Lindberg and Scheingold (1971).

ence when the members are agreed on the identity of the enemy and wish to insure each other against him. (Haas, 1969b: 94)

For the United States, the external enemy was, of course, the Soviet Union. Although this was historically true for the other members of NATO as well, in other American-sponsored mutual security systems, notably the OAS and SEATO, differences of opinion about the enemy became a source of political controversy among the coalition partners. The growing polycentrism in NATO during the 1960s and 1970s can likewise be partially attributed to a decline in the perception of a common external threat among the alliance's members.

If the Soviet Union was the common threat stimulating creation of NATO, the United States (and, to a lesser but more immediate extent, a reunited West Germany) was the perceived enemy of the Warsaw Pact. Thus the two principal Cold War alliance systems were created to enhance mutual security because each faced an enemy that fostered insecurity. The alliances may have contributed to global security by assuring the effective operation of a deterrence system based on a delicately tuned balance of terror. But neither alliance is appropriately interpreted as an institutional approach to the problem of war that has effectively transformed the underlying causes of interstate violence.

Have other regional organizations fared better as conflict-resolving mechanisms? At least some evidence suggests that the answer is yes. Joseph S. Nye's (1971) *Peace in Parts* identifies nineteen conflicts involving members of the OAS, OAU, and Arab League between 1945 and 1970 "in which people were killed or there was a high probability that such fighting would have occurred if the organization had not become involved." In roughly a third of these nineteen cases, regional organization involvement helped settle the conflict, and in seven of the sixteen cases involving fighting the relevant organization helped to end the hostilities (Nye, 1971: 170). The organizations were least successful in dealing with primarily internal-conflict situations.

The inability to deal with internal conflict is troublesome, since these situations have become pervasive. Nor is the success rate the organizations experienced in coping with other types of conflict overwhelming. On the other hand, these data are roughly comparable to those found for international organizations generally. Of the sixty-five successful attempts to resolve interstate conflict arising between 1919 and 1975 using peaceful procedures of settlement, international organizations were involved roughly a third of the time (K. J. Holsti, 1977: 487).

In the long run international organizations, particularly at the regional level, may contribute to the building of security communities in which the expectation of peaceful modes of conflict resolution ultimately becomes more widespread than the expectation of violence. The processes through which such metamorphoses might occur are addressed by the functional and neofunctional approaches to peace.

Political Integration and the Functional Approach to Peace

Political integration refers either to the process or the product of efforts to build new political communities. Usually these are assumed to be supranational institutional structures transcending the nation-state.[28] Integration theorists therefore frequently focus attention on international organizations and on the question of how they might be transformed from instruments *of* states to structures *over* them. Functionalism and neofunctionalism are bodies of theory specifically directed toward this question.

Functionalism in its various manifestations is not an argument for a frontal attack on the nation-state, proposing that it be replaced by some form of world government. *World federalists*, however, do advocate this approach. They argue for a world government in which political and military power would be transferred from competitive nation-states to a central authority that would monopolize the use of force, and hence suppress war-threatening conflict throughout the globe. Federalists suppose this transformation will occur because people will see (presumably before it is too late) that the benefits of transferring power and loyalty to a world government outweigh the costs. The transfer would thus be a rational act; survival would be valued more highly than relative national advantage, and people would act according to the calculation that destruction can be averted by dismantling the multistate system that produces war.[29]

Critics of the federalist plan argue that it is based on rather naive assumptions (see Claude, 1971, for an elaboration). Included is the assumption that governments are bad, but people good, wise, and enlightened. "People" are therefore assumed to be eager "to

28. Compare Deutsch et al. (1957), where "integrated" communities are characterized by the absence of intracommunity warfare and the expectation of peaceful resolution of conflict rather than by the presence of supranational structures.

29. See Barr (1953) for an example of world federalist logic. Advocates of world peace through world law (such as Clark and Sohn, 1966) are sometimes classified as world federalists.

take the federalist plunge" even though their governments may resist it. In an age of nationalism such an assumption may be unwarranted.[30] That necessity will lead to global institutional innovation
is also questionable—the need for something will not automatically
bring it into existence. Aversion to war and raised consciousness
about its dangers do not guarantee replacement of the system presumed to cause violence. Even if it did, the expectation that world
government could be created quickly is unrealistic.

Functionalism differs from federalism by focusing on immediate self-interest and by not requiring that a transfer of authority to
supranational institutions occur immediately. *Classical functionalism* (Mitrany, 1966 and 1975) focuses, not on creation of a world federal structure with all its constitutional paraphernalia, but rather
on building "peace by pieces" through transnational organizations
that focus on the "sharing of sovereignty" rather than on its surrender.

The functionalists' peace plan addresses not the immediate
sources of national insecurity but transnational cooperation in technical areas, primarily social and economic, as a means to promote
the "good life." Technical experts rather than professional diplomats are the agents linking states across national boundaries by
bridging various strata of social need. Functionalists assume that
habits of cooperation learned in one technical area will eventually
spill over into another, especially if the experience proves to be mutually beneficial. To enhance the probability that cooperative endeavors will prove rewarding and not frustrating, functionalists
recommend that less difficult tasks be tackled first, those where nations are already in agreement. The successful mastering of one
problem will then encourage attacking another. If the process continues unabated, ties among nations will multiply and collaboration
will culminate in the transfer of sovereign authorities to supranational, welfare-oriented institutions. "Hence, the mission of functionalism is to make peace possible by organizing particular layers
of human social life in accordance with their particular requirements, breaking down the artificialities of the zoning arrangements
associated with the principle of sovereignty" (Claude, 1971).

Functionalism assumes that war originates in poverty, misery,
and despair. If these conditions that afflict human welfare can be
eliminated, the incentive for military rivalry will recede (akin to Sig-

---

30. This does not mean, however, that the nation-state will always be the dominant form of political organization. In the long haul of history, the nation-state is of
relatively recent origin. Prior to its creation in 1648, other political forms dominated,
such as city-states in ancient Greece, empire under Rome, and quasiworld government in Europe under the Church.

mund Freud's contention that "all that produces ties of sentiment between man and man must serve as war's antidote"). Technical experts are preferable to professional diplomats for achieving the transformation because the latter are overly protective of the prerogatives of sovereignty to the detriment of enhancing human welfare. In this sense functionalism is an international version of the "politics is dirty" proposition.

The father of functionalism, David Mitrany (1966; the essay was originally published in 1943), argues that functionalism is *A Working Peace System* because it is based on self-interest:

> Functionalism proposes not to squelch but to utilize national selfishness; it asks governments not to give up sovereignty which belongs to their peoples but to acquire benefits for their peoples which were hitherto unavailable, not to reduce their power to defend their citizens but to expand their competence to serve them. It intimates that the basic requirement for peace is that states have the wit to cooperate in pursuit of national interests that coincide with those of other states rather than the will to compromise national interests that conflict with those of others. (Claude, 1971: 386)

Functionalism draws its historical insights from the formation of the universal public unions in the 1800s (such as the Universal Postal Union) and from the growth of international organizations in the twentieth century. It helps explain some of the early organizational ideology underlying the activities of the specialized agencies of the United Nations. And it provides insight into the reasons behind the growth of IGOs and INGOs alike, seeing the latter as providing essential support to the former's efforts to promote transnational collaboration in solving technical problems (Jacobson, 1979).

Although in its original formulation functionalism does not deal with multinational corporations, it is tempting to speculate that MNCs may propel the transformation of world politics in a manner consistent with functionalist logic. Individuals who manage global corporations often think and talk of themselves "as a revolutionary class" possessing a holistic, cosmopolitan vision of the earth that stands as a direct challenge to traditional nationalism (Barnet and Müller, 1974). This ideology, and the corresponding slogan "down with the borders," is based on the assumptions that the world can be managed as an integrated unit, that global corporations can serve as agents of social change, that governments interfere unnecessarily with the free flow of capital and technology, and that the MNCs can function to mediate disputes and facilitate compromise between contending states.

As a theory of peace and world order, however, functionalism may not adequately take into account some important political realities. First, the assumption it makes about the causes of war is questionable. Do poverty and despair cause war, or does war cause poverty and despair (Claude, 1971)? Indeed, may not material deprivation sometimes breed—instead of aggression—apathy, anomie, and hostility without recourse to violence (Gurr, 1970)? Why should we assume the functionalist theory of war is more accurate than the many other explanations of global violence?

Second, functionalism assumes that political differences between nations will be eroded by the habits of cooperation learned by experts organized transnationally to cope with technical problems. The reality is that technical cooperation is often more severely impacted by political considerations than the other way around. The withdrawal from and subsequent reentry of the United States into the International Labor Organization (ILO) because of the politicized nature of the organization dramatized the primacy of politics. Indeed, functionalism makes the naive assumption that technical (functional) undertakings and political affairs can be separated. They cannot. If technical cooperation becomes as important to state welfare as functionalists argue it will, states will nevertheless not step aside. Welfare and power cannot be separated, because the solution of economic and social problems cannot be divorced from political considerations. Whether the authority and competency of transnational institutions can readily be expanded at the expense of national governments is therefore doubtful. Thus, as one critic put it, functionalism "in its pure form, and on a global scale, . . . is an idea whose time has passed" (Keohane, 1978). Or is it an idea whose time has not yet come?

Neofunctionalists share the intellectual traditions of functionalism, but they differ from classical functionalists on the question of politics. Classical functionalism is sometimes regarded as essentially a nonpolitical (social-psychological) approach to the solution of political problems. *Neofunctionalism*, in contrast, explicitly emphasizes the political factors involved in the process of merging formerly independent states.

> Neo-functionalism holds that political institutions and policies should be crafted so that they lead to further integration through the process of . . . "the expansive logic of sector integration." For example, as [first] president of the ECSC [European Coal and Steel Community], [Jean] Monnet sought to use the integration of the coal and steel markets of the six member countries as a lever to promote the integration of their social security and transport policies, arguing that such action was es-

sential to eliminate distortions in coal and steel prices. Finally, the neo-functionalism of Monnet and others has as its ultimate goal . . . the creation of a federal state. (Jacobson, 1979: 72)

Neofunctionalism thus proposes to reach its ultimate goal of a supranational community not by avoiding controversial issue areas but by stressing cooperation in areas that are politically controversial. It proposes to hurdle political obstacles standing in the way of cooperation by demonstrating the benefits common to all members of a potential political union.

Western Europe is the preeminent example of the application of neofunctionalist principles to the development of an integrated political community. Within a single generation, cooperation across European boundaries has led to economic union and to the creation of common institutions that may ultimately lead to the development of political unity among the member countries of the European Community. Whether political union is realized depends not only on continued economic integration, but also on the integration of social and economic sectors (see Nye, 1971; and Keohane and Nye, 1975). Politics may intrude upon the process of realizing ultimate political union. The historical record of Europe's efforts to build the community now in place demonstrates the many points at which politics can impede—or accelerate—the integrative process (see Feld, 1979). Nevertheless, Western Europe has already achieved the characteristics of a pluralistic security community, one where the expectation of war has receded in one of the historically most violence-prone regions of the world.

European integration has served as a model for neofunctionalist logic in other regions of the world. Parts of Latin America, Africa, Asia, and Eastern Europe have engaged in institution-building efforts sometimes comparable to the European experiment (see Nye, 1967 and 1971; Cochrane, 1969; Lindberg and Scheingold, 1971; Kegley and Howell, 1975; and Kuhlman, 1976). However, because integration is a multidimensional phenomenon, involving the political and social as well as the economic systems, there is no guarantee that the "logic of sector integration" will proceed automatically. Spillover, involving either the deepening of ties in one sector or their expansion to another so as to assure member satisfaction with the integration process may propel further integration (Schmitter, 1969). But there is no inherent expansive momentum in integration schemes. Spill-back (when a regional integration scheme fails, as in the case of the East African Community) and spill-around (when a regional integration scheme stagnates or its activities become encapsulated) are also empirical possibilities.

The difficulty that other world regions have experienced in achieving the same level of institution building as Western Europe suggests something about the complexity of creating new political communities. Furthermore, the paradox that political integration in some portions of the globe is proceeding at the same time that *disintegration* characterizes others is noteworthy. A United States of Europe may be in its nascent stages, but Northern Ireland, Great Britain, South Africa, and Canada are being pressured by centrifugal political forces that threaten to fragment them. Thus societies may either amalgamate or decay; there is no reason to expect integrative processes, once under way, to continue by the pull of their own momentum.

The factors associated with successful integration efforts are many and their mixture complex. It is not enough that two countries purposely choose to interact cooperatively for the integrative process to commence. Research indicates that the probability that such cooperative behavior will culminate in integration is remote in the absence of geographical proximity, similar political systems, favorable public opinion, cultural homogeneity, similar experiences in historical and internal social development, regime stability, similar levels of military preparedness and economic capabilities, bureaucratic compatibilities, and previous collaborative endeavors (Cobb and Elder, 1970; Deutsch, 1975). Although not all of these conditions must be present for integration to occur, the absence of more than a few will considerably diminish the chances of success. The integration of two or more societies, let alone the entire world, is, in short, not an easily accomplished goal. Evidence to date in fact suggests that the integration of nation-states into larger political communities may be peculiarly relevant to advanced industrial societies, but have doubtful applicability to the Third World. Hence, contemporary properties of the globe are simply not conducive to the rapid amalgamation of the polities that comprise the world's political system.

LAW, ORGANIZATION, AND WORLD ORDER

It is revealing that theories of the contribution of international law and organization to conflict regulation perceive the problem of war as connected fundamentally to the deficiencies built into the state-system itself. The schemes devised for a more peaceful world address the inadequacies of the nation-state and the inability of governments to meet the challenges posed by the emergence of a truly interdependent world; they see the international system underdeveloped, underinstitutionalized, and in a latent state of anarchy. Although the contributions that law and organization have made to altering this situation have, to date, been marginal, as long-term historical processes their importance should not be minimized. Inis L. Claude makes a cogent argument regarding the process of organizing internationally:

> Particular *organizations* may be nothing more than playthings of power politics and handmaidens of national ambitions. But international *organization*, considered as an historical process, represents a secular trend toward the systematic development of an enterprising quest for political means of making the world safe for human habitation. It may fail, and peter out ignominiously. But if it maintains the momentum that it has built up in the twentieth century, it may yet effect a transformation of human relationships on this planet which will at some indeterminate point justify the assertion that the world has come to be governed—that mankind has become a community capable of sustaining order, promoting justice, and establishing the conditions of that good life which Aristotle took to be the supreme aim of politics. (Claude, 1971: 447–448, emphasis added)

Somewhat ironically, the prior actions of sovereign states in their pursuit of national interests have carried world politics into a new era of global interdependence. Interdependence constitutes perhaps the greatest threat to the survival of the state and its sovereign autonomy (outside of nuclear extinction). The force of expanding interdependence changes many of the questions and nearly all of the classic answers. Complex interdependence is characterized by the same kinds of tight interstate linkages associated with a state of integration. But interdependence is not synonymous with integration (Haas, 1976; Keohane and Nye, 1975). Integration implies a deliberate effort to link policy issues. Interdependence suggests linkage occurs whether states want it or not.

Under these emergent conditions, the classical focus of states on military power seems increasingly questionable. The search for political substitutes for force through international law and transnational institutions proceeds. But a quiet if revolutionary transformation in global politics may be unfolding, one which makes political probes for peace more compelling in the face of the dangers posed by modern warfare. All those who think about war wish to avoid it. The incentives created for the prevention of war in an age of interdependence may make the ancient dream of a global community more likely. But until human effort and power are organized on the globe more effectively for the security of all, and legal and political institutions are developed to protect it, it is doubtful that peace will become a property of this transforming world.

Part V

WORLD POLITICS
IN TRANSITION

Fourteen

Macropolitics in Transition: The Analysis of Global Transformation

Trend is not destiny.

René Dubos, 1975

The world is round, crowded, shrinking. Everything is related to everything else. Communication is global, the environment is a unity, inflation is indivisible, war anywhere is worry everywhere.

Harland Cleveland, 1976

The forces propelling change in world politics are multifaceted and deeply rooted. Among them are unprecedented numbers of national political units with internal characteristics significantly different from those in the past; new kinds of subnational and transnational actors; and more people. Many of these political actors pursue often unconventional world political objectives, thus producing novel cleavages and controversies. The capabilities of global actors have changed drastically, making human extinction possible and economic modes of exercising influence increasingly practicable. Technological innovations have changed the value priorities which surround foreign policy planning and the means by which external goals are pursued. Long-standing patterns of relationships among the central units in world politics—from coalition configurations and power distributions to status hierarchies and income rankings—have been fundamentally challenged.

These changes are recorded on a global agenda crowded with new issues and problems and in the new vocabulary of policy rhetoric that has arisen to discuss them. Moreover, the global system has been knit together into a complex web of interdependence, making the political interconnections among transnational actors qualitatively different from those exhibited previously. The accelerated pace of world political change can be added to this list of world political developments. And the unparalleled dangers and challenges of the present add an element of urgency to world affairs. As U Thant warned, if current trends continue, the future of life on earth could be endangered. Perhaps this explains why, given the present state of global politics, contemplations of the future seem to be increasingly punctuated by the language of desperation (Falk, 1979).

The preceding discussion of these developments has treated these trends, together with the factors that surround them, as major elements underlying the transformation of world politics. The convergence of so many of these trends in the last quarter of the twentieth century suggests that the transformation of world politics is well under way—that, indeed, it may already be an accomplished fact.

Compelling as this impression is, it assumes a common understanding about the elements that distinguish change or evolution from transformation. It assumes, in other words, a consensus about the distinctions between changes that seems inevitable with the passage of time (including long-term changes as well as temporary fluctuations) and the kinds of changes that culminate in a fundamental shift from one configuration of world political forces into another. Furthermore, it assumes that the changes occurring in world politics are more potent than the forces promoting continuity.

In seeking to identify the interactive effects among global trends and to assess their implications for world political processes as a way of probing the elements of political transformation, four broad issues command particular attention. First, what is meant by the term *global transformation* and how do we detect it? Second, where should we search to locate the sources of change in world politics? Third, what concepts or analogues describe the global predicament and its sources, and what do they portend for the possibilities of managing global change? This chapter will focus on the first three of these questions. Then, in the concluding chapter, the fourth question will be examined as a way of speculating about whether the transformation of world politics is indeed occurring, and, if so, whether it will continue. Then, in the concluding chapter, we will ask what implications are to be drawn from these ideas for world politics today and for its probable evolution in the future.

THE NATURE OF GLOBAL TRANSFORMATION:
AN EXAMINATION OF DIFFERENT TYPES

What does it mean to assert that world politics are undergoing profound change? What is transformation? How can it be detected? It may seem facile to describe today's international system as one marked by change. Yet, change is inherent in world politics. Change has occurred in *every* historical period. It is useful, therefore, to think of a transformation as the culmination of piecemeal developments that produce a qualitative difference in the overall conduct of politics across borders. In fact, however, the direction and force of transnational changes are rarely uniform. Only infrequently are consistent trends discernible, permitting the observer to declare with confidence that a prevailing international system is disappearing and a new one emerging. The developments monitored in this book suggest that several categories of change might be at work simultaneously. Three possibilities warrant discussion: discontinuity, continuity, and the interaction between them.

Discontinuity

A potentially revolutionary restructuring of world politics has been portended by numerous signs—the scarcity of energy and other resources, the deterioration of the environment, the proliferation of weapons, the overpopulation of the world, the emergence of new kinds of global actors, the fragmentation of the bipolar world, the resurgence of superpower rivalry, and the continuing conflict between rich and poor. The milieu created by these momentous trends, many of which represent sharp discontinuities from the past, suggests that the contemporary period is perhaps more conducive to a basic reshaping of world politics—a transformation—than at any time since the end of World War II. The significance of emergent discontinuities can be best appreciated by inspecting them in light of a long dynamic perspective. A comparison of global trends reveals that different rates of global change are possible. Some global attributes change so fast that they can be labeled revolutionary in both rapidity and scope. Others fluctuate widely in the short run, but within confined limits. Still others move so glacially that they appear not to be trends at all. It is easy, given these differences, to confuse a temporary interruption with an enduring alteration. Change may be either ephemeral or recurrent. The former signals a discontinuity, the latter a potential transformation. To differentiate ephemeral change from continuing change requires tracing a change against the backdrop of long periods of observation. Thus, detecting real transformations or historical watersheds in world politics is hazardous (Aron, 1958). The so-called breakpoints of international systems do not fall neatly into easily defined periods so that we know that one system has truly ended and a new one has commenced.[1]

1. This distinction assumes, of course, that we are speaking only of global changes that are major, touching many other features of world politics. The distinction is important because a "small" but "permanent" change is hardly equivalent to a "transformation." The disagreement among analysts about the dates of prior trans-

The major turning points in world history are usually identified with major wars, in part because their effects are so catastrophic that preexisting international arrangements are disrupted, perhaps destroyed. World Wars I and II are often seen as fundamental breaks with the past, each of which set in motion a transformation of world politics.

Other watersheds are delimited by the advent of major techno-logical developments, such as the splitting of the atom, which pre-cipitated fundamental changes in the capabilities of states to cause widespread destruction. More subtle but equally seminal transfor-mations in world politics may be triggered by the cumulative impact of incremental developments, such as the disintegration of colonial empires and the consequent creation of new states, or the effects of the emergence of new resource scarcities.

Regardless of the criteria employed to delineate chronological transformations in world politics and to distinguish momentary dis-ruptions of prevailing tendencies from a metamorphosis, it is im-portant that the differentiation be made (Hoffmann, 1960). Other-wise any random fluctuation, unexpected accident, or short-term perturbation might be mistaken for a transformation. And because foreign policy decision makers base their judgments in part on a reading of long-term developments, any misinterpretation could be potentially dangerous.

Continuity

Although change is endemic to world politics, some political fea-tures have endured for centuries. Because we live in a period of diz-zying world political change, it is easy to become preoccupied with unfolding departures from previous patterns and yet blinded to what is constant. Although today nothing may seem the same as yes-terday, some things most certainly are.

The obvious illustration of the relatively stable in world politics is the perpetuation of the territorial nation-state and the corre-sponding support of the principle of sovereignty that has rational-ized this form of political organization for over three centuries. Whether the nation-state, born in 1648 to cope with then emergent political conditions, is equipped to deal adequately with the prob-lems posed by contemporary global circumstances is questionable. In the age of intercontinental missiles, no national government is able to make credible its claim to protect its citizens from foreign

---

formations in world politics testifies to the problems posed. See Rosecrance (1963); Coplin (1980); K. J. Holsti (1977); Kaplan (1957); and Hoffmann (1961) for examples and discussions of alternate periodizations of world politics.

attack. Nor are most governments able to manage successfully their economies in a world where borders cannot insulate one country's internal condition from economic developments in another. It seems that "nation-states, even as global powers, are not devices best suited for attacking the complex problems of a world system . . ." (Modelski, 1978). The adequacy of the state-system is increasingly questioned (Herz, 1976; Boulding, 1962), but it has survived, nevertheless.

Paralleling the persistence of the nation-state has been maintenance of many of the central norms of the global political culture. The reluctance to construct political institutions that would transcend nation-states and to empower them with supranational authority remains endemic. The absence of formal world government, the continued reliance of system members on self-help measures to achieve political objectives (including the use of violence without international mandate), and the continuing derivation of international legal norms and obligations from custom as well as from formal consent—all reflect and reinforce the continuity of the existing global political culture. This continuity has led some (such as Bull, 1977) to describe international society as anarchical if not also archaic.

The persistence through time of various hierarchies in world politics provides another striking illustration of the view that global politics are laced with continuing structural features. The perpetuation of the economic hierarchy that divides the rich from the poor, the political hierarchy that separates the rulers from the subordinates, the resource hierarchy that renders some as suppliers and others as dependencies, and the military hierarchy that pits the strong against the weak—all continue to shape the relations of nations. The particular nations populating various strata in these pecking orders have changed during the past four decades, but the preservation of the underlying structural inequalities constitutes a potent force inhibiting change in world politics. Although it is still accurate to think in terms of change and transformation, the periodic conflicts stimulated by hierarchical conditions remind us of the importance of continuities in affecting the way emergent global controversies are played out.

The Interplay of Continuity and Discontinuity

Because change and constancy coexist, global trends often move in divergent directions. Thus the impression that in world politics everything changes while everything lasts seems somehow warranted. Global transformation, both its prospects and probabilities, is inevitably influenced by *interaction* of the continuous and the discontinuous.

It is in the vortex of stable properties and changing characteristics that the ultimate direction of world politics is determined. Interaction between the continuous and the discontinuous may thus produce different kinds of systemic changes.[2] Three possible outcomes can be mentioned.

First, the international system may exhibit *equilibrium*. Because trend and transformation are not synonymous, the forces of change and continuity may balance one another to produce, not transformation, but a kind of kinetic equilibrium (like a motor running but going nowhere). The result is a dynamic system fraught with movement but characterized by maintenance of its essential parameters. Stated differently, countervailing trends may combine to preserve the central properties of the system within confined limits of variation, producing fluidity at the same time that the patterns of relations in world politics are prevented from deviating substantially from their equilibrium or steady state (see Liska, 1957).

Social systems maintain their steady states through what are called self-regulatory or *homeostatic* mechanisms.[3] The existence of "system-maintenance" mechanisms makes global transformations statistically rare (McClelland, 1966); these mechanisms retard the impact of transforming agents and thus promote only incremental adaptations from the status quo. System-maintenance mechanisms operate in complex interaction with one another, much like a thermostat maintains the temperature in a room within confined limits of variation.

A variety of regulatory devices built into the standard framework of world politics collectively brakes systemic transformations and preserves systemic stability. Examples of system-maintenance mechanisms that inhibit global transformation include international legal norms, past treaty agreements and other commitments, ties within and among international and supranational organizations, and strategic balances of power. The homeostatic propensities of complex systems thus encourage recurrent patterns of world politics, steering world political developments along a relatively even path and preventing erratic deviations from the general course. The

2. In the terminology of futures studies, investigation of the various effects that trends have on one another is called "cross-impact analysis." Cross-impact analysis has gained currency because some of the hardest issues are "polycentric policy problems"—problems for which solutions have often unwelcome implications for other problems.

3. In domestic political systems, for example, educational institutions often promote system maintenance through the socialization process that transmits the supportive values of the system (the political culture) from one generation to the next.

obstacles to transformation exerted by these self-adjusting mechanisms should not be underestimated. Because of the force of these constraints, the basic properties of world politics manifest considerable durability and resilience, even in the face of system-transforming challenges and changes.

Despite the obstacles to change posed by the agents of pattern maintenance, trends may interact *cumulatively* to propel world politics into a new and transformed steady state. Using the vocabulary of futures studies, global trends and constants may cohere to produce an envelope curve—one that aggregates several subsidiary developments—capable of producing a new pattern of world political relationships. Thus "threshold effects" may propel international politics into a transformed shape; the slow accumulation of small changes that by themselves have no apparent impact may open the way for a substantial transformation in the overall arrangement of world political processes.

Despite the short-run resistance of global politics to transformation, in the long run cumulatively inspired transforming forces can be potent. The growth of interstate interdependence through transnational exchange is an inviting illustration. While the "high politics" of strategic posturing continues to command the world's headlines, the effects of transnational travel, communication, investment, trade, and the like have been operating quietly behind the scenes to reshape the global environment. The emerging importance of "low politics" can be attributed to the cumulative impacts registered by these developments. Whether the additive effects of these compound changes have reached a threshold point, capable of spilling over to produce a fundamentally transformed world politics, is problematic. The potential for such transformation is, nonetheless, evident, and in many important respects these developments have already considerably transformed the texture of world political behavior. The growth of the number of people on the globe and the observed consequences for international relations provides another example of the long-run impact of cumulative change.

Incremental transformation through cumulative and compound changes should not be seen as somehow inevitable, however. Trends in world politics rarely unfold in a constant, linear directions. In the long run, persistence forecasting (pointing to automatic eventual transformation) usually fails because the conditions that coalesce to produce a given trend rarely persist (see Russett, 1969). Conditions change. As they change, they produce different effects from those observable at any given moment. Historical trends sometimes exhaust themselves; others stabilize, or perhaps even reverse themselves as natural or man-made obstacles interrupt their evolutionary path. We can predict with certainty, for instance, that world population growth will *not* continue unabated indefinitely; it *must* stabilize or decline fairly soon (in decades, as these things are conventionally measured). Nor is it probable that the prevailing patterns of energy production and consumption will remain a feature of global politics as the world enters the twenty-first century. Thus, a final alternate mode of change in world politics is possible. This is the capacity for international systems to exhibit, over time, *reversibility*.

Reversibility suggests that future global politics may emulate their distant past. Indeed, the historically minded observer of world affairs may encounter a sense of *déja vu*, because, over long temporal spans, *cycles* make today's changes look only like a reversion to the political characteristics dominant in an earlier historical period. This tendency may explain the maxim that most utopias are forms of nostalgia. Long cycles have been observed, for instance, in the shift of the global system between a phase like the present one, in which global problems have been addressed by reliance on national solutions, and a phase in which global problems have been confronted by transnational institutions (Modelski, 1978). To the extent that such long cycles are operative in world politics, the long-term historical interaction between forces of continuity and change "holds within itself the seeds of its own dissolution" (Modelski, 1978).

The possibility of such cyclical alterations in world politics exists even now. There are some, for instance, who claim that the world of 1980 was much like that of 1936 and that apparent changes may soon give way to the reassertion of long-standing patterns. What this portends for the world's political future is uncertain, however. Observers differ about which cyclical fluctuation is the more probable. Some see world politics as a jungle of all against all, with a consequent fragmentation of political authority into even smaller parcels. Others see world politics reverting to the ecclesiastical kind of quasiworld government some perceived to have been operative in Europe during the Middle Ages. Some see science and technology as the forces propelling the pendulum into an as yet unfathomable future of abundance and affluence. Others see the pendulum moving back toward the stone age.

To summarize, world politics consists of interacting continuities and discontinuities. Clearly it is difficult to predict which of these forces will dominate the future. But in seeking to do so it is also clear that we must think in multicausal terms. No trend or trouble stands alone; all are interacting simultaneously. Mental images of the sort that "X is behind everything" can only be partially true at best. Each factor is connected to the rest in a tight set of linkages that promise to grow even tighter as the world becomes more interdependent. Unraveling the Gordian complexity of relationships among all factors and forces that culminate to produce the conglomeration that we call world politics may be difficult, but we must acknowledge the can of worms for what it is. We dare not delude ourselves into thinking that simple mental models posturing as reality capture it adequately. We can, at best, only approximate comprehension of the realities of world politics. But we must try. A true but complicated idea always has less chance of succeeding than one which is false and simple, as Alexis de Tocqueville observed. Humankind's ability to free the future from the paralyzing grip of the past may be contingent upon its ability to entertain complicated ideas for a complicated world.

THE SOURCES OF SYSTEMIC TRANSFORMATION

Each chapter in this book perhaps conveys the impression that the trend or issue discussed therein constitutes the key to understanding the multiple problems that afflict the future of world politics. Insufficient food, too many people, energy scarcities, the widening gap between rich and poor, the evolution of the East-West conflict, the militarization of the entire globe, the incidence of civil and interstate war—each looks like a principal mover of the world's political conduct and a chief cause of its afflictions.

The admonition that the future of world politics will flow from multiple causes suggests, however, that transformation in world politics depends on how a multiplicity of discordant global trends simultaneously affect each other. The future course of global conditions is thus highly problematic. It depends on how changes and continuities eventually coalesce. But in a sense this conclusion begs the important question. It avoids consideration of the sources from which transformation in world politics may derive, a consideration crucial to grasping the nature of global transformation. If the developments described in preceding chapters are to be understood in their entirety, three additional analytic ideas must also be appreciated.

Historical (In)determinism

The study of global trends has become fashionable. In part this is because the often breathtaking pace of global developments commands attention, elicits fear, and demands control. These conditions invite the faulty inference that transformations occur by themselves, that history somehow moves irresistibly by the force of its own momentum.

Especially when the status quo appears obsolete and change appears inevitable, the reification of change is tempting. The future may appear to be predetermined by the gravity of history. *Historical determinism*, among other claims, contends that history dictates its own pace and the course of subsequent developments.[4] Once set in motion, sheer momentum perpetuates continual motion, and history advances in a self-sustained fashion. From this perspective, the transformation of world politics may appear to be moving toward a preordained destiny in response to a collection of predetermined fatalistic trends.

A corollary of this image is the equally dubious proposition that human destiny has an overall purpose. Such teleological reasoning is not compatible with scientific thinking, of course. It argues that a purpose can be attributed to nature, that a master design is in operation, and that therefore any development can be meaningfully interpreted as an inevitable consequence of the overall scheme of things programmed by nature. Thus the American expansion of its borders on and beyond the continent merely accorded to a preordained plan ("manifest destiny"); and the Soviets, like their czarist predecessors, are motivated by "nature's design" to seek a warmwater port.

In the view of modern science, neither historical determinism nor teleological explanation is a fruitful way of understanding trends and transformations in world politics. Both deny free will.[5] Thus they run counter to an indisputable fact—that change is inevitably a product of human choice, of human action and inaction. What people have elected to do has shaped the world we presently inhabit. Accordingly, events are not predetermined according to some master plan; if they were, the study of human life and society would be a wasted activity, and no one would have any incentive to try to make things different.

It is more fruitful to recognize that the transformation of world politics has and will continue to be determined by the collective impact of individual and group behaviors, bounded as they are by eco-

4. The ideas associated with historical determinism are actually complicated and varied. Generally historical determinism maintains the view that there exist certain types of factors—God, reason, class struggle, or whatever—which guide historical change in certain patterns or preordained ways.

5. Historical determinism need not, however, deny free choice altogether; it can also maintain that choices are constrained by the factors which determine history. This was the position of Karl Marx, for instance.

logical opportunities and constraints. Nature does not act. Humans do. Different mixtures of human choice alone have the capacity to modify prevailing tendencies. "Things are in the saddle, And ride mankind," Emerson reflected. This metaphor conveys the image that no one is in control, that developments themselves determine the human condition. In actuality, mankind is in the saddle, riding things. International circumstances are a product of human actions, including visceral responses as well as reasoned choices. Humankind makes its own fate (see Childe, 1962).

Change in world politics may therefore be neither autonomous nor automatic. Because trends do not dictate human destiny, historical transformations are not a necessity. Historical developments impose circumstantial limits that constrain the free exercise of choice, but history itself does not have its own motion which moves a trend along a designated trajectory. Trends are not "natural" laws (Popper, 1957). What makes political behavior central to the globe's future condition is that such behavior places world politics in a human context, underscoring the fact that human fate is conditioned by the way people allocate values through political conduct. Perhaps this axiom is the reason why Aristotle called politics the master science.

Microperspectives on Macropolitics

If the transformation of world politics is a function of human choice, then clearly individuals matter. Parenting a child, purchasing a foreign-produced car, writing an overseas pen pal, saluting a flag, traveling abroad, voting for a jingoistic politician—each of these individual actions affects, however imperceptibly, the quality of life on earth. Vast impersonal forces may appear to rule the world, but Walt Whitman was helpful in reminding us that even in politics and metaphysics, sooner or later we come down to one single, solitary soul (cited in Falk, 1975a).

We can easily underestimate the contribution individuals make to the direction of global trends. But, indeed, we are all responsible—"we are all of us, consciously or unconsciously, waking or sleeping, building the unity of man or plotting the end of the world" (Edmund Taylor cited in Cleveland, 1976). The trends and continuities that will propel the world into the next century are shaped by the activities of all now, for better or for worse. The sentiment stressing the importance of individuals in international relations is captured in the preamble of the UNESCO Constitution: "Since wars begin in the minds of men, it is in the minds of men that the defenses of peace must be constructed."

Although the role of the individual in world politics cannot be denied (see Kelman, 1970), the causal linkage between individual actions and the overall state of the world is extraordinarily difficult to describe and explain. The structure of the global system may be conditioned by the cumulative, interactive effects of individuals' choices, but macroprocesses are not tied directly to microbehaviors. *How* these microparts fit together to shape the whole is therefore most complicated. Why world political trends assume a shape that no one fully anticipated may be due to the inability to trace how individual acts interrelate to affect outcomes. The system looks unplanned and its effects malevolent because individual acts are not coordinated. Surprise is frequent because the process that combines the parts into the whole is beyond the scrutiny of even the most gifted observer.

Understanding trends and transformations in world politics is complicated by this analytic difficulty. A microperspective yields a worm's-eye view of the world. A macroperspective provides a bird's-eye view of global developments. But how to get from the former to the latter has eluded scholarship. This difficulty introduces a final analytic point relevant to studying the sources of global transformation.

Levels of Analysis

All people may contribute individually to the macro trends under way in the world arena, but they do not contribute equally and their impacts are not uniform. The actions of some actors are relatively more potent in shaping world politics than the actions of others. Thus we cannot in a simple way employ reductionist logic, which seeks to locate all world developments in individual choices. Instead, we must discriminate among the relative contribution of these choices in terms of their ability to influence global circumstances.

Two facts underscore this necessity. First, political clout in the global system is distributed unevenly. Hence, the best place to look for the major forces of systemic transformation is in those sectors where power is concentrated. Who are the most influential, and how do they exercise their influence? Second, individual choice is typically exercised in a group context. Decisions reached are therefore affected strongly by the collective needs, values, and preferences of the groups to which individuals belong. These empirical facts of social life make it important to study world politics by reference, not just to individuals, but to the various groups and collectivities they form and to the significant reference groups to which humans habitually defer. We must, in other words, approach world politics by studying the variety of collectivities to which people extend their loyalty, from small special-interest groupings to larger entities like nation-states.

This analytic prescription is conventionally referred to as "the level-of-analysis problem" in the study of international relations (Singer, 1961). It emphasizes the necessity of explaining developments in world politics in terms of the impact exerted by actors at various levels of aggregation and draws attention to the implications for understanding world politics that result from emphasizing different levels. Also by scholarly convention, these actors can be categorized according to the relative size and scope of their composition.

At the smallest level, of course, is the so-called idiosyncratic or individual level of analysis—the personal characteristics of each human being, from the average citizen to the head of a state. At a second level are the regimes that govern nation-states as well as various sub-national groupings of individuals, including pressure groups, voluntary associations, political parties, occupational groupings (organized labor, white-collar workers), and the like. At the systemic level are the over 160 nation-states found in interaction with one another around the globe. These sometimes combine on a regional scale to form IGOs, INGOs, and multinational business enterprises, including, for example, such regional collectivities as the EEC, NATO, and the Warsaw Pact. At this level also are those global actors purporting universality, such as the United Nations. The systemic or international level of analysis also includes all those macro properties that influence the actors comprising the global arena, such as international law, the distribution of power, and the amount of alliance aggregation and war extant in a given historical period.

This conception recommends that transformations in world politics be attributed not to any one of these levels of analysis, but to outcomes stemming from all of them. Because there are interdependencies and interconnections across levels, this also means that any global development can be traced to forces operating at each level. The behavior of any one nation, for instance, will be affected by the dispositions of its leaders, the domestic political and social conditions within it, and the state of its external environment and the kinds of stimuli it receives from abroad. Similarly, any future increase or relaxation of worldwide international tension will be governed in part by how actors at *each* level choose to act internationally today.

To understand the future of world politics, therefore, it is necessary to consider the contribution made by *all* actors, at *all* levels of analysis. This does not require that we regard everyone's impact on the state of the total system as equal. It merely requires an awareness of the interdependencies among various levels (although *how* various levels fit into the larger pattern of macroprocesses may be unknown). And it suggests that the potency of any level may vary depending on the global situation at hand. That is, the relative importance of actors and factors at each level will depend upon, and be affected by, the nature of the international circumstance being considered. Some acts and levels will assume powerful influence in some situations and become relatively immaterial in others. The immediate relevance of OPEC to the world political economy and its relative unimportance for the strategic military balance is illustrative.

One conclusion derived from the level-of-analysis problem in the study of world politics is that exclusive attention to the nation-state in world affairs is unwarranted. As this book has sought to make clear, other kinds of actors have emerged, and their actions are making substantial contributions to the evolution of world political conditions.

Nonetheless, the traditional state-centric focus is understandable. Political power remains embedded primarily in the central decision-making institutions of the national units that make up the international system, especially the superpowers. This underscores the continuing importance of analyzing comparatively the foreign policies of nation-states. Until global or regional collective problem-solving institutions amass greater power over nation-states, human destiny will continue to be shaped significantly by government-to-government relationships. Under current global circumstances, the transformation of world politics will continue to be mediated primarily through the decisions of those entrusted with authoritative decision making for the political units they govern.

Qualitative Evaluations of Quantitative Transformations

The nature of trends and transformations in world politics already under way invites still another kind of analytic question—the normative one of how the transformations occurring and the continuities persisting should be judged. Are they for the better or worse? Should global changes inspire optimism or evoke pessimism? Are they good or evil?

The contemporary facts defining the global condition do not provide a consistent message. Selective human perception and value discrepancies point to alternative scenarios and disparate evaluations. Assessments differ because they are focused on different dimensions of world politics, and those attributes are judged according to personal value systems. Evaluations about the stage of the world in the evolutionary process also differ because people hold different conceptions of a preferred end product. The range of assessments itself attests to the level of confusion that trends and transformations in world politics elicit. Two categories of value assessment warrant special consideration because of the important questions they raise about continuity and change in world politics.

The first is the image of global *progress*. For some (for example, Kahn, 1976), the future inspires confidence and hope, not despair. These optimists contend that degradation and decay in future global conditions are unlikely. On the contrary, many trends are favorable. For instance, the standard of living enjoyed by a considerable proportion of humanity far surpasses that enjoyed by even the most advantaged in even the recent past. Dismal worldwide trends such as overpopulation, food shortages, and violence are partially offset by the presence of regional and national countertrends. Despite the friction between contending nations and the dangers posed by the destructiveness of their weapons, for instance, the superpowers have avoided war for well over three decades, and their crisis-management capabilities have improved considerably. Such assessments thus take comfort in recalling the world's impressive track record in successfully coping with previous challenges; indeed, all previous predictions of apocalyptic doom have proven unfounded in the searchlight of subsequent periods.

According to the interpretation that today's problems do not necessarily mean greater problems tomorrow, the last fifth of the twentieth century is pregnant with possibilities, not just unprecedented troubles. Equipped with raised social consciousness about global problems and new tools of science and technology, humankind's prospects for improvement appear better than ever before.

Futurists subscribing to this perspective appreciate the extent to which material progress is contingent upon the present implementation of political solutions. The *real* problem is that the progress under way in some quarters of the globe is not dispersed evenly; correspondingly, the problems afflicting the world's population do not touch everybody to the same degree. Political thinkers have long believed that the maintenance of severe welfare differentials within and between countries breeds instability and violence. Reducing these differences in order to provide the greatest number with the greatest good is not only the greatest challenge, it is also a precondition for the amelioration of the human condition. For the absence of stability and peace will surely impair humanity's ability to control change for the better by reversing those trends already on the downswing. Optimists also argue, however, that within the pervasive inequalities presently characterizing the global system will be found the building blocks for the creation of institutions capable of assuring a more just and peaceful international environment.

A second perspective is that of global *regress*. Optimists view the future through the present with hope. But others assess the global condition and its prospects quite differently. For such pessimists, we live in a system characterized by scarcity and fear. If you can look at the future without trepidation, they believe, you are an exception. Indeed, if you are unaware of the challenges posed, you must be blind. Paranoia is a heightened state of awareness. If you are not at least somewhat paranoid about the trends emanating from prevailing circumstances, then surely you do not understand the direction in which the world is heading.

From the perspective of global regress, the signs point toward a period of diminishing expectations, deteriorating conditions, and, in general, dismal prospects. Already we live with unimaginable brutality. For the majority of humankind, poverty, hunger, and degradation are everyday experiences. Violence is an ever present danger, and the expectation of a better life an unknown or forgotten hope. Efforts to control arms are failing, and, as a result, even personal survival is precarious. Because the world shows no evidence of mounting a meaningful response to the dangers it confronts, the human prospect is dim (Heilbroner, 1975). In the words of the title of a recent book, the future resides in a present characterized by *A Choice of Catastrophes* (Asimov, 1979).

The despondency of these pessimistic observers is rooted in a cluster of assumptions. Apocalypse is around the corner, if not already here, because the unaddressed trends threatening the world have reached the point where they are now impossible to reverse. The dispersion of weapons, the proliferation of nuclear know-how, the depletion of the world's resources and destruction of its ecosystem, the unabated growth of the world's teeming billions alongside relative declines in its available food—all point to real, perhaps insurmountable, hazards. The dangers exert a compound effect on one another as well, making the effort to control any one an obstacle to the control of the others. Each decision not only opens alternatives; it also forecloses others. In short, global trends constitute a time bomb, and the time required to make adaptive adjustments is rapidly ticking away.

Although the scenarios of the pessimists differ, the outcomes are all grim (Galtung, 1980). Options have narrowed. The pace of change itself inhibits the implementation of solutions. The earth imposes real limits that no technology can escape without toying with the natural limits imposed by nature. Indeed, technology itself may contribute to problems, not solutions—"what man makes unmakes man," Norman Cousins has contended. In sum, it may be too late: the existing problems dwarf the remedies, the adequacy of the prevailing international system is a delusion, and the probabilities that humankind will collaborate peacefully to reorder the planet's political system are remote. As sober an observer as U Thant once remarked that unless global problems are managed soon, they will reach "such staggering proportions that they will be beyond our capacity to control."

THREE PERSPECTIVES ON THE GLOBAL CONDITION

Whether present global afflictions portend that the world is headed on a long slide toward complete ruin, or whether instead they provide opportunities for renewed growth and stability, is open to question. Optimists and pessimists share dissatisfaction about the contemporary global condition and a sense of urgency about its future. Where their evaluations differ are in whether and how an appropriate response can be mounted against the dangers posed. From either perspective, apocalyptic choices are undoubtedly faced. Like a rudderless ship without sail or compass, the global community finds itself in an uncharted and turbulent whirlpool of change. Whether it can survive and chart a safe passage to a new future is problematic.

Embedded in the recent historical record of world politics—and in the logic that sustains it—are several tendencies that appear nearly universal. These are the general processes that inhere in the patterned responses of different actors to similar circumstantial or environmental stimuli. Hence, these processes facilitate an understanding of the sources and consequences of many of the global trends and troubles discussed in preceding chapters by providing common conceptual denominators for assessing the recurrent behavioral responses of myriad actors to diverse international conditions. At the same time they provide insight into the prospects for controlling global change.

Let us attempt to grasp the roots of the globe's contemporary afflictions by considering three closely related conceptual perspectives: the "tragedy of the commons," the "ecological perspective," and "complex interdependence."

The Tragedy of the Global Commons

"We are living through an era of the most extensive and intensive political change in human history," observed Zbigniew Brzezinski, noting that "Never before at one time have so many nations and peoples been subjected to so many political upheavals [and] so many competing political ideologies." Why is this period of history characterized by upheaval and competition at unprecedented levels? Why are conflicts more heated, war chests larger, national debts bigger, poverty more pervasive, ideological antagonisms more hostile, and optimism about the world's future more difficult to find?

A popular and compelling explanation of the global predicament is provided by the so-called *tragedy of the commons* metaphor, which locates some of the determinants of the world's afflictions and offers tragic predictions of its future. This concept was first articulated in 1833 by the English political economist William Foster Lloyd, and more recently popularized and extended to contemporary world problems by Garrett Hardin in a well-known article appearing in *Science* magazine in 1968.[6] The central questions asked through the analogy are, "what is the likely human response to conditions of scarcity" and "what are the likely consequences"?

The commons metaphor sees the shape of the world mediated through the cumulative effects of individual decisions. It argues that how people exercise their freedom of choice matters most. By stressing individual action and especially the importance of personal motivations, it speaks to the evolution of systems (like the global one) where formal government is minimal and latitude for individual choice defended.

Like other political realists, Lloyd and Hardin see human behavior driven by the search for self-advantage and personal benefit. This drive is most pronounced and prevalent, they contend, when people perceive themselves to be in competition for limited resources that are held in common.

If individuals are interested primarily in advancing their personal welfare (although not necessarily at the expense of others), what consequences should be anticipated for the group of which they are a part? In a world of finite resources and unregulated choice, the predictable product is the creation of problems for all.

What is the logical basis for this conclusion? Consider, as Lloyd did, what was observable in nineteenth-century English villages where the village green was typically common property and all individual herdsmen were permitted to graze their cattle on it. Sharing of the common grazing area worked well as long as the number of cattle did not exceed the land's carrying capacity, for if that oc-

6. The interpretation provided here is derived from Hardin and Baden (1977); Brown (1978); Soroos (1977); Schelling (1978); and Starr (1978).

curred the pasture would be ruined and the number of cattle it could support would decline drastically.

Which development—protection of the commons, or its destruction—is more probable in a system of unconstrained (sovereign) choice? The answer rests in the response of individual herdsmen, as shaped by their personal motivations. In the nineteenth-century English village, the incentives were powerful for individual herdsmen to increase the size of their herds as much as possible; only in this way could they maximize their individual gain. If pushed, individual herdsmen might have conceded that the collective interest of all would· be served if individuals' herds were reduced in size, so that the commons could be preserved. But self-constraint—voluntary reduction by one herdsman of the number of his own cattle to relieve the pressure on the common village green—lacked appeal. There was, indeed, no guarantee that others would follow suit. On the other hand, the addition of one more animal to the village green would produce personal gain whose costs would be borne by everyone. Hence rational economic behavior in such a system encouraged each man to increase without limit the size of his herd. It discouraged self-sacrifice for the common welfare. And ultimately the inevitable consequence materialized: the collective impact of each effort to maximize gains was to place more cattle on the village green than it could sustain. "Ruin is the destination toward which all men rush, each pursuing his own best interest in a society that believes in the freedom of the commons" (Hardin, 1977).

Now the English common green can be likened to the planet's system, where once again individual choices may have unintended but tragic collective consequences. If everyone chooses to act selfishly, to try to extract as many available goods for himself as possible, ultimately the collective interest suffers and the basis for the welfare of *all* members of the community is destroyed. The lesson, in short, is that individual behavior guided by narrow self-interest sums to collective disaster.

It is precisely this tendency which leads futurists to gloomy predictions about the globe. The tragedy of the commons is also the tragedy of world politics. Individuals seldom show an inclination to sacrifice for the welfare of the whole in order to preserve the benefits derived from retention of their part of that whole. The problem persists, Hardin warns, because people deny the destructive consequences of their selfish behavior, and because the system disguises those consequences until that destruction becomes irreversible. Further, Hardin claims, it is too much to expect people suddenly to discover the dangers of personal or national selfishness, and the rewards of self-denial, and voluntarily to sacrifice personal interests for the needs of the global society of which they are members.

The metaphor of the commons is useful.[7] It suggests that under global conditions of expanding populations, rising expectations, and diminishing resources, disaster is probable. In the context of scarcity and fear, the pressures for selfish individual behavior are extraordinary, the consequences predictable. We live in a world insecure about its future. Humankind's collective future may be shaped—perhaps ruined—by the cumulative impact exerted by the disparate choices of the more than four billion individuals organized into scores of territorially based units sharing a common sphere called earth.

The ubiquity of the commons behavior is apparent throughout the globe. The story of citizens putting private motives above public concerns is a familiar one. The tendency of governments to place national welfare above global welfare (see Johansen, 1980) and to see in others' success only their own failure is prevalent. From the parochial vantage point of narrow self-interest, world politics resemble a simple zero-sum game of pure conflict: what one side wins, the other loses. But in an interdependent world, it can be disastrously dysfunctional for both individuals and governments to think about non-zero-sum global circumstances in a zero-sum manner.

Consider three examples. In the area of arms races, no one nation can increase its sense of security when any other nation obtains military superiority—the quest for superiority by one diminishes the security of all, including, ironically, that of the country militarily stronger than all others, because efforts to achieve superiority have a way of breeding costly arms races.

Second, in the area of economic competition, national efforts to solve economic problems at the expense of others—through protectionist policies aimed at reducing imports through tariffs, quotas, and the like—have tended to precipitate retaliatory counteractions with an eventual consequence all too tragic. When an open international marketplace is closed, few benefit, most suffer. The world depression of the 1930s, precipitated in part by a prolonged and infectious spiral of protectionism, stands as a grim reminder of what happens when some nations seek self-advantage by exploiting the rest.

7. Schelling (1978) observes that the commons image has become widely used as a kind of shorthand "for situations in which people so impinge on each other in pursuing their own interests that collectively they might be better off if they could be restrained, but no one gains individually by self-restraint." He goes on to point out that "the commons are a special but widespread case out of a broader class of situations in which some of the costs or damages of what people do occur beyond their purview, and they either don't know or don't care about them." See Schelling (1978: 112–115)

A third example of the destructive international consequences of self-serving behavior can be found in the short-sightedness that governs the politics of pollution of the planet. The free-rider syndrome—the temptation to pass along the costs of environmental protection and control to others, and to assume that it is appropriate for some to let the rest be responsible for problems that are shared—is an all too evident form of behavior threatening to turn the world's seas into cesspools. Again the principle is illustrated: when most people seek to benefit only themselves, the effect is that all suffer. Although people seem to assume otherwise, in reality there is no such thing as a free ride.

Within nations, of course, governments have routinely intervened to regulate the proclivities of selfish citizens when that selfishness entails clear social costs. Governments seek to protect the common welfare by imposing constraints on individuals' freedom to act selfishly and destructively. Laws are enacted to proscribe such behavior, and sanctions are leveled against lawbreakers, as exemplified by the universal prohibition of the "freedom" to steal from others. In this sense, nations everywhere regulate man's selfish inclinations internally by restricting freedoms, by placing limits on permissible types of behavior. The sacrifice of freedom is rationalized by the higher good of societal stability and preservation, akin to the philosopher Jean Jacques Rousseau's adage that "man must be forced to be free." There are no societies that fail to legislate social behavior, nor are there any that do not try to regulate their economies. Indeed, no government permits a truly "free" enterprise system to operate. An unrestrained market mechanism is too costly and dangerous a luxury for any government to tolerate.

Globally, of course, there are no meaningful institutional constraints on the sovereign right of nations to act selfishly toward others to the detriment of the welfare of the rest. The sovereign right to act independently in relations among nations is steadfastly defended in international law. In the realm of foreign policy some still speak of freedom of choice, and anarchical freedom remains a defining characteristic of global politics. It is precisely because the sovereign principle of independent foreign policy action is preserved that the commons metaphor is so appropriate for understanding world politics. Like the English commons, the arena of world politics is not regulated by a formal authority empowered to protect the common welfare of the members comprising the global community.

---

for a further clarification of the special commons case and the broader class of situations for which the commons imagery has become widely used.

In the absence of a worldwide mechanism to deter humankind from its most destructive instincts—lust for power and greed for material goods, whether necessary or unnecessary—the roots of many aspects of the global predicament are not difficult to locate. The world may be in the shape it is because the general welfare has not been adequately protected by the "invisible hand" of global anarchy (Orr and Soroos, 1979). Indeed, the danger of permitting the unfettered pursuit of national advantage is one of the prominent lessons of recent history. Unbridled sovereign freedom and the invisible hand of unrestrained competition have visibly failed to avert an impending disaster.

On the other hand, the specter of a colossal superstate arising to manage global affairs is hardly more comforting. Concentrating power in the hands of a global actor may only accelerate the degree of injustice and the pace of destruction (Bull, 1977), for, as Lord Acton observed, absolute power corrupts absolutely. Who could regulate such an all-powerful regulator? Who would police a potentially oppressive peacekeeper? Is either path toward the control of global transformation—continued international anarchy or some form of centralized institution—a desirable means to the ends of global order and justice?

The Ecological Perspective

The metaphor of the tragedy of the commons is intimately linked to the ecological perspective on world problems. The ecological perspective (see Sprout and Sprout, 1968; Pirages, 1978) interprets the global environment as a unified ecosystem of delicately and tightly integrated components. Every global circumstance derives from the conjunction of environmental circumstances and human initiatives. Human conduct on the earth shapes the entire human habitat, just as nature shapes the activities of humans.

The emphasis of ecologists on the interrelatedness of biological, economic, political, social, technological, geographic, and other elements of the globe's subsystems is obviously pertinent to today's problems. For instance, the ecological perspective commands appreciation of the extent to which the fate of humankind is contingent upon the viability of the earth's biosystem that makes life itself possible. This obvious but often ignored principle underscores the fact that nature imposes limits, that the carrying capacity of the planet—its ability to support human and other life forms—is not infinite. The earth has finite nonrenewable resources and can sustain only a limited offtake of renewable resources. A finite earth places limits on the numbers it can sustain and the consumption associated with interminable economic growth. If too many people are born or too many resources to support them extracted, the ecosystem will surely be destroyed and life as we know it will cease. The spoiling of the earth through environmental degradation affects every corner of the globe, and, ecologists note, all are potential desecrators of the global environment.

The conduct of relations among nations is vitally affected by the earth's environmental constraints. The location of resources influences how people will live and the rate at which their economies can grow. Because resources are not distributed evenly, some people may be better off than others. Because some communities in a global environment of unequals are better equipped to extract available resources than others, disparities in power differentials invariably widen. And because resources are scarce, competition among nations for acquisition of the earth's bounty recurs.

In an era of growing population, the politics of distribution have assumed increasing importance in the relations of people. Because the carrying capacity of the earth is tied directly to the propagation and consumption behavior that people exhibit (moderated somewhat by applicable levels of technology operating within given economic constraints), the behavioral questions raised are necessarily political ones. Who is to get how much of what, and by what means? The question becomes acute in the context of increased scarcities (Ophuls, 1977). The existence of limits to growth (Meadows et al., 1974) makes the politics of a crowded world increasingly affected by approaching limits.

Because the earth is finite and its resources limited, the struggle for what is available often becomes intense as well as recurrent.[8] The interplay of North and South, much of the intercourse between East and West, and a considerable portion of the efforts of governments to impose limits on the desires of their own populations can be attributed to operative ecological constraints and the consequences for choice that they impose.

In the past, global ecological changes occasionally led to the disappearance of entire empires and to the ascendance of others. Ecological modifications expanded the size of governments, enlarged their regulation of citizens' behavior, and encouraged foreign military adventurism. Will future developments mirror these consequences? Inasmuch as the human appetite for resources shows no

8. This applies domestically as well as internationally. See Bell (1973) for a critical examination of the "crisis of capitalism" that locates the causes of the woes currently faced by many Western democratic societies in the inability of governments any longer to provide the increments in income or welfare to which their citizens believe they have become entitled. These arguments are expanded to the global level in Bell (1977).

sign of diminishing, ecological factors promise to color the issues dominant in world politics even more in the future. The conjunction of growth and constraint has already made the vulnerability of the earth's precarious ecosystem a transnational political issue.

Ecological principles help explain why the behavior of one transnational actor affects the well-being and survivability of others. Like billiard balls on a confined surface, movement by one ball generates a reaction elsewhere. What happens to one element ultimately has consequences for other elements and the surface as a whole. This metaphor does not insist that all parts of the functioning system are equal. In world politics some units are big, others small; some rich, others poor. Nonetheless, the fates of all are intertwined in interdependent relationships. As a worldview, the billiard-ball metaphor contends that the pattern of interaction among components is responsible for the evolutionary condition of the entire planet.

Foreign policy interactions are generally believed to conform to the action-reaction principle (see Rosecrance, 1963). Although nation-states are legally free to choose whatever they think serves their national interest, they rarely utilize the range of options available. Instead, the options are restricted by choice. The natural environment imposes limits on what can realistically be done, but nations also voluntarily constrain their behavior along a spectrum of fairly continuous patterns. Systems theory contends that a nation's general pattern or range of behavior abroad is influenced most by inputs received from its external environment. The most potent of these are the volume and type of behavior that others direct toward a nation. The action-reaction syndrome is consistent with this postulate. By extension, this also means that relations between nations tend to become *reciprocal*, especially when pairs of nations are in frequent interaction. When actions and communications are exchanged between bargaining actors, the kind and quantity of behavior received by one tend to be returned similarly to the other.[9]

The propensity for actions to provoke similar reactions from their targets can be discerned in the exchanges surrounding many of the controversies examined in this book. "Like for like" and "tit for tat" are clearly exhibited in the evolution of East-West competi-

· 9. The principle of reciprocity is a central hypothesis of social psychological exchange theory (Thibaut and Kelly, 1959; Gouldner, 1960; Malinowski, 1969). The notion that behavior exchanges between nations are reciprocal is also supported by many studies in international relations (Hollist, 1975; Kegley, Richardson, and Agnew, 1981; Tanter, 1974; North et al., 1963), and is a core element of international law (Levi, 1974b; Kelsen, 1968). The idea also enjoys a rich folklore, ranging from Biblical admonitions ("do unto others as you would have them do unto you") to contemporary statements in mass culture (such as the Beatles: "and in the end, the love you make is equal to the love you take").

tion, where the behavior of one protagonist has predicted the subsequent reaction of the other. Similar exchanges have been exhibited between North and South, where the revolt of the poor against the rich has provoked a counterreaction of rich against poor. The self-perpetuating dynamic of the global arms race is animated by similar reciprocal exchanges (Richardson, 1960a); each increase in armaments justifies additional arms acquisitions by those whose sense of security has been diminished and who view reciprocal retaliatory increases as the means of restoring the *status quo ante*. What is restored, of course, is not the preexisting military balance but the presence of an arms spiral.

The ecological precept of action-reaction processes applies to intercultural *images* as well as interstate behaviors. The major battle of ideas embodied in transnational ideological conflicts shows this tendency—crusading fervor within one movement often arouses antagonistic crusades by others. Ideologies breed their antitheses, and ideological crusades stimulate the rise of opposing belief systems. War between Christian and Muslim or Catholic and Protestant is an emblem of this phenomenon in world affairs. Communism versus capitalism is the obvious contemporary example.

That many global disputes are rooted in perceptual antagonisms finds much support (Jervis, 1976). Especially when relationships are hostile, distrust and suspicion between conflicting parties tend to arise, as each sees the other as the other sees its opponent. That is, mirror images emerge. This syndrome is especially evident in the images of each other maintained by the Soviets and Americans in the course of the East-West conflict. But it applies to many other relationships as well.

When mirror images develop in international conflicts, self-righteous perceptions often lead to actions and responses that are ethnocentrically judged as constructive, whereas an adversary's actions are perceived negatively and culpably ("the problem is their fault—they caused it"). This tends to exacerbate considerably the difficulties of conflict resolution; self-righteousness and paranoia are incompatible with the control of conflict. Thus mirror images often lead to self-fulfilling prophecies; predictions promote the behavior predicted.[10] George F. Kennan has noted the consequence of these tendencies in the context of international relations: "It is an undeniable privilege of every man to prove himself in the right in the thesis that the world is his enemy, for if he reiterates it frequently enough and makes it the background of his conduct, he is bound

10. An obvious illustration: when inflation is predicted, people increase their spending today to avoid tomorrow's increased costs, thereby contributing to the conditions that stimulate the anticipated price increases. Thus the prediction becomes the father of its fulfillment, and the future is shaped by how it is anticipated.

to be right." In quoting this observation, Boulding (1975) adds that "if for 'enemy' we read 'friend' in this statement, the proposition seems to be equally true but much less believed." In his memoirs Henry A. Kissinger provides a graphic portrayal of these processes and vividly illustrates their potential ecological consequences. The following passage describes how the United States and the Soviet Union react to each other:

> The superpowers often behave like two heavily armed blind men, feeling their way around a room, each believing himself in mortal peril from the other, whom he assumes to have perfect vision . . . each tends to ascribe to the other side a consistency, foresight and coherence that its own experience belies. Of course, over time even two blind men can do enormous damage to each other, not to speak of the room. (Kissinger, 1979: 522)

Ecological consciousness suggests that responsibility for the deterioration of relationships between transnational actors cannot be assigned exclusively to only one. If it takes two to make a fight, it also takes two to resolve one. Cognizance of the reciprocal give-and-take principle suggests that any problem results from *mutual* contributions, and that give and take must accompany the search for the reconciliation of differences. Compromise is essential, and it is imperative to emphasize that the impulse to engage in reprisal is potentially suicidal in the nuclear age. The slogan "no substitute for victory" is, ecologists warn, a recipe for disaster in an interconnected planet. Ecological logic would conclude that "what Dean Rusk aptly called the 'football stadium psychology' of diplomacy, in which someone wins or loses each day" (Sorensen, 1965) is simply inappropriate as a control mechanism for global problems.

The implications of ecological perspectives on world affairs can be summarized in the following propositions. The world is inseparable. It is a mosaic. Every part of the global puzzle is intertwined with every other. Each action breeds a reaction. Every actor's behavior is conditioned by the actions taken toward that actor, and by how those actions are perceived. All acts have social and environmental consequences; what is done by each molds the kind of environment that all inherit. Global problems are thus rooted in the collective actions of all nations and of the individuals who inhabit them; hence, no problem can be solved by unilateral national action. Each nation needs others, and all must solve their policy problems with the participation of the others affected. Immutable environmental constraints on problem solving require mutable policy solutions. Thus people are responsible for their future and for the environment in which they reside. Humanity as a collectivity is in charge of its common global fate.

Complex Interdependence

The relevance of the ecological perspective is intimately related to the dramatic increase in the extent to which nations of the world find themselves linked to one another in complex, interdependent relationships. Nearly all of the global trends monitored in this book are touched by this extraordinary property of contemporary politics. Indeed, interdependence is perhaps the most salient concept underlying the profound transnationalization under way in world politics.

The manifestations of complex interdependence are perhaps most immediate and visible in the international political economy. National political authorities in one nation are no longer able to insulate their sovereign jurisdictions from the effects of economic policies engineered by political authorities or by private-sector actors located abroad. But other transnational linkages have also become part of what it means to live in an interdependent world. Military alliances have become entangling and permanent. Heads of state visit each other with such frequency that the practice of summitry and shuttle diplomacy are now commonplace. Private citizens increasingly participate in intercultural experiences, whether by mail and telecommunications or through business travel and tourism. National economies have become internationalized, as trade and capital flows among them have expanded geometrically. And energy transfers across borders determine the relative comfort and economic well-being of people residing in widely separated sectors of the globe. In short, action anywhere seemingly touches somebody or something somewhere else.

Global interdependence is likely to continue to describe the world political system, at least in the short run. This prediction can be made because systemic-transforming events are statistically rare. Other things being equal, the immediate future will resemble the immediate past; in the absence of a nuclear holocaust or catastrophic global accident, tomorrow's global attributes may be predicted to resemble today's. Global interdependence therefore makes for a world whose immediate shape can be safely predicted. But it also means that particular events will often be unanticipated, and a sense of surprise will prevail.

The long run is less certain. Resurgent nationalism, the drive to acquire military capabilities in order to preserve national security, the ever present protectionist sentiment regarding international economic matters, and the urge to develop independence from foreign sources of critical raw materials all point toward a world characterized by national efforts to minimize the domestic impact that complex international interdependence necessarily implies.

It seems unlikely that nations will be able to extricate themselves easily from their complex involvement in the affairs of others. Autarky or national self-sufficiency seems unlikely in a rapidly growing world already characterized by food and resource scarcities. And no country on earth is able to hide from the shadow cast by the threat of nuclear weapons. Nevertheless, the search for national independence in an interdependent world promises to introduce even greater uncertainty into an already uncertain world.

Recognizing the dangers inherent in making predictions about the future of an uncertain world, some speculations consistent with a continuation of global interdependence can nevertheless be offered. One is the possibility of a gradual but steadily increasing worldwide *cultural consolidation*. Certainly cultural diversity will not be eliminated, but its degree may erode. Emerging in the place of cultural diversity may be what Kenneth Boulding has described as a superculture manifested in a global sweep of skyscrapers, airports, universities, movies, and rock music.

> Nairobi looks like Wichita; Moscow is beginning to look like Dallas; Johannesburg looks like Tulsa; Tokyo and London are beginning to look like New York; and even Paris has broken down and built a skyscraper. All airports are the same airport, and Avis and Hertz have conquered the world (Boulding, 1974).

When the same songs are popular worldwide, when the same books make the best-seller lists in national capitals simultaneously, and when the fads that determine how people clothe themselves are the same everywhere, every place is next door to any place. It is not farfetched to think of interdependence as the state of global affairs that acts as a catalyst to the emergence of a global political culture.

Interdependence mounts other challenges more immediately relevant to foreign policy decision makers. As national fates become increasingly interlocked, the incidence and intensity of international conflict can be expected to increase (Knorr and Trager, 1977) because disputes arise from interactions among parties in contact. Interactions produce disagreements over a variety of issues, including authority (who is to have power over whom) and the allocation of valued things (who is to get how much of what, and by what means and at what costs). Hence the level of international conflict can be expected to grow more frequent as the level of transnational exchange increases. In part this is also due to a resurgence of nationalistic sentiment, even in the face of forces that undermine it.

Conflict stimulated by interdependence is not necessarily something to be feared, however. Conflict can serve many positive purposes, including cooperation as opposed to violence. It can bring antagonistic parties together, clarify their values, promote communication among them, and sensitize them to the mutual benefits of compromise. Thus the level of conflict that the global system is likely to experience may broaden opportunities as well as increase dangers. Adlai E. Stevenson warned that we should "not hold the vision of a world without conflict." But, he continued, "We do hold the vision of a world without war—and this inevitably requires an alternative system for coping with conflict."

The challenge to war as an instrument of conflict resolution implies a challenge to the nation-state, because war is often an instrument of national policy. Interdependence also challenges the state system because it poses a direct challenge to nationalism. Should nationalistic thinking (loyalty to the nation before all other objects of potential affection) erode, the climate for the conduct of world politics would be altered fundamentally. Zbigniew Brzezinski, writing prior to the events with which he had to grapple as national security adviser to President Carter, termed the demise of nationalism as a force in world politics *the* major divide that separates the past from the future. Because of this erosion, humankind presently straddles the threshold *Between Two Ages:*

> A new pattern of international politics is emerging. The world is ceasing to be an arena in which relatively self-sustained, "sovereign," and homogeneous nations interact, collaborate, clash, or make war. . . . Transnational ties are gaining in importance, while the claims of nationalism, though still intense, are nevertheless becoming diluted. This change, naturally, has gone further in the most advanced countries, but no country is now immune to it. The consequence is a new era—an era of the global political process. (Brzezinski, 1970: 275)

Subsequent events in Iran and Afghanistan in particular may have altered Brzezinski's views of nationalistic sentiment. But the processes challenging nationalism persist. The role played by transnational nonstate actors in shaping national and international policies is particularly pertinent. A former American policy maker, George Ball (1967), observed with respect to multinational corporations, for example, that "Those who manage great enterprises have ceased to think in the classical pattern of producing goods for the home market and exporting the surplus overseas. Today they operate and think on a worldwide scale." The thinking is revolutionary, as described in the words of one transnational corporate manager:

> For business purposes, the boundaries that separate one nation from another are no more real than the equator. They are merely convenient demarcations of ethnic, linguistic, and cultural entities. They do not define business requirements or consumer trends. . . . The world outside the home country is no longer viewed as a series of disconnected customers and prospects for its products, but as an extension of a single market. (Barnet and Müller, 1974: 14)

To be sure, a global vision that sees national borders as relatively meaningless is a significant departure from conventional ways of thinking about the world and its politics.

If interdependence challenges nationalism and the inclination to think in terms of national borders, it certainly challenges the suitability of national solutions to global problems. "Today . . . we understand, far better than ever before, our common destiny," remarked Secretary of State Cyrus Vance before the United Nations General Assembly, adding that "no nation, acting alone, can assure its people peace and economic security, and . . . the future of each of our nations depends upon the future of all our nations."

Such a view is unassailable. Few problems can any longer be defined as domestic or local, for their characteristics and potential solutions are shaped by conditions transcending national boundaries. For instance, the solution to the challenges of the population-food equation, of the ideological incompatibilities that divide East and West, of environmental degradation, and of arms races and war can only be met effectively through cooperative endeavors between nations. According to the logic of interdependence, the ecological perspective, and the tragedy of the global commons, neither security nor prosperity can be acquired through individual national actions. As Secretary of State Henry A. Kissinger remarked, "We are stranded between old conceptions of political conduct and a wholly new conception, between the inadequacy of the nation-state and the emerging imperative of global community" (cited in Falk, 1976). This imperative undermines the continued attachment to narrow self-interests and questions the wisdom of those not willing to think in terms of global interests.

If the perception that global problems require global solutions is as widespread as it appears, and if the forces undermining local solutions to national and transnational issues are so potent, then the obvious inability of the world community to devise the solutions so necessary as well as beneficial to all poses a perplexing question.

In one sense the answer to this curious "why not" question has been formulated throughout the preceding chapters as they dealt with more or less discrete issues. In a larger sense, however, the query asks not what are the political interests that impede political solutions to particular problems, but rather, whether the obstacles to effective policy making are so widespread that global change is beyond management? The importance of the question is dictated by the assumption made in nearly all proposals for reform, namely, that controlling the transformation of world politics is not beyond the capacity of people. Asking "why not" to an imagined world that has never been can be liberating. But this sentiment assumes that efficacious strategies for engineering the transition from the present world to a preferred one are available (see Johanson, 1978; North, 1976; and Falk, 1975).

IS GLOBAL CHANGE BEYOND CONTROL?

If the future is generally an extension of the past, then many facets of the probable future pose undeniable dangers. In general, however, the future has few political advocates. To be sure, there are those in academic circles who can persuasively argue the future *ought* to be considered. But for most politicians the future is near-term and its requirements clear-cut—winning the next election, or averting an impending coup. In neither process do future generations figure prominently.

Even if politicians and policy makers were able to look beyond their immediate problems, the complexities introduced by global interdependence often produce unintended consequences as policy makers create conditions that were not part of their intent. Such developments arise, and surprise recurs, because complex interdependence makes it nearly impossible to discern the causal chain that connects the interdependent parts. Andrew Scott provides one compelling illustration of the unintended consequences of foreign-policy choice:

> The Bretton Woods system was designed to foster increased trade, the improvement of payments procedures, and economic development. It succeeded in accomplishing these objectives. It also "accomplished" a number of other things that were not intended—it furthered inequality between developed and less-developed nations, it contributed to the build-up of international debt, it provided the institutional framework within which an extraordinary growth of multinational enterprises took place, it tied global economic conditions to domestic and foreign

policy decisions of the United States, [and] by contributing to the increase of trade it also contributed to the growth of interdependence and to the vulnerability of the global economic system to disruption. (Scott, 1979: 2–3)

Hence interdependence has narrowed the options available to policy planners and expanded the risks associated with each option. Under these circumstances, determining what is in the interest of humanity is not simple. Even conditions once believed to be altogether desirable, such as growth, are now questioned (see Schumacher, 1973). Growth, like cancer, has begun to appear to be a path to death.

Collectively the manifestations and consequences of complex interdependence present formidable obstacles to wise policy planning. The first step in doing good, the ancient Greek philosophers believed, is to know what is good. The overlap of actors, issues, and interests obscures identification of what is good. Every good has its costs, and every policy option risks unintended consequences elsewhere. Choice is often between the lesser of evils. The obstacles to rational policy planning are expressed well in mass culture by the popularity of Murphy's notorious laws—the precepts that nothing is as simple as it looks, that everything takes longer to complete than imagined, and that whatever can go wrong will go wrong.

The paradox of complex interdependence is that it has simultaneously enlarged responsibilities and expanded the issues to be confronted while narrowing the available options and spreading thin the attention of leaders. Because choice among crisp alternatives no longer exists, trade-offs abound. The concept of foreign policy choice itself may now be obsolete, replaced by the ever increasing frequency of situations posing dilemmas, not alternatives.[11] Ration-

11. The failure of the Carter administration to shape promised new departures in American foreign policy—most noteworthy in the areas of human rights, reduction of the massive levels of U.S. military spending in conjunction with ratification of the SALT treaty, decrease of American arms sales abroad, bringing a halt to the spread of nuclear weapons, and courting the friendship while enhancing the welfare of the Third World—reveals the extent to which these goals are intertwined, and how the pursuit of any one may undermine the prospect of realizing the others. Most of these goals "had" to be jettisoned. Why? Courting allies in the Third World necessarily required dealing with some repressive regimes. Halting nuclear proliferation meant asking others to give up the energy source perceived to be the easiest path to modernization. Reducing armament shipments abroad can weaken the defensive capabilities of Third World countries vulnerable to attack. Garnering domestic support for the SALT II agreement required a sharp increase in overall U.S. defense spending. And so it goes. Each policy endeavor becomes an obstacle to the pursuit of others. The momentum found in the foreign policies of many of the world's major countries in the past decade—the impression that nothing can be done, that new policies are almost impossible to initiate—can be explained in part by the tug and pull exerted by the cross-pressures of entangled issues, actors, and developments. Governments are ex-

al policy formulation is "bounded" (Simon, 1957) by circumstantial obstacles; freedom of choice is greatly constrained.[12] And the political barriers to meaningful choice grow more formidable with each incremental increase in global complexity.

What this assessment suggests is that the complex metamorphoses of emergent global paradoxes may have outrun the ability to keep pace. Global complexity means that it is more difficult, not less, to implement needed global reforms. The signs are everywhere. National actors seem to muddle through problems as crises emerge, rather than to act purposively to mold the world to preferred plans. A Band-Aid approach that deals with symptoms, not causes, is usually taken. Policies proposing comprehensive or radical solutions are avoided because they are the most controversial politically. Instead trial and error, ad hoc, and incremental approaches (Braybrooke and Lindblom, 1963) that retain old approaches to new realities tend to be pursued. The world seems to be surprised on an increasingly regular basis as problems appear for which no one seems prepared. Each future day appears to produce yet new future shocks (Toffler, 1970). Bureaucracies created to deal with traditional issues appear unequipped and overwhelmed by the repeated advent of international circumstances that appear novel.

So is the transformation of world politics beyond the capacity of any actor or set of actors to control? If what can still be done is less than what could once be done, is the management of world politics for the better largely precluded? Under contemporary world conditions, must foreign policy at its best involve only a choice between the lesser of evils?

These are apocalyptic questions. They ask that we think some uncomfortable thoughts—whether humankind can control its fate, can steer the direction of the global transformation that may well determine the course of human destiny.

---

traordinarily subject to these kinds of pressures. Many of the limits to foreign policy adaptation are not imaginary. The requirements of issue-area trade-offs are real.

12. For an extensive examination of the constraints on American foreign policy inhibiting change and promoting policy continuity, see Kegley and Wittkopf (1979).

Fifteen

The Global Predicament:
Ten Questions for a Tense Era

> If we could first know *where* we are, and *whither* we are tending, we could better judge *what* to do, and *how* to do it.
>
> Abraham Lincoln, 1858

> If present trends continue, the world in 2000 will be more crowded, more polluted, less stable ecologically, and more vulnerable to disruption than the world we live in now. Serious stresses involving population, resources, and environment are clearly visible ahead. Despite greater material output, the world's people will be poorer in many ways than they are today.
>
> *The Global 2000 Report to the President*, 1980

The trends and transformations described in this book provoke questions. They do not provide clear answers. What they suggest about the meaning of world politics is open to alternative interpretations that will likely be colored by the vantage point of the observer.

The transformation of world politics poses challenges to the wisdom of old beliefs. These changes require unconventional questions about conventional ideas. In this final chapter ten questions are posed. These questions are linked to the preceding discussion; how they are answered by those presently holding power may influence significantly the kind of world that will unfold.

1. Are Most Maps of the World Obsolete?

Our vision of the world is conditioned by how our mental maps are drawn. Maps depict global space, and the way they are usually charted carries assumptions about how the world should be viewed. As simplified models, they are inherently inadequate, because simplification entails selection, and selection distorts reality. Nonetheless, maps are messages, and the cartographical conceptions they convey shape thinking about global realities.

The changes that are sweeping the world raise questions about the usefulness of most conventionally drawn world maps. Most maps still picture the world as stable and static. They show borders as real, not as transparent inventions of man. Borders are *political* symbols. But present-day political reality is a world of permeable borders and movement, in which people, goods, and services are linked. Borders are penetrated and transcended by the flow of goods, by the passage of people, by communication on airwaves, by airborne traffic, and by space satellites. Because change, turmoil, and mobility are striking characteristics of contemporary life, static worldviews are misleading. How well is humankind served by the conventional image of a world divided into homogeneous, competitive territorial units?

2. Are Nation-States Obsolete?

"A myth" is what John F. Kennedy called "the untouchability of national sovereignty." Henry Kissinger labeled the nation-state "inadequate" and the emergence of a global community an "imperative." Implicit in these views is an attack on the utility of the nation-state as a political entity, capable of adequately handling global challenges.

Auguste Comte argued that societal institutions are created to address problems and meet human needs; they disappear when they can no longer perform these functions. Nation-states are being challenged from within, where national economies are breaking down into regional or sectoral parts (Toffler, 1980) and absorbed from without in transnational linkages. Their legitimacy is questioned because of their inability to perform their most vital function—protecting their citizens from foreign aggression. In the age of weapons of mass extinction, no nation can make credible its claim to guarantee the common defense. The nation-state's primary *raison d'être* may no longer exist (Herz, 1976).

Indeed, the nation-state's managerial capabilities everywhere, irrespective of form of government, are under critical scrutiny. Lack of faith in governmental efficiency has reached epidemic proportions. No government is immune from attacks by its own citizens for its inability to protect its population or improve its life. Making war, preserving peace, maintaining domestic stability, providing for the general welfare, ensuring a just distribution of income, engineering economic growth, controlling inflation, preserving civil liberties—in few countries are citizens completely satisfied with the workings of their governments.

The growth of interstate interdependence may provide a compelling explanation of this worldwide trend. Under circumstances where one nation's condition is dependent on many others, may the efficient management of internal conditions and global circumstances be beyond the control of any government acting alone? May the independent sovereign national unit be ill-suited to the prevailing demands of global interdependence?

3. Is Complex Interdependence a Blessing or a Curse?

Global interdependence—a development encompassing nearly every aspect of world politics—poses perhaps the greatest threat to the nation-state. It has expanded the range of global issues while simultaneously making their management more difficult. Whether in the long run interdependence will prove to be a blessing or a curse is, therefore, problematic.

From one perspective, global interdependence may prove to be a blessing, for the diverse components of the globe may be drawn inexorably together in pursuit of mutual survival and welfare. Awareness of the common destiny of all may compel cooperation among states and command efforts to resolve national differences for the good of all. In this sense, global optimists see the challenges facing the world as forces which, ironically, may bring the world together for the first time. Noninvolvement in these challenges is no longer a realistic policy alternative. Similarly, the utility of violent conflict will diminish, for the willingness of people to fight those on whom their continued welfare rests can be expected to decline. At a minimum, so this reasoning contends, conflict between interdependent states will be limited because few nations will be able to disentangle themselves from the transnational ties that bind them together. From this perspective, then, the continued tightening of interstate linkages is to be welcomed, for it strengthens the seams that hold together the fragile tapestry of international relations.

But from another, more pessimistic, perspective, global interdependence may prove to be a force that prevents the world from effectively addressing the many problems confronting it. Advocates of this view propose, for example, that global interdependence does not necessarily carry with it global organization, regardless how compelling the need for centralized coordination may be. The absence of a spirit of community among nations still remains, and there is ample evidence in the contemporary world of a continued craving for the autonomy that nation-states allegedly once possessed. Under conditions of scarcity, the temptation to use force to satisfy what are perceived to be necessary national wants may not be resisted. Indeed, frustration over the inability to sever dependency relationships may in fact lead to war, not to peace.

Thus, the web of tightening global interdependence foretells both danger and opportunity. If, on balance, the advantages of interdependence outweigh the disadvantages, then the means for accelerating its development should be used in such a way as to benefit the greatest number. Conversely, if global interdependence on balance poses a challenge to human welfare, security, and survival, then the means for containing and perhaps reversing its effects need to be found. But is the capacity to realize either goal within the power of a disorganized and fragmented world community?

4. What Is "The National Interest"?

Assuming the continuation (if not the efficacy) of nation-states in the global system, what should their policy goals be? What is the national interest? This question has preoccupied policy makers for centuries as they have debated the meaning of national interest. In earlier times, the classic assumption was that a state, as an autonomous entity, should do whatever necessary to promote its internal welfare, protect itself from external attack, and preserve its basic values and way of life.

Similar goals are sought today, but the choices for their realization are not nearly as obvious as they seemingly were once. In an age of trade-offs, does the quest for narrow self-advantage carry unacceptable costs? Will the drive for power result in destruction? When every nation is dependent on others for its welfare, is not a search for autonomy self-defeating? Perhaps the historic tendency to define the national interest chauvinistically (my country, right or wrong) carries unacceptable costs domestically as well as internationally.

In the past, those questioning the prevailing definitions of the national interest seldom were applauded for their criticisms. But perhaps the need to question is awakening globally. Increasingly advocacy of more sophisticated definitions of national self-interest can be heard. The imperative was expressed by Margaret Mead in her reflection that "substantially we all share the same atmosphere today, and we can only save ourselves by saving other people also. There is no longer a contradiction between patriotism and concern for the world . . ." (cited in Cleveland, 1976). This idea was also voiced by Cyrus Vance in a speech before the UN General Assembly, when he observed that "more than ever cooperative endeavors among nations are a matter not only of idealism but of direct self-interest."

Years ago, the eminent political realist E. H. Carr (1939) articulated his convictions about the realism of idealism when he observed that self-interest is not served by standing in opposition to the general interests of mankind. Is this challenge to the traditional zero-sum concept of the national interest gaining strength? May not greater belief in the value of "one for all" help create an "all for one" world? Does not the world at large have a collective interest in the control of parochially defined national interests?

5. Are Certain Kinds of Military Power Impotent?

This seemingly curious query is raised with increasing frequency. Its roots are found in a number of assumptions about the transforming role of military force in world politics. For instance, given the destructiveness of both conventional and nuclear weapons, it finds expression among those who ask whether modern weapons are too dangerous to be employed. It finds expression in questions concerning the control of weapons: Is proper control possible? Is accidental holocaust avoidable? It is even inherent in the concern of those who question the deterrent value of military power. Do arms deter attack by others? Or instead, because of the fear, distrust, and threats they elicit, might weapons ironically invite preemptive attacks by suspicious adversaries on whom they are targeted? Because security is a psychological phenomenon, is it necessarily augmented by the acquisition of more weapons of war?

To be sure, the majority of mankind continues to assume that preparation for war is the best route to the maintenance of peace. It may be decades before this assumption is seriously questioned by enough people to mobilize efforts to reduce the level of expenditures for the instruments of war. Old habits die hard, especially when threats and fears persist.

Policy debate has not often centered on the issue of whether arms should be acquired. Such debate of necessity *does* center on questions concerning the price of weapons. What priorities should be attached to military expenditures compared to other needs? How much military strength is necessary to assure peace? Are there thresholds beyond which the addition of greater destructive power is meaningless and its costs prohibitive? In seeking national security through military might, is it possible that over the long run the economic burdens will become so great that the economy and resources that those arms are meant to safeguard will be undermined? Can even the most prosperous and advantaged nation afford to expend large proportions of its national treasure in peacetime for military preparations?

Another compelling challenge to the belief in military power finds expression in the proposition that military power has declined in its capacity to confer influence on its possessor. "The paradox of contemporary military strength," Henry A. Kissinger observed, is that "the capacity to destroy is difficult to translate into a plausible threat even against countries with no capacity for retaliation." The threat of force is often not very credible. Military power is rendered impotent by its very strength. Whether it can be used as a mode of leverage in bargaining is therefore thrown into question.

Weapons *may* perform a deterrent function. But if increasingly costly military strength can no longer be used to extract compliance from others, then weapons will have lost their capacity to function as a basis—or a substitute—for diplomacy, and the militarily powerful will no longer be able to command influence. And if military power is impotent, why pay the price of vigilance? Inasmuch as no increase in military capacity is likely to be sufficient to make a nation invulnerable, escalating military build-ups can only be assessed in terms of other consequences. That these are often counterproductive was reflected in U Thant's observation that "The massive sums devoted to armaments do not increase international or human security or happiness. On the contrary, they serve to feed the escalating arms race, to increase insecurity, and to multiply the risks to human survival" (cited in Finlay and Hovet, 1975).

The experience of the United States during the Vietnam war is consistent with the argument that military power does not equal political influence. Vietnam demonstrated in a vivid and disturbing manner that superior firepower did not enable a powerful nation to "get the other fellow to comply" with its preferences. Vietnam was a test of the thesis that force yields influence, and the results showed the inadequacies of military might in molding behavior. To many observers, Vietnam illustrated the impracticality of seeking military solutions to political problems in the contemporary world.

However, there is much inherent in the system of global politics that resists the logic of this lesson. The things that hurt, instruct, Benjamin Franklin noted. It took as costly an event as Vietnam to demonstrate the inability of a vastly superior military power to enforce its will on a small and weak country. But the lesson, like the memory of the war itself, may easily fade with the disappearance of the pain it produced. Must the world be hurt before it can be instructed? Is it not disturbing to think of the costs that may have to be paid again in order to relearn that weapons cannot solve many of the world's problems? Nor can comfort be taken in the picture of two superpowers (in John F. Kennedy's words) "both racing to alter that uncertain balance of terror that stays the hand of mankind's final war."

These observations point, of course, to the potential ascendance of nonmilitary modes of exercising influence. Is it perhaps no accident, especially as the web of international economic interdependence has tightened, that the utility of nonmilitary instruments of influence have asumed a new importance in world politics?

6. Is War Obsolete?

Perhaps Walter Millis is correct in predicting that "the threat of war, as it becomes increasingly less credible and less usable, is bound to become less and less prominent in international affairs" (cited in AFSC, 1967). Empirically, however, it is obvious that war is *not* obsolete. War has been traditionally regarded as a foreign policy option of last resort—when all else fails and a state cannot obtain its perceived objectives by other means, force of arms might be tried. The recurrent incidence of war in the contemporary period attests to the persistence of this perception.

This is not to say that war as an institution is necessarily permanent, however, nor to assert that it will always be a dominant component of global politics. In the long run, institutions often wither away when they cease to serve their intended purpose. Could this trend already be under way with regard to war? As the number of nations has steadily climbed, the number of wars between them has remained stable or even declined. This runs counter to the laws of probability. More wars should be expected, other things being equal. But they have *not* become more frequent, and, since World War II, they have been confined largely to battles between and within the emerging nations. The most advanced military powers have avoided war with one another and have been directly involved in Third World engagements infrequently.

The economic costs of warfare have risen. The human and material costs of modern warfare have also risen astronomically, even prohibitively, with the increasing destructiveness of strategic weapons. These weapons continue to be dispersed rapidly throughout the globe. In combination, it is possible that these trends portend the eventual obsolescence of warfare and its gradual disappearance as a human activity.

Of course, whether the proverbially unthinkable use of today's weapons will make war itself unthinkable is problematic. It may be, instead, that the eventual disappearance of war will stem from another, more frightening source—the possibility that war will disappear because the use of weapons will obliterate humankind. There will *not* be a third *world* war, for in the aftermath of such an engagement there would be little left of the *world*. John F. Kennedy noted that the next world war would last only hours: "No matter who fired first or was annihilated last, there will be no 'winners' . . . The world is very different now. For man holds in his mortal hands the power to abolish all forms of human life."

The only puzzle is when and by what means war will become obsolete. "The choice is either nonviolence or nonexistence," Martin Luther King, Jr., noted. An understanding of this reality cannot but change how relations between rationally behaving nations will be conducted. For, again in Kennedy's words, "The world has long since passed the time when armed conflict can be the solution to international problems . . . [because the destructiveness of modern weapons] changes all the answers and all the questions."

7. Is Empire Dead?

Since mankind first began to roam the planet, the possibility that some would attain hegemony over others has been feared. Much of world history has been written in terms of dreams of world conquest, the quest of peoples for world domination, and the efforts of others to prevent it.

Changing realities can change both the dreamer and the dream. Whether global conquest or the overthrow of the system remains a possibility or even a desire in the contemporary world is questionable. Occasionally borders do change and territory does shift hands through annexation. But the pursuit of territorial expansionism and of empire is noticeably infrequent over the long run. If anything, change in borders occurs more often as a result of national disintegration than of territorial expansion.

Is empire dead? Is the age of territorial imperialism over? Many continue to think and act as if nations are actively planning to extend their influence over others. But the past forty years of international politics have witnessed a trend on the part of the great powers to relinquish their possessions and dismantle their empires. Since World War II, the forceful acquisition and integration by great powers of territory beyond the confines of their historic boundaries has been noticeably absent in world affairs.[1]

1. The Soviet intervention into Afghanistan in 1979 represents one possible exception, although the permanence of the Soviet occupation of that strife-torn, impoverished country cannot be assumed. The general postwar pattern was noted by President Carter, who observed that "The subjugation of Afghanistan represents the first direct intrusion of Soviet Armed Forces beyond the borders of the Warsaw Pact nations since the Second World War."

Why the quest for empire may be passing from the scene (if, indeed, it is) is unclear. Boulding (1978) provides a plausible explanation: empire did not benefit the imperial powers materially. William Langer, writing in the early 1960s, when the decolonization process was at its peak, argued similarly:

> It is highly unlikely that the modern world will revert to the imperialism of the past. History has shown that the nameless fears which in the late nineteenth century led to the most violent outburst of expansionism were largely unwarranted. The Scandinavian states and Germany since Versailles have demonstrated that economic prosperity and social well-being are not dependent on the exploitation of other peoples, while better distribution of wealth in the advanced countries has reduced if not obviated whatever need there may have been to seek abroad a safety-valve for the pressures building up at home. Even in the field of defense, the old need for overseas bases or for the control of adjacent territories is rapidly being outrun. (Langer, 1962: 129)

Bidding farewell to empire may be premature, but "it is certainly true that there has been over the past century a marked alteration of mood, reflecting greater sensitivity to human suffering and a greater readiness to assume responsibility for the weak and helpless," Langer observed. (Prophetically, perhaps, the Soviet Union was the one country Langer exempted from his observations.)

If imperialism, empire-building, and territorial acquisition are no longer in a nation's self-interest, should great powers so prodigiously prepare against the alleged hegemonic aims of others? Is it necessary for that assumption to form the cornerstone of defense policy?

8. What Price Preeminence?

Although the presumed desire for world conquest may be little more than a carry-over from a previous period of international politics, national competition for *status* in the international pecking order remains a central feature of the global political arena. Prestige, respect, and wealth—these remain the core values of many societies and the central goals for which they strive internationally.

In a materialistic world, the search for status has led more to competition for economic, military, and political ascendance than it has to competition for territorial acquisition. In the context of interdependence and scarcity, the competition for access to resources presumed to assure economic growth has necessarily been keen. To remain or become first in the international political system means flirting with the political and economic means for bending the world to one's will. Pressures for policies of domination are therefore created. Our age is one of conflict, to be sure, and much of the struggle and tension that characterize relations among nations (and other types of transnational actors) testifies to the continued pursuit of primacy in the world arena.

The potential long-term consequences of this competition are not entirely favorable, for gross differentials of power and wealth are a constant source of strain. Inequality among nations and military contests between them have been the prices associated with the pursuit of prominence. The perpetuation of poverty within some nations, often exacerbated by their exploitation by other nations, has been another. Instability produced by the divisiveness of rising expectations and diminishing prospects is a third. In struggles among unequals, some nations are victimized. Alienation, resentment, and oppression are among the by-products of inequality. The ethics of a global arrangement that perpetuates unequal divisions is certainly questionable. Those viewing the situation from a global perspective have indeed asked if *The Crime of World Power* (Aliano, 1978) is not made evident by these circumstances.

However deplorable the overall situation may be (especially to the disadvantaged), the pursuit of preeminence remains. The appropriateness of the search for status in the international hierarchy has seldom been challenged. Will challengers remain silent? To be questioned as the world moves forward in time is the wisdom of pursuing top-dog status. The problems of primacy are numerous, the disadvantages of advantage many. With leadership comes the burden of responsibility and the necessity of setting the pace (Hoffmann, 1978). Preponderant nations are often the target of other nations' resentment, envy, hostility, fear, and blame. Preeminent nations invariably are tempted to shape the destiny of others, to study them in their own values. Rulers of the world seldom are able to rule their own spirit, as John Quincy Adams warned.

It seems likely that the quest for preeminence will be more seriously questioned in national capitals as the costs of top-dog status are given more consideration.[2] Debate of that issue, however, may not be taken seriously by some, because to nearly every nation the one predicament worse than being preeminent is becoming subject to the vagaries of another power. A policy issue for the future is whether the acquisition and maintenance of planetary preeminence is in any nation's long-term interests, or if the maintenance of a soci-

---

2. For discussions of the implications—and advantages—of being number two in the international pecking order, see Iklé (1979) and Howell (1980).

ety of unequals produces a world environment safe for any nation, including those at the apex of power and wealth.[3]

9. An End to Ideology?

World politics has traditionally been viewed largely through the conceptual lens of some transnational ideological system. Ideological beliefs command the loyalties of many individuals, shaping their orientation to and interpretation of world events. The psychological need for a systematic worldview is persuasive and is not likely to diminish. As a consequence world politics undoubtedly will continue to be colored by ideological rhetoric and logic. Moreover, competition among contending isms has conventionally comprised a significant component of world politics. Much of post-World War II international politics can appropriately be interpreted as an ideological contest—between communism and its opponents and, increasingly, between the belief systems of the advantaged and the disadvantaged.

Attention to this dimension can obscure its diminished importance, however. Ideological forces may be in decline as a significant factor in international politics; the present age could be a transitional one in which "the end of ideology" is in sight. Polycentric tendencies within the communist world and the decline of cohesion within the Atlantic alliance may be symptoms of the deterioration of the capacity of ideological systems to command loyalties and to shape the response of actors toward issues. No less an ideologically attuned observer than Zbigniew Brzezinski has labeled the waning of ideological conflicts among developed nations one of the most significant changes in world politics. In reference to the ideological movement believed by most Americans to possess almost unlimited powers, Brzezinski argued in 1967:

> Communism, the principal, and until recently the most militant, revolutionary ideology of our day, is dead—communism is dead as an ideology in the sense that it is no longer capable of mobilizing unified global support. On the contrary, it is increasingly fragmented by conflicts among constituent units and parties. This has contributed to ideological disillusionment among its members. Communist states, Communist movements, and Communist subversion are still very important on the international scene, but Communist ideology as a vital force is no longer with us. (Brzezinski, 1967: 376)

The potential decline of ideology as an organizing force in world politics—giving way, according to Brzezinski and others, to a "prob-

---

3. The idea that the pursuit of equality was in everyone's eventual self-interest was contained in John F. Kennedy's observation that if the many who are poor cannot be helped, the few who are rich cannot be saved.

lem-solving," engineering approach to social change, presumably emphasizing pragmatics over abstractions—challenges many assumptions that conventionally orient nations toward the world. If ideology is dead, do policies designed to eliminate ideologies make any sense? Cannot active opposition to an ideological movement have the paradoxical effect of strengthening it, thus stalling (although perhaps not reversing) its long-run tendency toward deterioration and fragmentation? Indeed, is an ideological orientation toward an ideologically powerless world warranted?

The possibility that trends will reverse themselves cannot be safely ignored, however, for people have a tendency to turn to all-encompassing belief systems in times of crisis and uncertainty. As developments in the Persian Gulf and elsewhere in the 1980s suggest, world politics might be taken back to a time when ideological antagonisms and ancient religious animosities once again assert themselves. Will such antagonisms again become a potent force, even an obsession, to an extent that even the technocratically oriented industrial countries will be unable to ignore or control them?

10. What Is Progress?

This rarely examined question promises to command attention as policy makers deal with a world of rapid change. At the heart of the question is whether in an era of diminishing natural resources and rapidly expanding populations progress can any longer be equated with economic growth. The possibility that science and the technology it produces may now be creating more problems than they solve is already evident in advanced industrial countries.

"A rise in the GNP," Kenneth Boulding (1978) notes, "does not necessarily mean things are better; it may only mean that some things are bigger." But a rise in GNP can have sharply different consequences for people presently living in poor societies compared with those in rich societies. For the inhabitants of most Third World countries, growth in GNP may mean more food, better housing, better education, and an increased standard of living.[4] Because most people living in the First World already have these basic amenities, additional increments of income usually lead to the satisfaction of relatively trivial needs.

The impact on the global system of continued striving for growth is nevertheless substantial. "The incremental person in poor

4. This assumes that increases in output will not go only to those in developing societies who are already rich, and that most people in these societies still have not been able to satisfy their basic needs. The conclusion follows from the economic law of diminishing marginal utility, which says that people will meet their most pressing needs first and successively less pressing needs with additional increments of income.

countries contributes negligibly to production, but makes few demands on world resources," observes Herman Daly (1973). By contrast, "the incremental person in the rich country contributes to his country's GNP, and to feed his high standard of living contributes greatly to depletion of the world's resources and pollution of its spaces." In both cases, then, continued population growth is detrimental—for poor societies, because it inhibits increases in per capita income and welfare; for rich societies, because it further burdens the earth's delicate ecological system.

An alternative to perpetual growth for the world's rich nations is pursuit of a *steady-state* economy, wherein a constant stock of capital and population, combined with as modest a rate of production and consumption of goods as possible, is sought (Daly, 1973). Since most advanced industrial nations have already approached zero population growth, or steady state, realizing zero economic growth will require profoundly altered attitudes toward production and consumption. It will also require an alteration in attitudes toward cultural norms regarding leisure and satisfaction. The durability of goods will have to be maximized and junk will have to be recycled. The profit motive that sustains the perceived need for growth to satisfy the craving for items that are not really necessary (for which demand is often created through advertising) will have to be scrapped. Domestic political systems will have to devise means of managing conflict other than by doling out increments of an ever expanding pie—for in a steady-state economy the pie will no longer be growing.

These prescriptions pose profound challenges to the very foundations on which much of Western civilization has been built. But is there any alternative? Can growth in a finite world proceed infinitely? How many fish can be taken from a fishery before the offtake exceeds the fishery's maximum sustainable yield? How long can a finite energy source sustain ever increasing rates of consumption before automobiles sputter to a stop, industries grind to a halt, and lights go out? How many pollutants can be dumped into the atmosphere before irreparable environmental damage is done? And ultimately, how many people can a delicately balanced ecosystem support?

THE CONTINUING TRANSFORMATION OF WORLD POLITICS

The foregoing list of perplexing questions and related dilemmas could be readily expanded. In a period of rapid global change and increasingly complex international interdependence, policy prerogatives are often diminished. The temptation to sacrifice long-term welfare to the exigencies of the moment is therefore strong. Still, there is a compelling need to question goals and the means for realizing them.

The preceding questions are likely to erupt in policy debates time and again, for global transformation itself renders old approaches to new circumstances questionable and poses new questions that must be addressed. In fact, in framing these questions we have purposely focused on the puzzles and seeming contradictions that lie at the core of international politics as it has traditionally been conceptualized and conducted. The potential for present trends to accelerate, move in divergent directions, or reverse themselves make all forms of conventional wisdom suspect. The failure to acknowledge the existence of important global trends and transformations may indeed risk making humanity a victim of its own prevailing orthodoxies.

From the vantage point of the early 1980s, the new decade conveys the inescapable impression of being one that will usher into world politics a breakpoint in history. The world seems to be undergoing a fundamental restructuring. Previously established patterns and relationships seem to have been interrupted, perhaps permanently. Trends point to possible new departures in world affairs and to the likely eruption of unanticipated events that may have profound consequences for the global system. Something revolutionary, not simply novel, may be happening.

Juxtaposed against the revolutionary is the persistent—the obstinate durability of established rituals, instilled rules, entrenched institutions, and ingrained customs. These may serve to resist the pull of some of the revolutionary transformations under way, providing changes do not coalesce to reinforce each other cumulatively. Change and persistence coexist uneasily in world politics, and it is this intertwined mixture that makes the future direction of the international system so uncertain.

If a new world politics is in the process of unfolding, that process cannot be ·regarded as complete. A new structure has not emerged to replace the preexisting one. Hence the global system as it presently exists defies characterization. It is clearly moving, but discordantly and in seemingly divergent directions. Because the path to the future has not yet assumed recognizable definition, the description of the present as an age *in transformation* is most compelling.

And, it is not hyperbole to label the present condition of world politics as one of *crisis*. To be sure, the instabilities in world politics make for a condition of crisis in the sense that the present convulsions will lead, inexorably, to decisive change. The world stands at the threshold of either progress or disaster. Although crises need not be resolved negatively and a change in direction may augur positively, grounds for optimism do not abound (Deutsch, 1979; Blaney, 1979). Many global trends point ominously to a planet on the brink of a new dark age (see Stavrianos, 1976). The potential for future international discord and deterioration is great. The scope of emerging problems staggers the imagination. The crises these trends represent pose, in short, an inescapable challenge.

But global destiny is not predetermined. Although "it is the business of the future to be dangerous" (Whitehead, 1929), the magnitude of the present crisis should not blind us to the possibility of progress. New opportunities for liberation from the world's present plight are extant as well as are new dangers. These opportunities do not doom mankind to a future of defeat.

Two fundamental races govern the path between the world that is and the world that will be. The first is the race between knowledge and oblivion. Ignorance is the greatest obstacle to global progress and justice. Advances in scientific and technological knowledge have far outpaced knowledge about how the social and political problems they have generated can be managed. Global trends are moving far more rapidly than our awareness of them, and faster than our understanding of the processes by which the potentially catastrophic train of events the globe presently exhibits has been set in motion. A trend that nobody at first takes seriously, or one that nobody knows how to reverse, may lead to a crisis. A revolution in knowledge to match the pace of revolutionary transformations in world politics may therefore present the ultimate challenge. "The splitting of the atom," Albert Einstein warned, "has changed everything save our modes of thinking, and thus we drift toward unparalleled catastrophe. Unless there is a fundamental change in their attitudes toward one another as well as their concept of the future, the world will face unprecedented disaster."

"Knowledge is our destiny," Jacob Bronowski noted. If the world is to engineer a future of promise for itself, it must acquire more sophisticated knowledge. Sophistication requires seeing the world in terms of the individual parts that make up the total system of world politics and that collectively shape the political evolution of the world. The temptation to picture others according to our images of ourselves and to project onto them our own aims and values must be overcome. Conventional wisdom must be challenged. The belief that there is a simple formula for a better tomorrow must be discarded. The limits of rational choice and the political obstacles to reform must be acknowledged. Toleration, even the pursuit, of ambiguity is essential.

Second, the future of world politics—and of humankind—rests on a race between the ability of nations to act in concert to protect their communal destiny and the forces militating against transnational collaboration. What is being tested is the capacity of the world to summon the political will to implement those reforms necessary to meet global challenges.

"Since there is now a risk of mankind destroying itself," former West German Chancellor Willy Brandt warned, "this risk must be met by new methods." Can new methods be found? Can a comprehensive reordering of international priorities be effected in time to deter global annihilation? Or are the obstacles to adaptive global restructuring insurmountable and the rush toward self-destruction unstoppable? Mankind only raises those questions it can solve, Karl Marx speculated. Are the world's political problems beyond solution?

Ironically, the magnitude of the problems faced may be the source for their resolution (akin to Jean Monnet's prophecy that "the international situation will have to become much worse before radical steps can be taken to improve it"). All the apocalyptic dangers that thinkers have always feared and forecast are risked. Perhaps global conditions are approaching that point of deterioration where resistance to reform can now be overcome politically. As Henry A. Kissinger noted in this context, "with all the dislocations that we are now experiencing there also exists an extraordinary opportunity to form for the first time in history a truly global society, carried by the principle of interdependence."

But will that opportunity be seized? Will humankind join together to address global problems and enhance transcendant common interests? Can it, in Jean Monnet's phrase, "put [its] problems on one side of the table and all of us on the other?" Whether humankind will be victim or victor may well depend on the answer.

In facing an uncertain global future, the moving words of President Kennedy describe a posture we might well assume:

> However close we sometimes seem to that dark and final abyss, let no man of peace and freedom despair. For he does not stand alone . . .
>
> Together we shall save our planet or together we shall perish in its flames. Save it we can, and save it we must, and then shall we earn the eternal thanks of mankind.

References

ABOLFATHI, FARID, JOHN J. HAYES, AND RICHARD E. HAYES. (1979) "Trends in United States Response to International Crises," pp. 57–85 in Charles W. Kegley, Jr., and Patrick J. McGowan (eds.), *Challenges to America*. Beverly Hills, Calif.: Sage Publications.

ABRAHAMSSON, BERNHARD J. (1975) "The International Oil Industry," pp. 73–88 in Joseph S. Szyliowicz and Bard E. O'Neill (eds.), *The Energy Crisis and U.S. Foreign Policy*. New York: Praeger.

ADDO, HERB. (1981) "Foreign Policy Strategies for Achieving the NIEO: A Third World Perspective," forthcoming in Charles W. Kegley, Jr., and Patrick J. McGowan (eds.), *The Political Economy of Foreign Policy Behavior*. Beverly Hills, Calif.: Sage Publications.

AFSC [American Friends Service Committee]. (1967) *In Place of War*. New York: Grossman.

AKEHURST, MICHAEL. (1970) *A Modern Introduction to International Law*. New York: Atherton.

ALGER, CHADWICK F. (1965) "Personal Contact in Intergovernmental Organizations," pp. 523–547 in Herbert C. Kelman (ed.), *International Behavior*. New York: Holt, Rinehart and Winston.

ALIANO, RICHARD A. (1978) *The Crime of World Power*. New York: Putnam.

ALPEROVITZ, GAR. (1970) *Cold War Essays*. Garden City, N.Y.: Doubleday-Anchor.

_____. (1967) *Atomic Diplomacy: Hiroshima and Potsdam*. New York: Vintage Books.

ALSOP, JOSEPH, AND DAVID JORAVSKY. (1980) "Was the Hiroshima Bomb Necessary? An Exchange," *The New York Review of Books* 28 (October 23): 37–42.

AMBROSE, STEPHEN E. (1980) *Rise to Globalism*. Baltimore: Penguin.

ANGELL, ROBERT C. (1979) *The Quest for World Order*. Ann Arbor: University of Michigan Press.

———. (1965) "An Analysis of Trends in International Organizations," Peace Research Society (International), *Papers*, Vol. 3: 185–195.

ARAD, RUTH W., AND UZI B. ARAD. (1979) "Scarce Natural Resources and Potential Conflict," pp. 23–85 in Ruth W. Arad et al., *Sharing Global Resources*. New York: McGraw-Hill.

———, RACHEL MCCULLOCK, JOSÉ PIÑERA, AND ANN L. HOLLICK. (1979) *Sharing Global Resources*. New York: McGraw-Hill.

ARON, RAYMOND. (1958) "Evidence and Inference in History," *Daedalus* 87 (Fall): 11–39.

ASCH, SEYMOUR E. (1951) "Effects of Group Pressure Upon the Modification and Distortion of Judgment," pp. 117–190 in Harold Guetzkow (ed.), *Groups, Leadership and Men*. Pittsburgh: Carnegie.

ASIMOV, ISAAC. (1979) *A Choice of Catastrophes*. New York: Simon and Schuster.

AZAR, EDWARD E. (1973) *Probe for Peace: Small State Hostilities*. Minneapolis: Burgess.

———, AND THOMAS J. SLOAN. (1975) *Dimensions of Interaction: A Source Book for the Study of the Behavior of 31 Nations from 1948 Through 1973*. Occasional Paper No. 8, International Studies Association. Pittsburgh: University Center for International Studies, University of Pittsburgh.

BALL, GEORGE W. (ed.) (1975) *Global Companies: The Political Economy of World Business*. Englewood Cliffs, N.J.: Prentice-Hall.

BALL, GEORGE W. (1967) "The Promise of the Multinational Corporation," *Fortune* 75 (June 1): 80.

BARKUN, MICHAEL. (1968) *Law Without Sanctions: Order in Primitive Societies and the World Community*. New Haven: Yale University Press.

BARNET, RICHARD J. (1980a) "The World's Resources: I—The Lean Years," *The New Yorker* 56 (March 17): 45–48 et passim.

———. (1980b) "The World's Resources: III—Human Energy," *The New Yorker* 56 (April 7) 46–56 et passim.

———. (1979) "Challenging the Myths of National Security," *New York Times Magazine*, April 1.

———. (1977) *The Giants: Russia and America*. New York: Simon and Schuster.

———, AND RONALD E. MÜLLER. (1974) *Global Reach: The Power of the Multinational Corporations*. New York: Simon and Schuster.

BARR, STRINGFELLOW. (1953) *Citizens of the World*. Garden City, N.Y.: Doubleday.

BEER, FRANCIS A. (1974) *How Much War in History: Definitions, Estimates, Extrapolations and Trends*. Sage Professional Papers in International Studies, Vol. 3, series no. 02–030. Beverly Hills, Calif.: Sage Publications.

BELL, DANIEL. (1977) "The Future World Disorder: The Structural Context of Crises," *Foreign Policy* 27 (Summer): 109–135.

____. (1973) *The Coming of Post-Industrial Society.* New York: Basic Books.

BENNETT, A. LeRoy. (1980) *International Organizations.* Englewood Cliffs, N.J.: Prentice-Hall.

BERES, LOUIS RENÉ. (1978) "The Nuclear Threat of Terrorism," *International Studies Notes* 5 (Spring): 14–17.

BERGSTEN, C. FRED. (1973) "The Threat from the Third World," *Foreign Policy* 11 (Summer): 102–124.

____, THOMAS HORST, AND THEODORE MORAN. (1978) *American Multinationals and American Interests.* Washington, D.C.: Brookings Institution.

BERKOWITZ, LEONARD, AND ANTHONY LePAGE. (1970) "Weapons as Aggression-Eliciting Stimuli," pp. 132–144 in Edwin I. Megaree and Jack E. Kokanson (eds.), *The Dynamics of Aggression.* New York: Harper & Row.

BERKOWITZ, MORTON, P. G. BOCK, AND VINCENT J. FUCCILLO. (1977) *The Politics of American Foreign Policy.* Englewood Cliffs, N.J.: Prentice-Hall.

BERTELSEN, JUDY S. (ed.) (1977) *Nonstate Nations in International Politics.* New York: Praeger.

BETTS, RICHARD K. (1977) "Paranoids, Pygmies, Pariahs & Nonproliferation," *Foreign Policy* 26 (Spring): 157–183.

BHAGWATI, JAGDISH N. (1972) "Economics and World Order from the 1970's to 1990's: The Key Issues," pp. 1–42 in Jagdish N. Bhagwati (ed.), *Economics and World Order.* New York: Free Press.

BIERCE, AMBROSE. (1925) *The Devil's Dictionary.* New York: Boni.

BISHOP, WILLIAM. (1962) *International Law.* Boston: Little, Brown.

BLACKBURN, DONALD et al. (1973) *Restricted Engagement Options.* Vienna, Va.: BND Corporation, Nov. 30.

BLAINEY, GEOFFREY. (1973) *The Causes of War.* New York: Free Press.

BLAIR, BRUCE G., AND GARRY D. BREWER. (1977) "The Terrorist Threat to World Nuclear Programs," *Journal of Conflict Resolution* 21 (September): 379–403.

BLAKE, DAVID H., AND ROBERT S. WALTERS. (1976) *The Politics of Global Economic Relations.* Englewood Cliffs, N.J.: Prentice-Hall.

BLANEY, HARRY CLAY III. (1979) *Global Challenges: A World at Risk.* New York: New Viewpoints/Franklin Watts.

BLECHMAN, BARRY M., AND STEPHEN S. KAPLAN, WITH DAVID K. HALL, WILLIAM B. QUANDT, JEROME N. SLATER, ROBERT M. SLUSSER, AND PHILIP WINDSOR. (1978) *Force without War.* Washington, D.C.: The Brookings Institution.

BLOCK, FRED L. (1977) *The Origins of International Economic Disorder.* Berkeley: University of California Press.

BOULDING, KENNETH E. (1978) *Stable Peace.* Austin: University of Texas Press.

____. (1975) "National Images and International Systems," pp. 347–360 in

William D. Coplin and Charles W. Kegley, Jr. (eds.), *Analyzing International Relations*. New York: Praeger.

———. (1974) "What Went Wrong, if Anything, Since Copernicus?," *Science and Public Affairs* 17 (January): 17–23.

———. (1962) *Conflict and Defense: A General Theory*. New York: Harper & Row.

———, AND TAPAN MUKERJEE (eds.) (1972) *Economic Imperialism*. Ann Arbor: University of Michigan Press.

BOUTHOUL, GASTON, AND RENÉ CARRÈRE. (1978) "A List of the 366 Major Armed Conflicts of the Period 1740–1974," *Peace Research* 10 (July): 83–108.

BOZEMAN, ADDA B. (1971) *The Future of Law in a Multicultural World*. Princeton: Princeton University Press.

———. (1960) *Politics and Culture in International History*. Princeton: Princeton University Press.

BRAYBROOKE, DAVID, AND CHARLES LINDBLOM. (1963) *A Strategy of Decision*. New York: Free Press.

BRECHER, MICHAEL. (1977) "Toward a Theory of International Crisis Behavior," *International Studies Quarterly* 21 (March): 39–74.

BRENNER, MICHAEL J. (1979) "Carter's Bungled Promise," *Foreign Policy* 36 (Fall): 89–101.

———. (1973) "The Problem of Innovation and the Nixon-Kissinger Foreign Policy," *International Studies Quarterly* 17 (September): 255–294.

BRIERLY, JAMES L. (1944) *The Outlook for International Law*. Oxford: Clarendon.

BRINTON, CRANE. (1965) *The Anatomy of Revolution*. New York: Vintage.

BRONFENBRENNER, URIE. (1975) "The Mirror Image in Soviet-American Relations," pp. 161–166 in William D. Coplin and Charles W. Kegley, Jr. (eds.), *Analyzing International Relations*. New York: Praeger.

BROWN, LESTER R. (1979) *Resource Trends and Population Policy: A Time for Reassessment*. Worldwatch Paper 29 (May). Washington, D.C.: Worldwatch Institute.

———. (1978) *The Twenty-Ninth Day*. New York: Norton.

———. (1974) *By Bread Alone*. New York: Praeger.

———. (1972) *World Without Borders*. New York: Vintage.

———, PATRICIA L. MCGRATH, AND BRUCE STOKES. (1976) *Twenty-Two Dimensions of the Population Problem*. Worldwatch Paper 5 (March). Washington, D.C.: Worldwatch Institute.

BROWN, PETER G., AND HENRY SHUE (eds.) (1977) *Food Policy*. New York: Free Press.

BROWN, SEYOM. (1977) "A Cooling-off Period for U.S.-Soviet Relations," *Foreign Policy* 28 (Fall): 3–21.

BROWNLIE, IAN. (1973) *Principles of Public International Law*. London: Clarendon.

BRZEZINSKI, ZBIGNIEW. (1972) "How the Cold War Was Played," *Foreign Affairs* 52 (October): 181–209.

——. (1970) *Between Two Ages: America's Role in the Technotronic Era*. New York: Viking.

——. (1967) "The Implications of Change for U.S. Foreign Policy," *Department of State Bulletin* 57 (July 3): 19–23.

——, AND SAMUEL P. HUNTINGTON. (1964) *Political Power: USA/USSR*. New York: Viking.

BUENO DE MESQUITA, BRUCE. (1975a) "The Effect of Systemic Polarization on the Probability and Duration of War." Paper presented at the Annual Meeting of the International Studies Association, Washington, D.C., February 19–22.

——. (1975b) "Measuring Systemic Polarity," *Journal of Conflict Resolution* 19 (June): 187–216.

BULL, HEDLEY. (1977) *The Anarchical Society: A Study of Order in World Politics*. New York: Columbia University Press.

BUNDY, WILLIAM P. (1977) "Elements of National Power," *Foreign Affairs* 56 (October): 1–26.

BURNEY, MAHMUD A. (1979) "A Recognition of Interdependence: UNCTAD V," *Finance and Development* 16 (September): 15–18.

BUTTERWORTH, ROBERT LYLE. (1976) *Managing Interstate Conflict, 1945–74: Data with Synopses*. Pittsburgh: University Center for International Studies, University of Pittsburgh.

BYWATER, MARION. (1975) "The Lomé Convention," *European Community* 184 (March): 5–9.

CAMERON, DAVID R. (1978) "The Expansion of the Public Economy: A Comparative Analysis," *American Political Science Review* 72 (December): 1243–1261.

CAPLOW, THEODORE. (1973) "Are the Rich Countries Getting Richer and the Poor Countries Poorer?," pp. 44–54 in Steven L. Spiegel (ed.), *At Issue: Politics in the Global Arena*. New York: St. Martin's.

CAPORASO, JAMES A., AND MICHAEL D. WARD. (1979) "The United States in an Interdependent World: The Emergence of Economic Power," pp. 139–170 in Charles W. Kegley, Jr., and Patrick J. McGowan (eds.), *Challenges to America*. Beverly Hills, Calif.: Sage Publications.

CARR, E. H. (1966) *International Relations Between the Two World Wars, 1919–1939*. New York: Harper & Row.

——. (1939) *The Twenty-Years' Crisis, 1919–1939: An Introduction to the Study of International Relations*. London: Macmillan.

CATTELL, RAYMOND B. (1949) "The Dimensions of Culture Patterns by Factorization of National Characteristics," *Journal of Abnormal and Social Psychology* 44 (October): 443–469.

CENTRAL INTELLIGENCE AGENCY. (1980) "International Terrorism in 1979." A Report Prepared by the National Foreign Assessment Center. Washington, D.C.: Director of Public Affairs, Central Intelligence Agency (April).

_____. (1977) *The International Energy Situation: Outlook to 1985.* Washington, D.C.: Central Intelligence Agency.

CHILDE, V. GORDON. (1962) *Man Makes Himself.* New York: Mentor.

CHOUCRI, NAZLI. (1972) "Population, Resources, and Technology: Political Implications of the Environmental Crisis," *International Organization* 26 (Spring): 175–212.

_____, AND ROBERT C. NORTH. (1975) *Nations in Conflict.* San Francisco: Freeman.

CHRISTENSEN, CHERYL. (1978) "World Hunger: A Structural Approach," *International Organization* 32 (Summer): 745–774.

CHRISTOPHER, WARREN. (1978) "Agenda for International Economic Issues," Bureau of Public Affairs, United States Department of State, Current Policy No. 25 (June 22).

CLARK, GRENVILLE, AND LOUIS B. SOHN. (1966) *World Peace Through World Law.* Cambridge: Harvard University Press.

CLAUDE, INIS L., JR. (1971) *Swords into Plowshares.* New York: Random House.

_____. (1967) *The Changing United Nations.* New York: Random House.

_____. (1962) *Power and International Relations.* New York: Random House.

CLAUSEWITZ, KARL VON. (1976) *On War.* Edited and translated by Michael Howard and Peter Paret. Princeton: Princeton University Press.

CLEVELAND, HARLAN. (1976) *The Third Try at World Order.* New York: Aspen Institute for Humanistic Studies.

CLINE, RAY S. (1975) *World Power Assessment: A Calculus of Strategic Drift.* Washington, D.C.: Georgetown University Center for Strategic and International Studies.

CLUTTERBUCK, RICHARD. (1975) *Living with Terrorism.* London: Faber and Faber.

COBB, ROGER, AND CHARLES ELDER. (1970) *International Community.* New York: Harcourt Brace and World.

COCHRANE, JAMES D. (1969) *Politics of Regional Integration: The Central American Case.* New Orleans: Tulane University Press.

COHEN, BENJAMIN J. (1979) "Europe's Money, America's Problem," *Foreign Policy* 35 (Summer): 31–47.

_____. (1973) *The Question of Imperialism.* New York: Basic Books.

COLLINS, JOHN N. (1973) "Foreign Conflict Behavior and Domestic Disorder in Africa," pp. 251–293 in Jonathan Wilkenfeld (ed.), *Conflict Behavior and Linkage Politics.* New York: David McKay.

Commission on Transnational Corporations. (1979) "Supplementary Material on the Issue of Defining Transnational Corporations," UN Doc. E/C.10/58, United Nations Economic and Social Council (March 23). New York: United Nations.

———. (1978) *Transnational Corporations in World Development: A Re-Examination*. UN Doc. E/C.10/38, United Nations Economic and Social Council (March 20). New York: United Nations.

CONNELLY, PHILIP, AND ROBERT PERLMAN. (1975) *The Politics of Scarcity*. London: Oxford University Press.

COOPER, CHESTER L. (1978) "Nuclear Hostages," *Foreign Policy* 32 (Fall): 127–135.

COOPER, RICHARD N. (1979) "International Energy Problems," Bureau of Public Affairs, United States Department of State, Current Policy No. 74 (July 17).

COPELAND, MILES. (1969) *The Game of Nations*. New York: Simon and Schuster.

COPLIN, WILLIAM D. (1980) *Introduction to International Politics*. Englewood Cliffs, N.J.: Prentice-Hall.

———. (1975) "International Law and Assumptions about the State System," pp. 270–279 in William D. Coplin and Charles W. Kegley, Jr. (eds.), *Analyzing International Relations*. New York: Praeger.

———. (1969) "Current Studies of the Functions of International Law," pp. 149–207 in James A. Robinson (ed.), *Political Science Annual*. Indianapolis: Bobbs-Merrill.

———. (1966) *The Functions of International Law*. Chicago: Rand McNally.

———, AND CHARLES W. KEGLEY, JR. (eds.) (1975) *Analyzing International Relations*. New York: Praeger.

COSER, LEWIS. (1956) *The Functions of Social Conflict*. London: Routledge and Kegan Paul.

COTTAM, RICHARD W., AND GERALD GALLUCCI. (1977) *The Rehabilitation of Power in International Relations*. Pittsburgh: University of Pittsburgh Center for International Studies, University of Pittsburgh.

COULOUMBIS, THEODORE A., AND JAMES H. WOLFE. (1978) *Introduction to International Relations*. Englewood Cliffs, N.J.: Prentice-Hall.

CUTLER, LLOYD N. (1978) *Global Interdependence and the Multinational Firm*. Headline Series 239 (April). New York: Foreign Policy Association.

DALY, HERMAN E. (1977) *Steady-State Economics*. San Francisco: Freeman.

———. (1973) "Introduction," pp. 1–29 in Herman E. Daly (ed.), *Toward a Steady-State Economy*. San Francisco: Freeman.

DARMSTADTER, JOEL, AND HANS H. LANDSBERG. (1976) "The Economic Background," pp. 15–37 in Raymond Vernon (ed.), *The Oil Crisis*. New York: Norton.

DAVIES, JAMES C. (1962) "Toward a Theory of Revolution," *American Sociological Review* 27 (February): 5–19.

DE BLOCH, JEAN. (1898) *The Future of War*. New York: Doubleday and Mc-Clure.

DEHIO, LUDWIG. (1962) *The Precarious Balance*. Translated by Charles Fullman. New York: Knopf.

DENTON, FRANK, AND WARREN PHILLIPS. (1971) "Some Patterns in the History of Violence," pp. 327–338 in Claggett G. Smith (ed.), *Conflict Resolution*. Notre Dame, Ind.: University of Notre Dame Press.

DEUTSCH, KARL W. (1979) *Tides Among Nations*. New York: Free Press.

_____. (1975) "The Growth of Nations: Some Recurrent Patterns of Political and Social Integration," pp. 306–319 in William D. Coplin and Charles W. Kegley, Jr. (eds.), *Analyzing International Relations*. New York: Praeger.

_____. (1971) "The Probability of International Law," pp. 57–83 in Karl W. Deutsch and Stanley Hoffmann (eds.), *The Relevance of International Law*. Cambridge, Mass.: Schenkman Publishing.

_____. (1970) *Politics and Government: How People Decide Their Fate*. New York: Houghton-Mifflin.

_____, AND J. DAVID SINGER. (1975) "Multipolar Power Systems and International Stability," pp. 320–337 in William D. Coplin and Charles W. Kegley, Jr. (eds.), *Analyzing International Relations*. New York: Praeger.

_____, AND RICHARD L. MERRITT. (1965) "Effects of Events on National and International Images," pp. 132–187 in Herbert C. Kelman (ed.), *International Behavior*. New York: Holt, Rinehart and Winston.

_____, SIDNEY A. BURRELL, ROBERT A. KANN, MAURICE LEE, JR., MARTIN LICHTERMAN, RAYMOND E. LINDGREN, FRANCIS L. LOEWENHEIM, AND RICHARD W. VAN WAGENEN. (1957) *Political Community and the North Atlantic Area*. Princeton: Princeton University Press.

DEVISSCHER, CHARLES. (1957) *Theory and Reality in Public International Law*. Princeton: Princeton University Press.

DEWEY, EDWARD R. (1964) *The 177 Year Cycle in War, 600 B.C.–A.D. 1957*. Pittsburgh: Foundation for the Study of Cycles.

DIRENZO, GORDON J. (ed.) (1974) *Personality and Politics*. Garden City, N.Y.: Doubleday-Anchor.

DISARM EDUCATION FUND. (1978) *Newsletter*. New York: The Disarm Education Fund.

DOUGHERTY, JAMES E., AND RICHARD L. PFALTZGRAFF, JR. (1971) *Contending Theories of International Relations*. Philadelphia: Lippincott.

DRUCKER, PETER F. (1974) "Multinationals and Developing Countries: Myths and Realities," *Foreign Affairs* 53 (October): 121–134.

DUBOS, RENÉ. (1975) "Trend is Not Destiny," *New York Times*, November 10, 11.

DULLES, JOHN FOSTER. (1939) *War, Peace, and Change*. New York: Harper.

DUNN, LEWIS A. (1979) "Half Past India's Bang," *Foreign Policy* 36 (Fall): 71–89.

Easton, David. (1969) "The New Revolution in Political Science," *American Political Science Review* 63 (December): 1051–1061.

Easton, Stewart C. (1964) *The Rise and Fall of Western Colonialism*. New York: Praeger.

Eckaus, Richard S. (1977) *Appropriate Technologies for Developing Countries*. Washington, D.C.: National Academy of Science.

Eckholm, Erik P. (1976) *Losing Ground*. New York: Norton.

Ecklund, George N. (1980) "OPEC Crude: 'Real' Prices Haven't Gone Up Since 1974," *World Oil* 190 (January): 119–122.

Eckstein, Harry. (1972) "On the Etiology of Internal Wars," pp. 9–30 in Ivo K. Feierabend, Rosalind L. Feierabend, and Ted Robert Gurr (eds.), *Anger, Violence, and Politics*. Englewood Cliffs, N.J.: Prentice-Hall.

Eddy, Sherwood, and Kirby Page. (1924) *The Abolition of War*. New York: George H. Doran.

Ehrlich, Paul R., Anne H. Ehrlich, and John P. Holdren. (1977) *Ecoscience*. San Francisco: Freeman.

Einstein, Albert. (1946) Radio Address of May 29, published in pp. 124–127 in Arthur Weinberg and Lila Weinberg (eds.), *Instead of Violence*. Boston: Beacon Press, 1963.

Ekirch, Arthur A., Jr. (1966) *Ideas, Ideals, and American Diplomacy*. New York: Appleton-Century-Crofts.

Etzioni, Amitai. (1968) "Toward a Sociological Theory of Peace," pp. 403–428 in Leon Bramson and George W. Goethals (eds.), *War*. New York: Basic Books.

Ewing, David W. (1974) "The Corporation as Peacemonger," pp. 150–157 in Peter A. Toma, Andrew Gyorgy, and Robert S. Jordan (eds.), *Basic Issues in International Relations*. Boston: Allyn and Bacon.

Falk, Richard A. (1979) "The Clear and Present Danger of World War III," *Transition* 4 (November): 1–2.

———. (1978) *Nuclear Policy and World Order: Why Denuclearization*. New York: Institute for World Order.

———. (1976) *Future Worlds*. Headline Series 229 (February). New York: Foreign Policy Association.

———. (1975) *A Study of Future Worlds*. New York: Free Press.

———. (1971) "The Relevance of Political Context to the Nature and Functioning of International Law," pp. 177–202 in Karl W. Deutsch and Stanley Hoffmann (eds.), *The Relevance of International Law*. Garden City, N.Y.: Doubleday-Anchor.

———. (1970) *The Status of Law in International Society*. Princeton: Princeton University Press.

———. (1968) *Legal Order in a Violent World*. Princeton: Princeton University Press.

———. (1965) "World Law and Human Conflict," pp. 227–249 in Elton B. Mc-

Neil (ed.), *The Nature of Human Conflict*. Englewood Cliffs, N.J.: Prentice-Hall.

———. (1964) *The Role of Domestic Courts in the International Legal Order*. Syracuse: Syracuse University Press.

———. (1962) "Historical Tendencies, Modernizing and Revolutionary Nations, and the International Legal Order," pp. 128–160 in Saul H. Mendlovitz (ed.), *Legal and Political Problems of World Order*. New York: The Fund for Education Concerning World Peace Through World Law.

———, AND SAUL H. MENDLOVITZ (eds.) (1973) *Regional Politics and World Order*. San Francisco: Freeman.

FEDDER, EDWIN H. (1968) "The Concept of Alliance," *International Studies Quarterly* 12 (March): 65–286.

FEIERABEND, IVO K., ROSALIND L. FEIERABEND, AND TED ROBERT GURR (eds.) (1972) *Anger, Violence, and Politics*. Englewood Cliffs, N.J.: Prentice-Hall.

FELD, WERNER J. (1979) *International Relations: A Transnational Approach*. Sherman Oaks, Calif.: Alfred.

———. (1972) *Nongovernmental Forces and World Politics*. New York: Praeger.

FERRIS, WAYNE H. (1973) *The Power Capabilities of Nation-States*. Lexington, Mass.: Heath.

FINKELSTEIN, LAWRENCE S. (1980) "The IR of IGOs." Paper presented at the Annual Meeting of the International Studies Association, Los Angeles, March 19–22.

———. (1974) "International Organizations and Change," *International Studies Quarterly* 18 (December): 485–520.

FINLAY, DAVID J., AND THOMAS J. HOVET, JR. (1975) *7304: International Relations on the Planet Earth*. New York: Harper & Row.

FINLAYSON, JOCK A., AND MARK W. ZACHER. (1980) "The United Nations and Collective Security: Retrospect and Prospect." Paper presented at the Annual Meeting of the International Studies Association, Los Angeles, March 19–22.

FISHER, ROGER. (1969) *International Conflict for Beginners*. New York: Harper & Row.

FISHLOW, ALBERT, CARLOS F. DÍAZ-ALEJANDRO, RICHARD R. FAGEN, AND ROGER D. HANSEN. (1978) *Rich and Poor Nations in the World Economy*. New York: McGraw-Hill.

FOOD AND AGRICULTURE ORGANIZATION OF THE UNITED NATIONS. (1977) *The Fourth FAO World Food Survey*. Rome: Food and Agriculture Organization of the United Nations.

———. (n.d.) *Billions More to Feed*. Rome: Food and Agriculture Organization of the United Nations.

FOREIGN POLICY ASSOCIATION. (1979) *Great Decisions '78*. New York: Foreign Policy Association.

FRANK, JEROME D. (1967) *Sanity and Survival.* New York: Random House.

FREMLIN, J. H. (1964) "How Many People Can the World Support?," *New Scientist* 24 (October 29): 285–287.

FREUD, SIGMUND. (1968) "Why War," pp. 71–80 in Leon Bramson and George W. Goethals (eds.), *War.* New York: Basic Books.

FRIED, JOHN H. E. (1971) "International Law—Neither Orphan Nor Harlot, Neither Jailer Nor Never-Never Land," pp. 124–176 in Karl W. Deutsch and Stanley Hoffmann (eds.), *The Relevance of International Law.* New York: Doubleday-Anchor.

FRIEDHEIM, ROBERT L. (1965) "The 'Satisfied' and 'Dissatisfied' States Negotiate International Law," *World Politics* 18 (October): 20–41.

FROMKIN, DAVID. (1977) "The Strategy of Terrorism," pp. 128–141 in Steven L. Spiegel (ed.), *At Issue: Politics in the World Arena.* New York: St. Martin's.

GADDIS, JOHN LEWIS. (1972) *The United States and the Origins of the Cold War.* New York: Columbia University Press.

GALL, NORMAN. (1976) "Atoms for Brazil, Dangers for All," *Foreign Policy* 23 (Summer): 155–201.

GALTUNG, JOHAN. (1980) *The True Worlds.* New York: Free Press.

GAMSON, WILLIAM A., AND ANDRE MODIGLIANI. (1971) *Untangling the Cold War.* Boston: Little, Brown.

GARDNER, LLOYD C. (1970) *Architects of Illusion.* Chicago: Quadrangle.

GASTIL, RAYMOND D. (1980) "The Comparative Survey of Freedom–X," *Freedom At Issue* 54 (January–February): 3–15.

——. (1978) "The Comparative Survey of Freedom–VIII," *Freedom at Issue* 44 (January–February): 3–19.

GELB, LESLIE H. (1979) "The Future of Arms Control: A Glass Half Full," *Foreign Policy* 36 (Fall): 21–32.

——. (1976) "What Exactly Is Kissinger's Legacy?" *New York Times Magazine* (October 31): 13–15 et passim.

GEORGE, ALEXANDER L., AND RICHARD SMOKE. (1974) *Deterrence in American Foreign Policy: Theory and Practice.* New York: Columbia University Press.

GILBERT, G. M. (1950) *The Psychology of Dictatorship.* New York: Ronald.

GILPIN, ROBERT. (1975a) "Three Models of the Future," *International Organization* 29 (Winter): 37–60.

——. (1975b) *U.S. Power and the Multinational Corporation.* New York: Basic Books.

The Global 2000 Report to the President. (1980a) Vol. 1: Entering the Twenty-First Century. Washington, D.C.: Government Printing Office.

The Global 2000 Report to the President. (1980b) Vol. II: The Technical Report. Washington, D.C.: Government Printing Office.

GLOVER, EDWARD. (1946) *War, Sadism, and Pacifism*. Cambridge: Allen and Unwin.

GOLDMANN, KJELL. (1973) "East-West Tension in Europe, 1946–1970: A Conceptual Analysis and a Quantitative Description," *World Politics* 26 (October): 106–125.

———, AND JOHAN LAGERKRANZ. (1977) "Neither Tension Nor Détente: East-West Relations in Europe, 1971–1975," *Cooperation and Conflict*, Vol. 12, No. 4: 251–264.

GOODMAN, ALLEN E. (1975) "The Causes and Consequences of Détente, 1949–1973." Paper presented to the National Security Education Seminar, Colorado College, Colorado Springs, Colorado (July).

GORDON, LINCOLN. (1979) *Growth Policies and the International Order*. New York: McGraw-Hill.

GOULD, WESLEY L. (1957) *An Introduction to International Law*. New York: Harper.

GOULDNER, ALVIN WARD. (1960) "The Norm of Reciprocity," *American Sociological Review* 25 (April): 161–178.

GRAHAM, THOMAS R. (1979) "Revolution in Trade Politics," *Foreign Policy* 26 (Fall): 49–63.

GRANT, JAMES P. (1978) *Disparity Reduction Rates in Social Indicators*. Washington, D.C.: Overseas Development Council.

GREEN, PHILIP. (1966) *Deadly Logic: The Theory of Nuclear Deterrence*. Columbus: Ohio State University Press.

GREGG, ROBERT W. (1977) "The Apportioning of Political Power," pp. 69–80 in David A. Kay (ed.), *The Changing United Nations*. Proceedings of The Academy of Political Science, vol. 32, no. 4. New York: The Academy of Political Science.

GRIEVES, FOREST L. (1977) *Conflict and Order*. Boston: Houghton Mifflin.

GROOM, A. J. R., AND C. R. MITCHELL. (1978) *International Relations Theory: A Bibliography*. London: Francis Pinter.

GROTIUS, HUGO. (1625) *De Jure Belli ac Pacis*. Translated by F. W. Kelsy. Reprinted in 1925. Oxford: Carnegie Endowment for International Peace.

GRUHN, ISEBILL V. (1976) "The Lomé Convention: Inching Toward Interdependence," *International Organization* 30 (Spring): 241–262.

GULICK, EDWARD VOSE. (1955) *Europe's Classical Balance of Power*. Ithaca, N.Y.: Cornell University Press.

GURR, TED ROBERT. (1970) *Why Men Rebel*. Princeton: Princeton University Press.

HAAS, ERNST B. (1976) "Turbulent Fields and the Theory of Regional Integration," *International Organization* 30 (Spring): 173–212.

———. (1969a) "Collective Security and the Future International System," pp. 226–316 in Richard A. Falk and Cyril E. Black (eds.), *The Future of the International Legal Order*, Vol. I. Princeton: Princeton University Press.

_____. (1969b) *Tangle of Hopes*. Englewood Cliffs, N.J.: Prentice-Hall.

_____. (1968) *Beyond the Nation State*. Stanford, Calif.: Stanford University Press.

_____. (1962) "Dynamic Environment and Static System," pp. 257–309 in Morton A. Kaplan (ed.), *The Revolution in World Politics*. New York: Wiley.

_____. (1953a) "The Balance of Power: Prescription, Concept, or Propaganda?," *World Politics* 5 (July): 442–477.

_____. (1953b) "The Balance of Power as a Guide to Policy Making," *Journal of Politics* 15 (August): 370–398.

HAAS, MICHAEL. (1970) "International Subsystems: Stability and Polarity," *American Political Science Review* 64 (March): 98–123.

HAMMARSKJÖLD, DAG. (1965) "Introduction to the Annual Report of the Secretary-General on the Work of the Organization, 16 June 1959–15 June 1960," pp. 399–409 in Joel Larus (ed.), *From Collective Security to Preventive Diplomacy*. New York: Wiley.

HANRIEDER, WOLFRAM F. (1978) "Dissolving International Politics: Reflections on the Nation-State," *American Political Science Review* 72 (December): 1276–1287.

HANSEN, ROGER D. (1979) *The North-South Stalemate*. New York: McGraw-Hill.

_____. (1976) *The U.S. and World Development: Agenda for Action 1976*. New York: Praeger.

HARDIN, GARRETT. (1977) "The Tragedy of the Commons," pp. 16–30 in Garrett Hardin and John Baden (eds.), *Managing the Commons*. San Francisco: Freeman.

_____. (1974) "Lifeboat Ethics: The Case Against Helping the Poor," *Psychology Today* 8 (September): 38–43, 123–126.

_____. (1968) "The Tragedy of the Commons," *Science* 162 (December 13): 1243–1248.

_____, AND JOHN BADEN, eds. (1977) *Managing the Commons*. San Francisco: Freeman.

HARF, JAMES E., DAVID G. HOOVLER, AND THOMAS E. JAMES, JR. (1974) "Systemic and External Attributes in Foreign Policy Analysis," pp. 235–250 in James N. Rosenau (ed.), *Comparing Foreign Policies*. New York: Halsted.

HARKAVY, OSCAR. (1975) "A Prescription for International Assistance to Population Programs in the Developing World," pp. 128–134 in William D. Coplin and Charles W. Kegley, Jr. (eds.), *Analyzing International Relations*. New York: Praeger.

HART, JEFFREY A. (1978) "The New International Economic Order Negotiations: From the Sixth Special Session to the End of the North-South Dialogue." Paper presented at the Meeting of the Peace Science Society, Boca Raton, Florida, April 6–7.

HARWOOD, RICHARD. (1979) "Will SALT Impede World's Race Toward Nuclear Death?," as reprinted in *The State* (Columbia, S.C.), June 10, pp. 1 et passim.

HAUPT, ARTHUR, AND THOMAS KANE. (1978) *Population Handbook*. Washington, D.C.: Population Reference Bureau.

HAYES, DENIS. (1977) *Rays of Hope: The Transition to a Post-Petroleum World*. New York: Norton.

HAYTER, TERESA. (1971) *Aid as Imperialism*. Baltimore: Penguin.

HEENAN, DAVID A., AND WARREN J. KEEGAN. (1979) "The Rise of Third World Multinations," *Harvard Business Review* 57 (January–February): 101–109.

HEILBRONER, ROBERT L. (1977) "The Multinational Corporation and the Nation-State," pp. 338–352 in Steven L. Spiegel (ed.), *At Issue: Politics in the World Arena*. New York: St. Martin's.

_____. (1975) *An Inquiry into the Human Prospect*. New York: Norton.

HERMANN, CHARLES F. (1972) "Some Issues in the Study of International Crisis," pp. 3–17 in Charles F. Hermann (ed.), *International Crises*. New York: Free Press.

HERZ, JOHN H. (1976) *The Nation-State and the Crisis of World Politics*. New York: McKay.

HIGGINS, BENJAMIN, AND JEAN DOWNING HIGGINS. (1979) *Economic Development of a Small Planet*. New York: Norton.

HINSLEY, F. H. (1963) *Power and the Pursuit of Peace*. Cambridge: Cambridge University Press.

HIRSCH, FRED. (1976) "Is there a New International Economic Order?," *International Organization* 30 (Summer): 521–531.

HOEBEL, E. ADAMSON. (1961) *The Law of Primitive Man*. Cambridge: Harvard University Press.

HOFFMANN, STANLEY. (1978) *Primacy or World Order*. New York: McGraw-Hill.

_____. (1975) "Notes on the Elusiveness of Modern Power," *International Journal* 30 (Spring): 183–206.

_____. (1971) "International Law and the Control of Force," in Karl W. Deutsch and Stanley Hoffmann (eds.), *The Relevance of International Law*. Garden City, N.Y.: Doubleday-Anchor.

_____. (1968) *Gulliver's Troubles, or the Setting of American Foreign Policy*. New York: McGraw-Hill.

_____. (1961) "International Systems and International Law," pp. 205–237 in Klaus Knorr and Sidney Verba (eds.), *The International System*. Princeton: Princeton University Press.

_____. (1960) *Contemporary Theory in International Politics*. Englewood Cliffs, N.J.: Prentice-Hall.

HOLLIST, W. LADD. (1975) "Reciprocal Exchange in International Transactions." Paper presented at the Annual Meeting of the International Studies Association, Washington, D.C. (February 19–22).

HOLMES, JOHN W. (1977) "A Non-American Perspective," pp. 30–43 in David A. Kay (ed.), *The Changing United Nations*. Proceedings of The Academy of Political Science, Vol. 32, No. 4. New York: The Academy of Political Science.

HOLSTI, K. J. (1977) *International Politics: A Framework for Analysis*. Englewood Cliffs, N.J.: Prentice-Hall.

_____. (1970) "National Role Conception in the Study of Foreign Policy." *International Studies Quarterly* 14 (September): 233–309.

_____. (1966) "Resolving International Conflicts," *Journal of Conflict Resolution* 10 (September): 272–296.

HOLSTI, OLE R. (1979) "Global Food Problems and Soviet Agriculture," pp. 150–175 in David W. Orr and Marvin S. Soroos (eds.), *The Global Predicament: Ecological Perspectives on World Order*. Chapel Hill: University of North Carolina Press.

_____. (1975) "The Belief System and National Images: A Case Study," pp. 22–33 in William D. Coplin and Charles W. Kegley, Jr. (eds.), *Analyzing International Relations*. New York: Praeger.

_____. (1972) *Crisis Escalation War*. Montreal: McGill-Queen's University Press.

_____, AND JAMES N. ROSENAU. (1979) "America's Foreign Policy Agenda: The Post-Vietnam Beliefs of American Leaders," pp. 231–268 in Charles W. Kegley, Jr. and Patrick J. McGowan (eds.), *Challenges to America*. Beverly Hills, Calif.: Sage Publications.

HOLZMAN, FRANKLIN, AND RICHARD PORTES. (1978) "The Limits of Pressure," *Foreign Policy* 32 (Fall): 80–90.

HOOLE, FRANCIS A., AND DINA A. ZINNES (eds.) (1976) *Quantitative International Politics*. New York: Praeger.

HOPKINS, RAYMOND F., AND DONALD J. PUCHALA. (1978) "Perspectives on the International Relations of Food," *International Organization* 32 (Summer): 581–616.

HOPPLE, GERALD W., PAUL J. ROSSA, AND JONATHAN WILKENFELD. (1980) "Threats and Foreign Policy: The Overt Behavior of States in Conflict," pp. 19–53 in Patrick J. McGowan and Charles W. Kegley, Jr. (eds.), *Threats, Weapons, and Foreign Policy*. Beverly Hills, Calif.: Sage Publications.

HOROWITZ, DAVID. (1971) "The Cold War Continues, 1945–1948," pp. 42–74 in Michael Parenti (ed.), *Trends and Tragedies in American Foreign Policy*. Boston: Little, Brown.

HORST, PAUL. (1963) *Matrix Algebra for Social Scientists*. New York: Holt, Rinehart and Winston.

HOWE, JAMES W., AND JOHN W. SEWELL. (1975) "Triage and Other Challenges to Helping the Poor Countries Develop," pp. 55–71 in James W. Howe,

The U.S. and World Development: Agenda for Action 1975. New York: Praeger.

HOWELL, LLEWELLYN D. (1980) "Why the United States *Should* Be Number Two in the International Power Hierarchy." Paper delivered at the Annual Meeting of the International Studies Association, Los Angeles (March 19–22).

HUNTINGTON, SAMUEL P. (1978) "Trade, Technology, and Leverage: Economic Diplomacy," *Foreign Policy* 32 (Fall): 63–80.

——. (1973) "Transnational Organizations in World Politics," *World Politics* 25 (April): 333–368.

INKLE, FRED CHARLES. (1979) *What It Means to Be Number Two.* Washington, D.C.: Ethics and Public Policy Center.

International Economic Report of the President. (1976) Washington, D.C.: Government Printing Office.

——. (1975) Washington, D.C.: Government Printing Office.

JACOBSEN, KURT. (1969) "Sponsorships in the United Nations: A System Analysis," *Journal of Peace Research*, no. 3, pp. 235–256.

JACOBSON, HAROLD K. (1979) *Networks of Interdependence.* New York: Knopf.

JAMES, WILLIAM. (1968) "The Moral Equivalent of War," pp. 21–31 in Leon Bramson and George Goethals (eds.), *War.* New York: Basic Books.

JANIS, IRVING. (1972) *Victims of Groupthink: A Psychological Study of Foreign-Policy Decisions and Fiascoes.* Boston: Houghton Mifflin.

JENKINS, BRIAN M. (1978) "International Terrorism: Trends and Potentialities," *Journal of International Affairs* 32 (Spring/Summer): 115–124.

JERVIS, ROBERT. (1976) *Perception and Misperception in International Politics.* Princeton: Princeton University Press.

——. (1969) "Hypotheses on Misperception," pp. 239–254 in James N. Rosenau (ed.), *International Politics and Foreign Policy.* New York: Free Press.

JOHANSEN, ROBERT C. (1980) *The National Interest and the Human Interest.* Princeton: Princeton University Press.

——. (1978) *Toward a Dependable Peace: A Proposal for an Appropriate Security System.* New York: Institute for World Order.

JONES, JOSEPH MARION. (1964) *The Fifteen Weeks.* New York: Harcourt Brace and World.

JORDAN, ROBERT C. (1980) *The Role of Actors in Global Issues.* Columbia, S.C.: Consortium for International Studies Education, International Studies Association.

JUNN, ROBERT S. (1980) "Voting in the United Nations Security Council." Paper presented at the Annual Meeting of the International Studies Association, Los Angeles (March 19–22).

KAHN, HERMAN. (1976) *The Next 200 Years.* New York: Morrow.

———. (1965) *On Escalation: Metaphors and Scenarios.* Baltimore: Penguin.

———. (1960) *On Thermonuclear War.* Princeton: Princeton University Press.

KAPLAN, MORTON A. (1975) "Models of International Systems," pp. 257–269 in William D. Coplin and Charles W. Kegley, Jr. (eds.), *Analyzing International Relations.* New York: Praeger.

———. (1957) *Systems and Process in International Politics.* New York: Wiley.

———, AND NICHOLAS DeB. KATZENBACH. (1961) *The Political Foundations of International Law.* New York: Wiley.

———. (ed.) (1968) *New Approaches to International Relations.* New York: St. Martin's.

KATZENSTEIN, PETER J. (1975) "International Interdependence: Some Long-term Trends and Recent Changes," *International Organization* 29 (Autumn): 1021–1034.

KAY, DAVID A. (1970a) "Instruments of Influence in the United Nations Political Process," pp. 92–107 in David A. Kay (ed.), *The United Nations Political System.* New York: Wiley.

———. *The New Nations in the United Nations, 1960–1967.* New York: Columbia University Press.

KEGLEY, CHARLES W., JR. (1980) "Measuring Transformation in the Global Legal System," in Nicholas G. Onuf (ed.), *Law-making in the Global Community.* Durham: North Carolina Academic Press.

———. (1975) "Measuring the Growth and Decay of Transnational Norms Relevant to the Control of Violence: A Prospectus for Research," *Denver Journal of International Law and Policy* 5 (Fall): 425–439.

———, NEIL R. RICHARDSON, AND ANN C. AGNEW. (1981) "Symmetry and Reciprocity as Characteristics of Dyadic Foreign Policy Behavior," *Social Science Quarterly* 62 (March): forthcoming.

———, GREGORY A. RAYMOND, AND RICHARD A. SKINNER. (1980) "A Comparative Analysis of Nuclear Armament," pp. 231–255 in Patrick J. McGowan and Charles W. Kegley, Jr. (eds.), *Threats, Weapons, and Foreign Policy.* Beverly Hills, Calif.: Sage Publications.

———, AND PATRICK J. McGOWAN. (1979) "Environmental Change and the Future of American Foreign Policy," pp. 13–33 in Charles W. Kegley, Jr., and Patrick J. McGowan (eds.), *Challenges to America.* Beverly Hills, Calif.: Sage Publications.

———, AND EUGENE R. WITTKOPF. (1979) *American Foreign Policy: Pattern and Process.* New York: St. Martin's.

———, NEIL R. RICHARDSON, AND GUNTER RICHTER. (1978) "Conflict at Home and Abroad: An Empirical Extension," *Journal of Politics* 40 (August): 742–752.

———, AND LLEWELLYN D. HOWELL. (1975) "The Dimensionality of Regional Integration: Construct Validation in the Southeast Asian Context," *International Organization* 29 (Autumn): 997–1020.

KELMAN, HERBERT C. (1973) "Violence Without Moral Restraint," *Journal of Social Issues* 29 (4): 25–61.

____. (1970) "The Role of the Individual in International Relations," *Journal of International Affairs* 24 (1): 1–17.

KELSEN, HANS. (1968) *Principles of International Law.* New York: Holt, Rinehart and Winston.

____. (1945) *General Theory of Law and State.* Translated by A. Weldberg. Cambridge: Harvard University Press.

KENDE, ISTVAN. (1978) "Wars of Ten Years (1967–1976)," *Journal of Peace Research* 15 (3): 227–241.

____. (1971) "Twenty-Five Years of Local Wars," *Journal of Peace Research* 8 (1): 5–22.

KENNAN, GEORGE F. (1976) "The United States and the Soviet Union, 1917–1976," *Foreign Affairs* 54 (July): 670–690.

____. (1967) *Memoirs.* Boston: Little, Brown.

____. (1961) *Russia and the West under Lenin and Stalin.* Boston: Little, Brown.

____. (1956) "Overdue Changes in Our Foreign Policy," *Harper's* 213 (August): 27–33.

____. (1954) *Realities of American Foreign Policy.* Princeton: Princeton University Press.

____. (1951) *American Diplomacy, 1900–1950.* New York: Mentor.

____. ("X") (1947) "The Sources of Soviet Conduct," *Foreign Affairs* 25 (July): 566–582.

KENNEDY, EDWARD M. (1977) "The Empty Pork Barrel: Unemployment and the Pentagon Budget," news release, February 13.

KEOHANE, ROBERT O. (1978) "Review of *The Functional Theory of Politics* by David Mitrany," *American Political Science Review* 72 (June): 805–806.

____. (1969) "Who Cares About the General Assembly?," *International Organization* 23 (Winter): 141–149.

____. (1966) "Political Influence in the General Assembly," *International Conciliation* No. 557 (March): 1–64.

____, AND JOSEPH S. NYE. (1977) *Power and Interdependence.* Boston: Little, Brown.

____. (1975) "International Interdependence and Integration," pp. 363–414 in Fred I. Greenstein and Nelson W. Polsby (eds.), *International Politics: Handbook of Political Science,* Vol. 8. Reading, Mass.: Addison-Wesley.

____. (1973) "World Politics and the International Economic System," pp. 115–180 in C. Fred Bergsten (ed.), *The Future of the International Economic Order.* Lexington, Mass.: Heath.

____ (eds.) (1971) "Transnational Relations and World Politics," *International Organization* 25 (Summer): 329–358.

KIM, SAMUEL S. (1979) *China, the United Nations, and World Order.* Princeton: Princeton University Press.

KINDLEBERGER, CHARLES P. (1977a) *America in the World Economy.* Headline Series 237, October. New York: Foreign Policy Association.

————. (1977b) "U.S. Foreign Economic Policy, 1976–1977," *Foreign Affairs* 55 (January): 395–417.

————. (1969) *American Business Abroad.* New Haven: Yale University Press.

KISER, JOHN W. (1978) "What Gap? Which Gap?," *Foreign Policy* 32 (Fall): 90–94.

KISSINGER, HENRY A. (1979) *White House Years.* Boston: Little, Brown.

————. (1977) *American Foreign Policy.* New York: Norton.

————. (1974) "Statement of U.S.-Soviet Relations," News Release of the Bureau of Public Affairs, Department of State Special Report (September 19).

————..(1973) "Secretary Kissinger at *Pacim in Terris,*" News Release of the Bureau of Public Affairs, Department of State (October 10).

————. (1964) *A World Restored.* New York: Grosset & Dunlap.

————. (1957) *Nuclear Weapons and Foreign Policy.* New York: Harper.

KLINGBERG, FRANK L. (1979) "Cyclical Trends in American Foreign Policy Moods and Their Policy Implications," pp. 37–55 in Charles W. Kegley, Jr., and Patrick J. McGowan (eds.), *Challenges to America.* Beverly Hills, Calif.: Sage Publications.

————. (1970) "Historical Periods, Trends, and Cycles in International Relations," *Journal of Conflict Resolution* 14 (December): 505–512.

KLITGAARD, ROBERT E. (1978) "Sending Signals," *Foreign Policy* 32 (Fall): 103–106.

KLUCKHOHN, CLYDE. (1944) "Anthropological Research and World Peace," pp. 143–152 in L. Bryson, Laurence Finkelstein, and Robert M. MacIver (eds.), *Approaches to World Peace.* New York: Conference on Science, Philosophy, and Religion.

KNORR, KLAUS. (1976) "The Limits of Economic and Military Power," pp. 229–243 in Raymond Vernon (ed.), *The Oil Crisis.* New York: Norton.

————. (1973) *Power and Wealth.* New York: Basic Books.

————, AND FRANK TRAGER (eds.) (1977) *Economic Issues and National Security.* Lawrence: Regents Press of Kansas.

————, AND JAMES N. ROSENAU (eds.) (1969) *Contending Approaches to International Politics.* Princeton: Princeton University Press.

————, AND SIDNEY VERBA (eds.) (1961) *The International System.* Princeton: Princeton University Press.

KOLKO, JOYCE, AND GABRIEL KOLKO. (1972) *The Limits of Power.* New York: Harper & Row.

KORBONSKI, ANDRZEJ. (1973) "Theory and Practice of Regional Integration: The Case of Comecon," pp. 152–175 in Richard A. Falk and Saul H.

Mendlovitz (eds.), *Regional Politics and World Order.* San Francisco: Freeman.

KRASNER, STEPHEN D. (1979) "The Tokyo Round: Particularistic Interests and Prospects for Stability in the Global Trading System," *International Studies Quarterly* 23 (December): 491–531.

———. (1978) *Defending the National Interest.* Princeton: Princeton University Press.

———. (1976) "State Power and the Structure of International Trade," *World Politics* 28 (April): 317–347.

———. (1974) "Oil is the Exception," *Foreign Policy* 14 (Spring): 68–84.

KUHLMAN, JAMES A. (1976) "Eastern Europe," pp. 444–465 in James N. Rosenau, Kenneth W. Thompson, and Gavin Boyd (eds.), *World Politics.* New York: Free Press.

KUHN, THOMAS S. (1970) *The Structure of Scientific Revolutions.* Chicago: University of Chicago Press.

LaBARR, D. F., AND J. DAVID SINGER (eds.) (1976) *The Study of International Politics.* Santa Barbara, Calif.: Clio Press.

LANDSBERG, HANS H. ET AL. (1979) *Energy: The Next Twenty Years.* Cambridge, Mass.: Ballinger Publishing.

LANGER, WILLIAM L. (1962) "Farewell to Empire," *Foreign Affairs* 41 (October): 115–130.

LASSWELL, HAROLD D., AND MYRES S. McDOUGAL. (1966–1967) "Jurisprudence in Policy-Oriented Perspective," *University of Florida Law Journal* 19 (Winter): 486–513.

LEGG, KEITH R., AND JAMES F. MORRISON. (1971) *Politics and the International System: An Introduction.* New York: Harper & Row.

LENCZOWSKI, GEORGE. (1976) "The Oil-Producing Countries," pp. 59–72 in Raymond Vernon (ed.), *The Oil Crisis.* New York: Norton.

LEONTIEF, WASSILY ET AL. (1977) *The Future of the World Economy.* New York: Oxford University Press.

LERCHE, CHARLES O., JR., AND ABDUL A. SAID. (1979) *Concepts of International Politics.* Englewood Cliffs, N.J.: Prentice-Hall.

LEVINSON, DANIEL J. (1964) "Idea Systems in the Individual and in Society," pp. 297–318 in George K. Zollschan and Walter Hirsch (eds.), *Explorations in Social Change.* Boston: Houghton Mifflin.

LEVY, WALTER J. (1978–1979) "The Years that the Locust Hath Eaten: Oil Policy and OPEC Development Prospects," *Foreign Affairs* 57 (Winter): 287–305.

LEVI, WERNER. (1974a) "International Law in a Multicultural World," *International Studies Quarterly* 18 (December): 417–450.

———. (1974b) *International Politics.* Minneapolis: University of Minnesota Press.

LEWIS, W. ARTHUR. (1978) *The Evolution of the International Economic Order.* Princeton: Princeton University Press.

LEWIS, KEVIN N. (1979) "The Prompt and Delayed Effects of Nuclear War," *Scientific American* 241 (July): 35–47.

LIEBERMAN, SEYMOUR. (1965) "The Effects of Changes in Roles on the Attitudes of Role Occupants," pp. 155–168 in J. David Singer (ed.), *Human Behavior and International Politics.* Chicago: Rand McNally.

LIJPHART, AREND. (1974) "The Structure of the Theoretical Revolution in International Relations," *International Studies Quarterly* 18 (March): 42–49.

LILLICH, RICHARD B. (1972) "Domestic Institutions," pp. 384–424 in Cyril E. Black and Richard A. Falk (eds.), *The Future of the International Legal Order.* Princeton: Princeton University Press.

LINDBERG, LEON N., AND STUART A. SCHEINGOLD (eds.) (1971) *Regional Integration.* Cambridge: Harvard University Press.

LISKA, GEORGE. (1968) *Alliances and the Third World.* Baltimore: Johns Hopkins Press.

_____. (1957) *International Equilibrium.* Cambridge: Harvard University Press.

LISSITZYN, OLIVER J. (1963) "International Law in a Divided World," *International Conciliation*, No. 542 (March): 3–69.

LITTLE, RICHARD. (1975) *Intervention: External Involvement in Civil Wars.* Totowa, N.J.: Rowman and Littlefield.

LORENZ, KONRAD. (1963) *On Aggression.* New York: Harcourt Brace and World.

LOVELL, JOHN P. (1970) *Foreign Policy in Perspective.* New York: Holt, Rinehart and Winston.

LUARD, EVAN. (1976) *Types of International Society.* New York: Free Press.

_____. (1968) *Conflict and Peace in the Modern International System.* Boston: Little, Brown.

MAHONEY, ROBERT B., JR., AND RICHARD P. CLAYBERG. (1980) "Images and Threats: Soviet Perceptions of International Crises, 1946–1975," pp. 55–81 in Patrick J. McGowan and Charles W. Kegley, Jr. (eds.), *Threats, Weapons, and Foreign Policy.* Beverly Hills, Calif.: Sage Publications.

MALINOWSKI, BRONISLAW. (1969) "The Principle of Give and Take," pp. 73–76 in Louis A. Coser and B. Rosenberg (eds.), *Sociological Theory.* New York: Macmillan.

MANSBACH, RICHARD W., YALE H. FERGUSON, AND DONAL E. LAMPERT. (1976) *The Web of World Politics.* Englewood Cliffs, N.J.: Prentice-Hall.

MASTERS, ROGER D. (1969) "World Politics as a Primitive Political System," pp. 104–118 in James N. Rosenau (ed.), *International Politics and Foreign Policy.* New York: Free Press.

McCLELLAND, CHARLES A. (1972) "The Beginning, Duration, and Abatement of International Crises," pp. 83–108 in Charles F. Hermann (ed.), *International Crises.* New York: Free Press.

_____. (1966) *Theory and the International System.* New York: Macmillan.

McCLOSKY, HERBERT. (1967) "Personality and Attitude Correlates of Foreign Policy Orientation," pp. 51–109 in James N. Rosenau (ed.), *Domestic Sources of Foreign Policy.* New York: Free Press.

McCULLOCH, RACHEL, AND JOSÉ PIÑERA. (1979) "Alternative Commodity Trade Regimes," pp. 105–167 in Ruth W. Arad et al., *Sharing Global Resources.* New York: McGraw-Hill.

McDOUGAL, MYRES S., AND HAROLD D. LASSWELL. (1959) "The Identification and Appraisal of Diverse Systems of Public Order," *American Journal of International Law* 53 (January): 1–29.

McGOWAN, PATRICK J., AND CHARLES W. KEGLEY, JR. (eds.) (1980) *Threats, Weapons, and Foreign Policy.* Beverly Hills, Calif.: Sage Publications.

McLAUGHLIN, MARTIN M. (1979a) *The United States and World Development: Agenda 1979.* New York: Praeger.

——. (1979b) "The United States in the North-South Dialogue: A Survey," pp. 77–113 in Martin M. McLaughlin, *The United States and World Development: Agenda 1979.* New York: Praeger.

McNAMARA, ROBERT S. (1977) "Population and International Security," *International Security* 2 (Fall): 25–55.

McNEIL, ELTON B. (1965) "The Future of Human Conflict," pp. 309–315 in Elton B. McNeil (ed.), *The Nature of Human Conflict.* Englewood Cliffs, N.J.: Prentice-Hall.

MEAD, MARGARET. (1968) "Warfare is Only an Invention—Not a Biological Necessity," pp. 270–274 in Leon Bramson and George W. Goethals (eds.), *War.* New York: Basic Books.

MEADOWS, DONELLA H., DENNIS L. MEADOWS, JØRGEN RANDERS, AND WILLIAM W. BEHRENS III. (1974) *The Limits to Growth.* New York: New American Library.

MICKOLAS, EDWARD F. (1976) "Negotiating for Hostages," *Orbis* 19 (Winter): 1309–1325.

MILBURN, THOMAS W. (1972) "The Management of Crisis," pp. 259–280 in Charles F. Hermann (ed.), *International Crises.* New York: Free Press.

Mining and Minerals Policy, 1979. (1979) Annual Report of the Secretary of the Interior Under the Mining and Minerals Policy Act of 1970. Washington, D.C.: Government Printing Office.

MITRANY, DAVID. (1975) *The Functional Theory of Politics.* New York: St. Martin's.

——. (1966) *A Working Peace System.* Chicago: Quadrangle.

MODELSKI, GEORGE. (1981) "The Theory of Long Cycles and U.S. International Economic Policy," forthcoming in Charles W. Kegley, Jr., and Patrick J. McGowan (eds.), *The Political Economy of Foreign Policy Behavior.* Beverly Hills, Calif.: Sage Publications.

—— (ed.) (1979) *Transnational Corporations and World Order.* San Francisco: Freeman.

——. (1978) "The Long Cycle of Global Politics and the Nation-State," *Comparative Studies in Society and History* 20 (April): 214–235.

MORAN, THEODORE H. (1975) *Multinational Corporations and the Politics of Dependence.* Princeton: Princeton University Press.

MORAWETZ, DAVID. (1977) *Twenty-five Years of Economic Development, 1950 to 1975.* Washington, D.C.: The World Bank.

MORGAN, DAN. (1979) *Merchants of Grain.* New York: Viking.

MORGAN, PATRICK M. (1975) *Theories and Approaches to International Politics.* New Brunswick, N.J.: Transaction Books.

MORGENTHAU, HANS J. (1973) *Politics Among Nations.* New York: Knopf.

_____. (1969) "Historical Justice and the Cold War," *New York Review of Books* 13 (July 10): 10–17.

_____. (1967) *Politics Among Nations.* New York: Knopf.

_____. (1948) *Politics Among Nations.* New York: Knopf.

MORRIS, DESMOND. (1969) *The Human Zoo.* New York: Dell.

MORSE, EDWARD L. (1976) *Modernization and the Transformation of International Relations.* New York: Free Press.

MOUNTAIN, MAURICE J. (1978) "Technology Exports and National Security," *Foreign Policy* 32 (Fall): 95–103.

MOYNIHAN, DANIEL P. (1975) "The United States in Opposition," *Commentary* 59 (March): 31–44.

_____, WITH SUZANNE WEAVER. (1978) *A Dangerous Place.* Boston: Little, Brown.

MÜLLER, RONALD. (1973–1974) "Poverty is the Product," *Foreign Policy* 13 (Winter): 71–103.

MYRDAL, GUNNAR. (1955) *Realities and Illusions in Regard to Inter-Governmental Organizations.* London: Oxford University Press.

NAGEL, STUART S. (1969) *The Legal Process from a Behavioral Perspective.* Homewood, Ill.: Dorsey Press.

NEF, JOHN U. (1968) *War and Human Progress.* New York: Norton.

NELSON, STEPHAN D. (1974) "Nature/Nurture Revisited," *International Studies Quarterly* 18 (June): 285–335.

NIEBUHR, REINHOLD. (1947) *Moral Man and Immoral Society.* New York: Scribners.

NIXON, RICHARD M. (1980) *The Real War.* New York: Warner Books.

NOGEE, JOSEPH L. (1975) "Polarity: An Ambiguous Concept," *Orbis* 28 (Winter): 1193–1224.

NORMAN, COLIN. (1979) *Knowledge and Power: The Global Research and Development Budget.* Worldwatch Paper 31, July. Washington, D.C.: Worldwatch Institute.

NORTH, ROBERT C. (1976) *The World that Could Be.* New York: Norton.

_____, OLE R. HOLSTI, M. GEORGE ZANINOVICH, AND DINA A. ZINNES. (1963) *Content Analysis.* Evanston, Ill.: Northwestern University Press.

NORTHRUP, F. S. C. (1952) *The Taming of Nations.* New York: Macmillan.

Novak, Jeremiah. (1979) "The Geopolitics of the Dollar," *Worldview* 22 (May): 23–26, 35–36.

Nove, Alec. (1978) *East-West Trade: Problems, Prospects, Issues.* The Washington Papers, vol. 6, no. 53. Beverly Hills, Calif.: Sage Publications.

Nussbaum, Arthur. (1961) *A Concise History of the Law of Nations.* New York: Macmillan.

Nye, Joseph S., Jr. (1979) "We Tried Harder (and Did More)," *Foreign Policy* 36 (Fall): 101–104.

____. (1974) "Multinational Corporations in World Politics," *Foreign Affairs* 53 (October): 153–175.

____. (1971) *Peace in Parts.* Boston: Little, Brown.

____ (ed.) (1968) *International Regionalism.* Boston: Little, Brown.

____. (1967) "Central American Regional Integration," *International Conciliation* 562 (March).

____, and Robert O. Keohane. (1971) "Transnational Relations and World Politics: An Introduction," *International Organization* 25 (Summer): 329–349.

Olsen, Mancur. (1971) "Rapid Growth as a Destabilizing Force," pp. 215–227 in James C. Davies (ed.), *When Men Revolt and Why.* New York: Free Press.

Onuf, Nicholas G. (1980) *Law-Making in the Global Community.* Durham: Carolina Academic Press.

Ophuls, William. (1977) *Ecology and the Politics of Scarcity.* San Francisco: Freeman.

Organski, A. F. K. (1968) *World Politics.* New York: Knopf.

Orr, David, and Marvin S. Soroos (eds.) (1979) *The Global Predicament: Ecological Perspectives on World Order.* Chapel Hill: University of North Carolina Press.

Osgood, Robert E. (1968) *Alliances and American Foreign Policy.* Baltimore: Johns Hopkins Press.

Paddock, William, and Paul Paddock. (1967) *Famine—1975.* Boston: Little, Brown.

Parenti, Michael. (1980) *Democracy for the Few.* New York: St. Martin's.

____. (1969) *The Anti-Communist Impulse.* New York: Random House.

Parry, Clive. (1968) "The Function of Law in the International Community," pp. 1–54 in Max Sorensen (ed.), *Manual of Public International Law.* New York: St. Martin's.

Pastusiak, Longin. (1978) "Objective and Subjective Premises of Détente," *Polish Round Table* 8: 53–72.

Paterson, Thomas G. (1979) *On Every Front: The Making of the Cold War.* New York: Norton.

Paynton, C., and R. Blackey (eds.) (1971) *Why Revolution?* Cambridge, Mass.: Schenkman.

PELEG, ILAN. (1980) "Military Production in Third World Countries," pp. 209–230 in Patrick J. McGowan, and Charles W. Kegley, Jr. (eds.), *Threats, Weapons, and Foreign Policy*. Beverly Hills, Calif.: Sage Publications.

PENROSE, EDITH. (1976) "The Development of Crisis," pp. 39–57 in Raymond Vernon (ed.), *The Oil Crisis*. New York: Norton.

PENTLAND, CHARLES. (1976) "International Organizations," pp. 624–659 in James N. Rosenau, Kenneth W. Thompson, and Gavin Boyd (eds.), *World Politics*. New York: Free Press.

PIERRE, ANDREW J. (1976) "The Politics of International Terrorism," *Orbis* 19 (Winter): 1251–1269.

PIRAGES, DENNIS. (1978) *The New Context for International Relations: Global Ecopolitics*. North Scituate, Mass.: Duxbury.

PLANO, JACK C., AND ROBERT E. RIGGS. (1967) *Forging World Order*. New York: Macmillan.

PLISCHKE, ELMER. (1978) "Microstates: Lilliputs in World Affairs," *The Futurist* 12 (February): 19–25.

POPPER, KARL R. (1957) *The Poverty of Historicism*. Boston: Beacon.

POPULATION REFERENCE BUREAU. (1976) *World Population Growth and Response, 1965–1975*. Washington, D.C.: Population Reference Bureau.

PORTES, RICHARD. (1978) "East, West, and South: The Role of the Centrally Planned Economies in the International Economy." Discussion Paper Number 630, Harvard Institute of Economic Research, Harvard University (June).

———. (1977) "East Europe's Debt to the West: Interdependence is a Two-Way Street," *Foreign Affairs* 55 (July): 751–782.

PREBISCH, RAÚL. (1964) *Towards a New Trade Policy for Development*. New York: United Nations.

PREEG, ERNEST H. (1976) "Economic Blocs and U.S. Foreign Policy," pp. 271–283 in William C. Vocke (ed.), *American Foreign Policy*. New York: Free Press.

PRUITT, DEAN G. (1965) "Definition of the Situation as a Determinant of International Action," pp. 393–432 in Herbert C. Kelman (ed.), *International Behavior*. New York: Holt, Rinehart and Winston.

———, AND RICHARD C. SNYDER (eds.) (1969) *Theory and Research on the Causes of War*. Englewood Cliffs, N.J.: Prentice-Hall.

PUCHALA, DONALD J. (1973) *International Politics Today*. New York: Dodd, Mead.

QUESTER, GEORGE H. (1971a) *Nuclear Diplomacy*. New York: Dunellen.

——— (ed.) (1971b) *Power, Action, and Interaction*. Boston: Little, Brown.

RAPOPORT, ANATOL. (1964) *Strategy and Conscience*. New York: Schocken Books.

———. (1960) *Fights, Games and Debates*. New York: Basic Books.

RAYMOND, GREGORY A. (1980) *Conflict Resolution and the Structure of the State System: An Analysis of Arbitrative Settlements.* Montclair, N.J.: Allanheld, Osmun and Co.

____. (1978) *Arbitration, Military Capability, and Major Power War, 1815–1914: A Systems Approach to Evaluation Research.* Carlisle Barracks, Pa.: U.S. Army War College.

____. (1977) "The Transnational Rules Indicator Project: An Interim Report," *International Studies Notes* 4 (Spring): 12–16.

RICHARDSON, LEWIS F. (1960a) *Arms and Insecurity.* Pittsburgh: Boxwood Press.

____. (1960b) *Statistics of Deadly Quarrels.* Chicago: Quadrangle.

RIENOW, ROBERT, AND LEANA RIENOW. (1967) *Moment in the Sun.* New York: Dial.

RIGGS, ROBERT E. (1978) "The United States and the Diffusion of Power in the Security Council," *International Studies Quarterly* 22 (December): 513–544.

____. (1977) "One Small Step for Functionalism: UN Participation and Congressional Attitude Change," *International Organization* 31 (Summer): 515–539.

RIKER, WILLIAM H. (1962) *The Theory of Political Coalitions.* New Haven: Yale University Press.

ROHN, PETER H. (1976) *Treaty Profiles.* Santa Barbara, Calif.: Clio Books.

____. (1974) *World Treaty Index.* 5 vol. Santa Barbara, Calif.: American Bibliographical Center-Clio Press.

____. (1970) *Institutions in Treaties.* Syracuse, N.Y.: The Maxwell School of Syracuse University.

____. (1968) "The United Nations Treaty Series Project," *International Studies Quarterly* 12 (September): 174–195.

ROKEACH, MILTON. (1960) *The Open and Closed Mind.* New York: Basic Books.

ROSECRANCE, RICHARD N. (1966) "Bipolarity, Multipolarity, and the Future," *Journal of Conflict Resolution* 10 (September): 314–327.

____. (1963) *Action and Reaction in World Politics.* Boston: Little, Brown.

____, A. ALEXANDROFF, W. KOEHLER, J. KROLL, S. LAQUEUR, AND J. STOCKER. (1977) "Whither Interdependence?," *International Organization* 31 (Summer): 425–471.

____, AND ARTHUR STEIN. (1973) "Interdependence: Myth or Reality?," *World Politics* 24 (October): 1–27.

ROSEN, STEVEN J. (ed.) (1973) *Testing the Theory of the Military-Industrial Complex.* Lexington, Mass.: Heath.

ROSEN, STEVEN J., AND WALTER S. JONES. (1980) *The Logic of International Relations.* Cambridge, Mass.: Winthrop.

ROSENAU, JAMES N. (1980) *The Scientific Study of Foreign Policy.* New York: Nichols.

_____. (1971) *The Scientific Study of Foreign Policy.* New York: Free Press.

_____ (ed.) (1969) *International Politics and Foreign Policy.* New York: Free Press.

_____. (1966) "Pre-Theories and Theories of Foreign Policy," pp. 27–92 in R. Barry Farrell (ed.), *Approaches of Comparative and International Politics.* Evanston, Ill.: Northwestern University Press.

ROSTOW, EUGENE V. (1968) *Law, Power, and the Pursuit of Peace.* New York: Harper & Row.

ROTHSCHILD, EMMA. (1980) "Boom and Bust," *The New York Review of Books* 27 (April 3): 31–34.

ROTHSTEIN, ROBERT L. (1979) *Global Bargaining: UNCTAD and the Quest for a New International Economic Order.* Princeton: Princeton University Press.

ROWE, EDWARD T. (1974a) "Aid and Coups d'État," *International Studies Quarterly* 18 (June): 239–255.

_____. (1974b) *Strengthening the United Nations: A Study of the Evolution of Member State Commitments.* Sage Professional Papers in International Studies, Vol. 3, Series no. 02–031. Beverly Hills, Calif.: Sage Publications.

_____. (1969) "Changing Patterns in the Voting Success of Member States in the United Nations General Assembly: 1945–1966," *International Organization* 23 (Spring): 231–253.

RUMMEL, RUDOLPH J. (1963) "Dimensions of Conflict Behavior Within and Between Nations," *General Systems Yearbook* 8: 1–50.

RUSSELL, FRANK M. (1936) *Theories of International Relations.* New York: Appleton-Century-Crofts.

RUSSETT, BRUCE M. (1978) "The Marginal Utility of Income Transfers to the Third World," *International Organization* 32 (Autumn): 913–928.

_____. (1969) "The Ecology of Future International Politics," pp. 93–103 in James N. Rosenau (ed.), *International Politics and Foreign Policy.* New York: Free Press.

_____. (1967) *International Regions and the International System.* Chicago: Rand McNally.

_____. (1965) *Trends in World Politics.* New York: Macmillan.

SAMPSON, ANTHONY. (1978) "Want to Start a War?," *Esquire* (March 1): 59–62 et passim.

_____. (1973) *The Sovereign State of ITT.* New York: Stein & Day.

SAMUELS, NATHANIEL. (1970) "American Business and International Investment Flows," *Department of State Bulletin* 62 (January 12): 33–38.

SCHECHTER, MICHAEL G. (1979) "The Common Fund: A Test Case for the New International Economic Order." Paper presented at the Annual Conference of the International Studies Association/South, Athens, Georgia, October 4–6.

SCHELLING, THOMAS C. (1978) *Micromotives and Macrobehavior.* New York: Norton.

_____. (1966) *Arms and Influence.* New Haven: Yale University Press.

_____. (1960) *The Strategy of Conflict.* Cambridge: Harvard University Press.

SCHERTZ, LYLE. (1977) "World Needs: Shall the Hungry Be with Us Always?," pp. 13–35 in Peter G. Brown, and Henry Shue (eds.), *Food Policy.* New York: Free Press.

SCHLESINGER, ARTHUR M., JR. (1967) "Origins of the Cold War," *Foreign Affairs* 46 (October): 22–52.

SCHMITTER, PHILIPPE C. (1969) "Three Neo-Functional Hypotheses About International Integration," *International Organization* 23 (Winter): 161–166.

SCHNEIDER, BARRY R. (1972) "Escalation and Crisis Concepts," Mimeo., Department of Political Science, Wabash College.

SCHNEIDER, WILLIAM. (1976) *Food, Foreign Policy, and Raw Materials Cartels.* New York: Crane, Russak.

SCHUMACHER, E. F. (1973) *Small is Beautiful.* New York: Harper & Row.

SCOLNICK, JOSEPH M., JR. (1974) "An Appraisal of Studies of the Linkage Between Domestic and Internal Conflict," *Comparative Political Studies* 6 (January): 485–509.

SCOTT, ANDREW M. (1979) "Science and Surprise: The Role of the Inadvertent in International Affairs." Paper presented at the Annual Meeting of the International Studies Association/South, Athens, Georgia, October 4–6.

SEEVERS, GARY L. (1978) "Food Markets and Their Regulation," *International Organization* 32 (Summer): 721–743.

SEWELL, JOHN W. (1980) *The United States and World Development: Agenda 1980.* New York: Praeger.

_____. (1979) "Can the North Prosper Without Growth and Progress in the South?," pp. 45–76 in Martin M. McLaughlin, *The United States and World Development: Agenda 1979.* New York: Praeger.

_____. (1977) *The United States and World Development: Agenda 1977.* New York: Praeger.

SHERRY, MICHAEL. (1977) *Preparing for the Next War.* New Haven: Yale University Press.

SHONFIELD, ANDREW. (1980) "The World Economy 1979," *Foreign Affairs.* Special issue *America and the World 1979.* Vol. 58, No. 3: 596–621.

SIBLEY, MULFORD Q. (1963) "Unilateral Disarmament," pp. 112–140 in Robert A. Goldwin (ed.), *America Armed.* Chicago: Rand McNally.

SIMON, HERBERT A. (1957) *Administrative Behavior.* New York: Macmillan.

SIMPSON, SMITH. (1967) *Anatomy of the State Department.* Boston: Houghton Mifflin.

SINGER, HANS W., AND JAVED A. ANSARI. (1977) *Rich and Poor Countries.* Baltimore: Johns Hopkins Press.

SINGER, J. DAVID. (1963) "Inter-Nation Influence: A Formal Model," *American Political Science Review* 57 (June): 420–430.

———. (1961) "The Level-of-Analysis Problem in International Relations," pp. 77–92 in Klaus Knorr and Sidney Verba (eds.), *The International System.* Princeton: Princeton University Press.

———. (1960) "Theorizing About Theory in International Politics," *Journal of Conflict Resolution* 4 (December): 431–442.

SINGER, J. DAVID (ed.) (1968) *Quantitative International Politics.* New York: Free Press.

———. (ed.) (1965) *Human Behavior and International Politics.* Chicago: Rand McNally.

SINGER, J. DAVID, AND MELVIN SMALL (eds.) (1979) *The Correlates of War: I.* New York: Free Press.

———. (1975) "War in History and in the State of the World Message," pp. 220–248 in William D. Coplin and Charles W. Kegley, Jr. (eds.), *Analyzing International Relations.* New York: Praeger.

———. (1972) *The Wages of War, 1816–1965: A Statistical Handbook.* New York: Wiley.

———. (1969) "National Alliance Commitments and War Involvement, 1815–1945," pp. 513–542 in James N. Rosenau (ed.), *International Politics and Foreign Policy.* New York: Free Press.

———. (1968) "Alliance Aggregation and the Onset of War, 1815–1945," pp. 247–285 in J. David Singer (ed.), *Quantitative International Politics.* New York: Free Press.

SINGER, J. DAVID, AND MICHAEL WALLACE. (1970) "Intergovernmental Organization and the Preservation of Peace, 1916–1964: Some Bivariate Relationships," *International Organization* 24 (Summer): 520–547.

SIVARD, RUTH LEGER. (1979a) *World Energy Survey.* Leesburg, Va.: World Priorities.

———. (1979b) *World Military and Social Expenditures 1979.* Leesburg, Va.: World Priorities.

———. (1977a) *World Military and Social Expenditures 1977.* Leesburg, Va.: WMSE Publications.

———. (1977b) *Military Budgets and Social Needs: Setting World Priorities.* Public Affairs Committee, Public Affairs Pamphlet No. 551 (October).

———. (1976) *World Military and Social Expenditures 1976.* Leesburg, Va.: WMSE Publications.

SIVERSON, RANDOLPH M. (1979) "War and Change in the International System." Paper presented to the Annual Meeting of the International Studies Association/West, Portland, Oregon, March 22–24.

SKJELSBAEK, KJELL. (1971) "The Growth of International Nongovernmental Organization in the Twentieth Century," *International Organization* 25 (Summer): 420–445.

SLOAN, STEPHEN, AND RICHARD KEARNEY. (1978) "Non-Territorial Terrorism," *Conflict* 1 (1): 131–144.

SMALL, MELVIN, AND J. DAVID SINGER. (1979) "Conflicts in the International System, 1816–1977: Historical Trends and Policy Futures," pp. 89–115 in Charles W. Kegley, Jr., and Patrick J. McGowan (eds.), *Challenges to America*. Beverly Hills, Calif.: Sage Publications.

_____. (1972) "Patterns in International Warfare, 1816–1965," pp. 121–131 in James F. Short, Jr., and Marvin E. Wolfgang (eds.), *Collective Violence*. Chicago: Aldine-Atherton.

SMART, IAN. (1976) "Uniqueness and Generality," pp. 259–281 in Raymond Vernon (ed.), *The Oil Crisis*. New York: Norton.

SMITH, COLIN, AND SHYAM BHATIA. (1980) "Stealing the Bomb for Pakistan: Nuclear Proliferation and Dr. Khan's 'Mission Impossible,'" *World Press Review* 27 (March): 26–28.

SMOKE, RICHARD. (1977) *War: Controlling Escalation*. Cambridge: Harvard University Press.

_____. (1975) "National Security Affairs," pp. 247–362 in Fred I. Greenstein and Nelson W. Polsby (eds.), *International Politics. Handbook of Political Science*, Vol. 8. Reading, Mass.: Addison-Wesley.

SNYDER, GLENN H. (1972) "Crisis Bargaining," pp. 217–256 in Charles F. Hermann (ed.), *International Behavior*. New York: Free Press.

_____. (1969) "The Balance of Power and the Balance of Terror," pp. 114–126 in Dean G. Pruitt and Richard C. Snyder (eds.), *Theory and Research on the Causes of War*. Englewood Cliffs, N.J.: Prentice-Hall.

_____. (1960) "Balance of Power in the Nuclear Age," *Journal of International Affairs* 14 (1): 21–34.

_____, AND PAUL DIESING. (1977) *Conflict Among Nations: Bargaining, Decision-Making, and System Structure in International Crisis*. Princeton: Princeton University Press.

SNYDER, RICHARD C. (1955) "Toward Greater Order in the Study of International Politics," *World Politics* 7 (April): 461–468.

SONDERMANN, FRED A. (1957) "The Study of International Relations, 1956 Version," *World Politics* 9 (October): 102–111.

SORENSEN, MAX. (1968) *Manual of Public International Law*. New York: St. Martin's.

SORENSEN, THEODORE C. (1965) *Kennedy*. New York: Bantam.

SOROKIN, PITIRIM A. (1937) *Social and Cultural Dynamics*. New York: American Book.

SOROOS, MARVIN S. (1977) "The Commons and Lifeboat as Guides for International Ecological Policy," *International Studies Quarterly* 21 (December): 647–674.

Spanier, John. (1975) *Games Nations Play*. New York: Praeger.

Spero, Joan Edelman. (1977) *The Politics of International Economic Relations*. New York: St. Martin's.

Sprout, Harold, and Margaret Sprout. (1971) *Toward a Politics of the Planet Earth*. New York: Van Nostrand.

——. (1968) *An Ecological Paradigm for the Study of International Politics*. Research Monograph 30, Center of International Studies. Princeton: Princeton University.

Stanley, J., and M. Pearton. (1972) *The Arms Trade with the Third World*. New York: Humanities Press.

Starr, Harvey. (1978) "Collective Goods Approaches to Alternative World Structures." Paper presented at the Annual Meeting of the International Studies Association, Washington, D.C., February 24–28.

Stavrianos, L. S. (1976) *The Promise of the Coming Dark Age*. San Francisco: Freeman.

Stein, Arthur. (1976) "Conflict and Cohesion: A Review of the Literature," *Journal of Conflict Resolution* 20 (March): 143–172.

Stern, Ernest, and Wouter Tims. (1976) "The Relative Bargaining Strength of the Developing Countries," pp. 6–50 in Ronald G. Ridker (ed.), *Changing Resource Problems of the Fourth World*. Washington, D.C.: Resources for the Future.

Stobaugh, Robert, and Daniel Yergin. (1980) "Energy: An Emergency Telescoped," *Foreign Affairs*. Special issue *America and the World 1979*. Vol. 58, No. 3: 563–595.

——. (1979) "After the Second Shock: Pragmatic Energy Strategies," *Foreign Affairs* 57 (Spring): 836–871.

Stockholm International Peace Research Institute. (1976) *Armaments and Disarmament in the Nuclear Age*. Stockholm: Stockholm International Peace Research Institute.

Stockton, Richard. (1932) *Inevitable War*. New York: Perth Press.

Stoessinger, John G. (1977) *The United Nations and the Superpowers: China, Russia, and America*. New York: Random House.

Strange, Susan. (1971) "The Politics of International Currencies," *World Politics* 23 (January): 215–231.

Streeten, Paul. (1974) "World Trade in Agricultural Commodities and the Terms of Trade with Industrial Goods," pp. 207–223 in Nurul Islam (ed.), *Agricultural Policy in Developing Countries*. London: Macmillan.

Stuyt, A. M. (1972) *Surveys of International Arbitrations, 1794–1970*. Leiden, Netherlands: A. W. Sijthoff.

Sullivan, Michael P. (1976) *International Relations: Theories and Evidence*. Englewood Cliffs, N.J.: Prentice-Hall.

Sumner, William Graham. (1968) "War," pp. 205–228 in Leon Bramson and George W. Goethals (eds.), *War*. New York: Basic Books.

TANNENBAUM, FRANK. (1979) "The Survival of the Fittest," pp. 180–186 in George Modelski (ed.), *Transnational Corporations and World Order.* San Francisco: Freeman.

TANTER, RAYMOND. (1974) *Modelling and Managing International Conflicts.* Beverly Hills, Calif.: Sage Publications.

———. (1966) "Dimensions of Conflict Behavior With and Between Nations, 1958–1960," *Journal of Conflict Resolution* 10 (March): 143–164.

———, AND RICHARD ULLMAN (eds.) (1972) *Theory and Policy in International Relations.* Princeton: Princeton University Press.

TAYLOR, CHARLES L., AND MICHAEL C. HUDSON. (1972) *World Handbook of Political and Social Indicators.* New Haven: Yale University Press.

TAYLOR, TREVOR (ed.) (1978) *Approaches and Theory in International Relations.* New York: Longman.

THIBAUT, JOHN W., AND HAROLD H. KELLY. (1959) *The Social Psychology of Groups.* New York: Wiley.

THIEL, MICHAEL F. (1979) "World Oil and OPEC: The Razor's Edge," *World Oil* 189 (October): 123–124 et passim.

THOMPSON, KENNETH W. (1960) *Political Realism and the Crisis of World Politics.* Princeton: Princeton University Press.

———. (1958) "The Limits of Principle in International Politics," *Journal of Politics* 20 (August): 437–467.

TOCQUEVILLE, ALEXIS DE. (1969) *Democracy in America.* Garden City, N.Y.: Doubleday-Anchor.

———. (1955) *The Old Regime and the French Revolution.* Translated by S. Gilbert. Garden City, N.Y.: Doubleday-Anchor.

TODARO, MICHAEL P. (1977) *Economic Development in the Third World.* New York: Longman.

TOFFLER, ALVIN. (1980) *The Third Wave.* New York: Morrow.

———. (1970) *Future Shock.* New York: Random House.

TOYNBEE, ARNOLD J. (1947) *A Study of History.* New York: Oxford University Press.

TRB. (1978) "A Bigger Bang," *The New Republic* 178 (May 27): 2.

TRIFFIN, ROBERT. (1978–79) "The International Role and Fate of the Dollar," *Foreign Affairs* 57 (Winter): 269–286.

TUCKER, ROBERT W. (1980) "America in Decline: The Foreign Policy of 'Maturity,'" *Foreign Affairs.* Special issue *America and the World 1979.* Vol. 58, No. 3: 449–484.

TUGWELL, REXFORD GUY. (1971) *Off Course: From Truman to Nixon.* New York: Praeger.

TUNG, WILLIAM L. (1968) *International Law in an Organizing World.* New York: Crowell.

U.S. ARMS CONTROL AND DISARMAMENT AGENCY. (1979a) *Arms Control 1978.* Washington, D.C.: Government Printing Office.

_____. (1979b) *World Military Expenditures and Arms Transfers 1968–1977.* Washington, D.C.: Government Printing Office.

_____. (1978a) *Arms Control 1977.* Washington, D.C: Government Printing Office.

_____. (1978b) *World Military Expenditures and Arms Transfers, 1967–1976.* Washington, D.C.: Government Printing Office.

U.S. DEPARTMENT OF COMMERCE. (1980) "U.S. Trade Status with Communist Countries." International Trade Administration, Office of East-West Policy and Planning (August 26).

_____. (1979) *Selected Trade and Economic Data of the Centrally Planned Economies, June.* Washington, D.C.: Government Printing Office.

_____. (1978) *Selected Trade and Economic Data of the Centrally Planned Economies, December 1977.* Washington, D.C.: Government Printing Office.

U.S. DEPARTMENT OF ENERGY. (1980a) Energy Information Administration. *International Petroleum Annual 1978.* Washington, D.C.: Government Printing Office.

_____. (1980b) Energy Information Administration. *Monthly Energy Review,* April.

U.S. DEPARTMENT OF STATE. (1979a) *Salt II Basic Guide.* Washington, D.C.: Government Printing Office.

_____. (1979b) *The Strategic Arms Limitation Talks.* Washington, D.C.: Government Printing Office.

_____. (1979c) "U.S. Policy Toward the Soviet Union," Bureau of Public Affairs, Office of Public Communication (February).

_____. (1978a) "World Population: The Silent Explosion—Part 3," *Department of State Bulletin* 78 (December): 44–47.

_____. (1978b) "World Population: The Silent Explosion—Part 2," *Department of State Bulletin* 78 (November): 1–8.

_____. (1978c) "World Population: The Silent Explosion—Part 1," *Department of State Bulletin* 78 (October): 45–54.

U.S. OFFICE OF TECHNOLOGY ASSESSMENT. (1979) *The Effects of Nuclear War.* Washington, D.C.: Government Printing Office.

VAN DYKE, VERNON. (1966) *International Politics.* New York: Appleton-Century-Crofts.

VARON, BENSION, AND KENJI TAKEUCHI. (1974) "Developing Countries and Non-Fuel Minerals," *Foreign Affairs* 52 (April): 497–510.

VAUPEL, JAMES W., AND JOAN P. CURHAN. (1969) *The Making of Multinational Enterprise: A Sourcebook of Tables Based on a Study of 187 Major U.S. Manufacturing Corporations.* Boston: Division of Research, Graduate School of Business Administration, Harvard University.

VERBA, SIDNEY. (1961) "Assumption of Rationality and Non-Rationality in Models of the International System," *World Politics* 14 (October): 93–117.

VERNON, RAYMOND. (1979) "The Fragile Foundations of East-West Trade," *Foreign Affairs* 57 (Summer): 1035–1051.

_____. (1976) "An Introduction," pp. 1–14 in Raymond Vernon (ed.), *The Oil Crisis*. New York: Norton.

_____. (1971) *Sovereignty at Bay*. New York: Basic Books.

VOLGY, THOMAS J. (1974) "Reducing Conflict in International Politics: The Impact of Structural Variables," *International Studies Quarterly* 18 (June): 179–210.

_____, AND JON E. QUISTGARD. (1974) "Correlates of Organizational Rewards in the United Nations: An Analysis of Environmental and Legislative Variables," *International Organization* 28 (Spring): 179–205.

VON GLAHN, GERHARD. (1976) *Law Among Nations*. New York: Macmillan.

WALLACE, MICHAEL D. (1971) "Power, Status, and International War," *Journal of Peace Research* 8 (1): 23–35.

_____, AND J. DAVID SINGER. (1970) "Intergovernmental Organization in the Global System, 1915–1964: A Quantitative Description," *International Organization* 24 (Spring): 239–287.

WALTER, EUGENE VICTOR. (1969) *Terror and Resistance*. New York: Oxford University Press.

WALTZ, KENNETH N. (1979) *Theory of International Politics*. Reading, Mass.: Addison-Wesley.

_____. (1975) "Theory of International Relations," pp. 1–85 in Fred I. Greenstein and Nelson W. Polsby (eds.), *International Politics. Handbook of Political Science*, Vol. 8. Reading, Mass.: Addison-Wesley.

_____. (1971) "The Stability of the Bipolar World," pp. 333–342 in William D. Coplin and Charles W. Kegley, Jr. (eds.), *A Multi-Method Introduction to International Politics*. Chicago: Markham.

_____. (1970) "The Myth of National Interdependence," pp. 205–223 in Charles P. Kindleberger (ed.), *The International Corporation*. Cambridge: M.I.T. Press.

_____. (1954) *Man, the State, and War*. New York: Columbia University Press.

WALZER, MICHAEL. (1977) *Just and Unjust Wars*. New York: Basic Books.

WEIGERT, KATHLEEN MAAS, AND ROBERT E. RIGGS. (1969) "Africa and United Nations Elections: An Aggregate Data Analysis," *International Organization* 23 (Winter): 1–19.

WELCH, WILLIAM. (1970) *American Images of Soviet Foreign Policy*. New Haven: Yale University Press.

WELLS, DONALD A. (1967) *The War Myth*. New York: Pegasus.

WELTMAN, JOHN J. (1974) "On the Obsolescence of War," *International Studies Quarterly* 18 (December): 395–416.

WHEATON, HENRY. (1846) *Elements of International Law*. Philadelphia: Lea and Blanchard.

WHITE, IRVIN L. (1974) "International Law," pp. 251–269 in Michael Haas (ed.), *International Systems*. New York: Chandler.

WHITEHEAD, ALFRED NORTH. (1929) *Science and the Modern World.* New York: Macmillan.

WIESNER, JEROME B., AND HERBERT F. YORK. (1964) "National Security and the Nuclear Test-Ban," *Scientific American* 211 (October): 27–35.

WIGHT, MARTIN. (1968) "The Balance of Power," pp. 149–175 in Herbert Butterfield and Martin Wight (eds.), *Diplomatic Investigations.* Cambridge: Harvard University Press.

WILKINS, MIRA. (1976) "The Oil Companies in Perspective," pp. 159–178 in Raymond Vernon (ed.), *The Oil Crisis.* New York: Norton.

WILLETTS, PETER. (1978) *The Non-Aligned Movement.* New York: Nichols.

WILLRICH, MASON. (1975) Energy and World Politics. New York: Free Press.

WINBERG, ALAN R. (1979) "Resource Politics: The Future of International Markets for Raw Materials," pp. 178–194 in David W. Orr and Marvin S. Soroos (eds.), *The Global Predicament: Ecological Perspectives on World Order.* Chapel Hill: University of North Carolina Press.

WITTKOPF, EUGENE R. (1976) "Correlates of Political Success in the UN General Assembly, 1946–1970: An Intra-Organizational Perspective." Paper presented at the Annual Meeting of the International Studies Association, Toronto, February 25–29.

———. (1975) "Soviet and American Political Success in the United Nations General Assembly, 1946–70," pp. 179–204 in Charles W. Kegley, Jr. et al. (eds.), *International Events and the Comparative Analysis of Foreign Policy.* Columbia: University of South Carolina Press.

———. (1972) "A Statistical Classification of International Inter-Governmental Organizations." Paper presented at the Annual Meeting of the International Studies Association, Dallas, March 15–18.

WOHLSTETTER, ALBERT. (1976–77) "Spreading the Bomb Without Quite Breaking the Rules," *Foreign Policy* 25 (Winter): 88–96, 145–179.

World Armaments and Disarmament: SIPRI Yearbook 1980. (1980) London: Taylor & Francis.

World Bank Atlas. (1979) Washington, D.C.: World Bank.

World Development Report, 1979. (1979) New York: Oxford University Press for the World Bank.

"World Trends: Surplus to Shortage in One Easy Lesson." (1979) *World Oil* 189 (August 15): 61–64.

WRIGGINS, W. HOWARD. (1978) "Third World Strategies for Change: The Political Context of North-South Interdependence," pp. 19–117 in W. Howard Wriggins and Gunnar Adler-Karlsson, *Reducing Global Inequities.* New York: McGraw-Hill.

WRIGGINS, W. HOWARD, AND GUNNAR ADLER-KARLSSON. (1978) *Reducing Global Inequities.* New York: McGraw-Hill.

WRIGHT, QUINCY. (1955) *The Study of International Relations.* New York: Appleton-Century-Crofts.

———. (1953) "The Outlawry of War and the Law of War," *American Journal of International Law* 47: 365–376.

____. (1942) *A Study of War*. Chicago: University of Chicago Press.

Wu, Yuan-li. (1973) *Raw Material Supply in a Multipolar World*. New York: Crane, Russak.

Yalem, Ronald J. (1972) "Tripolarity and the International System," *Orbis* 15 (Winter): 1051–1063.

Yearbook of International Organizations, 1978. (1978) Brussels: Union of International Associations.

Yergin, Daniel. (1977) "Politics and Soviet-American Trade: The Three Questions," *Foreign Affairs* 55 (April): 517–538.

Ziegler, David W. (1977) *War, Peace, and International Politics*. Boston: Little, Brown.

Zinnes, Dina A. (1976) *Contemporary Research in International Relations: A Perspective and a Critical Appraisal*. New York: Free Press.

____, Robert C. North, and Howard E. Koch, Jr. (1961) "Capability, Threat, and the Outbreak of War," pp. 469–482 in James N. Rosenau (ed.), *International Politics and Foreign Policy*. New York: Free Press.

____, and Jonathan Wilkenfeld. (1971) "An Analysis of Foreign Conflict Behavior of Nations," pp. 167–213 in Wolfram F. Hanrieder (ed.), *Comparative Foreign Policy*. New York: David McKay.

____, Joseph L. Zinnes, and Robert D. McClure. (1972) "Hostility in Diplomatic Communication," pp. 139–161 in Charles F. Hermann (ed.), *International Crises*. New York: Free Press.

Index

Note: Page numbers in italics refer to material in figures, tables, or boxes.